1,001
BEST
LOW-CARB
RECIPES

Delicious, Healthy, Easy-to-make
Recipes for Cutting Carbs

EDITED BY

Sue Spitler WITH **Linda R. Yoakam, MS, RD**

S
SURREY
BOOKS

AGATE

CHICAGO

Nutritional analyses: Linda R. Yoakam, R.D., M.S.
Printed in the United States of America.

Cover photos (clockwise from top left of front cover): Shutterstock; iStock.com/Elena Danileiko; Brave New Pictures; iStock.com/Carla McMahon; Rick Browne; iStock.com/amberto4ka. (spine): iStock.com/Elena Danieleiko. (back cover): Brave New Pictures.

Library of Congress Cataloging-in-Publication Data

1,001 low-carb recipes for life
1,001 best low-carb recipes : delicious, healthy, easy-to-make recipes for cutting carbs / edited by Sue Spitler with Linda R. Yoakam.
    pages cm. -- (1,001)
    Includes index.
    Summary: "A collection of low-carbohydrate recipes for the home cook"-- Provided by publisher.
    Revision of: 1,001 low-carb recipes for life / edited by Sue Spitler with Linda R. Yoakam. c2004.
    Includes index.
    ISBN 978-1-57284-184-0 (paperback) -- ISBN 978-1-57284-770-5 (ebook) -- ISBN 1-57284-770-0 (ebook)
    1. Low-carbohydrate diet--Recipes. I. Spitler, Sue. II. Yoakam, Linda R. III. Title: One thousand one low-carb recipes.
    RM237.73.A15 2016
    641.5›6383--dc23

                            2015031870

10 9 8 7 6 5 4 3 2   17 18 19 20 21 22

Surrey Books is an imprint of Agate Publishing. Agate books are available in bulk at discount prices. Agatepublishing.com

Contents

Acknowledgments

A heartfelt thank you to all who helped in the creation of *1,001 Best Low-Carb Recipes*—

Chef Pat Molden for her fine culinary skills, Linda Yoakam, R.D., M.S., for her guidance and nutritional analyses, Gene DeRoin for his editing expertise, Anna Layton for her multi-tasking help, and publisher Susan Schwartz for her support and encouragement.

Introduction

Judging by magazines at checkout stands, cookbooks on bookstore shelves, and the buzz around workplace watercoolers, low-carbohydrate eating is widely popular. But low-carb diet plans may also be confusing because no standard for what constitutes "low-carb" exists and because no consensus has been reached on the value of one diet plan over another.

Additionally, many who follow the diet-book plans for low-carb eating do so incorrectly. They eat too many foods with few health benefits (such as big steaks with blue cheese sauce) or excessive amounts of certain foods (such as bigger steaks with lots of blue cheese sauce). Others, in their crusade against carbs, needlessly eliminate foods that are inherently healthful and provide variety in the diet (such as non-starchy vegetables and many fruits).

So before you commit yourself body and soul to a low-carb regimen, take a few minutes to read the following information about healthful—and successful—low-carb eating. After all, no diet or eating plan will work, not even low carb, if you can't stay on it for lack of variety or if long-term health concerns arise.

1,001 Best Low-Carb Recipes was not written to be yet another "diet" book. It is written for people like you, who have already chosen to follow a low-carb diet plan. But be advised that your eating plan should be under the guidance of a physician or registered dietitian, and be sure to read this short introduction on nutrients and the role they play in maintaining health. With a fuller understanding of what nutrients are and how each impacts your body, you can use *1,001 Best Low-Carb Recipes* to enjoy delicious recipes that help you lower and control carbs, control or lose weight, manage blood sugars, and lower the risk of heart disease.

How a Low-Carb Diet Works

Let's start with basic nutrition. There are many kinds of nutrients, of which carbohydrates, or "carbs" for short, is just one. Other nutrients include proteins, fats, vitamins, minerals, and water. For the purposes of this book, we are concerned only with the nutrients that contain calories. These are: carbohydrates, fats, and protein. Whether trying to lose or maintain weight, improve blood sugar control, or prevent heart disease, calories count first, no matter what form they are in: carbs, fats, or proteins. And depending on your health goals, the idea is to find the balance of calories and nutrients that works best for you. No one diet works for all people.

Carbohydrates are the body's primary and preferred source of energy. When you eat carbs, the body converts them into glucose, or blood sugar, which the body's cells use for fuel. Think of your body as a car, with fuel, or blood sugar, being added at the gas pump. When the fuel enters your body, a hormone called insulin unlocks the body's cells and allows the fuel to be absorbed.

Carbohydrates contain four calories per gram. They can come in a simple form called sugar, commonly found in foods such as candy, soda pop, cakes, pies, cookies, and ice cream. Carbohydrates can also come in more complex forms, sometimes called starches, like bread, grains, vegetables, and fruits. And finally, carbohydrates come in an indigestible form called fiber, or roughage. Fiber is found in foods such as whole grains, fruits, and vegetables and is important because it helps to slow and regulate sugar entering the bloodstream. Fiber also provides other health benefits: it helps reduce cholesterol, aids digestion, and prevents constipation and possibly colon cancer.

People with diabetes must carefully control the carbs they eat to avoid blood sugar highs and lows. Using the car analogy again, when too much fuel enters the body too quickly, blood sugars can "spill" out into the bloodstream, raising levels. Too much blood sugar can also cause the cells to become resistant to insulin. If you are overweight by as little as 20 pounds or have too much blood sugar or insulin resistance, it can lead to a host of health problems, up to and including prediabetes, diabetes with all of its complications, and raised triglycerides (blood lipids or fats) that are implicated in heart disease.

After carbohydrates, fats are the body's secondary choice for energy, and they are also the preferred form of calories for storing body fat. Fat has nine calories per gram, or more than twice as many calories per gram as carbs. Fat calories, however, do not raise blood sugar. Fat in a meal actually helps control weight because it increases digestion time and makes you feel full. When you eat fats, some will be used for energy, but excess amounts will be stored as body fat.

The fat calories you eat, if chosen wisely, can help prevent heart disease. For example, saturated fats and cholesterol in the diet are associated with heart disease, while foods high in omega 3 fatty acids, such as salmon and walnuts, are associated with improved heart health. Some fats, such as hydrogenated fats found in margarine, shortenings, and many packaged foods, contain trans-fatty acids, a form of fat associated with many health problems, including heart disease.

Your body's least favorite source of energy is protein because it takes longer to be converted into glucose. Proteins, with four calories per gram, are essential for growth and maintenance of muscle mass, but watch out for the fat that lurks within proteins, not only for weight control but also for your heart's health. When you eat protein it enters the small intestine where it is broken down into molecules of amino acids. These are absorbed into the bloodsteam and sent to the liver where some are converted into glucose, or blood sugar. However, the process takes some time and is not a major contributor to high blood sugar. Some of the amino acids are used to build new protein.

Three keys to long-term weight control and good health can be clearly stated: balance the amounts of carbohydrate, protein, and fat that your body needs to function properly; eat healthful foods, such as carbs high in fiber and healthy fats; and burn excess calories by activity and exercise.

Keeping Carbs Low

How low is a low-carb diet? There is no standard definition. Registered dietitians recommend a *minimum* of 130 grams of total carbohydrate daily, that is, the minimum required for normal functioning of the brain and nervous system. Because the long-term effects of following a very low-carbohydrate diet are still unknown, we would not advocate eating fewer than 130 grams of carbohydrate daily, which can be considered "low" compared to the Dietary Reference Intake-recommended amount of 45–65% of total calories from carbohydrates (45% of a 2000-calorie diet is 225 grams of carbohydrate; 65% is 325 grams of carbohydrate).

The following sample menu is an example of an eating plan based on 130 grams of carbohydrate a day.

(Italic indicates recipe in book)

MEAL	ONE SERVING	PAGE NO.	NET CARBS (GMS)	MEAL TOTALS
Breakfast	½ Fresh Grapefruit		6.4	
	Bacon & Egg Breakfast Pizza	18	18	24.4
Lunch	*Gyros Burger*	267	21.5	
	Greek Islands Salad	396	7.8	
	Fresh Grapes		16.8	
	Iced Tea		0	46.1
Dinner	*Flounder Florentine*	293	16.6	
	Microwave Bulgur Pilaf à l'Orange	373	12.6	
	Green Beans in Mustard Sauce	328	7.1	
	Key Lime Pie	473	12.4	
	Milk		11.7	60.4
	DAY TOTAL NET CARBS (GMS)			130.9

Net Carbs and The Glycemic Index

New research in carbohydrate metabolism indicates that not all carbs are created equal. We also took "Net Carbs" and the "Glycemic Index" into account when we developed the recipes for *1,001 Best Low-Carb Recipes*.

The net carb is based on the belief that fiber sources of carbohydrate are not absorbed by the body and therefore are calorie-free, do not affect blood sugars, and do not contribute to weight gain. Since this is the case, fiber carbs can be subtracted from the total carbohydrate count of a recipe or food. The total carbohydrates minus the fiber carbohydrates leaves the "net" carbs available to the body. This difference between the total carbs and fiber is also known as "impact carbs," as these are the carbs that have an "impact" on the body. In this book we chose to use the term "net carbs," and this figure is provided with each recipe.

In addition, some carbohydrates increase blood sugar faster than other carbohydrates. The speed at which carbs are converted to blood sugar has been measured for some foods and is called the glycemic index. The higher the G.I. number, the faster the carbs change to blood sugar. With high G.I. foods, the rapid rise in blood sugar causes insulin, a hormone produced in the pancreas, to peak, resulting in a rapid drop in blood sugar, which then leads to hunger, snacking, and overeating. The lower the G.I. number, the slower the carbs change into blood sugar and the less insulin is released, which results in less overeating.

White bread and white sugar get the highest G.I. value of 100. When you choose carbohydrate foods to complement recipes in this book, pick those with both low net carbs and low glycemic indexes. For example, if rice is served with a stir-fry recipe, brown rice would be the better choice since it has a G.I. of 50 compared to 56 for white rice. Or, if breakfast includes fruit, 1/2 of a grapefruit has a lower G.I. than a banana.

The chart below lists a variety of commonly consumed foods with known glycemic indexes. The total carbohydrate, net carbohydrate, and glycemic index are listed for each. All values are for 100-gram amounts, which is approximately 1/2 cup.

Carbohydrate, Net Carbohydrate, and Glycemic Index for Common Foods[1]

FOOD ITEM (100 GMS)	TOTAL CARBS (GMS)	NET CARBS (GMS)	GLYCEMIC INDEX (G.I.)
Apples	15.2	12.5	38
Apple Juice	11.7	11.6	40
Apricots	11.1	8.7	57
Bananas	23.4	21.0	52
Cantaloupe	8.4	7.6	65
Cherries	13.7	11.4	22
Grapefruit	7.7	6.4	25
Grapefruit Juice	9.2	9.1	48
Grapes	17.8	16.8	43
Oranges	11.8	9.4	42

continued on following page

[1]Revised International Table of Glycemic Index (GI) and Glycemic Load (GL) Values 2002; based on *American Journal of Clinical Nutrition*, pgs. 5-56, July 2002.

Continued: Carbohydrate, Net Carbohydrate, and Glycemic Index for Common Foods

FOOD ITEM (100 GMS)	TOTAL CARBS (GMS)	NET CARBS (GMS)	GLYCEMIC INDEX (G.I.)
Orange Juice	10.4	10.2	52
Peaches	11.1	9.1	42
Pears	15.1	12.7	38
Strawberries	7.0	4.7	40
Watermelon	7.2	6.7	72
Baked Beans	19.4	14.6	56
Kidney Beans	22.8	16.4	28
Lentils	20.1	10.4	26
Macaroni	28.4	27.1	47
Spaghetti	28.3	26.6	38
Pearled Barley, dry	77.7	62.1	29
All Bran Cereal	74.2	41.9	38
100% Whole-Grain Bread	41.2	26.5	51
Cornmeal, dry	77.7	70.3	69
Couscous, cooked	23.2	21.8	65
Oat Bran	66.2	50.8	55
Brown Rice, cooked	23.0	21.2	50
White Rice, cooked	28.2	27.8	56
Shredded Wheat	82.5	71.6	75

Choose the Right Ingredients

In developing recipes for this book, we were careful to select carbs with low glycemic indexes and have, where possible, used whole-grain pastas rather than white semolina flour pastas, whole wheat flour rather than all-purpose white flour, brown rice instead of white rice, and brown sugar or sugar substitute instead of white sugar.

Fat in a meal helps control weight by increasing the time it takes to digest that meal, thus delaying the onset of hunger. Fat works with the low-glycemic foods to help improve your sense of fullness and satisfaction, which is why the recipes in this book mostly use full-fat products. As a bonus, full-fat foods frequently have fewer carbohydrates than the lower-fat products.

Also, we chose to use natural fats, like butter, in order to avoid trans-fatty acids, which are associated with LDL ("bad") cholesterol and heart disease. On the other hand, monounsaturated fats, the kind associated with HDL ("good") cholesterol, are considered healthy for the heart. These include olive oil, flax seeds and their oil, and walnuts and their oil; fatty fish like salmon or mackerel also contain monounsaturated fat. Olive oil and canola oil are used for most of the recipes in this book because of their monounsaturated fat content.

Nutritional Data

1,001 Best Low-Carb Recipes is an invaluable guide to preparing healthy, low-carbohydrate meals for your family. The delicious recipes can be used successfully with any low-carbohydrate diet plan already being followed.

We have provided nutritional information for each recipe in this book, but remember that nutritional data are not always infallible. The nutritional analyses were derived by using computer software highly regarded by nutritionists and dietitians, but they are meant only as guidelines. Figures are based on actual laboratory values of ingredients, so results may vary slightly, depending on the brand or manufacturer of an ingredient used.

Ingredients noted as "optional" or "to taste" or "as garnish" are not included in the nutritional analyses. When alternate choices or amounts of ingredients are given, the ingredient or amount listed first was used for analysis. Similarly, data is based on the first number of servings shown, where a range is given. Nutritional analyses are also based on the cooking instructions given; other procedures will invalidate data.

Other factors that can affect the accuracy of nutritional data include variability in sizes, weights, and measures of fruits, vegetables, and other foods. There is also a possible 20 percent error factor in the nutritional labeling of prepared foods.

If you have any health problems that require strict dietary requirements, it is important to consult a physician, dietitian, or nutritionist before using recipes in this or any other cookbook. Also, if you are a diabetic or require a diet that restricts calories, fat, or sodium, remember that nutritional data might be accurate for the recipe as written but not for the food you cooked due to the variables explained above.

We hope you'll enjoy the delicious low-carb recipes we've created for you. It's easy to stay with your plan for diet and exercise if the food you eat tastes wonderful, isn't it?

—Linda R. Yoakam, R.D., M.S.

ONE

Breakfast and Breads

Breakfast Shake

4 servings (about 1 cup each)

1 large banana, cut into chunks
1 cup sugar-free cranberry juice
1 cup reduced-fat milk
1 cup halved strawberries
¼ cup wheat germ
4 ice cubes

Per Serving
Net Carbohydrate (gm): 16.6
Calories: 106
Fat (gm): 2.1
Saturated fat (gm): 0.9
Cholesterol (mg): 4.9
Sodium (mg): 34
Protein (gm): 4.2
Carbohydrate (gm): 19.1

1. Process all ingredients in blender until smooth.

Variation:

Orange-Cantaloupe Cooler—Make recipe as above, substituting 2 cups cubed cantaloupe for the banana and strawberries, and orange juice for the cranberry juice.

Tofruity

4 servings (about 1 cup each)

½ package (14-ounce size) light silken tofu, drained
1 cup cubed, peeled, and pitted mango
1 cup raspberries, *or* halved strawberries
1 cup orange juice
3–4 ice cubes

Per Serving
Net Carbohydrate (gm): 14.6
Calories: 88
Fat (gm): 0.8
Saturated fat (gm): 0.1
Cholesterol (mg): 0
Sodium (mg): 43
Protein (gm): 4
Carbohydrate (gm): 14.6

1. Process all ingredients in blender or food processor until smooth.

Variation:

Pink Passion Smoothie—Make recipe as above, substituting watermelon for the mango, strawberries for the raspberries, and cranberry juice for the orange juice.

Honey-Walnut Yogurt

2 servings

2 cups plain yogurt
¼–½ cup walnut pieces
2–4 teaspoons honey

Per Serving
Net Carbohydrate (gm): 24
Calories: 274
Fat (gm): 13.6
Saturated fat (gm): 3.4
Cholesterol (mg): 14.7
Sodium (mg): 172
Protein (gm): 15.2
Carbohydrate (gm): 25.1

1. Spoon yogurt into bowls; sprinkle with walnuts and drizzle with honey.

Best Breakfast Oatmeal

4 servings

3 cups water
1½ cups quick-cooking oats
¼ cup dried cranberries, *or* dried fruit bits
¼ cup toasted slivered almonds
Ground cinnamon
¼ cup sugar-free pancake syrup
¼ cup light cream

Per Serving
Net Carbohydrate (gm): 26.5
Calories: 217
Fat (gm): 9.3
Saturated fat (gm): 2.4
Cholesterol (mg): 9.9
Sodium (mg): 28
Protein (gm): 6.2
Carbohydrate (gm): 30.6

1. Heat water to boiling in large saucepan; stir in oatmeal. Reduce heat and simmer, stirring occasonally, until thickened, 2 to 3 minutes.

2. Spoon oatmeal into bowls; sprinkle with cranberries, almonds, and cinnamon. Drizzle with syrup and cream.

Omelet Puff with Vegetable Mélange

2 servings

4 egg whites
¼ cup water
1 egg
¼ teaspoon dried tarragon leaves
¼ teaspoon salt
¼ teaspoon pepper
Vegetable Mélange (recipe follows)

Per Serving
Net Carbohydrate (gm): 4.8
Calories: 124
Fat (gm): 6.1
Saturated fat (gm): 1.3
Cholesterol (mg): 106.2
Sodium (mg): 436
Protein (gm): 11.2
Carbohydrate (gm): 6.2

1. Beat egg whites in large bowl until foamy; mix in water at high speed, beating until stiff but not dry peaks form.

2. Beat egg, tarragon, salt, and pepper at high speed in small bowl until thick and lemon colored. Fold egg white mixture into egg mixture.

3. Cook egg mixture in greased skillet over medium to medium-low heat until bottom of omelet is light brown, about 5 minutes. Transfer to oven and bake at 325 degrees, uncovered, until omelet is puffed and light brown. Loosen edge of omelet with spatula; slide onto serving platter, carefully folding omelet in half. Spoon Vegetable Mélange over omelet.

Vegetable Mélange

makes about 1½ cups

1 cup sliced zucchini
⅓ cup sliced onion
⅔ cup sliced green bell pepper
1 medium tomato, cut into wedges
1–2 tablespoons olive oil
1–2 tablespoons water

1. Sauté vegetables in oil in medium skillet 3 to 5 minutes. Add water; cook, covered, over medium-low heat until tender, about 5 minutes.

Eggs Napoleon

6 servings

3 English muffins, halved, toasted
Spinach leaves, as garnish
6 slices tomato
6 poached eggs
Cream Cheese Hollandaise Sauce (recipe follows)
Paprika, as garnish
Chopped parsley leaves, as garnish

Per Serving
Net Carbohydrate (gm): 15.2
Calories: 271
Fat (gm): 17.8
Saturated fat (gm): 9.3
Cholesterol (mg): 248
Sodium (mg): 377
Protein (gm): 11.3
Carbohydrate (gm): 16.1

1. Top English muffin halves with spinach leaves and tomato slices. Top each with a poached egg.

2. Spoon Cream Cheese Hollandaise Sauce over eggs; sprinkle with paprika and parsley.

Cream Cheese Hollandaise Sauce

makes about 1½ cups

6 ounces cream cheese
⅓ cup sour cream
3–4 tablespoons reduced-fat milk
1–2 teaspoons lemon juice
½–1 teaspoon Dijon-style mustard
½ teaspoon ground turmeric

1. Heat all ingredients in small saucepan over medium-low to low heat until melted and smooth, stirring constantly.

Variation:

Eggs Benedict—Make recipe as above, substituting 2 to 3 slices warm Canadian bacon for the spinach and tomatoes. Sprinkle top of each serving with 1 slice crisply fried, crumbled bacon.

Basque-Style Eggs

4 servings

Peperonata (recipe follows)
1 cup chopped tomato
6 eggs
2 tablespoons reduced-fat milk
Salt and pepper, to taste

Per Serving
Net Carbohydrate (gm): 9.9
Calories: 193
Fat (gm): 11.3
Saturated fat (gm): 2.8
Cholesterol (mg): 318.9
Sodium (mg): 106
Protein (gm): 11.3
Carbohydrate (gm): 12.6

1. Make Peperonata, adding chopped tomato during last 10 minutes of cooking time.

2. Beat eggs and milk. Move Peperonata to side of skillet; add eggs. Cook until eggs are set, stirring occasionally. Gently stir eggs into Peperonata; season to taste with salt and pepper.

Peperonata

makes about 1½ cups

1 cup sliced onion
1 cup sliced red bell pepper
1 cup sliced green bell pepper
4–6 cloves garlic, minced
1–2 tablespoons olive oil
¼ cup water

1. Cook onion, peppers, and garlic in oil in large skillet over medium heat 5 minutes. Add water; cook, covered, over medium-low to low heat until vegetables are very tender and creamy, 20 to 25 minutes, stirring occasionally.

Cheddar Cheese Soufflé

4 servings

1–2 tablespoons grated Parmesan cheese
1 cup reduced-fat milk
3 tablespoons all-purpose flour
1 tablespoon chopped chives
½ teaspoon dried marjoram leaves
½ teaspoon dry mustard
¼ teaspoon cayenne pepper
1–2 pinches ground nutmeg
3 egg yolks
¼ cup (1 ounce) shredded Cheddar cheese
Salt and white pepper, to taste
3 egg whites
¼ teaspoon cream of tartar

Per Serving
Net Carbohydrate (gm): 8.1
Calories: 146
Fat (gm): 7.9
Saturated fat (gm): 3.7
Cholesterol (mg): 172.8
Sodium (mg): 144.4
Protein (gm): 9.8
Carbohydrate (gm): 8.3

1. Sprinkle a lightly greased 1-quart soufflé dish with Parmesan cheese. Attach an aluminum foil collar to dish, extending foil 3 inches above top of dish; lightly grease inside of collar.

2. Mix milk and flour until smooth in small saucepan; mix in chives, marjoram, dry mustard, cayenne, and nutmeg. Heat to boiling, whisking constantly; boil until thickened, about 1 minute, whisking constantly. Whisk about ½ cup mixture into egg yolks in small bowl; whisk egg mixture back into saucepan. Add cheese and cook over low heat until melted, whisking constantly. Season to taste with salt and white pepper.

3. Beat egg whites until foamy in medium bowl; add cream of tartar and beat into stiff, but not dry, peaks. Stir ⅓ of the egg whites into cheese mixture; fold cheese mixture into remaining whites in bowl. Spoon into prepared soufflé dish. Bake at 350 degrees until soufflé is puffed, browned, and just set in the center, 35 to 40 minutes. Serve immediately.

Variation:

Pepper-Jack Soufflé—Make recipe as above, substituting pepper-jack cheese for the Cheddar cheese and 3 tablespoons finely chopped cilantro, 1 tablespoon dried onion flakes, and ½ teaspoon ground cumin for the chives, marjoram, and dry mustard. Serve with hot or mild salsa.

Quiche Lorraine

6 servings

2–3 tablespoons unseasoned dry bread crumbs
¼ cup finely chopped onion
1 tablespoon butter
¾ cup reduced-fat milk
½ can (12-ounce size) evaporated milk
2 eggs
¼ cup sour cream
¼ teaspoon salt
⅛ teaspoon cayenne pepper
⅛ teaspoon ground nutmeg
1 cup (4 ounces) shredded Swiss cheese
1 tablespoon flour
3 slices bacon, fried crisp, crumbled

Per Serving
Net Carbohydrate (gm): 8.5
Calories: 230
Fat (gm): 15.8
Saturated fat (gm): 8.4
Cholesterol (mg): 111.5
Sodium (mg): 315
Protein (gm): 12.6
Carbohydrate (gm): 8.8

1. Sprinkle a lightly greased 8-inch pie pan with bread crumbs.

2. Sauté onion in butter in small skillet until tender, 3 to 5 minutes, and reserve. Mix milks, eggs, sour cream, salt, cayenne, and nutmeg in medium bowl until smooth. Toss cheese with flour; stir into milk mixture. Stir in bacon and onion. Pour into prepared pie pan and bake at 350 degrees until set in the center and a sharp knife inserted near center comes out clean, about 40 minutes. Cool quiche on wire rack 5 minutes before cutting.

Variation:

Spinach Quiche—Drain ½ package (10-ounce size) frozen, thawed spinach between paper toweling. Prepare recipe as above, adding spinach to onion in skillet and cooking over medium to medium-low heat until mixture is quite dry, 3 to 4 minutes. Proceed as above.

Vegetable Frittata with Parmesan Toast

4 servings

1 small poblano chili, *or* green bell pepper, chopped
¼ cup thinly sliced green onions and tops
2 cups sliced mushrooms
2 cloves garlic, minced
2 tablespoons olive oil
¼ cup water
6 eggs
¼ cup reduced-fat milk
⅓ cup (3 ounces) shredded Cheddar cheese
¼ teaspoon salt
⅛ teaspoon pepper
2 slices multigrain bread, cut diagonally into halves
2 tablespoons shredded Parmesan cheese

Per Serving
Net Carbohydrate (gm): 12
Calories: 336
Fat (gm): 23.1
Saturated fat (gm): 8.5
Cholesterol (mg): 344.2
Sodium (mg): 494
Protein (gm): 19.5
Carbohydrate (gm): 13.6

1. Sauté vegetables in oil in large skillet 5 minutes; add water and simmer, covered, over medium heat until vegetables are tender and liquid is absorbed, about 5 minutes.

2. Beat together eggs and milk; mix in cheese, salt, and pepper. Pour mixture over vegetables and cook without stirring, uncovered, over medium-low heat until egg is set and lightly browned on bottom, about 10 minutes.

3. Broil frittata 6 inches from heat source until cooked on top, 3 to 4 minutes; invert frittata onto serving plate.

4. Sprinkle bread with Parmesan cheese; broil 6 inches from heat source until browned, 2 to 3 minutes. Serve with frittata.

Vegetable Hash and Eggs

4 servings

1 cup chopped red, *or* green, bell pepper
¼ cup chopped green onions and tops
1–2 tablespoons olive, *or* canola, oil
2 cups cubed, cooked unpeeled Idaho potatoes
1 cup cubed zucchini
¾ cup halved cherry tomatoes
½–1 teaspoon dried thyme leaves
Salt and pepper, to taste
4 eggs

Per Serving
Net Carbohydrate (gm): 17.9
Calories: 192
Fat (gm): 8.7
Saturated fat (gm): 2.1
Cholesterol (mg): 212.5
Sodium (mg): 71
Protein (gm): 8.5
Carbohydrate (gm): 20.8

1. Sauté bell pepper and onions in oil in large skillet 3 to 4 minutes; add potatoes and zucchini and cook over medium heat until potatoes are browned and zucchini is tender, stirring frequently. Add tomatoes and thyme; cook 2 to 3 minutes longer. Season to taste with salt and pepper.

2. Move hash to side of skillet; add eggs to center of skillet. Cook, covered, over low heat until eggs are cooked, 3 to 4 minutes; season to taste with salt and pepper. Serve from skillet, or transfer to serving platter.

Sweet Potato and Ham Hash with Poached Eggs

4 servings

¼ cup sliced green onions and tops
½ cup chopped red bell pepper
1–2 tablespoons canola oil
2 cups cubed, cooked sweet potatoes
8 ounces cubed lean smoked ham
1 teaspoon dried rosemary leaves
½ teaspoon dried thyme leaves
Salt and pepper, to taste
4 poached, *or* fried, eggs

Per Serving
Net Carbohydrate (gm): 16.1
Calories: 280
Fat (gm): 13.4
Saturated fat (gm): 3.5
Cholesterol (mg): 244.4
Sodium (mg): 968
Protein (gm): 20.3
Carbohydrate (gm): 18.9

1. Sauté green onions and bell pepper in oil in large skillet 2 to 3 minutes. Add sweet potatoes, ham, and herbs; cook over medium heat until potatoes and ham are lightly browned. Season to taste with salt and pepper. Cook, uncovered, until vegetables are browned and tender, about 10 minutes. Spoon hash onto plates; top each serving with an egg.

Rajas with Eggs

4 servings

1½ cups sliced poblano chilies, *or* green bell peppers
½ cup sliced onion
2 tablespoons canola oil
2 cups cubed, peeled and cooked Idaho potatoes
Salt and pepper, to taste
4 fried, *or* poached, eggs
½ cup mild, *or* hot, salsa

Per Serving
Net Carbohydrate (gm): 28.4
Calories: 285
Fat (gm): 14.4
Saturated fat (gm): 2.5
Cholesterol (mg): 211.1
Sodium (mg): 408
Protein (gm): 10.1
Carbohydrate (gm): 31.1

1. Sauté chilies and onion in oil in large skillet until softened, about 5 minutes; add potatoes and cook over medium heat until onion and potatoes are browned, 5 to 8 minutes. Season to taste with salt and pepper. Top each serving with an egg; serve with salsa.

Huevos Rancheros

6 servings

Vegetable cooking spray
6 corn tortillas (6-inch)
6–12 eggs, fried
Salt and pepper, to taste
Chili-Tomato Sauce (recipe follows)

Per Serving
Net Carbohydrate (gm): 26.5
Calories: 232
Fat (gm): 7.8
Saturated fat (gm): 2
Cholesterol (mg): 211.1
Sodium (mg): 1275
Protein (gm): 9.7
Carbohydrate (gm): 32.6

1. Spray both sides of tortillas lightly with cooking spray; cook in large skillet over medium heat until browned, about 1 minute on each side. Arrange tortillas on serving plates and top with eggs. Season to taste with salt and pepper. Spoon Chili-Tomato Sauce over.

Chili-Tomato Sauce

makes about 2 cups

2 cups cubed tomatoes
⅓ cup finely chopped onion
1 serrano, *or* jalapeño, chili, seeds and veins discarded, minced
1 clove garlic, minced
1–2 teaspoons light olive oil
Salt, to taste

1. Process tomatoes in food processor or blender until almost smooth.

2. Sauté onion, chili, and garlic in oil in medium skillet until tender, 3 to 4 minutes. Add tomatoes and heat to boiling; cook over medium to medium-high heat until mixture thickens to a medium sauce consistency, 5 to 8 minutes. Season to taste with salt; serve warm.

Eggs Scrambled with Crisp Tortilla Strips

6 servings

3 corn tortillas (6-inch), cut into 2 x ½-inch strips
Vegetable cooking spray
6 eggs
¼ cup reduced-fat milk
Salt and pepper, to taste
6 tablespoons crumbled Mexican white cheese, *or*
    farmer's cheese
6 tablespoons finely chopped cilantro
¾ cup mild, *or* hot, salsa

Per Serving
Net Carbohydrate (gm): 8.9
Calories: 149
Fat (gm): 8
Saturated fat (gm): 3.3
Cholesterol (mg): 222
Sodium (mg): 402
Protein (gm): 9.1
Carbohydrate (gm): 9.6

1. Spray tortilla strips lightly with cooking spray; cook in skillet over medium to medium-high heat until browned and crisp.

2. Beat eggs and milk until foamy; pour over tortilla strips in skillet. Cook over medium to medium-low heat until eggs are cooked, stirring occasionally. Season to taste with salt and pepper; sprinkle with cheese and cilantro. Serve with salsa.

Mexican Scrambled Eggs with Chorizo

6 servings

1 cup chopped tomato
½ cup sliced green onions and tops
2–3 teaspoons finely chopped serrano, *or* jalapeño, chilies
2 small cloves garlic, minced
4 ounces chorizo, finely chopped
1 tablespoon olive oil
6–8 eggs
3 tablespoons reduced-fat milk
Salt and pepper, to taste
¾ cup mild, *or* hot, salsa
6 corn, *or* flour, tortillas (6 inch)

Per Serving
Net Carbohydrate (gm): 15.9
Calories: 263
Fat (gm): 15.4
Saturated fat (gm): 4.8
Cholesterol (mg): 229.7
Sodium (mg): 566
Protein (gm): 13
Carbohydrate (gm): 17.8

1. Sauté tomato, green onions, chilies, garlic, and chorizo in oil in large skillet until vegetables are tender and chorizo is cooked, about 5 minutes.

2. Beat together eggs and milk until foamy; add to skillet and cook over medium to medium-low heat until eggs are cooked, stirring occasionally; season to taste with salt and pepper. Serve with salsa and tortillas.

Pinto Bean Cheesecake with Chili Tomato Sauce

10 servings

4 flour tortillas (6 inch)
3 packages (8 ounces each) cream cheese, room temperature
6 eggs
1 can (15 ounces) pinto beans, rinsed, drained
½ jalapeño chili, finely chopped
2 tablespoons finely chopped onion
2 cloves garlic, minced
2 teaspoons Worcestershire sauce
2 teaspoons ground cumin
½ teaspoon dried oregano leaves
½ teaspoon chili powder
½ teaspoon salt
½ teaspoon cayenne pepper
Chili-Tomato Sauce (see p. 9)

Per Serving
Net Carbohydrate (gm): 18.2
Calories: 292
Fat (gm): 15.6
Saturated fat (gm): 8.8
Cholesterol (mg): 159.4
Sodium (mg): 669
Protein (gm): 13.9
Carbohydrate (gm): 21.4

1. Lightly grease 9-inch springform pan and line with overlapping tortillas.

2. Beat cream cheese in large bowl until fluffy; beat in eggs. Mix in remaining ingredients, except Chili-Tomato Sauce, and pour into pan.

Bake at 300 degrees until center is set and sharp knife inserted halfway between center and edge of cheesecake comes out almost clean, 1¾ to 2 hours. Cool to room temperature on wire rack. Refrigerate overnight.

3. Cook wedges of cheesecake in greased skillet over medium-low heat until browned on both sides. Serve with Chili-Tomato Sauce.

Dutch Pancake with Berries

6 servings

4 eggs
¾ cup reduced-fat milk
¾ cup whole wheat pastry flour
1 tablespoon brown sugar
¼ teaspoon salt
2 tablespoons butter
1 cup halved small strawberries
½ cup raspberries
½ cup blueberries
Maple-Flavored Syrup (recipe follows)

Per Serving
Net Carbohydrate (gm): 22.9
Calories: 225
Fat (gm): 10.5
Saturated fat (gm): 5.3
Cholesterol (mg): 160.5
Sodium (mg): 220
Protein (gm): 7.7
Carbohydrate (gm): 26.3

1. Whisk all ingredients, except butter, berries, and Maple-Flavored Syrup, in large bowl until almost smooth (batter will be slightly lumpy).

2. Melt butter in large skillet with ovenproof handle until bubbly; pour in batter. Bake, uncovered, at 425 degrees until pancake is puffed and browned, 20 to 25 minutes (do not open door during first 15 minutes).

3. Cut pancake into 6 wedges and place on serving plates. Spoon combined berries over and serve with Maple-Flavored Syrup.

Maple-Flavored Syrup

makes 1 cup

1 cup apple juice
2½ teaspoons cornstarch
1¾ teaspoons Equal for Recipes®, *or* 6 packets Equal®
1 tablespoon butter
½–¾ teaspoon maple extract

1. Mix apple juice, cornstarch, and Equal® in small saucepan; heat to boiling. Boil, stirring, until thickened, about 1 minute. Add butter and maple extract, stirring until butter is melted. Serve warm; refrigerate remaining syrup.

Variation:

Ham 'n Egg Pancake Puff—Make recipe as above, deleting berries and Maple-Flavored Syrup. Sauté 1 pound cubed smoked ham and ¼ cup sliced green onions and tops in 1 tablespoon canola oil in large skillet until lightly browned. Add 6 to 9 beaten eggs to skillet and cook over medium heat, stirring occasionally, until cooked. Serve over warm pancake wedges.

Buttermilk Buckwheat Pancakes

4 servings

1 cup reduced-fat buttermilk
1 egg
1 tablespoon canola oil
½ cup whole wheat pastry flour
⅓ cup buckwheat flour
1 tablespoon packed light brown sugar
1 teaspoon baking powder
½ teaspoon baking soda
½ teaspoon salt
1 teaspoon grated orange rind
½–1 cup sugar-free pancake syrup, *or* Maple-Flavored Syrup (see p. 11), warm

Per Serving
Net Carbohydrate (gm): 29.4
Calories: 204
Fat (gm): 6.1
Saturated fat (gm): 1.2
Cholesterol (mg): 55.7
Sodium (mg): 694
Protein (gm): 7.9
Carbohydrate (gm): 32.8

1. Mix buttermilk, egg, and oil in medium bowl; add remaining ingredients, except pancake syrup, and beat until almost smooth.

2. Pour batter into lightly greased large skillet, using about ¼ cup batter for each pancake. Cook over medium heat until bubbles form in pancakes and they are browned on the bottoms, 3 to 5 minutes. Turn pancakes; cook until browned on other side, 3 to 5 minutes.

3. Serve pancakes with syrup.

Fried Cornmeal Mush

4 servings

4 cups water
1 cup yellow cornmeal
¼ teaspoon salt
1–2 tablespoons butter
½–1 cup sugar-free pancake syrup

Per Serving
Net Carbohydrate (gm): 24.7
Calories: 147
Fat (gm): 4.1
Saturated fat (gm): 2
Cholesterol (mg): 8.2
Sodium (mg): 229
Protein (gm): 2.5
Carbohydrate (gm): 27

1. Heat water to boiling in large saucepan; gradually stir in cornmeal and salt. Reduce heat and simmer, stirring frequently, until mixture is thickened, about 5 minutes. Pour into greased loaf pan, 7 x 4 inches, and cool. Refrigerate until firm, 3 to 4 hours or overnight.

2. Remove cornmeal from loaf pan and cut into 8 slices. Melt butter in large skillet; add cornmeal slices and cook over medium heat until browned, 3 to 4 minutes on each side. Serve with syrup.

Variation:

Blueberry Cornmeal Mush—Make recipe as above, adding 1 tablespoon grated orange rind to cornmeal mixture and omitting syrup. Sprinkle browned cornmeal mush slices with powdered sugar; spoon ⅓ cup blueberries over each serving.

Polenta Spoon Bread

8 servings

2 tablespoons minced garlic
1 medium red bell pepper, chopped
1 tablespoon olive oil
3 egg yolks
2½ cups reduced-fat milk
1 cup polenta, *or* yellow cornmeal
1½ teaspoons salt
1 teaspoon Italian seasoning
⅛–¼ teaspoon red pepper flakes
2 tablespoons melted butter
¼ cup (1 ounce) grated Parmesan cheese
3 egg whites, beaten to stiff peaks

Per Serving
Net Carbohydrate (gm): 15.8
Calories: 182
Fat (gm): 9.5
Saturated fat (gm): 4.2
Cholesterol (mg): 96
Sodium (mg): 581
Protein (gm): 7.5
Carbohydrate (gm): 17.2

1. Sauté garlic and bell pepper in oil in small skillet until tender, 2 to 3 minutes. Cool.

2. Whisk egg yolks and milk until smooth in medium saucepan; heat to boiling, whisking constantly. Whisk in polenta and salt gradually; reduce heat to medium and whisk in bell pepper mixture, Italian seasoning, and pepper flakes. Simmer 2 minutes, stirring constantly with wooden spoon. Remove from heat; stir in butter and cheese.

3. Fold egg whites into polenta mixture; pour into greased 2-quart soufflé dish or casserole. Bake at 375 degrees until puffed and golden, about 30 minutes. Delicious served with ham or bacon slices.

Granola Bread

1 loaf (20 servings)

1 package active dry yeast
⅓ cup warm water (110–115 degrees)
1 tablespoon light brown sugar
⅔ cup buttermilk
1¾–2¼ cups whole wheat pastry flour, divided
½ cup soy flour
1 teaspoon baking powder
½ teaspoon salt
1 tablespoon butter, softened
¾ cup low-fat granola
Buttermilk, for glaze

Per Serving
Net Carbohydrate (gm): 11.1
Calories: 74
Fat (gm): 1.6
Saturated fat (gm): 0.5
Cholesterol (mg): 2
Sodium (mg): 109
Protein (gm): 3
Carbohydrate (gm): 13

1. Mix yeast, warm water, and brown sugar in large mixer bowl; let stand 5 minutes. Add buttermilk, 1¾ cups whole wheat flour, soy flour, baking powder, salt, and butter, mixing on low speed until smooth. Mix in granola and enough remaining whole wheat flour to make smooth dough (dough will be slightly sticky).

2. Knead dough on floured surface until smooth and elastic, about 5 minutes. Roll into a rectangle 18 x 10 inches. Roll up, beginning at short end; press each end to seal. Place, seam side down, in greased 9 x 5-inch loaf pan. Let rise, covered, in warm place until double in size, about 1 hour.

3. Brush top of loaf with buttermilk. Bake at 375 degrees until loaf is golden and sounds hollow when tapped, 40 to 45 minutes. Remove from pan and cool on wire rack.

English Muffin Bread

1 loaf (16 servings)

1–2 teaspoons yellow cornmeal
2–2½ cups whole wheat pastry flour, divided
½ cup quick-cooking oats
1 package active dry yeast
1 teaspoon salt
1¼ cups reduced-fat milk
1 tablespoon honey
¼ teaspoon baking soda

Per Serving
Net Carbohydrate (gm): 12.8
Calories: 76
Fat (gm): 0.9
Saturated fat (gm): 0.3
Cholesterol (mg): 1.5
Sodium (mg): 176
Protein (gm): 3.3
Carbohydrate (gm): 15

1. Sprinkle greased 8 x 4 x 2-inch loaf pan with cornmeal.

2. Combine 1½ cups flour, oats, yeast, and salt in large bowl. Heat milk and honey in small saucepan until warm (110–120 degrees); stir in baking soda. Add milk mixture to flour mixture, mixing until smooth. Stir in enough remaining 1 cup flour to make a thick batter. Pour into prepared pan. Let rise, covered, in warm place until double in size, 45 to 60 minutes.

3. Bake at 400 degrees until bread is golden and sounds hollow when tapped, 25 to 30 minutes. Remove from pan immediately and cool on wire rack.

Variation:

Raisin Bread—Do not coat loaf pan with cornmeal. Stir 1 teaspoon cinnamon and 4 cups chopped raisins into batter; pour into greased 9 x 4 x 2-inch loaf pan and bake as above.

Vinegar Biscuits

12 servings (1 each)

¾ cup reduced-fat milk
¼ cup cider vinegar
1¾ cups whole wheat pastry flour
¼ cup soy flour
1½ teaspoons baking soda
1 teaspoon cream of tartar
½ teaspoon salt
3 tablespoons vegetable shortening, melted

Per Serving
Net Carbohydrate (gm): 12.2
Calories: 104
Fat (gm): 4
Saturated fat (gm): 1
Cholesterol (mg): 1.2
Sodium (mg): 263
Protein (gm): 3.5
Carbohydrate (gm): 14.5

1. Mix milk and vinegar in glass measure. Combine flours, baking soda, cream of tartar, and salt in medium bowl; add milk mixture and shortening, mixing until blended.

2. Knead dough on generously floured surface 1 to 2 minutes. Pat dough into ½ inch thickness; cut into 12 biscuits with 3-inch-round cutter. Bake on greased cookie sheet at 425 degrees until golden, 10 to 12 minutes.

Variation:

Parmesan-Chive Biscuits—Stir 3 to 4 tablespoons finely chopped chives into dough in Step 1. Lightly brush tops of biscuits with melted butter and sprinkle generously with grated Parmesan cheese. Bake as above.

Cheese-Caraway Scones

6 servings (1 each)

1 cup whole wheat pastry flour
¼ cup yellow cornmeal
1½ teaspoons baking powder
¼ teaspoon salt
1 tablespoon butter, softened
1 tablespoon canola oil
¼ cup (1 ounce) shredded Cheddar cheese
1 egg, lightly beaten
⅓ cup reduced-fat milk
2 teaspoons caraway seeds
Paprika

Per Serving
Net Carbohydrate (gm): 16.8
Calories: 165
Fat (gm): 7.6
Saturated fat (gm): 2.9
Cholesterol (mg): 46.9
Sodium (mg): 289
Protein (gm): 6
Carbohydrate (gm): 19.9

1. Combine flour, cornmeal, baking powder, and salt in large bowl; stir in butter, oil, and cheese, mixing until mixture is crumbly. Stir in combined egg and milk, mixing until blended; mix in caraway seeds.

2. Knead dough into ball on floured board. Roll out into 7-inch circle and cut into 8 wedges. Dust top of each wedge with a little paprika. Arrange wedges in greased 9-inch pie pan. Bake at 375 degrees until scones are browned, 15 to 20 minutes.

Variation:

Bacon-Chive Scones—Make recipe as above, substituting smoked mozzarella cheese for the Cheddar cheese, and adding ¼ cup crumbled cooked bacon and 2 tablespoons chopped chives to the dough in Step 1.

Cornmeal and Pimiento Muffins

12 servings (1 muffin each)

¾ cup reduced-fat milk
¼ cup plain yogurt
3 tablespoons maple syrup
2 eggs
1 cup whole wheat pastry flour
¾ cup yellow cornmeal
½ teaspoon baking soda
½ teaspoon salt
¼ cup well drained, chopped pimiento

Per Serving
Net Carbohydrate (gm): 16
Calories: 99
Fat (gm): 1.7
Saturated fat (gm): 0.6
Cholesterol (mg): 36.9
Sodium (mg): 175
Protein (gm): 3.8
Carbohydrate (gm): 17.9

1. Combine milk, yogurt, maple syrup, and eggs in large bowl, blending well. Stir in combined flour, cornmeal, baking soda, and salt, mixing just until blended; mix in pimiento.

2. Spoon batter into greased muffin tins. Bake at 375 degrees until muffins are golden and toothpick inserted in center comes out clean, 15 to 20 minutes. Cool in tins 5 minutes; invert on wire rack and cool.

Banana Bran Muffins

24 servings (1 muffin each)

1½ cups whole wheat pastry flour
1½ cups unprocessed bran
2 teaspoons baking soda
2 teaspoons ground cinnamon
1 teaspoon ground nutmeg
½ teaspoon salt
1 egg
1 egg white
½ cup honey
½ cup buttermilk
½ cup water
1 small ripe banana, mashed
1 teaspoon vanilla extract
Grated rind of 1 orange, optional

Per Serving
Net Carbohydrate (gm): 12.5
Calories: 66
Fat (gm): 0.6
Saturated fat (gm): 0.2
Cholesterol (mg): 9.1
Sodium (mg): 164
Protein (gm): 2.3
Carbohydrate (gm): 15.2

1. Combine flour, bran, baking soda, cinnamon, nutmeg, and salt in medium bowl; stir in combined remaining ingredients, mixing until just blended.

2. Pour batter into greased muffin tins, filling half full. Bake at 400 degrees until muffins are browned and toothpick inserted in center comes out clean, about 15 minutes. Cool in tins 5 minutes; invert and cool on wire racks.

Brown Rice Muffins

12 servings (1 each)

1 cup reduced-fat milk
4 tablespoons butter, melted
2 eggs, beaten
1 cup cooked brown rice
1½ cups whole wheat pastry flour
3 tablespoons baking powder
1 tablespoon packed light brown sugar
½ teaspoon salt

Per Serving
Net Carbohydrate (gm): 15.5
Calories: 133
Fat (gm): 5.7
Saturated fat (gm): 3.1
Cholesterol (mg): 48
Sodium (mg): 527
Protein (gm): 4.2
Carbohydrate (gm): 17.8

1. Mix milk, butter, eggs, and rice in large bowl. Add combined flour, baking powder, brown sugar, and salt, mixing just until dry ingredients are moistened.

2. Spoon batter into 12 greased muffin cups. Bake at 400 degrees until muffins are browned, 20 to 25 minutes. Remove from pans and cool on wire racks.

High-Energy Muffins

12 servings (1 muffin each)

1 can (15 ounces) pinto beans, rinsed, drained
¼ cup reduced-fat milk
2 tablespoons butter, softened
⅓ cup packed light brown sugar
1 egg
1 egg white
1 teaspoon vanilla
¾ cup whole wheat pastry flour
½ teaspoon baking soda
½ teaspoon salt
¾ teaspoon ground cinnamon
¼ cup raisins

Per Serving
Net Carbohydrate (gm): 17.2
Calories: 119
Fat (gm): 3
Saturated fat (gm): 1.5
Cholesterol (mg): 23.6
Sodium (mg): 290
Protein (gm): 3.9
Carbohydrate (gm): 20

1. Process beans and milk in food processor until mixture is smooth. Beat butter, brown sugar, eggs, and vanilla in medium bowl until smooth; beat in bean mixture. Add combined flour, baking soda, salt, and cinnamon, mixing just until blended. Mix in raisins.

2. Spoon mixture into 12 greased muffin cups. Bake at 375 degrees until toothpicks inserted in centers come out clean, 20 to 25 minutes. Cool muffins in pans 5 minutes; remove and cool on wire racks.

Bacon and Egg Breakfast Pizza

6 servings

1 cup pizza sauce
Whole Wheat Pizza Dough (see p. 445)
½ cup sliced green bell pepper
¼ cup thinly sliced onion
1 cup (4 ounces) mozzarella cheese
2 eggs
6 slices bacon, fried crisp, crumbled

Per Serving
Net Carbohydrate (gm): 18
Calories: 219
Fat (gm): 9.4
Saturated fat (gm): 3.9
Cholesterol (mg): 88.5
Sodium (mg): 355
Protein (gm): 13.1
Carbohydrate (gm): 21.7

1. Spread pizza sauce evenly over pizza dough; sprinkle with green pepper, onion, and cheese. Bake at 425 until pizza is lightly browned, 15 to 20 minutes.

2. Remove pizza from oven. Break eggs into center of pizza; stir with a fork and quickly spread over pizza. Sprinkle with bacon. Return to oven and bake until eggs are cooked, 2 to 3 minutes.

TWO

Soups, Chowders, and Chilis

Quick Chicken Stock

makes about 2 quarts

1 pound boneless, skinless chicken breast, cubed
1 teaspoon olive oil
2½ quarts water
2 ribs celery, with leaves, halved
4 large onions, with skins, quartered
4 medium carrots, halved
1 small turnip, quartered
2 bay leaves
6 cloves garlic
8 black peppercorns
10 fresh, *or* 2 teaspoons dried, sage leaves
1 sprig thyme

Per Serving
Net Carbohydrate (gm): 1.2
Calories: 15
Fat (gm): 0.7
Saturated fat (gm): 0.1
Cholesterol (mg): 3.1
Sodium (mg): 6
Protein (gm): 1.3
Carbohydrate (gm): 1.2

1. Sauté chicken in oil in large saucepan until well-browned, about 10 minutes. Add remaining ingredients and heat to boiling; reduce heat and simmer, covered, 1 hour, skimming any foam from surface.

2. Strain stock through double layer of cheesecloth, discarding meat and vegetables. Cool before refrigerating. Remove congealed fat from surface of stock.

Rich Chicken Stock

makes about 4 quarts

1 chicken (about 4 pounds), cut up
2 pounds chicken necks and wings
1 veal knuckle, cracked, optional
2 medium onions, studded with several whole cloves
6 medium carrots, quartered
2 medium leeks, white parts only, cut into 1-inch pieces
3 ribs celery, including leaves, cut into 1-inch pieces
½ teaspoon dried thyme leaves
½ teaspoon dried tarragon leaves
1 clove garlic, peeled
10 black peppercorns
6 sprigs parsley
5 quarts water
1 cup dry white wine, optional

Per Serving
Net Carbohydrate (gm): 0.8
Calories: 39
Fat (gm): 0.8
Saturated fat (gm): 0.2
Cholesterol (mg): 1
Sodium (mg): 36
Protein (gm): 4.9
Carbohydrate (gm): 0.8

1. Combine all ingredients in stockpot or large Dutch oven and heat to boiling. Reduce heat and simmer, covered, 3 to 4 hours, skimming any foam from surface.

2. Strain stock through double layer of cheesecloth, discarding bones, meat, and vegetables. Cool before refrigerating. Remove congealed fat from surface of stock.

Variation:

Roasted Chicken Stock—Place chicken, chicken bones, veal knuckle, and vegetables in large roasting pan. Roast at 425 degrees until well browned, about 30 minutes. Transfer to stockpot and complete recipe as above.

Beef Stock

makes about 3½ quarts

2 pounds beef short ribs, *or* other meaty beef bones
2 pounds beef marrow bones, cut into pieces
1 pound cubed beef chuck, fat trimmed
1 large onion, quartered
1 clove garlic, peeled
4 medium carrots, quartered
10 black peppercorns
1 bay leaf
1 teaspoon dried thyme leaves
3 sprigs parsley
3 ribs celery, quartered
4 quarts water
1 cup dry red wine, optional

Per Serving
Net Carbohydrate (gm): 1.3
Calories: 16
Fat (gm): 0.5
Saturated fat (gm): 0.3
Cholesterol (mg): 3
Sodium (mg): 42
Protein (gm): 2.7
Carbohydrate (gm): 0.6

1. Combine all ingredients in stockpot or large Dutch oven and heat to boiling. Reduce heat and simmer, covered, 5 to 6 hours, skimming any foam from surface.

2. Strain stock through double layer of cheesecloth, discarding bones, meat, and vegetables. Cool before refrigerating. Remove congealed fat from surface of stock.

Variation:

Brown Beef Stock—Place bones and meat in large roasting pan. Roast at 425 degrees until well browned, about 45 minutes. Transfer to stockpot and complete recipe as above.

Fish Stock

makes about 1½ quarts

2–3 pounds fish bones from non-oily fish such as
    haddock, whitefish, flounder
1 large onion, sliced
1 carrot, sliced
1 rib celery, sliced
2 bay leaves
8 black peppercorns
½ teaspoon salt
½ teaspoon white pepper
2 quarts water
1 cup dry white wine, optional

Per Serving
Net Carbohydrate (gm): 0.3
Calories: 17
Fat (gm): 0.1
Saturated fat (gm): 0
Cholesterol (mg): 0
Sodium (mg): 191
Protein (gm): 2.8
Carbohydrate (gm): 0.3

1. Combine all ingredients in large saucepan and heat to boiling. Reduce heat and simmer 30 minutes, skimming foam from surface.

2. Strain through double layer of cheesecloth, discarding bones and vegetables. Cool before refrigerating.

Basic Vegetable Stock

makes about 2 quarts

1 large onion, coarsely chopped
1 large leek, white part only, cut into 1-inch pieces
1 large carrot, cut into 1-inch pieces
1 rib celery, cut into 1-inch pieces
½ teaspoon canola oil
2 quarts water
1 cup dry white wine, *or* water
1 quart mixed chopped vegetables (broccoli, green beans, cabbage,
    tomatoes, summer or winter squash, bell peppers, mushrooms, etc.)
6 parsley sprigs
1 bay leaf
4 whole allspice
1 tablespoon black peppercorns
2 teaspoons bouquet garni

Per Serving
Net Carbohydrate (gm): 1.8
Calories: 12
Fat (gm): 0.4
Saturated fat (gm): 0
Cholesterol (mg): 0
Sodium (mg): 12
Protein (gm): 0.4
Carbohydrate (gm): 1.8

1. Sauté onion, leek, carrot, and celery in oil in stockpot or large Dutch oven, 5 minutes. Add water, wine, and chopped vegetables. Tie herbs in cheesecloth bag and add to pot. Heat to boiling; reduce heat and simmer, covered, 1½ to 2 hours.

2. Strain stock, pressing lightly on vegetables to extract all juices; discard solids. Cool before refrigerating or freezing.

Asparagus Lemon Soup

6 servings (about ¾ cup each)

1 quart Quick, *or* Rich, Chicken Stock (see p. 20), *or*
    canned chicken broth
⅓ cup orzo, *or* other small soup pasta
3 cups thinly sliced asparagus
2 eggs, lightly beaten
¼ cup lemon juice
¼ cup sliced green onions and tops
Salt and pepper, to taste

Per Serving
Net Carbohydrate (gm): 10.2
Calories: 87
Fat (gm): 2.4
Saturated fat (gm): 0.6
Cholesterol (mg): 72.9
Sodium (mg): 28
Protein (gm): 5.6
Carbohydrate (gm): 11.8

1. Heat stock to boiling in large saucepan. Add orzo; reduce heat and simmer 5 minutes. Stir in asparagus and heat to boiling. Reduce heat and simmer until asparagus and orzo are tender, about 7 minutes.

2. Heat soup to boiling. Rapidly stir in eggs and cook 1 minute. Remove from heat. Add lemon juice and green onions; season to taste with salt and pepper.

Spinach Soup

10 servings (about 1 cup each)

½ cup thinly sliced leek (white part only)
½ cup thinly sliced carrot
½ cup thinly sliced celery
1 tablespoon olive oil
2 quarts Quick, *or* Rich, Chicken Stock (see p. 20), *or* canned chicken broth
2 pounds fresh, *or* frozen thawed, spinach
Salt and pepper, to taste
½ cup grated Parmesan cheese

Per Serving
Net Carbohydrate (gm): 3.4
Calories: 71
Fat (gm): 3.5
Saturated fat (gm): 1.1
Cholesterol (mg): 5.6
Sodium (mg): 158
Protein (gm): 5.5
Carbohydrate (gm): 6.3

1. Sauté leek, carrot, and celery in oil in large saucepan until tender. Add stock and heat to boiling. Add spinach and cook, uncovered, for 2 minutes until spinach wilts. Process in food processor or blender until smooth. Return soup to saucepan and heat until hot; season to taste with salt and pepper. Ladle soup into bowls; sprinkle with cheese.

Mushroom Soup

6 servings (about 1⅓ cups each)

1 ounce dried porcini mushrooms
1 cup boiling water
2 cups sliced white mushrooms
½ cup thinly sliced onion
1½ tablespoons minced garlic
2 teaspoons butter
2 teaspoons flour
1 quart Quick, *or* Rich, Chicken Stock (see p. 20), *or* canned chicken broth
⅓ cup dry white wine, *or* chicken broth
1 tablespoon chopped fresh, *or* 1 teaspoon dried, rosemary leaves
2–3 tablespoons lemon juice
½ cup chopped parsley
Salt and pepper, to taste

Per Serving
Net Carbohydrate (gm): 6.8
Calories: 66
Fat (gm): 2.1
Saturated fat (gm): 1
Cholesterol (mg): 5.7
Sodium (mg): 24
Protein (gm): 2.8
Carbohydrate (gm): 7.9

1. Soak porcini in boiling water in small bowl until softened, about 20 minutes. Carefully remove porcini with slotted spoon. Strain liquid through double layer of cheesecloth and reserve. Pick through porcini carefully, rinsing if necessary to remove grit. Chop coarsely.

2. Sauté white mushrooms, onion, and garlic in butter in large saucepan until lightly browned, about 5 minutes. Sprinkle with flour and cook 1 minute. Stir in stock, wine, rosemary, porcini, and 2 tablespoons reserved porcini liquid; heat to boiling. Reduce heat and simmer until mushrooms are tender, about 10 minutes.

3. Stir in lemon juice and parsley; season to taste with salt and pepper.

Mushroom Soup Danielle

4 servings

1 pound mushrooms
1 tablespoon butter
1½ tablespoons all-purpose flour
1 quart Beef Stock (see p. 21), *or* canned beef broth
1 tablespoon light soy sauce
2 tablespoons dry sherry
1 teaspoon lemon juice
Salt and pepper, to taste
3 tablespoons chopped chives

Per Serving
Net Carbohydrate (gm): 8
Calories: 89
Fat (gm): 3.5
Saturated fat (gm): 2
Cholesterol (mg): 8.5
Sodium (mg): 166
Protein (gm): 4.3
Carbohydrate (gm): 9.5

1. Slice 4 large mushroom caps and reserve. Chop up remaining mushrooms and stems. Sauté chopped mushrooms in butter in large saucepan until mushrooms are tender and juices almost evaporated, about 8 minutes. Sprinkle with flour and cook 1 minute. Add stock and soy sauce; heat to boiling. Reduce heat and simmer 5 minutes.

2. Process in blender or food processor until smooth. Return to saucepan and heat to simmering. Add sliced mushroom caps to soup; simmer 5 minutes. Stir in sherry and lemon juice. Season to taste with salt and pepper; sprinkle with chives.

Celery Soup with Fennel

6 servings

½ cup boiling water
1 teaspoon fennel seeds
3 cups sliced celery
½ cup sliced green onions and tops
1 small garlic clove, minced
1 tablespoon olive oil
1 quart Quick, *or* Rich, Chicken Stock (see p. 20), *or* canned chicken broth
2½ tablespoons uncooked quick-cooking brown rice
3 tablespoons finely chopped fresh chives
Salt and white pepper, to taste
Finely chopped chives, as garnish
Plain yogurt, as garnish

Per Serving
Net Carbohydrate (gm): 6.7
Calories: 66
Fat (gm): 3
Saturated fat (gm): 0.4
Cholesterol (mg): 2.1
Sodium (mg): 60
Protein (gm): 2.2
Carbohydrate (gm): 8.6

1. Pour boiling water over fennel seeds in small bowl; reserve.

2. Sauté celery, onions, and garlic in oil in large saucepan until onions are tender, about 4 minutes. Add stock, rice, and chives; heat to boiling. Reduce heat and simmer, covered, until celery and rice are tender, about 20 minutes.

3. Process in blender or food processor until smooth.

4. Drain fennel seeds stirring liquid into soup; discard seeds. Season to taste with salt and white pepper. Refrigerate until chilled. Garnish with chives and yogurt.

Celery-Tomato Soup

8 servings

4 cups thinly sliced celery
2 cups finely chopped onions
1 tablespoon olive oil
1 can (28 ounces) whole tomatoes, undrained, pureed
3 cups reduced-sodium fat-free chicken, *or* vegetable, broth
½ cup dry white wine, *or* chicken broth
¼ cup finely chopped parsley
1 teaspoon dried marjoram leaves
¼ teaspoon dried thyme leaves
¼ teaspoon dried tarragon leaves
1 teaspoon sugar
Salt and pepper, to taste

Per Serving
Net Carbohydrate (gm): 7.1
Calories: 83.8
Fat (gm): 2.5
Saturated fat (gm): 0.3
Cholesterol (mg): 9.4
Sodium (mg): 296
Protein (gm): 4.4
Carbohydrate (gm): 9.7

1. Sauté celery and onion in oil in large saucepan until onion is tender, about 8 minutes. Add remaining ingredients, except salt and pepper. Heat to boiling; reduce heat and simmer, covered, 10 minutes or until celery is tender. Season to taste with salt and pepper.

Herbed Tomato Soup

6 servings (about 1½ cups each)

4 green onions and tops, sliced
4 cloves garlic, minced
1 teaspoon olive oil
10 cups chopped, peeled and seeded tomatoes, divided
2½ cups Quick, *or* Rich, Chicken Stock (see p. 20), *or* canned chicken broth
½ cup dry white wine, *or* chicken broth
¼ cup chopped fresh, *or* 1½ teaspoons dried, basil leaves
1 bay leaf
2 teaspoons sugar
¼ cup chopped parsley
Salt and pepper, to taste

Per Serving
Net Carbohydrate (gm): 9.9
Calories: 79
Fat (gm): 1.7
Saturated fat (gm): 0.2
Cholesterol (mg): 1.3
Sodium (mg): 24
Protein (gm): 2.6
Carbohydrate (gm): 12.5

1. Sauté green onions and garlic in oil in large saucepan until transparent, about 2 minutes. Reserve 2 cups tomatoes; process remaining tomatoes in food processor or blender until smooth; stir into saucepan and cook 5 minutes. Stir in stock, wine, basil, bay leaf, and sugar. Heat to boiling; reduce heat and simmer, uncovered, 30 minutes.

2. Stir in reserved 2 cups tomatoes; heat to boiling. Reduce heat and simmer, uncovered, 5 minutes. Stir in parsley; discard bay leaf, and season to taste with salt and pepper.

Note: To peel tomatoes, place them, a few at a time, in a pan of boiling water for about 30 seconds. Remove and slip off skins. Halve the tomatoes and remove seeds.

Easy Gazpacho

4 servings

2 cans (14½ ounces each) plum tomatoes, undrained
1 small clove garlic, minced
2 tablespoons chopped green onions and tops, *or* chives
1 cup diced, peeled and seeded cucumber
½ cup chopped celery
½ cup diced green bell pepper
2 tablespoons chopped parsley
2–3 drops hot pepper sauce
1–2 teaspoons red wine vinegar
Salt and pepper, to taste

Per Serving
Net Carbohydrate (gm): 9.7
Calories: 57
Fat (gm): 0.4
Saturated fat (gm): 0.1
Cholesterol (mg): 0
Sodium (mg): 316
Protein (gm): 2.8
Carbohydrate (gm): 13

1. Process tomatoes and liquid with garlic in blender or food processor until smooth. Transfer to mixing bowl and add remaining ingredients except salt and pepper. Chill, covered, several hours. Season to taste with salt and pepper.

Gazpacho with Avocado Sour Cream

6 servings (about 1½ cups each)

5 cups chopped, seeded tomatoes
2 cups tomato juice
2 cloves garlic
2 tablespoons lime juice
1 teaspoon dried oregano leaves
1 cup coarsely chopped seedless cucumber
1 cup chopped yellow bell pepper
1 cup chopped celery
6 green onions and tops, thinly sliced, divided
2 tablespoons finely chopped cilantro
Salt and pepper, to taste
Avocado Sour Cream (recipe follows)
Hot pepper sauce, optional

Per Serving
Net Carbohydrate (gm): 11
Calories: 102
Fat (gm): 4.8
Saturated fat (gm): 1.5
Cholesterol (mg): 3.6
Sodium (mg): 43
Protein (gm): 3.2
Carbohydrate (gm): 15

1. Reserve 1 cup tomatoes; process remaining tomatoes, tomato juice, garlic, lime juice, and oregano in food processor or blender until smooth.

2. Mix tomato mixture, reserved 1 cup tomatoes, cucumber, bell pepper, celery, 5 green onions, and cilantro in large bowl; season to taste with salt and pepper. Refrigerate until chilled, 3 to 4 hours.

3. Serve soup in chilled bowls; top each with a dollop of Avocado Sour Cream and sprinkle with remaining green onion. Pass around the hot pepper sauce.

Avocado Sour Cream

makes about ⅔ cup

½ cup chopped avocado
¼ cup sour cream
2 tablespoons reduced-fat milk
Salt and white pepper, to taste

1. Process the first three ingredients in food processor until smooth; season to taste with salt and white pepper.

Crunchy Vegetable Soup

4 servings

1½ cups cut (1-inch) asparagus (6 ounces)
¾ cup coarsely chopped carrot
½ cup coarsely chopped celery
2 tablespoons coarsely chopped onion
½ cup sliced mushrooms
1 cup reduced-sodium fat-free chicken, *or* vegetable, broth
1 cup plain yogurt
Pinch dried tarragon leaves
Dash cayenne pepper
Salt and black pepper, to taste

Per Serving
Net Carbohydrate (gm): 7.4
Calories: 74
Fat (gm): 1.5
Saturated fat (gm): 0.6
Cholesterol (mg): 9.9
Sodium (mg): 121
Protein (gm): 6.6
Carbohydrate (gm): 9.3

1. Process vegetables and broth in blender or food processor until finely chopped. Pour into medium saucepan. Heat to boiling; reduce heat and simmer, 6 to 8 minutes or until vegetables are crisp-tender. Stir in yogurt, tarragon, and cayenne pepper; season to taste with salt and black pepper.

Note: Other combinations of vegetables can be used for this soup, such as broccoli, cauliflower, cucumbers, and radishes.

Egg Drop Soup

4 servings

1 quart Rich Chicken Stock (see pg. 26), *or*
    canned chicken broth
1½ tablespoons cornstarch
3 tablespoons cold water
2 green onions and tops, chopped
2 eggs, lightly beaten
Salt and white pepper, to taste

Per Serving
Net Carbohydrate (gm): 4.2
Calories: 90
Fat (gm): 3.3
Saturated fat (gm): 0.8
Cholesterol (mg): 107.2
Sodium (mg): 69
Protein (gm): 8.2
Carbohydrate (gm): 4.4

1. Heat stock to boiling in medium saucepan. Mix cornstarch and water; add to broth and stir until thickened. Stir in green onions. Remove from heat and stir in eggs with a fork. Season with salt and white pepper to taste.

Chinese Snow Pea Soup

4 servings

1 quart reduced-sodium fat-free chicken broth
¼ cup minced green onions and tops
¼ cup finely chopped carrots
1 clove garlic, minced
1 teaspoon grated gingerroot
1 teaspoon light soy sauce
¼ cup sliced mushrooms
1 cup sliced snow peas
4 ounces firm tofu, cut into ½-inch cubes (1 cup)
Sliced green onion and top, as garnish

Per Serving
Net Carbohydrate (gm): 2.9
Calories: 82
Fat (gm): 2.8
Saturated fat (gm): 0.2
Cholesterol (mg): 25
Sodium (mg): 299
Protein (gm): 10.2
Carbohydrate (gm): 3.9

1. Combine broth, minced green onions, carrots, garlic, gingerroot, and soy sauce in medium saucepan; heat to boiling. Reduce heat and simmer, covered, 5 minutes. Add mushrooms and simmer 5 minutes. Add snow peas and tofu and simmer 1 minute. Garnish with sliced green onion.

Thai Fish Soup

4 servings

1½ quarts Fish Stock (see p. 21), *or* reduced-sodium
    fat-free chicken broth
2 teaspoons reduced-sodium soy sauce
1 teaspoon minced garlic
1 teaspoon minced gingerroot
Pinch ground Szechwan peppercorns, optional
½ pound flounder, *or* other lean white fish, fillets, ground
½ teaspoon salt
½ teaspoon pepper
1 cup sliced mushrooms
½ cup sliced snow peas
2 tablespoons chopped cilantro
Salt and pepper, to taste

Per Serving
Net Carbohydrate (gm): 2.1
Calories: 89
Fat (gm): 0.9
Saturated fat (gm): 0.2
Cholesterol (mg): 27.1
Sodium (mg): 709
Protein (gm): 15.9
Carbohydrate (gm): 2.6

1. Combine stock, soy sauce, garlic, gingerroot, and peppercorns in large saucepan; heat to boiling. Reduce heat and simmer, covered, 5 minutes.

2. Mix ground fish, ½ teaspoon salt, and ½ teaspoon pepper; shape into 1-inch balls. Heat soup to boiling; drop fish balls into soup. Simmer until fish balls float to the surface, about 5 minutes. Stir in mushrooms, snow peas, and cilantro; simmer until snow peas are crisp-tender, 2 to 3 minutes. Season to taste with salt and pepper.

Greek Lemon-Rice Soup

4 servings

3½ cups reduced-sodium fat-free chicken broth
¼ cup uncooked quick-cooking brown rice
2 large cloves garlic, minced
¼–⅓ cup fresh lemon juice
1 egg, lightly beaten
2 tablespoons finely chopped parsley
Salt and white pepper, to taste

Per Serving
Net Carbohydrate (gm): 10.5
Calories: 107
Fat (gm): 2.9
Saturated fat (gm): 0.5
Cholesterol (mg): 75
Sodium (mg): 237
Protein (gm): 8.8
Carbohydrate (gm): 11

1. Heat broth to boiling in medium saucepan; stir in rice and garlic. Reduce heat and simmer, covered, until rice is tender, about 20 minutes.

2. Mix lemon juice and egg in small bowl; slowly stir into soup. Stir in parsley; season to taste with salt and white pepper.

Roasted Red Peppers Soup

4 servings

¾ cup chopped onion
½ small jalapeño chili, minced
1 clove garlic, minced
1 tablespoon canola oil
1 jar (5 ounces) roasted red bell peppers, drained
¾ cup tomato juice
1 can (14½ ounces) reduced-sodium vegetable, *or*
    chicken, broth
¼ teaspoon dried marjoram leaves
Salt and pepper, to taste
¼ cup sour cream
1 small green onion and top, thinly sliced

Per Serving
Net Carbohydrate (gm): 10.4
Calories: 103
Fat (gm): 6.2
Saturated fat (gm): 1.8
Cholesterol (mg): 5.3
Sodium (mg): 443
Protein (gm): 1.6
Carbohydrate (gm): 11.4

1. Sauté onion, jalapeño chili, and garlic in oil in medium saucepan until tender.

2. Process onion mixture, roasted peppers, and tomato juice in blender or food processor until smooth. Return mixture to saucepan and add broth and marjoram; heat to boiling. Reduce heat and simmer, covered, 15 minutes. Season to taste with salt and pepper.

3. Serve soup warm, or refrigerate and serve cold. Top each serving with a dollop of sour cream and sprinkle with green onion.

Note: Use jarred roasted peppers for this soup, or roast 2 medium red bell peppers. To roast peppers: cut in half and discard seeds. Place, skin sides up, on foil-lined pan. Broil 4 inches from heat source until skins are blackened. Place peppers in plastic bag for 5 minutes to loosen skins, then peel and discard skins.

Cream of Broccoli Soup

6 servings (about 1 cup each)

½ cup chopped onion
3 cloves garlic, minced
1 tablespoon olive oil
2 pounds broccoli, cut into 1-inch pieces (8 cups)
½ teaspoon dried thyme leaves
⅛ teaspoon ground nutmeg
3½ cups reduced-sodium fat-free chicken broth
⅓ cup whipping cream
Salt and white pepper, to taste
6 tablespoons sour cream
2–3 teaspoons lemon juice

Per Serving
Net Carbohydrate (gm): 5.8
Calories: 168
Fat (gm): 11.2
Saturated fat (gm): 5
Cholesterol (mg): 38.1
Sodium (mg): 199
Protein (gm): 9.5
Carbohydrate (gm): 10.7

1. Sauté onion and garlic in oil in large saucepan until tender, 3 to 5 minutes. Stir in broccoli, thyme, and nutmeg; cook 2 minutes longer.

2. Add broth to saucepan; heat to boiling. Reduce heat and simmer, covered, until broccoli is very tender, about 10 minutes.

3. Process soup in food processor or blender until smooth. Return soup to saucepan; add cream and cook over medium heat until hot. Season to taste with salt and white pepper. Pour soup into bowls. Mix sour cream and lemon juice; swirl about 1 tablespoon of mixture into each bowl of soup.

Cream of Cauliflower Soup with Cheese

6 servings (about 1 cup each)

½ cup chopped onion
2 cloves garlic, minced
1 tablespoon butter
2 tablespoons all-purpose flour
3½ cups reduced-sodium fat-free chicken broth
3 cups cauliflower florets (12 ounces)
1 cup cubed, peeled, and cooked Idaho potato
¼ cup whipping cream
¾ cup (3 ounces) shredded Cheddar cheese
Salt and white pepper, to taste
Ground mace, *or* nutmeg, as garnish

Per Serving
Net Carbohydrate (gm): 6.8
Calories: 188
Fat (gm): 11.5
Saturated fat (gm): 6.6
Cholesterol (mg): 48.6
Sodium (mg): 277
Protein (gm): 9.9
Carbohydrate (gm): 12.1

1. Sauté onion and garlic in butter in large saucepan until tender, about 5 minutes. Stir in flour; cook 1 minute longer. Add broth, cauliflower, and potato; heat to boiling. Reduce heat and simmer, covered, until vegetables are tender, 10 to 15 minutes.

2. Remove about half the vegetables from the soup with a slotted spoon and reserve. Process remaining soup in food processor or blender until smooth. Return soup to saucepan; stir in reserved vegetables, cream, and cheese. Cook over low heat until cheese is melted, 3 to 4 minutes, stirring frequently. Season to taste with salt and white pepper.

3. Pour soup into bowls; sprinkle lightly with mace.

Variations:

Fennel Bisque with Walnuts—Make soup as above, substituting 1 large leek, sliced, for the onion, and 2 large fennel bulbs, sliced, for the cauliflower. Complete soup as above, omitting Cheddar cheese. Ladle soup into bowls; sprinkle with 3 ounces crumbled blue cheese and ¼ cup chopped toasted walnuts.

Cream of Turnip Soup—Make soup as above, substituting chopped turnips for the cauliflower and Swiss, Gouda, *or* Havarti, cheese for the Cheddar; add ½ teaspoon dried thyme leaves.

Herbed Cucumber Soup

6 servings

½ cup chopped onion
1 tablespoon canola oil
8 cups chopped, peeled, seeded cucumbers
3 tablespoons flour
1 quart reduced-sodium fat-free chicken, *or*
    vegetable, broth
1 teaspoon dried mint leaves, *or* dill weed
⅓ cup whipping cream
Salt and white pepper, to taste
Paprika, as garnish
6 thin slices cucumber

Per Serving
Net Carbohydrate (gm): 7.1
Calories: 135
Fat (gm): 8.5
Saturated fat (gm): 3.3
Cholesterol (mg): 34.9
Sodium (mg): 176
Protein (gm): 6.6
Carbohydrate (gm): 8.7

1. Sauté onion in oil in medium saucepan until tender, about 3 minutes. Add cucumbers and cook over medium heat 5 minutes; stir in flour and cook 1 to 2 minutes longer.

2. Add broth to saucepan; heat to boiling. Reduce heat and simmer, covered, 10 minutes. Process soup in food processor or blender until smooth; stir in mint and cream; season to taste with salt and pepper. Cool; refrigerate until chilled, 3 to 4 hours.

3. Pour soup into bowls; sprinkle lightly with paprika and top each with a cucumber slice.

Summer Squash Soup

6 servings (about 1¼ cups each)

½ cup chopped shallots, *or* onion
¼ cup sliced green onions and tops
2 cloves garlic, minced
1 tablespoon olive oil
4 cups chopped zucchini, *or* yellow summer squash
1 cup cubed, peeled Idaho potato
1 quart reduced-sodium fat-free chicken broth
1 cup chopped kale, *or* spinach leaves
1 teaspoon dried tarragon leaves
¼ cup whipping cream
Salt and cayenne pepper, to taste
6 thin slices zucchini
6 thin slices yellow summer squash

Per Serving
Net Carbohydrate (gm): 8.2
Calories: 129
Fat (gm): 7.2
Saturated fat (gm): 2.7
Cholesterol (mg): 30.4
Sodium (mg): 181
Protein (gm): 6.9
Carbohydrate (gm): 10.1

1. Sauté shallots, green onions, and garlic in oil in large saucepan until tender, about 5 minutes. Add chopped zucchini and potato; sauté until lightly browned, about 5 minutes.

2. Add broth, kale, and tarragon to saucepan; heat to boiling. Reduce heat and simmer, covered, until vegetables are tender, 10 to 15 minutes.

3. Process soup in food processor or blender until smooth; return to saucepan. Stir in cream; season to taste with salt and cayenne pepper. Heat and serve warm, or refrigerate and serve chilled. Serve soup in bowls, garnished with a slice each of zucchini and summer squash.

Variation:

Squash and Fennel Bisque—Make soup as above, adding 1 fennel bulb, sliced, and 1 cup sliced celery in Step 1, and substituting spinach for kale in Step 2. Omit tarragon. Thin with additional broth if necessary.

Creamy Tomato-Vegetable Soup

6 servings (about 1⅓ cups each)

⅔ cup finely chopped onion
⅔ cup chopped green bell pepper
½ cup chopped celery
1 large garlic clove, minced
1 tablespoon butter
2 tablespoons all-purpose flour
1 quart reduced-sodium fat-free chicken broth
1½ cups small cauliflower florets
2 cups diced zucchini
¼ cup dry sherry, optional
¼ cup finely chopped parsley
1 teaspoon dried basil leaves
¼ teaspoon dried thyme leaves
1 can (8 ounces) tomato sauce
¾ cup whipping cream
Salt and cayenne pepper, to taste

Per Serving
Net Carbohydrate (gm): 8.8
Calories: 200
Fat (gm): 14.1
Saturated fat (gm): 8.2
Cholesterol (mg): 63.2
Sodium (mg): 444
Protein (gm): 7.6
Carbohydrate (gm): 11.5

1. Sauté onion, bell pepper, celery, and garlic in butter in large saucepan until onion is tender, about 5 minutes. Sprinkle with flour and cook 1 minute longer. Add broth, cauliflower, zucchini, sherry, and herbs; heat to boiling. Reduce heat and simmer, covered, until vegetables are tender, about 10 minutes.

2. Stir in tomato sauce and cream; simmer 2 to 3 minutes. Season to taste with salt and cayenne pepper.

Two-Tomato Soup

6 servings (about 1¼ cups each)

½ cup chopped onion
½ cup sliced celery
⅓ cup chopped carrot
2 teaspoons minced garlic
1 tablespoon olive oil
1 quart reduced-sodium fat-free chicken broth
1 quart chopped ripe tomatoes, *or*
   1 can (28 ounces) whole tomatoes, undrained
⅓ cup sun-dried tomatoes (not in oil)
1–2 teaspoons dried basil leaves
½ cup whipping cream
Salt and pepper, to taste

Per Serving
Net Carbohydrate (gm): 8
Calories: 163
Fat (gm): 11.2
Saturated fat (gm): 5
Cholesterol (mg): 44.1
Sodium (mg): 259
Protein (gm): 6.9
Carbohydrate (gm): 10.4

1. Sauté onion, celery, carrot, and garlic in oil in large saucepan until tender; about 5 minutes. Add broth, tomatoes, sun-dried tomatoes, and basil; heat to boiling. Reduce heat and simmer, covered, until vegetables are tender, 10 to 15 minutes.

2. Process soup in food processor or blender until smooth; return to saucepan. Stir in cream and cook over medium heat until hot through, 3 to 5 minutes. Season to taste with salt and pepper.

Lightly Creamed Vegetable Soup

6 servings (about 1⅓ cups each)

1 cup chopped green bell pepper
1 cup chopped red bell pepper
1 cup sliced yellow summer squash
1 cup thinly sliced carrots
1 cup thinly sliced celery
⅔ cup thinly sliced onion
1 clove garlic, minced
1½ tablespoons butter
¼ cup all-purpose flour
1 quart reduced-sodium fat-free chicken broth
1 bay leaf
Pinch ground cloves
Salt and pepper, to taste
½ cup whipping cream
Freshly ground nutmeg, as garnish

Per Serving
Net Carbohydrate (gm): 9.8
Calories: 181
Fat (gm): 11.7
Saturated fat (gm): 6.5
Cholesterol (mg): 52.3
Sodium (mg): 231
Protein (gm): 7
Carbohydrate (gm): 12.3

1. Sauté vegetables in butter in large saucepan until onion is tender, 8 to 10 minutes. Stir in flour and cook 1 minute; stir in broth, bay leaf, and cloves. Heat to boiling; reduce heat and simmer, covered, until vegetables are tender, 10 to 15 minutes. Discard bay leaf. Season to taste with salt and pepper.

2. Whip the cream in small bowl until doubled in volume and stir into soup just before serving. Pour soup into bowls; sprinkle lightly with nutmeg.

Lime-Scented Vegetable Soup

6 servings (about 1¼ cups each)

2 cups sliced carrots
1 cup chopped red bell pepper
¾ cup sliced celery
⅓ cup sliced green onions and tops
6 cloves garlic, minced
1 small jalapeño chili, finely chopped
1 tablespoon canola oil
1½ quarts reduced-sodium fat-free chicken broth
½–¾ cup lime juice
½ teaspoon ground cumin
Salt and pepper, to taste
1 cup chopped tomato
½ cup chopped, seeded cucumber
½ cup chopped avocado
3–4 tablespoons finely chopped cilantro

Per Serving
Net Carbohydrate (gm): 8.6
Calories: 136
Fat (gm): 6.6
Saturated fat (gm): 0.6
Cholesterol (mg): 25
Sodium (mg): 283
Protein (gm): 8.8
Carbohydrate (gm): 11.9

1. Sauté carrots, bell pepper, celery, green onions, garlic, and jalapeño chili in oil in large saucepan until lightly browned, about 5 minutes.

2. Add broth, lime juice, and cumin to saucepan; heat to boiling. Reduce heat and simmer, covered, until vegetables are tender, 10 to 15 minutes. Season to taste with salt and pepper.

3. Pour soup into bowls; add tomato, cucumber, and avocado to each bowl. Sprinkle with cilantro.

Tangy Zucchini Soup

4 servings

⅔ cup finely chopped onion
1 small clove garlic, minced
2 cups diced zucchini
½ cup diced, peeled potato
3 cups reduced-sodium fat-free chicken broth
2 tablespoons chopped parsley
¼ teaspoon dry mustard
Dash cayenne pepper
½ cup buttermilk
½ cup whipping cream
Salt and white pepper, to taste
Thinly sliced zucchini, as garnish

Per Serving
Net Carbohydrate (gm): 9
Calories: 187
Fat (gm): 12.7
Saturated fat (gm): 7.1
Cholesterol (mg): 61.1
Sodium (mg): 236
Protein (gm): 8.3
Carbohydrate (gm): 10.6

1. Combine onion, garlic, zucchini, potato, broth, parsley, mustard, and cayenne pepper in large saucepan; heat to boiling. Reduce heat and simmer, covered, until potato is very tender, about 15 minutes.

2. Process in blender or food processor until smooth; transfer to serving bowl. Stir in buttermilk and cream; season to taste with salt and white pepper. Refrigerate until chilled. Garnish with sliced zucchini.

Asian Mushroom Soup with Noodles

6 servings

Per Serving
Net Carbohydrate (gm): 13.9
Calories: 189
Fat (gm): 5.3
Saturated fat (gm): 0.4
Cholesterol (mg): 0.7
Sodium (mg): 125
Protein (gm): 12.5
Carbohydrate (gm): 19

3 cups boiling water
1 ounce dried shiitake mushrooms
2 pounds cremini mushrooms, sliced, divided
½ cup minced onion
1 clove garlic, minced
¼ teaspoon dried thyme leaves
2 tablespoons canola oil
1 quart Rich Chicken Stock (p. 20), *or* reduced-sodium fat-free chicken broth
½ cup dry white wine, *or* chicken broth
2 ounces soba noodles
1 cup trimmed snow peas
⅓ cup thinly sliced radishes
1 tablespoon red wine vinegar
2 tablespoons finely chopped parsley
Salt and pepper, to taste

1. Pour boiling water over dried mushrooms in bowl and let stand until softened, about 15 minutes. Drain; strain liquid through fine strainer and reserve. Coarsely chop mushrooms and stems.

2. Sauté shiitake mushrooms, half of the cremini mushrooms, onion, garlic, and thyme in oil in large saucepan until soft, 5 to 8 minutes. Add stock, wine, and reserved mushroom liquid; heat to boiling. Reduce heat and simmer, covered, 30 minutes.

3. Strain soup, discarding mushrooms. Add remaining half of the cremini mushrooms, noodles, snow peas, radishes, vinegar, and parsley; simmer, uncovered, until noodles are cooked, about 5 minutes. Season to taste with salt and pepper.

Chinese Pork and Watercress Soup

4 servings

4 ounces boneless pork loin, fat trimmed,
    cut into 1 x ¼-inch strips
1 small clove garlic, minced
1 tablespoon chopped gingerroot
2 teaspoons toasted sesame oil
5 cups Quick, *or* Rich, Chicken Stock (see p. 20), *or*
    canned chicken broth
4 green onions and tops, quartered lengthwise and
    cut into 1-inch pieces
1 tablespoon dry sherry
2 teaspoons reduced-sodium soy sauce
½ cup cooked brown rice
1½ cups loosely packed, stemmed watercress (1½ ounces)
Salt and pepper, to taste

Per Serving
Net Carbohydrate (gm): 8.4
Calories: 121
Fat (gm): 4.8
Saturated fat (gm): 1
Cholesterol (mg): 20.4
Sodium (mg): 116
Protein (gm): 9.2
Carbohydrate (gm): 9.5

1. Sauté pork, garlic, and gingerroot in oil in large saucepan until lightly browned, about 3 minutes. Stir in stock, green onions, sherry, soy sauce, and rice; heat to boiling. Reduce heat and simmer, covered, until pork is cooked, about 5 minutes.

2. Stir in watercress; remove from heat and let stand until watercress is wilted, about 30 seconds. Season to taste with salt and pepper; serve immediately.

Hot Sour Soup

6 servings (about 1 cup each)

½ ounce dried Chinese black mushrooms (shiitake)
¾ cup boiling water
1 quart reduced-sodium fat-free chicken broth
½ cup bamboo shoots
¼ cup white distilled vinegar
2 tablespoons reduced-sodium tamari soy sauce
1 tablespoon finely chopped gingerroot
½–1 teaspoon Szechwan peppercorns or red pepper flakes
1 tablespoon cornstarch
3 tablespoons water
1½ cups cubed light extra-firm tofu (6 ounces)
1 cup cubed roast pork loin (½-inch cubes)
Salt, cayenne, and black pepper, to taste
1 egg, lightly beaten
1–2 teaspoons dark sesame oil
Sliced green onion, as garnish
Sour Sauce (recipe follows)

Per Serving
Net Carbohydrate (gm): 8.3
Calories: 144
Fat (gm): 5.4
Saturated fat (gm): 1.4
Cholesterol (mg): 67.2
Sodium (mg): 521
Protein (gm): 14.1
Carbohydrate (gm): 8.9

1. Combine mushrooms and boiling water in small bowl; let stand until mushrooms are softened, 15 to 20 minutes. Drain; reserving liquid. Slice mushrooms, discarding tough stems.

2. Combine broth, mushrooms, reserved liquid, bamboo shoots, vinegar, soy sauce, gingerroot, and peppercorns in large saucepan; heat to boiling. Reduce heat and simmer, uncovered, 10 minutes. Heat soup to boiling; mix cornstarch and water and stir into soup. Boil until thickened, about 1 minute, stirring constantly.

3. Stir tofu and pork into soup; simmer, covered, 5 minutes. Season to taste with salt, cayenne, and black pepper. Just before serving, stir egg slowly into soup; stir in sesame oil.

4. Pour soup into bowls; sprinkle with green onion and add Sour Sauce as desired.

Sour Sauce

makes about ⅓ cup

3 tablespoons white distilled vinegar
1 tablespoon reduced-sodium tamari soy sauce
2 tablespoons sugar

1. Mix all ingredients; refrigerate until serving time.

Beet Borscht

8 servings (about 1¼ cups each)

2 cups julienned, peeled fresh beets
1 tablespoon canola oil
6 cups shredded red cabbage (about 1 small head)
1 cup julienned carrots
1 clove garlic, minced
1½ quarts reduced-sodium fat-free beef broth
1 bay leaf
2 teaspoons packed dark brown sugar
1–2 tablespoons cider vinegar
6 ounces thinly sliced reduced-sodium reduced-fat smoked sausage
Salt and pepper, to taste
½ cup sour cream
Thin lemon slices, as garnish

Per Serving
Net Carbohydrate (gm): 10.8
Calories: 130
Fat (gm): 5.4
Saturated fat (gm): 2.1
Cholesterol (mg): 14.7
Sodium (mg): 351
Protein (gm): 8.4
Carbohydrate (gm): 13.2

1. Sauté beets in oil in large saucepan 2 to 3 minutes; stir in cabbage, carrots, garlic, broth, bay leaf, sugar, and vinegar. Heat to boiling; reduce heat and simmer, uncovered, 30 minutes or until vegetables are tender, adding sausage during last 10 minutes of cooking time. Discard bay leaf; season to taste with salt and pepper.

2. Serve soup in bowls; garnish with dollops of sour cream and lemon slices.

Note: For convenience, 2 cups canned, drained, shredded beets can be substituted for the fresh beets; reduce cooking time to 10 to 15 minutes.

Russian Borscht

12 servings

1½ quarts reduced-sodium fat-free beef broth
2 pounds lean beef stew meat, cubed (½-inch)
2 bay leaves
1 teaspoon dried thyme leaves
4 cups thinly sliced cabbage
2 cups shredded beets
2 cups shredded carrots
1 cup chopped onion
1 cup shredded turnip
1 can (14½ ounces) diced tomatoes with roasted garlic, undrained
1 tablespoon packed light brown sugar
3–4 tablespoons red wine vinegar
Salt and pepper, to taste
Dill Sour Cream (recipe follows)

Per Serving
Net Carbohydrate (gm): 7.7
Calories: 196
Fat (gm): 7.9
Saturated fat (gm): 3.6
Cholesterol (mg): 45.8
Sodium (mg): 279
Protein (gm): 20.8
Carbohydrate (gm): 10.2

1. Combine broth, stew meat, bay leaves, and thyme in large saucepan and heat to boiling; reduce heat and simmer, covered, until meat is tender, about 1½ hours.

2. Stir in vegetables, tomatoes and liquid, and sugar and heat to boiling; reduce heat and simmer, covered, until vegetables are tender, about 20 minutes. Season to taste with vinegar, salt, and pepper; discard bay leaves. Serve in bowls, drizzled with Dill Sour Cream.

Dill Sour Cream

makes about ¾ cup

¾ cup sour cream
1 tablespoon dried dill weed
2–3 tablespoons reduced-fat milk

1. Mix all ingredients, using enough milk to make a thick, pourable consistency.

Brandied Onion Soup

8 servings (about 1 cup each)

4 cups thinly sliced onions
2 cloves garlic, minced
1 tablespoon butter
1 tablespoon olive oil
2 tablespoons all-purpose flour
2 quarts Brown Beef Stock (see p. 21), *or* canned beef broth
2–4 tablespoons brandy, optional
Salt and pepper, to taste
1 cup shredded Parmesan cheese

Per Serving
Net Carbohydrate (gm): 8.8
Calories: 116
Fat (gm): 6.1
Saturated fat (gm): 2.9
Cholesterol (mg): 11.6
Sodium (mg): 192
Protein (gm): 5.2
Carbohydrate (gm): 10.3

1. Cook onions and garlic in butter and oil in large saucepan over medium-low heat until golden, 15 to 20 minutes. Add flour and cook 1 minute longer. Stir in stock and heat to boiling; reduce heat and simmer, covered, 35 to 45 minutes. Add brandy; season to taste with salt and pepper.

2. Ladle soup into bowls and sprinkle each serving with 2 tablespoons cheese.

Three-Onion Soup with Mushrooms

6 servings (about 1½ cups each)

3 cups thinly sliced onions
1½ cups thinly sliced leeks (white parts only)
½ cup chopped shallots, *or* green onions and tops
1 tablespoon butter
1 teaspoon packed light brown sugar
2 cups sliced mushrooms
6½ cups reduced-sodium fat-free chicken broth
Salt and pepper, to taste

Per Serving
Net Carbohydrate (gm): 9.8
Calories: 121
Fat (gm): 3.9
Saturated fat (gm): 13
Cholesterol (mg): 32.6
Sodium (mg): 300
Protein (gm): 9.6
Carbohydrate (gm): 12.1

1. Cook onions, leeks, and shallots in butter in large saucepan, covered, over medium-low heat 15 minutes. Stir in sugar; continue cooking, uncovered, until onion mixture is golden, about 10 minutes longer.

2. Stir mushrooms into onion mixture; cook over medium heat until tender, about 5 minutes. Add broth and heat to boiling; reduce heat and simmer, uncovered, 15 minutes. Season to taste with salt and pepper.

Matzo Ball Soup with Vegetables

6 servings (about 2 cups each)

2 quarts Rich Chicken Stock (see p. 20), *or*
    canned chicken broth
½ cup sliced celery
½ cup diced carrot
1 cup peas
1 cup small broccoli florets
Matzo Balls (recipe follows)
Salt and pepper, to taste

Per Serving
Net Carbohydrate (gm): 14.5
Calories: 167
Fat (gm): 4.4
Saturated fat (gm): 0.5
Cholesterol (mg): 36.8
Sodium (mg): 212
Protein (gm): 12
Carbohydrate (gm): 17.2

1. Combine all ingredients, except Matzo Balls, salt, and pepper, in large saucepan; heat to boiling. Reduce heat and simmer, covered, until vegetables are tender, about 20 minutes. Add Matzo Balls to soup; simmer, covered, 5 minutes. Season to taste with salt and pepper.

Matzo Balls

makes 1 dozen

1 egg
2 egg whites
1 tablespoon canola oil
½ cup plus 1 tablespoon matzo meal
¼ teaspoon salt
2½ tablespoons Rich Chicken Stock (see p. 20), *or* fat-free chicken broth

1. Combine all ingredients, mixing well; chill, covered, 1 hour. Form dough into 12 balls; drop into simmering water and cook 30 to 35 minutes. Remove with slotted spoon and drain.

Stracciatelle with Tiny Meatballs

8 servings (about 1½ cups each)

1 quart Quick, *or* Rich, Chicken Stock (see p. 20),
    or chicken broth
2 cups water
½ cup broken whole wheat spaghetti, *or* small soup pasta
½ cup thinly sliced carrot
½ cup chopped celery
¼ cup chopped onion
2 quarts sliced spinach (8 ounces)
2 tablespoons chopped parsley
Turkey Meatballs (recipe follows)
Salt and pepper, to taste
2 eggs, lightly beaten
Shredded Parmesan cheese, as garnish

Per Serving
Net Carbohydrate (gm): 8.8
Calories: 106
Fat (gm): 2.4
Saturated fat (gm): 0.7
Cholesterol (mg): 66.1
Sodium (mg): 158
Protein (gm): 11.3
Carbohydrate (gm): 10.9

1. Combine Chicken Broth, water, spaghetti, vegetables, and parsley in large saucepan and heat to boiling. Drop Turkey Meatballs into boiling broth. Reduce heat and simmer 15 minutes or until meatballs and pasta are done. Season to taste with salt and pepper.

2. Slowly pour eggs into soup, stirring gently. Ladle soup into bowls; garnish with Parmesan cheese.

Turkey Meatballs

makes 24 small meatballs

8 ounces ground lean turkey
2 tablespoons unseasoned dry bread crumbs
1 teaspoon grated Parmesan cheese
2 teaspoons chopped parsley
¼ cup finely minced onion
2 tablespoons tomato paste

1. Mix all ingredients; form into small meatballs using about 2 teaspoons of mixture for each.

Minestrone

6 servings (about 1⅔ cups each)

1 cup sliced carrots
½ cup chopped onion
½ cup chopped celery
½ cup sliced fennel bulb
2 cloves garlic, minced
1 tablespoon olive oil
5 cups reduced-sodium fat-free beef broth
1 can (15 ounces) garbanzo beans, rinsed, drained
1 cup sugar snap peas (4 ounces)
1 cup sliced zucchini (4 ounces)
1 cup broccoli florets (4 ounces)
2 teaspoons Italian herb blend
1 cup diced, seeded tomatoes (4 ounces)
¼ cup finely chopped parsley
Salt and pepper, to taste
6 tablespoons shredded Parmesan cheese

Per Serving
Net Carbohydrate (gm): 14.2
Calories: 164
Fat (gm): 4.8
Saturated fat (gm): 1.2
Cholesterol (mg): 3.6
Sodium (mg): 409
Protein (gm): 11.7
Carbohydrate (gm): 20.2

1. Sauté carrots, onion, celery, fennel, and garlic in oil in large saucepan until onion is tender, about 5 minutes. Add broth, beans, peas, zucchini, broccoli, and herbs; heat to boiling. Reduce heat and simmer, covered, until vegetables are tender, 10 to 15 minutes. Stir in tomatoes and parsley; season to taste with salt and pepper. Pour soup into bowls; sprinkle with cheese.

Garden Harvest Soup

6 servings (about 1½ cups each)

1 cup thinly sliced onion
1 cup chopped red bell pepper
1 cup chopped yellow bell pepper
½ cup sliced carrot
2 cloves garlic, minced
1 tablespoon olive oil
5 cups reduced-sodium fat-free chicken broth
1½ cups whole-kernel corn
1 cup cut (1-inch) green beans
1 cup sliced zucchini
1 cup sliced yellow summer squash
2 teaspoons Italian herb blend
Salt and pepper, to taste
¼ cup whipping cream
Finely chopped parsley, as garnish

Per Serving
Net Carbohydrate (gm): 13.7
Calories: 165
Fat (gm): 7.6
Saturated fat (gm): 2.7
Cholesterol (mg): 34.5
Sodium (mg): 225
Protein (gm): 9
Carbohydrate (gm): 17.2

1. Sauté onion, bell peppers, carrot, and garlic in oil in large saucepan until lightly browned, about 8 minutes. Add broth, corn, green beans, zucchini, squash, and herb blend; heat to boiling. Reduce heat and simmer, covered, until vegetables are tender, about 15 minutes. Season to taste with salt and pepper.

2. Whip the cream in medium bowl until soft peaks form; stir into soup just before serving. Pour soup into bowls; sprinkle with parsley.

Tortellini Soup with Kale

8 servings (about 1½ cups each)

1 cup sliced leeks (white parts only), *or* green onions and tops
3 cloves garlic, minced
1 tablespoon olive oil
3 quarts Basic Vegetable Stock (see p. 22), *or*
    canned vegetable broth
2 cups packed coarsely chopped kale
1 cup sliced mushrooms
½ package (9-ounce size) mushroom, *or* herb, tortellini
Salt and white pepper, to taste

Per Serving
Net Carbohydrate (gm): 12.8
Calories: 101
Fat (gm): 3.6
Saturated fat (gm): 0.7
Cholesterol (mg): 8.5
Sodium (mg): 90
Protein (gm): 4.1
Carbohydrate (gm): 14

1. Sauté leeks and garlic in oil in large saucepan until leeks are tender, about 5 minutes. Add stock and heat to boiling; stir in kale and mushrooms. Reduce heat and simmer, covered, 5 minutes.

2. Add tortellini to saucepan; simmer, uncovered, until tortellini are al dente, about 7 minutes. Season to taste with salt and white pepper.

Spicy North African Chicken Soup

6 servings

2 cups coarsely chopped onions
1 cup thinly sliced celery
2 large cloves garlic, minced
½ teaspoon red pepper flakes
1 tablespoon olive oil
1½ quarts Quick, *or* Rich, Chicken Stock (see p. 20), *or*
    canned chicken broth
1 pound boneless, skinless chicken breast, cubed (½-inch)
⅓ cup bulgur wheat
1 can (14½ ounces) no-added-salt stewed tomatoes, undrained
1 cinnamon stick
2 large bay leaves
1 teaspoon dried thyme leaves
⅛ teaspoon ground cloves
Salt and pepper, to taste

Per Serving
Net Carbohydrate (gm): 13.4
Calories: 189
Fat (gm): 4.3
Saturated fat (gm): 0.7
Cholesterol (mg): 46.9
Sodium (mg): 78
Protein (gm): 21.3
Carbohydrate (gm): 17.2

1. Sauté onions, celery, garlic, and red pepper flakes in oil in large saucepan until onions are soft, about 10 minutes. Add remaining ingredients, except salt and pepper, and heat to boiling. Reduce heat and simmer, covered, 25 to 30 minutes or until bulgur is tender. Discard cinnamon stick and bay leaves; season to taste with salt and pepper.

West African Curried Chicken Soup

6 servings

1 cup chopped celery
¾ cup finely chopped onion
1 clove garlic, minced
2 teaspoons peanut oil
1–2 teaspoons mild curry powder
3 tablespoons all-purpose flour
1 quart Quick Chicken Stock (see p. 20), *or* canned chicken broth
1 can (8 ounces) crushed pineapple in juice, undrained
1 pound boneless, skinless chicken breast, cooked, cubed (½-inch)
¾ cup reduced-fat milk

Per Serving
Net Carbohydrate (gm): 12.5
Calories: 172
Fat (gm): 4
Saturated fat (gm): 1.2
Cholesterol (mg): 50.1
Sodium (mg): 71
Protein (gm): 20.3
Carbohydrate (gm): 13.6

1. Sauté celery, onion, and garlic in oil in large saucepan until onion is soft, about 5 minutes; stir in curry powder and flour and stir over medium heat 1 minute. Add stock and heat to boiling; reduce heat and simmer, covered, 20 minutes.

2. Stir in pineapple and juice, chicken, and milk; remove from heat and cool. Refrigerate until chilled.

Mexican-Style Chicken and Lime Soup

8 servings (about 1⅔ cups each)

1 cup chopped onion
1 cup chopped green bell pepper
2 teaspoons canola, *or* olive, oil
2 quarts Quick, *or* Rich, Chicken Stock (see p. 20), *or*
    canned chicken broth
1½ pounds boneless, skinless chicken breast, cubed (¾-inch)
2 cups chopped, peeled and seeded tomatoes
1 cup whole kernel corn
1 cup diced zucchini
¼ cup chopped cilantro
¼–⅓ cup lime juice
Salt and pepper, to taste
Vegetable cooking spray
4 corn tortillas, each cut into 10 wedges
8 thin lime slices

Per Serving
Net Carbohydrate (gm): 14
Calories: 185
Fat (gm): 3.4
Saturated fat (gm): 0.5
Cholesterol (mg): 52.4
Sodium (mg): 76.2
Protein (gm): 23
Carbohydrate (gm): 16.4

1. Sauté onion and bell pepper in oil in large saucepan until tender, about 5 minutes. Add stock, chicken, tomatoes, corn, and zucchini; heat to boiling. Reduce heat and simmer, covered, 20 minutes. Add cilantro and lime juice; season to taste with salt and pepper.

2. Spray large skillet with cooking spray; heat over medium heat until hot. Add tortilla wedges and spray with cooking spray; cook over medium heat, tossing occasionally, until crisp, about 5 minutes. Place in soup bowls; ladle soup over. Float lime slices on top of soup.

Chicken and Chilies Soup

6 servings (about 1 cup each)

1 cup finely chopped onion
½ cup chopped celery
1 large clove garlic, minced
1 teaspoon canola oil
2 tablespoons all-purpose flour
1 quart reduced-sodium fat-free chicken broth
1 cup cubed cooked chicken breast
1 can (4 ounces) chopped green chilies, rinsed, drained
1½ cups small cauliflower florets
1 cup cubed zucchini
Salt and pepper, to taste
¾ cup (3 ounces) shredded mild Cheddar cheese
Chopped chives, as garnish

Per Serving
Net Carbohydrate (gm): 4.6
Calories: 159
Fat (gm): 7.3
Saturated fat (gm): 3.3
Cholesterol (mg): 49.5
Sodium (mg): 353
Protein (gm): 16.2
Carbohydrate (gm): 6.6

1. Sauté onion, celery, and garlic in oil in large saucepan until onion is tender, about 5 minutes; sprinkle with flour and cook 1 minute longer. Add broth, chicken, chilies, cauliflower, and zucchini; heat to boiling. Reduce heat and simmer, covered, until vegetables are tender, about 10 minutes.

2. Season to taste with salt and pepper. Add cheese, stirring until melted. Sprinkle each serving with chives.

Pasilla Black Bean Soup

6 servings (about 1 cup each)

1 cup chopped onion
1 cup chopped carrots
1 jalapeño chili, chopped
4 cloves garlic, chopped
1 tablespoon olive oil
6 pasilla chilies, stems and seeds removed, torn into pieces
¾ teaspoon dried oregano leaves
½ teaspoon ground cumin
¼ teaspoon dried thyme leaves
1 quart reduced-sodium fat-free chicken broth
1 can (14½ ounces) diced tomatoes, undrained
1 can (15 ounces) black beans, rinsed, drained
Salt and pepper, to taste
Chopped cilantro, as garnish

Per Serving
Net Carbohydrate (gm): 14.9
Calories: 168
Fat (gm): 4.5
Saturated fat (gm): 0.3
Cholesterol (mg): 16.7
Sodium (mg): 354
Protein (gm): 10.2
Carbohydrate (gm): 21.1

1. Sauté onion, carrots, jalapeño chili, and garlic in oil in large saucepan until onion is tender, about 5 minutes. Add pasilla chilies, oregano, cumin, and thyme; cook, covered, 5 minutes.

2. Add broth, tomatoes and liquid, and beans to saucepan; heat to boiling. Reduce heat and simmer, covered, 10 minutes. Process soup in food processor or blender until smooth. Season to taste with salt and pepper. Sprinkle with cilantro.

Quick Manhattan Clam Chowder

6 servings (about 1⅓ cups each)

1 cup chopped onion
1 cup chopped celery and leaves
½ cup chopped red bell pepper
1 clove garlic, minced
2 tablespoons butter
2 cans (6½ ounces each) chopped clams, undrained
1 can (14½ ounces) stewed tomatoes, undrained
2 cups tomato juice
1 cup water
1 cup cubed, peeled potato (½-inch)
1 teaspoon dried thyme leaves
1 bay leaf
Salt and pepper, to taste

Per Serving
Net Carbohydrate (gm): 15.9
Calories: 192
Fat (gm): 5.6
Saturated fat (gm): 2.7
Cholesterol (mg): 52.1
Sodium (mg): 620
Protein (gm): 17.9
Carbohydrate (gm): 18.4

1. Sauté onion, celery, bell pepper, and garlic in butter in large saucepan until tender, about 5 minutes.

2. Stir in clams and liquid, tomatoes and liquid, and remaining ingredients, except salt and pepper. Heat to boiling; reduce heat and simmer, covered, until potato is tender, about 10 minutes. Discard bay leaf; season to taste with salt and pepper.

Clam Bisque

4 servings (about 1 cup each)

1 tablespoon grated onion
2 teaspoons butter
1 tablespoon all-purpose flour
½ teaspoon celery salt
2 cups reduced-fat milk
1 cup reduced-sodium fat-free chicken broth, *or* water
1 can (6½ ounces) minced clams, undrained
Salt and pepper, to taste
1 tablespoon chopped parsley

Per Serving
Net Carbohydrate (gm): 9.7
Calories: 180
Fat (gm): 7.4
Saturated fat (gm): 3.9
Cholesterol (mg): 59.7
Sodium (mg): 385
Protein (gm): 17.8
Carbohydrate (gm): 9.8

1. Sauté onion in butter in medium saucepan 1 minute; stir in flour and celery salt and cook 1 minute longer. Stir in milk and broth; heat to boiling. Boil, stirring, 1 minute. Stir in clams and liquid; cook over medium heat 2 to 3 minutes. Season to taste with salt and pepper. Stir in parsley.

Note: Substitute canned lobster, crab meat, *or* shrimp for the clams to create a different bisque.

Mussel Soup with Saffron

4 servings

1¼ cups bottled clam juice
¾ cup water
⅔ cup dry white wine, *or* clam juice
2½ pounds mussels, scrubbed
⅓ cup julienned carrot
⅓ cup julienned celery
1 large clove garlic, minced
4 green onions and tops, julienned
2 teaspoons olive oil
1 bay leaf
10 saffron threads, finely crumbled
¼ cup finely chopped, peeled and seeded tomatoes
Salt and cayenne pepper, to taste
Finely chopped chives, *or* parsley, as garnish

Per Serving
Net Carbohydrate (gm): 13.1
Calories: 305
Fat (gm): 8.7
Saturated fat (gm): 1.5
Cholesterol (mg): 79.4
Sodium (mg): 1328
Protein (gm): 39.4
Carbohydrate (gm): 14.1

1. Combine clam juice, water, and wine in large saucepan; heat to boiling. Add mussels; reduce heat, and simmer, covered, 5 minutes or until shells open. Drain and reserve cooking liquid. Remove mussels from shells and reserve; discard shells and any unopened mussels.

2. Sauté carrot, celery, garlic, and green onions in oil in large saucepan 5 minutes. Stir in reserved mussel liquid, bay leaf, and saffron and heat to boiling. Reduce heat and simmer, covered, 10 minutes.

3. Add tomatoes and reserved mussels and simmer 2 minutes. Discard bay leaf; season to taste with salt and cayenne pepper. Garnish each serving with chopped chives.

Shrimp Bisque

4 servings (about 1 cup each)

¾ cup chopped onion
2 teaspoons butter
12 ounces peeled, deveined uncooked shrimp
3 tablespoons all-purpose flour
3 tablespoons tomato paste
2 teaspoons curry powder
¼ teaspoon paprika
3 cups reduced-sodium fat-free chicken broth
½ cup whipping cream
Salt and cayenne pepper, to taste
¾ cup chopped tomato

Per Serving
Net Carbohydrate (gm): 11.3
Calories: 299
Fat (gm): 16.2
Saturated fat (gm): 8.5
Cholesterol (mg): 194.6
Sodium (mg): 447
Protein (gm): 25
Carbohydrate (gm): 13.3

1. Sauté onion in butter in large saucepan until tender, about 5 minutes; stir in shrimp and sauté until pink and curled, about 5 minutes. Sprinkle with flour and cook 1 minute longer. Stir in tomato paste, curry powder, and paprika and cook 1 minute. Stir in broth and heat to boiling, stirring until thickened, 1 to 2 minutes.

2. Process soup in blender or food processor until almost smooth. Return soup to saucepan; stir in cream and simmer 2 to 3 minutes. Season to taste with salt and cayenne pepper. Sprinkle each serving with tomato.

Artichoke Bisque with Shrimp

6 servings (about 1 cup each)

⅓ cup sliced green onions and tops
2 tablespoons butter
¼ cup all-purpose flour
3 cups Quick, *or* Rich, Chicken Stock (see p. 20), *or*
    canned chicken broth
1¾ cups reduced-fat milk
1 can (14 ounces) artichoke hearts, rinsed, drained, divided
¾ cup whipping cream
12 ounces peeled, deveined small shrimp
Pinch nutmeg
Salt and cayenne pepper, to taste

Per Serving
Net Carbohydrate (gm): 13.4
Calories: 287
Fat (gm): 18
Saturated fat (gm): 9.9
Cholesterol (mg): 145.3
Sodium (mg): 343
Protein (gm): 17.4
Carbohydrate (gm): 14.5

1. Sauté green onions in butter until tender, about 3 minutes. Sprinkle with flour and cook 2 minutes longer, stirring constantly. Stir in stock and milk and heat to boiling; boil, stirring constantly, until thickened.

2. Process half the artichoke hearts in food processor or blender until smooth. Stir into soup and heat to boiling.

3. Quarter the remaining artichoke hearts and stir into soup. Stir in cream, shrimp, and nutmeg; simmer until shrimp are cooked and soup is hot, about 5 minutes. Season to taste with salt and cayenne pepper.

Oyster and Mushroom Bisque

4 servings (about 1 cup each)

4 cups sliced mushrooms (8 ounces)
1 tablespoon butter
1 tablespoon all-purpose flour
1 cup reduced-sodium fat-free chicken broth
1 egg yolk
⅔ cup reduced-fat milk
⅓ cup whipping cream
1 pint oysters, undrained
3 tablespoons dry sherry, *or* whipping cream
Salt and white pepper, to taste

Per Serving
Net Carbohydrate (gm): 11.7
Calories: 268
Fat (gm): 15.5
Saturated fat (gm): 7.5
Cholesterol (mg): 152.9
Sodium (mg): 236
Protein (gm): 16.9
Carbohydrate (gm): 12.5

1. Sauté mushrooms in butter in medium saucepan until tender, about 5 minutes; stir in flour and cook 1 minute longer. Process mushrooms, chicken broth, and egg yolk in food processor or blender until smooth; return mixture to saucepan and stir in milk and cream. Cook, stirring constantly, over medium heat until lightly thickened; do not boil.

2. Add oysters and liquor to saucepan and cook over low heat, stirring, until edges of oysters curl, 1 to 2 minutes. Stir in sherry; season to taste with salt and white pepper.

Squash and Scallop Soup

6 servings

1 cup chopped celery
½ cup chopped onion
1 tablespoon butter
3 tablespoons all-purpose flour
1 cup reduced-fat milk
2 cups reduced-sodium fat-free chicken broth
2 cups cubed, peeled butternut, *or* Hubbard, squash (½-inch)
¼ teaspoon ground ginger
1 pound bay scallops
1–2 teaspoons low-sodium Worcestershire sauce
Salt and white pepper, to taste

Per Serving
Net Carbohydrate (gm): 13.6
Calories: 178
Fat (gm): 5.8
Saturated fat (gm): 1.4
Cholesterol (mg): 41
Sodium (mg): 464
Protein (gm): 17.1
Carbohydrate (gm): 14.2

1. Sauté celery and onion in butter in large saucepan until tender, about 5 minutes; sprinkle with flour and cook 1 to 2 minutes longer. Stir in milk, broth, squash, and ginger. Heat to boiling; reduce heat and simmer, covered, until squash is tender, about 20 minutes.

2. Stir in scallops; simmer until scallops are tender, about 5 minutes. Stir in Worcestershire sauce; season to taste with salt and white pepper.

Spicy Crab and Scallop Chowder

4 servings

¾ cup chopped onion
½ cup chopped celery
2 teaspoons Cajun seasoning
1 tablespoon butter
1½ cups Fish Stock (see p. 21), *or* clam juice
1 can (14 ounces) stewed tomatoes, undrained
1 can (4 ounces) lump crabmeat, drained
8 ounces bay scallops
¼ cup whipping cream
Salt and pepper, to taste

Per Serving
Net Carbohydrate (gm): 8.8
Calories: 205
Fat (gm): 10.9
Saturated fat (gm): 5.4
Cholesterol (mg): 72
Sodium (mg): 587
Protein (gm): 16.1
Carbohydrate (gm): 10.7

1. Sauté onion, celery, and Cajun seasoning in butter in large saucepan until softened, about 5 minutes. Add stock, and stewed tomatoes and liquid. Heat to boiling; simmer 2 minutes.

2. Stir in crabmeat and scallops; simmer until scallops are tender and opaque, about 3 minutes. Stir in cream; heat until hot (do not boil). Season to taste with salt and pepper.

Sherried Crab Meat Soup

4 servings (about 1½ cups each)

Per Serving
Net Carbohydrate (gm): 6.4
Calories: 157
Fat (gm): 2.4
Saturated fat (gm): 1
Cholesterol (mg): 86.9
Sodium (mg): 436
Protein (gm): 22.3
Carbohydrate (gm): 6.9

1½ cups Fish Stock (see p. 21), *or* reduced-sodium
    fat-free chicken broth
1 cup sliced celery
2 cans (6½ ounces each) crab meat, drained, divided
1 cup reduced-fat milk
¼ teaspoon ground mace
1 tablespoon cornstarch
3 tablespoons dry sherry, *or* water
Salt and cayenne pepper, to taste
Thinly sliced celery, as garnish

1. Combine stock, celery, and 1 can crab meat in large saucepan. Heat to boiling; reduce heat and simmer, covered, until celery is tender, about 10 minutes. Process mixture in food processor or blender until smooth; return to saucepan.

2. Stir in milk and mace and heat to boiling; stir in combined cornstarch and sherry and stir until thickened. Stir in remaining 1 can crab meat; reduce heat and simmer 2 to 3 minutes. Season to taste with salt and cayenne pepper. Serve soup in bowls; garnish with sliced celery.

Egg Drop Crab Soup

6 servings (about 1 cup each)

Per Serving
Net Carbohydrate (gm): 13
Calories: 145
Fat (gm): 4.1
Saturated fat (gm): 0.7
Cholesterol (mg): 112.7
Sodium (mg): 486
Protein (gm): 14.1
Carbohydrate (gm): 14.2

4 green onions and tops, sliced
2 teaspoons minced garlic
1 teaspoon minced gingerroot
1–2 teaspoons dark sesame oil
1 quart reduced-sodium fat-free chicken broth
1 can (15 ounces) cream-style corn
1 can (6 ounces) crabmeat, drained
Salt and pepper, to taste
2 eggs, lightly beaten
1 tablespoon chopped cilantro

1. Sauté green onions, garlic, and gingerroot in oil in large saucepan 2 minutes. Stir in broth, corn, and crabmeat. Heat to boiling; reduce heat and simmer 5 minutes. Season to taste with salt and pepper. Slowly stir eggs into soup. Stir in cilantro.

Ginger Fish Soup

4 servings

1 quart reduced-sodium fat-free chicken broth
1 cup water
1 tablespoon reduced-sodium soy sauce
1 tablespoon minced gingerroot
1 teaspoon minced garlic
1 ounce whole wheat angel hair pasta, *or* spaghetti, broken
12 ounces skinless fish fillets (flounder, whitefish, *or* perch), cut into ½-inch slices
6 ounces small peeled, deveined shrimp
1½ cups thinly sliced, peeled and seeded cucumber
1 cup sliced mushrooms
4 cups packed spinach leaves, sliced
Salt and cayenne pepper, to taste
¼ cup sliced green onions and tops

Per Serving
Net Carbohydrate (gm): 7.9
Calories: 249
Fat (gm): 7.2
Saturated fat (gm): 0.9
Cholesterol (mg): 138.7
Sodium (mg): 509
Protein (gm): 35.1
Carbohydrate (gm): 10

1. Heat broth, water, soy sauce, gingerroot, and garlic to boiling in large saucepan; stir in pasta. Reduce heat and simmer, uncovered, until pasta is al dente, about 4 minutes.

2. Stir in fish, shrimp, cucumber, and mushrooms and simmer, uncovered, until fish flakes with a fork, about 2 minutes. Stir in spinach. Season to taste with salt and cayenne pepper. Sprinkle each serving with green onions.

Cantonese Fish Soup

4 servings

1 quart Fish Stock (see p. 21), *or* canned chicken broth
1 pound haddock, *or* other lean white fish fillets,
    cut into 1-inch strips
2 tablespoons dry white wine, *or* Fish Stock
2 teaspoons minced fresh gingerroot
3 green onions and tops, minced
½ teaspoon dark sesame oil
1 cup sliced spinach leaves
Salt and pepper, to taste

Per Serving
Net Carbohydrate (gm): 1.1
Calories: 131
Fat (gm): 1.5
Saturated fat (gm): 0.2
Cholesterol (mg): 64.3
Sodium (mg): 276
Protein (gm): 24.7
Carbohydrate (gm): 1.6

1. Heat stock to boiling in a large saucepan; add remaining ingredients, except salt and pepper. Reduce heat and simmer, uncovered, until fish is tender and flakes with a fork, about 5 minutes. Season to taste with salt and pepper.

Niçoise Fish Soup

8 servings

1 cup chopped onion
1 tablespoon minced garlic
1 tablespoon olive oil
3 cups water
1 cup bottled clam juice
2 cups chopped tomatoes
½ teaspoon dried thyme leaves
½ teaspoon crushed fennel seeds
½ teaspoon ground turmeric
1 bay leaf
2 pounds deboned assorted firm lean fish (halibut, haddock, red snapper, cod, etc.),
    cut into 1-inch chunks
Salt and cayenne pepper, to taste

Per Serving
Net Carbohydrate (gm): 3.4
Calories: 159
Fat (gm): 4.5
Saturated fat (gm): 0.6
Cholesterol (mg): 36.2
Sodium (mg): 266
Protein (gm): 26.3
Carbohydrate (gm): 4.4

1. Sauté onion and garlic in oil in large saucepan until tender, about
5 minutes. Stir in water, clam juice, tomatoes, and herbs. Heat to boiling;
reduce heat and simmer, covered, 10 minutes. Discard bay leaf.

2. Add fish and heat to boiling; reduce heat and simmer until fish flakes
with a fork, about 5 minutes. Season to taste with salt and cayenne pepper.

Caldo de Pescado

10 servings

2 cups chopped onions
1 cup chopped red bell pepper
3 cloves garlic, minced
1 tablespoon olive oil
3 cups Fish Stock (see p. 21), *or* bottled clam juice
1 can (28 ounce) crushed red tomatoes, undrained
1 cup cubed, unpeeled red potatoes
1 teaspoon grated orange rind
¼ teaspoon ground turmeric
1 pound Pacific rockfish fillets, *or* other firm fish, cut into 1-inch strips
12 ounces red snapper fillets, cut into 1-inch strips
12 ounces small shrimp, peeled, deveined
1 cup whole kernel corn
Salt and cayenne pepper, to taste

Per Serving
Net Carbohydrate (gm): 11.2
Calories: 186
Fat (gm): 3.4
Saturated fat (gm): 0.6
Cholesterol (mg): 80
Sodium (mg): 413
Protein (gm): 25.3
Carbohydrate (gm): 13.8

1. Sauté onions, bell pepper, and garlic in olive oil in large saucepan until
onion is soft, about 8 minutes. Add stock, tomatoes and liquid, potatoes,
orange rind, and turmeric and heat to boiling. Reduce heat and simmer,
covered, 15 to 20 minutes. Add seafood and corn; cook until fish is tender
and flakes with a fork, about 5 minutes. Season to taste with salt and
cayenne pepper.

Sopa Azteca

4 servings

Vegetable cooking spray
2 corn tortillas, cut into thin strips
1 cup sliced red onion
4 cloves garlic, minced
½ teaspoon cumin seeds
½ teaspoon crushed red pepper
1 tablespoon olive oil
1½ quarts Fish Stock (see p. 21), *or* canned chicken broth
12 ounces red snapper, *or* other lean white fish fillets, cut into 1-inch pieces
¼ cup minced cilantro
¼ cup chopped avocado
Lime juice, to taste
Salt, to taste
6 tablespoons (1½ ounces) shredded Cheddar cheese

Per Serving
Net Carbohydrate (gm): 9.2
Calories: 243
Fat (gm): 10
Saturated fat (gm): 3.2
Cholesterol (mg): 42.1
Sodium (mg): 430
Protein (gm): 25.8
Carbohydrate (gm): 11.1

1. Spray large saucepan with cooking spray; heat over medium heat until hot. Cook tortillas over medium heat until crisp, spraying with additional cooking spray as needed. Remove from saucepan and reserve.

2. Sauté onion, garlic, cumin, and red pepper in oil in saucepan until onion is tender, about 5 minutes. Add stock and red snapper; heat to boiling; reduce heat and simmer, uncovered, until fish is tender and flakes with a fork, about 5 minutes.

3. Stir in cilantro and avocado; season to taste with lime juice and salt. Sprinkle each serving with cheese and reserved tortilla strips.

Cioppino Mediterranean

6 servings

¼ cup chopped green bell pepper
2 tablespoons finely chopped onion
1 clove garlic, minced
1 tablespoon olive oil
2 cans (16 ounces each) whole tomatoes, undrained, chopped
1 can (6 ounces) tomato paste
1 cup water
½ cup dry red wine, *or* bottled clam juice
3 tablespoons chopped parsley
1 teaspoon dried oregano leaves
1 teaspoon dried basil leaves
1 pound fillet of sole, cut into bite-sized pieces
1 pound shrimp, peeled, deveined
1 can (6½ ounces) minced clams, undrained
Salt and pepper, to taste

Per Serving
Net Carbohydrate (gm): 13
Calories: 279
Fat (gm): 5.3
Saturated fat (gm): 0.8
Cholesterol (mg): 170.1
Sodium (mg): 457
Protein (gm): 38.5
Carbohydrate (gm): 16.1

1. Sauté bell pepper, onion, and garlic in oil in large saucepan until tender, about 5 minutes. Add remaining ingredients, except seafood, salt, and pepper, and heat to boiling. Reduce heat and simmer, covered, 20 minutes.

2. Add sole, shrimp, and clams and liquor and simmer until sole is tender and flakes with a fork, about 5 minutes. Season to taste with salt and pepper.

Kakavia

12 servings

4 cups chopped onions
1½ cups chopped carrots
1 cup chopped celery
1 cup sliced leeks (white parts only)
1 tablespoon minced garlic
2 tablespoons olive oil
1 can (14½ ounces) diced tomatoes, undrained
1 quart water
1 cup dry white wine, *or* bottled clam juice
3 tablespoons lemon juice
4 pounds fish fillets (striped bass, flounder, grouper, *or* red snapper), cut into
    bite-sized pieces
24 littleneck or cherrystone clams, scrubbed
24 medium shrimp, peeled, deveined
24 mussels, scrubbed
3 bay leaves
½ teaspoon dried thyme leaves
¼ cup minced parsley
Salt and pepper, to taste

Per Serving
Net Carbohydrate (gm): 12
Calories: 332
Fat (gm): 8
Saturated fat (gm): 1.4
Cholesterol (mg): 177
Sodium (mg): 390
Protein (gm): 45.1
Carbohydrate (gm): 14.2

1. Sauté onions, carrots, celery, leeks, and garlic in oil in large saucepan until onions are tender, about 10 minutes.

2. Add tomatoes and liquid, water, wine, and lemon juice; heat to boiling. Add remaining ingredients, except parsley, salt, and pepper; reduce heat and simmer, covered, until fish is tender and clams and mussels open, about 10 minutes. Discard bay leaves and any unopened clams and mussels. Stir in parsley; season to taste with salt and pepper.

Mediterranean-Style Shrimp Vegetable Soup

6 servings (about 1½ cups each)

2 cups sliced mushrooms
1 cup chopped onion
½ cup chopped red bell pepper
3 cloves garlic, minced
1 tablespoon olive oil
1 can (16 ounces) whole tomatoes, undrained,
    coarsely chopped
1 can (8 ounces) tomato sauce
2 pounds shrimp, peeled, deveined
2 cups reduced-sodium vegetable, *or* chicken, broth
½ cup dry white wine, *or* clam juice
1 cup bottled clam juice
2 strips orange rind (3 x ½ inch)
2 bay leaves
1 teaspoon dried marjoram leaves
¼ teaspoon fennel seeds, crushed
Salt and pepper, to taste

Per Serving
Net Carbohydrate (gm): 9.1
Calories: 245
Fat (gm): 5.6
Saturated fat (gm): 0.8
Cholesterol (mg): 229.8
Sodium (mg): 656
Protein (gm): 36.1
Carbohydrate (gm): 11.7

1. Sauté mushrooms, onion, bell pepper, and garlic in oil in large saucepan until vegetables are tender, 8 to 10 minutes. Add remaining ingredients, except salt and pepper; heat to boiling. Reduce heat and simmer, covered, 10 minutes. Discard bay leaves; season to taste with salt and pepper.

Herbed Broccoli-Chicken Soup

6 servings (about 1 cup each)

3 cans (15 ounces each) reduced-sodium fat-free chicken broth
4 cloves garlic, minced
2–3 teaspoons dried thyme leaves
3 cups small broccoli florets
12 ounces cubed, cooked skinless chicken breast
1 cup uncooked whole wheat rotini, *or* other whole wheat pasta
2–3 tablespoons lemon juice
Salt and pepper, to taste

Per Serving
Net Carbohydrate (gm): 13.9
Calories: 204
Fat (gm): 3.5
Saturated fat (gm): 0.6
Cholesterol (mg): 65.8
Sodium (mg): 367
Protein (gm): 26.7
Carbohydrate (gm): 16.9

1. Heat chicken broth, garlic, and thyme to boiling in medium saucepan; stir in broccoli, chicken, and rotini. Reduce heat and simmer, uncovered, until broccoli is tender and pasta is al dente, about 10 minutes.

2. Stir in lemon juice; season to taste with salt and pepper.

Chicken-Rice Soup

8 servings (about 1¾ cups each)

1 cup finely chopped onion
1 cup thinly sliced carrots
1 cup thinly sliced celery
1 large garlic clove, minced
2 teaspoons canola oil
2 quarts reduced-sodium fat-free chicken broth
2 pounds boneless, skinless chicken breast
¾ cup shredded parsnip
¾ cup shredded turnip
½ cup brown basmati rice
2 bay leaves
¾ teaspoon dried thyme leaves
½ teaspoon dried tarragon leaves
Salt and pepper, to taste

Per Serving
Net Carbohydrate (gm): 13.8
Calories: 253
Fat (gm): 4.5
Saturated fat (gm): 0.5
Cholesterol (mg): 90.7
Sodium (mg): 336
Protein (gm): 34.9
Carbohydrate (gm): 16.3

1. Sauté onion, carrots, celery, and garlic in oil in large saucepan until onion is tender, about 5 minutes. Add remaining ingredients except salt and pepper. Heat to boiling; reduce heat and simmer, covered, 45 minutes, or until rice is tender.

2. Lift out chicken; remove meat, cut into bite-sized pieces, and return to soup. Discard bay leaves; season to taste with salt and pepper.

Chicken and Vegetable Chowder

8 servings (about 1½ cups each)

2 cups chopped zucchini
1 cup chopped carrots
¾ cup chopped onion
¾ cup chopped green bell pepper
½ cup chopped celery
2 cloves garlic, minced
2 tablespoons butter
1½ pounds skinless, boneless chicken breast, cubed (1-inch)
¼ cup all-purpose flour
1 quart reduced-sodium fat-free chicken broth
1 teaspoon dried thyme leaves
1 bay leaf
¾ cup whipping cream
¼ cup chopped parsley
Salt and pepper, to taste

Per Serving
Net Carbohydrate (gm): 7.5
Calories: 260
Fat (gm): 13.3
Saturated fat (gm): 7.4
Cholesterol (mg): 100.8
Sodium (mg): 222
Protein (gm): 25.2
Carbohydrate (gm): 9.4

1. Sauté vegetables in butter in large saucepan until tender, about 8 minutes; stir in chicken and sauté until lightly browned, about 5 minutes. Sprinkle with flour and cook 2 minutes longer. Stir in broth and herbs. Heat to boiling; reduce heat and simmer until chicken is tender, about 15 minutes.

2. Stir in cream and simmer until hot, 2 to 3 minutes; stir in parsley. Discard bay leaf; season to taste with salt and pepper.

Tex-Mex Chicken Chowder

6 servings

2 cups diced zucchini
½ cup finely chopped onion
1 clove garlic, chopped
1 tablespoon butter
1 cup cubed, cooked chicken breast
3 cups reduced-fat milk
2 cups (8 ounces) shredded pepper-Jack cheese
Salt and pepper, to taste

Per Serving
Net Carbohydrate (gm): 7.9
Calories: 285
Fat (gm): 18.9
Saturated fat (gm): 12
Cholesterol (mg): 80.5
Sodium (mg): 350
Protein (gm): 20.7
Carbohydrate (gm): 8.6

1. Sauté zucchini, onion, and garlic in butter in large saucepan until tender, about 5 minutes; add chicken and milk and heat to boiling. Reduce heat and simmer, covered, 5 minutes. Reduce heat to low and gradually add cheese, stirring until melted. Do not boil. Season to taste with salt and pepper.

Cheesy Chicken Corn Chowder

6 servings

½ cup finely chopped onion
1 tablespoon butter
4 cups cubed, cooked chicken breast (1 pound)
1 can (15 ounces) cream-style corn
1 cup diced zucchini
3 cups reduced-fat milk
1½ cups (6 ounces) shredded Cheddar cheese
Salt and pepper, to taste

Per Serving
Net Carbohydrate (gm): 19.3
Calories: 379
Fat (gm): 18.1
Saturated fat (gm): 10.5
Cholesterol (mg): 110.4
Sodium (mg): 506
Protein (gm): 34.6
Carbohydrate (gm): 20.6

1. Sauté onion in butter in large saucepan until tender, about 5 minutes; add chicken, corn, zucchini, and milk and heat to boiling. Reduce heat and simmer, covered, 5 minutes. Reduce heat to low and gradually add cheese, stirring until melted. Do not boil. Season to taste with salt and pepper.

Sopa de Casa

6 servings (about 1⅓ cups each)

1 cup chopped onion
½ jalapeño chili, minced
2 large cloves garlic, minced
1 tablespoon canola oil
1 pound boneless, skinless chicken breast,
    cut into ¾-inch pieces
2½ cups frozen whole kernel corn, thawed, divided
2½ cups reduced-sodium fat-free chicken broth
¼ cup whipping cream
1 can (4 ounces) chopped green chilies, undrained
1 cup chopped tomato
¾ teaspoon dried oregano leaves
¼ teaspoon ground cumin
¾ cup (3 ounces) shredded Monterey Jack cheese
Salt and pepper, to taste

Per Serving
Net Carbohydrate (gm): 14.9
Calories: 286
Fat (gm): 12.4
Saturated fat (gm): 5.3
Cholesterol (mg): 82.9
Sodium (mg): 318
Protein (gm): 26.6
Carbohydrate (gm): 18.1

1. Sauté onion, jalapeño chili, and garlic in oil in large saucepan until tender, about 3 minutes. Add chicken and cook over medium heat until chicken is browned, about 5 minutes.

2. Process 1½ cups corn and chicken broth in food processor or blender until smooth; stir into saucepan. Stir in remaining 1 cup corn, cream, chilies, tomato, and herbs and heat to boiling. Reduce heat and simmer, covered, 10 minutes; add cheese, stirring until melted. Season to taste with salt and pepper.

Indian Spinach Soup with Chicken

6 servings

2 pounds boneless, skinless chicken breast, cubed (½-inch)
1 cup chopped onion
½ teaspoon cumin seeds
2 teaspoons canola oil
2 large cloves garlic, minced
1½ tablespoons mild, *or* hot, curry powder
2 teaspoons ground coriander
½ teaspoon ground cardamom
1½ quarts reduced-sodium fat-free chicken broth
1½ cups cubed, peeled potatoes
1 package (10 ounces) frozen chopped spinach, thawed
1 cup chopped tomatoes
Salt and pepper, to taste

Per Serving
Net Carbohydrate (gm): 10.7
Calories: 292
Fat (gm): 5.3
Saturated fat (gm): 0.7
Cholesterol (mg): 112.6
Sodium (mg): 431
Protein (gm): 44.8
Carbohydrate (gm): 14.1

1. Sauté chicken, onion, and cumin seeds in oil in large saucepan until onion begins to brown, about 5 minutes. Add garlic and spices and sauté 1 minute longer. Add broth and potatoes; heat to boiling. Reduce heat and simmer, covered, until potatoes are tender, 10 to 15 minutes. Add spinach and tomatoes; simmer, covered 5 minutes. Season to taste with salt and pepper.

Lentil-Vegetable Soup

4 servings

½ cup chopped onion
½ cup chopped carrot
½ cup chopped celery
½ cup chopped lean smoked ham
⅛–¼ teaspoon red pepper flakes
1 tablespoon olive oil
½ cup dried lentils
1 quart reduced-sodium fat-free chicken broth
1 can (14½ ounce) stewed tomatoes, undrained
Salt and pepper, to taste

Per Serving
Net Carbohydrate (gm): 13.9
Calories: 214
Fat (gm): 5.9
Saturated fat (gm): 1
Cholesterol (mg): 31.3
Sodium (mg): 754
Protein (gm): 17.8
Carbohydrate (gm): 23.6

1. Sauté onion, carrot, celery, ham, and red pepper flakes in oil in large saucepan until onion is browned, about 5 minutes. Stir in lentils and broth; heat to boiling. Reduce heat and simmer 30 minutes, or until lentils are just tender.

2. Add tomatoes and liquid; simmer 10 minutes. Season to taste with salt and pepper.

Chicken-Vegetable Soup with Pasta

4 servings

1 pound boneless, skinless chicken breast, cubed (½-inch)
1 cup chopped onion
1 cup sliced celery
½ cup sliced carrot
3 cloves garlic, minced
1 teaspoon dried thyme leaves
½ teaspoon dried oregano leaves
1 tablespoon olive oil
1 quart reduced-sodium fat-free chicken broth
1 cup water
½ cup broken whole wheat spaghetti, uncooked
⅓ cup frozen peas
2 cups sliced escarole, *or* spinach, leaves
Salt and pepper, to taste
2 tablespoons grated Parmesan cheese

Per Serving
Net Carbohydrate (gm): 10.8
Calories: 275
Fat (gm): 7.3
Saturated fat (gm): 1.4
Cholesterol (mg): 92.7
Sodium (mg): 397
Protein (gm): 37.1
Carbohydrate (gm): 13.9

1. Sauté chicken, onion, celery, carrot, garlic, and herbs in oil in large saucepan until lightly browned, about 8 minutes.

2. Add broth and water; heat to boiling. Stir in pasta, peas, and escarole. Reduce heat and simmer, uncovered, until pasta is al dente, about 7 minutes. Season to taste with salt and pepper. Spoon soup into bowls; sprinkle with cheese.

Beef, Barley, and Vegetable Soup

8 servings

1½ pounds lean beef stew meat, fat trimmed
2 tablespoons olive oil
1 cup chopped onion
⅔ cup sliced celery
½ cup chopped carrot
1 clove garlic, minced
1 tablespoon all-purpose flour
1 quart water
2 cups reduced-sodium fat-free beef broth
½ teaspoon dried marjoram leaves
½ teaspoon dried thyme leaves
1 bay leaf
1 can (14½ ounces) diced tomatoes, undrained
1 cup cut green beans (1-inch)
1 cup cubed parsnips
½ cup frozen peas
⅓ cup quick-cooking barley
Salt and pepper, to taste

Per Serving
Net Carbohydrate (gm): 11.9
Calories: 238
Fat (gm): 9.6
Saturated fat (gm): 2.8
Cholesterol (mg): 45.5
Sodium (mg): 279
Protein (gm): 22.2
Carbohydrate (gm): 15.5

1. Cook beef in oil in large saucepan over medium heat until browned, 8 to 10 minutes. Add onion, celery, carrot, and garlic; cook 5 minutes. Stir in flour; cook 1 minute longer.

2. Add water, broth, and herbs to saucepan; heat to boiling. Reduce heat and simmer, covered, until beef is very tender, 1 to 1½ hours.

3. Add remaining ingredients, except salt and pepper. Heat to boiling; reduce heat and simmer, covered, until vegetables are cooked and barley is tender, about 10 minutes. Discard bay leaf; season to taste with salt and pepper.

Creole Beef and Barley Soup

6 servings

1 pound lean ground beef
1 cup chopped onion
2 large garlic cloves, minced
1 tablespoon olive, *or* canola, oil
3 cups shredded cabbage
1 cup sliced celery
1 cup sliced carrots
¼ cup pearl barley
1½ quarts Brown Beef Stock (see p. 21), *or* canned beef broth
1 tablespoon Creole seasoning blend
1 teaspoon chili powder
½ teaspoon dry mustard
1 can (14½ ounces) no-salt-added stewed tomatoes
Salt, to taste

Per Serving
Net Carbohydrate (gm): 14.2
Calories: 273
Fat (gm): 14.6
Saturated fat (gm): 4.9
Cholesterol (mg): 51.2
Sodium (mg): 102
Protein (gm): 17.1
Carbohydrate (gm): 18.6

1. Cook beef, onion, and garlic in oil in large saucepan over medium heat until beef is browned, about 5 minutes. Drain fat.

2. Stir in remaining ingredients, except tomatoes and salt; heat to boiling. Reduce heat and simmer, covered, 40 minutes; add tomatoes and simmer 10 minutes or until barley is tender. Season to taste with salt.

Hearty Beef and Vegetable Soup

8 servings (about 1½ cups each)

1 quart Brown Beef Stock (see p. 21), *or* canned beef broth
2 cups tomato juice
3 cups shredded green, *or* red, cabbage
1 cup thinly sliced onion
1 cup thinly sliced carrots
1 cup thinly sliced mushrooms
1 cup cubed (½-inch) unpeeled potato
4 cups cubed cooked lean beef roast, *or* steak (1 pound)
2 tablespoons raisins
1 tablespoon packed light brown sugar
1 teaspoon caraway seeds
1 teaspoon paprika
2–3 teaspoons vinegar
Salt and pepper, to taste
Dill Sour Cream (see p. 39)

Per Serving
Net Carbohydrate (gm): 13.8
Calories: 271
Fat (gm): 15.3
Saturated fat (gm): 6.8
Cholesterol (mg): 57.4
Sodium (mg): 65
Protein (gm): 17.7
Carbohydrate (gm): 16.3

1. Combine all ingredients, except salt, pepper, and Dill Sour Cream, in large saucepan. Heat to boiling; reduce heat and simmer, covered, until vegetables are tender, about 20 minutes. Season to taste with salt and pepper. Ladle into bowls; top with dollops of Dill Sour Cream.

Meaty Minestrone

10 servings (about 1⅔ cups each)

Per Serving
Net Carbohydrate (gm): 15.7
Calories: 282
Fat (gm): 12.8
Saturated fat (gm): 4.1
Cholesterol (mg): 48.5
Sodium (mg): 195
Protein (gm): 22.7
Carbohydrate (gm): 20.6

1½ pounds lean beef stew meat, cubed (½-inch)
1 cup chopped onion
1 cup sliced carrots
½ cup sliced celery
2 cloves garlic, minced
1 tablespoon olive oil
1½ quarts Beef Stock (see p. 21), *or* canned beef broth
1 tablespoon Italian herb blend
1 bay leaf
1 can (15 ounces) Great Northern beans, rinsed, drained
1 can (14½ ounces) diced tomatoes, undrained
8 ounces Italian-style turkey sausage, cooked, drained, sliced
1 package (10 ounces) frozen Romano (Italian) green beans
2 ounces uncooked whole wheat rotini, *or* shell pasta
Salt and pepper, to taste
Shredded Parmesan cheese, as garnish

1. Sauté beef, onion, carrots, celery, and garlic in oil in large saucepan until lightly browned, about 10 minutes. Stir in stock and herbs; heat to boiling. Reduce heat and simmer, covered, until meat is tender, about 1 hour.

2. Stir in remaining ingredients, except salt, pepper, and cheese. Heat to boiling; reduce heat and simmer, covered, until pasta is al dente, about 15 minutes. Discard bay leaf; season to taste with salt and pepper. Serve soup in bowls; sprinkle with Parmesan cheese.

Sausage and Lentil Soup

10 servings (about 1½ cups each)

Per Serving
Net Carbohydrate (gm): 12.5
Calories: 211
Fat (gm): 9.9
Saturated fat (gm): 3
Cholesterol (mg): 18.3
Sodium (mg): 227
Protein (gm): 11.8
Carbohydrate (gm): 21.4

12 ounces reduced-sodium reduced-fat Italian-style
    turkey sausage, casing removed
1½ cups chopped onions
¾ cup chopped carrots
8 ounces dried lentils
3 quarts Beef Stock (see p. 21), *or* canned beef broth
1 can (28 ounces) diced tomatoes, undrained
½ teaspoon dried marjoram leaves
½ teaspoon dried thyme leaves
1 bay leaf
2–3 teaspoons lemon juice
Salt and pepper, to taste

1. Cook sausage in large saucepan over medium heat until browned; drain and crumble with a fork. Add onions and carrots; sauté until lightly browned, about 5 minutes.

2. Add lentils, stock, tomatoes and liquid, and herbs to saucepan and heat to boiling. Reduce heat and simmer, covered, until lentils are tender, about 45 minutes. Discard bay leaf; season to taste with lemon juice, salt, and pepper.

Veggie Noodle Soup

6 servings (about 1¾ cups each)

1 cup chopped celery
1 cup chopped carrots
½ cup chopped parsnip
½ cup chopped onion
1 tablespoon canola, *or* olive, oil
2 quarts Rich Chicken Stock (see p. 20), *or*
    canned chicken broth
1 cup small broccoli florets
½ cup cut green beans
½ cup frozen peas
½ teaspoon dried thyme leaves
½ teaspoon dried rosemary leaves
2 ounces uncooked egg noodles
2 cups shredded, cooked chicken breast
Salt and pepper, to taste

Per Serving
Net Carbohydrate (gm): 13.5
Calories: 221
Fat (gm): 5.4
Saturated fat (gm): 0.7
Cholesterol (mg): 46.2
Sodium (mg): 120
Protein (gm): 23.3
Carbohydrate (gm): 17

1. Sauté celery, carrots, parsnip, and onion in oil in large saucepan until tender, about 8 minutes. Stir in stock, broccoli, green beans, peas, and herbs; heat to boiling.

2. Stir in noodles and chicken; reduce heat and simmer until noodles are tender, 7 to 10 minutes. Season to taste with salt and pepper.

Country Chicken Noodle Soup

8 servings

1 stewing chicken, cut up (about 4 pounds)
3 quarts water
1 onion, quartered
1 teaspoon dried marjoram leaves
1 bay leaf
1½ cups sliced carrots
1 cup frozen whole kernel corn
1 cup frozen peas
Country Noodles (recipe follows)
¼ cup chopped parsley
Salt and pepper, to taste

Per Serving
Net Carbohydrate (gm): 18.5
Calories: 317
Fat (gm): 9.6
Saturated fat (gm): 2.4
Cholesterol (mg): 116.3
Sodium (mg): 220
Protein (gm): 34.7
Carbohydrate (gm): 21.2

1. Place chicken, water, onion, marjoram, and bay leaf in large saucepan. Heat to boiling; reduce heat and simmer, covered, until chicken is tender, about 1 hour. Strain broth and return to saucepan; skim off fat. Remove meat from chicken, discarding skin and bones; cut meat into small cubes and add to broth.

2. Stir carrots, corn, and peas into saucepan; heat to boiling. Reduce heat and simmer, covered, until carrots are almost tender, about 10 minutes. Unroll Country Noodles and drop into soup; simmer until noodles are tender, 3 to 5 minutes. Stir in parsley; season to taste with salt and pepper.

Country Noodles

1 cup whole wheat flour
1 egg
1 tablespoon water
¼ teaspoon salt

1. Place flour in medium bowl. Make a well in center; add egg, water, and salt to well and beat with fork to combine. Gradually mix flour into egg mixture with fork until dough is formed. Knead dough on floured surface until smooth, kneading in additional flour if dough is sticky. Let dough stand, covered, at room temperature 1 hour.

2. Roll dough on lightly floured surface to ⅛-inch thickness. Loosely roll up dough like a jelly roll; cut into scant ⅓-inch slices.

Microwave Chicken Chili

4 servings (about 1½ cups each)

12 ounces ground chicken breast
⅓ cup chopped onion
1 small clove garlic, minced
1 can (14 ounces) stewed tomatoes, undrained
¼ teaspoon ground cumin
1 teaspoon chili powder
1 can (15 ounces) pinto beans, rinsed, drained
Salt and pepper, to taste

Per Serving
Net Carbohydrate (gm): 16.9
Calories: 300
Fat (gm): 11.8
Saturated fat (gm): 0.2
Cholesterol (mg): 0
Sodium (mg): 665
Protein (gm): 24.7
Carbohydrate (gm): 23.4

1. Combine chicken, onion, and garlic in 2-quart glass casserole; microwave, loosely covered, on High power until chicken is cooked, about 4 minutes. Drain; crumble chicken with a fork.

2. Stir in remaining ingredients, except salt and pepper; microwave, covered, on Medium power 10 minutes, stirring halfway through cooking time. Season to taste with salt and pepper.

Big Red Chili

6 servings (about 1½ cups each)

1½ pounds ground beef sirloin
1 cup chopped red onion
1 cup chopped red bell pepper
1 can (28 ounces) crushed tomatoes, undrained
1 can (15 ounces) red kidney beans, rinsed, drained
2 tablespoons red wine vinegar
2 tablespoons chili powder
¼ teaspoon ground allspice
⅔ cup mild, *or* medium, picante sauce
Salt and pepper, to taste

Per Serving
Net Carbohydrate (gm): 17.5
Calories: 272
Fat (gm): 6.1
Saturated fat (gm): 1.8
Cholesterol (mg): 68.6
Sodium (mg): 780
Protein (gm): 29.6
Carbohydrate (gm): 25.4

1. Cook beef in large saucepan over medium heat until browned, about 8 minutes; drain fat and crumble with a fork. Add onion and bell pepper and sauté until tender, about 5 minutes. Add remaining ingredients, except picante sauce, salt, and pepper; heat to boiling. Reduce heat and simmer, covered, 20 minutes. Add picante sauce; simmer, covered, 5 to 10 minutes longer. Season to taste with salt and pepper.

Variation:

Farmhouse Chili—Make recipe as above, substituting home-style turkey sausage for the ground beef and tomato juice for the picante sauce. Decrease chili powder to 1 tablespoon. Omit allspice; add 1 to 2 tablespoons maple syrup and ½ teaspoon each ground cumin and dried sage leaves.

South-of-the-Border Chili

6 servings (about 1 cup each)

½ cup chopped onion
¼ cup sliced green onions and tops
½ cup chopped red bell pepper
1 small jalapeño chili, seeded, finely chopped
2 cloves garlic, minced
1 tablespoon canola oil
1 pound boneless, skinless chicken breast, cut into ¾-inch pieces
1 can (10¾ ounces) reduced-sodium reduced-fat cream of chicken soup
½ cup tomato sauce
1 cup reduced-fat milk
1 can (4 ounces) chopped green chilies, drained
1 tablespoon chili powder
½ teaspoon ground cumin
Salt and pepper, to taste
½ cup (2 ounces) shredded Monterey Jack cheese

Per Serving
Net Carbohydrate (gm): 8.8
Calories: 218
Fat (gm): 8.6
Saturated fat (gm): 2.9
Cholesterol (mg): 61.2
Sodium (mg): 583
Protein (gm): 23.3
Carbohydrate (gm): 10.9

1. Sauté onions, bell pepper, jalapeño chili, and garlic in oil in large saucepan 5 minutes; add chicken and cook until browned, 5 to 8 minutes.

2. Stir in remaining ingredients, except salt, pepper, and cheese; heat to boiling. Reduce heat and simmer, covered, until chicken is tender, 8 to 10 minutes. Season to taste with salt and pepper. Sprinkle each serving with cheese.

White Chili

8 servings

2 cups chopped red, *or* green, bell peppers
2 cups chopped onions
2 cloves garlic, minced
2 teaspoons minced gingerroot
2 jalapeño chilies, minced
1 teaspoon dried thyme leaves
1 teaspoon dried oregano leaves
1 tablespoon canola oil
1½ pounds boneless, skinless chicken breast, cubed (¾-inch)
2 tablespoons all-purpose flour
2 cups reduced-sodium fat-free chicken broth
2 cans (15 ounces each) Great Northern beans, rinsed, drained
Salt and pepper, to taste
Green Tomato Salsa (recipe follows)
Sour cream, as garnish

Per Serving
Net Carbohydrate (gm): 17.1
Calories: 246
Fat (gm): 4
Saturated fat (gm): 0.5
Cholesterol (mg): 55.5
Sodium (mg): 282
Protein (gm): 27.8
Carbohydrate (gm): 24.3

1. Sauté peppers, onions, garlic, gingerroot, chilies, thyme, and oregano in oil in large saucepan until onions are tender, about 8 minutes. Add chicken and sauté until browned, about 5 minutes; sprinkle with flour and cook 1 to 2 minutes longer.

2. Add broth and beans to saucepan; heat to boiling. Reduce heat and simmer, uncovered, until chicken is tender, about 10 minutes. Season to taste with salt and pepper. Serve with Green Tomato Salsa and sour cream.

Green Tomato Salsa

makes about ¾ cup

8 ounces Mexican green tomatoes (tomatillos)
⅓ cup chopped onion
1 clove garlic, minced
1 tablespoon finely chopped cilantro
1 teaspoon minced jalapeño chili
¼ teaspoon ground cumin
⅛ teaspoon sugar
Salt, to taste

1. Remove and discard husks from green tomatoes; simmer in water to cover in large saucepan until tender, 5 to 8 minutes. Cool; drain, reserving liquid.

2. Process tomatoes, onion, garlic, cilantro, jalapeño chili, cumin, and sugar in food processor, using pulse technique, until almost smooth, adding enough reserved liquid to make medium dipping consistency. Season to taste with salt.

Pork Chili with Greens

8 servings (about 1½ cups each)

2 pounds ground lean pork, *or* turkey
2 cans (15 ounces each) kidney beans, rinsed, drained
2 cans (16 ounces each) whole tomatoes, undrained, chopped
½ cup chopped onion
½ teaspoon ground cinnamon
½ teaspoon ground cumin
8 cups coarsely chopped kale (8 ounces)
Salt and pepper, to taste

Per Serving
Net Carbohydrate (gm): 16.6
Calories: 290
Fat (gm): 7
Saturated fat (gm): 2.3
Cholesterol (mg): 68.7
Sodium (mg): 438
Protein (gm): 31.6
Carbohydrate (gm): 25.4

1. Cook pork in large saucepan over medium-high heat until browned, about 10 minutes; drain well. Stir in remaining ingredients, except kale, salt, and pepper. Heat to boiling; reduce heat and simmer, covered, 45 minutes.

2. Stir kale into soup; simmer uncovered 10 minutes. Season to taste with salt and pepper.

Tip: For a chili that is even lower in carbohydrates, use spinach in place of kale.

Chili con Carne

8 servings (about 1 cup each)

1 pound lean ground beef
1½ cups chopped onions
1 cup chopped green bell pepper
2 cloves garlic, minced
1 tablespoon canola oil
1–2 tablespoons chili powder
2 teaspoons dried cumin
1 teaspoon dried oregano leaves
¼ teaspoon ground cloves
2 cans (14½ ounces each) whole tomatoes, no-salt-added,
    undrained, coarsely chopped
1 can (6 ounces) tomato paste
¾ cup reduced-sodium fat-free beef broth
1 tablespoon packed light brown sugar
2–3 teaspoons unsweetened cocoa
1 can (15 ounces) pinto beans, rinsed, drained
Salt and pepper, to taste
½ cup (2 ounces) shredded Cheddar cheese
½ cup thinly sliced green onions and tops
½ cup sour cream

Per Serving
Net Carbohydrate (gm): 18.4
Calories: 312
Fat (gm): 16.5
Saturated fat (gm): 6.8
Cholesterol (mg): 50.9
Sodium (mg): 302
Protein (gm): 18.5
Carbohydrate (gm): 24.6

1. Cook ground beef, onions, bell pepper, and garlic in oil in large saucepan over medium heat until meat is brown and vegetables are tender, about 10 minutes. Add chili powder, cumin, oregano, and cloves; cook 1 to 2 minutes longer.

2. Add tomatoes and liquid, tomato paste, broth, brown sugar, and cocoa to beef mixture. Heat to boiling; reduce heat and simmer, covered, 1 hour. Stir in beans and simmer, uncovered, until slightly thickened. Season to taste with salt and pepper.

3. Spoon chili into bowls; sprinkle with 1 tablespoon each of cheese, green onions, and sour cream.

Chili Rio Grande

12 servings (about 1½ cups each)

1 quart chopped onions
1 tablespoon canola oil
2 pounds lean pork, cubed
1 pound lean ground beef
2 tablespoons minced garlic
¼ cup chili powder
1 tablespoon ground cumin
2 teaspoons dried oregano leaves
2 cans (16 ounces each) whole tomatoes, undrained, chopped
1¾ cups reduced-sodium fat-free beef broth
1 can (12 ounces) beer, *or* tomato juice
1 can (4 ounces) chopped green chilies
2 cans (15 ounces each) pinto beans, rinsed, drained
Salt and pepper, to taste

Per Serving
Net Carbohydrate (gm): 15.8
Calories: 325
Fat (gm): 12.5
Saturated fat (gm): 4.1
Cholesterol (mg): 71.3
Sodium (mg): 302
Protein (gm): 29.1
Carbohydrate (gm): 22.4

1. Sauté onions in oil in large saucepan until golden brown, about 20 minutes. Add meats and cook until brown, about 10 minutes. Stir in garlic, chili powder, cumin, and oregano and cook 2 minutes longer.

2. Stir in tomatoes and liquid, broth, beer, and chilies. Heat to boiling; reduce heat and simmer, covered, until pork is very tender, about 1½ hours, stirring occasionally. Stir in beans and cook, uncovered, until thickened, about 10 minutes. Season to taste with salt and pepper.

THREE

Poultry

Chicken Fricassee

6 servings

6 boneless, skinless chicken breast halves (6 ounces each)
1 tablespoon canola oil
1 cup sliced onion
1½ cups cut carrots (1-inch pieces)
1½ cups cut celery (1-inch pieces)
2 cloves garlic, minced
3 tablespoons all-purpose flour
3½ cups reduced-sodium fat-free chicken broth
2 bay leaves
1 teaspoon lemon juice
½ teaspoon packed brown sugar
Pinch ground cloves
2 tablespoons chopped parsley
Salt and pepper, to taste

Per Serving
Net Carbohydrate (gm): 8.3
Calories: 279
Fat (gm): 5.4
Saturated fat (gm): 0.7
Cholesterol (mg): 113.2
Sodium (mg): 273
Protein (gm): 44.7
Carbohydrate (gm): 10.4

1. Sauté chicken in oil in Dutch oven until browned, about 8 minutes. Remove from pot. Add vegetables to Dutch oven; sauté until lightly browned, about 5 minutes. Stir in flour and cook 1 minute longer.

2. Return chicken to Dutch oven. Add broth, bay leaves, lemon juice, brown sugar, and cloves. Heat to boiling; reduce heat and simmer, covered, until chicken is tender, about 20 minutes. Simmer, uncovered, until sauce is thickened to medium consistency, about 5 minutes. Discard bay leaves. Stir in parsley and season to taste with salt and pepper.

Sunday Chicken

6 servings

1 cup thinly sliced onion
1 cup sliced celery
2 teaspoons minced garlic
1 teaspoon dried thyme leaves
2 tablespoons olive oil
3 pounds chicken pieces (bone-in)
¾ cup reduced-sodium fat-free chicken broth
½ cup dry vermouth, *or* chicken broth
1½ cups cubed (1 inch) new potatoes
Salt and pepper, to taste
¼ cup chopped parsley

Per Serving
Net Carbohydrate (gm): 9.9
Calories: 416
Fat (gm): 25.5
Saturated fat (gm): 6.5
Cholesterol (mg): 109.6
Sodium (mg): 134
Protein (gm): 28.7
Carbohydrate (gm): 11.6

1. Sauté onion, celery, garlic, and thyme in oil until softened, about 3 minutes. Add chicken and cook until browned on all sides, about 8 minutes. Add broth and vermouth; heat to boiling. Reduce heat and simmer, covered, 20 minutes.

2. Add potatoes and simmer, covered, until chicken and potatoes are tender, about 20 minutes. Season to taste with salt and pepper; sprinkle with parsley.

Chicken Stew with Parsley Dumplings

6 servings

1 cup chopped onion
1 cup sliced carrots
½ cup sliced celery
1 tablespoon butter
3 cups reduced-sodium fat-free chicken broth, divided
1½ pounds boneless, skinless chicken breasts, cubed
½ teaspoon dried sage leaves
½ cup frozen peas
2 tablespoons finely chopped parsley
⅓ cup whole wheat flour
Salt and pepper, to taste
Parsley Dumplings (recipe follows)

Per Serving
Net Carbohydrate (gm): 19.4
Calories: 305
Fat (gm): 7.9
Saturated fat (gm): 3.8
Cholesterol (mg): 93
Sodium (mg): 451
Protein (gm): 34.3
Carbohydrate (gm): 23.5

1. Sauté onion, carrots, and celery in butter in large saucepan until lightly browned, about 5 minutes. Add 2½ cups chicken broth, chicken, and sage; heat to boiling. Reduce heat and simmer, covered, until chicken is cooked and vegetables are tender, 10 to 15 minutes.

2. Stir peas and parsley into stew; heat to boiling. Mix flour and remaining ½ cup chicken broth; stir into stew. Boil, stirring constantly, until thickened, 1 to 2 minutes. Season to taste with salt and pepper.

3. Spoon Parsley Dumplings dough into 6 mounds on top of boiling chicken and vegetables (do not drop directly into liquid). Reduce heat and simmer, covered, 10 minutes. Simmer, uncovered, 10 minutes longer.

Parsley Dumplings

¾ cup whole wheat pastry flour
1 teaspoon baking powder
¼ teaspoon salt
1½ tablespoons butter
⅓ cup reduced-fat milk
1 tablespoon finely chopped parsley

1. Combine flour, baking powder, and salt in small bowl. Cut in butter with pastry blender until mixture resembles coarse crumbs. Stir in milk to make a soft dough; stir in parsley.

Royal Palace Chicken

4 servings

4 boneless, skinless chicken breast halves (5 ounces each)
3 tablespoons all-purpose flour
1 teaspoon paprika
½ teaspoon dry mustard
1 tablespoon canola oil
½ cup dry white wine, *or* chicken broth
¼ cup water
1 cup peeled pearl onions
¾ cup halved baby carrots
½ teaspoon dried thyme leaves
Salt and pepper, to taste
Duchess Potatoes (recipe follows)
1 tablespoon melted butter

Per Serving
Net Carbohydrate (gm): 26.7
Calories: 414
Fat (gm): 13.9
Saturated fat (gm): 5.6
Cholesterol (mg): 156.4
Sodium (mg): 426
Protein (gm): 36.7
Carbohydrate (gm): 30.1

1. Coat chicken with combined flour, paprika, and dry mustard. Sauté chicken in oil in large skillet until browned on both sides, 5 to 8 minutes. Remove and reserve.

2. Add wine, water, onions, carrots, and thyme to skillet; heat to boiling. Reduce heat and simmer, covered, 10 minutes. Add chicken and simmer, covered, until chicken is tender, about 20 minutes. Season to taste with salt and pepper.

3. Spoon chicken mixture into oven-proof serving dish. Spoon Duchess Potatoes around the edge of dish. Brush with butter; bake at 475 degrees until potatoes are golden brown, about 8 minutes.

Duchess Potatoes

makes about 2 cups

2½ cups cubed, peeled Idaho potatoes, cooked
2 tablespoons whipping cream
2 tablespoons sour cream
½ teaspoon salt
Dash white pepper
1 egg yolk, beaten

1. Mash potatoes until smooth, gradually adding cream. Mix in sour cream, salt, white pepper, and egg yolk.

Garden Stew with Chicken

6 servings

6 boneless, skinless chicken breast halves (5 ounces each)
1 tablespoon olive oil
1½ cups cubed (1-inch) onions
8 ounces shiitake, *or* white, mushrooms, sliced
1 small jalapeño chili, finely chopped
1 tablespoon all-purpose flour
2 cups reduced-sodium fat-free chicken broth
2 cups sliced zucchini
1 cup cubed (¼ inch) turnips
8 ounces baby carrots, halved
2 cups chopped, seeded tomatoes
½ cup chopped cilantro
Salt and pepper, to taste

Per Serving
Net Carbohydrate (gm): 14.5
Calories: 280
Fat (gm): 5.2
Saturated fat (gm): 0.9
Cholesterol (mg): 95.9
Sodium (mg): 199
Protein (gm): 40
Carbohydrate (gm): 18.3

1. Cook chicken in oil in large skillet over medium heat until browned on both sides, about 10 minutes. Remove from skillet.

2. Add onions, mushrooms, and jalapeño chili to skillet; sauté 5 minutes. Stir in flour; cook 1 minute longer.

3. Add broth, reserved chicken, zucchini, turnips, and carrots to skillet; heat to boiling. Reduce heat and simmer, covered, until chicken and vegetables are tender, 10 to 12 minutes. Add tomatoes and cilantro; season to taste with salt and pepper.

Chicken with Sherried Vegetable Sauce

4 servings

4 boneless, skinless chicken breast halves (5 ounces each)
1 tablespoon olive oil
¾ cup very thinly sliced leeks (white parts only)
½ cup chopped onion
⅓ cup chopped shallots
1 cup chopped mushrooms
½ cup dry sherry, *or* chicken broth
2 cups reduced-sodium fat-free chicken broth
1½ cups chopped tomatoes
1 tablespoon dried thyme leaves
1 bay leaf
Salt and pepper, to taste
¼ cup drained capers

Per Serving
Net Carbohydrate (gm): 11.6
Calories: 302
Fat (gm): 6.4
Saturated fat (gm): 1
Cholesterol (mg): 94.6
Sodium (mg): 468
Protein (gm): 38.6
Carbohydrate (gm): 14

1. Cook chicken in oil in large skillet until browned on both sides, about 8 minutes. Remove chicken and reserve. Sauté onion, leeks, shallots, and mushrooms in skillet until very soft, about 7 minutes. Add sherry; cook over high heat until liquid is almost evaporated, 2 minutes.

2. Add broth, tomatoes, thyme, and bay leaf to skillet; heat to boiling. Reduce heat and simmer, uncovered, until tomato is very soft, about 10 minutes; discard bay leaf. Process mixture in food processor or blender until smooth.

3. Return sauce and chicken to skillet; heat to boiling. Reduce heat and simmer, covered, until chicken is cooked through, about 10 minutes. Season to taste with salt and pepper; stir in capers.

Crisp Oven-Fried Chicken

6 servings

2 eggs
¼ cup whipping cream
6 skinless chicken breast halves (bone-in) (6 ounces each)
¼ cup all-purpose flour
1 cup finely crushed bran flakes cereal
¾ cup unseasoned dry bread crumbs
⅓ cup grated Parmesan cheese
½ teaspoon dried rosemary leaves, crumbled
¼ teaspoon dried thyme leaves
Salt and pepper, to taste

Per Serving
Net Carbohydrate (gm): 23.3
Calories: 319
Fat (gm): 9
Saturated fat (gm): 4.2
Cholesterol (mg): 150.1
Sodium (mg): 387
Protein (gm): 32.6
Carbohydrate (gm): 26.2

1. Beat eggs and cream in shallow bowl until blended. Coat chicken breasts with flour; dip them in egg mixture, then coat generously with combined bran flakes, bread crumbs, cheese, and herbs.

2. Place chicken, meat sides up, in lightly greased baking pan; sprinkle lightly with salt and pepper. Bake at 350 degrees until chicken is browned and juices run clear, 45 to 60 minutes.

Microwave Chicken Crunch

6 servings

3 pounds chicken pieces
1 cup buttermilk
2 cups corn flakes cereal, finely crushed
½ teaspoon garlic powder
½ teaspoon paprika
½ teaspoon dried thyme leaves
¼ teaspoon salt
¼ teaspoon pepper

Per Serving
Net Carbohydrate (gm): 9.9
Calories: 351
Fat (gm): 21
Saturated fat (gm): 6.1
Cholesterol (mg): 108.1
Sodium (mg): 287
Protein (gm): 28.7
Carbohydrate (gm): 10.3

1. Dip chicken pieces in buttermilk. Coat chicken with combined remaining ingredients. Place in 12-inch glass baking dish, with thicker pieces toward outside.

2. Microwave, loosely covered, on High, 7 to 8 minutes. Turn chicken and rotate dish. Microwave on High until chicken is cooked through, 6 to 8 minutes.

Poached Chicken with Spring Vegetables

4 servings

2 pounds chicken pieces (bone-in)
2 quarts water
⅔ cup sliced green onions and tops
⅔ cup cut celery (1-inch pieces)
8 ounces small whole mushrooms
3 garlic cloves, minced
1 tablespoon olive oil
1 tablespoon all-purpose flour
½ pound small new potatoes, unpeeled, quartered
1 cup baby carrots
1 cup cut asparagus (1-inch pieces)
2 sprigs fresh, *or* ½ teaspoon dried, thyme leaves
1 teaspoon fresh, *or* ½ teaspoon dried, marjoram leaves
½ teaspoon fresh, *or* pinch dried, sage leaves
Salt and pepper, to taste

Per Serving
Net Carbohydrate (gm): 18.9
Calories: 389
Fat (gm): 13.6
Saturated fat (gm): 3.2
Cholesterol (mg): 118.5
Sodium (mg): 141
Protein (gm): 43.5
Carbohydrate (gm): 23

1. Place chicken and water in large saucepan; heat to boiling. Reduce heat and simmer until very tender, about 30 minutes. Remove chicken and reserve 2 cups stock. Remove meat from chicken, cut into bite-sized pieces, and reserve; discard skin and bones.

2. Sauté green onions, celery, mushrooms, and garlic in oil in large saucepan until lightly browned, about 8 minutes. Sprinkle with flour and cook 1 minute longer; add 2 cups reserved stock and heat to boiling, stirring until thickened. Add potatoes, carrots, asparagus, and herbs; simmer until vegetables are almost tender, about 15 minutes. Add reserved chicken; simmer until vegetables are tender, about 5 minutes. Season to taste with salt and pepper.

Chicken Stew with Sunflower Seed Dumplings

8 servings

1 cup thinly sliced onion
¾ cup sliced celery
1 tablespoon canola oil
3 pounds skinless chicken breasts and thighs (bone-in)
¾ cup reduced-sodium fat-free chicken broth
½ cup dry vermouth, *or* water
1 teaspoon minced garlic
½ teaspoon dried thyme leaves
1 cup baby carrots
1 cup cut green beans
Salt and pepper, to taste
Sunflower Seed Dumplings (recipe follows)

Per Serving
Net Carbohydrate (gm): 14.2
Calories: 270
Fat (gm): 8.5
Saturated fat (gm): 2.8
Cholesterol (mg): 86.3
Sodium (mg): 341
Protein (gm): 27.2
Carbohydrate (gm): 17.6

1. Sauté onion and celery in oil in Dutch oven until onion is tender, about 5 minutes. Add chicken, broth, vermouth, garlic, and thyme; heat to boiling. Reduce heat and simmer, covered, until chicken is tender, 30 to 40 minutes, adding carrots and beans during last 15 minutes. Season to taste with salt and pepper.

2. Spoon Sunflower Seed Dumplings dough into 8 mounds on top of boiling stew. Reduce heat and simmer, covered, 10 minutes; uncover and simmer until dumplings are dry on top, about 10 minutes.

Sunflower Seed Dumplings

makes 8 dumplings

1 cup whole wheat pastry flour
2 teaspoons baking powder
¼ teaspoon salt
2 tablespoons butter
1 tablespoon toasted sunflower seeds
½ cup reduced-fat milk

1. Combine flour, baking powder, and salt in medium bowl. Cut in butter with pastry blender until mixture resembles coarse crumbs. Stir in sunflower seeds. Mix in milk, forming a soft dough.

Baked Chicken and Stuffing

6 servings

3 cups whole wheat croutons
1 cup reduced-sodium fat-free chicken broth
⅔ cup chopped carrots
½ cup chopped celery
½ cup chopped onion
1 teaspoon dried marjoram leaves
½ teaspoon dried thyme leaves
1 can (10½ ounces) reduced-sodium reduced-fat cream of mushroom soup
½ cup reduced-fat milk
3 tablespoons chopped parsley
⅛ teaspoon pepper
6 boneless, skinless chicken breast halves (4 ounces each)

Per Serving
Net Carbohydrate (gm): 17
Calories: 239
Fat (gm): 3.7
Saturated fat (gm): 1
Cholesterol (mg): 74.4
Sodium (mg): 423
Protein (gm): 30.6
Carbohydrate (gm): 18.6

1. In a large bowl, combine croutons, broth, carrots, celery, onion, and herbs. Spoon stuffing mixture down center of lightly greased 13 x 9-inch baking dish.

2. Mix soup, milk, parsley, and pepper in medium bowl; spoon ½ of soup mixture along edges of dish. Place chicken breasts over soup, overlapping if necessary. Pour remaining soup mixture over chicken.

3. Bake at 400 degrees, covered, 20 minutes; uncover and bake until chicken is cooked through, about 10 minutes longer.

Chicken Breasts with Vegetable Stuffing

6 servings

Vegetable Stuffing (recipe follows)
6 skinless chicken breast halves (bone-in) (8 ounces each)
1 tablespoon butter, softened
1 teaspoon dried basil leaves
1 teaspoon dried thyme leaves
Salt and pepper, to taste
Minced parsley, as garnish

Per Serving
Net Carbohydrate (gm): 18.3
Calories: 392
Fat (gm): 7.8
Saturated fat (gm): 3.4
Cholesterol (mg): 146.7
Sodium (mg): 527
Protein (gm): 56.6
Carbohydrate (gm): 20.4

1. Spoon Vegetable Stuffing into 13 x 9-inch baking dish; arrange chicken breasts, bone sides down, on top. Spread butter over chicken and sprinkle with basil, thyme, salt, and pepper. Bake, covered, at 350 degrees until chicken is cooked, 45 to 60 minutes. Sprinkle with parsley.

Vegetable Stuffing

makes about 4 cups

2 cups chopped onions
1 cup chopped celery
1 cup finely chopped cabbage
⅓ cup chopped carrot
1 tablespoon butter
3 cups herb-seasoned bread stuffing mix
2 tablespoons chopped parsley
1 cup reduced-sodium fat-free chicken broth
Salt and pepper, to taste

1. Sauté vegetables in butter in large skillet until tender, about 8 minutes. Stir in stuffing mix and parsley; add broth and mix well. Season to taste with salt and pepper.

Roast Chicken with Cornbread Dressing

6 servings

1 roasting chicken (about 3 pounds)
2 tablespoons canola oil, divided
1½ teaspoons dried rosemary leaves, divided
1½ cups thinly sliced celery
¾ cup chopped onion
¼ cup coarsely chopped pecans
¾ teaspoon dried sage leaves
¼ teaspoon dried thyme leaves
3 cups cornbread stuffing mix
1½ cups reduced-sodium fat-free chicken broth
Salt and pepper, to taste
1 egg, lightly beaten

Per Serving
Net Carbohydrate (gm): 11.2
Calories: 463
Fat (gm): 30.4
Saturated fat (gm): 6.9
Cholesterol (mg): 148.1
Sodium (mg): 362
Protein (gm): 31.7
Carbohydrate (gm): 14.7

1. Rub chicken with 1 tablespoon oil; sprinkle with 1 teaspoon rosemary. Roast chicken on rack in roasting pan at 375 degrees until meat thermometer inserted in thickest part of thigh, away from bone, registers 170 degrees (chicken leg will move freely and juices will run clear), about 1½ hours. Let chicken stand 10 minutes before carving.

2. While chicken is cooking, sauté celery, onion, and pecans in remaining 1 tablespoon oil until vegetables are tender, about 5 minutes. Stir in sage, thyme, and remaining ½ teaspoon rosemary; cook over medium heat 1 to 2 minutes.

3. Add vegetable mixture to stuffing mix in large bowl; add chicken broth and toss. Season to taste with salt and pepper. Mix in egg. Spoon dressing into greased 2-quart casserole. Bake, covered, in oven with chicken during last 30 to 45 minutes roasting time.

Variation:

Pork Chops with Bread Dressing—Make dressing as above in Steps 2 and 3, substituting whole wheat stuffing mix for the cornbread mix, and walnuts for the pecans. Trim fat from 6 loin pork chops (about 5 ounces each); cook in lightly greased skillet until well browned, about 5 minutes on each side. Arrange pork chops on top of dressing in casserole. Bake, covered, at 350 degrees until pork chops are tender, 30 to 40 minutes.

Chicken-in-the-Pot

8 servings

1 large stewing chicken (about 5 pounds)
Water, to cover
3½ quarts water
1 large onion, quartered
3 cups sliced carrots, divided
3 cups thinly sliced leeks (white parts only), divided
3 cups sliced celery, divided
8 sprigs parsley
1 cup quartered mushrooms
½ pound peeled pearl onions
Salt and pepper, to taste

Per Serving
Net Carbohydrate (gm): 11.6
Calories: 457
Fat (gm): 22.7
Saturated fat (gm): 6.3
Cholesterol (mg): 139.2
Sodium (mg): 188
Protein (gm): 46.1
Carbohydrate (gm): 15.5

1. Clean chicken and truss legs and wings; place in stockpot, add water to cover, and heat to boiling. Reduce heat and simmer, covered, 5 minutes; remove chicken and discard water.

2. Return chicken to pot with 3½ quarts water and heat to boiling; reduce heat and simmer, covered, 1 hour, occasionally skimming foam that rises to the surface.

3. Add quartered onion, 1 cup carrots, 1 cup leeks, 1 cup celery, and parsley; simmer, covered, 1 hour, or until chicken is tender. Remove chicken and cut into serving pieces. Strain broth, discarding vegetables.

4. Combine broth, chicken, and remaining vegetables in pot and simmer, covered, until vegetables are tender, about 20 minutes; season to taste with salt and pepper.

Tip: If you can find a nice stewing hen for this recipe, you will be rewarded with a wealth of old-fashioned flavor.

Honey-Mustard Chicken Stew

4 servings

1 pound boneless, skinless chicken breast, cubed (1 inch)
1 cup chopped onion
1 tablespoon olive oil
1¾ cups reduced-sodium fat-free chicken broth
2 tablespoons honey
1 tablespoon Dijon mustard
1–2 teaspoons curry powder
2 cups small cauliflower florets
⅔ cup sliced carrots
Salt and pepper, to taste

Per Serving
Net Carbohydrate (gm): 14.3
Calories: 248
Fat (gm): 5.7
Saturated fat (gm): 0.9
Cholesterol (mg): 76.7
Sodium (mg): 293
Protein (gm): 31
Carbohydrate (gm): 17

1. Sauté chicken and onion in oil in large skillet until lightly browned, about 8 minutes. Add remaining ingredients, except salt and pepper, and heat to boiling. Reduce heat and simmer, covered, until chicken is tender, about 15 minutes. Simmer, uncovered, until stew has thickened slightly, about 5 minutes. Season to taste with salt and pepper.

Napa Valley Braised Chicken

4 servings

1 pound boneless, skinless chicken breast, cut into strips
1 clove garlic, minced
2 tablespoons chopped onion
1 tablespoon canola oil
2 tablespoons all-purpose flour
½ cup reduced-sodium fat-free chicken broth
¼ cup dry sherry, *or* chicken broth
2 tablespoons chopped parsley
1 bay leaf
1 cup white seedless grapes, halved
Salt and pepper, to taste

Per Serving
Net Carbohydrate (gm): 11.5
Calories: 228
Fat (gm): 5.2
Saturated fat (gm): 0.7
Cholesterol (mg): 68.8
Sodium (mg): 93
Protein (gm): 27.9
Carbohydrate (gm): 12.2

1. Sauté chicken, garlic, and onion in oil in large skillet until chicken is browned, about 5 minutes; sprinkle with flour and cook 1 minute longer. Add remaining ingredients, except grapes, salt, and pepper, and heat to boiling. Reduce heat and simmer, covered, 5 minutes. Add grapes and simmer until chicken is tender, 5 to 10 minutes; season to taste with salt and pepper.

Tarragon-Mustard Chicken Stew

4 servings

1 pound boneless, skinless chicken breast, cubed (1 inch)
1 cup chopped onion
1 cup chopped celery
1 tablespoon olive oil
1½ cups reduced-sodium fat-free chicken broth
2 tablespoons Dijon mustard
2 teaspoons packed brown sugar
1 teaspoon lemon juice
2½ teaspoons dried tarragon leaves
2 teaspoons cornstarch
¼ cup water
Salt and white pepper, to taste

Per Serving
Net Carbohydrate (gm): 7.1
Calories: 214
Fat (gm): 5.4
Saturated fat (gm): 0.8
Cholesterol (mg): 75.1
Sodium (mg): 354
Protein (gm): 29.5
Carbohydrate (gm): 8.4

1. Sauté chicken, onion, and celery in oil in large saucepan until lightly browned, about 8 minutes. Add broth, mustard, brown sugar, lemon juice, and tarragon; heat to boiling. Reduce heat and simmer, covered, until chicken is tender, about 10 minutes.

2. Heat to boiling; stir in combined cornstarch and water. Boil, stirring until thickened, 1 to 2 minutes. Season to taste with salt and white pepper.

Apple Cider Chicken

6 servings

2 pounds chicken pieces (bone-in)
1 tablespoon canola oil
2 cups thickly sliced, unpeeled firm cooking apples
3 tablespoons all-purpose flour
1½ cups apple cider
½ teaspoon dried rosemary leaves
½ teaspoon dried thyme leaves
½ cup whipping cream
Salt and pepper, to taste
2 tablespoons chopped parsley

Per Serving
Net Carbohydrate (gm): 8.4
Calories: 414
Fat (gm): 26.8
Saturated fat (gm): 8.4
Cholesterol (mg): 120.1
Sodium (mg): 85
Protein (gm): 27.3
Carbohydrate (gm): 9.5

1. Cook chicken in oil in Dutch oven over medium-high heat until browned on all sides, about 8 minutes; remove chicken from pan.

2. Add apples to Dutch oven and sauté until beginning to brown, 2 to 3 minutes. Sprinkle with flour and cook 1 to 2 minutes longer. Add cider, rosemary, and thyme and heat to boiling, stirring constantly. Return chicken to Dutch oven. Bake, tightly covered, at 375 degrees until chicken is tender, about 45 minutes.

3. Arrange chicken and apples on serving platter. Heat pan juices to boiling; boil until slightly thickened, about 5 minutes. Add cream; stir over medium heat until hot. Season to taste with salt and pepper. Pour sauce over chicken. Sprinkle with parsley.

Orange-Apple Chicken

4 servings

4 boneless, skinless chicken breast halves (6 ounces each)
¼ cup all-purpose flour
1 teaspoon lemon-pepper
½ teaspoon salt
½ teaspoon garlic powder
2 tablespoons canola oil
⅓ cup cubed apple
⅓ cup apple juice
⅓ cup no-sugar-added orange marmalade
Chopped parsley, as garnish

Per Serving
Net Carbohydrate (gm): 17.7
Calories: 325
Fat (gm): 9
Saturated fat (gm): 1
Cholesterol (mg): 98.6
Sodium (mg): 460
Protein (gm): 40.3
Carbohydrate (gm): 18.6

1. Coat chicken with combined flour, lemon-pepper, salt, and garlic powder. Sauté chicken in oil in large skillet until browned, about 5 minutes on each side. Stir in apple, apple juice, and marmalade; simmer, uncovered, until sauce is thickened and chicken is tender, about 5 minutes. Sprinkle with parsley.

Hearty Chicken and Lentil Stew

6 servings

4 thin slices bacon, cut into 2-inch pieces
3 pounds chicken pieces (bone-in)
1 cup dried lentils
¾ cup chopped onion
½ cup sliced celery
1 large clove garlic, minced
1 cup reduced-sodium fat-free chicken broth
½ cup dry white wine, *or* water
1 can (14½ ounces) diced tomatoes, undrained
1 teaspoon dried thyme leaves
Salt and pepper, to taste
1 tablespoon chopped parsley

Per Serving
Net Carbohydrate (gm): 12.3
Calories: 345
Fat (gm): 6.9
Saturated fat (gm): 1.9
Cholesterol (mg): 107.6
Sodium (mg): 431
Protein (gm): 43
Carbohydrate (gm): 23.2

1. Sauté bacon in Dutch oven until crisp; remove bacon and reserve. Drain all but 2 teaspoons bacon fat from Dutch oven; add chicken and sauté until browned on all sides, about 10 minutes.

2. Add reserved bacon and remaining ingredients, except salt, pepper, and parsley; heat to boiling. Reduce heat and simmer, covered, until chicken and lentils are tender, about 40 minutes, adding water if needed for desired consistency. Season to taste with salt and pepper; sprinkle with parsley.

Slow-Cooker Creole Chicken

4 servings

1 cup reduced-sodium fat-free chicken broth
1 can (6 ounces) tomato paste
2 cups thinly sliced cabbage
1 cup chopped onion
1 cup chopped green bell pepper
2 large cloves garlic, minced
1 tablespoon lemon juice
1 tablespoon Worcestershire sauce
1 tablespoon packed light brown sugar
2 teaspoons Dijon mustard
3–4 drops hot pepper sauce
2 teaspoons dried thyme leaves
1 bay leaf
2½ pounds chicken breast halves, skinned (bone-in)
Salt and pepper, to taste

Per Serving
Net Carbohydrate (gm): 17.8
Calories: 304
Fat (gm): 3
Saturated fat (gm): 0.6
Cholesterol (mg): 109.1
Sodium (mg): 659
Protein (gm): 46.2
Carbohydrate (gm): 22.4

1. Combine chicken broth and tomato paste in slow cooker; mix until smooth. Add remaining ingredients, except salt and pepper, and mix well; cover and cook on High 1 hour. Cook on Low until chicken is tender, 5 to 6 hours.

2. Remove chicken and cut meat into strips, discarding bones; stir back into slow cooker. Discard bay leaf; season to taste with salt and pepper.

Slow-Cooker Coq au Vin

6 servings

2½ pounds chicken pieces (bone-in)
1 tablespoon butter
⅔ cup sliced green onions and tops
1 clove garlic, minced
1 cup peeled pearl onions
8 ounces small mushrooms
1½ cups quartered small new potatoes
1 cup reduced-sodium fat-free chicken broth
¾ cup Burgundy wine, *or* chicken broth
1 teaspoon dried thyme leaves
Salt and pepper, to taste

Per Serving
Net Carbohydrate (gm): 11
Calories: 396
Fat (gm): 18.8
Saturated fat (gm): 5.8
Cholesterol (mg): 114.4
Sodium (mg): 175
Protein (gm): 37.4
Carbohydrate (gm): 13.7

1. Cook chicken in butter in large skillet until browned on all sides, about 10 minutes. Stir in green onions and garlic and sauté 2 minutes. Place chicken mixture in slow cooker with remaining ingredients, except salt and pepper; cover and cook on Low 8 to 10 hours, until chicken is very tender. Season to taste with salt and pepper.

Chicken Vesuvio

8 servings

8 boneless, skinless chicken breast halves (6 ounces each)
4 cups unpeeled red potato wedges
¼ cup chopped green onions and tops
¼ cup lemon juice
3 tablespoons olive oil
1 tablespoon minced garlic
1 tablespoon chopped fresh, *or*
    1 teaspoon dried, rosemary leaves
1 tablespoon chopped fresh, *or*
    1 teaspoon dried, oregano leaves
2 cups sliced mushrooms
¼ cup sliced pitted black olives

Per Serving
Net Carbohydrate (gm): 11.2
Calories: 285
Fat (gm): 7.6
Saturated fat (gm): 1.3
Cholesterol (mg): 98.6
Sodium (mg): 147
Protein (gm): 40.7
Carbohydrate (gm): 12.4

1. Arrange chicken and potatoes in lightly greased 13 x 9-inch baking pan. Top with combined green onions, lemon juice, olive oil, garlic, rosemary, and oregano.

2. Bake chicken and potatoes, covered, at 400 degrees 25 minutes. Add mushrooms and olives to pan. Bake, covered, until chicken is cooked through and potatoes are tender, about 20 minutes.

Breast of Chicken in Porcini Sauce

4 servings

¼ ounce dried porcini, *or* shiitake, mushrooms
½ cup hot water
2 ounces white mushrooms, sliced
¼ cup chopped onion
2 tablespoons olive oil, divided
2 cups chopped, peeled and seeded plum tomatoes
½ cup reduced-sodium fat-free chicken broth
⅓ cup dry white wine, *or* chicken broth
1 tablespoon chopped fresh, *or* ½ teaspoon dried, rosemary leaves
1 tablespoon chopped fresh, *or* 1 teaspoon dried, basil leaves
1 tablespoon chopped fresh, *or* 1 teaspoon dried, oregano leaves
Salt and pepper, to taste
4 boneless, skinless chicken breast halves (6 ounces each)

Per Serving
Net Carbohydrate (gm): 5.7
Calories: 298
Fat (gm): 9.4
Saturated fat (gm): 1.5
Cholesterol (mg): 101.7
Sodium (mg): 130
Protein (gm): 41.7
Carbohydrate (gm): 7.4

1. Soak porcini mushrooms in hot water until soft, about 10 minutes; strain, reserving liquid. Slice mushrooms, discarding tough stems.

2. Sauté porcini, white mushrooms, and onion in 1 tablespoon oil in medium skillet until tender, about 5 minutes. Add reserved porcini liquid, tomatoes, broth, wine, and herbs. Heat to boiling; boil until slightly thickened, about 5 minutes. Season to taste with salt and pepper.

3. Cook chicken in remaining 1 tablespoon oil in large skillet until browned, about 5 minutes on each side. Add mushroom mixture to skillet; simmer, covered, until chicken is cooked through, about 5 minutes.

Chicken with Sherried Mushroom Sauce

4 servings

4 boneless, skinless chicken breast halves (6 ounces each)
2 tablespoons olive oil
1 cup mushroom caps
2 cloves garlic, minced
3 tablespoons all-purpose flour
1½ cups reduced-sodium fat-free chicken broth
½ cup dry sherry, *or* chicken broth
1 teaspoon dried thyme leaves
1 teaspoon dried tarragon leaves
Salt and pepper, to taste
½ cup (2 ounces) grated Parmesan cheese
2 tablespoons chopped parsley

Per Serving
Net Carbohydrate (gm): 8.4
Calories: 381
Fat (gm): 12.5
Saturated fat (gm): 3.4
Cholesterol (mg): 115.8
Sodium (mg): 372
Protein (gm): 47.5
Carbohydrate (gm): 9

1. Cook chicken in oil in large skillet over medium heat until browned, about 3 minutes on each side. Transfer chicken to glass baking dish.

2. Add mushrooms and garlic to skillet and sauté until lightly browned, about 3 minutes; sprinkle with flour and cook 1 minute longer. Add broth, sherry, tarragon, and thyme. Heat to boiling, stirring until smooth and slightly thickened. Season to taste with salt and pepper.

3. Pour mushroom sauce over chicken; sprinkle with cheese. Bake, uncovered, at 350 degrees until chicken is cooked through, about 30 minutes. Sprinkle with parsley.

Cajun Chicken

4 servings

4 boneless, skinless chicken breast halves (6 ounces each)
1 tablespoon melted butter
Cajun Seasoning (recipe follows)

Per Serving
Net Carbohydrate (gm): 1.5
Calories: 223
Fat (gm): 5.3
Saturated fat (gm): 2.5
Cholesterol (mg): 106.8
Sodium (mg): 266
Protein (gm): 39.7
Carbohydrate (gm): 2.1

1. Brush both sides of chicken with butter; sprinkle with Cajun Seasoning, pressing mixture onto chicken.

2. Grill chicken over medium-hot coals, or broil 6 inches from heat source, until chicken is cooked and juices run clear, about 5 minutes on each side.

Cajun Seasoning

makes about 2 tablespoons

2 teaspoons paprika
1 teaspoon onion powder
1 teaspoon garlic powder
½ teaspoon dried thyme leaves
½ teaspoon dried oregano leaves
½ teaspoon cayenne pepper
½ teaspoon black pepper
¼ teaspoon salt

1. Mix all ingredients; store in airtight container until ready to use.

Note: Packaged Cajun seasoning can be purchased, but we particularly like our homemade blend! The spice blend is also delicious on grilled steaks or portobello mushrooms.

Cajun Mustard-Grilled Chicken

4 servings

4 boneless, skinless chicken breast halves (6 ounces each)
1 tablespoon butter, melted
1 tablespoon Cajun Seasoning (see above), *or*
    purchased Cajun seasoning
Cajun Mustard Baste (recipe follows)
4 slices Jarlsberg, *or* Swiss, cheese (about 3 ounces)

Per Serving
Net Carbohydrate (gm): 3.5
Calories: 376
Fat (gm): 18.4
Saturated fat (gm): 9.2
Cholesterol (mg): 138.2
Sodium (mg): 644
Protein (gm): 47
Carbohydrate (gm): 4.5

1. Dip chicken in butter; sprinkle both sides with Cajun Seasoning. Grill chicken over medium-hot coals until almost cooked through, 5 to 8 minutes on each side, brushing with Cajun Mustard Baste during cooking. Top with cheese; cook until cheese melts, about 2 minutes.

Cajun Mustard Baste

makes about ½ cup

⅓ cup finely chopped green onions
2 cloves garlic, minced
2 tablespoons butter
¼ cup spicy brown mustard
¼ cup chopped cilantro
1 tablespoon Cajun Seasoning (see p. 88), *or* purchased Cajun seasoning

1. Sauté green onions and garlic in butter in small skillet until tender, about 2 minutes; stir in remaining ingredients.

Jamaican Jerk Chicken

8 servings

3 pounds chicken pieces (bone-in)
Jamaican Jerk Sauce (recipe follows)
3 cups cooked brown rice, warm
1 cup diced mango

Per Serving
Net Carbohydrate (gm): 30.4
Calories: 532
Fat (gm): 30.1
Saturated fat (gm): 8
Cholesterol (mg): 123.3
Sodium (mg): 161
Protein (gm): 31.7
Carbohydrate (gm): 32.9

1. Combine chicken and Jamaican Jerk Sauce in glass baking dish, turning to coat. Refrigerate, covered, several hours or overnight, turning several times.

2. Grill chicken over hot coals until done, 5 to 8 minutes on each side. Combine rice and mango; serve with chicken.

Jamaican Jerk Sauce

makes about 2 cups

⅔ cup cubed onion
10 cloves garlic
¼ cup chopped pimiento
¼ cup honey
2–4 tablespons sliced pickled jalapeño chilies
2 tablespoons olive oil
1 tablespoon Worcestershire sauce
1 teaspoon hot pepper sauce
1 teaspoon dried thyme leaves
1 teaspoon ground cinnamon
½ teaspoon ground nutmeg
½ teaspoon black pepper
¼ teaspoon cayenne pepper

1. Process all ingredients in food processor or blender until smooth.

Grilled Chicken with Gingered Tomato Relish

6 servings

6 boneless, skinless chicken breast halves (6 ounces each)
2 tablespoons olive oil
1 tablespoon minced garlic
1 tablespoon minced gingerroot
Gingered Tomato Relish (recipe follows)

Per Serving
Net Carbohydrate (gm): 8
Calories: 263
Fat (gm): 6.7
Saturated fat (gm): 1.2
Cholesterol (mg): 98.6
Sodium (mg): 97
Protein (gm): 40
Carbohydrate (gm): 9

1. Coat chicken on both sides with combined oil, garlic, and gingerroot. Grill chicken over hot coals until done, about 5 minutes on each side. Place chicken on serving platter; top with Gingered Tomato Relish.

Gingered Tomato Relish

makes about 1½ cups

1½ cups chopped, seeded tomatoes
½ cup finely chopped zucchini
¼ cup finely chopped carrot
¼ cup finely chopped onion
2 tablespoons finely chopped gingerroot
2 tablespoons packed dark brown sugar
1 tablespoon cider vinegar
Salt and pepper, to taste

1. Combine all ingredients, except salt and pepper, in medium skillet. Cook, covered, over medium heat until tomatoes are soft and mixture is bubbly. Simmer, uncovered, until excess liquid is gone, about 10 minutes. Season to taste with salt and pepper.

Maple-Mustard Chicken Thighs

4 servings

⅓ cup maple syrup
2 tablespoons Dijon mustard
1 tablespoon mayonnaise
8 boneless, skinless chicken thighs (about 1¼ pounds)
8 thin slices bacon

Per Serving
Net Carbohydrate (gm): 18.1
Calories: 356
Fat (gm): 15.8
Saturated fat (gm): 4.5
Cholesterol (mg): 129.9
Sodium (mg): 545
Protein (gm): 32
Carbohydrate (gm): 18.1

1. Combine maple syrup, mustard, and mayonnaise in small bowl; dip chicken in syrup mixture, coating well. Wrap chicken thighs with bacon, securing with toothpicks. Place on aluminum foil-lined baking sheet. Bake at 425 degrees until juices run clear and bacon is crisp, about 25 minutes, turning once.

Chicken Limone

4 servings

4 boneless, skinless chicken breast halves (6 ounces each), pounded thin
¼ cup all-purpose flour
2 tablespoons olive oil
⅓ cup dry white wine, *or* chicken broth
¼ cup lemon juice
1 tablespoon chopped parsley
Salt and pepper, to taste
Lemon slices, as garnish

Per Serving
Net Carbohydrate (gm): 7.2
Calories: 292
Fat (gm): 8.8
Saturated fat (gm): 1.4
Cholesterol (mg): 98.6
Sodium (mg): 90
Protein (gm): 40.2
Carbohydrate (gm): 7.5

1. Coat chicken with flour. Sauté chicken in oil in large skillet until cooked through, 2 to 3 minutes on each side; remove from skillet.

2. Add wine and lemon juice to skillet; heat to boiling. Boil until liquid is reduced by half, about 3 minutes, stirring and scraping up browned bits from skillet. Stir in parsley and season to taste with salt and pepper. Return chicken to skillet and cook 1 to 2 minutes, turning pieces to coat with juices.

3. Arrange chicken on serving platter; pour juices over chicken and garnish with lemon slices.

Microwave Lemon Chicken

4 servings

4 boneless, skinless chicken breast halves (6 ounces each), pounded to ½ inch thickness
Salt and pepper, to taste
¼ cup reduced-sodium fat-free chicken broth
2 cloves garlic, minced
2 tablespoons lemon juice
1 tablespoon butter
2 tablespoons chopped parsley
Paprika, to taste
4 slices lemon, as garnish

Per Serving
Net Carbohydrate (gm): 2
Calories: 223
Fat (gm): 5.2
Saturated fat (gm): 2.4
Cholesterol (mg): 108.3
Sodium (mg): 137
Protein (gm): 40.1
Carbohydrate (gm): 2.7

1. Sprinkle chicken lightly with salt and pepper and place in glass baking dish. Combine broth, garlic, lemon juice, and butter, and pour over chicken. Microwave, loosely covered, on High until juices run clear when chicken is pierced with a fork, about 6 minutes.

2. Sprinkle chicken with parsley and paprika. Garnish with lemon slices.

Microwave Chicken Dijon

4 servings

4 boneless, skinless chicken breast halves (6 ounces each),
    pounded to ½ inch thickness
2 tablespoons Dijon mustard
2 tablespoons mayonnaise
½ teaspoon pepper
½ teaspoon paprika
Chopped chives, as garnish

Per Serving
Net Carbohydrate (gm): 0.4
Calories: 245
Fat (gm): 7.5
Saturated fat (gm): 1.4
Cholesterol (mg): 102.6
Sodium (mg): 300
Protein (gm): 39.4
Carbohydrate (gm): 0.5

1. Arrange chicken in glass baking dish; mix mustard, mayonnaise, pepper, and paprika in small bowl. Spread tops of chicken with half the mustard mixture.

2. Microwave, loosely covered, on High 3 minutes. Turn chicken and spread with remaining mustard mixture. Cover and microwave on High 3 minutes or until chicken is cooked through. Sprinkle with chives.

Lemon-Sage Chicken Breasts

4 servings

4 boneless, skinless chicken breast halves (6 ounces each)
¼ cup lemon juice
8 large fresh sage leaves
½ teaspoon dried Italian seasoning
Salt and pepper, to taste
1 tablespoon olive oil
4 slices lemon, as garnish

Per Serving
Net Carbohydrate (gm): 2.1
Calories: 223
Fat (gm): 5.4
Saturated fat (gm): 1
Cholesterol (mg): 98.6
Sodium (mg): 89
Protein (gm): 39.5
Carbohydrate (gm): 2.8

1. Toss chicken with lemon juice and sage leaves in glass baking dish or bowl. Let stand, covered, 30 minutes. Remove chicken and pat dry; reserve marinade. Sprinkle chicken with Italian seasoning, salt, and pepper.

2. Sauté chicken in oil in large skillet until browned on one side, about 5 minutes. Turn chicken; add reserved marinade to skillet, and cook, covered, until chicken is browned on bottom and no longer pink in the center, about 8 minutes.

3. Slice chicken diagonally into ½-inch slices and arrange on platter. Pour pan juices and sage leaves over chicken; garnish with lemon slices.

Rosemary-Plum Chicken

6 servings

6 boneless, skinless chicken breast halves (4 ounces each)
¼ cup all-purpose flour
1 teaspoon paprika
2 tablespoons butter
½ cup no-sugar-added red plum jam
¼ cup dry white wine, *or* water
2 tablespoons Dijon-style mustard
1½ teaspoons dried rosemary leaves, crushed
Salt and pepper, to taste

Per Serving
Net Carbohydrate (gm): 12.3
Calories: 208
Fat (gm): 3.6
Saturated fat (gm): 1.7
Cholesterol (mg): 71.2
Sodium (mg): 196
Protein (gm): 26.9
Carbohydrate (gm): 13

1. Coat chicken with combined flour and paprika; sauté in butter in large skillet until browned on both sides, about 10 minutes. Stir in combined jam, wine, mustard, and rosemary; heat to boiling. Reduce heat and simmer, covered, until chicken is cooked, about 20 minutes. Season to taste with salt and pepper.

Dijon Chicken au Gratin

6 servings

6 boneless, skinless chicken breast halves (5 ounces each)
1 cup sliced zucchini
1 cup sliced red bell pepper
¼ cup Dijon mustard
½ cup dry white wine, *or* chicken broth
1 cup unseasoned dry bread crumbs
½ cup grated Parmesan cheese
1 tablespoon dried tarragon leaves
Salt and pepper, to taste

Per Serving
Net Carbohydrate (gm): 14.8
Calories: 292
Fat (gm): 4.8
Saturated fat (gm): 2
Cholesterol (mg): 87.4
Sodium (mg): 586
Protein (gm): 38.4
Carbohydrate (gm): 16

1. Place chicken breasts in lightly greased 13 x 9-inch baking pan. Arrange zucchini and bell pepper on top of chicken. Mix mustard and wine in small bowl until smooth; pour over vegetables and chicken. Combine remaining ingredients, except salt and pepper; sprinkle evenly over entire dish. Sprinkle lightly with salt and pepper.

2. Bake, covered, at 350 degrees 20 minutes; uncover and bake until chicken is tender, about 10 minutes longer.

Chicken, Pasta, and Vegetables au Gratin

6 servings

1 cup sliced mushrooms
1 cup cubed zucchini
½ cup shredded carrot
¼ cup sliced green onions and tops
4 tablespoons butter
¼ cup all-purpose flour
2 cups reduced-fat milk
Salt and pepper, to taste
3 cups cubed, cooked chicken breasts
2 cups cooked whole wheat rotini
½ cup (2 ounces) shredded Swiss, *or* mozzarella cheese

Per Serving
Net Carbohydrate (gm): 20.5
Calories: 342
Fat (gm): 14.9
Saturated fat (gm): 8.2
Cholesterol (mg): 90.6
Sodium (mg): 194
Protein (gm): 29.5
Carbohydrate (gm): 22.7

1. Sauté mushrooms, zucchini, carrot, and green onions in butter in medium saucepan until tender, about 5 minutes. Sprinkle with flour and cook 1 minute longer. Stir in milk and heat to boiling, stirring until thickened; season to taste with salt and pepper.

2. Combine chicken and rotini in lightly greased 11 x 7-inch baking dish. Pour vegetable mixture over; top with cheese. Bake at 350 degrees until cheese is browned and sauce is bubbly, about 25 minutes.

Confetti Chicken Roll-ups

4 servings

1 cup frozen whole kernel corn
1 cup finely chopped green bell pepper
3 tablespoons diced pimientos
½ cup (2 ounces) shredded Monterey Jack cheese
1 cup cooked brown rice
4 boneless, skinless chicken breast halves (6 ounces each), pounded thin
Salt and pepper, to taste

Per Serving
Net Carbohydrate (gm): 19.5
Calories: 337
Fat (gm): 7
Saturated fat (gm): 3.3
Cholesterol (mg): 111
Sodium (mg): 170
Protein (gm): 45.5
Carbohydrate (gm): 22.2

1. Combine corn, bell pepper, pimientos, cheese, and rice in medium bowl. Spoon ¼ of the vegetable-rice mixture on each chicken breast, leaving a ¼-inch border on all sides. Roll up each breast, beginning with the short side; secure with toothpicks.

2. Place chicken breasts seam sides down in lightly greased baking pan. Sprinkle lightly with salt and pepper. Bake, covered, 20 minutes at 325 degrees. Uncover and bake until rolls are browned and juices run clear, about 10 minutes longer.

Carolina Chicken and Bean Pilau

8 servings

6 slices bacon
2½ pounds boneless, skinless chicken breast, cubed
1 cup chopped onion
1 cup chopped green bell pepper
1 cup chopped celery
1 teaspoon chopped garlic
1 teaspoon dried thyme leaves
2 bay leaves
½ teaspoon cayenne pepper
3 tablespoons all-purpose flour
1 quart reduced-sodium fat-free chicken broth
1 can (15 ounces) pinto beans, rinsed, drained
¾ cup quick-cooking brown rice
1 cup sliced carrots
Salt and pepper, to taste

Per Serving
Net Carbohydrate (gm): 24.5
Calories: 356
Fat (gm): 6.5
Saturated fat (gm): 1.7
Cholesterol (mg): 99.7
Sodium (mg): 472
Protein (gm): 43
Carbohydrate (gm): 29.2

1. Cook bacon in Dutch oven until crisp; remove, crumble, and reserve. Cook chicken in bacon fat over medium heat until well-browned, about 8 minutes. Remove chicken and reserve. Add onion, green pepper, celery, and garlic to Dutch oven and sauté until very tender, about 10 minutes. Stir in thyme, bay leaves, cayenne pepper, and flour; cook over medium heat until flour is beginning to brown, about 5 minutes, stirring frequently.

2. Stir in broth; heat to boiling, stirring until smooth. Stir in reserved chicken and bacon, beans, rice, and carrots. Heat to boiling; reduce heat and simmer, covered, until rice is tender, about 20 minutes. Let stand, covered, 10 minutes. Remove bay leaves and season to taste with salt and pepper.

Chicken and Vegetable Crepes

4 servings (2 each)

1 pound boneless, skinless chicken breast, cubed (½ inch)
1 tablespoon butter
1½ cups thinly sliced cabbage
¾ cup thinly sliced celery
½ cup thinly sliced green bell pepper
½ cup sliced mushrooms
⅓ cup chopped green onions and tops
2 teaspoons packed light brown sugar
2 tablespoons water
2–3 teaspoons lemon juice
Salt and pepper, to taste
Crepes (see p. 370), warm
Cream Cheese Hollandaise Sauce (see p. 4)

Per Serving
Net Carbohydrate (gm): 25.1
Calories: 521
Fat (gm): 28.8
Saturated fat (gm): 16.6
Cholesterol (mg): 243.7
Sodium (mg): 498
Protein (gm): 37.7
Carbohydrate (gm): 28.6

1. Sauté chicken in butter in large skillet until browned, about 5 minutes; add cabbage, celery, bell pepper, mushrooms, green onions, sugar, and water. Cook, covered, over medium heat until cabbage and mushrooms are wilted, about 5 minutes. Cook, uncovered, until vegetables are tender, about 5 minutes longer. Season to taste with lemon juice, salt, and pepper.

2. Spoon chicken mixture along centers of crepes; roll up and arrange, seam sides down, on serving plates. Serve with Cream Cheese Hollandaise Sauce.

Chicken and Cabbage Strudel

6 servings

1 pound boneless, skinless chicken breast, cubed (½ inch)
3 tablespoons canola oil, divided
1 cup sliced leeks (white parts only)
3 cloves garlic, minced
3 cups thinly sliced cabbage
1 cup sliced mushrooms
½ cup thinly sliced fennel bulb
1 cup reduced-sodium fat-free chicken broth
½ cup dry white wine, *or* chicken broth
1 teaspoon anise seeds, crushed
½ teaspoon caraway seeds, crushed
¾ cup cooked brown rice
¼ cup dark raisins
Salt and pepper, to taste
6 sheets frozen fillo pastry, thawed
2 egg whites, lightly beaten
Fresh Tomato and Herb Sauce (recipe follows)

Per Serving
Net Carbohydrate (gm): 30.3
Calories: 339
Fat (gm): 9.9
Saturated fat (gm): 1.1
Cholesterol (mg): 48
Sodium (mg): 239
Protein (gm): 24.4
Carbohydrate (gm): 34.5

1. Sauté chicken in 1 tablespoon oil in large saucepan until browned, about 5 minutes; add leeks and garlic and sauté 3 minutes longer. Add cabbage, mushrooms, fennel, broth, wine, and anise and caraway seeds; cook, covered, until cabbage wilts, about 5 minutes. Cook, uncovered, over medium heat until cabbage begins to brown, about 10 minutes. Stir in rice and raisins; season to taste with salt and pepper. Cool.

2. Lay 1 sheet fillo on clean surface; cover remaining fillo with damp towel to keep from drying. Combine egg whites and remaining 2 tablespoons oil in small bowl; brush lightly on fillo. Top with 2 more sheets fillo, brushing each with oil mixture. Spoon ½ of cabbage mixture across dough, 2 inches from short edge; roll up and place, seam-side down, on greased cookie sheet. Flatten roll slightly; brush with oil mixture. Repeat with remaining fillo pastry and cabbage mixture.

3. Bake at 375 degrees until strudels are golden, 35 to 45 minutes. Cool 5 to 10 minutes before cutting. Trim ends of strudels, cutting diagonally. Cut strudels diagonally into serving pieces. Arrange on plates. Serve with Fresh Tomato and Herb Sauce.

Fresh Tomato and Herb Sauce

makes about 2½ cups

3 cups chopped, peeled and seeded tomatoes
¼ cup chopped onion
2 cloves garlic, minced
¼ cup dry red wine
1 tablespoon tomato paste
2 teaspoons packed light brown sugar
2 tablespoons finely chopped fresh, *or* 1½ teaspoons dried, thyme leaves
1 bay leaf
3–4 tablespoons finely chopped fresh, *or* 1½ teaspoons dried, basil leaves
⅛ teaspoon crushed red pepper
Salt and pepper, to taste

1. Combine all ingredients, except basil, red pepper, salt, and pepper, in large saucepan; heat to boiling. Reduce heat and simmer, covered, 5 minutes. Simmer, uncovered, until sauce is reduced to medium consistency, about 20 minutes.

2. Stir in basil and red pepper and simmer 5 to 10 minutes longer. Discard bay leaf; season to taste with salt and pepper.

Spaghetti Squash Stuffed with Chicken and Vegetables

4 servings

2 medium spaghetti squash (about 2 pounds each),
    cut lengthwise into halves, seeded
1 pound boneless, skinless chicken breast, cubed
1 cup chopped onion
1 cup chopped red, *or* green, bell pepper
⅔ cups diagonally sliced carrots
2 cups quartered mushrooms
½ cup sliced celery
2 cloves garlic, minced
1 tablespoon olive oil
2 teaspoons all-purpose flour
1 cup coarsely chopped tomatoes
½ cup reduced-sodium fat-free chicken broth
1 teaspoon dried marjoram leaves
Salt and pepper, to taste
2 green onions and tops, thinly sliced

Per Serving
Net Carbohydrate (gm): 23.8
Calories: 294
Fat (gm): 6.7
Saturated fat (gm): 1.1
Cholesterol (mg): 68.8
Sodium (mg): 158
Protein (gm): 31.4
Carbohydrate (gm): 29.8

1. Place squash halves, cut sides down, in large baking pan; add ½ inch water. Bake, covered, at 350 degrees until squash is tender, 30 to 40 minutes. Scrape pulp into large bowl, separating strands with fork; reserve shells.

2. Sauté chicken, onion, bell pepper, carrots, mushrooms, celery, and garlic in oil in large skillet until chicken is light brown, about 8 minutes. Stir in flour and cook 1 minute longer.

3. Add tomatoes, broth, and marjoram to skillet; heat to boiling. Cook, covered, until chicken and vegetables are tender, about 10 minutes. Season to taste with salt and pepper.

4. Toss chicken mixture with spaghetti squash; spoon mixture into reserved squash shells. Sprinkle with green onions.

Chicken Oscar

6 servings

6 boneless, skinless chicken breast halves (5 ounces each), pounded to ¼ inch thickness
¾ cup unseasoned dry bread crumbs
2 cups seasoned croutons, *or* stuffing mix
½ cup reduced-sodium fat-free chicken broth
24 thin stalks asparagus
¾ cup (3 ounces) shredded provolone cheese

Per Serving
Net Carbohydrate (gm): 17
Calories: 326
Fat (gm): 8.5
Saturated fat (gm): 3
Cholesterol (mg): 93.9
Sodium (mg): 456
Protein (gm): 41.5
Carbohydrate (gm): 18.7

1. Coat chicken with bread crumbs; place in lightly greased 13 x 9-inch baking pan. Combine croutons and broth in medium bowl; spoon mixture onto center of each chicken breast.

3. Place asparagus on top of stuffing. Bake, covered, at 350 degrees until asparagus and chicken are tender, about 30 minutes. Uncover and place cheese atop asparagus; bake until cheese melts, about 5 minutes longer.

Chicken Cordon Bleu

6 servings

4 ounces sliced Swiss cheese
3 ounces sliced lean smoked ham
6 boneless, skinless chicken breast halves (5 ounces each), pounded thin
¼ cup all-purpose flour
2 eggs, lightly beaten
⅓ cup unseasoned dry bread crumbs
1 tablespoon canola oil

Per Serving
Net Carbohydrate (gm): 9
Calories: 374
Fat (gm): 18
Saturated fat (gm): 5.1
Cholesterol (mg): 173.9
Sodium (mg): 396
Protein (gm): 41
Carbohydrate (gm): 9.3

1. Layer cheese and ham on each chicken breast, cutting to fit. Roll up chicken breasts and secure with toothpicks. Coat chicken rolls lightly with flour; dip in eggs and coat with bread crumbs.

2. Cook rolls in oil in large skillet over medium heat until browned on all sides, 8 to 10 minutes. Place chicken in baking pan. Bake at 350 degrees, uncovered, until cooked through, about 20 minutes.

Chicken Saltimbocca

6 servings

6 boneless, skinless chicken breast halves (6 ounces each), pounded to ½ inch thickness
6 thin slices boiled ham
1 cup chopped, seeded tomatoes
1 teaspoon dried oregano leaves
⅓ cup unseasoned dry bread crumbs
¼ cup (1 ounce) shredded mozzarella cheese
2 tablespoons minced parsley

Per Serving
Net Carbohydrate (gm): 5.5
Calories: 249
Fat (gm): 4
Saturated fat (gm): 1.4
Cholesterol (mg): 111.2
Sodium (mg): 438
Protein (gm): 44.8
Carbohydrate (gm): 6.1

1. Place chicken on lightly greased baking pan. Top with ham slices; top ham with combined tomato and oregano. Bake at 350 degrees, loosely covered, 10 minutes. Sprinkle with combined bread crumbs, cheese, and parsley; bake until chicken is cooked through, about 10 minutes.

Ham and Chicken Bake

6 servings

8 ounces lean ham, cubed (½ inch)
8 ounces cooked chicken breast, cubed (½ inch)
¾ cup finely chopped red bell pepper
½ cup finely chopped onion
1 can (15 ounces) cream-style corn
2 cups frozen mixed vegetables
½ cup reduced-fat milk
1½ teaspoons bouquet garni
1 cup whole wheat croutons, coarsely crushed
3 tablespoons butter, melted
1–2 teaspoons Worcestershire sauce

Per Serving
Net Carbohydrate (gm): 23
Calories: 285
Fat (gm): 10.3
Saturated fat (gm): 5
Cholesterol (mg): 66.7
Sodium (mg): 902
Protein (gm): 23.5
Carbohydrate (gm): 26.7

1. Combine ham, chicken, bell pepper, onion, corn, vegetables, milk, and bouquet garni in lightly greased 2-quart casserole. Sprinkle croutons over the top. Drizzle with combined butter and Worcestershire sauce. Bake, uncovered, at 350 degrees until brown and bubbly, about 35 minutes.

Chicken, Vegetable, and Goat Cheese Casserole

6 servings

2 cups cut asparagus (1½-inch pieces)
1 cup broccoli florets
1 package (6¼ ounces) quick-cooking long-grain
  and wild rice
6 cups cubed, cooked chicken breast
4 ounces cream cheese, cubed
¾ cup (3 ounces) shredded mozzarella cheese
4 ounces goat cheese, crumbled
Salt and pepper, to taste

Per Serving
Net Carbohydrate (gm): 23.9
Calories: 509
Fat (gm): 19.3
Saturated fat (gm): 10.6
Cholesterol (mg): 160.3
Sodium (mg): 804
Protein (gm): 56.3
Carbohydrate (gm): 25.8

1. Cook asparagus and broccoli in boiling water to cover, 4 minutes. Drain well.

2. Cook rice according to package directions, using ½ the spice packet. Mix rice, chicken, vegetables, and cheeses; season to taste with salt and pepper. Spoon into 1½-quart casserole.

3. Bake, covered, at 375 degrees until casserole is hot and cheese is melted, about 20 minutes.

Chicken and Broccoli Casserole

6 servings

1¾ cups herb-seasoned whole wheat stuffing mix
3 tablespoons butter, melted
1 can (10¾ ounces) reduced-sodium, reduced-fat cream
  of chicken soup
3 cups cubed, cooked chicken breast
½ cup reduced-fat milk
2 cups frozen chopped broccoli, thawed
3 tablespoons minced onion
¼ teaspoon pepper

Per Serving
Net Carbohydrate (gm): 17.1
Calories: 287
Fat (gm): 11.5
Saturated fat (gm): 4.9
Cholesterol (mg): 74.9
Sodium (mg): 784
Protein (gm): 25.7
Carbohydrate (gm): 19

1. Combine stuffing mix and butter in medium bowl; spoon 1 cup stuffing mixture into lightly greased 2-quart casserole. Combine remaining ingredients in large bowl; pour into casserole and top with remaining ¾ cup stuffing mixture.

2. Bake at 425 degrees 20 to 25 minutes or until golden brown and bubbly. Let stand 5 minutes before serving.

Chicken Divan

6 servings

½ cup mayonnaise
¼ cup all-purpose flour
2½ cups reduced-fat milk
1 cup (4 ounces) shredded sharp Cheddar cheese
Salt and pepper, to taste
1 package (16 ounces) frozen cut broccoli, thawed
½ cup (2 ounces) grated Parmesan cheese, divided
1½ pounds roasted skinless chicken breast, cut into ¼-inch slices

Per Serving
Net Carbohydrate (gm): 11.1
Calories: 499
Fat (gm): 26.9
Saturated fat (gm): 8.5
Cholesterol (mg): 133.9
Sodium (mg): 542
Protein (gm): 48.8
Carbohydrate (gm): 13.6

1. Whisk mayonnaise and flour in medium saucepan over low heat until smooth. Gradually whisk in milk; whisk constantly over medium-high heat until mixture boils and thickens. Add Cheddar cheese, whisking until melted. Season to taste with salt and pepper.

2. Arrange broccoli in lightly greased 12 x 8-inch baking dish. Spoon half the sauce over; sprinkle with half the Parmesan cheese. Top with chicken, remaining sauce, and remaining Parmesan cheese. Bake, uncovered, at 375 degrees until hot and bubbly, about 25 minutes.

Spanish Chicken and Rice

6 servings

1 pound boneless, skinless chicken breast, cubed
1 tablespoon olive oil
1 cup chopped onion
2 cloves garlic, minced
2½ cups reduced-sodium fat-free chicken broth
½ cup dry sherry, *or* chicken broth
1 cup diced green bell pepper
1 cup diced red bell pepper
¼ teaspoon crushed saffron threads
Dash cayenne pepper
1 cup quick-cooking brown rice
1 cup frozen peas
Salt and pepper, to taste

Per Serving
Net Carbohydrate (gm): 21
Calories: 266
Fat (gm): 4.5
Saturated fat (gm): 0.6
Cholesterol (mg): 54.2
Sodium (mg): 281
Protein (gm): 24.7
Carbohydrate (gm): 25.4

1. Sauté chicken in oil in large saucepan until lightly browned, about 5 minutes. Stir in onion and garlic and sauté until onion is tender, about 5 minutes.

2. Add remaining ingredients, except peas, salt, and pepper, and heat to boiling. Reduce heat and simmer, covered, until rice is tender, 20 to 25 minutes, stirring in peas during last 5 minutes of cooking time. Season to taste with salt and pepper.

Chicken à la King over Toast

4 servings

½ cup chopped green bell pepper
2½ tablespoons butter
1½ cups sliced mushrooms
⅓ cup whole wheat flour
1¼ cups reduced-sodium fat-free chicken broth
1¼ cups reduced-fat milk
2 tablespoons dry sherry, optional
2 cups cubed, cooked chicken breast
½ cup frozen peas
1 jar (2 ounces) chopped pimiento, rinsed, drained
Salt and pepper, to taste
4 slices whole-grain bread, toasted
Minced parsley, as garnish

Per Serving
Net Carbohydrate (gm): 24.1
Calories: 363
Fat (gm): 12.4
Saturated fat (gm): 6.4
Cholesterol (mg): 93.9
Sodium (mg): 346
Protein (gm): 31.7
Carbohydrate (gm): 31.4

1. Sauté bell pepper in butter in large saucepan 2 to 3 minutes. Add mushrooms and sauté until tender, about 4 minutes longer (do not brown). Stir in flour; cook over medium-low heat, stirring constantly, 1 minute.

2. Stir broth, milk, and sherry into saucepan; heat to boiling, stirring constantly until thickened, about 1 minute. Stir in chicken, peas, and pimiento; cook until hot through, 3 to 4 minutes. Season to taste with salt and pepper.

3. Cut toast into triangles; arrange on plates. Top with chicken mixture and sprinkle with parsley.

Variation:

Ham and Eggs à la King—Make recipe as above, substituting 8 ounces cubed, trimmed lean smoked ham for the chicken; add 2 chopped hard-cooked eggs.

Chicken Stew Paprikash

4 servings

1 pound boneless, skinless chicken breast, cut into thin strips
1 cup finely chopped onion
2 cloves garlic, minced
1 tablespoon canola oil
1 cup chopped green bell pepper
2 cups sliced mushrooms
1 can (14½ ounces) stewed tomatoes, undrained
1 tablespoon paprika
1 teaspoon poppy seeds
½ cup sour cream
Salt and pepper, to taste

Per Serving
Net Carbohydrate (gm): 14.6
Calories: 289
Fat (gm): 10.9
Saturated fat (gm): 3.9
Cholesterol (mg): 76.2
Sodium (mg): 297
Protein (gm): 30.2
Carbohydrate (gm): 17.7

1. Sauté chicken, onion, and garlic in oil in large saucepan until chicken is browned, about 5 minutes. Add bell pepper and mushrooms and sauté 5 minutes longer.

2. Add tomatoes and liquid, paprika, and poppy seeds and heat to boiling; reduce heat and simmer, covered, until chicken is tender, about 10 minutes. Stir in sour cream; simmer 1 minute longer. Season to taste with salt and pepper.

Ginger-Orange Chicken and Squash Stew

6 servings

1½ pounds boneless, skinless chicken breasts, cubed
1½ cups chopped green bell peppers
1 cup chopped onion
2 cloves garlic, minced
1 tablespoon olive oil
3 cups cubed (½ inch), peeled butternut squash
1½ cups cubed (½ inch), peeled Idaho potatoes
1 can (14½ ounces) diced tomatoes, undrained
2 cups reduced-sodium fat-free chicken broth
½ cup orange juice
¼ teaspoon ground ginger
1 cup sour cream
2 tablespoons minced parsley
1 tablespoon grated orange rind
Salt and pepper, to taste

Per Serving
Net Carbohydrate (gm): 24.7
Calories: 337
Fat (gm): 11.1
Saturated fat (gm): 4.9
Cholesterol (mg): 88.1
Sodium (mg): 387
Protein (gm): 32.4
Carbohydrate (gm): 27.1

1. Sauté chicken, peppers, onion, and garlic in oil in large saucepan until browned, about 10 minutes. Add squash, potatoes, tomatoes and liquid, broth, orange juice, and ginger; heat to boiling. Reduce heat and simmer, uncovered, until chicken and vegetables are tender, about 25 minutes.

2. Stir in sour cream, parsley, and orange rind; season to taste with salt and pepper.

Chicken Stew Athenos

4 servings

1 pound boneless, skinless chicken breast, cubed (¾-inch)
1 tablespoon olive oil
1 can (14 ounces) stewed tomatoes, undrained
1 tablespoon lemon juice
2 teaspoons minced garlic
1 cinnamon stick
1 bay leaf
¼ cup dry sherry, *or* chicken broth
Salt and pepper, to taste
½ cup crumbled feta cheese

Per Serving
Net Carbohydrate (gm): 7.6
Calories: 255
Fat (gm): 8.9
Saturated fat (gm): 3.6
Cholesterol (mg): 82.2
Sodium (mg): 292
Protein (gm): 30
Carbohydrate (gm): 8.9

1. Sauté chicken in oil in large saucepan until lightly browned, about 5 minutes. Add remaining ingredients, except salt, pepper, and cheese. Heat to boiling; reduce heat and simmer, covered, until chicken is cooked through, about 15 minutes. Discard bay leaf and cinnamon stick and season to taste with salt and pepper. Spoon into bowl; sprinkle with cheese.

Quick Chicken and Vegetables

6 servings

1½ pounds boneless, skinless chicken breast, cubed (½-inch)
1 cup sliced carrots
¾ cup chopped onion
2 teaspoons minced garlic
1 tablespoon olive oil
1 can (15 ounces) navy beans, rinsed, drained
2 cups reduced-sodium fat-free chicken broth, divided
1 can (16 ounces) Italian-style zucchini with mushrooms in tomato sauce
1 cup frozen peas
2 teaspoons dried Italian seasoning
Salt and pepper, to taste

Per Serving
Net Carbohydrate (gm): 19.5
Calories: 309
Fat (gm): 5.8
Saturated fat (gm): 0.8
Cholesterol (mg): 74
Sodium (mg): 745
Protein (gm): 37
Carbohydrate (gm): 26.8

1. Sauté chicken, carrots, onion, and garlic in oil in large saucepan until chicken is browned, about 8 minutes. Process navy beans with 1 cup broth in blender or food processor until smooth; add to chicken and vegetables in saucepan. Add remaining 1 cup broth, zucchini, peas, and Italian seasoning.

2. Heat to boiling. Reduce heat and simmer, uncovered, until chicken is tender, about 8 minutes. Season to taste with salt and pepper.

Alfredo Chicken Stew

4 servings

1 pound boneless, skinless chicken breast, cubed
3 tablespoons butter
¼ cup sliced green onions and tops
1 teaspoon minced garlic
¼ cup all-purpose flour
1 teaspoon dried basil leaves
2 cups reduced-fat milk
½ cup whipping cream
1 cup cut up (1½-inch) asparagus
½ cup frozen tiny peas
½ cup (2 ounces) shredded Parmesan cheese
Salt and pepper, to taste

Per Serving
Net Carbohydrate (gm): 16
Calories: 471
Fat (gm): 27.1
Saturated fat (gm): 16.3
Cholesterol (mg): 149.1
Sodium (mg): 430
Protein (gm): 37.9
Carbohydrate (gm): 18.3

1. Sauté chicken in butter in large saucepan until lightly browned, about 5 minutes; add the green onions and garlic and sauté 3 minutes longer. Stir in flour and basil and cook 1 minute longer; stir in milk and cream. Heat to boiling, stirring until thickened, about 1 minute.

2. Stir in asparagus and peas; reduce heat and simmer, covered, until chicken and asparagus are cooked, about 10 minutes. Add cheese, stirring until melted; season to taste with salt and pepper.

Lemon Chicken Stew

6 servings

2 pounds boneless, skinless chicken breast, cubed
1 jalapeño chili, minced
2 cloves garlic, minced
1 tablespoon olive oil
2 cans (14½ ounces each) diced tomatoes, undrained
2 cups fresh, *or* frozen, broccoli florets
¼–⅓ cup lemon juice
¼ cup finely chopped fresh, *or* 2 tablespoons dried, basil leaves
Salt and pepper, to taste
½ cup (2 ounces) shredded Parmesan cheese

Per Serving
Net Carbohydrate (gm): 5.8
Calories: 254
Fat (gm): 6.2
Saturated fat (gm): 2.1
Cholesterol (mg): 92.9
Sodium (mg): 652
Protein (gm): 40
Carbohydrate (gm): 7.7

1. Sauté chicken, jalapeño chili, and garlic in oil in large saucepan until lightly browned, about 5 minutes. Stir in tomatoes and liquid, broccoli, and lemon juice; heat to boiling. Reduce heat and simmer, uncovered, until chicken and broccoli are cooked, about 10 minutes.

2. Stir in basil; season to taste with salt and pepper. Spoon into serving bowl; sprinkle with Parmesan cheese.

Chicken Stew Provençal

4 servings

1½ pounds boneless, skinless chicken breast, cubed (1-inch)
1 tablespoon minced garlic
1 tablespoon olive oil
1 can (28 ounces) whole tomatoes, undrained,
    coarsely chopped
2 cups thinly sliced, peeled potatoes
1 cup dry white wine, *or* chicken broth
1½ teaspoons herbes de Provence
Salt and pepper, to taste
Finely chopped basil leaves, as garnish

Per Serving
Net Carbohydrate (gm): 22
Calories: 364
Fat (gm): 5.7
Saturated fat (gm): 1
Cholesterol (mg): 98.6
Sodium (mg): 389
Protein (gm): 42.6
Carbohydrate (gm): 25.4

1. Sauté chicken and garlic in oil in large saucepan until chicken is browned, about 5 minutes. Add remaining ingredients, except salt, pepper, and basil; heat to boiling. Reduce heat and simmer, covered, 20 minutes or until chicken and potatoes are tender. Season to taste with salt and pepper; sprinkle each serving with basil.

Picnic Chicken Stew

8 servings

2 pounds boneless, skinless chicken breast, cubed
1 cup chopped onion
1 cup chopped red bell pepper
2 cloves garlic, minced
1 tablespoon canola oil
1 can (15 ounces) vegetarian baked beans
1 can (15 ounces) garbanzo beans, rinsed, drained
1 can (14½ ounces) diced tomatoes, undrained
2 teaspoons chili powder
½ teaspoon dried thyme leaves
Salt and pepper, to taste

Per Serving
Net Carbohydrate (gm): 22.1
Calories: 278
Fat (gm): 4.1
Saturated fat (gm): 0.6
Cholesterol (mg): 65.7
Sodium (mg): 457
Protein (gm): 32.3
Carbohydrate (gm): 29

1. Sauté chicken, onion, bell pepper, and garlic in oil in large saucepan until lightly browned, about 8 minutes. Stir in remaining ingredients, except salt and pepper; heat to boiling. Reduce heat and simmer, uncovered, until chicken is tender, about 8 minutes. Add salt and pepper to taste.

Orange-Scented Chicken Stew

4 servings

2 cups thinly sliced onions
2 tablespoons chopped garlic
2 tablespoons olive oil
1 teaspoon ground cinnamon
½ teaspoon ground ginger
1½ pounds boneless, skinless chicken breast, cut into strips
1 can (15 ounces) red beans, rinsed, drained
1 cup reduced-sodium fat-free chicken broth
¼ cup orange juice
1 tablespoon grated orange rind
½ cup chopped parsley
Salt and cayenne pepper, to taste

Per Serving
Net Carbohydrate (gm): 19.1
Calories: 399
Fat (gm): 9.8
Saturated fat (gm): 1.5
Cholesterol (mg): 104.8
Sodium (mg): 521
Protein (gm): 48.2
Carbohydrate (gm): 28.4

1. Cook onions and garlic in oil in large skillet over low heat, covered, until very tender, about 15 minutes; stir in spices and cook 1 minute longer. Stir in chicken and cook over medium-high heat until browned, about 8 minutes.

2. Stir in remaining ingredients, except parsley, salt, and cayenne pepper, and heat to boiling. Reduce heat and simmer, uncovered, until chicken is tender, about 5 minutes. Stir in parsley; season to taste with salt and cayenne pepper.

Chicken Skillet with Sun-Dried Tomatoes and Olives

4 servings

½ cup chopped onion
½ cup chopped green bell pepper
1 tablespoon olive oil
1½ pounds boneless, skinless chicken breast, cubed (1-inch)
1 cup cubed zucchini
1 can (14½ ounces) Italian-seasoned diced tomatoes, undrained
1 teaspoon dried marjoram leaves
3 tablespoons chopped sun-dried tomatoes
2 tablespoons chopped, black, *or* Greek, olives
Salt and pepper, to taste

Per Serving
Net Carbohydrate (gm): 7.8
Calories: 266
Fat (gm): 6.1
Saturated fat (gm): 1.1
Cholesterol (mg): 98.6
Sodium (mg): 655
Protein (gm): 41.3
Carbohydrate (gm): 10

1. Sauté onion and bell pepper in oil in large skillet until tender, about 5 minutes; add chicken and sauté until lightly browned, about 5 minutes. Stir in remaining ingredients, except salt and pepper. Heat to boiling; reduce heat and simmer, uncovered, until chicken is tender and sauce is thickened, about 5 minutes. Season to taste with salt and pepper.

Lisbon Chicken Stew

4 servings

1½ pounds boneless, skinless chicken breast, cubed (¾-inch)
1 cup chopped onion
1 teaspoon olive oil
1 can (15 ounces) garbanzo beans, rinsed, drained
1 can (14½ ounces) reduced-sodium fat-free chicken broth
1 can (14½ ounces) diced tomatoes, undrained
2 cups packed fresh spinach leaves
Pinch ground cinnamon
Salt and pepper, to taste
¼ cup slivered almonds, toasted

Per Serving
Net Carbohydrate (gm): 17.3
Calories: 392
Fat (gm): 9.3
Saturated fat (gm): 1
Cholesterol (mg): 109.3
Sodium (mg): 860
Protein (gm): 50.8
Carbohydrate (gm): 24.2

1. Sauté chicken and onion in oil in large saucepan until lightly browned, about 8 minutes. Add beans, broth, and tomatoes and liquid. Heat to boiling; reduce heat and simmer, covered, 10 minutes. Stir in spinach and cinnamon, and simmer 10 minutes longer; season to taste with salt and pepper. Spoon stew into bowls; sprinkle with almonds.

Chicken Breasts with Sauerkraut

6 servings

⅓ cup dry red wine, *or* reduced-sodium fat-free chicken broth
¼ cup canola oil
1 clove garlic, minced
½ teaspoon paprika
¼ cup chopped parsley
¼ teaspoon pepper
6 boneless, skinless chicken breast halves (6 ounces each)
3 cups prepared sauerkraut
1 teaspoon caraway seeds

Per Serving
Net Carbohydrate (gm): 2.6
Calories: 301
Fat (gm): 11.3
Saturated fat (gm): 1.2
Cholesterol (mg): 98.6
Sodium (mg): 841
Protein (gm): 40.5
Carbohydrate (gm): 5.7

1. Combine wine, oil, garlic, paprika, pepper, and parsley in large glass bowl; add chicken and toss well. Let stand, covered, 30 minutes, or refrigerate several hours, turning occasionally.

2. Broil chicken 6 inches from heat source until cooked through, about 5 minutes on each side.

3. Heat sauerkraut and caraway seeds to boiling in large skillet; reduce heat and simmer, uncovered, 5 minutes. Spoon sauerkraut onto serving platter; arrange chicken on top.

Chicken Paprikash

4 servings

1 pound boneless, skinless chicken breast, cubed (1-inch)
1 tablespoon butter
1 cup chopped onion
4 cloves garlic, minced
2 tablespoons all-purpose flour
½ cup reduced-sodium fat-free chicken broth
¼ cup dry white wine, *or* chicken broth
1 cup chopped, seeded tomato
1½ teaspoons paprika
½ cup sour cream
Salt and white pepper, to taste

Per Serving
Net Carbohydrate (gm): 9.5
Calories: 264
Fat (gm): 10
Saturated fat (gm): 5.4
Cholesterol (mg): 87.6
Sodium (mg): 141
Protein (gm): 29.4
Carbohydrate (gm): 11.1

1. Sauté chicken in butter in large saucepan until beginning to brown. Add onion and garlic and sauté until lightly browned, about 5 minutes. Sprinkle with flour and cook 1 minute longer. Add chicken broth, wine, tomato, and paprika and heat to boiling; reduce heat and simmer, covered, until chicken is tender, 15 to 20 minutes. Stir in sour cream and cook until hot, 2 to 3 minutes. Season to taste with salt and white pepper.

Microwave Chicken Paprikash

4 servings

1½ pounds chicken tenders
1 cup finely chopped onion
1 cup chopped green bell pepper
2 cloves garlic, minced
1 tablespoon canola oil
1 cup sliced mushrooms
1 cup canned stewed tomatoes
2½ teaspoons sweet Hungarian paprika
1 teaspoon poppy seeds
¼ cup sour cream
Salt and pepper, to taste

Per Serving
Net Carbohydrate (gm): 9.4
Calories: 307
Fat (gm): 9.9
Saturated fat (gm): 2.7
Cholesterol (mg): 103.7
Sodium (mg): 217
Protein (gm): 42.1
Carbohydrate (gm): 11.8

1. Microwave chicken in glass baking dish, loosely covered, on High until cooked through, about 5 minutes; reserve.

2. Microwave onion, green pepper, garlic, and oil in 2-quart glass casserole, covered, on High 3 minutes. Add mushrooms and microwave, covered, on High 2 minutes longer. Stir in reserved chicken, tomatoes, paprika, and poppy seeds. Microwave on High, loosely covered, until hot through, about 3 minutes. Let stand, covered, 5 minutes; stir in sour cream. Season to taste with salt and pepper.

Slow-Cooker Chicken with Mushrooms and Wine

6 servings

1¼ cups dry red wine, *or* chicken broth
1 can (6 ounces) tomato paste
1 tablespoon Worcestershire sauce
1 cup chopped onion
1 cup coarsely shredded carrots
8 ounces mushrooms, sliced
2 cloves garlic, minced
2 teaspoons dried Italian seasoning
¼ teaspoon dry mustard
1 bay leaf
2½ pounds chicken breast halves, skinned (bone-in)
Salt and pepper, to taste

Per Serving
Net Carbohydrate (gm): 10.6
Calories: 227
Fat (gm): 1.8
Saturated fat (gm): 0.4
Cholesterol (mg): 69
Sodium (mg): 332
Protein (gm): 30.3
Carbohydrate (gm): 13.3

1. Combine wine, tomato paste, and Worcestershire sauce in slow cooker; stir until smooth. Add remaining ingredients, except salt and pepper. Cover and cook on High 1 hour. Cook on Low 5 to 6 hours or until chicken is tender.

2. Remove chicken and cut into strips, discarding bones; stir back into slow cooker. Discard bay leaf; season to taste with salt and pepper.

Braised Chicken Sorrento

6 servings

2½ pounds chicken pieces (bone-in)
1 tablespoon olive oil
¾ cup chopped onion
1 clove garlic, chopped
5 cups chopped, peeled and seeded tomatoes
1 cup sliced mushrooms
¼ cup pitted black olives
1 can (6 ounces) tomato paste
2 teaspoons sugar
1 teaspoon dried Italian seasoning
½ teaspoon dried tarragon leaves
Pinch ground nutmeg
2 cups sliced zucchini
1 cup sliced red bell pepper
Salt and pepper, to taste

Per Serving
Net Carbohydrate (gm): 14.8
Calories: 370
Fat (gm): 18.6
Saturated fat (gm): 4.7
Cholesterol (mg): 92.8
Sodium (mg): 369
Protein (gm): 33
Carbohydrate (gm): 19.2

1. Cook chicken in oil in large skillet over medium heat until browned on all sides, about 10 minutes. Stir in onion and garlic and cook 3 minutes longer. Stir in tomatoes, mushrooms, olives, tomato paste, sugar, herbs, and nutmeg; heat to boiling. Reduce heat and simmer, covered, until chicken is almost tender, about 25 minutes.

2. Stir in zucchini and bell pepper; simmer until vegetables and chicken are tender, about 8 minutes. Season to taste with salt and pepper.

Chicken with Mediterranean Tomato-Caper Sauce

8 servings

8 boneless, skinless chicken breast halves (6 ounces each)
2 tablespoons olive oil
1 teaspoon dried oregano leaves
½ teaspoon ground cumin
¼ teaspoon ground cinnamon
½ teaspoon salt
¼ teaspoon pepper
Mediterranean Tomato-Caper Sauce (recipe follows)
Fresh oregano, *or* basil, leaves, as garnish

Per Serving
Net Carbohydrate (gm): 7.6
Calories: 255
Fat (gm): 5.7
Saturated fat (gm): 1
Cholesterol (mg): 98.6
Sodium (mg): 611
Protein (gm): 40.5
Carbohydrate (gm): 9.3

1. Toss chicken with combined oil, oregano, cumin, cinnamon, salt, and pepper. Broil chicken, 6 inches from heat source, until cooked, about 5 minutes on each side. Slice chicken diagonally and arrange on plates; top with sauce. Garnish with fresh oregano.

Mediterranean Tomato-Caper Sauce

makes about 2 cups

1 can (16 ounces) tomato sauce
2 teaspoons minced garlic
1 teaspoon dried oregano leaves
1 teaspoon ground cumin
1 teaspoon ground coriander
1 teaspoon paprika
Pinch ground cinnamon
Pinch ground cloves
2 teaspoons lime juice
¼ cup golden raisins
1 tablespoon drained capers
Salt and pepper, to taste

1. Combine all ingredients, except capers, salt, and pepper, in medium saucepan. Heat to boiling; reduce heat and simmer, covered, 10 minutes. Stir in capers; season to taste with salt and pepper.

Chicken Marengo

6 servings

6 boneless, skinless chicken breast halves (6 ounces each)
¼ cup all-purpose flour
1 tablespoon olive oil
2 cups sliced mushrooms
½ cup chopped onion
3 cloves garlic, minced
1¾ cups reduced-sodium fat-free chicken broth
½ cup dry white wine, *or* chicken broth
3 tablespoons tomato paste
2 tablespoons grated orange rind
1 teaspoon dried tarragon leaves
1 teaspoon dried thyme leaves
Salt and pepper, to taste

Per Serving
Net Carbohydrate (gm): 7.8
Calories: 275
Fat (gm): 4.9
Saturated fat (gm): 0.9
Cholesterol (mg): 105.9
Sodium (mg): 229
Protein (gm): 43.2
Carbohydrate (gm): 9.1

1. Coat chicken breasts with flour. Sauté in oil in Dutch oven until browned, about 5 minutes each side. Remove chicken. Add mushrooms, onion, and garlic to Dutch oven; sauté until tender, about 5 minutes.

2. Add broth, wine, tomato paste, orange rind, and herbs to Dutch oven; heat to boiling. Add chicken and bake, loosely covered, at 350 degrees until chicken is tender, 30 to 40 minutes. Season to taste with salt and pepper.

Chicken, Fennel, and Spaghetti with Sun-dried Tomato Pesto

6 servings

2 cups thinly sliced fennel bulb
1 tablespoon olive oil
¼ cup dry white wine, *or* chicken broth
Sun-Dried Tomato Pesto (recipe follows)
8 ounces whole wheat spaghetti, *or*
    angel hair pasta, cooked, warm
Salt and pepper, to taste
6 boneless, skinless chicken breast halves (6 ounces each)

Per Serving
Net Carbohydrate (gm): 28.2
Calories: 457
Fat (gm): 14.9
Saturated fat (gm): 2.8
Cholesterol (mg): 101.2
Sodium (mg): 231
Protein (gm): 47.1
Carbohydrate (gm): 32.7

1. Sauté fennel in oil in large skillet 2 to 3 minutes. Cook, covered, over medium-low heat until softened, about 10 minutes. Stir in wine and simmer, covered, until wine is almost gone and fennel is tender, about 15 minutes.

2. Spoon fennel mixture and Sun-Dried Tomato Pesto over spaghetti in serving bowl and toss. Season to taste with salt and pepper.

3. Sprinkle chicken lightly with salt and pepper. Broil chicken, 6 inches from heat source until cooked, about 5 minutes on each side. Spoon spaghetti on to serving plates; top with chicken.

Sun-Dried Tomato Pesto

makes about 1 cup

⅓ cup sun-dried tomatoes (not in oil)
⅓ cup very hot water
⅓ cup packed basil leaves
1 clove garlic
¼ cup olive oil
¼ cup grated Parmesan cheese

1. Soak tomatoes in hot water in bowl until softened, about 5 minutes. Drain, reserving liquid.

2. Process tomatoes and remaining ingredients in food processor or blender, adding enough reserved liquid to make a smooth, spoonable paste.

Chicken Piccata

6 servings

6 boneless, skinless chicken breast halves (5 ounces each), pounded to ¼ inch thickness
½ cup whole wheat flour, divided
2 tablespoons butter, divided
1 can (14½ ounces) reduced-sodium fat-free chicken broth
½ cup dry white wine, *or* chicken broth
2 tablespoons lemon juice
1 tablespoon finely chopped parsley
2 teaspoons drained capers

Per Serving
Net Carbohydrate (gm): 8.3
Calories: 257
Fat (gm): 6.3
Saturated fat (gm): 3
Cholesterol (mg): 100.2
Sodium (mg): 216
Protein (gm): 35.9
Carbohydrate (gm): 8.6

1. Coat chicken with 6 tablespoons flour. Cook chicken in 1 tablespoon butter in large skillet over medium heat until browned and no longer pink in center, about 3 minutes on each side. Remove chicken from skillet.

2. Melt remaining 1 tablespoon butter in skillet; stir in remaining 2 tablespoons flour and cook over medium heat 1 to 2 minutes. Stir in chicken broth, wine, and lemon juice; heat to boiling, stirring constantly. Reduce heat and simmer, uncovered, until thickened to a medium sauce consistency, about 10 minutes. Stir in parsley and capers.

3. Return chicken to sauce; cook over medium-low heat until chicken is hot through, about 2 minutes.

Chicken, Mushroom, and Tomatoes with Polenta

6 servings

8 ounces mushrooms, sliced
½ cup chopped onion
⅓ cup shredded carrot
2 cloves garlic, minced
2 teaspoons olive oil
6 chicken breast halves (3 pounds) (bone-in)
2 cans (14½ ounces each) diced tomatoes, undrained
1 can (8 ounces) tomato sauce
2 tablespoons tomato paste
1 teaspoon packed brown sugar
1 teaspoon dried basil leaves
1 teaspoon dried thyme leaves
Salt and pepper, to taste
Microwave Polenta (recipe follows)

Per Serving
Net Carbohydrate (gm): 24.8
Calories: 318
Fat (gm): 5.2
Saturated fat (gm): 1.6
Cholesterol (mg): 86.4
Sodium (mg): 1192
Protein (gm): 37.9
Carbohydrate (gm): 29

1. Sauté mushrooms, onion, carrot, and garlic in oil in Dutch oven until lightly browned, about 8 minutes. Add remaining ingredients, except salt, pepper, and Microwave Polenta; heat to boiling. Reduce heat and simmer, covered, until chicken is tender, about 35 minutes. Remove chicken and cut meat into 1-inch strips, discarding bones. Return chicken to Dutch oven; season to taste with salt and pepper. Serve over Microwave Polenta.

Microwave Polenta

makes about 3 cups

4 cups water
¾ cup yellow cornmeal
½ cup chopped onion
2 teaspoons butter
½ teaspoon salt
½ teaspoon pepper

1. Combine all ingredients in 2½-quart microwave-safe casserole. Cook, uncovered, on High power 6 minutes, stirring occasionally. Remove and stir with wire whisk until smooth. Cover and cook on High 6 to 7 minutes longer. Remove from microwave and let stand, covered, 3 to 4 minutes.

Chicken Alfredo

6 servings

6 boneless, skinless chicken breast halves (5 ounces each)
2 cloves garlic, minced
Paprika
Alfredo Sauce (recipe follows)
1 tablespoon finely chopped fresh, *or*
    1 teaspoon dried, basil leaves

Per Serving
Net Carbohydrate (gm): 8.8
Calories: 360
Fat (gm): 18.1
Saturated fat (gm): 10.7
Cholesterol (mg): 136
Sodium (mg): 461
Protein (gm): 38.4
Carbohydrate (gm): 9

1. Rub chicken with garlic; sprinkle generously with paprika. Place chicken in baking pan and bake at 350 degrees until juices run clear, about 25 minutes. Spoon Alfredo Sauce over chicken; sprinkle with basil.

Alfredo Sauce

makes about 2 cups

3 tablespoons butter
¼ cup all-purpose flour
2 cups reduced-fat milk
½ cup whipping cream
⅓ cup (1½ ounces) shredded Parmesan cheese
⅛ teaspoon ground nutmeg
½ teaspoon salt
¼ teaspoon pepper

1. Melt butter in medium saucepan; stir in flour. Cook over medium heat 1 minute, stirring constantly. Stir in milk and cream; heat to boiling, stirring constantly until thickened, about 2 minutes.

2. Reduce heat to low and stir in remaining ingredients; cook until cheese is melted, 1 to 2 minutes.

Chicken Breasts with Rosemary

4 servings

2 tablespoons olive oil, divided
2 teaspoons balsamic vinegar
1 teaspoon minced garlic
1 tablespoon grated lemon rind
¼ teaspoon salt
⅛ teaspoon pepper
4 boneless, skinless chicken breast halves (5 ounces each)
⅓ cup dry white wine, *or* chicken broth
1 tablespoon finely chopped fresh, *or*
    1 teaspoon dried, crumbled, rosemary leaves
½ cup diced, seeded tomato

Per Serving
Net Carbohydrate (gm): 2
Calories: 239
Fat (gm): 8.5
Saturated fat (gm): 1.4
Cholesterol (mg): 82.1
Sodium (mg): 223
Protein (gm): 33
Carbohydrate (gm): 2.5

1. Combine 1 tablespoon oil, vinegar, garlic, lemon rind, salt, and pepper in medium bowl; add chicken, tossing to coat. Let stand 10 minutes, or refrigerate, covered, several hours.

2. Cook chicken in remaining 1 tablespoon olive oil in large skillet over medium-high heat until browned on both sides, about 5 minutes on each side. Add remaining ingredients and heat to boiling; reduce heat and simmer, covered, until chicken is cooked through, about 10 minutes.

Tuscan Chicken Stew

6 servings

1 cup reduced-sodium fat-free chicken broth, hot
1 ounce dried porcini, *or* shiitake, mushrooms
6 boneless, skinless chicken breast halves
   (about 5 ounces each)
2 tablespoons all-purpose flour
2 tablespoons olive oil
½ cup dry white wine, *or* chicken broth
1 can (14 ounces) Italian-seasoned tomato sauce
Salt and pepper, to taste

Per Serving
Net Carbohydrate (gm): 9.1
Calories: 284
Fat (gm): 7.8
Saturated fat (gm): 1.1
Cholesterol (mg): 91.8
Sodium (mg): 343
Protein (gm): 38
Carbohydrate (gm): 11

1. Pour broth over mushrooms in small bowl; let stand until softened, about 10 minutes. Drain mushrooms, reserving broth. Slice mushrooms, discarding tough stems.

2. Coat chicken with flour; sauté in oil in large skillet until browned, about 5 minutes on each side. Stir in wine, tomato sauce, reserved broth, and mushrooms; heat to boiling. Reduce heat and simmer, covered, until chicken is tender, about 20 minutes. Remove lid and cook over medium-high heat until slightly thickened, about 5 minutes. Season to taste with salt and pepper.

Wine-Glazed Chicken with Ravioli and Asparagus

4 servings

4 boneless, skinless chicken breast halves (4 ounces each)
2 tablespoons butter
Salt and pepper, to taste
2 cups reduced-sodium fat-free chicken broth
1 cup dry white wine, *or* chicken broth
1 cup orange juice
¼ teaspoon crushed red pepper
1 pound asparagus, cut into 1-inch pieces
1 package (9 ounces) fresh mushroom ravioli, cooked, warm

Per Serving
Net Carbohydrate (gm): 27.2
Calories: 414
Fat (gm): 11.2
Saturated fat (gm): 5.3
Cholesterol (mg): 112.2
Sodium (mg): 401
Protein (gm): 38.6
Carbohydrate (gm): 30.6

1. Cook chicken in butter in large skillet over medium heat until chicken is no longer pink in center, about 8 minutes on each side. Sprinkle lightly with salt and pepper. Remove chicken and reserve.

2. Heat broth, wine, orange juice, and crushed red pepper to boiling in skillet; boil, uncovered, 10 minutes or until liquid is reduced to about ½ cup.

3. Add asparagus to skillet; cook, covered, over medium heat until crisp-tender, 3 to 4 minutes. Add ravioli and reserved chicken; cook until hot through, about 2 minutes longer. Season to taste with salt and pepper.

Speedy Chicken and Ravioli

4 servings

1 pound boneless, skinless chicken breast, cubed (½-inch)
¾ cup chopped onion
2 teaspoons minced garlic
1 tablespoon olive oil
¾ cup canned kidney beans, rinsed, drained
1 cup cubed tomato
½ teaspoon dried thyme leaves
1 package (9 ounces) fresh sun-dried tomato ravioli, cooked, warm
Salt and pepper, to taste

Per Serving
Net Carbohydrate (gm): 24.8
Calories: 359
Fat (gm): 9.9
Saturated fat (gm): 3.2
Cholesterol (mg): 94.2
Sodium (mg): 385
Protein (gm): 36.7
Carbohydrate (gm): 29.9

1. Sauté chicken, onion, and garlic in oil in large skillet until browned, 5 to 8 minutes. Stir in beans, tomato, and thyme; cook 2 minutes longer. Stir in ravioli and cook until chicken is cooked through, about 3 minutes longer. Season to taste with salt and pepper.

Chicken Cacciatore with Ziti

4 servings

1 pound boneless, skinless chicken breast, cubed (¾-inch)
1 tablespoon olive oil
½ cup chopped shallots, *or* green onions and tops
1 can (14½ ounces) diced tomatoes with
    roasted garlic, undrained
¼ cup dry red wine, *or* chicken broth
1 cup sliced zucchini
1 teaspoon dried Italian seasoning
Salt and pepper, to taste
4 ounces whole wheat ziti, *or* rotini, cooked, warm

Per Serving
Net Carbohydrate (gm): 27.3
Calories: 307
Fat (gm): 5.2
Saturated fat (gm): 0.9
Cholesterol (mg): 65.7
Sodium (mg): 440
Protein (gm): 32.6
Carbohydrate (gm): 31.1

1. Sauté chicken in oil in large saucepan until lightly browned, about 5 minutes. Add shallots; sauté until tender, about 3 minutes. Add remaining ingredients, except salt, pepper, and ziti; heat to boiling. Reduce heat and simmer, covered, until chicken is tender, about 15 minutes; season to taste with salt and pepper. Serve over pasta.

Chicken and Pasta Skillet

4 servings

½ cup chopped onion
½ cup chopped green bell pepper
1 tablespoon olive oil
1 pound boneless, skinless chicken breast, cubed (1-inch)
3 ounces whole wheat rotini, cooked
1½ cups cubed zucchini
1 can (15½ ounces) Italian-seasoned diced tomatoes, undrained
1 teaspoon dried marjoram leaves
3 tablespoons chopped, softened sun-dried tomatoes
2 tablespoons chopped Greek olives
Salt and pepper, to taste

Per Serving
Net Carbohydrate (gm): 22.6
Calories: 282
Fat (gm): 5.7
Saturated fat (gm): 1
Cholesterol (mg): 65.7
Sodium (mg): 660
Protein (gm): 31.5
Carbohydrate (gm): 26.7

1. Sauté onion and bell pepper in olive oil in large skillet until tender, about 4 minutes; add chicken and cook until lightly browned, about 5 minutes. Stir in remaining ingredients, except salt and pepper. Heat to boiling; reduce heat and simmer, uncovered, until chicken is cooked and sauce is thickened, about 10 minutes. Season to taste with salt and pepper.

Chicken Marinara

4 servings

2 cups chopped onions
1½ cups chopped celery
1 clove garlic, minced
¼ teaspoon crushed red pepper flakes
1½ pounds boneless, skinless chicken breast, cubed
1 tablespoon olive oil
1 can (15 ounces) crushed tomatoes
2 cups chopped zucchini
2 teaspoons dried Italian seasoning
Salt and pepper, to taste

Per Serving
Net Carbohydrate (gm): 15.6
Calories: 288
Fat (gm): 5.9
Saturated fat (gm): 1
Cholesterol (mg): 98.6
Sodium (mg): 383
Protein (gm): 42
Carbohydrate (gm): 16.8

1. Sauté onions, celery, garlic, red pepper, and chicken in oil in large saucepan until lightly browned. Add tomatoes, zucchini, and Italian seasoning; heat to boiling. Reduce heat and simmer, covered, 10 minutes. Simmer, uncovered, until chicken is tender and sauce is thickened, about 10 minutes. Season to taste with salt and pepper.

Tomato-Chicken Stew

6 servings

1½ pounds boneless, skinless chicken breast, cubed
1 cup sliced onion
2 cloves garlic, minced
1 tablespoon olive oil
1 can (14½ ounces) diced tomatoes, undrained
1½ cups reduced-sodium fat-free chicken broth
½ cup dry white wine, *or* water
¼ cup tomato paste
2 teaspoons lemon juice
1 bay leaf
1 teaspoon dried oregano leaves
½ teaspoon dried thyme leaves
2 cups sliced mushrooms
1 can (15 ounces) Great Northern beans, rinsed, drained
Salt and pepper, to taste

Per Serving
Net Carbohydrate (gm): 18.2
Calories: 290
Fat (gm): 4.5
Saturated fat (gm): 0.8
Cholesterol (mg): 72
Sodium (mg): 434
Protein (gm): 35.3
Carbohydrate (gm): 23.5

1. Sauté chicken, onion, and garlic in oil in Dutch oven until browned, about 10 minutes. Add remaining ingredients, except mushrooms, beans, salt, and pepper; heat to boiling. Reduce heat and simmer, covered, 10 minutes. Add mushrooms and beans; simmer, uncovered, until chicken is tender and sauce has thickened, about 10 minutes. Discard bay leaf; season to taste with salt and pepper.

Quick Chicken Peperonata

4 servings

1½ pounds boneless, skinless chicken breast, cubed (1-inch)
1 teaspoon minced garlic
1 tablespoon olive oil
2 cups frozen stir-fry pepper blend
1 can (15 ounces) chunky Italian-seasoned tomato sauce
Salt and pepper, to taste
¼ cup grated Parmesan cheese

Per Serving
Net Carbohydrate (gm): 8.8
Calories: 312
Fat (gm): 8.9
Saturated fat (gm): 1.9
Cholesterol (mg): 102.5
Sodium (mg): 550
Protein (gm): 44
Carbohydrate (gm): 12.3

1. Sauté chicken and garlic in oil in large skillet until lightly browned, about 6 minutes. Push chicken to side of pan; add stir-fry pepper blend and cook until softened, 3 to 4 minutes. Stir in tomato sauce. Heat to boiling; reduce heat and simmer, covered, until chicken is cooked through, about 10 minutes. Season to taste with salt and pepper; sprinkle with Parmesan cheese.

Hunter's Stew

4 servings

1½ pounds boneless, skinless chicken breast, cubed (1-inch)
¼ cup all-purpose flour
1½ tablespoons olive oil
1½ cups chopped onions
1 cup diced red bell pepper
1 cup diced green bell pepper
½ cup chopped carrot
2 large cloves garlic, minced
1 can (14½ ounces) diced tomatoes, undrained
1½ cups reduced-sodium fat-free chicken broth
¼ cup tomato paste
1 teaspoon dried thyme leaves
1 teaspoon dried marjoram leaves
Salt and pepper, to taste

Per Serving
Net Carbohydrate (gm): 19.9
Calories: 360
Fat (gm): 8.1
Saturated fat (gm): 1.3
Cholesterol (mg): 107.9
Sodium (mg): 508
Protein (gm): 45.8
Carbohydrate (gm): 24.8

1. Toss chicken with flour; sauté in oil in Dutch oven until browned, about 8 minutes. Stir in onions, bell peppers, carrot, and garlic; sauté until vegetables begin to brown, about 5 minutes.

2. Add remaining ingredients, except salt and pepper; heat to boiling. Reduce heat and simmer, covered, until chicken is tender, about 20 minutes. Season to taste with salt and pepper.

Orange Chicken and Vegetables

6 servings

6 boneless, skinless chicken breast halves (4 ounces each)
1 tablespoon olive oil
1 cup thinly sliced onion
½ cup chopped red bell pepper
2 cloves garlic, chopped
1 tablespoon all-purpose flour
1 cup chopped, seeded tomatoes
½ teaspoon dried marjoram leaves
¼ teaspoon dried thyme leaves
1 piece cinnamon stick (1 inch)
1 cup reduced-sodium fat-free chicken broth
½ cup orange juice
1 tablespoon grated orange rind
1 cup sliced carrots
1 cup cut green beans (1 inch pieces)
Salt and pepper, to taste

Per Serving
Net Carbohydrate (gm): 9.4
Calories: 204
Fat (gm): 4.2
Saturated fat (gm): 0.7
Cholesterol (mg): 69.9
Sodium (mg): 113
Protein (gm): 29
Carbohydrate (gm): 12

1. Cook chicken in oil in large skillet over medium heat until browned, about 5 minutes on each side. Arrange chicken in 12 x 9-inch glass baking dish.

2. Add onion, bell pepper, and garlic to skillet and sauté until tender, about 5 minutes. Stir in flour; cook over medium heat 1 minute. Add tomatoes, marjoram, thyme, and cinnamon stick; sauté 1 to 2 minutes longer.

3. Add broth, orange juice, and rind to skillet; heat to boiling. Reduce heat and simmer, uncovered, 5 minutes. Arrange carrots and beans around chicken; pour broth mixture over. Bake, covered, at 350 degrees until chicken is tender, about 30 minutes. Season to taste with salt and pepper.

Chicken with Red Wine

4 servings

4 boneless, skinless chicken breast halves (5 ounces each)
1 tablespoon olive oil
1 cup chopped onion
2 large cloves garlic, minced
1 tablespoon all-purpose flour
¾ cup reduced-sodium fat-free chicken broth
¾ cup dry red wine
1½ teaspoons dried oregano leaves
½ teaspoon dried thyme leaves
1 bay leaf
Salt and pepper, to taste

Per Serving
Net Carbohydrate (gm): 5.6
Calories: 252
Fat (gm): 5.5
Saturated fat (gm): 0.9
Cholesterol (mg): 86.8
Sodium (mg): 125
Protein (gm): 35
Carbohydrate (gm): 6.8

1. Cook chicken in oil in large skillet until browned on both sides, about 8 minutes. Stir in onion and garlic and sauté until tender, about 5 minutes; sprinkle with flour and cook 1 minute longer.

2. Add remaining ingredients, except salt and pepper; heat to boiling. Reduce heat and simmer, uncovered, until chicken is tender and sauce is slightly thickened, about 20 minutes. Discard bay leaf; season to taste with salt and pepper.

United Nations Chicken

4 servings

4 boneless, skinless chicken breast halves (6 ounces each)
Salt and pepper, to taste
1 tablespoon olive oil
½ cup chopped onion
¼ cup chopped green bell pepper
Sauce of your choice (recipes follow)

Per Serving
Net Carbohydrate (gm): 1.8
Calories: 226
Fat (gm): 5.4
Saturated fat (gm): 1
Cholesterol (mg): 98.6
Sodium (mg): 89
Protein (gm): 39.6
Carbohydrate (gm): 2.3

1. Sprinkle chicken lightly with salt and pepper. Sauté chicken in oil in large skillet until browned, about 5 minutes on each side. Add onion and bell pepper and sauté until chicken is cooked and vegetables are tender, about 5 minutes.

2. Serve chicken with desired sauce.

Sauces for United Nations Chicken (all serve 4)

Sauce Athenos

makes about ½ cup

¾ cup reduced-sodium fat-free chicken broth
2 tablespoons lemon juice
1 tablespoon grated lemon peel
1 teaspoon dried oregano leaves
8 sliced black olives

Per Serving
Net Carbohydrate (gm): 1
Calories: 22
Fat (gm): 1.3
Saturated fat (gm): 0.1
Cholesterol (mg): 4.7
Sodium (mg): 124
Protein (gm): 1.5
Carbohydrate (gm): 1.7

1. Heat all ingredients, except olives, to boiling in small saucepan; boil until reduced to about ½ cup, about 5 minutes. Spoon over chicken; sprinkle with olives.

Sauce Parisian

makes about 2 cups

⅓ cup reduced-sodium fat-free chicken broth
⅓ cup dry red wine
½ pound mushrooms, sliced
½ cup frozen, *or* jarred, drained pearl onions
1 teaspoon dried thyme leaves
2 tablespoons chopped parsley

Per Serving
Net Carbohydrate (gm): 3.3
Calories: 39
Fat (gm): 0.3
Saturated fat (gm): 0
Cholesterol (mg): 2.1
Sodium (mg): 28
Protein (gm): 2.4
Carbohydrate (gm): 4.6

1. Heat broth and wine to boiling in large skillet; add mushrooms, reduce heat and simmer, covered, until mushrooms are wilted, about 5 minutes. Stir in onions and thyme; cook, uncovered, over medium heat until liquid is almost evaporated, about 5 minutes. Spoon over chicken; sprinkle with parsley.

Sauce Italiano

makes about ½ cup

½ cup yogurt
½ cup chopped, seeded tomato
1 tablespoon fresh, *or* 1 teaspoon dried, basil leaves
1 tablespoon fresh, *or* 1 teaspoon dried, oregano leaves
Dash pepper
4 anchovies, optional

Per Serving
Net Carbohydrate (gm): 3.1
Calories: 25
Fat (gm): 0.6
Saturated fat (gm): 0.3
Cholesterol (mg): 1.8
Sodium (mg): 24
Protein (gm): 1.8
Carbohydrate (gm): 3.3

1. Heat all ingredients, except anchovies, over low heat in small saucepan until warm. Spoon over chicken; top with anchovies.

Sauce Mexicali

makes about 1 cup

¼ cup finely chopped onion
1 small jalapeño chili, minced
2 teaspoons canola oil
1 teaspoon chili powder
½ cup chopped, seeded tomato
¾ cup reduced-sodium fat-free chicken broth
⅓ cup sour cream
2 teaspoons finely chopped cilantro

Per Serving
Net Carbohydrate (gm): 2.4
Calories: 74
Fat (gm): 6.1
Saturated fat (gm): 2.3
Cholesterol (mg): 11.7
Sodium (mg): 64
Protein (gm): 2.3
Carbohydrate (gm): 3.2

1. Sauté onion and jalapeño chili in oil in small skillet until tender, 2 to 3 minutes. Stir in chili powder and tomato; cook 1 to 2 minutes. Stir in broth and heat to boiling; reduce heat and simmer until reduced to about ½ cup, about 5 minutes. Add sour cream and cilantro; stir over low heat until warm. Spoon over chicken.

Sauce Oriental

makes about 2 cups

⅓ cup reduced-sodium fat-free chicken broth
½ pound mushrooms, sliced
½ cup sliced water chestnuts
½ cup sliced green onions and tops
3 tablespoons sesame seeds, toasted

Per Serving
Net Carbohydrate (gm): 4.7
Calories: 69
Fat (gm): 3.7
Saturated fat (gm): 0.5
Cholesterol (mg): 2.1
Sodium (mg): 27
Protein (gm): 3.8
Carbohydrate (gm): 7

1. Heat broth, mushrooms, water chestnuts, and green onions to boiling in large skillet; reduce heat and simmer, covered, until mushrooms are wilted, about 5 minutes. Cook, uncovered, over medium heat until liquid is almost evaporated, about 5 minutes. Spoon over chicken; sprinkle with sesame seeds.

Ginger Chicken with Oranges

8 servings

8 boneless, skinless chicken breast halves (6 ounces each)
½ cup orange juice concentrate, thawed
1 teaspoon ground ginger
½ teaspoon pepper
1 orange, peeled, sliced
1 cup orange juice
2 tablespoons honey
2 tablespoons grated orange rind
1 tablespoon cornstarch

Per Serving
Net Carbohydrate (gm): 17.2
Calories: 260
Fat (gm): 2.1
Saturated fat (gm): 0.6
Cholesterol (mg): 98.6
Sodium (mg): 90
Protein (gm): 40.2
Carbohydrate (gm): 18.2

1. Place chicken in lightly greased shallow baking dish. Brush with combined orange juice concentrate, ginger, and pepper. Arrange orange slices on top of chicken. Bake, covered, at 350 degrees 15 minutes. Uncover and bake until juices run clear, about 10 minutes longer.

2. Combine remaining ingredients in small saucepan and cook, stirring constantly until thickened. Pour sauce over chicken.

Chicken Stew, Catalan Style

6 servings

3 pounds chicken pieces (bone-in)
2 tablespoons olive oil, divided
2 cups finely chopped onions
1 clove garlic, minced
1½ cups chopped, peeled, and seeded tomatoes
½ cup tomato sauce
½ cup dry white wine, *or* chicken broth
2 teaspoons dried basil leaves
1 bay leaf
2 cups cubed eggplant
2 cups sliced zucchini
2 cups chopped green, *or* red, bell peppers
2 tablespoons chopped cilantro
2 tablespoons chopped parsley
Salt and pepper, to taste

Per Serving
Net Carbohydrate (gm): 10.8
Calories: 417
Fat (gm): 25.7
Saturated fat (gm): 6.6
Cholesterol (mg): 106.4
Sodium (mg): 214
Protein (gm): 29.2
Carbohydrate (gm): 14.9

1. Cook chicken in 1 tablespoon oil in Dutch oven until browned on all sides, about 10 minutes; remove chicken and reserve.

2. Sauté onions and garlic in Dutch oven until tender, about 5 minutes. Add reserved chicken, tomatoes, tomato sauce, wine, basil, and bay leaf; heat to boiling. Reduce heat and simmer, covered, 30 minutes.

3. Sauté eggplant, zucchini, and peppers in remaining 1 tablespoon oil in large skillet until lightly browned. Add to Dutch oven and simmer, uncovered, until chicken is tender, about 10 minutes. Discard bay leaf. Stir in cilantro and parsley; season to taste with salt and pepper.

Chicken with Almonds

4 servings

2 pounds chicken pieces
2 tablespoons butter
¼ cup chopped onion
2 cloves garlic, chopped
2 tablespoons all-purpose flour
1 tablespoon tomato paste
1½ cups reduced-sodium fat-free chicken broth
2 tablespoons dry sherry, *or* chicken broth
1 teaspoon dried tarragon leaves
¼ cup slivered almonds
¾ cup sour cream
Salt and pepper, to taste

Per Serving
Net Carbohydrate (gm): 7.6
Calories: 479
Fat (gm): 32.9
Saturated fat (gm): 12.9
Cholesterol (mg): 146
Sodium (mg): 290
Protein (gm): 34.3
Carbohydrate (gm): 9.1

1. Cook chicken in butter in large skillet until browned on all sides, about 10 minutes; remove from pan. Sauté onion and garlic in skillet until tender, about 4 minutes; stir in flour and tomato paste and cook 1 minute longer. Stir in broth, sherry, and tarragon. Heat to boiling, stirring until thickened.

2. Return chicken to skillet. Add almonds and heat to boiling; reduce heat and simmer, covered, until chicken is tender, about 40 minutes.

3. Place chicken on serving platter. Stir sour cream into sauce; heat until warm. Season to taste with salt and pepper. Pour sauce over chicken.

Chicken Madrid

4 servings

4 boneless, skinless chicken breast halves (5 ounces each)
¾ cup sliced onion
1 tablespoon canola oil
1 can (14½ ounces) reduced-sodium stewed tomatoes, undrained
½ can (15-ounce size) quartered artichoke hearts, drained
Salt and pepper, to taste
Orange Cilantro Rice (recipe follows)

Per Serving
Net Carbohydrate (gm): 25.2
Calories: 349
Fat (gm): 8.2
Saturated fat (gm): 0.9
Cholesterol (mg): 82.1
Sodium (mg): 384
Protein (gm): 37.9
Carbohydrate (gm): 29.9

1. Sauté chicken and onion in oil in large skillet until chicken is browned, about 5 minutes on each side. Add tomatoes and liquid and artichoke hearts. Heat to boiling; reduce heat and simmer, covered, until chicken is tender, about 20 minutes. Season to taste with salt and pepper. Serve over Orange Cilantro Rice.

Orange Cilantro Rice

makes about 2 cups

½ cup sliced green onions and tops
2 teaspoons canola oil
¾ cup quick-cooking brown rice
1 tablespoon grated orange rind
1½ cups water
2 tablespoons chopped cilantro
Salt, to taste

1. Sauté onions in oil in medium saucepan until tender, about 3 minutes. Add rice and orange rind and cook over medium heat until lightly browned, about 2 minutes. Stir in water. Heat to boiling; reduce heat and simmer, covered, until rice is tender, about 20 minutes. Stir in cilantro and season to taste with salt.

Arroz con Pollo

6 servings

2 pounds boneless, skinless chicken breast, cubed (1-inch)
2 tablespoons olive oil
1 cup chopped onion
2 cloves garlic, minced
2½ cups reduced-sodium fat-free chicken broth
½ cup dry sherry, *or* reduced-sodium fat-free chicken broth
1 cup chopped green bell pepper
1 cup chopped red bell pepper
½ teaspoon saffron threads, optional, *or* ½ teaspoon ground turmeric
Dash cayenne pepper
¾ cup quick-cooking brown rice
½ cup fresh, *or* frozen, peas
Salt and pepper, to taste

Per Serving
Net Carbohydrate (gm): 24.4
Calories: 374
Fat (gm): 7.8
Saturated fat (gm): 1.2
Cholesterol (mg): 98
Sodium (mg): 187
Protein (gm): 41.3
Carbohydrate (gm): 27.4

1. Sauté chicken in oil in Dutch oven until browned, about 5 minutes; add onion and garlic and sauté until onion is tender, about 3 minutes longer.

2. Add remaining ingredients, except salt and pepper. Heat to boiling; reduce heat and simmer, covered, 20 minutes or until rice is tender. Season to taste with salt and pepper.

Med-Rim Chicken Stew

4 servings

1 pound boneless, skinless chicken breast, cubed
⅓ cup whole wheat flour
1 teaspoon dried thyme leaves
1 teaspoon dried rosemary leaves
1 teaspoon dried tarragon leaves
1 cup sliced mushrooms
¼ cup chopped onion
1 clove garlic, crushed
2 tablespoons olive oil
1 cup quartered plum tomatoes
1 cup dry white wine, *or* reduced-sodium fat-free chicken broth
¼ cup sliced black olives
Salt and pepper, to taste

Per Serving
Net Carbohydrate (gm): 11.7
Calories: 293
Fat (gm): 9.4
Saturated fat (gm): 1.5
Cholesterol (mg): 65.7
Sodium (mg): 141
Protein (gm): 28.5
Carbohydrate (gm): 13.4

1. Toss chicken with flour and herbs in small bowl. Sauté chicken, mushrooms, onion, and garlic in oil in large skillet until chicken is browned. Add tomatoes, wine, and olives; simmer, covered, until chicken is tender, about 20 minutes. Simmer, uncovered, until sauce is slightly thickened, about 5 minutes. Season to taste with salt and pepper.

Mediterranean Chicken

6 servings

2¼ pounds chicken pieces (bone-in)
1 tablespoon olive oil
3 cloves garlic, minced
½ cup dry white wine, *or* water
¼ cup balsamic vinegar
1 cup chopped, seeded plum tomatoes
3 tablespoons sliced Greek, *or* other black, olives
1 tablespoon dried rosemary leaves
2 tablespoons chopped fresh, *or* 1 tablespoon dried, oregano leaves
Salt and pepper, to taste

Per Serving
Net Carbohydrate (gm): 5.1
Calories: 204
Fat (gm): 6.4
Saturated fat (gm): 1.3
Cholesterol (mg): 83.2
Sodium (mg): 116
Protein (gm): 25.9
Carbohydrate (gm): 5.8

1. Sauté chicken in oil in large skillet until browned on all sides, about 10 minutes. Remove chicken and reserve.

2. Sauté garlic in skillet until tender, about 2 minutes. Add wine; heat to boiling. Boil until reduced by half, about 3 minutes. Add reserved chicken and remaining ingredients, except salt and pepper; heat to boiling. Reduce heat and simmer, covered, until chicken is tender, about 25 minutes. Season to taste with salt and pepper.

Grecian Chicken

4 servings

2 pounds chicken pieces (bone-in)
1 tablespoon butter, melted
3 tablespoons dried oregano leaves
1¼ teaspoons garlic powder
¼ teaspoon salt
¼ teaspoon pepper
½ cup fresh lemon juice
½ cup dry white wine, *or* reduced-sodium fat-free chicken broth
1 teaspoon Worcestershire sauce
1 tablespoon cornstarch
¼ cup water

Per Serving
Net Carbohydrate (gm): 6.2
Calories: 376
Fat (gm): 24.1
Saturated fat (gm): 7.9
Cholesterol (mg): 114.6
Sodium (mg): 264
Protein (gm): 27.3
Carbohydrate (gm): 7.8

1. Arrange chicken, skin-sides up, in 12 x 7-inch glass baking dish. Brush chicken with combined butter, oregano, garlic powder, salt, and pepper. Bake, covered, at 375 degrees 30 minutes.

2. Combine lemon juice, wine, and Worcestershire sauce; pour over chicken. Cover and bake until chicken is tender, about 20 minutes. Place chicken on serving platter.

3. Heat baking dish juices to boiling; stir in combined cornstarch and water. Boil, stirring, until thickened, 1 to 2 minutes. Pour sauce over chicken.

Chicken with Spinach and Pine Nuts

4 servings

2 cloves garlic, minced
¼ cup pine nuts
1 tablespoon olive oil
10 ounces fresh baby spinach
2 teaspoons balsamic vinegar
Salt and pepper, to taste
4 boneless, skinless chicken breast halves (5 ounces each),
    pounded to ¼ inch thickness

Per Serving
Net Carbohydrate (gm): 1.1
Calories: 245
Fat (gm): 9.6
Saturated fat (gm): 1.6
Cholesterol (mg): 82.1
Sodium (mg): 158
Protein (gm): 36.9
Carbohydrate (gm): 2.2

1. Sauté garlic and pine nuts in oil in large skillet 1 to 2 minutes; add spinach. Cook, covered, until spinach is just wilted, about 4 minutes. Stir in vinegar; season to taste with salt and pepper.

2. Broil chicken 6 inches from heat source until cooked through, about 3 minutes on each side. Spoon spinach mixture onto plates and top with chicken.

Grilled Chicken Breasts with Fennel

6 servings

¼ cup fennel seeds, optional
6 boneless, skinless chicken breast halves (6 ounces each)
2 tablespoons olive oil, divided
Salt and pepper, to taste
2 large bulbs fennel, thickly sliced,
   steamed until crisp-tender

Per Serving
Net Carbohydrate (gm): 3.3
Calories: 250
Fat (gm): 6.7
Saturated fat (gm): 1.1
Cholesterol (mg): 98.6
Sodium (mg): 129
Protein (gm): 40.2
Carbohydrate (gm): 5.7

1. Sprinkle fennel seeds, if using, on hot coals. Brush 1 tablespoon oil on chicken breasts and sprinkle lightly with salt and pepper. Grill chicken over medium-hot coals until cooked through, 5 to 8 minutes on each side.

2. Brush remaining 1 tablespoon oil on fennel slices and sprinkle lightly with salt and pepper. Grill fennel until browned, 2 to 3 minutes on each side. Arrange fennel on serving platter; top with chicken.

Moroccan Chicken with Chickpeas

8 servings

½ cup chopped onion
2 cloves garlic
2 tablespoons chopped parsley
1 teaspoon ground turmeric
1 teaspoon ground ginger
¼ teaspoon cayenne pepper
1 tablespoon lemon juice
4 pounds chicken pieces (bone-in)
1 can (14½ ounces) reduced-sodium fat-free chicken broth
1 cinnamon stick
1 bay leaf
1 can (15 ounces) chickpeas, rinsed, drained
1 cup sliced onion
½ cup raisins
Salt, to taste

Per Serving
Net Carbohydrate (gm): 20.2
Calories: 288
Fat (gm): 5.3
Saturated fat (gm): 1.2
Cholesterol (mg): 105.2
Sodium (mg): 304
Protein (gm): 35.5
Carbohydrate (gm): 23.7

1. Process chopped onion, garlic, parsley, turmeric, ginger, cayenne pepper, and lemon juice in food processor or blender until almost smooth. Brush mixture over chicken and refrigerate, covered, 1 hour or overnight.

2. Combine chicken and marinade, chicken broth, cinnamon stick, and bay leaf in large saucepan; heat to boiling. Reduce heat and simmer, covered, until chicken is tender, about 50 minutes, adding chickpeas, sliced onion, and raisins 10 minutes before end of cooking time. Discard cinnamon stick and bay leaf; season to taste with salt.

Mexican Chicken, Pork, and Pineapple Stew

6 servings

1 pound boneless, skinless chicken breast,
   cubed (1½-inches)
12 ounces pork tenderloin, cubed (1½ inches)
2 tablespoons canola oil
2 tablespoons slivered almonds
1 tablespoon sesame seeds
1 piece cinnamon stick (1 inch)
3 ancho chilies, stems, seeds, and veins discarded
1 cup cubed, seeded tomatoes
1¾ cups reduced-sodium fat-free chicken broth, divided
1 cup cubed jicama
1 cup cubed fresh, *or* canned, drained, pineapple
1 small ripe plantain, cut into ½-inch pieces
Salt and pepper, to taste

Per Serving
Net Carbohydrate (gm): 16.4
Calories: 316
Fat (gm): 10.7
Saturated fat (gm): 1.4
Cholesterol (mg): 87.6
Sodium (mg): 147
Protein (gm): 34.3
Carbohydrate (gm): 21.1

1. Cook chicken and pork in oil in large skillet over medium heat until browned, about 8 minutes. Remove from skillet and reserve.

2. Add almonds, sesame seeds, and cinnamon stick to skillet. Cook over medium heat until almonds and sesame seeds are toasted, 3 to 4 minutes; transfer almond mixture to blender container. Add chilies and tomatoes to skillet and cook over medium heat until chilies are soft, about 2 minutes; transfer to blender. Add 1 cup broth to blender and process until mixture is smooth.

3. Return chili mixture to skillet and cook over medium heat until slightly thickened, 4 to 5 minutes. Add meat, remaining ¾ cup broth, jicama, and fruit; heat to boiling. Reduce heat and simmer, covered, until meat is tender, about 30 minutes. Season to taste with salt and pepper.

Chicken with Picante Salsa

6 servings

2½ pounds chicken thighs (bone-in)
1 teaspoon garlic powder
Picante Salsa (recipe follows)
2 cups cooked brown rice, warm

Per Serving
Net Carbohydrate (gm): 17.1
Calories: 335
Fat (gm): 18
Saturated fat (gm): 5
Cholesterol (mg): 99.2
Sodium (mg): 117
Protein (gm): 23
Carbohydrate (gm): 19.2

1. Sprinkle chicken with garlic powder and arrange in baking pan. Spoon about ½ cup Picante Salsa over chicken. Bake, loosely covered, at 375 degrees until chicken is cooked through, 50 to 60 minutes. Arrange chicken on rice on serving platter. Serve with remaining Picante Salsa.

Picante Salsa

makes about 2 cups

1½ cups finely chopped, seeded tomatoes
½ cup chopped onion
¼ cup finely chopped cilantro
2 jalapeño chilies, minced
¼ cup tomato juice

1. Combine all ingredients.

Green Salsa Chicken

6 servings

6 boneless, skinless chicken breast halves (5 ounces each)
1 tablespoon canola oil
⅓ cup chopped onion
1 clove garlic, chopped
2 cups mild, *or* hot, green salsa
3 cups packed sliced romaine lettuce leaves
½ cup reduced-sodium fat-free chicken broth
¼ cup sour cream
2 tablespoons chopped cilantro
Salt and pepper, to taste

Per Serving
Net Carbohydrate (gm): 4.8
Calories: 235
Fat (gm): 6.3
Saturated fat (gm): 1.7
Cholesterol (mg): 93.2
Sodium (mg): 552
Protein (gm): 37.1
Carbohydrate (gm): 6.3

1. Cook chicken in oil in large skillet over medium heat until browned on both sides, about 8 minutes. Stir in onion and garlic; cook 2 minutes longer.

2. Process salsa, lettuce, and broth in food processor or blender until almost smooth. Add to skillet; heat to boiling. Reduce heat and simmer, covered, until chicken is tender and juices run clear, about 30 minutes.

3. Stir in sour cream; simmer 1 minute. Stir in cilantro; season to taste with salt and pepper.

Microwave Chicken El Paso

2 servings

12 ounces chicken tenders
3 tablespoons lemon juice
1 cup thinly sliced onion
1 cup thinly sliced red, *or* green, bell pepper
2 teaspoons finely chopped jalapeño chili, *or*
    ½ teaspoon crushed red pepper flakes
2 cloves garlic, minced
1 teaspoon olive oil
1½ teaspoons dried oregano leaves
1 teaspoon ground cumin
Salt and pepper, to taste
2 tablespoons finely chopped cilantro, *or* parsley

Per Serving
Net Carbohydrate (gm): 12.2
Calories: 286
Fat (gm): 5.6
Saturated fat (gm): 1.1
Cholesterol (mg): 98.5
Sodium (mg): 100
Protein (gm): 41.8
Carbohydrate (gm): 16.5

1. Toss chicken and lemon juice in small glass baking dish; reserve. Microwave remaining ingredients, except salt, pepper, and cilantro, in 2-quart glass casserole, loosely covered, on High, until peppers are crisp-tender, about 4 minutes, stirring once.

2. Microwave chicken in baking dish, loosely covered, on High until cooked through, about 4 minutes, stirring halfway through cooking time. Stir chicken into vegetables; microwave on High until hot, about 1 minute. Season to taste with salt and pepper; sprinkle with cilantro.

Santa Fe Chicken

6 servings

6 boneless, skinless chicken breast halves (6 ounces each)
2 teaspoons ground cumin, divided
1 teaspoon garlic salt
1 tablespoon canola oil
1 cup canned black beans, rinsed, drained
1 cup whole kernel corn
⅔ cup picante sauce
½ cup diced red bell pepper
2–4 tablespoons chopped cilantro

Per Serving
Net Carbohydrate (gm): 11
Calories: 278
Fat (gm): 4.7
Saturated fat (gm): 0.7
Cholesterol (mg): 98.6
Sodium (mg): 613
Protein (gm): 42.8
Carbohydrate (gm): 14.3

1. Season chicken with 1 teaspoon cumin and the garlic salt. Cook chicken in oil in large skillet over medium heat until browned, about 4 minutes on each side.

2. Combine beans, corn, picante sauce, bell pepper, and remaining 1 teaspoon cumin; spoon over chicken in skillet. Heat to boiling; reduce heat and simmer, covered, until chicken is cooked through, about 10 minutes. Sprinkle with cilantro.

Quick Chicken Chili

6 servings

1 cup chopped onion
3 cloves garlic, minced
3 tablespoons chili powder
1 teaspoon ground cumin
1 tablespoon canola oil
1 can (14½ ounces) crushed tomatoes, undrained
4 cups cubed, cooked chicken breast
1 can (15 ounces) red kidney beans, rinsed, drained
Salt and pepper, to taste
¾ cup (3 ounces) shredded Monterey Jack cheese

Per Serving
Net Carbohydrate (gm): 13.2
Calories: 325
Fat (gm): 10.6
Saturated fat (gm): 4.1
Cholesterol (mg): 84.3
Sodium (mg): 605
Protein (gm): 35.8
Carbohydrate (gm): 20.9

1. Sauté onion, garlic, chili powder, and cumin in oil in large skillet until onion is tender, about 5 minutes. Add tomatoes; heat to boiling. Reduce heat and simmer, uncovered, 5 minutes. Stir in chicken and beans, and cook until hot through, about 5 minutes. Season to taste with salt and pepper. Serve in bowls; sprinkle with cheese.

Speedy Chili with Chicken

6 servings

4 cups shredded, cooked chicken breast
1 can (14 ounces) stewed tomatoes, undrained
1 can (15½ ounces) pinto beans, rinsed, drained
¾ cup mild picante sauce
2 ancho chilies, softened, chopped
2 tablespoons dried onion flakes
½ teaspoon crushed red pepper
1 teaspoon paprika
3 tablespoons chopped cilantro
Salt, to taste

Per Serving
Net Carbohydrate (gm): 20
Calories: 304
Fat (gm): 6.4
Saturated fat (gm): 1.5
Cholesterol (mg): 79.3
Sodium (mg): 844
Protein (gm): 35.2
Carbohydrate (gm): 26.5

1. Combine all ingredients, except cilantro and salt, in large saucepan. Heat to boiling; reduce heat and simmer, covered, 5 minutes. Stir in cilantro and season to taste with salt.

Chicken Mole

6 servings

6 skinless chicken breast halves (bone-in) (6 ounces each)
1 tablespoon canola oil
Mole Sauce (recipe follows)
3 tablespoons finely chopped cilantro

Per Serving
Net Carbohydrate (gm): 7.6
Calories: 328
Fat (gm): 12.5
Saturated fat (gm): 1.5
Cholesterol (mg): 100.7
Sodium (mg): 121
Protein (gm): 43
Carbohydrate (gm): 10.8

1. Cook chicken in oil in large skillet over medium heat until browned, about 8 minutes. Arrange in large baking pan.

2. Spoon Mole Sauce over chicken; bake, loosely covered, until chicken is tender and no longer pink in the center, about 25 minutes. Arrange chicken on serving platter; sprinkle with cilantro.

Mole Sauce

makes about 1½ cups

2 mulato chilies
2 ancho chilies
2 pasilla chilies
Boiling water
1 tablespoon slivered almonds
1 tablespoon pumpkin seeds
1 tablespoon sesame seeds
1 tablespoon raisins
2 whole peppercorns
2 whole cloves
⅛ teaspoon coriander seeds
1½-inch piece cinnamon stick
¼ cup chopped onion
2 cloves garlic, finely chopped
2 teaspoons canola oil
½ small tomato, chopped
½ small (6-inch) corn tortilla, torn into pieces
½–¾ cup reduced-sodium fat-free chicken broth
1 tablespoon unsweetened cocoa
Salt, to taste

1. Cook chilies in dry skillet over medium heat until softened; remove and discard stems, seeds, and veins. (If chilies are already soft, the cooking step can be omitted.) Pour boiling water over chilies to cover in bowl; let stand 10 to 15 minutes. Drain, reserving ¾ cup liquid.

2. Cook almonds, pumpkin seeds, sesame seeds, raisins, and spices in small, dry skillet over medium heat until toasted, 1 to 2 minutes, stirring constantly; remove from skillet.

3. Sauté onion and garlic in oil in small skillet until tender, 2 to 3 minutes.

4. Process chilies, almond mixture, onion mixture, and tomato in blender until chopped. Add reserved chili liquid and tortilla; process, adding enough chicken broth to make smooth, thick mixture.

5. Transfer mixture to large skillet; stir in cocoa and remaining chicken broth. Heat to boiling; reduce heat and simmer, uncovered, until thick, about 5 minutes, stirring frequently. Season to taste with salt.

Chicken and Cheese Rellenos

6 servings

6 large poblano chilies
2–3 quarts water
1 cup chopped onion
½ cup shredded carrot
1 clove garlic, chopped
2 tablespoons canola oil, divided
1 pound boneless, skinless chicken breast, cooked, shredded
½ cup whole kernel corn
½ teaspoon ground cumin
½ teaspoon dried thyme leaves
½ cup (2 ounces) shredded Monterey Jack cheese
½ cup (2 ounces) shredded Cheddar cheese
Salt and pepper, to taste
Chili Tomato Sauce (recipe follows)

Per Serving
Net Carbohydrate (gm): 16.5
Calories: 264
Fat (gm): 10.4
Saturated fat (gm): 3.3
Cholesterol (mg): 57.1
Sodium (mg): 466
Protein (gm): 25.9
Carbohydrate (gm): 19.1

1. Cut stems from tops of chilies; remove and discard seeds and veins. Heat water to boiling in large saucepan; add peppers. Reduce heat and simmer, uncovered, 2 to 3 minutes, until peppers are slightly softened. Drain well and cool.

2. Sauté onion, carrot, and garlic in 2 teaspoons oil until tender, 3 to 5 minutes. Add chicken, corn, and herbs; cook over medium heat 1 to 2 minutes. Remove from heat; stir in cheeses. Season to taste with salt and pepper.

3. Stuff peppers with mixture. Heat remaining 4 teaspoons oil in large skillet until hot; sauté peppers over medium heat until tender and browned on all sides, about 8 minutes. Serve with Chili Tomato Sauce.

Chili Tomato Sauce

makes 1 cup

1 cup tomato sauce
2 tablespoons water
1–1½ tablespoons chili powder
1 clove garlic
Salt and pepper, to taste

1. Combine tomato sauce, water, chili powder, and garlic in small saucepan; heat to boiling. Reduce heat and simmer, uncovered, 2 to 3 minutes. Season to taste with salt and pepper.

Cancun Chicken Loaf

4 servings

1 pound ground chicken
½ cup finely chopped onion
¼ cup tomato sauce
¼ cup canned chopped green chilies
¼ cup quick-cooking rolled oats
1 egg, lightly beaten
1 tablespoon toasted sunflower seeds
1 teaspoon garlic powder
½ teaspoon dried thyme leaves
¼ teaspoon ground coriander
½–1 teaspoon salt
¼ teaspoon pepper

Per Serving
Net Carbohydrate (gm): 6.1
Calories: 235
Fat (gm): 12
Saturated fat (gm): 0.6
Cholesterol (mg): 53.1
Sodium (mg): 352
Protein (gm): 23
Carbohydrate (gm): 8

1. Mix all ingredients in large bowl; shape into loaf in greased baking pan. Bake at 350 degrees until cooked to 165 degrees on meat thermometer, about 1 hour.

Chiliquile Casserole

8 servings

6 corn tortillas (6 inch)
Vegetable cooking spray
1 cup thinly sliced green bell pepper
1–2 teaspoons minced jalapeño chili
2 cups enchilada sauce
1 can (15 ounces) black beans, rinsed, drained
1½ cups diced zucchini
4 cups shredded, cooked chicken breast
1 cup thinly sliced tomato
Jalapeño con Queso Sauce (recipe follows)
Medium, *or* hot, salsa, optional

Per Serving
Net Carbohydrate (gm): 23
Calories: 359
Fat (gm): 13.5
Saturated fat (gm): 6.4
Cholesterol (mg): 80.4
Sodium (mg): 927
Protein (gm): 33.4
Carbohydrate (gm): 27.1

1. Spray both sides of tortillas lightly with cooking spray; cook in small skillet over medium-high heat to brown lightly, 30 to 60 seconds per side. Cool slightly; cut into ½-inch strips.

2. Spray small skillet with cooking spray; heat over medium heat until hot. Sauté bell pepper and jalapeño chili until tender, 2 to 3 minutes; stir in enchilada sauce and heat until hot.

3. Arrange ⅓ of the tortilla strips in bottom of 2-quart casserole; top with ½ cup black beans, ½ cup zucchini, 1¼ cups chicken, ⅓ cup tomato slices, and ⅔ cup Jalapeño con Queso Sauce. Repeat layers 2 times.

4. Bake, uncovered, at 350 degrees until hot through, 25 to 30 minutes. Serve with salsa.

Jalapeño con Queso Sauce

makes about 2 cups

Vegetable cooking spray
1 teaspoon finely chopped jalapeño chili
1 teaspoon ground cumin
½ teaspoon dried oregano leaves
8 ounces pasteurized processed cheese product, cubed
⅓ – ½ cup reduced-fat milk
1¼ cups (5 ounces) shredded Cheddar cheese

1. Spray medium saucepan with cooking spray; heat over medium heat until hot. Sauté jalapeño chili until tender, about 2 minutes; stir in cumin and oregano.

2. Add processed cheese product; cook over low heat, stirring frequently, until melted. Stir in ⅓ cup milk and Cheddar cheese. Stir in additional milk if needed for desired consistency, cooking until hot, 1 to 2 minutes.

Chicken Enchiladas Mole

4 servings

3 cups shredded, cooked chicken breast
½ cup (2 ounces) shredded Cheddar cheese
½ cup sliced green onions and tops
4 tablespoons sour cream
¼ cup finely chopped cilantro
4 corn tortillas (6 inch)
Mole Sauce (see p. 134)

Per Serving
Net Carbohydrate (gm): 23.4
Calories: 425
Fat (gm): 16.6
Saturated fat (gm): 6.3
Cholesterol (mg): 104
Sodium (mg): 253
Protein (gm): 41.7
Carbohydrate (gm): 30

1. Combine chicken, cheese, green onions, sour cream, and cilantro in medium bowl. Spoon chicken mixture along centers of tortillas. Roll up and place, seam sides down, in baking pan. Spoon Mole Sauce over tortillas.

2. Bake, loosely covered, at 350 degrees until enchiladas are hot through, 20 to 30 minutes.

Chicken Flautas with Tomatillo Sauce

4 servings

½ cup chopped tomato
¼ cup chopped onion
2–4 tablespoons finely chopped poblano chili, *or* green bell pepper
½ teaspoon ground cumin
¼ teaspoon dried thyme leaves
2 tablespoons canola oil, divided
2 cups shredded, cooked chicken breast
2 tablespoons finely chopped cilantro
Salt and pepper, to taste
4 corn tortillas (6 inch)
Tomatillo Sauce (recipe follows)
4 tablespoons crumbled Mexican white cheese, *or* farmer's cheese
¼ cup sour cream

Per Serving
Net Carbohydrate (gm): 20
Calories: 343
Fat (gm): 16.8
Saturated fat (gm): 4.5
Cholesterol (mg): 67.8
Sodium (mg): 190
Protein (gm): 25.4
Carbohydrate (gm): 23.8

1. Sauté tomato, onion, poblano chili, cumin, and thyme in 1 tablespoon oil in large skillet until onion is tender, about 5 minutes. Add chicken and cilantro; cook 2 to 3 minutes. Season to taste with salt and pepper.

2. Spoon chicken mixture onto tortillas; roll up and fasten with toothpicks. Cook flautas over medium to medium-high heat in remaining 1 tablespoon oil until browned on all sides, about 5 minutes.

3. Arrange flautas on plates; spoon Tomatillo Sauce over. Sprinkle with cheese; top with sour cream.

Tomatillo Sauce

makes about 1 cup

¾ pound Mexican green tomatoes (tomatillos)
¼ cup chopped onion
1 clove garlic, minced
½ small serrano chili, minced
2 tablespoons finely chopped cilantro
1 teaspoon canola oil
2–3 teaspoons packed light brown sugar
Salt and white pepper, to taste

1. Remove and discard husks from tomatoes; simmer tomatoes, covered, in 1 inch water in large saucepan until tender, 5 to 8 minutes. Cool; drain.

2. Process tomatoes, onion, garlic, serrano chili, and cilantro in food processor or blender, using pulse technique, until almost smooth. Heat oil in large skillet over medium heat until hot. Add sauce and "fry" over medium heat until slightly thickened, about 5 minutes; season to taste with brown sugar, salt, and pepper.

Chicken Tacos with Poblano Chili Sauce

8 servings

3 arbol, *or* New Mexico, chilies, stems, seeds, and veins discarded
Hot water
1 cup chopped zucchini
½ cup finely chopped onion
3 cloves garlic, minced
2 tablespoons finely chopped cilantro
1 teaspoon dried marjoram leaves
1 teaspoon dried oregano leaves
2 tablespoons canola oil, divided
3 cups shredded, cooked chicken breast
Poblano Chili Sauce, divided (recipe follows)
Salt and cayenne pepper, to taste
8 corn tortillas (6 inch)
½ cup sour cream

Per Serving
Net Carbohydrate (gm): 17.4
Calories: 238
Fat (gm): 9.8
Saturated fat (gm): 2.5
Cholesterol (mg): 45.7
Sodium (mg): 98
Protein (gm): 18.7
Carbohydrate (gm): 20.5

1. Cover arbol chilies with hot water in small bowl; let stand until softened, 10 to 15 minutes. Drain; chop finely.

2. Sauté zucchini, onion, garlic, and herbs in 1 tablespoon oil until tender, about 5 minutes. Stir in chicken, arbol chilies, and ½ cup Poblano Chili Sauce. Cook over medium heat until hot; season to taste with salt and cayenne pepper.

3. Spoon chicken mixture along centers of tortillas; fold in half. Cook tacos in remaining 1 tablespoon oil until browned on both sides. Serve with remaining Poblano Chili Sauce and sour cream.

Poblano Chili Sauce

makes about 2 cups

1½ cups chopped tomatoes
½ cup chopped poblano chili, stem, seeds, and veins discarded
½ cup chopped onion
2 cloves garlic, minced
1–2 tablespoons chili powder
2 teaspoons canola oil
Salt and pepper, to taste

1. Sauté tomatoes, poblano chili, onion, garlic, and chili powder in oil until chili and onion are very tender, 8 to 10 minutes.

2. Process mixture in food processor or blender until smooth; season to taste with salt and pepper.

Chicken Fajitas

4 servings

1 pound boneless, skinless chicken breast, cut into strips
Fajita Marinade (recipe follows)
1 tablespoon olive oil
1 cup sliced red bell pepper
1 cup sliced onion
1 teaspoon ground cumin
½ teaspoon dried marjoram leaves
Salt and pepper, to taste
4 small (6 inch) flour tortillas, warm
2 tablespoons finely chopped cilantro
1 cup hot, *or* mild, salsa
½ cup sour cream

Per Serving
Net Carbohydrate (gm): 27.8
Calories: 364
Fat (gm): 12.3
Saturated fat (gm): 4.5
Cholesterol (mg): 76.3
Sodium (mg): 688
Protein (gm): 30.8
Carbohydrate (gm): 30.8

1. Combine chicken and Fajita Marinade in glass bowl, tossing to coat. Refrigerate, covered, 1 to 2 hours.

2. Cook chicken in oil in large skillet over medium heat until browned and no longer pink in the center, 5 to 8 minutes; move chicken to side of pan. Add bell pepper and onion; cook over medium heat until tender, about 5 minutes. Sprinkle chicken and vegetables with cumin and marjoram; season to taste with salt and pepper.

3. Spoon chicken and vegetable mixture onto tortillas; sprinkle with cilantro, top with salsa and sour cream, and roll up.

Fajita Marinade

makes about ¼ cup

3 tablespoons lime juice
2 cloves garlic
¾ teaspoon dried oregano leaves
¼ teaspoon ground allspice
¼ teaspoon black pepper

1. Mix all ingredients.

Note: For grilled fajitas, leave chicken breasts whole and cut peppers and onions in half. Grill over hot coals, then slice before serving.

Fajita Pitas

4 servings

1 pound chicken tenders
1½ cups thinly sliced red, *or* green, bell peppers
1 cup thinly sliced onion
1½ teaspoons ground cumin
¾ teaspoon dried oregano leaves
⅛ teaspoon crushed red pepper
1 tablespoon canola oil
2 whole wheat pitas, cut into halves, warm
½ cup mild, *or* medium, salsa
4 tablespoons sour cream

Per Serving
Net Carbohydrate (gm): 21.8
Calories: 309
Fat (gm): 8.9
Saturated fat (gm): 2.4
Cholesterol (mg): 70.9
Sodium (mg): 312
Protein (gm): 31.2
Carbohydrate (gm): 26.7

1. Sauté chicken, bell pepper, onion, cumin, oregano, and red pepper flakes in oil in large skillet until chicken is cooked through and vegetables are crisp-tender, about 8 minutes. Serve chicken mixture in pitas; top with salsa and sour cream.

Chicken Tostadas with Hot Green Salsa

6 servings

6 corn tortillas (6 inch)
3 cups shredded, cooked skinless chicken breast, warm
1 cup shredded lettuce
1 cup chopped tomatoes
Hot Green Salsa (recipe follows)
6 tablespoons sour cream

Per Serving
Net Carbohydrate (gm): 16.2
Calories: 223
Fat (gm): 6
Saturated fat (gm): 2.3
Cholesterol (mg): 59.1
Sodium (mg): 194
Protein (gm): 23.4
Carbohydrate (gm): 19.5

1. Cook tortillas in lightly greased skillet over medium heat until golden brown on both sides. Arrange tortillas on serving plates; top each with chicken, lettuce, and tomatoes; top with Hot Green Salsa and sour cream.

Hot Green Salsa

makes about 1½ cups

1 can (12 ounces) tomatillos, drained
½ cup chopped onion
¼ cup packed cilantro sprigs
2 jalapeño chilies, seeded
3 cloves garlic, halved
¼ teaspoon salt

1. Process all ingredients in food processor until finely chopped.

Chicken Burritos with a Bite

8 servings

1½ pounds ground chicken
1 tablespoon canola oil
1 cup chopped onion
½ teaspoon ground cumin
½ teaspoon garlic powder
½ teaspoon dried oregano leaves
1 can (15 ounces) pinto beans, rinsed, drained
1 can (4 ounces) chopped hot, *or* mild, green chilies
8 flour tortillas, warm (6 inch)
½ cup (2 ounces) shredded Cheddar cheese

Per Serving
Net Carbohydrate (gm): 40.7
Calories: 433
Fat (gm): 15.9
Saturated fat (gm): 2.8
Cholesterol (mg): 7.4
Sodium (mg): 601
Protein (gm): 24.9
Carbohydrate (gm): 46.2

1. Cook chicken in oil in large skillet over medium heat until browned, crumbling with a fork, about 8 minutes; stir in onion, cumin, garlic powder, and oregano and cook 3 to 4 minutes longer. Stir in beans and chilies; simmer until hot through, about 5 minutes. Spoon chicken mixture onto tortillas and sprinkle with cheese; roll up, tucking in edges.

Curried Chicken and Apples

6 servings

6 boneless, skinless chicken breast halves (6 ounces each)
2 tablespoons canola oil
1 cup chopped onion
1 cup coarsely chopped, peeled cooking apples
1 cup sliced carrots
1 tablespoon minced garlic
1½ tablespoons curry powder
1 teaspoon ground ginger
2 tablespoons all-purpose flour
2 cups reduced-sodium fat-free chicken broth
Salt and pepper, to taste
1 cup plain yogurt

Per Serving
Net Carbohydrate (gm): 11.3
Calories: 314
Fat (gm): 8.1
Saturated fat (gm): 1.3
Cholesterol (mg): 109.4
Sodium (mg): 209
Protein (gm): 44.9
Carbohydrate (gm): 13.6

1. Cook chicken in oil in Dutch oven over medium heat until browned, about 10 minutes. Remove chicken and reserve. Add onion, apple, carrots, and garlic and sauté 5 minutes; stir in curry powder, ginger, and flour and cook 2 minutes longer.

2. Stir in broth and reserved chicken; heat to boiling. Reduce heat and simmer, covered, until chicken is tender, about 20 minutes. Season to taste with salt and pepper; stir in yogurt.

Tandoori Chicken with Orange Cilantro Rice

4 servings

⅓ cup plain yogurt
1 small jalapeño chili, minced
1 tablespoon finely chopped cilantro, *or* parsley
2 teaspoons minced garlic
1 teaspoon minced gingerroot
1 teaspoon grated lime rind
2 teaspoons paprika
1½ teaspoons ground cumin
1 teaspoon ground coriander
2 pounds skinless chicken pieces (bone-in)
Orange Cilantro Rice (see p. 126)

Per Serving
Net Carbohydrate (gm): 28.7
Calories: 345
Fat (gm): 8.2
Saturated fat (gm): 1.7
Cholesterol (mg): 101.1
Sodium (mg): 109
Protein (gm): 35.1
Carbohydrate (gm): 31

1. Combine all ingredients, except chicken and Orange Cilantro Rice, in small bowl. Spread surfaces of chicken with yogurt mixture; place in shallow glass baking dish and refrigerate 3 to 4 hours, or overnight.

2. Place chicken on lightly greased grill rack over medium hot coals. Grill, covered, until chicken is cooked and juices run clear, about 8 minutes on each side. Or, place chicken in greased, aluminum foil-lined baking pan and roast at 350 degrees until juices run clear, 30 to 45 minutes. Serve with Orange Cilantro Rice.

Curry-Ginger Chicken

10 servings

2 cups chopped onions
2 cloves garlic, finely chopped
2 tablespoons canola, *or* peanut, oil
Ginger Spice Blend (recipe follows)
5 pounds chicken pieces
2 cups chopped, peeled and seeded tomatoes
1½ cups frozen peas
½ cup plain yogurt
¼ cup chopped cilantro
Salt and pepper, to taste

Per Serving
Net Carbohydrate (gm): 7.1
Calories: 249
Fat (gm): 8
Saturated fat (gm): 1.5
Cholesterol (mg): 100.6
Sodium (mg): 123
Protein (gm): 33.5
Carbohydrate (gm): 9.8

1. Sauté onions and garlic in oil in Dutch oven until tender, about 5 minutes; stir in Ginger Spice Blend and sauté 2 minutes longer. Stir in chicken and cook over medium heat 5 minutes.

2. Stir in tomatoes; heat to boiling. Reduce heat and simmer, covered, until chicken is tender, about 40 minutes. Stir in peas and yogurt; simmer until hot. Stir in cilantro and season to taste with salt and pepper.

Ginger Spice Blend

makes about ¼ cup

2 tablespoons finely chopped gingerroot
1 tablespoon sesame seeds
2 teaspoons coriander seeds
1 teaspoon cumin seeds
1 teaspoon ground turmeric
¼ teaspoon crushed red pepper
¼ teaspoon fennel seeds

1. Process all ingredients in food processor or blender until smooth.

Tandoori Chicken Kabobs

4 servings

1½ pounds boneless, skinless chicken breast halves,
    cubed (1½-inch)
2 tablespoons plain yogurt
2 teaspoons lemon juice
1 teaspoon curry powder
¼ teaspoon turmeric
¼ teaspoon ground cumin
1½ cups cubed onions
1½ cups tomato wedges

Per Serving
Net Carbohydrate (gm): 0.5
Calories: 231
Fat (gm): 2.5
Saturated fat (gm): 0.7
Cholesterol (mg): 99
Sodium (mg): 102
Protein (gm): 41.1
Carbohydrate (gm): 9.5

1. Combine chicken, yogurt, lemon juice, curry powder, turmeric, and cumin in medium bowl, tossing to coat well. Let stand 30 minutes.

2. Thread chicken, onions, and tomatoes on skewers. Grill kabobs over hot coals until done, about 8 minutes, turning frequently.

Creamy Chicken Curry

4 servings

1 cup cubed, unpeeled tart apple
½ cup chopped onion
1 clove garlic, minced
1 teaspoon curry powder
¼ teaspoon ground ginger
1 tablespoon peanut, *or* canola, oil
2 tablespoons all-purpose flour
1¼ cup reduced-sodium fat-free chicken broth
⅓ cup heavy cream
2 cups cubed, cooked chicken
¼ cup raisins
Salt and pepper, to taste

Per Serving
Net Carbohydrate (gm): 16.4
Calories: 309
Fat (gm): 16.2
Saturated fat (gm): 6.5
Cholesterol (mg): 93.3
Sodium (mg): 137
Protein (gm): 22.8
Carbohydrate (gm): 18.2

1. Sauté apple, onion, garlic, curry powder, and ginger in oil in large skillet until tender, about 5 minutes. Stir in flour; cook 1 to 2 minutes longer.

2. Stir in broth and cream; heat to boiling, stirring until thickened, about 3 minutes. Stir in chicken and raisins; cook 2 to 3 minutes longer. Season to taste with salt and pepper.

Curried Chicken and Vegetable Stew

4 servings

1 pound boneless, skinless chicken breast, cubed
½ cup chopped onion
2 cloves garlic
1 tablespoon peanut, *or* canola, oil
3 cups cauliflower florets
1 cup cubed (½ inch) potato
1 cup sliced carrots
1½ cups reduced-sodium fat-free chicken broth
¾ teaspoon ground turmeric
¼ teaspoon dry mustard
¼ teaspoon ground cumin
¼ teaspoon ground coriander
1 tablespoon all-purpose flour
2 tablespoons cold water
1 cup chopped, seeded tomato
2 tablespoons finely chopped parsley
1–2 tablespoons lemon juice
Salt, cayenne, and black pepper, to taste

Per Serving
Net Carbohydrate (gm): 17
Calories: 270
Fat (gm): 5.9
Saturated fat (gm): 1
Cholesterol (mg): 75.1
Sodium (mg): 196
Protein (gm): 32.6
Carbohydrate (gm): 21.9

1. Sauté chicken, onion, and garlic in oil in large saucepan until chicken is browned, about 5 minutes. Add cauliflower, potato, carrots, broth, spices, and herbs; heat to boiling. Reduce heat and simmer, covered, until chicken and vegetables are tender, about 15 minutes.

2. Heat mixture to boiling. Mix flour and water; stir into boiling mixture. Cook, stirring constantly, until thickened. Stir in tomato, parsley, and lemon juice; simmer 2 to 3 minutes longer. Season to taste with salt, cayenne, and black pepper.

Kashmir Chicken Stew

6 servings

1½ cups chopped onions
1 cup chopped red bell pepper
2 teaspoons minced garlic
¼ teaspoon crushed red pepper
2 tablespoons peanut, *or* canola, oil
1½ pounds boneless, skinless chicken breast, cubed (1-inch)
1 teaspoon ground cumin
1 teaspoon ground cinnamon
1 can (15 ounces) navy beans, rinsed, drained
1 can (14½ ounces) stewed tomatoes, undrained
⅓ cup raisins
Salt and pepper, to taste

Per Serving
Net Carbohydrate (gm): 25.5
Calories: 318
Fat (gm): 6.4
Saturated fat (gm): 1.2
Cholesterol (mg): 65.7
Sodium (mg): 510
Protein (gm): 33.2
Carbohydrate (gm): 31.6

1. Sauté onions, bell pepper, garlic, and red pepper in oil in large saucepan 2 to 3 minutes. Add chicken, cumin, and cinnamon; sauté until chicken is lightly browned, about 5 minutes.

2. Add remaining ingredients, except salt and pepper; heat to boiling. Reduce heat and simmer, covered, until chicken is tender, about 10 minutes. Season to taste with salt and pepper.

Caribbean Chicken Stew

6 servings

1½ pounds boneless, skinless chicken breast, cubed
½ cup finely chopped onion
1 tablespoon peanut oil
1 bay leaf
1 tablespoon curry powder
¼ teaspoon crushed red pepper
1½ cups reduced-sodium fat-free chicken broth
1 cup chopped mixed dried fruit (apples, pears, peaches, raisins, apricots, etc.)
1 tablespoon packed light brown sugar
2 teaspoons lemon juice
Salt and pepper, to taste
¼ cup chopped, dry-roasted cashews

Per Serving
Net Carbohydrate (gm): 20.8
Calories: 271
Fat (gm): 6.9
Saturated fat (gm): 1.3
Cholesterol (mg): 72
Sodium (mg): 125
Protein (gm): 29.8
Carbohydrate (gm): 23.4

1. Sauté chicken and onion in oil in large saucepan until chicken is browned, about 8 minutes. Add remaining ingredients, except salt, pepper, and cashews; heat to boiling. Reduce heat and simmer, covered, until chicken is tender, about 20 minutes. Season to taste with salt and pepper; spoon into serving bowl and sprinkle with cashews.

Coconut Chicken Stew

6 servings

2 pounds boneless, skinless chicken breast, cubed
¼ cup sliced green onions and tops
1 clove garlic, minced
2 teaspoons minced gingerroot
2 teaspoons peanut, *or* canola, oil
2 cups frozen mixed stir-fry vegetables
1 can (15 ounces) red beans, rinsed, drained
1 cup light unsweetened coconut milk
1 cup reduced-sodium fat-free chicken broth
1 tablespoon cornstarch
2 tablespoons lime juice
Salt and cayenne pepper, to taste
Finely chopped cilantro, as garnish

Per Serving
Net Carbohydrate (gm): 12.2
Calories: 280
Fat (gm): 5.8
Saturated fat (gm): 2.1
Cholesterol (mg): 91.8
Sodium (mg): 543
Protein (gm): 40.1
Carbohydrate (gm): 16.3

1. Sauté chicken, green onions, garlic, and gingerroot in oil in large skillet until lightly browned, about 5 minutes. Stir in stir-fry vegetables, beans, coconut milk, and broth; heat to boiling. Reduce heat and simmer, uncovered, until chicken is cooked, about 10 minutes.

2. Heat stew to boiling; stir in combined cornstarch and lime juice. Boil until thickened, about 1 minute; season to taste with salt and cayenne pepper and stir in cilantro.

Island Stew, Sweet-and-Sour

6 servings

2 pounds chicken tenders
1 tablespoon peanut, *or* canola, oil
3 cups sliced red, yellow, and green bell peppers
½ cup sliced onion
2 teaspoons minced garlic
2 teaspoons minced gingerroot
1–2 jalapeño chilies, finely chopped
3 cups reduced-sodium fat-free chicken broth
1 can (8 ounces) pineapple chunks in juice, drained, juice reserved
1 tablespoon packed light brown sugar
2–3 teaspoons curry powder
2–3 tablespoons apple cider vinegar
2 tablespoons cornstarch
1 can (15 ounces) black beans, rinsed, drained
Salt and pepper, to taste

Per Serving
Net Carbohydrate (gm): 22.8
Calories: 341
Fat (gm): 5.6
Saturated fat (gm): 1
Cholesterol (mg): 100
Sodium (mg): 435
Protein (gm): 43.1
Carbohydrate (gm): 27.8

1. Cook chicken in oil in large skillet over medium heat until browned, about 8 minutes. Remove from skillet.

2. Add bell peppers, onion, garlic, gingerroot, and jalapeño chilies to skillet; sauté 5 minutes. Stir in broth, pineapple, sugar, curry powder, vinegar, and chicken; heat to boiling. Reduce heat and simmer, uncovered, until chicken is tender, about 5 minutes.

3. Heat mixture to boiling. Mix cornstarch and reserved pineapple juice; stir into boiling mixture. Boil, stirring until mixture is thickened, about 1 minute. Stir in beans; cook over medium heat 2 minutes longer. Season to taste with salt and pepper.

Sherried Chicken Stir-Fry

4 servings

Per Serving
Net Carbohydrate (gm): 9.9
Calories: 216
Fat (gm): 3
Saturated fat (gm): 0.5
Cholesterol (mg): 72
Sodium (mg): 897
Protein (gm): 29.9
Carbohydrate (gm): 11.7

1 pound boneless, skinless chicken breast, cubed
1 teaspoon dark sesame oil
1 cup chopped onion
1 cup sliced snow peas
½ cup chopped red bell pepper
1 teaspoon minced garlic
1 teaspoon minced gingerroot
1 cup reduced-sodium fat-free chicken broth
¼ cup dry sherry, *or* water
1½ tablespoons cornstarch
3–4 tablespoons soy sauce
¼ cup sliced green onions and tops

1. Sauté chicken in oil in large skillet until browned, about 5 minutes; stir in onion, snow peas, bell pepper, garlic, and gingerroot. Sauté 5 minutes; stir in broth and sherry. Heat to boiling. Simmer, covered, until chicken is tender, about 15 minutes. Stir in combined cornstarch and soy sauce; simmer until thickened. Sprinkle with green onions.

Thai-Spiced Chicken and Carrot Stew

4 servings

Per Serving
Net Carbohydrate (gm): 7.2
Calories: 194
Fat (gm): 3
Saturated fat (gm): 0.5
Cholesterol (mg): 76.4
Sodium (mg): 390
Protein (gm): 30.9
Carbohydrate (gm): 9.3

1 pound boneless, skinless chicken breast, cubed (½-inch)
1½ cups diagonally sliced carrots
1 tablespoon minced gingerroot
1 tablespoon minced garlic
1 can (14½ ounces) reduced-sodium fat-free chicken broth
1 tablespoon light soy sauce
¾ cup sliced green onions and tops
1 tablespoon Thai peanut sauce, *or*
    1 tablespoon peanut butter and ½ teaspoon crushed red pepper
1 teaspoon packed light brown sugar
½ teaspoon dark sesame oil

1. Combine chicken, carrots, gingerroot, garlic, broth, and soy sauce in large saucepan. Heat to boiling; reduce heat and simmer, covered, until chicken is cooked and carrots are tender, about 15 minutes.

2. Add remaining ingredients; simmer, uncovered, 5 minutes longer.

Luau Chicken

6 servings

1½ pounds boneless, skinless chicken breast, cubed
3 tablespoons all-purpose flour
1 tablespoon canola oil
8 ounces mushrooms, sliced
¾ cup diagonally sliced carrots
½ cup thinly sliced red onion
1 clove garlic, minced
1 cup reduced-sodium fat-free chicken broth
½ cup unsweetened pineapple juice
2–3 tablespoons rice, *or* cider, vinegar
2–3 tablespoons soy sauce
1 cup thin tomato wedges
1 cup frozen peas
Salt and pepper, to taste

Per Serving
Net Carbohydrate (gm): 12.9
Calories: 232
Fat (gm): 4.3
Saturated fat (gm): 0.6
Cholesterol (mg): 69.9
Sodium (mg): 303
Protein (gm): 31.3
Carbohydrate (gm): 16

1. Coat chicken with flour; cook in oil in large skillet over medium heat until browned, about 8 minutes. Add mushrooms, carrots, onion, and garlic and sauté 5 minutes.

2. Stir in broth, pineapple juice, vinegar, and soy sauce; heat to boiling. Reduce heat and simmer, uncovered, until chicken is cooked and sauce has thickened, about 10 minutes.

3. Stir in tomato wedges and peas; cook 3 to 4 minutes longer. Season to taste with salt and pepper.

Sherried Pineapple Chicken Stew

6 servings

1 cup chopped onion
1 cup chopped green bell pepper
1 tablespoon peanut, *or* canola, oil
2 pounds boneless, skinless chicken breast, cubed (1 inch)
1 can (8 ounces) crushed pineapple, undrained
¾ cup reduced-sodium fat-free chicken broth
2 tablespoons soy sauce
1 tablespoon packed light brown sugar
2 teaspoons rice vinegar
½ teaspoon ground ginger
¼ cup dry sherry
1 tablespoon all-purpose flour
Salt and pepper, to taste

Per Serving
Net Carbohydrate (gm): 13.2
Calories: 262
Fat (gm): 4.4
Saturated fat (gm): 0.9
Cholesterol (mg): 90.7
Sodium (mg): 456
Protein (gm): 37
Carbohydrate (gm): 14.5

1. Sauté onion and bell pepper in oil in large saucepan until tender, about 5 minutes. Stir in remaining ingredients, except sherry, flour, salt, and pepper; heat to boiling. Reduce heat and simmer, covered, until chicken is tender, about 10 minutes.

2. Heat stew to boiling; stir in combined sherry and flour. Boil, stirring, until thickened, about 1 minute. Season to taste with salt and pepper.

Stir-Fry Chicken with Broccoli

6 servings

¼ cup light soy sauce
1½ tablespoons dry sherry, *or* lemon juice
¾ teaspoon ground ginger
2 pounds boneless, skinless chicken breast, cubed (1-inch)
1 tablespoon peanut, *or* canola, oil
2 cups small broccoli florets
1 cup sliced mushrooms
½ cup sliced celery
½ cup sliced green onions and tops
½ cup chopped red bell pepper
1 large clove garlic, crushed

Per Serving
Net Carbohydrate (gm): 4.1
Calories: 221
Fat (gm): 4.3
Saturated fat (gm): 0.9
Cholesterol (mg): 87.6
Sodium (mg): 434
Protein (gm): 37.5
Carbohydrate (gm): 5.8

1. Combine soy sauce, sherry, ginger, and chicken in medium glass bowl. Let stand 10 minutes.

2. Stir-fry chicken mixture in oil in wok or large skillet over medium-high heat until browned, about 7 minutes. Push chicken to side of wok; stir in remaining ingredients and stir-fry until broccoli is crisp-tender, about 3 minutes. Stir in chicken; stir-fry until chicken is cooked through, about 4 minutes.

Chicken-Vegetable Stir-Fry

4 servings

1 tablespoon peanut, *or* canola, oil
1 pound boneless, skinless chicken breast, cut into strips
1 cup sliced green onions and tops
1 cup sliced red bell pepper
2–3 teaspoons minced gingerroot
1 teaspoon minced garlic
3 cups thinly sliced Chinese cabbage
2 cups fresh, *or* canned, drained bean sprouts
1 can (15 ounces) pinto beans, rinsed, drained
¾ cup reduced-sodium fat-free chicken broth, *or* water
1–2 tablespoons tamari soy sauce
2 teaspoons cornstarch

Per Serving
Net Carbohydrate (gm): 18.1
Calories: 306
Fat (gm): 6.2
Saturated fat (gm): 1.2
Cholesterol (mg): 70.4
Sodium (mg): 683
Protein (gm): 36.3
Carbohydrate (gm): 27.2

1. Heat oil in wok or large skillet over medium-high heat until hot. Add chicken and stir-fry until browned, about 5 minutes; add green onions, bell pepper, gingerroot, and garlic and stir-fry 1 minute. Stir in Chinese cabbage, bean sprouts, and beans and stir-fry until cabbage is slightly wilted, about 3 minutes. Stir in combined remaining ingredients and heat to boiling; simmer until thickened, about 1 minute.

Cantonese Chicken with Mushrooms

6 servings

2 pounds boneless, skinless chicken breast, cubed
6 dried shiitake mushrooms, softened, cut into strips,
    stems discarded
3 tablespoons soy sauce
2 tablespoons oyster sauce
2 tablespoons dry sherry, optional
2 teaspoons minced garlic
2 teaspoons minced gingerroot
1½ tablespoons cornstarch
1 teaspoon dark sesame oil
½ teaspoon packed brown sugar
4 green onions (green parts only), cut into 2-inch lengths
2 teaspoons peanut, *or* canola, oil

Per Serving
Net Carbohydrate (gm): 6.6
Calories: 218
Fat (gm): 4.1
Saturated fat (gm): 0.8
Cholesterol (mg): 87.6
Sodium (mg): 741
Protein (gm): 36.1
Carbohydrate (gm): 7.4

1. Combine all ingredients, except green onions and peanut oil, in large glass bowl; toss well. Let stand, covered, at room temperature 30 minutes or refrigerate several hours.

2. Cook green onions in peanut oil in wok or large skillet over medium-high heat 1 minute. Add chicken mixture and stir-fry until chicken is cooked through, about 8 minutes.

Chicken China Moon

4 servings

2 tablespoons soy sauce
2 tablespoons packed brown sugar
1 tablespoon sesame seeds, toasted
2 teaspoons finely chopped gingerroot
4 boneless, skinless chicken breast halves (6 ounces each),
    pounded to ½ inch thickness
2 tablespoons chopped green onion

Per Serving
Net Carbohydrate (gm): 7.9
Calories: 231
Fat (gm): 3.1
Saturated fat (gm): 0.7
Cholesterol (mg): 99.6
Sodium (mg): 606
Protein (gm): 40.2
Carbohydrate (gm): 8.4

1. Combine soy sauce, brown sugar, sesame seeds, and gingerroot in small bowl. Brush chicken with soy mixture. Grill chicken over medium hot coals, or broil 6 inches from heat source, until cooked through, about 4 minutes on each side; baste frequently with soy mixture. Sprinkle with green onion.

Microwave Chicken Chow Mein

4 servings

2 cups sliced mushrooms
1 cup diagonally sliced celery
1 cup thinly sliced green bell pepper
1 cup thin onion wedges
1 teaspoon peanut, *or* canola, oil
2 cups fresh bean sprouts
1 can (6 ounces) sliced water chestnuts, rinsed, drained
1 jar (2 ounces) chopped pimientos, drained
2 tablespoons soy sauce
½ cup reduced-sodium fat-free chicken broth
1 pound thinly sliced, cooked chicken breast

Per Serving
Net Carbohydrate (gm): 13.6
Calories: 223
Fat (gm): 3.1
Saturated fat (gm): 0.6
Cholesterol (mg): 68.8
Sodium (mg): 642
Protein (gm): 31.7
Carbohydrate (gm): 18.2

1. Microwave mushrooms in 2-quart glass casserole on High until tender, about 2 minutes. Stir in celery, green pepper, onion, and oil; microwave until celery is tender, 3 to 4 minutes, stirring once.

2. Stir in remaining ingredients, except chicken; microwave, loosely covered, on High 5 to 6 minutes, stirring twice. Stir in chicken and microwave, loosely covered, on High 1 minute longer. Let stand, covered, 5 minutes.

Sweet-and-Sour Chicken

8 servings

2 pounds chicken tenders
2 cups sliced carrots
1 cup diced green bell pepper
½ cup sliced green onions and tops
1 tablespoon peanut, *or* canola, oil
1 cup pineapple tidbits
1 can (15 ounces) red kidney beans, rinsed, drained
1 cup orange juice
2 tablespoons cornstarch
¼ cup soy sauce
¼ cup packed light brown sugar
¼ cup white distilled vinegar
Salt and pepper, to taste

Per Serving
Net Carbohydrate (gm): 22.7
Calories: 266
Fat (gm): 3.5
Saturated fat (gm): 0.7
Cholesterol (mg): 65.7
Sodium (mg): 770
Protein (gm): 30.3
Carbohydrate (gm): 27.9

1. Stir-fry chicken, carrots, green peppers, and green onions in oil in large skillet or wok over medium-high heat until chicken is browned, about 10 minutes.

2. Add pineapple and beans to skillet. Stir in combined remaining ingredients, except salt and pepper; heat to boiling. Reduce heat and simmer uncovered until chicken and vegetables are tender, about 10 minutes. Season to taste with salt and pepper.

Microwave Sesame-Soy Chicken

4 servings

2 cloves garlic, minced
1–2 teaspoons dark sesame oil
1 pound chicken tenders
¼ cup lemon juice
2 tablespoons soy sauce
2 tablespoons chopped cilantro
Salt and pepper, to taste

Per Serving
Net Carbohydrate (gm): 2.4
Calories: 149
Fat (gm): 2.9
Saturated fat (gm): 0.6
Cholesterol (mg): 65.6
Sodium (mg): 576
Protein (gm): 26.9
Carbohydrate (gm): 2.6

1. Microwave garlic and sesame oil in 1-quart glass casserole on High 1 minute. Add remaining ingredients, except cilantro, salt, and pepper. Stir to coat chicken; let stand 15 minutes.

2. Microwave, loosely covered, on High until chicken is cooked through, 4 to 6 minutes, stirring after 2 minutes. Stir in cilantro; season to taste with salt and pepper.

Cantonese Chicken

4 servings

1½ pounds chicken tenders
⅓ cup chopped green onions and tops
1 large clove garlic, minced
1 teaspoon finely chopped gingerroot
1 tablespoon peanut, *or* canola, oil
¼ cup soy sauce
3 tablespoons dry sherry, *or* chicken broth
1 teaspoon cider vinegar
2 tablespoons honey
1 tablespoon packed light brown sugar
¼ teaspoon cayenne pepper

Per Serving
Net Carbohydrate (gm): 15.1
Calories: 297
Fat (gm): 6
Saturated fat (gm): 1.3
Cholesterol (mg): 98.5
Sodium (mg): 1125
Protein (gm): 40.7
Carbohydrate (gm): 15.5

1. Stir-fry chicken, green onions, garlic, and gingerroot in oil in wok or large skillet over medium heat until chicken is browned, about 5 minutes. Stir in combined remaining ingredients and stir-fry until chicken is tender and sauce is slightly thickened, 3 to 4 minutes.

Chicken Salad with Avocado Mayonnaise

6 servings

4 cups coarsely shredded, *or* cubed, cooked chicken breasts
½ cup chopped red bell pepper
½ cup chopped celery
⅓ cup chopped green onions and tops
⅓ cup chopped cilantro
Avocado Mayonnaise (recipe follows)
Salt and pepper, to taste
Lettuce leaves, as garnish

Per Serving
Net Carbohydrate (gm): 2.3
Calories: 310
Fat (gm): 20.1
Saturated fat (gm): 3.3
Cholesterol (mg): 82.7
Sodium (mg): 176
Protein (gm): 28
Carbohydrate (gm): 3.9

1. Combine all ingredients, except salt, pepper, and lettuce, in large bowl, mixing well. Season to taste with salt and pepper. Serve on lettuce leaves.

Avocado Mayonnaise

makes about 1¼ cups

½ cup coarsely mashed avocado
½ cup mayonnaise
2–3 teaspoons minced jalapeño chili
2–3 tablespoons lime juice
2 teaspoons ground cumin

1. Mix all ingredients in small bowl.

Chicken with Bean Salad

4 servings

3 tablespoons white wine
1 tablespoon olive oil
1 teaspoon balsamic vinegar
¾ teaspoon dried oregano leaves
½ teaspoon dried tarragon leaves
1 can (15 ounces) Great Northern beans, rinsed, drained
½ cup chopped celery
½ cup chopped tomato
¼ cup chopped red onion
Salt and pepper, to taste
4 boneless, skinless chicken breast halves (5 ounces each), pounded to ¼ inch thickness

Per Serving
Net Carbohydrate (gm): 19.1
Calories: 326
Fat (gm): 5.6
Saturated fat (gm): 1.1
Cholesterol (mg): 82.1
Sodium (mg): 94
Protein (gm): 41
Carbohydrate (gm): 25.1

1. Whisk wine, oil, vinegar, and herbs in large bowl; stir in remaining ingredients, except salt, pepper, and chicken. Stir well; season to taste with salt and pepper.

2. Sprinkle chicken lightly with salt and pepper. Broil chicken 6 inches from heat source until cooked through, about 3 minutes on each side. Place chicken on serving plates; top with bean mixture.

Berry-Chicken Salad

6 servings

6 boneless, skinless chicken breast halves (4 ounces each)
Raspberry-Dijon Dressing (recipe follows), divided
4 ounces Bibb, *or* Boston, lettuce,
    torn into bite-sized pieces (4 cups)
2 ounces watercress, torn into bite-sized pieces (2 cups)
2 cups sliced mushrooms
1 can (15 ounces) quartered artichoke hearts, drained
Salt and pepper, to taste
⅓ cup raspberries
⅓ cup blueberries

Per Serving
Net Carbohydrate (gm): 5.2
Calories: 356
Fat (gm): 24.6
Saturated fat (gm): 2.8
Cholesterol (mg): 65.7
Sodium (mg): 326
Protein (gm): 27.5
Carbohydrate (gm): 9.1

1. Combine chicken and ⅓ cup Raspberry-Dijon Dressing in glass dish, tossing to coat. Let stand, covered, 30 minutes or refrigerate several hours. Broil chicken 6 inches from heat source until cooked through, about 5 minutes on each side.

2. Toss lettuce, watercress, mushrooms, and artichokes with remaining dressing in large bowl; season to taste with salt and pepper. Spoon onto serving plates. Cut warm chicken into diagonal slices and arrange on salad. Sprinkle with raspberries and blueberries.

Raspberry-Dijon Dressing

makes about ¾ cup

3 tablespoons raspberry vinegar
2 tablespoons minced shallots, *or* green onions
1 tablespoon Dijon mustard
½ cup olive oil

1. Whisk vinegar, shallots, and mustard in small bowl; gradually whisk in oil.

Tropical Chicken Salad with Banana Dressing

6 servings

4 cups cubed, cooked chicken breast
1 cup cubed, seeded cucumber
1 cup cubed cantaloupe
½ cup sliced celery
½ cup cubed pineapple
½ cup sliced, peeled kiwi fruit
Banana Dressing (recipe follows)
⅓ cup coarsely chopped macadamia nuts

Per Serving
Net Carbohydrate (gm): 10.9
Calories: 417
Fat (gm): 28.3
Saturated fat (gm): 4.7
Cholesterol (mg): 86.5
Sodium (mg): 212
Protein (gm): 28.8
Carbohydrate (gm): 13.2

1. Combine all ingredients, except Banana Dressing and nuts, in large bowl. Spoon Banana Dressing over and toss well. Sprinkle with nuts.

Banana Dressing

makes about 1½ cups

⅔ cup mayonnaise
⅔ cup sliced banana
2–3 tablespoons lime, *or* lemon, juice
1–2 tablespoons reduced-fat milk
1 tablespoon grated lime, *or* lemon, rind

1. Process all ingredients in blender or food processor until smooth.

Ginger Bean and Chicken Salad

6 servings

4 cups cubed, cooked chicken breast
2 cups cut green beans, cooked, cooled
1 cup diced red bell pepper
¼ cup sliced green onions and tops
1 can (15 ounces) pinto beans, rinsed, drained
1 can (15 ounces) black beans, rinsed, drained
Ginger Dressing (recipe follows)
Salt and pepper, to taste

Per Serving
Net Carbohydrate (gm): 29.8
Calories: 405
Fat (gm): 12.7
Saturated fat (gm): 1.6
Cholesterol (mg): 71.8
Sodium (mg): 493
Protein (gm): 35
Carbohydrate (gm): 38

1. Combine all ingredients, except Ginger Dressing, salt, and pepper, in large bowl. Drizzle with Ginger Dressing and toss to coat; season to taste with salt and pepper.

Ginger Dressing

makes about ¾ cup

⅓ cup no-sugar-added apricot preserves
¼ cup canola oil
3 tablespoons cider, *or* rice wine vinegar
2 tablespoons honey
1–2 teaspoons minced gingerroot

1. Mix all ingredients.

Orange-Glazed Cornish Hens

4 servings

2 Rock Cornish game hens (1–1½ pounds each)
1 tablespoon melted butter
Paprika
⅓ cup no-sugar-added orange marmalade
¼ cup sliced green onions and tops
1 clove garlic, chopped
2 tablespoons finely chopped parsley
2 tablespoons coarsely chopped pecans

Per Serving
Net Carbohydrate (gm): 8.9
Calories: 521
Fat (gm): 35.1
Saturated fat (gm): 10.3
Cholesterol (mg): 235.4
Sodium (mg): 144
Protein (gm): 39.6
Carbohydrate (gm): 9.9

1. Cut hens into halves with poultry shears and place, cut sides down, on rack in roasting pan. Brush with butter and sprinkle with paprika. Roast at 350 degrees until thickest parts are fork-tender and drumstick meat feels soft when pressed, 1 to 1¼ hours. Combine remaining ingredients in small bowl; baste frequently with marmalade mixture during last 30 minutes of cooking time.

Moroccan-Style Cornish Hens Stuffed with Couscous

8 servings

1½ cups chopped onions
1 cup chopped red, *or* green, bell pepper
1 cup chopped zucchini
2 tablespoons olive oil
⅓ cup raisins
3 tablespoons dry white wine, *or* water
1 tablespoon honey
2 teaspoons ground cinnamon
¾ teaspoon dried rosemary leaves
½ teaspoon saffron threads, optional, *or* ½ teaspoon ground turmeric
½ cup couscous, cooked
Salt and pepper, to taste
4 Rock Cornish game hens (1–1½ pounds each)
Apricot Glaze (recipe follows)

Per Serving
Net Carbohydrate (gm): 22.1
Calories: 276
Fat (gm): 7.4
Saturated fat (gm): 1.4
Cholesterol (mg): 109
Sodium (mg): 65.6
Protein (gm): 26.5
Carbohydrate (gm): 24.7

1. Sauté onions, bell pepper, and zucchini in oil in large skillet until tender and lightly browned, about 8 minutes; stir in raisins, wine, honey, cinnamon, rosemary, and saffron. Heat to boiling; reduce heat and simmer 1 minute. Stir in couscous; season to taste with salt and pepper.

2. Stuff hens with couscous mixture and place in roasting pan. Bake at 375 degrees until juices run clear when thighs are pierced with a fork, about 45 minutes, basting with Apricot Glaze during last 20 minutes of cooking time.

Apricot Glaze

makes about ¼ cup

¼ cup no-sugar-added apricot jam
¾ teaspoon ground cinnamon
¼ teaspoon ground turmeric, *or* ground cumin

1. Combine all ingredients.

Cajun Cornish Hens

4 servings

2 Rock Cornish game hens (1–1½ pounds each),
 split lengthwise
3 tablespoons all-purpose flour
2 tablespoons olive oil
2 cups chopped, seeded tomatoes
2 cups sliced mushrooms
1 cup sliced red bell pepper
1 cup cubed smoked ham
1 tablespoon Worcestershire sauce
2 teaspoons Cajun seasoning
Salt and pepper, to taste

Per Serving
Net Carbohydrate (gm): 11.4
Calories: 291
Fat (gm): 12
Saturated fat (gm): 2.9
Cholesterol (mg): 121.6
Sodium (mg): 494
Protein (gm): 31.9
Carbohydrate (gm): 13.9

1. Coat hens with flour. Cook hens in oil in large skillet or Dutch oven over medium-high heat until browned, about 3 minutes on each side. Stir in remaining ingredients, except salt and pepper. Heat to boiling; reduce heat and simmer, covered, 20 minutes. Uncover and simmer until hens are cooked and sauce is thickened, about 20 minutes longer. Season to taste with salt and pepper.

Blue Cheese-Pecan Cornish Hens

4 servings

1 cup finely chopped green onions
½ cup chopped pecans
1 clove garlic, chopped
1 tablespoon butter
½ cup (2 ounces) crumbled blue cheese
2 Rock Cornish game hens (1–1½ pounds each),
 split lengthwise
1 tablespoon olive oil
Salt and pepper, to taste

Per Serving
Net Carbohydrate (gm): 2.4
Calories: 358
Fat (gm): 25
Saturated fat (gm): 7.4
Cholesterol (mg): 130.1
Sodium (mg): 352
Protein (gm): 29.4
Carbohydrate (gm): 4.4

1. Sauté green onions, pecans, and garlic in butter in large skillet until lightly browned, about 4 minutes. Cool; stir in cheese.

2. Loosen skin from hens; stuff cheese mixture under skin. Brush with olive oil and sprinkle lightly with salt and pepper. Place hens on aluminum foil–lined baking pan and cook at 425 degrees, loosely covered, 15 minutes. Cook, uncovered, until juices run clear, about 20 minutes longer.

Grilled Cornish Hens with Fruit Sauce

6 servings

1 large lemon, cut into 6 wedges, divided
3 Rock Cornish game hens (1–1½ pounds each)
¼ cup whole cloves, soaked briefly in water, drained
Fruit Sauce (recipe follows)

Per Serving
Net Carbohydrate (gm): 8.5
Calories: 376
Fat (gm): 22
Saturated fat (gm): 6.1
Cholesterol (mg): 168.3
Sodium (mg): 181
Protein (gm): 29
Carbohydrate (gm): 8.8

1. Prepare barbecue grill for indirect grilling method.
Place 1 lemon wedge in cavity of each hen, and arrange hens, breast side up, on greased grill rack over drip pan. Sprinkle cloves over hot coals.

2. Grill hens, covered, over indirect heat 45 minutes or until joints move easily and juices run clear when hens are pierced in thigh with fork. Cut hens in half and place on serving platter. Discard cooked lemon wedges and garnish with remaining wedges. Serve with Fruit Sauce.

Fruit Sauce

makes about 1 cup

½ cup port wine, *or* no-sugar-added cranberry juice
½ cup no-sugar-added cranberry juice
¼ cup no-sugar-added cherry preserves
2 tablespoons fresh lemon juice
¼ teaspoon ground nutmeg
Salt and pepper, to taste

1. Combine all ingredients, except salt and pepper, in small saucepan and heat to boiling; reduce heat and simmer, uncovered, until slightly thickened, about 5 minutes. Season to taste with salt and pepper.

Grilled Cornish Hens with Papaya

6 servings

3 Rock Cornish game hens (1–1½ pounds each)
Papaya Basting Sauce (recipe follows)
3 tablespoons packed light brown sugar
2 teaspoons light rum
1 medium papaya (10–12 ounces), seeded, cut into 6 slices

Per Serving
Net Carbohydrate (gm): 16.9
Calories: 414
Fat (gm): 23.7
Saturated fat (gm): 6.6
Cholesterol (mg): 169.7
Sodium (mg): 108
Protein (gm): 29.6
Carbohydrate (gm): 18.8

1. Cut hens along backbone with poultry shears or kitchen scissors. Press firmly on breastbones until they crack and hens lay flat. Brush hens with Papaya Basting Sauce.

2. Prepare grill for indirect grilling method. When coals are hot, place hens, skin side up, on grill rack over drip pan. Grill, covered, about 20 minutes, turning every 4 minutes and brushing hens with additional basting sauce during cooking. Hens are done when juices run clear when thighs are pierced with fork. Pass remaining sauce at table or pour over hens before serving.

3. Five minutes before hens are done, mix sugar and rum and brush cut sides of papaya slices with mixture. Grill papaya slices until hot, about 1 minute on each side. Serve with hens.

Papaya Basting Sauce

makes about 1½ cups

1 cup cubed, peeled and seeded ripe papaya (10–12 ounces)
½ cup orange juice

1. Process papaya and orange juice in food processor or blender until smooth.

Home-Style Turkey Stew

4 servings

1 pound boneless, skinless turkey breast, cubed (¾ inch)
2 cups thin onion wedges
4 ounces mushrooms, halved
1 tablespoon olive oil
1 cup sliced carrots
1½ cups cubed (¾ inch) potatoes
1 can (14½ ounces) reduced-sodium fat-free chicken broth
1 teaspoon celery seeds
1 teaspoons dried thyme leaves
1 cup frozen peas
Salt and pepper, to taste

Per Serving
Net Carbohydrate (gm): 22.8
Calories: 309
Fat (gm): 5.3
Saturated fat (gm): 0.8
Cholesterol (mg): 81
Sodium (mg): 202
Protein (gm): 36.1
Carbohydrate (gm): 28.9

1. Sauté turkey, onions, and mushrooms in oil in large saucepan until lightly browned, about 8 minutes. Add remaining ingredients, except peas, salt, and pepper, and heat to boiling. Reduce heat and simmer, covered, until turkey and vegetables are tender, about 15 minutes.

2. Stir in peas; cook 3 to 4 minutes. Season to taste with salt and pepper.

Country Turkey Ragout with White Wine

4 servings

1½ pounds boneless, skinless turkey breast, cubed (1 inch)
¼ cup all-purpose flour
2 tablespoons olive oil
1 cup chopped onion
¾ cup chopped carrots
½ cup sliced celery
2 cloves garlic, minced
3 cups sliced mushrooms
1 can (14½ ounces) diced tomatoes, undrained
½ cup dry white wine, *or* chicken broth
¼ cup reduced-sodium fat-free chicken broth
½ teaspoon dried rosemary leaves
½ teaspoon dried sage leaves
Salt and pepper, to taste

Per Serving
Net Carbohydrate (gm): 15.4
Calories: 361
Fat (gm): 8.3
Saturated fat (gm): 1.3
Cholesterol (mg): 106.9
Sodium (mg): 435
Protein (gm): 46.4
Carbohydrate (gm): 18.7

1. Coat turkey with flour; sauté turkey in oil in large skillet until browned, about 8 minutes. Stir in onion, carrots, celery, and garlic and sauté until lightly browned, about 5 minutes.

2. Stir in remaining ingredients, except salt and pepper; heat to boiling. Reduce heat and simmer, covered, until turkey is tender, about 30 minutes. Season to taste with salt and pepper.

Turkey-Wild Rice Stew

4 servings

1½ pounds boneless, skinless turkey breast, cubed (2 inch)
1 cup chopped onion
1 tablespoon olive oil
3 cups reduced-sodium fat-free chicken broth
½ cup wild rice
1 cup sliced carrots
1 tablespoon chopped fresh, *or* 1 teaspoon dried, sage leaves
2 cups small broccoli florets
Salt and pepper, to taste

Per Serving
Net Carbohydrate (gm): 19.8
Calories: 365
Fat (gm): 6.1
Saturated fat (gm): 0.9
Cholesterol (mg): 124.1
Sodium (mg): 275
Protein (gm): 52.2
Carbohydrate (gm): 24

1. Sauté turkey and onion in oil in large saucepan until lightly browned, about 5 minutes. Stir in broth, wild rice, carrots, and sage. Heat to boiling; reduce heat and simmer, covered, until rice is tender, about 50 minutes, adding broccoli during last 5 minutes of cooking time. Season to taste with salt and pepper.

Turkey Stew with Apricots and Chilies

4 servings

1 cup chopped onion
2 garlic cloves, minced
1 tablespoon butter
1¼ cups reduced-sodium fat-free chicken broth
1 teaspoon ground cumin
¼ teaspoon ground coriander
¼ teaspoon ground allspice
¾ cup quartered dried apricots
¼ cup chopped canned green chilies
1 cup chopped seeded tomato
1 pound cooked turkey breast, cubed (½ inch)
Salt and pepper, to taste

Per Serving
Net Carbohydrate (gm): 23.5
Calories: 298
Fat (gm): 4.8
Saturated fat (gm): 2.2
Cholesterol (mg): 110.1
Sodium (mg): 233
Protein (gm): 38.4
Carbohydrate (gm): 25.5

1. Sauté onion and garlic in butter in large saucepan until onion is tender, about 5 minutes. Add remaining ingredients, except turkey, salt and pepper; heat to boiling. Reduce heat and simmer, uncovered, until lightly thickened, about 10 minutes. Add turkey and simmer until hot. Season to taste with salt and pepper.

Southwest Turkey Stew with Chili-Cheese Dumplings

5 servings

2 pounds boneless, skinless turkey breast, cubed (1 inch)
1 tablespoon canola, *or* safflower, oil
1 cup chopped green bell pepper
1 cup chopped red bell pepper
¾ cup chopped onion
1 jalapeño chili, minced
2 cloves garlic, minced
1 tablespoon chili powder
1 teaspoon ground cumin
1 can (14½ ounces) stewed tomatoes, undrained
1 cup reduced-sodium fat-free chicken broth
Salt and pepper, to taste
Chili Cheese Dumplings (recipe follows)

Per Serving
Net Carbohydrate (gm): 26.1
Calories: 473
Fat (gm): 15.5
Saturated fat (gm): 5.7
Cholesterol (mg): 150.3
Sodium (mg): 635
Protein (gm): 51.7
Carbohydrate (gm): 32.2

1. Sauté turkey in oil in large saucepan until browned, about 8 minutes; stir in bell peppers, onion, jalapeño chili, garlic, chili powder, and cumin. Sauté until onion is tender, about 5 minutes.

2. Stir in tomatoes and liquid, and broth. Heat to boiling; reduce heat and simmer, covered, 10 minutes. Season to taste with salt and pepper. Drop Chili-Cheese Dumplings dough onto stew; cook, uncovered, 10 minutes. Cook covered until dumplings are done, about 10 minutes longer.

Chili-Cheese Dumplings

makes 5 dumplings

⅔ cup whole wheat pastry flour
⅓ cup yellow cornmeal
1½ teaspoons baking powder
1 teaspoon chili powder
½ teaspoon salt
2 tablespoons butter
¼ cup (1 ounce) shredded Monterey Jack cheese
1 tablespoon finely chopped cilantro
½ cup reduced-fat milk

1. Combine flour, cornmeal, baking powder, chili powder, and salt in medium bowl; cut in butter with pastry blender until mixture resembles coarse crumbs. Mix in cheese and cilantro; stir in milk, forming a soft dough.

Turkey Stew, Milan Style

4 servings

1½ pounds boneless, skinless turkey breast, cubed (1 inch)
3 tablespoons all-purpose flour
1 tablespoon olive oil
¾ cup chopped onion
2 cloves garlic, minced
1 cup dry white wine, *or* chicken broth
1 cup reduced-sodium fat-free chicken broth
1 can (6 ounces) tomato paste
¾ cup halved baby carrots
¾ cup sliced celery
1 teaspoon dried thyme leaves
2 bay leaves
¼ cup chopped fresh parsley
2 tablespoons grated lemon rind
Salt and pepper, to taste

Per Serving
Net Carbohydrate (gm): 16.7
Calories: 359
Fat (gm): 5.4
Saturated fat (gm): 0.9
Cholesterol (mg): 111.6
Sodium (mg): 498
Protein (gm): 46.9
Carbohydrate (gm): 20.5

1. Coat turkey with flour; sauté in oil in Dutch oven until lightly browned, about 5 minutes. Stir in onion and garlic; sauté until onion is tender, about 5 minutes longer.

2. Stir in wine, broth, tomato paste, carrots, celery, thyme, and bay leaves. Heat to boiling; reduce heat and simmer, covered, until turkey is tender, about 30 minutes. Discard bay leaves. Stir in parsley and lemon rind; season to taste with salt and pepper.

Poached Turkey and Vegetables Gremolata

4 servings

½ cup reduced-sodium fat-free chicken broth
¼ cup dry white wine, *or* chicken broth
4 turkey breast cutlets (6 ounces each)
2 cups red potato wedges
1 cup baby carrots
1 cup halved green beans
1 cup cubed zucchini
Salt and pepper, to taste
Gremolata (recipe follows)

Per Serving
Net Carbohydrate (gm): 15.8
Calories: 321
Fat (gm): 6.5
Saturated fat (gm): 1.3
Cholesterol (mg): 105
Sodium (mg): 158
Protein (gm): 43.5
Carbohydrate (gm): 19.2

1. Heat broth and wine to boiling in large skillet; add turkey and vegetables. Reduce heat and simmer, covered, until turkey is cooked and vegetables are tender, 10 to 15 minutes. Arrange turkey and vegetables on platter; keep warm.

2. Heat pan juices to boiling; boil until reduced to ¼ cup, about 5 minutes. Season to taste with salt and pepper; spoon over turkey and vegetables. Top with Gremolata.

Gremolata

makes about ½ cup

1 cup packed parsley
2 cloves garlic
2 tablespoons lemon juice
1 tablespoon olive oil
1 tablespoon grated lemon rind

1. Process all ingredients in food processor or blender until smooth.

Turkey Teriyaki

4 servings

¼ cup dry sherry, *or* reduced-sodium fat-free chicken broth
2 cloves garlic, minced
2 tablespoons finely chopped gingerroot
2 tablespoons soy sauce
1 tablespoon Dijon-style mustard
1 tablespoon grated orange rind
1½ pounds skinless turkey breast, cut into strips
1 tablespoon peanut, *or* canola, oil
1 teaspoon dark sesame oil
2 cups sliced mushrooms
1 cup frozen peas, thawed

Per Serving
Net Carbohydrate (gm): 4.8
Calories: 271
Fat (gm): 5.8
Saturated fat (gm): 1.1
Cholesterol (mg): 105.4
Sodium (mg): 159
Protein (gm): 45
Carbohydrate (gm): 7.5

1. Combine sherry, garlic, gingerroot, soy sauce, mustard, and orange rind in large glass bowl; add turkey and toss to coat. Refrigerate, covered, 1 hour.

2. Stir-fry turkey mixture in peanut and sesame oils in wok or large skillet over medium-high heat 2 to 3 minutes. Add mushrooms and peas; stir-fry until turkey and mushrooms are cooked, about 5 minutes.

Turkey Cacciatore

4 servings

1 pound turkey breast cutlets
2 tablespoons all-purpose flour
1 teaspoon dried Italian seasoning
2 tablespoons olive oil
1 cup sliced mushrooms
1 cup cubed zucchini
1 can (14½ ounces) stewed tomatoes, undrained
Salt and pepper, to taste

Per Serving
Net Carbohydrate (gm): 15.5
Calories: 293
Fat (gm): 11.3
Saturated fat (gm): 2
Cholesterol (mg): 67.9
Sodium (mg): 523
Protein (gm): 30
Carbohydrate (gm): 17.9

1. Coat turkey pieces with combined flour and Italian seasoning; cook in oil in large skillet over medium-high heat until browned, about 5 minutes on each side. Remove from pan. Sauté mushrooms and zucchini in skillet until lightly browned, about 5 minutes.

2. Stir in tomatoes and liquid; heat to boiling. Add turkey. Reduce heat and simmer, covered, until turkey is cooked and mixture is slightly thickened, about 10 minutes. Season to taste with salt and pepper.

Turkey Divan

4 servings

3 cups cubed, cooked turkey, *or* chicken, breast
2 cups broccoli florets, cooked until crisp-tender
⅓ cup chopped onion
1 tablespoon butter
⅓ cup whole wheat flour
1 cup reduced-sodium fat-free chicken broth
½ cup whipping cream
¼ cup dry white wine, *or* chicken broth
¼–½ teaspoon dried savory leaves
¼ teaspoon dried marjoram leaves
2–3 pinches ground nutmeg
1 cup (4 ounces) shredded Swiss cheese
Salt, cayenne, and white pepper, to taste
¼ cup unseasoned dry bread crumbs

Per Serving
Net Carbohydrate (gm): 16.2
Calories: 432
Fat (gm): 17.9
Saturated fat (gm): 10.3
Cholesterol (mg): 155.8
Sodium (mg): 309
Protein (gm): 45.6
Carbohydrate (gm): 18.3

1. Arrange turkey and broccoli in 10 x 6-inch baking dish.

2. Sauté onion in butter in medium saucepan until tender, about 3 minutes. Mix flour and chicken broth until smooth; stir into saucepan with cream and wine. Heat to boiling, whisking constantly until thickened, about 1 minute. Reduce heat to low; add herbs and cheese, whisking until cheese is melted. Season to taste with salt, cayenne, and white pepper.

3. Pour sauce over turkey and broccoli in baking dish; sprinkle with bread crumbs. Bake at 350 degrees until bubbly, about 25 minutes.

Turkey Cutlets with Sage

4 servings

1 pound turkey breast cutlets
4 teaspoons red wine vinegar
2 teaspoons minced garlic
2 teaspoons dried sage leaves
Salt and pepper, to taste
½ cup whole wheat flour
1 tablespoon olive oil
½ cup reduced-sodium fat-free chicken broth
1 tablespoon lemon juice

Per Serving
Net Carbohydrate (gm): 6.6
Calories: 197
Fat (gm): 5.3
Saturated fat (gm): 1
Cholesterol (mg): 71
Sodium (mg): 85
Protein (gm): 28.5
Carbohydrate (gm): 7

1. Sprinkle both sides of turkey with combined vinegar, garlic, and sage. Place turkey between sheets of plastic wrap. Pound to about ¼ inch thickness with meat mallet. Sprinkle lightly with salt and pepper and coat with flour.

2. Heat oil in large skillet over medium-high heat; add half the cutlets and cook until browned on both sides and cooked through, about 5 minutes. Remove cutlets to serving platter; keep warm. Repeat with remaining cutlets.

3. Heat broth and lemon juice to boiling in skillet; cook until reduced by half. Pour mixture over cutlets; serve immediately.

Apricot-Glazed Turkey Cutlets

4 servings

4 turkey breast cutlets (6 ounces each),
    pounded to ¼ inch thickness
1 teaspoon paprika
¼ teaspoon cayenne pepper
1 tablespoon butter
1½ tablespoons no-sugar-added apricot preserves
2 teaspoons Dijon mustard
2 tablespoons chopped parsley
Salt and pepper, to taste

Per Serving
Net Carbohydrate (gm): 2.6
Calories: 235
Fat (gm): 5.6
Saturated fat (gm): 2.7
Cholesterol (mg): 110.1
Sodium (mg): 170
Protein (gm): 40.3
Carbohydrate (gm): 2.9

1. Sprinkle turkey with combined paprika and cayenne pepper. Sauté in butter in large skillet until cooked through, about 3 minutes on each side. Brush with combined preserves, mustard, and parsley; sprinkle lightly with salt and pepper.

Turkey Cutlets Marsala

4 servings

4 turkey breast cutlets (6 ounces each),
    pounded to ¼ inch thickness
¼ cup all-purpose flour
1 tablespoon butter
¼ cup dry white wine, *or* chicken broth
2 tablespoons Marsala wine, *or* dry sherry
1 teaspoon dried rosemary leaves
Salt and pepper, to taste

Per Serving
Net Carbohydrate (gm): 6.1
Calories: 266
Fat (gm): 5.6
Saturated fat (gm): 2.7
Cholesterol (mg): 110.1
Sodium (mg): 113
Protein (gm): 41
Carbohydrate (gm): 6.4

1. Coat turkey cutlets with flour. Sauté cutlets in butter in large skillet until cooked through, 2 to 3 minutes on each side. Place turkey on serving platter; keep warm.

2. Add wine, Marsala, and rosemary to skillet; simmer until reduced to a glaze, about 3 minutes, stirring brown bits from bottom of skillet. Season to taste with salt and pepper. Spoon sauce over turkey.

Peppercorn Turkey Cutlets

4 servings

4 turkey breast cutlets (6 ounces each),
    pounded to ¼ inch thickness
2 tablespoons coarsely crushed black, *or* green, peppercorns
1 tablespoon butter
½ cup dry white wine, *or*
    reduced-sodium fat-free chicken broth
1 tablespoon brandy, optional
Salt and pepper, to taste
1 tablespoon chopped parsley

Per Serving
Net Carbohydrate (gm): 0.9
Calories: 245
Fat (gm): 5.6
Saturated fat (gm): 2.7
Cholesterol (mg): 110.1
Sodium (mg): 114
Protein (gm): 40.3
Carbohydrate (gm): 1.3

1. Sprinkle both sides of turkey with peppercorns and press firmly onto surface of meat. Sauté turkey in butter in large skillet until cooked through, 2 to 3 minutes on each side. Place turkey on serving platter; keep warm.

2. Stir wine and brandy (if using) into skillet; simmer until reduced to a glaze, about 3 minutes, stirring brown bits from bottom of skillet. Season to taste with salt and pepper. Spoon glaze over turkey and sprinkle with parsley.

Tex-Mex Pitas with Texas Salsa

8 servings

1½ pounds ground turkey
1 cup chopped onion
1 tablespoon minced garlic
1 tablespoon canola oil
1 tablespoon chili powder
1 teaspoon ground cumin
1 teaspoon dried oregano leaves
¾ cup (3 ounces) shredded pepper-Jack cheese
4 whole wheat pita breads, cut into halves
Shredded lettuce, as garnish
Texas Salsa (recipe follows)
½ cup sour cream

Per Serving
Net Carbohydrate (gm): 16.1
Calories: 301
Fat (gm): 15.7
Saturated fat (gm): 5.9
Cholesterol (mg): 83.8
Sodium (mg): 309
Protein (gm): 22.4
Carbohydrate (gm): 20.3

1. Cook turkey, onion, and garlic in oil in large skillet until turkey is browned, about 8 minutes, crumbling turkey with a fork. Stir in chili powder, cumin, and oregano and cook 2 minutes longer; remove from heat and stir in cheese.

2. Spoon mixture into pita halves; top with lettuce, Texas Salsa, and sour cream.

Texas Salsa

makes about 2 cups

2 cups chopped, seeded tomato
½ cup thinly sliced green onions and tops
1 jalapeño chili, minced
¼ cup chopped cilantro
½ teaspoon celery seed
1 tablespoon red wine vinegar
Salt and pepper, to taste

1. Mix all ingredients, except salt and pepper, in medium bowl. Season to taste with salt and pepper.

Turkey Meatballs with Tomato-Basil Sauce

4 servings

1 pound ground turkey
¾ cup Italian-seasoned dry bread crumbs
½ cup white wine, *or* reduced-sodium fat-free chicken broth
⅔ cup chopped onion
1 egg
1 teaspoon dried basil leaves
1 teaspoon dried oregano leaves
½ teaspoon dried marjoram leaves
¼ teaspoon black pepper
Tomato-Basil Sauce (recipe follows)

Per Serving
Net Carbohydrate (gm): 20
Calories: 363
Fat (gm): 15.1
Saturated fat (gm): 3.7
Cholesterol (mg): 142.8
Sodium (mg): 810
Protein (gm): 25.7
Carbohydrate (gm): 23.7

1. Combine all ingredients, except Tomato-Basil Sauce, in large bowl, mixing well. Shape into 16 meatballs and arrange in lightly greased baking dish.

2. Bake at 350 degrees until meatballs are firm, about 15 minutes. Spoon Tomato-Basil Sauce over meatballs and bake, loosely covered, until meatballs are no longer pink in center and sauce is bubbly, about 20 minutes.

Tomato-Basil Sauce

makes about 2 cups

⅔ cup chopped onion
2 cloves garlic, chopped
1 teaspoon olive oil
1 can (28 ounces) diced tomatoes, undrained
¼ cup chopped fresh, *or* 2 tablespoons dried, basil leaves
1 tablespoon chopped fresh, *or* 1 teaspoon dried, oregano leaves
Salt and pepper, to taste

1. Sauté onion and garlic in oil in large saucepan until tender, about 5 minutes. Stir in remaining ingredients, except salt and pepper. Heat to boiling; reduce heat and simmer, uncovered, until thickened, about 30 minutes. Season to taste with salt and pepper.

Italian Turkey Burgers

4 servings

1 pound ground turkey
1 egg
½ teaspoon salt
¼ teaspoon pepper
¾ cup Italian-flavored dry bread crumbs, divided
2 tablespoons olive oil, divided
1 cup thinly sliced mushrooms
½ cup red wine, *or* reduced-sodium fat-free chicken broth
½ cup plain yogurt

Per Serving
Net Carbohydrate (gm): 13.8
Calories: 348
Fat (gm): 18.4
Saturated fat (gm): 4.1
Cholesterol (mg): 143.4
Sodium (mg): 811
Protein (gm): 25.4
Carbohydrate (gm): 14.6

1. Combine turkey, egg, salt, pepper, and ¼ cup bread crumbs; shape into 4 burgers. Coat burgers with remaining bread crumbs. Cook burgers in 1 tablespoon oil in large skillet over medium-low to medium heat until browned and no longer pink in the center, 5 to 8 minutes on each side.

2. While burgers are cooking, sauté mushrooms in remaining 1 tablespoon oil in medium skillet until tender, about 5 minutes. Stir in wine and heat to boiling; reduce heat and simmer, uncovered, until wine is almost evaporated. Stir in yogurt.

3. Place burgers on serving plates; spoon mushroom mixture over.

Sausage and Cheese Baked Potatoes

8 servings

4 Idaho potatoes (6–7 ounces each)
12 ounces turkey sausage
1 pound mozzarella cheese, cubed
¼ cup reduced-fat milk

Per Serving
Net Carbohydrate (gm): 22.5
Calories: 315
Fat (gm): 14
Saturated fat (gm): 7.3
Cholesterol (mg): 66.1
Sodium (mg): 616
Protein (gm): 23.3
Carbohydrate (gm): 25

1. Pierce potatoes several times with tip of sharp knife or fork. Set potatoes on baking sheet. Bake at 425 degrees 45 minutes to 1 hour or until tender.

2. Cook turkey sausage in medium saucepan over medium heat until browned, crumbling with a fork. Add cheese and milk; cook over medium-low heat, stirring frequently, until cheese is melted.

3. Split potatoes lengthwise, and fluff pulp with fork. Spoon topping over potatoes. Sprinkle with lettuce and tomato (not included in nutritional data).

Italian Sausage Stew

4 servings

1 pound Italian-style turkey sausage
2 cups thin onion wedges
1 tablespoon chopped garlic
1 jalapeño chili, thinly sliced
2 cups reduced-sodium fat-free chicken broth
1 can (14½ ounces) diced tomatoes, undrained
2 cups sliced zucchini
1½ teaspoons dried Italian seasoning
½ teaspoon crushed red pepper
Salt and pepper, to taste
¼ cup (1 ounce) shredded Parmesan cheese

Per Serving
Net Carbohydrate (gm): 11.2
Calories: 541
Fat (gm): 42
Saturated fat (gm): 15.8
Cholesterol (mg): 96.2
Sodium (mg): 1642
Protein (gm): 32.7
Carbohydrate (gm): 14.1

1. Sauté sausage, onions, garlic, and jalapeno chili in large saucepan until sausage is lightly browned, about 5 minutes. Remove sausage and cut into 1-inch pieces. Return to skillet.

2. Add remaining ingredients, except salt, pepper, and Parmesan cheese and heat to boiling. Reduce heat and simmer, covered, until zucchini is tender, about 8 minutes. Season to taste with salt and pepper. Sprinkle each serving with 1 tablespoon cheese.

Italian-Style Turkey Sausage and Fennel Stew

6 servings

1 pound mild, *or* hot, Italian-style turkey sausage
1 tablespoon olive oil
⅔ cup sliced onion
1 can (14½ ounces) diced tomatoes, undrained
1 cup reduced-sodium fat-free chicken broth
2 cups cubed (¾ inch), peeled butternut squash
1½ cups sliced (½ inch) fennel bulbs
1½ cups halved Brussels sprouts
½ teaspoon crushed red pepper
1 teaspoon dried Italian seasoning
Salt and pepper, to taste

Per Serving
Net Carbohydrate (gm): 15.9
Calories: 296
Fat (gm): 23.9
Saturated fat (gm): 7
Cholesterol (mg): 44
Sodium (mg): 692
Protein (gm): 12.7
Carbohydrate (gm): 12.9

1. Cook sausage in oil in large saucepan until browned, about 10 minutes; remove sausage and slice. Add onion to saucepan; sauté until tender, about 5 minutes.

2. Stir in tomatoes and liquid, broth, squash, fennel, and sliced sausage. Heat to boiling; reduce heat and simmer, covered, 10 minutes. Stir in Brussels sprouts, crushed red pepper, and Italian seasoning. Simmer until Brussels sprouts are tender, about 10 minutes. Season to taste with salt and pepper.

Italian-Style Bean and Vegetable Stew

6 servings

1½ pounds Italian-style turkey sausage, casings removed
2 cups chopped portobello mushrooms
1½ cups chopped onions
4 cloves garlic, minced
2 tablespoons olive oil
2 cups broccoli florets and sliced stems
1 cup sliced yellow summer squash
1 can (15 ounces) red kidney beans, rinsed, drained
1 can (14 ounces) diced tomatoes, undrained
1½ teaspoons dried Italian seasoning
¼ teaspoon dried thyme leaves
¼ teaspoon crushed red pepper
Salt and pepper, to taste

Per Serving
Net Carbohydrate (gm): 13.4
Calories: 466
Fat (gm): 36.8
Saturated fat (gm): 10.6
Cholesterol (mg): 59.7
Sodium (mg): 1093
Protein (gm): 20.4
Carbohydrate (gm): 20.5

1. Sauté sausage, mushrooms, onions, and garlic in oil in large saucepan until onions are tender, about 10 minutes, crumbling sausage with a fork as it cooks; drain excess fat. Add broccoli and squash; cook, covered, over medium heat 5 minutes.

2. Stir in beans, tomatoes and liquid, herbs, and red pepper; heat to boiling. Reduce heat and simmer, covered, until broccoli is tender, 5 to 8 minutes. Season to taste with salt and pepper.

Smoked Sausage and Peppers Stew

4 servings

3 cups thinly sliced red, green, and yellow bell peppers
1 cup thinly sliced onion
12 ounces smoked turkey sausage, thinly sliced
1 tablespoon olive oil
1 tablespoon all-purpose flour
¾ cup reduced-sodium fat-free chicken broth
3 cups sliced kale, *or* spinach
2 cups sliced red potatoes
½ cup quartered sun-dried tomatoes, softened
1 teaspoon dried thyme leaves
1 teaspoon dried marjoram leaves
Salt and pepper, to taste

Per Serving
Net Carbohydrate (gm): 28
Calories: 300
Fat (gm): 12.3
Saturated fat (gm): 2.5
Cholesterol (mg): 47
Sodium (mg): 888
Protein (gm): 19.5
Carbohydrate (gm): 33.3

1. Sauté bell peppers, onion, and sausage in oil in large skillet until peppers are crisp-tender, about 8 minutes; sprinkle with flour and cook 1 minute longer.

2. Add remaining ingredients, except salt and pepper, and heat to boiling; reduce heat and simmer, covered, until vegetables are tender, about 15 minutes. Season to taste with salt and pepper.

Smoky Pinto Bean Stew

6 servings

1½ pounds smoked turkey sausage, sliced
1 tablespoon olive oil
1 cup chopped onion
1 cup chopped green bell pepper
2 cups sliced zucchini
2 cloves garlic, minced
1 can (28 ounces) whole tomatoes, undrained, chopped
1 can (15 ounces) pinto beans, rinsed, drained
1½ cups fresh, *or* frozen, cut green beans
2 teaspoons dried oregano leaves
Salt and pepper, to taste

Per Serving
Net Carbohydrate (gm): 19.5
Calories: 306
Fat (gm): 13.5
Saturated fat (gm): 3.1
Cholesterol (mg): 56.4
Sodium (mg): 1280
Protein (gm): 23.8
Carbohydrate (gm): 26.8

1. Cook sausage in oil in large saucepan over medium-high heat until browned, about 4 minutes. Add onion, bell pepper, zucchini, and garlic; cook over medium heat until vegetables are lightly browned, about 5 minutes.

2. Add remaining ingredients, except salt and pepper; heat to boiling. Reduce heat and simmer, uncovered, until vegetables are tender, about 10 minutes. Season to taste with salt and pepper.

FOUR

Meats

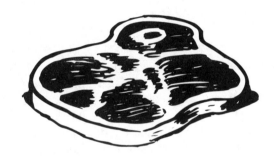

Mustard Roast Beef

6 servings

¼ cup no-sugar-added apricot preserves
¼ cup spicy brown mustard
1 tablespoon Worcestershire sauce
1 tablespoon light brown sugar
1 tablespoon prepared horseradish
1 teaspoon crushed caraway seeds
¼ teaspoon ground allspice
1 teaspoon crushed black peppercorns
1 boneless beef sirloin tip roast, fat trimmed (about 2 pounds)

Per Serving
Net Carbohydrate (gm): 7.3
Calories: 250
Fat (gm): 7.3
Saturated fat (gm): 2.5
Cholesterol (mg): 71.8
Sodium (mg): 264
Protein (gm): 33.9
Carbohydrate (gm): 7.8

1. Mix all ingredients except beef in small bowl. Spread mixture on all surfaces of meat. Place meat on rack in roasting pan. Roast at 350 degrees 40 to 50 minutes or until meat thermometer registers 140 degrees (medium) or 160 degrees (well-done).

Variation:

Crumb-Crusted Roast Beef—Make recipe as above omitting brown sugar, horseradish, caraway seeds, and allspice. Combine 1 cup fresh whole wheat bread crumbs, 2 teaspoons minced garlic, 1 teaspoon dried basil leaves, ½ teaspoon dried oregano leaves, and ¼ teaspoon dried marjoram leaves with the apricot preserves, mustard, Worcestershire sauce, and peppercorns in medium bowl. Pat crumb mixture onto roast. Roast as above.

Old-Fashioned Pot Roast

8 servings

1 boneless beef pot roast, fat trimmed (about 3 pounds)
1 tablespoon canola oil
Salt and pepper, to taste
2 cups onion wedges, divided
6 cloves garlic, minced
1 cup reduced-sodium fat-free beef broth
1 teaspoon dried thyme leaves
1 bay leaf
2 cups cubed (1½-inch), peeled potatoes
2 cups cut carrots (1½-inch)
2 cups cut parsnips (1½-inch)
¼ cup all-purpose flour
½ cup water

Per Serving
Net Carbohydrate (gm): 20
Calories: 497
Fat (gm): 28.4
Saturated fat (gm): 10.6
Cholesterol (mg): 111.1
Sodium (mg): 124
Protein (gm): 35
Carbohydrate (gm): 24.1

1. Cook meat in oil in Dutch oven over medium heat until browned, about 4 minutes on each side. Remove from pan and sprinkle lightly with salt and pepper. Add half the onions and all the garlic to the pan; sauté 2 to 3 minutes.

2. Return meat to pan. Add broth and herbs and heat to boiling. Transfer to oven and bake, covered, at 325 degrees until meat is fork-tender, 2¾ to 3 hours. Add remaining onions and vegetables to pan during last hour of cooking time. Arrange meat and vegetables on serving platter; discard bay leaf.

3. Pour meat juices into glass measure; spoon off and discard fat. Add water to juices, if necessary, to make 2 cups; heat to boiling in Dutch oven. Mix flour and ½ cup water; stir into boiling juices. Boil, whisking constantly, until thickened, about 1 minute; season to taste with salt and pepper. Serve gravy with pot roast and vegetables.

Variations:

Bourbon Pot Roast—Make recipe as above, omitting parsnips, and substituting ⅔ cup tomato juice and ⅓ cup bourbon for the beef broth. Add 1 teaspoon dry mustard and ½ teaspoon beef bouillon crystals with the tomato juice in Step 2.

Italian Pot Roast—Make recipe as above, omitting potatoes, carrots, parsnips, and flour. Substitute 1 cup dry red wine for the beef broth. Add 1 can (15 ounces) roasted garlic-seasoned diced tomatoes and juices, 1 can (6 ounces) tomato paste, and 1 teaspoon dried basil leaves in Step 2. Add ½ cup chopped carrot, ½ cup chopped celery, and 1 cup sliced mushrooms during last hour of cooking time. Serve over Polenta (see p. 374).

Slow-Cooker Pot Roast

6 servings

2 cups sliced, peeled potatoes
2 cups sliced carrots
2 cups sliced onions
¾ cup sliced celery and tops
½ teaspoon dried thyme leaves
½ teaspoon dried marjoram leaves
1 boneless beef chuck pot roast (about 3 pounds)
Salt and pepper, to taste
½ cup reduced-sodium fat-free beef broth

Per Serving
Net Carbohydrate (gm): 16.3
Calories: 565
Fat (gm): 33.4
Saturated fat (gm): 12.6
Cholesterol (mg): 145.2
Sodium (mg): 159
Protein (gm): 44.8
Carbohydrate (gm): 19.7

1. Put vegetables in slow-cooker and sprinkle with herbs. Season meat with salt and pepper and place in slow cooker. Add broth; cover and cook on Low 10 to 12 hours or on High 4 to 5 hours.

Variations:

German-Style Pot Roast—Add 3 or 4 sliced medium dill pickles, 1 teaspoon dried dill weed, and 1 tablespoon wine vinegar to slow-cooker with vegetables. Cook as above.

Italian-Style Pot Roast—Add 1 cup tomato sauce to slow-cooker with vegetables; substitute Italian seasoning for the thyme and marjoram. Cook as above.

Mexican-Style Pot Roast—Add ½ cup chopped green onions and tops, 1 tablespoon minced garlic, 1 cup beef broth, 2 tablespoons tomato paste, and 2 to 4 tablespoons chili powder to slow-cooker with vegetables. Cook as above.

Roast Beef Hash

4 servings

3 cups (12 ounces) shredded or cubed roasted lean beef
1½ cups cubed, peeled cooked potatoes
½ cup chopped green bell pepper
⅓ cup sliced green onions and tops
2 cloves garlic, minced
½ teaspoon dried marjoram leaves
¼ teaspoon dried thyme leaves
1 tablespoon olive oil
Salt and pepper, to taste

Per Serving
Net Carbohydrate (gm): 12.4
Calories: 241
Fat (gm): 8.6
Saturated fat (gm): 2.2
Cholesterol (mg): 66.3
Sodium (mg): 61
Protein (gm): 25.7
Carbohydrate (gm): 14.1

1. Sauté all ingredients, except salt and pepper, in oil in large skillet until well-browned, about 15 minutes, stirring occasionally. Season to taste with salt and pepper.

Variation:

Corned Beef Hash—Make recipe as above, substituting corned beef for roast beef. Use only lean parts of the corned beef and trim all fat.

Steak au Poivre

4 servings

2 teaspoons coarsely crushed black peppercorns
4 beef tenderloin steaks (5 ounces each), fat trimmed
Salt, to taste
2 teaspoons butter
⅓ cup brandy
¼ cup sour cream

Per Serving
Net Carbohydrate (gm): 0.9
Calories: 473
Fat (gm): 34.5
Saturated fat (gm): 14.9
Cholesterol (mg): 110
Sodium (mg): 97
Protein (gm): 26.1
Carbohydrate (gm): 1.2

1. Press peppercorns into steak, using about ¼ teaspoon per side; sprinkle lightly with salt. Sauté steaks in butter in large skillet over medium-high heat to desired degree of doneness, 3 to 4 minutes on each side for medium. Remove steaks to serving plates.

2. Add brandy to skillet; heat to boiling. Boil until reduced to about 2 tablespoons, 2 to 3 minutes, scraping bottom of skillet to loosen cooked particles. Stir in sour cream and cook over low heat 1 to 2 minutes. Spoon sauce over steaks.

Note: A mixture of white, pink, green, and black peppercorns can be used.

Filet Mignon Stroganoff

4 servings

4 beef tenderloin steaks (5 ounces each)
2 teaspoons butter
Salt and pepper, to taste
3 cups sliced mushrooms
¾ cup chopped red bell pepper
½ teaspoon dried marjoram leaves
¼ teaspoon dried thyme leaves
4 tablespoons cream cheese
⅓ cup sour cream

Per Serving
Net Carbohydrate (gm): 3.8
Calories: 478
Fat (gm): 37.9
Saturated fat (gm): 17.3
Cholesterol (mg): 124.7
Sodium (mg): 134
Protein (gm): 29
Carbohydrate (gm): 5.1

1. Cook steaks in butter in large skillet over medium-high heat to desired degree of doneness (about 3 minutes on each side for medium). Season to taste with salt and pepper; remove to serving platter and keep warm.

2. Add mushrooms and bell pepper to skillet and sauté until mushrooms are tender, about 5 minutes. Stir in herbs and cream cheese and stir until melted; stir in sour cream and cook until heated through. Season to taste with salt and pepper. Spoon mushroom mixture over steaks.

Tournedos Béarnaise

4 servings

4 slices (¾ inch thick) whole-grain French bread
2 teaspoons olive oil
1 clove garlic, cut in half
4 beef tenderloin steaks (5 ounces each)
2 teaspoons butter
Salt and pepper, to taste
Mock Béarnaise Sauce (recipe follows)

Per Serving
Net Carbohydrate (gm): 11
Calories: 542
Fat (gm): 41.2
Saturated fat (gm): 18.3
Cholesterol (mg): 129.4
Sodium (mg): 166
Protein (gm): 29.8
Carbohydrate (gm): 12.5

1. Brush both sides of bread slices with oil; place on cookie sheet and broil 4 inches from heat source until browned, 1 to 2 minutes on each side. Rub bread slices with garlic.

2. Cook steaks in butter in large skillet over medium-high heat to desired degree of doneness (about 3 minutes on each side for medium). Season to taste with salt and pepper.

3. Arrange steaks on bread slices; spoon Mock Béarnaise Sauce over.

Mock Béarnaise Sauce

makes about ¾ cup

1 package (3 ounces) cream cheese
3 tablespoons sour cream
1 tablespoon reduced-fat milk
1 tablespoon minced shallot
1–2 teaspoons tarragon vinegar, *or* lemon juice
½ teaspoon Dijon mustard
¾ teaspoon dried tarragon leaves
2 generous pinches ground turmeric
Salt and white pepper, to taste

1. Heat all ingredients in small saucepan over medium-low to low heat until melted and smooth, stirring constantly. Serve immediately.

Grilled Steak and Vegetables with Creamy Horseradish Sauce

6 servings

6 boneless beef eye of round, *or*
    sirloin, steaks (6 ounces each)
2 large cloves garlic, halved
Salt and pepper, to taste
3 medium tomatoes, halved
1 large red onion, cut into ½-inch slices
Creamy Horseradish Sauce (recipe follows)

Per Serving
Net Carbohydrate (gm): 4.9
Calories: 384
Fat (gm): 22.9
Saturated fat (gm): 7.7
Cholesterol (mg): 108.3
Sodium (mg): 163
Protein (gm): 37
Carbohydrate (gm): 6

1. Rub both sides of steaks with cut sides of garlic; sprinkle with salt and pepper. Grill steaks, tomato halves, and onion slices over hot coals until steaks are desired degree of doneness, 5 to 8 minutes per side for medium. Turn onion slices when browned on the bottom. Remove onion slices and tomatoes when tender. Serve with Creamy Horseradish Sauce.

Creamy Horseradish Sauce

makes about ¾ cup

½ cup sour cream
¼ cup mayonnaise
1–2 tablespoons prepared horseradish

1. Mix all ingredients; cover and refrigerate until serving time.

Grilled Steak with Tomato-Tarragon Sauce

4 servings

1½ pounds boneless beef sirloin, *or*
    eye of round, steak, fat trimmed
1 tablespoon canola oil
2 tablespoons red wine vinegar
1 tablespoon chopped fresh, *or*
    1 teaspoon dried, tarragon leaves
Tomato-Tarragon Sauce (recipe follows)

Per Serving
Net Carbohydrate (gm): 6.9
Calories: 423
Fat (gm): 27.7
Saturated fat (gm): 9.2
Cholesterol (mg): 110.4
Sodium (mg): 153
Protein (gm): 34.2
Carbohydrate (gm): 8.1

1. Brush both sides of steaks with combined oil, vinegar, and tarragon; refrigerate 1 hour. Discard marinade.

2. Grill steak over medium-hot coals to desired degree of doneness, about 5 minutes on each side for medium, depending upon thickness of meat. Slice steak into thin strips, across the grain, and serve with Tomato-Tarragon Sauce.

Tomato-Tarragon Sauce

makes about ¾ cup

¼ cup minced shallots
2 cloves garlic, minced
1 teaspoon canola oil
¾ cup tomato puree
2 tablespoons tarragon vinegar
2 teaspoons brown sugar
½ teaspoon dried tarragon leaves
Salt and pepper, to taste

1. Sauté shallots and garlic in oil in small saucepan until tender, 2 to 3 minutes. Add remaining ingredients, except salt and pepper, and heat to boiling; reduce heat and simmer, uncovered, 5 minutes. Season to taste with salt and pepper.

Chicken-Fried Steak

6 servings

6 boneless beef eye of round steaks (4 ounces each)
2 tablespoons all-purpose flour
1 egg, lightly beaten
¼ cup reduced-fat milk
½ cup seasoned dry bread crumbs
1 tablespoon butter
Salt and pepper, to taste
Cream Gravy (see p. 218)

Per Serving
Net Carbohydrate (gm): 12.4
Calories: 308
Fat (gm): 15.1
Saturated fat (gm): 7
Cholesterol (mg): 116
Sodium (mg): 270
Protein (gm): 28.2
Carbohydrate (gm): 12.8

1. Pound steaks with flat side of mallet to ¼ inch thickness. Coat steaks lightly with flour; dip in combined egg and milk and coat with bread crumbs.

2. Cook steaks in butter in large skillet over medium heat until browned, about 5 minutes on each side. Cover and cook over very low heat until steaks are tender, 30 to 40 minutes, turning occasionally. Season to taste with salt and pepper. Serve with Cream Gravy.

Beef Steaks with Tomatillo and Avocado Sauce

6 servings

¾ cup thinly sliced onion
1 tablespoon canola oil
6 boneless beef eye of round steaks (4 ounces each)
Salt and pepper, to taste
1 cup (½ recipe) Tomatillo Sauce (see p. 138)
2 tablespoons mashed avocado
2 tablespoons sour cream

Per Serving
Net Carbohydrate (gm): 5.8
Calories: 250
Fat (gm): 13.1
Saturated fat (gm): 3.9
Cholesterol (mg): 65.5
Sodium (mg): 54
Protein (gm): 24.9
Carbohydrate (gm): 7.7

1. Sauté onion in oil in large skillet 2 to 3 minutes, until softened; reduce heat to medium-low and cook until onion is very soft, 5 to 8 minutes. Remove from skillet.

2. Add steaks to skillet; cook over medium heat to desired degree of doneness, 3 to 4 minutes on each side for medium. Season to taste with salt and pepper. Heat Tomatillo Sauce and avocado in small saucepan until hot; stir in sour cream.

3. Arrange steaks on serving platter; top with onions and spoon Tomatillo Sauce over.

Beef with Red and Green Stir-Fry

4 servings

2 cups sliced red onions
2 cups sliced red bell peppers
1 cup sliced celery
2 teaspoons minced garlic
1 teaspoon minced gingerroot
1 tablespoon peanut oil, divided
6 cups sliced Swiss chard, *or* spinach
2 cups reduced-sodium fat-free beef broth
2 tablespoons cornstarch
4 teaspoons tamari soy sauce, divided
½–¾ teaspoon hot chili paste
Salt and pepper, to taste
4 boneless beef eye of round steaks (4 ounces each)

Per Serving
Net Carbohydrate (gm): 13.4
Calories: 292
Fat (gm): 11.7
Saturated fat (gm): 3.6
Cholesterol (mg): 63.8
Sodium (mg): 609
Protein (gm): 29.5
Carbohydrate (gm): 17.4

1. Stir-fry onions, bell peppers, celery, garlic, and gingerroot in 2 teaspoons oil in wok or large skillet until crisp-tender, 3 to 4 minutes. Add Swiss chard and stir-fry until wilted, 1 to 2 minutes.

2. Combine broth, cornstarch, 2 teaspoons soy sauce, and chili paste; stir into wok. Heat to boiling; boil, stirring constantly, until thickened, about 1 minute. Season to taste with salt and pepper.

3. Brush beef with remaining 2 teaspoons soy sauce. Cook steaks in remaining 1 teaspoon oil in large skillet over medium-high heat to desired degree of doneness, 3 to 4 minutes on each side for medium.

4. Arrange beef on serving platter; spoon vegetable mixture over.

Stuffed Flank Steak Brazil

8 servings

1 beef flank steak (2 pounds), butterflied
¼ cup red wine vinegar
2 teaspoons minced garlic
2 teaspoons dried thyme leaves
1 teaspoon salt
Black Bean Filling (recipe follows)
2 cups loosely packed spinach leaves
4 whole thin carrots, cooked
3 hard-cooked eggs, quartered
4 cups reduced-sodium fat-free beef broth

Per Serving
Net Carbohydrate (gm): 14.6
Calories: 336
Fat (gm): 11.4
Saturated fat (gm): 4.5
Cholesterol (mg): 126.8
Sodium (mg): 817
Protein (gm): 35.3
Carbohydrate (gm): 20.7

1. Place meat flat on counter; cover with waxed paper and pound to an even thickness, using flat side of meat mallet. Sprinkle surfaces of meat with vinegar, garlic, thyme, and salt. Let stand while preparing Black Bean Filling, or transfer to jelly roll pan and refrigerate, covered, up to 12 hours.

2. Spread Black Bean Filling over meat; cover with spinach leaves. Place carrots about 3 inches apart on spinach, parallel to grain of meat; place egg quarters between carrots. Roll up meat, starting from short end, and tie with kitchen string at 2-inch intervals.

3. Place meat in roasting pan; pour broth around meat, adding water if necessary to come ⅓ of the way up the side of meat rolls. Cover tightly with lid or foil. Bake at 375 degrees 1 hour or until meat reaches internal temperature of 130 degrees. Place meat on platter and let stand 5 minutes before slicing. Or chill, slice, and serve cold.

Black Bean Filling

makes about 3 cups

1 cup boiling water
1 ancho chili
2 cans (15 ounces each) black beans, rinsed, drained
¼ cup chopped onion
¼ cup chopped parsley
1 teaspoon ground cumin

1. Pour water over ancho chili in small bowl and let stand until softened, about 10 minutes; drain. Remove and discard stem from chili. Puree chili in blender with a small amount of soaking water until smooth.

2. Coarsely mash beans in medium bowl; stir in chili puree, onion, parsley, and cumin.

Tip: Ask your butcher to butterfly the flank steak. Or, to butterfly flank steak, place on cutting board and, with sharp knife, cut in half horizontally to within ½ inch of the opposite long side.

Vegetable-Stuffed Flank Steak

6 servings

1 beef flank steak (1½ pounds)
1 cup Italian salad dressing
Vegetable Stuffing (recipe follows)
1 tablespoon olive oil
1 cup reduced-sodium fat-free beef broth

Per Serving
Net Carbohydrate (gm): 9.4
Calories: 430
Fat (gm): 30.9
Saturated fat (gm): 6.7
Cholesterol (mg): 45.5
Sodium (mg): 444
Protein (gm): 27.8
Carbohydrate (gm): 10.5

1. Pound flank steak with meat mallet until even thickness (scant ¾ inch thick). Using sharp knife, score steak diagonally in diamond pattern on both sides. Place steak in shallow glass baking dish; pour dressing over. Refrigerate, covered, 1½ to 2 hours, turning steak occasionally.

2. Remove steak from marinade; reserve marinade. Spread Vegetable Stuffing on steak, leaving 2-inch margin along sides. Roll up lengthwise, jelly roll style; secure edge with wooden picks or tie with kitchen string.

3. Cook meat in oil in large skillet until browned on all sides, about 8 minutes. Add broth and reserved marinade to skillet. Bake, covered, at 325 degrees 30 to 45 minutes or until meat thermometer registers 140 degrees (medium) or 160 degrees (well-done).

Vegetable Stuffing

makes about 1¼ cups

8 ounces mushrooms, sliced
½ cup chopped carrot
¼ cup thinly sliced celery
¼ cup thinly sliced green onions and tops
1 clove garlic, minced
2 teaspoons olive oil
¼ cup unseasoned dry bread crumbs
1½ teaspoons dried Italian seasoning
Salt and pepper, to taste

1. Sauté mushrooms, carrot, celery, green onions, and garlic in oil in large skillet until tender, about 5 minutes. Stir in bread crumbs and Italian seasoning; stir over medium heat until bread crumbs are browned, 2 to 3 minutes. Season to taste with salt and pepper.

Steak on a Stick

6 servings

2 pounds boneless beef eye of round, *or* sirloin, steak, cut into ¾-inch cubes
2 tablespoons olive oil
2 tablespoons dry red wine, *or* beef broth
1 clove garlic, minced
1 teaspoon dried rosemary leaves
¼ teaspoon pepper
¼ teaspoon brown sugar
1 large tomato, cut into 6 wedges

Per Serving
Net Carbohydrate (gm): 1.2
Calories: 301
Fat (gm): 17.5
Saturated fat (gm): 5.4
Cholesterol (mg): 85
Sodium (mg): 79
Protein (gm): 31.8
Carbohydrate (gm): 1.6

1. Toss beef in large glass bowl with remaining ingredients, except tomato. Let stand about 20 minutes, or refrigerate, covered, several hours.

2. Thread beef on skewers, with a tomato wedge on the end of each; place on broiler pan. Broil 6 inches from heat source to desired degree of doneness, about 5 minutes on each side for medium, brushing with remaining marinade.

Beef and Roasted Pepper Fajitas

4 servings (1 fajita each)

2 cups thinly sliced red, yellow, and green bell peppers
2 tablespoons olive oil, divided
½–1 teaspoon ground cumin
¼ teaspoon ground cloves
1 dried pasilla chili, stem, seeds, and veins discarded
1 pound boneless beef round steak, cut into thin strips
3 cloves garlic, minced
¼ small jalapeño chili, seeds and veins discarded, minced
Salt, to taste
4 flour tortillas (6 inch), warm
2 tablespoons finely chopped cilantro
¼ cup sour cream

Per Serving
Net Carbohydrate (gm): 21.7
Calories: 424
Fat (gm): 23.4
Saturated fat (gm): 7.4
Cholesterol (mg): 63.1
Sodium (mg): 216
Protein (gm): 27.7
Carbohydrate (gm): 25

1. Toss peppers in bowl with 1 tablespoon oil, cumin, and cloves; arrange on lightly greased aluminum foil-lined jelly roll pan. Bake at 425 degrees until tender and browned, 20 to 25 minutes.

2. Cover pasilla chili with hot water in small bowl; let stand until softened, about 15 minutes. Drain and chop.

3. Sauté beef, garlic, jalapeño, and pasilla chilies in remaining 1 tablespoon oil in large skillet until beef is desired doneness, about 5 minutes for medium. Season to taste with salt.

4. Spoon beef and bell pepper mixtures onto tortillas; sprinkle with cilantro, top with sour cream, and roll up.

Wok Steak Sweet-and-Sour

4 servings

1 tablespoon peanut oil
1 pound beef tenderloin, *or*
    flank steak, thinly sliced across grain
1 cup thinly sliced onion
1 cup sliced zucchini
½ pound snow peas, ends trimmed
½ pound mushrooms, sliced
½ can (8-ounce size) sliced water chestnuts, drained
1 tablespoon sesame seeds
⅔ cup sweet-sour sauce
Salt and pepper, to taste

Per Serving
Net Carbohydrate (gm): 21.3
Calories: 452
Fat (gm): 28.1
Saturated fat (gm): 9.9
Cholesterol (mg): 77.2
Sodium (mg): 186
Protein (gm): 25.1
Carbohydrate (gm): 25.3

1. Heat oil in wok or large skillet over medium-high heat until hot; add beef and stir-fry until browned, 3 to 4 minutes. Move beef to side of wok; add vegetables and stir-fry until crisp-tender, about 5 minutes. Add sesame seeds and sweet-sour sauce, stirring to combine; season to taste with salt and pepper.

Sukiyaki

8 servings

2 tablespoons peanut, *or* canola, oil
2 pounds boneless beef sirloin steak,
    sliced into very thin strips
¼ cup water
¼ cup packed brown sugar
2 tablespoons soy sauce
¼ cup sake (rice wine)
¼ teaspoon beef bouillon crystals
1 cup diagonally sliced carrots
1½ cups thinly sliced onions
6 green onions, cut into 1½-inch pieces
2 cups sliced mushrooms
4 cups sliced Chinese cabbage
1 cup bamboo shoots
1 package (5 ounces) bean thread noodles, cooked

Per Serving
Net Carbohydrate (gm): 27.2
Calories: 401
Fat (gm): 19.1
Saturated fat (gm): 6.6
Cholesterol (mg): 73.6
Sodium (mg): 578
Protein (gm): 25.3
Carbohydrate (gm): 30.6

1. Heat oil in wok or large skillet until hot; add beef and stir-fry until browned, 2 to 3 minutes. Combine water, sugar, soy sauce, sake, and bouillon; add half the soy mixture, carrots, and onions to wok and stir-fry 2 minutes. Add remaining soy mixture and remaining vegetables; stir-fry until cabbage is crisp-tender, about 5 minutes. Stir in noodles; cook 1 to 2 minutes longer.

Beef Oriental

6 servings

1 boneless beef round steak (about 1½ pounds)
1 tablespoon peanut, *or* canola, oil
¼ cup minced onion
2 cloves garlic, minced
¼ cup water
2 tablespoons soy sauce
1½ cups reduced-sodium fat-free beef broth
1 package (16 ounces) frozen broccoli florets
1 package (16 ounces) frozen cauliflower florets
3 cups sliced mushrooms
½ cup julienned carrot
½ cup sliced water chestnuts
½ cup chopped celery
Salt and pepper, to taste

Per Serving
Net Carbohydrate (gm): 7.4
Calories: 245
Fat (gm): 7.9
Saturated fat (gm): 2.1
Cholesterol (mg): 53.9
Sodium (mg): 492
Protein (gm): 31.4
Carbohydrate (gm): 12.2

1. Cook meat in oil in large skillet over medium-high heat until browned, about 5 minutes on each side. Add onion, garlic, water, and soy sauce; heat to boiling. Reduce heat and simmer, covered, until meat is almost tender, about 20 minutes. Remove meat and cut into bite-sized pieces.

2. Return meat to skillet with remaining ingredients, except salt and pepper. Heat to boiling; reduce heat and simmer, covered, until vegetables and meat are tender, about 15 minutes. Season to taste with salt and pepper.

Beef and Vegetable Lo Mein

6 servings

4 dried shiitake mushrooms
1 tablespoon finely chopped gingerroot
3 cloves garlic, minced
1 tablespoon sesame, *or* peanut, oil
1½ pounds boneless beef eye of round
    steak cut into ½-inch strips
2 cups small broccoli florets
1 cup sliced carrots
⅓ cup water
2 tablespoons dry sherry, *or* water
2 teaspoons cornstarch
1 tablespoon black bean paste
2 teaspoons light soy sauce
½ package (12-ounce size) fresh Chinese-style noodles, cooked

Per Serving
Net Carbohydrate (gm): 21
Calories: 382
Fat (gm): 17
Saturated fat (gm): 3.5
Cholesterol (mg): 49.2
Sodium (mg): 381
Protein (gm): 32.1
Carbohydrate (gm): 34

1. Place dried mushrooms in small bowl; pour hot water over to cover. Let stand until mushrooms are soft, about 15 minutes; drain. Slice mushrooms, discarding tough stems.

2. Stir-fry mushrooms, gingerroot, and garlic in oil in wok or large skillet 2 minutes. Add beef; stir-fry until beef is cooked, about 8 minutes. Remove all from wok.

3. Add broccoli and carrots to wok; stir-fry until vegetables are crisp-tender, 5 to 8 minutes. Remove from wok.

4. Combine water, sherry, and cornstarch; add to wok and heat to boiling. Boil, stirring constantly, until thickened, about 1 minute. Stir in black bean paste and soy sauce. Return beef and vegetable mixtures to wok; add noodles. Stir-fry over medium heat until hot through, 2 to 3 minutes.

Asian Beef With Sesame Noodles

6 servings

Per Serving
Net Carbohydrate (gm): 29.1
Calories: 469
Fat (gm): 24
Saturated fat (gm): 8.4
Cholesterol (mg): 97.6
Sodium (mg): 594
Protein (gm): 30.3
Carbohydrate (gm): 30.1

2 pounds boneless beef sirloin, cut into thin strips
1–2 tablespoons peanut, *or* canola, oil
1½ cups water
2 thin slices gingerroot
2 cloves garlic, halved
2 green onions and tops, cut into 1-inch pieces
2–4 tablespoons soy sauce
1 tablespoon packed light brown sugar
1 tablespoon cornstarch
2 tablespoons dry sherry, *or* water
Salt and pepper, to taste
Sesame Noodles (recipe follows)
1 tablespoon sesame seeds, toasted
Finely chopped cilantro, as garnish

1. Cook beef in peanut oil in large skillet over medium-high heat until browned, about 8 minutes. Add water, gingerroot, garlic, green onions, soy sauce, and sugar; heat to boiling. Reduce heat and simmer, covered, until beef is tender, about 30 minutes.

2. Heat stew to boiling; stir in combined cornstarch and sherry. Boil, stirring, until thickened, about 1 minute. Season to taste with salt and pepper. Serve over Sesame Noodles; sprinkle with sesame seeds and cilantro.

Sesame Noodles

makes 6 servings

½ package (12-ounce size) Asian noodles *or*
    thin whole wheat spaghetti, cooked, warm
2 teaspoons soy sauce
1 teaspoon sesame oil
1 green onion and top, thinly sliced

1. Toss warm noodles with remaining ingredients.

Thai Stir-Fry

6 servings

1½ pounds boneless beef round steak,
    cut into very thin strips
1 tablespoon peanut oil
¾ cup sliced green onions and tops
2 cups small broccoli florets
1 cup sliced red bell pepper
1 cup thinly sliced carrots
½ cup Thai peanut sauce
½ cup reduced-sodium fat-free beef broth
2 teaspoons cornstarch
¼ cup finely chopped cilantro
¼ cup coarsely chopped dry roasted peanuts

Per Serving
Net Carbohydrate (gm): 9.3
Calories: 283
Fat (gm): 11.9
Saturated fat (gm): 2.6
Cholesterol (mg): 64.5
Sodium (mg): 348
Protein (gm): 30.8
Carbohydrate (gm): 13.4

1. Sauté beef in oil in large skillet until browned, about 5 minutes; remove from skillet. Add green onions, broccoli, bell pepper, and carrots and sauté until crisp-tender, 4 to 5 minutes. Stir in peanut sauce; stir in combined broth and cornstarch and heat to boiling. Boil until thickened, about 1 minute; stir in beef.

2. Spoon mixture into serving bowl; sprinkle with cilantro and peanuts.

Thai-Style Beef and Pasta

6 servings

2 pounds boneless beef eye of round, *or*
    sirloin, steak, cut into ¼-inch strips
3 tablespoons teriyaki sauce
1 tablespoon peanut, *or* canola, oil
Satay Sauce (recipe follows)
4 ounces whole wheat vermicelli, *or*
    thin spaghetti, cooked, warm
1 cup chopped, seeded cucumber

Per Serving
Net Carbohydrate (gm): 15.7
Calories: 381
Fat (gm): 18.2
Saturated fat (gm): 5.8
Cholesterol (mg): 85
Sodium (mg): 363
Protein (gm): 35.8
Carbohydrate (gm): 17.8

1. Toss beef with teriyaki sauce in medium bowl. Heat oil in wok or large skillet over high heat until hot. Add beef and stir-fry until browned, about 5 minutes. Add beef and Satay Sauce to vermicelli and toss; sprinkle with cucumber.

Satay Sauce

makes about ⅓ cup

3 tablespoons teriyaki sauce
2 tablespoons peanut butter
1 tablespoon water
⅛–¼ teaspoon ground ginger
⅛–¼ teaspoon crushed red pepper

1. Combine all ingredients.

Teriyaki Beef and Broccoli

4 servings

1 pound boneless beef round steak, fat trimmed,
    cut into thin strips
1 cup thin onion wedges
1 tablespoon peanut, *or* canola, oil
1½ cups reduced-sodium fat-free beef broth
2 tablespoons teriyaki sauce
1 tablespoon minced gingerroot
¾ cup thinly sliced carrots
2 cups small broccoli florets

Per Serving
Net Carbohydrate (gm): 7
Calories: 300
Fat (gm): 16.4
Saturated fat (gm): 5.3
Cholesterol (mg): 70.1
Sodium (mg): 646
Protein (gm): 27.8
Carbohydrate (gm): 9.7

1. Sauté beef and onions in oil in large skillet until meat is lightly browned, 5 to 8 minutes. Add broth, teriyaki sauce, and gingerroot; heat to boiling. Reduce heat and simmer, covered, until beef is tender, about 25 minutes, adding carrots and broccoli during last 10 minutes.

Five-Spice Beef

4 servings

1½ pounds boneless beef round steak, cut into 1-inch strips
1 cup orange juice
1 cup reduced-sodium fat-free beef broth
1 tablespoon teriyaki sauce
1¼ teaspoons five-spice powder
1 cup thin onion wedges
2 ounces bean thread noodles
1 red bell pepper, thinly sliced
1 teaspoon Chinese chili sauce with garlic
2 cups sliced Napa cabbage

Per Serving
Net Carbohydrate (gm): 23
Calories: 444
Fat (gm): 19.8
Saturated fat (gm): 7.2
Cholesterol (mg): 105.1
Sodium (mg): 405
Protein (gm): 38.3
Carbohydrate (gm): 26.3

1. Heat beef, orange juice, broth, teriyaki sauce, five-spice powder, and onions to boiling in large saucepan. Reduce heat and simmer, covered, until beef is tender, about 25 minutes.

2. Soak bean thread noodles in hot water to cover in large bowl for 15 minutes; drain.

3. Stir bell pepper, chili sauce, and cabbage into beef mixture; simmer, uncovered, for 3 minutes. Stir noodles into beef mixture. Heat until hot, about 2 minutes.

Country Beef Stew

4 servings

1½ pounds lean beef stew meat, cubed (¾-inch)
1 tablespoon canola oil
½ cup chopped onion
½ cup chopped celery
2 cloves garlic, minced
1 cup reduced-sodium fat-free beef broth
½ cup dry red wine, *or* beef broth
1 tablespoon tomato paste
½ teaspoon dried thyme leaves
½ teaspoon dried rosemary leaves
1 bay leaf
1 cup cubed, peeled potato
1 cup sliced (1-inch) carrots
½ cup cubed parsnip, *or* turnip
½ cup frozen peas
2 tablespoons all-purpose flour
¼ cup cold water
Salt and pepper, to taste

Per Serving
Net Carbohydrate (gm): 19.4
Calories: 425
Fat (gm): 15.5
Saturated fat (gm): 4.8
Cholesterol (mg): 91
Sodium (mg): 220
Protein (gm): 41.3
Carbohydrate (gm): 24

1. Cook beef in oil in Dutch oven over medium-high heat until browned, about 8 minutes. Add onion, celery, and garlic; cook until tender, about 5 minutes.

2. Add broth, wine, tomato paste, and herbs to Dutch oven; heat to boiling. Reduce heat and simmer, covered, until beef is tender, 1½ to 2 hours. Add remaining vegetables during last 30 minutes of cooking time.

3. Heat stew to boiling. Mix flour and water and stir into stew; boil, stirring constantly, until thickened, 1 to 2 minutes. Discard bay leaf; season to taste with salt and pepper.

Traditional Beef Stew

4 servings

1½ pounds boneless beef round steak,
    cut into thin, 1-inch strips
2 cups onion wedges
1 tablespoon olive oil
1½ cups reduced-sodium fat-free beef broth
½ cup dry red wine, *or* beef broth
1 teaspoon unsweetened cocoa
1 cup cubed (½-inch) peeled potatoes
1 cup sliced carrots
2 cups cut green beans
Salt and pepper, to taste

Per Serving
Net Carbohydrate (gm): 18.2
Calories: 481
Fat (gm): 23
Saturated fat (gm): 7.7
Cholesterol (mg): 105.1
Sodium (mg): 159
Protein (gm): 40.1
Carbohydrate (gm): 23.4

1. Sauté beef and onions in oil in Dutch oven until beef is lightly browned, 8 to 10 minutes. Add broth, wine, and cocoa; heat to boiling. Reduce heat and simmer, covered, until meat is tender, 50 to 60 minutes, adding vegetables during last 20 minutes. Season to taste with salt and pepper.

Harvest Stew

8 servings

2½ pounds boneless beef round steak, cut into 1-inch cubes
2 tablespoons olive oil
½ cup chopped onion
2 tablespoons all-purpose flour
3 cups cubed (1-inch), peeled butternut, *or* acorn, squash
2 cups chopped, seeded tomatoes
1 cup reduced-sodium fat-free beef broth
1 teaspoon dried marjoram leaves
½ teaspoon dried savory leaves
½ teaspoon dried thyme leaves
3 cups cubed zucchini
Salt and pepper, to taste

Per Serving
Net Carbohydrate (gm): 10.7
Calories: 352
Fat (gm): 19.7
Saturated fat (gm): 8.4
Cholesterol (mg): 87.6
Sodium (mg): 95
Protein (gm): 31.5
Carbohydrate (gm): 12

1. Cook beef in oil in Dutch oven over medium-high heat until browned, about 8 minutes; add onion and cook until lightly browned, about 5 minutes. Add flour and cook 1 minute longer.

2. Add squash, tomatoes, broth, and herbs; heat to boiling. Reduce heat and simmer, covered, until beef is tender, about 1 hour, adding zucchini during last 10 minutes of cooking time. Season to taste with salt and pepper.

Family Favorite Beef Stew

8 servings

2½ pounds lean beef stew meat, cubed (1-inch)
1 tablespoon canola oil
1½ cups chopped onions
4 cloves garlic, minced
1 teaspoon dried basil leaves
½ teaspoon dried marjoram leaves
½ teaspoon dried thyme leaves
1 bay leaf
3 tablespoons all-purpose flour
1 can (14½ ounces) diced tomatoes, undrained
1½ cups reduced-sodium fat-free beef broth
2 cups cubed turnips
1½ cups cubed (½-inch), peeled potatoes
1½ cups cubed (½-inch) carrots
1 cup sliced celery
2–3 teaspoons Worcestershire sauce
Salt and pepper, to taste

Per Serving
Net Carbohydrate (gm): 15.1
Calories: 319
Fat (gm): 11.7
Saturated fat (gm): 3.9
Cholesterol (mg): 75.8
Sodium (mg): 329
Protein (gm): 33.9
Carbohydrate (gm): 18.2

1. Sauté beef in oil in Dutch oven over medium-high heat until browned, about 10 minutes. Stir in onions, garlic, and herbs; sauté until browned, about 5 minutes. Stir in flour; cook 1 minute longer.

2. Add tomatoes and liquid and broth; heat to boiling. Reduce heat and simmer, covered, until beef is tender, 1 to 1½ hours, adding vegetables during last 30 minutes of cooking time. Season to taste with Worcestershire sauce, salt, and pepper.

Chuck Wagon Stew With Dill Dumplings

8 servings

2 pounds cubed (¾-inch) beef round steak
½ cup chopped onion
1 tablespoon vegetable oil
1 can (15 ounces) diced tomatoes, undrained
¾ cup reduced-sodium fat-free beef broth
1½ cups sliced carrots
1 can (15 ounces) pinto beans, rinsed, drained
2–3 teaspoons Worcestershire sauce
Salt and pepper, to taste
¼ cup all-purpose flour
½ cup cold water
Dill Dumplings (recipe follows)

Per Serving
Net Carbohydrate (gm): 27.3
Calories: 421
Fat (gm): 18.7
Saturated fat (gm): 6.1
Cholesterol (mg): 71.3
Sodium (mg): 696
Protein (gm): 29.9
Carbohydrate (gm): 31.3

1. Sauté beef and onion in oil in large saucepan until beef is browned, 5 to 8 minutes. Add tomatoes and liquid and broth; heat to boiling. Reduce heat and simmer, covered, until beef is almost tender, about 45 minutes.

2. Add carrots and beans; simmer, covered, 5 minutes. Season to taste with Worcestershire sauce, salt, and pepper.

3. Heat stew to boiling; stir in combined flour and water. Boil, stirring, until thickened, about 1 minute. Drop Dill Dumplings dough by spoonfuls onto top of stew. Simmer, uncovered, 10 minutes; simmer, covered, until dumplings are dry, about 10 minutes.

Dill Dumplings

makes 8 dumplings

1½ cups all-purpose baking mix
2 teaspoons dried dill weed
½ cup reduced-fat milk

1. Mix baking mix, dill weed, and milk to form soft dough.

Slow-Cooker Beef Stew

6 servings

1½ pounds cubed (¾-inch) beef round steak
2 cups cubed (¾-inch), unpeeled red potatoes
1½ cups coarsely shredded cabbage
1 cup chopped onion
½ cup sliced carrots
¼ cup quick-cooking brown rice
1½ cups reduced-sodium fat-free beef broth
¾ cup dry red wine, *or* beef broth
¼ cup catsup
2 teaspoons brown sugar
½ tablespoon cider vinegar
2 garlic cloves, minced
1½ teaspoons dried thyme leaves
1 teaspoon chili powder
½ teaspoon dry mustard
Salt and pepper, to taste

Per Serving
Net Carbohydrate (gm): 20.1
Calories: 336
Fat (gm): 13.3
Saturated fat (gm): 4.8
Cholesterol (mg): 70.1
Sodium (mg): 240
Protein (gm): 26.7
Carbohydrate (gm): 22.4

1. Combine all ingredients, except salt and pepper, in slow-cooker and stir well. Cover and cook on High 1 hour. Stir and cook, covered, on Low until meat is tender, 6½ to 8 hours. Season to taste with salt and pepper.

Slow-Cooker Barbecued Beef and Bean Stew

6 servings

1½ cups finely chopped onions
1 can (8 ounces) tomato sauce
½ cup mild, *or* medium, salsa
2 tablespoons cider vinegar
1½ tablespoons packed dark brown sugar
1 tablespoon chili powder
2 teaspoons Worcestershire sauce
1 pound boneless beef round steak, cut into ¼-inch strips
2 cloves garlic, minced
2 cans (15 ounces each) kidney beans, rinsed, drained
Salt and pepper, to taste

Per Serving
Net Carbohydrate (gm): 23
Calories: 314
Fat (gm): 9.4
Saturated fat (gm): 3.3
Cholesterol (mg): 46.7
Sodium (mg): 817
Protein (gm): 24.3
Carbohydrate (gm): 34

1. Combine all ingredients, except salt and pepper, in slow-cooker and stir well; cover, and cook on High 1 hour. Reduce heat to Low and cook, covered, until beef is tender, 5 to 6 hours. Season to taste with salt and pepper.

Cubed Steak Stew

6 servings

1½ pounds beef cubed steaks, cut into 2 x ½-inch strips
3 tablespoons all-purpose flour
½ teaspoon garlic powder
1 tablespoon canola oil
1 cup thinly sliced onion
1 can (14½ ounces) diced tomatoes with
    Italian herbs, undrained
1 can (8 ounces) tomato sauce
1 cup cubed (½-inch), peeled potatoes
1 package (10 ounces) frozen peas and carrots
Salt and pepper, to taste

Per Serving
Net Carbohydrate (gm): 17.7
Calories: 343
Fat (gm): 15.4
Saturated fat (gm): 4.9
Cholesterol (mg): 70.1
Sodium (mg): 546
Protein (gm): 28
Carbohydrate (gm): 22.4

1. Coat beef with combined flour and garlic powder; cook in oil in large skillet over medium-high heat until browned, about 10 minutes. Add onion, tomatoes and liquid, and tomato sauce; heat to boiling. Reduce heat and simmer, uncovered, until meat is tender, about 30 minutes, adding potatoes and peas and carrots during last 10 minutes cooking time. Season to taste with salt and pepper.

Easy Beef Stew

4 servings

1 pound beef round steak, cubed (½-inch)
1 tablespoon canola oil
1 pound mushrooms, thinly sliced
¼ cup chopped onion
1 clove garlic, minced
2 cups reduced-sodium fat-free beef broth
1 tablespoon dried Italian seasoning
1½ tablespoons cornstarch
1 cup white wine, *or* beef broth
Salt and pepper, to taste

Per Serving
Net Carbohydrate (gm): 7.4
Calories: 340
Fat (gm): 16.6
Saturated fat (gm): 5
Cholesterol (mg): 70.1
Sodium (mg): 142
Protein (gm): 29.4
Carbohydrate (gm): 8.9

1. Cook beef in oil in large skillet until brown, about 8 minutes; add mushrooms, onion, and garlic and sauté 5 minutes. Stir in beef broth and Italian seasoning; heat to boiling. Reduce heat and simmer, covered, until beef is tender, about 40 minutes.

2. Heat stew to boiling; stir in combined cornstarch and wine. Simmer until thickened, about 3 minutes. Season to taste with salt and pepper.

Italian Beef Stew with Polenta

6 servings

2 pounds lean beef stew meat, cubed (1-inch)
1 tablespoon olive oil
1½ cups chopped onions
2 cloves garlic, minced
½ cup reduced-sodium fat-free beef broth
½ cup dry red wine, *or* beef broth
1 teaspoon dried oregano leaves
1 teaspoon dried thyme leaves
1 can (14½ ounces) Italian-seasoned diced tomatoes, undrained
Salt and pepper, to taste
Basic Polenta (see p. 374)

Per Serving
Net Carbohydrate (gm): 14.2
Calories: 332
Fat (gm): 11.2
Saturated fat (gm): 3.2
Cholesterol (mg): 71.5
Sodium (mg): 424
Protein (gm): 36.1
Carbohydrate (gm): 16.4

1. Cook beef in oil in Dutch oven over medium-high heat until browned, 10 to 12 minutes. Add onions and garlic, and cook until lightly browned, 3 to 4 minutes longer. Add remaining ingredients, except salt, pepper, and Basic Polenta, and simmer, covered, 1 to 1½ hours or until beef is tender. Season to taste with salt and pepper. Serve over Basic Polenta.

Wine-Braised Beef Stew

6 servings

1½ pounds boneless beef round steak, cubed (1-inch)
2 tablespoons all-purpose flour
1 tablespoon olive oil
2 cups sliced mushrooms
1 cup chopped onion
1 cup sliced celery
1 tablespoon minced garlic
1 cup reduced-sodium fat-free beef broth
1 can (15 ounces) tomato sauce
1 cup dry red wine, *or* beef broth
½ teaspoon dry mustard
1 teaspoon dried thyme leaves
2 large bay leaves
⅛ teaspoon celery seeds
12 baby carrots
1½ cups cubed, unpeeled red potatoes
Salt and pepper, to taste

Per Serving
Net Carbohydrate (gm): 16.2
Calories: 349
Fat (gm): 15.6
Saturated fat (gm): 5.1
Cholesterol (mg): 70.1
Sodium (mg): 548
Protein (gm): 27.3
Carbohydrate (gm): 19.2

1. Toss beef with flour; cook in oil in Dutch oven over medium-high heat until browned, 8 to 10 minutes. Add mushrooms, onion, celery, and garlic; sauté until onion is tender, about 5 minutes.

2. Add broth, tomato sauce, wine, dry mustard, and herbs and heat to boiling. Transfer to oven and bake at 350 degrees, covered, until beef is tender, 1 to 1½ hours, adding carrots and potatoes during last 30 minutes. Discard bay leaves; season to taste with salt and pepper.

Easy Beef Burgundy

6 servings

2 pounds boneless beef sirloin, cubed (1½-inch)
1 can (10¾ ounces) reduced-fat cream of mushroom soup
½ package (1-ounce size) onion soup mix
½ cup Burgundy, *or* other dry red wine
½ cup water
1 pound mushrooms, sliced
8 ounces frozen pearl onions
½ cup chopped green bell pepper
½ cup cubed tomatoes
Salt and pepper, to taste

Per Serving
Net Carbohydrate (gm): 11.4
Calories: 381
Fat (gm): 19.8
Saturated fat (gm): 7.6
Cholesterol (mg): 102
Sodium (mg): 489
Protein (gm): 32.9
Carbohydrate (gm): 13.6

1. Combine beef, mushroom soup, onion soup mix, wine, and water in Dutch oven; heat to boiling. Transfer to oven and cook, covered, at 325 degrees 2 hours, stirring occasionally. Add vegetables and cook, uncovered, until meat and mushrooms are tender and sauce is thickened, about 30 minutes longer. Season to taste with salt and pepper.

Beef Bourguignon Côte d'Or

6 servings

1½ pounds beef eye of round, cubed (1½-inch)
¼ cup all-purpose flour
1 tablespoon olive oil
1 cup Burgundy wine, *or* reduced-sodium beef broth
1 cup water
1 teaspoon dried marjoram leaves
1 teaspoon dried thyme leaves
2 bay leaves
1½ cups peeled pearl onions
3 cups cubed carrots
8 ounces small whole mushrooms
Salt and pepper, to taste

Per Serving
Net Carbohydrate (gm): 12.6
Calories: 304
Fat (gm): 12.2
Saturated fat (gm): 3.9
Cholesterol (mg): 63.6
Sodium (mg): 81.7
Protein (gm): 26.3
Carbohydrate (gm): 16.2

1. Coat beef with flour; sauté in oil in Dutch oven until browned on all sides, about 10 minutes. Add wine, water, and herbs; heat to boiling.

2. Transfer Dutch oven to oven and bake, covered, at 350 degrees until beef is very tender, about 2 hours. Add vegetables during last 30 minutes of cooking time. Discard bay leaves; season to taste with salt and pepper.

Beef Da Vinci

4 servings

1½ pounds boneless beef round steak, cubed (1-inch)
1 cup chopped onion
1 cup chopped green bell pepper
¼ cup chopped shallots, *or* green onions
1 tablespoon olive oil
1 can (14½ ounces) diced tomatoes, undrained
1 teaspoon beef bouillon crystals
1 teaspoon dried oregano leaves
½ teaspoon dried basil leaves
2 teaspoon garlic powder
2 cups sliced mushrooms
Salt and pepper, to taste
¼ cup chopped Italian parsley
¼ cup grated Parmesan cheese

Per Serving
Net Carbohydrate (gm): 11.4
Calories: 444
Fat (gm): 24.4
Saturated fat (gm): 8.5
Cholesterol (mg): 109
Sodium (mg): 702
Protein (gm): 40.4
Carbohydrate (gm): 14.3

1. Sauté beef, onion, bell pepper, and shallots in oil in large skillet until meat is browned, about 10 minutes. Add remaining ingredients, except salt, pepper, parsley, and Parmesan cheese. Heat to boiling; reduce heat and simmer, covered, until meat is tender, about 1 hour. Simmer, uncovered, until sauce is thickened, about 10 minutes longer. Season to taste with salt and pepper. Spoon into serving bowl; sprinkle with parsley and cheese.

Braised Beef with Rosemary

6 servings

1 cup finely chopped onion
1 large garlic clove, minced
1 tablespoon olive oil
1½ pounds beef stew meat, cubed (1-inch)
1½ tablespoons all-purpose flour
1¾ cup reduced-sodium fat-free chicken broth
½ cup dry sherry, *or* fat-free chicken broth
1 can (15 ounces) tomato sauce
1 teaspoon dried rosemary leaves
¼ teaspoon dried thyme leaves
1 bay leaf
1 teaspoon light brown sugar
1 cup sliced carrots
1 cup sliced celery
3 cups cut (1-inch) green beans
Salt and pepper, to taste

Per Serving
Net Carbohydrate (gm): 14.7
Calories: 313
Fat (gm): 11
Saturated fat (gm): 3.4
Cholesterol (mg): 67.9
Sodium (mg): 597
Protein (gm): 29.6
Carbohydrate (gm): 19.3

1. Sauté onion and garlic in oil in Dutch oven until onion is tender, about 5 minutes; stir in meat and cook until lightly browned, about 8 minutes. Sprinkle with flour and cook 2 minutes longer.

2. Add broth, sherry, tomato sauce, herbs, and sugar; heat to boiling. Reduce heat and simmer, covered, until meat is tender, 1 to 1½ hours, adding carrots, celery, and green beans during last 30 minutes. Simmer, uncovered, until sauce thickens, about 10 minutes. Discard bay leaf; season to taste with salt and pepper.

Orange-Scented Beef Stew

6 servings

1½ pounds beef stew meat, cubed (¾-inch)
1½ tablespoons canola oil
¾ cup reduced-sodium fat-free beef broth, divided
1 cup tomato juice
1 cup orange juice
Grated rind of 1 orange
2 teaspoons cornstarch
Salt and pepper, to taste
1½ cups cooked whole wheat spinach noodles, warm

Per Serving
Net Carbohydrate (gm): 15.5
Calories: 284
Fat (gm): 11.5
Saturated fat (gm): 3.3
Cholesterol (mg): 60.6
Sodium (mg): 235
Protein (gm): 27.6
Carbohydrate (gm): 17.1

1. Cook beef in oil in Dutch oven over medium-high heat until browned, about 8 minutes. Add ½ cup broth, tomato juice, and orange juice; heat to boiling. Reduce heat and simmer, covered, until beef is tender, about 1 hour.

2. Heat stew to boiling and stir in orange rind; stir in combined cornstarch and remaining ¼ cup broth. Boil, stirring, until thickened, 1 to 2 minutes. Season to taste with salt and pepper. Serve over noodles.

Pepper Steak

4 servings

3 cups sliced green bell peppers
2 cups sliced onions
4 cloves garlic, minced
1 tablespoon olive oil
1 pound beef eye of round steak, *or*
    boneless sirloin steak, cut into 3 x ¼-inch strips
2 tablespoons all-purpose flour
1¾ cups reduced-sodium fat-free beef broth
1 tablespoon tomato paste
1 teaspoon dried Italian seasoning
½ cup water
2 tablespoons cornstarch
1½ cups quartered cherry tomatoes
1–2 tablespoons Worcestershire sauce
Salt and pepper, to taste

Per Serving
Net Carbohydrate (gm): 21.7
Calories: 323
Fat (gm): 9.7
Saturated fat (gm): 2.4
Cholesterol (mg): 49.2
Sodium (mg): 184
Protein (gm): 33.2
Carbohydrate (gm): 26.2

1. Sauté bell peppers, onions, and garlic in oil in large skillet until tender, about 8 minutes; remove from pan and reserve.

2. Coat beef with flour and add to skillet; cook over medium heat until lightly browned, 3 to 5 minutes, stirring frequently. Add broth, tomato paste, and Italian seasoning; heat to boiling. Reduce heat and simmer, covered, until beef is tender, about 45 minutes, adding reserved peppers mixture during last 10 minutes.

3. Heat pepper steak mixture to boiling. Stir in combined water and cornstarch. Boil, stirring constantly, until thickened, about 1 minute. Stir in tomatoes and simmer 2 to 3 minutes. Season to taste with Worcestershire sauce, salt, and pepper.

Variation:

Sweet-Sour Pepper Steak—Make recipe as above, substituting 1½ cups snow peas for half of the bell peppers and soy sauce for the Worcestershire sauce. Stir in ¼ cup no-sugar-added apricot preserves, ½ cup sliced water chestnuts, and 2 to 3 teaspoons cider vinegar at the end of cooking time.

Sirloin in Stroganoff Sauce

6 servings

1½ pounds beef sirloin steak, cut into 1½ x ½-inch strips
1 tablespoon butter
4 cups sliced mushrooms
½ cup sliced onion
2 cloves garlic, minced
2 tablespoons all-purpose flour
1½ cups reduced-sodium fat-free beef broth
1 teaspoon Dijon-style mustard
¼ teaspoon dried thyme leaves
½ cup sour cream
¼ cup chopped parsley
Salt and pepper, to taste
Finely chopped parsley, as garnish

Per Serving
Net Carbohydrate (gm): 5.3
Calories: 315
Fat (gm): 20.5
Saturated fat (gm): 9.1
Cholesterol (mg): 85.7
Sodium (mg): 144
Protein (gm): 25.7
Carbohydrate (gm): 6.3

1. Sauté beef in butter in large skillet to desired doneness, about 8 minutes for medium; remove from pan. Add mushrooms, onion, and garlic to skillet; sauté until tender, 5 to 8 minutes. Stir in flour and cook, stirring, 1 to 2 minutes longer.

2. Add beef broth, mustard, and thyme. Heat to boiling; reduce heat and simmer, uncovered, until sauce is thickened and flavors have combined, about 10 minutes. Stir in beef, sour cream, and parsley and cook 2 to 3 minutes. Season to taste with salt and pepper. Serve, garnished with chopped parsley.

Beef Stroganoff

6 servings

8 ounces mushrooms, sliced
½ cup chopped onion
¼ cup dried shallots
1 clove garlic, minced
1 tablespoon butter
3 tablespoons all-purpose flour
¾ cup reduced-sodium fat-free chicken broth
½ cup reduced-fat milk
1½ pounds lean beef round steak, sliced into thin strips
1 tablespoon canola oil
1 cup plain yogurt
¼ cup minced chives
Salt and pepper, to taste

Per Serving
Net Carbohydrate (gm): 9.1
Calories: 329
Fat (gm): 19.2
Saturated fat (gm): 7.3
Cholesterol (mg): 85.6
Sodium (mg): 138
Protein (gm): 28.2
Carbohydrate (gm): 9.9

1. Sauté mushrooms, onion, shallots, and garlic in butter in medium saucepan until tender, about 5 minutes. Sprinkle with flour and cook 1 minute longer. Add chicken broth and milk; heat to boiling, stirring until thickened.

2. Sauté beef in oil in large skillet until meat is browned, about 8 minutes. Add mushroom mixture and simmer, covered, until meat is tender, about 15 minutes. Stir in yogurt and chives and cook until heated through. Season to taste with salt and pepper.

Paprika-Sirloin Stew with Sour Cream

4 servings

1 cup reduced-sodium fat-free beef broth
2 cups cut (1½-inch) Italian green beans
2 cups cubed (½-inch), unpeeled red potatoes
1 cup pearl onions, peeled
2 bay leaves
1 pound boneless beef sirloin steak, cut into 1 x ¼-inch strips
1 tablespoon canola oil
1 can (14½ ounces) diced tomatoes, undrained
1 tablespoon paprika
½ cup sour cream
Salt and pepper, to taste

Per Serving
Net Carbohydrate (gm): 19.8
Calories: 404
Fat (gm): 22.7
Saturated fat (gm): 8.8
Cholesterol (mg): 83.9
Sodium (mg): 465
Protein (gm): 27.3
Carbohydrate (gm): 24

1. Heat broth, beans, potatoes, onions, and bay leaves to boiling in large saucepan; reduce heat and simmer, covered, until vegetables are tender, about 10 minutes.

2. Sauté beef in oil in large skillet until lightly browned; stir into vegetable mixture. Stir in tomatoes and liquid and paprika. Simmer, uncovered, 5 minutes or until slightly thickened. Discard bay leaves. Stir in sour cream; season to taste with salt and pepper.

Hungarian-Style Beef Stew

6 servings

1½ pounds boneless beef round steak,
   cut into ½-inch strips
1 cup finely chopped onion
1 large garlic clove, minced
1 tablespoon canola oil
1½ cups reduced-sodium fat-free beef broth
½ cup dry red wine, *or* beef broth
1 can (15 ounces) tomato sauce
1 teaspoon dried thyme leaves
1 bay leaf
1 teaspoon paprika
¼ teaspoon dry mustard
1 cup sliced carrots
1 cup sliced celery
2 cups cubed (¾-inch), unpeeled red potatoes
½ cup sour cream
Salt and pepper, to taste

Per Serving
Net Carbohydrate (gm): 15.4
Calories: 362
Fat (gm): 18.7
Saturated fat (gm): 7
Cholesterol (mg): 77.1
Sodium (mg): 571
Protein (gm): 27.3
Carbohydrate (gm): 18.5

1. Sauté beef, onion, and garlic in oil in Dutch oven until beef is browned, about 10 minutes.

2. Stir in broth, wine, tomato sauce, herbs, paprika, and dry mustard and heat to boiling; reduce heat and simmer, covered, until meat is tender, about 45 minutes, adding vegetables during last 20 minutes. Stir in sour cream and heat until hot, about 3 minutes. Discard bay leaf; season to taste with salt and pepper.

Beef and Cabbage Goulash

4 servings

1 pound boneless beef round steak, cubed (½-inch)
1 tablespoon olive oil
3 cups thin onion wedges
1 cup chopped portobello mushrooms
1 can (14½ ounces) diced tomatoes, undrained
1 tablespoon paprika
1 teaspoon unsweetened cocoa
2 cups sliced cabbage
1 tablespoon caraway seeds
Salt and pepper, to taste

Per Serving
Net Carbohydrate (gm): 13.2
Calories: 336
Fat (gm): 16.9
Saturated fat (gm): 5.3
Cholesterol (mg): 70.1
Sodium (mg): 397
Protein (gm): 27.4
Carbohydrate (gm): 18.4

1. Sauté beef in oil in large saucepan until browned, about 5 minutes; add onions and mushrooms and sauté 5 minutes longer. Add tomatoes and liquid, paprika, and cocoa and heat to boiling; reduce heat and simmer, covered, until meat is tender, about 20 minutes.

2. Stir in cabbage and caraway seeds; cook until cabbage is wilted, about 5 minutes longer. Season to taste with salt and pepper.

Hungarian Goulash

6 servings

2 pounds boneless beef round steak, cubed (½-inch)
1 cup finely chopped onion
1 teaspoon minced garlic
2 tablespoons all-purpose flour
1½ teaspoons paprika
¼ teaspoon dried thyme leaves
1 bay leaf
1 can (14½ ounces) diced tomatoes, undrained
1 cup sour cream
Salt and pepper, to taste

Per Serving
Net Carbohydrate (gm): 7.4
Calories: 390
Fat (gm): 23.9
Saturated fat (gm): 10.5
Cholesterol (mg): 107.5
Sodium (mg): 310
Protein (gm): 33.4
Carbohydrate (gm): 8.5

1. Combine beef, onion, and garlic in small Dutch oven; sprinkle with flour, paprika, and thyme and toss to coat. Stir in bay leaf and tomatoes and liquid; heat to boiling.

2. Transfer to oven and bake, covered, at 325 degrees, until beef is tender, about 1½ hours. Stir in sour cream and bake, uncovered, until hot through, about 10 minutes. Discard bay leaf; season to taste with salt and pepper.

Variation:

Triple Threat Goulash—Make recipe as above, using ¾ pound each: cubed lean beef, pork, and veal in place of the beef round steak. Add 1 teaspoon caraway seeds and ½ teaspoon dried dill weed with the flour in Step 1. Add 8 ounces sliced mushrooms with the tomatoes in Step 1.

Middle Eastern Beef and Beans

6 servings

½ cup dry Great Northern beans
1 pound beef stew meat, cubed (1-inch)
1 cup chopped onion
2 large cloves garlic, minced
1 tablespoon olive oil
3½ cups reduced-sodium fat-free beef broth
¾ cup uncooked brown rice
1 teaspoon dried thyme leaves
¼ teaspoon ground cinnamon
2 bay leaves
1½ cups diced, peeled fresh tomatoes
Salt and pepper, to taste

Per Serving
Net Carbohydrate (gm): 27.4
Calories: 320
Fat (gm): 9.8
Saturated fat (gm): 3.2
Cholesterol (mg): 41.8
Sodium (mg): 147
Protein (gm): 25.2
Carbohydrate (gm): 32.5

1. Cover beans with 2 inches water in Dutch oven and heat to boiling. Boil 2 minutes; remove from heat and let stand, covered, 1 hour. Drain.

2. Cook beef, onion, and garlic in oil in Dutch oven over medium heat until beef is browned, about 10 minutes. Add beans and remaining ingredients, except tomatoes, salt, and pepper; heat to boiling. Reduce heat and simmer, covered, until meat and beans are tender, about 1 hour, adding water if stew becomes too dry.

3. Add tomatoes; heat to boiling. Reduce heat and simmer, uncovered, until sauce is thickened, about 5 minutes. Discard bay leaves; season to taste with salt and pepper.

Greek-Style Beef and Lentil Stew

6 servings

1 cup chopped onion
1 cup chopped green bell pepper
2 teaspoons minced garlic
1 tablespoon olive oil
2 cups cubed, peeled Idaho potatoes
1 cup dry lentils
1 can (14½ ounces) diced tomatoes, undrained
3 cups reduced-sodium fat-free beef broth
1 teaspoon dried oregano leaves
1 teaspoon dried mint leaves
½ teaspoon ground turmeric
½ teaspoon ground coriander
12 ounces cooked beef eye of round, cubed (¾-inch)
1 cup sliced zucchini
½ pound cut (1-inch) green beans
Salt and pepper, to taste

Per Serving
Net Carbohydrate (gm): 24.2
Calories: 317
Fat (gm): 5.5
Saturated fat (gm): 1.4
Cholesterol (mg): 39.1
Sodium (mg): 345
Protein (gm): 30.6
Carbohydrate (gm): 37.3

1. Sauté onion, bell pepper, and garlic in oil in large saucepan until tender, about 5 minutes. Add potatoes, lentils, tomatoes and liquid, broth, herbs, and spices; heat to boiling. Reduce heat and simmer, covered, 15 minutes.

2. Add beef, zucchini, and green beans; simmer, uncovered, until lentils and vegetables are tender and stew is thickened, 10 to 15 minutes. Season to taste with salt and pepper.

West African Beef Stew

8 servings

2 pounds beef stew meat, cubed (½-inch)
1 tablespoon olive oil
1 cup chopped onion, divided
3 tablespoons tomato paste
1 teaspoon ground coriander
1 teaspoon ground cumin
1 teaspoon garlic powder
2 cups cubed tomatoes
1 tablespoon crushed red pepper
2½ cups reduced-sodium fat-free beef broth
¾ cup uncooked brown rice
1 can (15 ounces) black beans, rinsed, drained
Salt, to taste

Per Serving
Net Carbohydrate (gm): 22.5
Calories: 329
Fat (gm): 10.4
Saturated fat (gm): 3.4
Cholesterol (mg): 60.6
Sodium (mg): 340
Protein (gm): 31
Carbohydrate (gm): 26.7

1. Cook meat in oil in Dutch oven over medium-high heat until browned, about 10 minutes. Stir in ½ cup onion, tomato paste, coriander, cumin, and garlic powder; cook over low heat until onion is tender, about 5 minutes, stirring frequently.

2. Process remaining ½ cup onion, tomatoes, and red pepper in food processor until smooth. Stir into beef mixture; stir in broth and rice and heat to boiling. Reduce heat and simmer, covered, 40 minutes.

3. Stir in beans; simmer until rice and meat are tender, about 20 minutes longer. Season to taste with salt.

Curried Beef Stew With Chive Dumplings

8 servings

2 pounds beef stew meat, cubed (¾-inch)
2 tablespoons peanut, *or* canola, oil
1½ cups chopped onions
3 tablespoons all-purpose flour
1½ teaspoons curry powder
2 cups reduced-sodium fat-free beef broth
1 cup coarsely chopped, seeded tomato
1 bay leaf
Salt and pepper, to taste
1 package (10 ounces) frozen peas
Chive Dumplings (recipe follows)

Per Serving
Net Carbohydrate (gm): 24.7
Calories: 384
Fat (gm): 15.7
Saturated fat (gm): 4.8
Cholesterol (mg): 62.3
Sodium (mg): 460
Protein (gm): 31.1
Carbohydrate (gm): 28

1. Cook beef in oil in Dutch oven over medium heat until browned, about 10 minutes; add onions and cook until tender, 5 to 8 minutes. Stir in flour and curry powder and cook 1 minute longer.

2. Add broth, tomato, and bay leaf and heat to boiling; reduce heat and simmer, covered, until beef is almost tender, about 1 hour. Discard bay leaf; season to taste with salt and pepper.

3. Stir peas into stew and heat to boiling; spoon Chive Dumplings dough onto top of stew. Cook, uncovered, 10 minutes; cook, covered, 10 minutes or until dumplings are dry.

Chive Dumplings

makes 8 dumplings

1⅔ cups all-purpose baking mix
2 tablespoons finely chopped chives
¼–½ teaspoon curry powder
⅔ cup reduced-fat milk

1. Combine baking mix, chives, and curry powder in bowl; mix in milk, forming a soft dough.

Beef and Ancho Chili Stew

6 servings

4–6 ancho chilies, stems, seeds, and veins discarded
2 cups boiling water
2 cups coarsely cubed tomatoes
2 pounds boneless beef round steak, cubed (¾-inch)
1 tablespoon olive oil
1 large onion, chopped
2 cloves garlic, minced
1 teaspoon minced serrano, *or* jalapeño, chili
1 teaspoon dried oregano leaves
1 teaspoon crushed cumin seeds
2 tablespoons all-purpose flour
Salt and pepper, to taste

Per Serving
Net Carbohydrate (gm): 9
Calories: 372
Fat (gm): 20.6
Saturated fat (gm): 6.7
Cholesterol (mg): 93.4
Sodium (mg): 84
Protein (gm): 33.6
Carbohydrate (gm): 12.8

1. Place ancho chilies in bowl; pour boiling water over. Let stand until chilies are softened, about 10 minutes. Process chilies with water and tomatoes in food processor or blender until smooth.

2. Cook beef in oil in Dutch oven or large saucepan over medium-high heat until browned, about 8 minutes. Add onion, garlic, serrano chili, and herbs and cook until onion is tender, about 5 minutes. Stir in flour; cook over medium heat 1 to 2 minutes longer.

3. Add ancho chili mixture; heat to boiling. Reduce heat and simmer, covered, until beef is tender, about 45 minutes. Season to taste with salt and pepper.

Beef and Bean Tacos

8 servings

1 cup chopped poblano chili
⅓ cup chopped onion
1 clove garlic, minced
1 bay leaf, crumbled
1 teaspoon olive oil
1 can (15 ounces) pinto beans, rinsed, drained
1 can (8 ounces) tomato sauce
Salt and pepper, to taste
Beef Filling (recipe follows)
8 flour tortillas (6 inch), warm
½ cup (2 ounces) shredded Cheddar cheese
½ cup sour cream
2 tablespoons finely chopped cilantro

Per Serving
Net Carbohydrate (gm): 27.4
Calories: 336
Fat (gm): 14.3
Saturated fat (gm): 5.7
Cholesterol (mg): 44.5
Sodium (mg): 559
Protein (gm): 20.4
Carbohydrate (gm): 31.9

1. Sauté poblano chili, onion, garlic, and bay leaf in oil in large skillet until onion is tender, about 5 minutes. Add beans and tomato sauce; heat until hot. Season to taste with salt and pepper.

2. Spoon bean mixture and Beef Filling onto tortillas; top with cheese, sour cream, and cilantro. Fold over.

Beef Filling

makes about 2 cups

1 pound boneless beef eye of round
2 teaspoons olive oil
1½ cups coarsely chopped tomatoes
½ teaspoon ground cinnamon
Salt and pepper, to taste

1. Cut beef into 2-inch cubes and place in saucepan with 2 inches of water. Heat to boiling. Reduce heat and simmer, covered, until beef is tender, 15 to 20 minutes; drain. Cool slightly; shred finely with fork.

2. Sauté beef in oil in medium skillet until beginning to brown, 3 to 4 minutes. Add tomatoes and cinnamon; cook until tomatoes are wilted. Season to taste with salt and pepper.

Beef and Vegetable Enchiladas

6 servings

2 cups chopped zucchini
1½ cups chopped tomatoes
½ cup chopped poblano chili, *or* green bell pepper
¼ cup thinly sliced green onions and tops
4 cloves garlic, minced
1 teaspoon minced jalapeño chili
1 teaspoon dried oregano leaves
1–2 teaspoons ground cumin
2 teaspoons olive oil
1½ pounds beef eye of round steak cooked, shredded
Salt and pepper, to taste
12 corn tortillas (6 inch)
Enchilada Sauce (recipe follows)
½ cup (2 ounces) shredded Cheddar cheese
3 tablespoons finely chopped cilantro

Per Serving
Net Carbohydrate (gm): 29.7
Calories: 415
Fat (gm): 17.1
Saturated fat (gm): 6.1
Cholesterol (mg): 73.5
Sodium (mg): 206
Protein (gm): 31.4
Carbohydrate (gm): 35.7

1. Sauté vegetables and herbs in oil in large skillet until vegetables are tender, about 10 minutes. Add beef; cook over medium heat until no excess juices remain, 5 to 8 minutes. Season to taste with salt and pepper.

2. Dip tortillas in Enchilada Sauce to coat lightly and fill each with about ⅓ cup beef mixture; roll up and place, seam sides down, in large baking pan. Spoon remaining Enchilada Sauce over enchiladas; sprinkle with cheese.

3. Bake enchiladas, uncovered, at 350 degrees 15 to 20 minutes. Sprinkle with cilantro.

Enchilada Sauce

makes about 2 cups

1 ancho chili, stem, seeds, and veins discarded
1½ cups chopped tomatoes
1 cup chopped red bell pepper
½ cup sliced green onions and tops
2 cloves garlic
½ teaspoon dried marjoram leaves
1 teaspoon olive oil
Salt, to taste

1. Cover ancho chili with boiling water in small bowl; let stand until softened, about 10 minutes. Drain. Process ancho chili and remaining ingredients, except oil and salt, in food processor or blender until almost smooth.

2. Cook tomato mixture in oil in large skillet over medium heat until thickened to a medium consistency, about 5 minutes. Season to taste with salt.

Mexican Hash

4 servings

1 pound boneless beef round steak, cubed (½-inch)
1 quart water
1 tablespoon olive oil
1 cup chopped tomato
2 cups chopped poblano chilies, *or* green bell peppers
¾ cup chopped onion
2 cups cubed (½-inch), peeled and cooked Idaho potatoes
Chili powder, to taste
Salt and pepper, to taste

Per Serving
Net Carbohydrate (gm): 22
Calories: 382
Fat (gm): 20.1
Saturated fat (gm): 7.1
Cholesterol (mg): 71.2
Sodium (mg): 65
Protein (gm): 26
Carbohydrate (gm): 24.6

1. Heat beef cubes and water to boiling in large saucepan; reduce heat and simmer, covered, until beef is tender, 30 to 45 minutes. Drain; shred beef.

2. Cook beef in oil in large skillet over medium-high heat until beginning to brown and crisp, about 5 minutes. Add tomato; cook over medium heat 5 minutes longer. Remove mixture from skillet and reserve.

3. Add poblano chilies and onion to skillet; cook until tender, 5 to 8 minutes. Add potatoes and cook until browned, about 5 minutes. Add reserved meat mixture to skillet; cook until hot, 3 to 4 minutes. Season to taste with chili powder, salt, and pepper.

Home-Style Meat Loaf

6 servings

1½ pounds extra-lean ground beef
1 cup quick-cooking oats
½ cup reduced-fat milk
½ cup chopped onion
¼ cup chopped green bell pepper
¼ cup catsup, *or* chili sauce
1 egg
1 clove garlic, minced
1 teaspoon dried Italian seasoning
¾ teaspoon salt
½ teaspoon pepper

Per Serving
Net Carbohydrate (gm): 12.9
Calories: 340
Fat (gm): 19.9
Saturated fat (gm): 7.5
Cholesterol (mg): 113.4
Sodium (mg): 506
Protein (gm): 25.2
Carbohydrate (gm): 14.7

1. Mix all ingredients in large bowl until well blended.

2. Pat mixture into ungreased loaf pan, 9 x 5 inches, or shape into a loaf in baking pan. Bake at 350 degrees until juices run clear and meat thermometer registers 170 degrees, about 1 hour. Let stand in pan 5 minutes; remove to serving plate.

Variations:

Stuffed Green Peppers—Cut 6 medium green bell peppers lengthwise into halves; discard seeds. Cook peppers in boiling water 3 minutes; drain well on paper toweling. Make meat mixture as above, substituting 1 cup cooked brown rice for the oats and tomato sauce for the catsup. Fill peppers with beef mixture and place in baking pan. Bake, covered, at 350 degrees until beef mixture is no longer pink in the center, about 45 minutes. Serve with tomato sauce, if desired.

Italian Meat Loaf—Make recipe as above, adding ¼ cup grated Parmesan cheese, ⅓ cup shredded mozzarella cheese, and 2 tablespoons chopped, pitted ripe olives to meat mixture. After baking, spread meat loaf with 2 tablespoons seasoned tomato sauce and sprinkle with 2 tablespoons each, Parmesan and shredded mozzarella cheeses. Let stand, loosely covered, 10 minutes.

Savory Cheese Meat Loaf—Make recipe as above, substituting ½ pound ground lean pork for ½ pound of the beef, and adding 1 package (3 ounces) cream cheese, ½ cup shredded Cheddar cheese, and 2 tablespoons Worcestershire sauce to meat mixture. Spread top of loaf with ¼ cup of catsup before baking. Sprinkle ¼ cup shredded Cheddar cheese on top of meat loaf after baking. Let stand, loosely covered, 10 minutes.

Chutney-Peanut Meat Loaf—Make recipe as above, substituting ½ cup chopped mango chutney for the catsup and adding ⅓ cup chopped peanuts, 1 teaspoon curry powder, and ¼ teaspoon ground ginger to meat mixture.

Mushroom Meat Loaf—Sauté 1½ cups sliced mushrooms with the onion, bell pepper, and garlic in 1 teaspoon olive oil in large skillet until browned, about 5 minutes; cool slightly. Add mushroom mixture and 1 to 2 teaspoons prepared horseradish to meat mixture.

Lemon Meat Loaf

6 servings

1½ pounds extra-lean ground beef
1 cup fresh whole wheat bread crumbs
1 egg
½ cup chopped onion
¼ cup chopped green bell pepper
1 clove garlic, minced
1 tablespoon lemon juice
1 tablespoon grated lemon rind
1 teaspoon Dijon mustard
½ teaspoon dried savory leaves
¾ teaspoon salt
½ teaspoon pepper
Egg Lemon Sauce (recipe follows)

Per Serving
Net Carbohydrate (gm): 8.8
Calories: 347
Fat (gm): 22.2
Saturated fat (gm): 8.9
Cholesterol (mg): 156.4
Sodium (mg): 499
Protein (gm): 25.8
Carbohydrate (gm): 9.7

1. Mix all ingredients, except Egg Lemon Sauce, in large bowl until well blended.

2. Pat mixture into ungreased loaf pan, 9 x 5 inches, or shape into a loaf in baking pan. Bake at 350 degrees until juices run clear and meat thermometer registers 170 degrees, about 1 hour. Let stand in pan 5 minutes; remove to serving plate. Serve with Egg Lemon Sauce.

Egg Lemon Sauce

makes about 1¼ cups

1 tablespoon butter
2 tablespoons all-purpose flour
½ cup reduced-sodium fat-free chicken broth
½ cup reduced-fat milk
1 egg, lightly beaten
2–3 tablespoons lemon juice
1 teaspoon grated lemon rind
Salt and white pepper, to taste

1. Melt butter in medium saucepan; whisk in flour and cook, whisking constantly, over medium heat 2 minutes. Whisk in broth and milk and cook over medium heat until mixture boils and thickens, about 3 minutes.

2. Whisk about ½ of the broth mixture into the egg; whisk mixture back into saucepan. Whisk constantly over medium heat 1 minute; do not boil. Add lemon juice and rind; season to taste with salt and white pepper.

Variation:

Sweet-Sour Ham Loaf—Make recipe as above, substituting ½ pound ground cooked ham for ½ pound of the ground beef and omitting lemon juice, lemon rind, savory, and Egg Lemon Sauce. Add 2 sweet pickles, chopped, ⅓ cup coarsely chopped almonds, ¼ cup chopped mixed dried fruit, ⅓ cup no-sugar-added apricot preserves, 2 tablespoons catsup, 1 tablespoon cider vinegar, and 2 teaspoons soy sauce to the mixture in Step 1.

All-American Meat Loaf

8 servings

1 pound extra-lean ground beef
1 pound ground turkey
1½ cups quick cooking oats
1 can (10¾ ounces) tomato soup
½ cup chili sauce
½ cup plain yogurt
½ cup chopped parsley
2 tablespoons dried onions
1 egg
2 tablespoons Worcestershire sauce
1 tablespoon garlic powder
¼ teaspoon ground allspice
¼ teaspoon pepper

Per Serving
Net Carbohydrate (gm): 20.4
Calories: 339
Fat (gm): 15.6
Saturated fat (gm): 5.2
Cholesterol (mg): 110.5
Sodium (mg): 547
Protein (gm): 25.6
Carbohydrate (gm): 23.7

1. Combine all ingredients in large bowl, mixing well. Shape into loaf in greased 13 x 9-inch baking pan.

2. Bake at 350 degrees, loosely covered, until loaf is no longer pink in the center, about 1 hour.

Microwave Meat Loaf

4 servings

1 pound extra-lean ground beef
¼ cup chopped green bell pepper
¼ cup chopped red bell pepper
¼ cup chopped onion
3 cloves garlic, minced
½ cup whole wheat bread crumbs
1 tablespoon soy sauce
1 tablespoon prepared mustard
¼ teaspoon salt
¼ teaspoon pepper
1 large dill pickle, chopped

Per Serving
Net Carbohydrate (gm): 5.5
Calories: 284
Fat (gm): 18.2
Saturated fat (gm): 7
Cholesterol (mg): 76.4
Sodium (mg): 764
Protein (gm): 22.6
Carbohydrate (gm): 6.8

1. Mix all ingredients in medium bowl; shape into round loaf, about 2 inches high, in 9-inch pie plate. Cover loosely with waxed paper. Microwave on high 3 to 4 minutes. Rotate plate and microwave on high until meat loaf is no longer pink in the center, 3 to 4 minutes more.

Beef and Rice-Stuffed Peppers

6 servings

1½ pounds extra-lean ground beef
1 can (14 ounces) diced tomatoes, drained
1 cup uncooked instant brown rice
½ teaspoon celery salt
1 teaspoon Worcestershire sauce
¼ teaspoon garlic powder
6 large green bell peppers, halved lengthwise, seeded

Per Serving
Net Carbohydrate (gm): 30.1
Calories: 411
Fat (gm): 18.7
Saturated fat (gm): 7.1
Cholesterol (mg): 76.3
Sodium (mg): 313
Protein (gm): 25.3
Carbohydrate (gm): 33.9

1. Mix ground beef, tomatoes, rice, celery salt, Worcestershire sauce, and garlic powder in large bowl until well blended.

2. Fill peppers with meat mixture; place in lightly greased 13 x 9-inch baking dish. Bake, covered, at 350 degrees until beef is cooked and peppers are very tender, about 45 minutes.

Grilled Stuffed Peppers

4 servings

1 pound lean ground beef
½ cup unseasoned dry bread crumbs
1 teaspoon ground ginger
3 cloves garlic, minced
½–1 teaspoon salt
¼ teaspoon pepper
⅔ cup finely chopped onion
¼ cup dry white wine, *or* milk
1–2 tablespoons light soy sauce
4 large red, *or* green, bell peppers, halved lengthwise, seeded

Per Serving
Net Carbohydrate (gm): 21.4
Calories: 363
Fat (gm): 18.6
Saturated fat (gm): 7.1
Cholesterol (mg): 76.3
Sodium (mg): 630
Protein (gm): 24.7
Carbohydrate (gm): 21.3

1. Combine all ingredients, except bell peppers, in medium bowl. Spoon beef mixture into pepper halves. Place on grill, meat sides down, and grill 3 to 4 minutes. Turn peppers and grill until meat is no longer pink in the center, 5 to 8 minutes (peppers will be charred). Or, broil 6 inches from heat source, meat sides down, until peppers are charred; turn and broil until meat is no longer pink in the center, about 5 minutes.

Salisbury Steaks with Mushroom Gravy

4 servings

1 pound extra-lean ground beef
2–4 tablespoons finely chopped onion
3 tablespoons water
½ teaspoon salt
¼ teaspoon pepper
2 teaspoons canola oil
Mushroom Gravy (recipe follows)

Per Serving
Net Carbohydrate (gm): 4.5
Calories: 326
Fat (gm): 23
Saturated fat (gm): 8.9
Cholesterol (mg): 84.6
Sodium (mg): 438
Protein (gm): 23.6
Carbohydrate (gm): 5.1

1. Mix ground beef, onion, water, salt, and pepper in medium bowl just until blended. Shape mixture into four oval patties.

2. Cook Salisbury steaks in oil in large skillet over medium heat to desired degree of doneness, 3 to 4 minutes per side for medium. Serve with Mushroom Gravy.

Mushroom Gravy

makes about 1¼ cups

1 cup sliced mushrooms
¼ cup finely chopped onion
1 tablespoon butter
2 tablespoons all-purpose flour
1 cup reduced-sodium fat-free beef broth
Salt and pepper, to taste

1. Sauté mushrooms and onion in butter in medium skillet until tender, about 5 minutes. Stir in flour; cook 1 to 2 minutes longer.

2. Add beef broth and heat to boiling; boil, stirring constantly, until thickened. Season to taste with salt and pepper.

Swedish Meatballs with Cream Gravy

4 servings

1 pound extra-lean ground beef
½ cup finely chopped onion
½ cup unseasoned dry bread crumbs
⅓ cup reduced-fat milk
1 egg
1 tablespoon minced parsley leaves
½–1 teaspoon dried dill weed
¼ teaspoon ground allspice
Pinch ground cardamom
½ teaspoon salt
⅛ teaspoon pepper
Cream Gravy (recipe follows)
Finely chopped fresh dill weed, *or* parsley, as garnish

Per Serving
Net Carbohydrate (gm): 17.5
Calories: 422
Fat (gm): 25.5
Saturated fat (gm): 11.1
Cholesterol (mg): 146.8
Sodium (mg): 669
Protein (gm): 28
Carbohydrate (gm): 18.4

1. Combine all ingredients, except Cream Gravy and fresh dill weed, in medium bowl; shape mixture into 24 meatballs. Bake meatballs in baking pan at 425 degrees until browned and no longer pink in the center, 15 to 20 minutes.

2. Arrange meatballs in serving bowl; pour Cream Gravy over and sprinkle with fresh dill weed.

Cream Gravy

makes about 1 cup

1 tablespoon butter
1½ tablespoons all-purpose flour
1 cup reduced-fat milk
½ teaspoon beef bouillon crystals
2 tablespoons sour cream
Salt and pepper, to taste

1. Melt butter in medium saucepan; stir in flour and cook over medium-low heat 1 minute, stirring constantly. Whisk in milk and bouillon crystals; heat to boiling. Boil, stirring constantly, until thickened, about 1 minute. Stir in sour cream and cook 1 to 2 minutes; season to taste with salt and pepper.

Meatballs 'n Pasta

4 servings

1 pound lean ground beef
1 egg, lightly beaten
¾ cup quick-cooking oats
3 tablespoons minced dried onions, divided
2 teaspoons Italian seasoning, divided
½ cup grated Romano cheese
1 can (15 ounces) diced tomatoes, undrained
1½ quarts reduced-sodium fat-free beef broth
2 ounces whole wheat rotini
2 cups small broccoli florets
2 cups cubed zucchini
Salt and pepper, to taste

Per Serving
Net Carbohydrate (gm): 24.3
Calories: 510
Fat (gm): 26.4
Saturated fat (gm): 10.5
Cholesterol (mg): 145.8
Sodium (mg): 811
Protein (gm): 39.4
Carbohydrate (gm): 29.5

1. Combine beef, egg, oats, 1 tablespoon onions, ½ teaspoon Italian seasoning, and Romano cheese in a bowl. Shape mixture into 16 meatballs. Cook meatballs in Dutch oven until brown on all sides, about 10 minutes.

2. Stir in tomatoes and liquid, broth, remaining 2 tablespoons onions and 1½ teaspoons Italian seasoning and heat to boiling. Reduce heat and simmer, uncovered, 5 minutes. Add rotini, broccoli, and zucchini; heat to boiling. Reduce heat and simmer, uncovered, 10 minutes or until pasta is *al dente*. Season to taste with salt and pepper.

Hearty Meatball 'n Veggie Stew

6 servings

Hearty Meatballs (recipe follows)
1 tablespoon olive, *or* canola, oil
1½ cups reduced-sodium fat-free beef broth
1 can (28 ounces) diced tomatoes, undrained
1½ teaspoons dried Italian seasoning
3 cups cubed zucchini
1 cup sliced carrots
½ cup frozen peas
2 tablespoons cornstarch
¼ cup cold water
Salt and pepper, to taste

Per Serving
Net Carbohydrate (gm): 17
Calories: 362
Fat (gm): 17.9
Saturated fat (gm): 6.2
Cholesterol (mg): 101.7
Sodium (mg): 967
Protein (gm): 28.5
Carbohydrate (gm): 20.3

1. Cook Hearty Meatballs in oil in Dutch oven over medium heat until browned, 5 to 8 minutes.

2. Add broth, tomatoes and liquid, and Italian seasoning; heat to boiling. Reduce heat and simmer, covered, 30 minutes, adding zucchini, carrots, and peas during last 15 minutes of cooking time.

3. Heat stew to boiling; stir in combined cornstarch and cold water. Boil, stirring, until stew is thickened, about 1 minute. Season to taste with salt and pepper.

Hearty Meatballs

makes 24

1½ pounds lean ground beef
⅓ cup finely chopped onion
1 egg
½ cup unseasoned dry bread crumbs
2 cloves garlic, minced
1–2 teaspoons beef bouillon crystals
½ teaspoon salt
¼ teaspoon pepper

1. Mix all ingredients; shape mixture into 24 meatballs.

Meatballs in Tomato Chili Sauce

4 servings

½ pound ground pork
½ pound extra-lean ground beef
1 egg
¼ cup unseasoned dry bread crumbs
½ cup finely chopped zucchini
¼ cup finely chopped onion
2 cloves garlic, minced
1 teaspoon minced jalapeño chili
½ teaspoon dried oregano leaves
¼ teaspoon dried thyme leaves
½ teaspoon salt
⅛ teaspoon pepper
1–2 pasilla chilies
1 teaspoon olive oil
1 can (28 ounces) diced tomatoes, undrained

Per Serving
Net Carbohydrate (gm): 11.7
Calories: 382
Fat (gm): 23.3
Saturated fat (gm): 8.4
Cholesterol (mg): 131.6
Sodium (mg): 748
Protein (gm): 24.9
Carbohydrate (gm): 14.5

1. Mix pork, beef, egg, bread crumbs, zucchini, onion, garlic, jalapeño chili, oregano, thyme, salt, and pepper. Shape mixture into 16 meatballs.

2. Cook pasilla chilies in oil in small skillet over medium heat until softened; discard stems, seeds, and veins. Process chilies and tomatoes with liquid in blender until smooth.

3. Heat tomato mixture to boiling in large saucepan; add meatballs. Reduce heat and simmer, covered, until meatballs are cooked and no longer pink in the center, about 10 minutes.

Ground Beef and Vegetables Stroganoff

8 servings

1½ pounds extra-lean ground beef
1½ cups thinly sliced onions
12 ounces mixed wild mushrooms
    (shiitake, oyster, enoki, cremini), sliced
2 cloves garlic, minced
¼ cup dry red wine, *or* beef broth
12 ounces broccoli florets and sliced stalks
1 cup light cream
2 tablespoons all-purpose flour
1½ teaspoons Dijon mustard
1 cup sour cream
½ teaspoon dried dill weed
Salt and white pepper, to taste

Per Serving
Net Carbohydrate (gm): 12.1
Calories: 358
Fat (gm): 24.3
Saturated fat (gm): 11.9
Cholesterol (mg): 87.6
Sodium (mg): 117
Protein (gm): 20
Carbohydrate (gm): 14.9

1. Cook ground beef in large skillet until browned, about 10 minutes; drain well. Add onions, mushrooms, and garlic to skillet and sauté until softened, about 5 minutes. Add wine and broccoli; heat to boiling. Reduce heat and simmer, covered, until broccoli is tender, 8 to 10 minutes.

2. Mix cream, flour, and mustard; stir into skillet. Heat to boiling; boil, stirring constantly, until thickened, about 1 minute. Reduce heat to low; stir in sour cream and dill weed and cook 1 to 2 minutes longer. Season to taste with salt and white pepper.

Ground Beef Goulash

6 servings (about 1⅓ cups each)

1½ pounds extra-lean ground beef
1 tablespoon canola oil
1½ cups chopped onions
1 cup chopped green bell pepper
1 cup chopped red bell pepper
2 cloves garlic, minced
1 tablespoon all-purpose flour
2 teaspoons paprika
1 teaspoon crushed caraway seeds
¾ cup water
1 can (14 ounces) sauerkraut, rinsed, drained
1 cup coarsely chopped tomato
1 cup sour cream
Salt and pepper, to taste
Minced parsley, as garnish

Per Serving
Net Carbohydrate (gm): 10.1
Calories: 395
Fat (gm): 27.1
Saturated fat (gm): 11.3
Cholesterol (mg): 90.4
Sodium (mg): 534
Protein (gm): 24.4
Carbohydrate (gm): 14.1

1. Cook ground beef in oil in large skillet until browned, about 8 minutes; add onions, bell peppers, and garlic and cook until onions are tender, about 8 minutes longer. Stir in flour, paprika, and caraway seeds; cook 1 to 2 minutes longer. Stir in water, sauerkraut, tomato, and sour cream; season to taste with salt and pepper.

2. Spoon mixture into 2-quart casserole. Bake, covered, at 350 degrees until hot and bubbly, 20 to 30 minutes. Sprinkle with parsley.

Corned Beef and Red Cabbage Stew

4 servings

12 ounces cubed (½-inch) cooked lean corned beef
1½ cups cubed (½-inch), unpeeled red potatoes
1½ cups sliced carrots
1 cup cubed (½-inch) turnips
1 can (14½ ounces) reduced-sodium
    fat-free chicken broth, divided
1 tablespoon apple cider vinegar
1 teaspoon pickling spice
1 pound red cabbage, coarsely sliced
1½ tablespoons all-purpose flour
Salt and pepper, to taste

Per Serving
Net Carbohydrate (gm): 19.9
Calories: 476
Fat (gm): 22
Saturated fat (gm): 5.4
Cholesterol (mg): 173.9
Sodium (mg): 1934
Protein (gm): 43.9
Carbohydrate (gm): 23.8

1. Combine corned beef, potatoes, carrots, turnips, 1¼ cups broth, vinegar, and pickling spice in large saucepan. Heat to boiling; reduce heat and simmer, covered, 10 minutes.

2. Add cabbage; simmer until vegetables are tender, about 5 minutes. Heat stew to boiling; stir in combined remaining ½ cup broth and flour. Boil, stirring, until thickened, about 1 minute. Season to taste with salt and pepper.

Veal Marsala with Mushrooms

4 servings

1½ pounds veal scaloppini, pounded thin
1 teaspoon dried rosemary leaves
Salt and pepper, to taste
1 tablespoon olive oil
3 cups sliced mushrooms
2 cloves garlic, minced
1 teaspoon cornstarch
⅓ cup reduced-sodium fat-free chicken broth
½ cup dry Marsala wine

Per Serving
Net Carbohydrate (gm): 3.1
Calories: 255
Fat (gm): 6.6
Saturated fat (gm): 1.4
Cholesterol (mg): 134.6
Sodium (mg): 117
Protein (gm): 38.5
Carbohydrate (gm): 3.9

1. Sprinkle veal with rosemary, salt, and pepper. Sauté veal in oil in large skillet until browned, 2 to 3 minutes on each side. Remove from skillet.

2. Add mushrooms and garlic to skillet; sauté until lightly browned, about 5 minutes. Stir in combined cornstarch, chicken broth, and wine; heat to boiling. Reduce heat and simmer, stirring, until thickened, 1 to 2 minutes. Return veal to skillet; cook until hot through, 1 to 2 minutes.

Veal Peperonata

4 servings

1½ pounds veal scaloppini, pounded thin
¼ cup all-purpose flour
1 tablespoon olive oil
2 cups thinly sliced red, yellow, and green bell peppers
3 cloves garlic, minced
1 tablespoon minced fresh, *or*
    1 teaspoon dried, basil leaves
1 teaspoon chopped fresh, *or* ½ teaspoon dried, rosemary leaves
1 teaspoon fresh, *or* ½ teaspoon dried, thyme leaves
1½ cups chopped, peeled and seeded tomatoes
1 cup reduced-sodium fat-free beef broth
½ cup dry red wine, *or* beef broth
6 pitted black olives, sliced
2 tablespoons lemon juice
Salt and pepper, to taste

Per Serving
Net Carbohydrate (gm): 13.6
Calories: 313
Fat (gm): 7.5
Saturated fat (gm): 1.5
Cholesterol (mg): 132.6
Sodium (mg): 200
Protein (gm): 39.8
Carbohydrate (gm): 16.3

1. Coat veal with flour. Sauté veal in oil in large skillet until browned, 2 to 3 minutes on each side; remove from skillet. Add bell peppers, garlic, and herbs to skillet; sauté until peppers are tender, 5 to 8 minutes. Remove from skillet.

2. Add tomatoes, broth, wine, and olives to skillet; heat to boiling. Reduce heat and simmer, uncovered, until thickened to a sauce consistency, about 10 minutes. Return veal and peppers to skillet; stir in lemon juice and season to taste with salt and pepper.

Veal with Honey-Dijon Mushrooms

4 servings

1½ pounds veal scaloppini, pounded thin
¼ cup all-purpose flour
Salt and pepper, to taste
1 tablespoon olive oil
Honey-Dijon Mushrooms (recipe follows)

Per Serving
Net Carbohydrate (gm): 19.1
Calories: 358
Fat (gm): 10.2
Saturated fat (gm): 1.8
Cholesterol (mg): 137.3
Sodium (mg): 203
Protein (gm): 40
Carbohydrate (gm): 20.4

1. Coat veal with flour; sprinkle lightly with salt and pepper. Sauté veal in oil in large skillet until browned, 2 to 3 minutes on each side. Spoon Honey-Dijon Mushrooms over veal; simmer until veal is cooked through, 3 to 4 minutes. Arrange veal on platter; spoon mushrooms over.

Honey-Dijon Mushrooms

makes about 1½ cups

2 cups sliced mushrooms
½ cup chopped onion
1 tablespoon olive oil
2 teaspoons all-purpose flour
¾ cup reduced-sodium fat-free chicken broth
½ cup dry white wine, *or* chicken broth
3 tablespoons lemon juice
2 tablespoons honey
2 teaspoons Dijon mustard
¼ cup minced chives
¼ cup chopped parsley
Salt and pepper, to taste

1. Sauté mushrooms and onion in oil in large skillet until tender, about 5 minutes. Sprinkle with flour and cook 1 minute more. Add broth, wine, lemon juice, honey, and mustard. Heat to boiling; boil, uncovered, until slightly thickened, about 5 minutes. Stir in chives and parsley; season to taste with salt and pepper.

Veal Piccata

4 servings

1½ pounds veal scaloppini, pounded thin
¼ cup all-purpose flour
1 tablespoon olive oil
1½ cups sliced mushrooms
½ cup dry white wine, *or* chicken broth
3 tablespoons lemon juice
3 tablespoons chopped fresh parsley
Salt and pepper, to taste

Per Serving
Net Carbohydrate (gm): 7.8
Calories: 270
Fat (gm): 6.5
Saturated fat (gm): 1.3
Cholesterol (mg): 132.6
Sodium (mg): 97
Protein (gm): 37.9
Carbohydrate (gm): 8.4

1. Coat veal with flour. Sauté in oil in large skillet until browned, about 2 minutes on each side; remove veal from skillet. Add mushrooms to skillet and sauté 3 to 4 minutes. Add wine and lemon juice and heat to boiling; return veal to skillet. Reduce heat and simmer until veal is tender and sauce is slightly thickened, 2 to 3 minutes. Sprinkle with parsley; season to taste with salt and pepper.

Veal and Mushroom Roulade

6 servings

1 pound mushrooms, sliced
1 cup sliced onion
2 cloves garlic, minced
2 tablespoons olive oil, divided
Salt and pepper, to taste
6 veal scaloppini (2 pounds), pounded thin
1 cup dry white wine, *or* chicken broth
1 cup reduced-sodium fat-free chicken broth

Per Serving
Net Carbohydrate (gm): 3.5
Calories: 266
Fat (gm): 7.6
Saturated fat (gm): 1.4
Cholesterol (mg): 122
Sodium (mg): 130
Protein (gm): 35.9
Carbohydrate (gm): 6

1. Sauté mushrooms, onion, and garlic in 1 tablespoon oil in large skillet until tender, 6 to 8 minutes. Season to taste with salt and pepper.

2. Sprinkle veal lightly with salt and pepper. Divide mushroom mixture among veal scallops and roll up, tying with kitchen string. Sauté rolls in remaining 1 tablespoon oil until browned on all sides, 3 to 4 minutes. Add wine and broth to skillet and heat to boiling; reduce heat and simmer, covered, 10 to 15 minutes or until veal is tender.

Herbed Veal Chops

6 servings

6 veal chops (about 8 ounces each)
1 tablespoon olive oil
½ cup dry white wine, *or* chicken broth
2 tablespoons minced parsley
½ teaspoon dried basil leaves
½ teaspoon dried sage leaves
Salt and pepper, to taste

Per Serving
Net Carbohydrate (gm): 0.2
Calories: 222
Fat (gm): 6.8
Saturated fat (gm): 1.6
Cholesterol (mg): 140.8
Sodium (mg): 119
Protein (gm): 34.4
Carbohydrate (gm): 0.3

1. Cook veal chops in oil in large skillet over medium-high heat until browned, 2 to 3 minutes on each side. Reduce heat to low and cook 8 minutes, turning several times. Add wine and herbs and heat to boiling; reduce heat and simmer, covered, until chops are tender, about 10 minutes more. Season to taste with salt and pepper. Arrange chops on platter; spoon wine mixture over.

Braised Veal Chops Milano

4 servings

4 veal chops (9 ounces each)
1 tablespoon butter
1 cup chopped onion
1 pound mushrooms, sliced
1 tablespoon all-purpose flour
1 tablespoon tomato paste
¾ cup reduced-sodium fat-free chicken broth
½ cup dry white wine, *or* chicken broth
1 teaspoon dried Italian seasoning
1 small bay leaf
½ cup sliced black olives
Salt and pepper, to taste
2 tablespoons minced parsley

Per Serving
Net Carbohydrate (gm): 10.4
Calories: 418
Fat (gm): 12.5
Saturated fat (gm): 4.1
Cholesterol (mg): 224.1
Sodium (mg): 441
Protein (gm): 57.4
Carbohydrate (gm): 13.4

1. Cook veal chops in butter in large skillet over high heat until browned, about 3 minutes on each side; transfer to shallow baking dish. In same skillet, sauté onion and mushrooms until tender, about 5 minutes; stir in flour and cook 2 to 3 minutes longer. Stir in remaining ingredients, except salt, pepper, and parsley, and heat to boiling. Reduce heat and simmer, covered, 5 minutes. Season to taste with salt and pepper.

2. Pour sauce over veal in baking dish. Bake, uncovered, at 325 degrees until veal is tender, about 20 minutes. Sprinkle with parsley.

Veal Sauvignon and Swiss Chard Ragout

4 servings

1½ pounds veal cutlets, fat trimmed,
    cut into 2 x ¼-inch strips
1 tablespoon olive oil
1 cup thinly sliced onion
1 teaspoon minced garlic
1 cup Sauvignon blanc, *or* other dry white wine
1 tablespoon tomato paste
1 teaspoon dried marjoram leaves
3 cups sliced Swiss chard, *or* spinach leaves
2 cups small cauliflower florets
Salt and pepper, to taste

Per Serving
Net Carbohydrate (gm): 6
Calories: 302
Fat (gm): 9
Saturated fat (gm): 2.1
Cholesterol (mg): 135.8
Sodium (mg): 233
Protein (gm): 36.5
Carbohydrate (gm): 8.6

1. Sauté veal in oil in large skillet until lightly browned, about 5 minutes; add onion and garlic and sauté until onion is tender, about 5 minutes longer.

2. Add wine, tomato paste, and marjoram and heat to boiling; reduce heat and simmer, covered, until veal is tender, about 10 minutes, adding Swiss chard and cauliflower during last 5 minutes. Season to taste with salt and pepper.

Wine-Braised Veal

4 servings

1½ pounds boneless veal loin, cut into 2 x ½ -inch strips
1 cup chopped onion
1 large garlic clove, minced
1 tablespoon olive oil
1 cup dry white wine
½ cup tomato sauce
½ teaspoon dried thyme leaves
Salt and pepper, to taste

Per Serving
Net Carbohydrate (gm): 5.3
Calories: 291
Fat (gm): 8.9
Saturated fat (gm): 2.1
Cholesterol (mg): 135.8
Sodium (mg): 313
Protein (gm): 35.3
Carbohydrate (gm): 6.5

1. Sauté veal, onion, and garlic in oil until browned, about 8 minutes. Add remaining ingredients, except salt and pepper, and heat to boiling; reduce heat and simmer, covered, until veal is tender, about 10 minutes. Season to taste with salt and pepper.

Veal and Vegetables Paprikash

6 servings

1½ pounds veal scaloppini, cut into 1-inch strips
1 tablespoon butter
3 cups thinly sliced cabbage
1½ cups sliced mushrooms
1 cup chopped onion
1 cup sliced zucchini
1 cup chopped, seeded tomatoes
¼ cup all-purpose flour
1 tablespoon paprika
1 cup reduced-sodium fat-free chicken broth
¾ cup sour cream
Salt and pepper, to taste

Per Serving
Net Carbohydrate (gm): 10.4
Calories: 262
Fat (gm): 11.3
Saturated fat (gm): 5.5
Cholesterol (mg): 110.7
Sodium (mg): 170
Protein (gm): 27.3
Carbohydrate (gm): 13

1. Cook veal in butter in large skillet until browned, 3 to 5 minutes; add vegetables and combined flour, paprika, and broth. Heat to boiling; reduce heat and simmer, covered, until veal is cooked and vegetables are tender, about 10 minutes. Stir in sour cream; season to taste with salt and pepper.

Veal Stew with Mushroom Sour Cream Sauce

8 servings

2 pounds boneless veal loin, cubed (1-inch)
3 cloves garlic, minced
1 teaspoon caraway seeds, crushed
¾ teaspoon anise seeds, crushed
2 bay leaves
1 cup reduced-sodium fat-free chicken broth
½ cup dry white wine, *or* chicken broth
1 small head cabbage, cut into 8 wedges
3 leeks (white parts only), cut into 1-inch pieces
Salt and pepper, to taste
8 ounces mushrooms, sliced
2 teaspoons butter
1 tablespoon all-purpose flour
½ cup sour cream
¼ cup chopped parsley

Per Serving
Net Carbohydrate (gm): 10.4
Calories: 276
Fat (gm): 8.8
Saturated fat (gm): 3.6
Cholesterol (mg): 124.3
Sodium (mg): 181
Protein (gm): 33.2
Carbohydrate (gm): 14.3

1. Combine veal, garlic, herbs, chicken broth, and wine in large Dutch oven; heat to boiling. Reduce heat and simmer, covered, until veal is very tender, about 1 hour, adding cabbage and leeks during last 20 minutes of cooking time. Discard bay leaves. Remove veal and vegetables to a shallow serving dish and sprinkle lightly with salt and pepper; keep warm. Strain cooking broth and reserve.

2. Sauté mushrooms in butter in medium saucepan until tender, about 5 minutes. Sprinkle with flour and cook 1 minute longer. Stir in reserved cooking broth and heat to boiling. Boil, stirring until thickened, about 1 minute. Stir in sour cream and parsley; season to taste with salt and pepper. Pour sauce over veal and vegetables.

Veal Stew with Sage

4 servings

1½ pounds boneless veal loin, cubed (½-inch)
1 tablespoon butter
1 cup sliced carrots
¾ cup chopped onion
¾ cup sliced celery
2 cloves garlic, chopped
½ teaspoon dried sage leaves
¼ teaspoon dried thyme leaves
1½ cups reduced-sodium fat-free chicken broth
½ cup dry white wine, *or* chicken broth
Salt and pepper, to taste

Per Serving
Net Carbohydrate (gm): 5.4
Calories: 289
Fat (gm): 9.2
Saturated fat (gm): 3.5
Cholesterol (mg): 153.4
Sodium (mg): 281
Protein (gm): 37.9
Carbohydrate (gm): 7.3

1. Sauté veal in butter in large skillet until lightly browned, about 5 minutes; remove and reserve. Sauté carrots, onion, celery, and garlic in skillet until lightly browned, about 5 minutes.

2. Stir in reserved veal and remaining ingredients, except salt and pepper; heat to boiling. Reduce heat and simmer, covered, until veal is cooked, about 30 minutes. Season to taste with salt and pepper.

Veal Stew Marsala

4 servings

1½ pounds boneless veal loin, cubed (¾-inch)
1 tablespoon olive oil
2 cups sliced mushrooms
2 cloves garlic, minced
⅓ cup reduced-sodium fat-free chicken broth
⅓ cup dry Marsala wine
½ teaspoon crushed dried rosemary leaves
1 teaspoon cornstarch
1 tablespoon water
Salt and pepper, to taste

Per Serving
Net Carbohydrate (gm): 2.4
Calories: 257
Fat (gm): 9
Saturated fat (gm): 2.1
Cholesterol (mg): 137.9
Sodium (mg): 147
Protein (gm): 36.1
Carbohydrate (gm): 3

1. Sauté veal in oil in large skillet until browned, about 5 minutes; stir in mushrooms and garlic and sauté until browned, about 5 minutes more. Stir in chicken broth, Marsala, and rosemary; heat to boiling. Reduce heat and simmer until meat is tender, about 20 minutes.

2. Heat stew to boiling; stir in combined cornstarch and water. Boil, stirring until thickened, 1 to 2 minutes. Season to taste with salt and pepper.

Braised Veal Shanks Mediterranean

6 servings

6 veal shanks (about 4 pounds)
2 tablespoons olive oil
1 cup chopped onion
1 cup chopped carrots
½ cup chopped celery
1 large clove garlic, minced
1½ cups reduced-sodium fat-free chicken broth
1 can (14½ ounces) diced tomatoes, undrained
2 tablespoons tomato paste
1 tablespoon fresh, *or* 1 teaspoon dried, thyme leaves
1 bay leaf
⅓ cup drained capers
⅓ cup sliced black olives
1 tablespoon chopped fresh, *or* 1 teaspoon dried, basil leaves
1 tablespoon packed brown sugar
Salt and pepper, to taste

Per Serving
Net Carbohydrate (gm): 9
Calories: 269
Fat (gm): 9.9
Saturated fat (gm): 1.7
Cholesterol (mg): 119.3
Sodium (mg): 738
Protein (gm): 32.6
Carbohydrate (gm): 11.5

1. Cook veal shanks in oil in Dutch oven over medium heat until well browned, about 10 minutes; remove from pan. Add onion, carrots, celery, and garlic to Dutch oven; sauté until lightly browned, about 5 minutes.

2. Return veal to Dutch oven. Stir in broth, tomatoes and liquid, tomato paste, thyme, and bay leaf. Heat to boiling; transfer to oven and bake, covered, at 350 degrees until veal is tender, about 2 hours.

3. Stir in capers, olives, basil, and sugar; discard bay leaf. Season to taste with salt and pepper.

Osso Bucco

6 servings

6 veal shanks (about 4 pounds), fat trimmed
¼ cup all-purpose flour
2 tablespoons olive oil
1 cup finely chopped carrots
1 cup chopped leeks, white parts only
3 cloves garlic, minced
2 cans (14½ ounces each) diced tomatoes, undrained
½ cup dry white wine, *or* chicken broth
1 teaspoon dried basil leaves
¾ teaspoon dried thyme leaves
2 bay leaves
Gremolata (see p. 242), divided
Salt and pepper, to taste
2½ cups cooked brown rice, warm

Per Serving
Net Carbohydrate (gm): 30.7
Calories: 378
Fat (gm): 9.7
Saturated fat (gm): 1.8
Cholesterol (mg): 113.1
Sodium (mg): 466
Protein (gm): 34.3
Carbohydrate (gm): 34.6

1. Coat veal shanks lightly with flour; cook in oil in Dutch oven over medium heat until browned, about 10 minutes. Add carrots, leeks, and garlic and sauté until vegetables are lightly browned, 3 to 5 minutes.

2. Add tomatoes and liquid, wine, and herbs; heat to boiling. Reduce heat and simmer, covered, until veal is tender, about 1½ hours. Stir in ¼ cup Gremolata. Discard bay leaves; season to taste with salt and pepper. Serve over rice; pass remaining Gremolata.

Stew with Three Meats

6 servings

1 pound boneless beef round steak, cubed (1-inch)
8 ounces boneless pork loin, cubed (1-inch)
8 ounces boneless veal loin, cubed (1-inch)
1 cup chopped onion
1 tablespoon canola oil
1 can (14½ ounces) diced tomatoes, undrained
1 cup reduced-sodium fat-free beef broth
1 teaspoon paprika
1 teaspoon dried thyme leaves
Salt and pepper, to taste

Per Serving
Net Carbohydrate (gm): 3.9
Calories: 286
Fat (gm): 13.9
Saturated fat (gm): 4.3
Cholesterol (mg): 100.6
Sodium (mg): 332
Protein (gm): 33.3
Carbohydrate (gm): 4.9

1. Sauté beef, pork, veal, and onion in oil in Dutch oven until browned, about 10 minutes. Add remaining ingredients, except salt and pepper, and heat to boiling; reduce heat and simmer, covered, 1 hour or until meats are tender. Season to taste with salt and pepper.

Meat and Vegetable Stew Madrid

12 servings

1 cup chopped onion
1 tablespoon minced garlic
1 tablespoon olive oil
2 pounds beef stew meat, cubed (1 inch)
1½ cups brown rice
2 quarts water
1 pound boneless, skinless chicken breast, cubed (1-inch)
8 ounces lean ham, cubed
8 ounces chorizo, cooked, cut into 1-inch pieces
1 cup sliced carrots
1 cup sliced leeks (white parts only)
2 cups chopped, seeded tomatoes
1 tablespoon tomato paste
2 teaspoons paprika
½ teaspoon ground cumin
1 pound fresh baby spinach leaves
Salt and pepper, to taste

Per Serving
Net Carbohydrate (gm): 21.5
Calories: 386
Fat (gm): 15.1
Saturated fat (gm): 4.9
Cholesterol (mg): 83.2
Sodium (mg): 635
Protein (gm): 37.4
Carbohydrate (gm): 23.8

1. Sauté onion and garlic in oil in Dutch oven until tender, about 5 minutes. Stir in beef and rice and cook, stirring, until beef and rice are lightly browned, about 5 minutes. Add water and heat to boiling. Reduce heat and simmer, covered, 30 minutes.

2. Stir in remaining ingredients, except spinach, salt, and pepper. Heat to boiling; reduce heat and simmer, covered, until meats and rice are tender, about 25 minutes. Stir in spinach; season to taste with salt and pepper.

Three-Meat Goulash

12 servings

1 pound mushrooms, sliced
1 cup chopped onion
½ cup thinly sliced green onions and tops
2 tablespoons canola oil
1 tablespoon paprika
1 teaspoon crushed caraway seeds
1 teaspoon dried dill weed
1 pound boneless beef round steak, cubed (¾-inch)
1 pound boneless pork loin, cubed (¾-inch)
1 pound veal loin, cubed (¾-inch)
1 cup reduced-sodium fat-free beef broth
1 quart chopped, seeded tomatoes
⅓ cup tomato paste
1 cup sour cream
3 tablespoons all-purpose flour
Salt and pepper, to taste

Per Serving
Net Carbohydrate (gm): 7.8
Calories: 273
Fat (gm): 14.5
Saturated fat (gm): 5.3
Cholesterol (mg): 84.5
Sodium (mg): 154
Protein (gm): 26
Carbohydrate (gm): 9.8

1. Sauté mushrooms, onion, and green onions in oil in large Dutch oven 5 minutes; stir in paprika, caraway seeds, and dill weed and cook 1 minute longer. Remove and reserve.

2. Add meats to Dutch oven; cook over medium heat until browned, about 10 minutes. Return mushroom mixture to Dutch oven. Stir in broth, tomatoes, and tomato paste; heat to boiling. Reduce heat and simmer, covered, until meats are tender, about 50 minutes.

3. Mix sour cream and flour and stir into stew; simmer, stirring until thickened, 2 to 3 minutes. Season to taste with salt and pepper.

Karelian Ragout

8 servings

1 pound boneless beef round steak, cubed (1-inch)
1 pound boneless pork loin, cubed (1-inch)
1 pound boneless lamb leg, cubed (1-inch)
⅓ cup whole wheat flour
1¼ teaspoon ground allspice
1 quart thinly sliced onions
1 quart reduced-sodium fat-free beef broth
1 teaspoon dried thyme leaves
2 bay leaves
Salt and pepper, to taste
¼ cup finely chopped parsley

Per Serving
Net Carbohydrate (gm): 9.6
Calories: 357
Fat (gm): 16.3
Saturated fat (gm): 6.4
Cholesterol (mg): 110.8
Sodium (mg): 171
Protein (gm): 39
Carbohydrate (gm): 11.4

1. Toss meats with combined flour and allspice. Layer meats and onions in Dutch oven; add broth, thyme, and bay leaves and heat to boiling. Reduce heat and simmer, covered, until meats are tender, about 1 hour. Discard bay leaves. Season to taste with salt and pepper and stir in parsley.

Two Meat-Two Mushroom Stew

6 servings

Per Serving
Net Carbohydrate (gm): 24.6
Calories: 356
Fat (gm): 8.9
Saturated fat (gm): 3.4
Cholesterol (mg): 113.2
Sodium (mg): 384
Protein (gm): 35.9
Carbohydrate (gm): 27.3

½ cup boiling water
3 medium dried shiitake mushrooms
½ cup sliced green onions and tops
½ teaspoon lightly crushed fennel seeds
1 tablespoon butter
1 pound boneless pork loin, cubed (¾-inch)
1 pound boneless veal loin, cubed (¾-inch)
2 tablespoons all-purpose flour
½ cup dry white wine, *or* chicken broth
2 teaspoons beef bouillon crystals
4 ounces small cremini, *or* white button, mushrooms, halved
Salt and pepper, to taste
3 cups cooked brown rice, warm
Finely chopped parsley, as garnish

1. Pour boiling water over dried mushrooms in small bowl; let stand until mushrooms are softened, 5 to 10 minutes. Drain, reserving liquid; strain liquid. Slice mushrooms into thin strips, discarding hard centers.

2. Sauté shittake mushrooms, green onions, and fennel seeds in butter in large saucepan 2 to 3 minutes; add meats and sauté until lightly browned, 5 to 8 minutes. Sprinkle with flour and cook 1 minute longer.

3. Add wine, bouillon, and reserved mushroom liquid to saucepan; heat to boiling. Reduce heat and simmer, covered, until meats are tender, about 40 minutes, adding cremini mushrooms during last 10 minutes of cooking time. Season to taste with salt and pepper. Serve over rice; sprinkle with parsley.

Two-Meat Goulash

8 servings

1½ pounds boneless beef round steak, cubed (¾-inch)
1½ pounds boneless pork loin, cubed (¾-inch)
2 tablespoons canola oil
1 cup chopped onion
2 cloves garlic, minced
½ teaspoon crushed caraway seeds
½ teaspoon crushed fennel seeds
2 tablespoons paprika
2 tablespoons all-purpose flour
2 bay leaves
1 cup reduced-sodium fat-free beef broth
1 can (14½ ounces) diced tomatoes, undrained
2 tablespoons tomato paste
8 ounces small mushrooms, cut into halves
½ cup sour cream
Salt and pepper, to taste

Per Serving
Net Carbohydrate (gm): 7
Calories: 378
Fat (gm): 19.9
Saturated fat (gm): 6.8
Cholesterol (mg): 111.1
Sodium (mg): 312
Protein (gm): 39.4
Carbohydrate (gm): 8.7

1. Sauté meats in oil in Dutch oven until browned, 5 to 8 minutes; add onion, garlic, caraway and fennel seeds and sauté until onion is tender, about 5 minutes. Stir in paprika, flour, and bay leaves and cook 1 minute longer.

2. Add beef broth, tomatoes and liquid, and tomato paste; heat to boiling. Reduce heat and simmer, covered, until meats are tender, about 50 minutes, adding mushrooms during last 10 minutes of cooking time. Stir in sour cream and simmer 5 minutes. Discard bay leaves and season to taste with salt and pepper.

Mock Chicken Legs

6 servings

1 pound pork tenderloin
8 ounces boneless beef sirloin steak, fat trimmed
¼ cup all-purpose flour
1 tablespoon butter
Salt and pepper, to taste
Cream Gravy (see p. 218)

Per Serving
Net Carbohydrate (gm): 7.4
Calories: 252
Fat (gm): 12.5
Saturated fat (gm): 6.1
Cholesterol (mg): 89.1
Sodium (mg): 175
Protein (gm): 25.5
Carbohydrate (gm): 7.6

1. Cut meats into 1-inch cubes; assemble on small wooden skewers, alternating kinds of meat. Coat meat with flour; let stand at room temperature 15 minutes.

2. Cook kabobs in butter in large skillet over medium to medium-low heat until well browned on all sides, about 10 minutes.

3. Add ½ inch water to skillet; heat to boiling. Reduce heat and simmer, covered, until meat is tender, 15 to 20 minutes. Remove from skillet; season to taste with salt and pepper. Serve with Cream Gravy.

Slow-Cooker Pork Roast

6 servings

1 boneless pork loin roast (2 pounds)
2 cloves garlic, cut into slivers
1 tablespoon chopped fresh, *or*
    2 teaspoons dried, rosemary leaves
1 tablespoon coarse ground pepper
Salt, to taste
1 tablespoon olive oil
2 cups sliced onions
2 bay leaves
1 cup hot water

Per Serving
Net Carbohydrate (gm): 4.5
Calories: 255
Fat (gm): 9.8
Saturated fat (gm): 2.9
Cholesterol (mg): 82.6
Sodium (mg): 57
Protein (gm): 33.8
Carbohydrate (gm): 5.8

1. Make slits in pork and insert slivers of garlic. Rub pork with rosemary and pepper; sprinkle lightly with salt. Cook pork in oil in large skillet over medium-high heat until browned on all sides, 8 to 10 minutes.

2. Arrange half the onions in bottom of slow-cooker. Add pork, remaining onions, bay leaves, and water. Cover and cook on Low until pork is tender and no longer pink in center, about 10 hours. Discard bay leaves.

Tip: To make gravy, blend 2 tablespoons cornstarch and ¼ cup water into smooth paste; stir into juices in slow-cooker. Cook, covered, on High until mixture boils and thickens, about 15 minutes.

Rosemary Roast Pork Tenderloin

4 servings

2 pork tenderloins (about 12 ounces each)
1 large clove garlic, cut into 10–12 slivers
1 tablespoon olive oil
1½ teaspoons crushed dried rosemary leaves
Salt and pepper, to taste

Per Serving
Net Carbohydrate (gm): 0.3
Calories: 230
Fat (gm): 8.2
Saturated fat (gm): 2.2
Cholesterol (mg): 109.6
Sodium (mg): 68
Protein (gm): 35.8
Carbohydrate (gm): 0.4

1. Cut small slits in pork and insert garlic slivers. Place pork in small roasting pan and brush with oil. Rub surface of pork with rosemary leaves. Sprinkle lightly with salt and pepper.

2. Roast pork at 425 degrees 20 to 30 minutes until meat thermometer inserted in center registers 160 degrees (slightly pink) or 170 degrees (well-done).

Note: Pork can be eaten slightly pink; it is safe to eat after the internal temperature has reached 140 degrees.

Pork Tenderloin with Apricot Stuffing

4 servings

1 pork tenderloin (about 1 pound)
1 can (8½ ounces) apricot halves, undrained
⅓ cup finely chopped celery
⅓ cup thinly sliced green onions and tops
⅛ teaspoon ground cinnamon
⅛ teaspoon pepper
2 cups herb-seasoned croutons
⅔ cup reduced-sodium fat-free chicken broth
1½ teaspoons cornstarch
⅛ teaspoon ground nutmeg

Per Serving
Net Carbohydrate (gm): 19.7
Calories: 270
Fat (gm): 7.2
Saturated fat (gm): 2.3
Cholesterol (mg): 78.7
Sodium (mg): 347
Protein (gm): 27.8
Carbohydrate (gm): 22.2

1. Slice tenderloin lengthwise, cutting to, but not through, opposite side. Spread tenderloin open and pound meat lightly with meat mallet to rectangle about 10 x 6 inches.

2. Drain apricots, reserving juice. Cut apricots into ½-inch cubes. Combine apricots, celery, green onions, cinnamon, pepper, and croutons in large bowl; pour broth over and toss.

3. Spread stuffing mixture evenly over tenderloin. Roll up meat, jelly roll style, starting from long side. Secure meat roll with wooden toothpicks or tie with kitchen string at 1-inch intervals. Cut meat into eight slices. Arrange slices in lightly greased 11 x 7-inch baking pan.

4. Add enough water to reserved apricot juice to make ¾ cup; mix with cornstarch and nutmeg in small saucepan. Whisk over medium heat until mixture boils and thickens, about 3 minutes. Pour over meat. Bake at 325 degrees, covered, until pork is cooked, about 40 minutes.

Pork Medallions with Apples and Sage

4 servings

1 pork tenderloin (about 1 pound), cut into ½-inch slices
2 cups sliced (½-inch), unpeeled apples
¼ cup finely chopped shallots, *or* green onions and tops
2 teaspoons butter
1 tablespoon all-purpose flour
¼ teaspoon dried sage leaves
1 cup plain yogurt
½ cup apple juice
Salt and pepper, to taste
1 tablespoon chopped chives

Per Serving
Net Carbohydrate (gm): 17.9
Calories: 250
Fat (gm): 6.5
Saturated fat (gm): 3.1
Cholesterol (mg): 82.2
Sodium (mg): 111
Protein (gm): 27.6
Carbohydrate (gm): 19.6

1. Arrange pork in greased 11 x 7-inch baking dish, overlapping slices; arrange apples on top of meat.

2. Sauté shallots in butter in small skillet until tender, about 2 minutes. Stir in flour and sage; cook 1 minute. Stir in yogurt and apple juice; heat to boiling, whisking until thickened. Season to taste with salt and pepper. Spoon sauce over pork and apples in baking dish; sprinkle with chives. Bake at 325 degrees, covered, until pork is tender, about 40 minutes.

Pork, Greens, and Caramelized Onions

4 servings

Per Serving
Net Carbohydrate (gm): 14.8
Calories: 312
Fat (gm): 11.6
Saturated fat (gm): 2.2
Cholesterol (mg): 91.8
Sodium (mg): 403
Protein (gm): 32.2
Carbohydrate (gm): 19.2

4 cups thinly sliced onions
2 tablespoons olive oil, divided
1 teaspoon packed brown sugar
3 cups reduced-sodium fat-free chicken broth
2 cups thinly sliced kale, mustard greens, *or* Swiss chard
2 cups thinly sliced curly endive, *or* spinach
¼ teaspoon salt
¼ teaspoon pepper
1 pork tenderloin (about 1 pound), cut into ¼-inch slices

1. Cook onions in 1 tablespoon oil in large skillet over medium heat 5 minutes; reduce heat to low and stir in sugar. Cook until onions are golden in color and very soft, about 20 minutes.

2. Stir chicken broth into onions; heat to boiling. Reduce heat and simmer, uncovered, until broth is reduced by ⅓, about 8 minutes. Add kale and endive; simmer, covered, until greens are wilted, 5 to 7 minutes. Simmer, uncovered, until broth is almost evaporated, about 5 minutes. Stir in salt and pepper.

3. Cook pork slices in remaining 1 tablespoon oil in large skillet over medium to medium-high heat until browned on both sides and no longer pink in center, about 5 minutes.

4. Spoon onion mixture onto serving platter; top with pork.

Rosemary-Sage Pork Medallions

4 servings

Per Serving
Net Carbohydrate (gm): 0.5
Calories: 219
Fat (gm): 8.5
Saturated fat (gm): 2.3
Cholesterol (mg): 101.4
Sodium (mg): 79
Protein (gm): 32.9
Carbohydrate (gm): 0.8

2 pork tenderloins (about 12 ounces each),
    cut into ½-inch slices
1 clove garlic, minced
1 teaspoon dried rosemary leaves
1 teaspoon dried sage leaves
1 tablespoon olive oil
2 teaspoons lemon juice
Salt and pepper, to taste

1. Sprinkle pork with combined garlic and herbs. Sauté pork in oil in large skillet until browned and no longer pink in the center, 3 to 4 minutes on each side. Sprinkle with lemon juice; sprinkle lightly with salt and pepper.

Bayou Pork Chops

4 servings

4 bone-in loin pork chops (7–8 ounces each)
1 tablespoon canola, *or* olive, oil
1 cup chopped onion
¾ cup thinly sliced green bell pepper
½ cup sliced celery
2 large cloves garlic, minced
1 can (14 ounces) stewed tomatoes, undrained
1 can (4 ounces) chopped green chilies
2 tablespoons chopped fresh parsley
Salt and pepper, to taste

Per Serving
Net Carbohydrate (gm): 16.1
Calories: 267
Fat (gm): 10.3
Saturated fat (gm): 2.3
Cholesterol (mg): 57.5
Sodium (mg): 626
Protein (gm): 23.2
Carbohydrate (gm): 20.3

1. Cook pork chops in oil in large skillet until browned, 3 to 4 minutes on each side. Remove from skillet.

2. Add onion, bell pepper, celery, and garlic to skillet; sauté until tender, 3 to 4 minutes. Stir in tomatoes and liquid and chilies; heat to boiling. Reduce heat and simmer, uncovered, 5 minutes. Add pork chops; simmer, covered, until pork chops are tender, about 20 minutes. Stir in parsley; season to taste with salt and pepper.

Pork Chops Parmesan

4 servings

3 tablespoons yellow cornmeal
3 tablespoons grated Parmesan cheese
½ teaspoon pepper
½ teaspoon dried basil leaves
4 bone-in loin pork chops (8 ounces each)
2 tablespoons olive oil
¼ cup chopped green onions and tops
1 clove garlic, minced
¼ teaspoon crushed fennel seeds
3 tablespoons chopped fresh parsley

Per Serving
Net Carbohydrate (gm): 1.6
Calories: 237
Fat (gm): 12.9
Saturated fat (gm): 3.4
Cholesterol (mg): 72
Sodium (mg): 139
Protein (gm): 26.3
Carbohydrate (gm): 2.2

1. Combine cornmeal, Parmesan cheese, pepper, and basil; coat pork chops with mixture. Cook pork chops in oil in large skillet over medium heat until browned, 3 to 4 minutes on each side. Add green onions, garlic, and fennel seeds; reduce heat to low and cook, covered, until pork chops are no longer pink in the center, 5 to 8 minutes, turning occasionally. Sprinkle with parsley.

Pork, Bell Pepper, and Onion Stew

4 servings

1 pork tenderloin (about 1 pound),
    cut into 2 x ½-inch strips
1 tablespoon olive oil
2 cups sliced red, orange, and green bell peppers
¾ cup thinly sliced red onion
1 teaspoon minced garlic
1 can (15 ounces) tomato sauce
2 tablespoons dry sherry, *or* water
1 teaspoon dried basil leaves
1 teaspoon dried thyme leaves
Salt and pepper, to taste

Per Serving
Net Carbohydrate (gm): 11.9
Calories: 235
Fat (gm): 7
Saturated fat (gm): 1.7
Cholesterol (mg): 73.1
Sodium (mg): 691
Protein (gm): 26.3
Carbohydrate (gm): 15.5

1. Cook pork in olive oil in large skillet over medium heat until browned, 5 to 8 minutes; remove from skillet. Add peppers, onion, and garlic to skillet and sauté until tender and lightly browned, about 5 minutes. Stir in reserved pork, tomato sauce, sherry, and herbs. Heat to boiling; reduce heat and simmer, covered, until pork is tender, about 10 minutes. Simmer, uncovered, until sauce is slightly thickened, 2 to 3 minutes longer. Season to taste with salt and pepper.

Pork and Summer Vegetable Ragout

4 servings

1 pork tenderloin (about 1 pound), cubed (¾-inch)
1 tablespoon olive oil
1 cup chopped onion
1 clove garlic, minced
1 can (16 ounces) tomato puree
2 cups sliced red, yellow, and green bell peppers
1½ cups thinly sliced zucchini
¼ cup dry sherry, *or* chicken broth
¾ teaspoon dried rosemary leaves
½ teaspoon dried sage leaves
1 bay leaf
Salt and pepper, to taste

Per Serving
Net Carbohydrate (gm): 14.6
Calories: 256
Fat (gm): 7.1
Saturated fat (gm): 1.7
Cholesterol (mg): 73.1
Sodium (mg): 736
Protein (gm): 27.1
Carbohydrate (gm): 19.2

1. Cook pork in oil in large skillet until browned, about 5 minutes; remove from skillet and reserve. Add onion and garlic to skillet and sauté until tender, about 5 minutes. Add reserved pork and remaining ingredients, except salt and pepper; heat to boiling. Reduce heat and simmer, covered, until meat is tender, about 15 minutes. Discard bay leaf; season to taste with salt and pepper.

Pork and Squash Ragout

4 servings

1 pork tenderloin (about 1 pound), cubed (¾-inch)
1 tablespoon butter
1½ cups chopped onions
1½ cups coarsely chopped green bell peppers
2 teaspoons minced garlic
1 tablespoon all-purpose flour
2 cups cubed (½-inch), peeled butternut squash
2 cans (14½ ounces each) diced tomatoes, undrained
¾ teaspoon dried Italian seasoning
Salt and pepper, to taste

Per Serving
Net Carbohydrate (gm): 22.3
Calories: 274
Fat (gm): 6.6
Saturated fat (gm): 3.1
Cholesterol (mg): 81.3
Sodium (mg): 743
Protein (gm): 27.8
Carbohydrate (gm): 25.7

1. Sauté pork in butter in large skillet until browned, about 8 minutes; remove from skillet. Add onions, bell peppers, and garlic to skillet and sauté until tender, about 8 minutes. Stir in flour; cook 1 minute longer.

2. Add pork and remaining ingredients, except salt and pepper; heat to boiling. Reduce heat and simmer 10 to 15 minutes. Season to taste with salt and pepper.

Rosemary Pork with White Beans and Artichokes

6 servings

2 pork tenderloins (12 ounces each), cubed (¾-inch)
2 cloves garlic, minced
1 tablespoon olive oil
1 tablespoon all-purpose flour
1 can (14½ ounces) diced tomatoes, undrained
1 can (14 ounces) artichoke hearts, rinsed, drained, quartered
1 can (15 ounces) cannellini, *or* navy, beans, rinsed, drained
⅔ cup fat-free reduced-sodium chicken broth
2 teaspoons dried rosemary leaves
2 teaspoons grated orange rind
Salt and pepper, to taste

Per Serving
Net Carbohydrate (gm): 14.4
Calories: 256
Fat (gm): 6
Saturated fat (gm): 1.5
Cholesterol (mg): 75.9
Sodium (mg): 635
Protein (gm): 29.7
Carbohydrate (gm): 18.7

1. Sauté pork and garlic in oil in large saucepan until lightly browned, about 8 minutes; sprinkle with flour and cook 1 minute longer.

2. Stir in remaining ingredients, except salt and pepper; heat to boiling. Reduce heat and simmer, covered, until pork is cooked, about 15 minutes. Season to taste with salt and pepper.

Peppered Pork Stew

4 servings

1 pork tenderloin (about 1 pound), cut into ½-inch slices
2 teaspoons coarsely crushed peppercorns
1 tablespoon butter
1 cup finely chopped onion
¼ cup chopped red bell pepper
1 clove garlic, minced
1½ cups reduced-sodium fat-free beef broth
½ cup dry white wine, *or* beef broth ¼ cup all-purpose flour
1 tablespoon red wine vinegar
Salt and pepper, to taste
¼ cup minced chives

Per Serving
Net Carbohydrate (gm): 9.8
Calories: 237
Fat (gm): 6.5
Saturated fat (gm): 3.1
Cholesterol (mg): 81.3
Sodium (mg): 140
Protein (gm): 27.4
Carbohydrate (gm): 11.3

1. Sprinkle pork slices with peppercorns, pressing into surface of meat. Sauté meat in butter in large skillet and cook until browned, 2 to 3 minutes on each side. Remove from skillet and reserve.

2. Add onion, bell pepper, and garlic to skillet and cook until tender, about 5 minutes. Add broth; heat to boiling. Return pork to skillet; reduce heat and simmer until pork is tender, about 10 minutes.

3. Heat stew to boiling; stir in combined wine, flour, and vinegar. Boil, stirring until thickened, 1 to 2 minutes. Season to taste with salt and pepper. Sprinkle with chives.

Orange Pork Ragout

4 servings

1 pound boneless pork loin, cut into 2 x ½-inch strips
1 tablespoon olive oil
3 cups sliced red, yellow, and green bell peppers
1 cup sliced onion
1½ cups orange juice
2 teaspoons light brown sugar
1 teaspoon dried thyme leaves
¼ teaspoon ground cloves
Salt and pepper, to taste

Per Serving
Net Carbohydrate (gm): 20.5
Calories: 303
Fat (gm): 12.5
Saturated fat (gm): 3.6
Cholesterol (mg): 71.9
Sodium (mg): 67
Protein (gm): 24.1
Carbohydrate (gm): 23.4

1. Sauté pork in oil in large skillet until lightly browned, about 5 minutes; remove and reserve. Add peppers and onion to skillet and sauté until tender, about 5 minutes. Add reserved pork and remaining ingredients, except salt and pepper, and heat to boiling. Reduce heat and simmer, covered, 10 minutes. Remove lid and simmer until pork is cooked and sauce thickened, about 10 minutes more. Season to taste with salt and pepper.

Pork Tenderloin Stew with Gremolata

4 servings

1 pork tenderloin (about 1 pound), cubed (1-inch)
2 teaspoons olive oil
4 shallots, thinly sliced
1 cup reduced-sodium fat-free beef broth
1 cup cubed (½-inch), peeled potatoes
1 can (15 ounces) diced tomatoes, undrained
Salt and pepper, to taste
Gremolata (recipe follows)

Per Serving
Net Carbohydrate (gm): 13.1
Calories: 227
Fat (gm): 5.7
Saturated fat (gm): 1.5
Cholesterol (mg): 73.1
Sodium (mg): 440
Protein (gm): 27.5
Carbohydrate (gm): 15.2

1. Cook pork in oil in large saucepan over medium heat until lightly browned, 5 to 8 minutes. Add shallots and sauté until shallots are tender, 2 to 3 minutes. Stir in broth and heat to boiling; reduce heat and simmer, covered, 10 minutes.

2. Add potatoes and tomatoes and liquid; simmer, covered, until pork and potatoes are tender, about 15 minutes. Season to taste with salt and pepper. Spoon stew into bowls; sprinkle with Gremolata.

Gremolata

makes about ½ cup

1 cup packed parsley sprigs
1–2 tablespoons grated lemon rind
4 large cloves garlic, minced

1. Process all ingredients in food processor until finely minced.

Pork Loin, Potato, and Cabbage Stew

4 servings

1½ pounds boneless pork loin, cut into 2 x ½-inch strips
½ pound Idaho potatoes, peeled, grated
1 can (14½ ounces) stewed tomatoes, undrained
1 can (8 ounces) tomato sauce
3 cups thinly sliced cabbage
½ cup finely chopped onion
2 cloves garlic, minced
1 tablespoon brown sugar
2 teaspoons balsamic vinegar
2 teaspoons dried thyme leaves
1 bay leaf
Salt and pepper, to taste

Per Serving
Net Carbohydrate (gm): 25.6
Calories: 347
Fat (gm): 7
Saturated fat (gm): 2.4
Cholesterol (mg): 106.6
Sodium (mg): 647
Protein (gm): 39.4
Carbohydrate (gm): 30.5

1. Combine all ingredients, except salt and pepper, in large saucepan; heat to boiling. Reduce heat and simmer, covered, until meat is tender, about 30 minutes. Discard bay leaf; season to taste with salt and pepper.

Pork Braised with Sauerkraut

4 servings

1 pound boneless pork loin, cubed (¾-inch)
2 teaspoons olive oil
1 pound red potatoes, unpeeled, cut into thin slices
1 cup chopped onion
1 can (14½ ounces) diced tomatoes, undrained
1 teaspoon caraway seeds
1 package (16 ounces) fresh sauerkraut, drained
¼ cup sour cream
Salt and pepper, to taste

Per Serving
Net Carbohydrate (gm): 22.2
Calories: 324
Fat (gm): 9.5
Saturated fat (gm): 3.5
Cholesterol (mg): 76.4
Sodium (mg): 1185
Protein (gm): 27.8
Carbohydrate (gm): 29.4

1. Cook pork in oil in large skillet over medium heat until browned, 5 to 8 minutes. Add remaining ingredients, except sour cream, salt, and pepper; heat to boiling. Reduce heat and simmer, covered, until meat and potatoes are tender, about 25 minutes. Stir in sour cream; season to taste with salt and pepper.

Finnish Pork Stew with Beets

4 servings

1 pound boneless pork loin, sliced into 2 x ½-inch strips
1 cup chopped onion
1 tablespoon canola oil
1 can (16 ounces) julienned beets, undrained
3 tablespoons cider vinegar
½ cup reduced-sodium fat-free beef broth
1½ teaspoons prepared horseradish
½ teaspoon dried thyme leaves
2 teaspoons cornstarch
¼ cup cold water
Salt and pepper, to taste

Per Serving
Net Carbohydrate (gm): 10.9
Calories: 230
Fat (gm): 8
Saturated fat (gm): 1.8
Cholesterol (mg): 71.1
Sodium (mg): 359
Protein (gm): 25.9
Carbohydrate (gm): 13.1

1. Cook pork and onion in oil in large skillet over medium heat until browned, about 5 minutes.

2. Drain beets, reserving ½ cup juice; stir juice into skillet with vinegar, broth, horseradish, and thyme. Heat to boiling; reduce heat and simmer, covered, until meat is tender, about 20 minutes.

3. Heat stew to boiling; stir in combined cornstarch and water. Boil, stirring until thickened, about 1 minute. Add drained beets and simmer, uncovered, 5 minutes. Season to taste with salt and pepper.

Mediterranean Curried Pork

6 servings

1 pork tenderloin (about 1 pound), cubed (¾-inch)
2 tablespoons olive oil, divided
1 small eggplant (about 12 ounces), unpeeled,
    cut into 1-inch pieces
1 cup sliced onion
½ cup chopped green bell pepper
½ cup sliced celery
2 cloves garlic, minced
1 tablespoon all-purpose flour
½ teaspoon ground cinnamon
½ teaspoon ground nutmeg
½ teaspoon ground cumin
¼ teaspoon curry powder
2 cans (14½ ounces each) diced tomatoes, undrained
2 cups cubed zucchini
1 can (15 ounces) garbanzo beans, rinsed, drained
3 tablespoons dark raisins
Salt and cayenne pepper, to taste

Per Serving
Net Carbohydrate (gm): 27.1
Calories: 296
Fat (gm): 7.9
Saturated fat (gm): 1.6
Cholesterol (mg): 48.7
Sodium (mg): 697
Protein (gm): 22.5
Carbohydrate (gm): 34.3

1. Cook pork in 1 tablespoon oil in large saucepan over medium heat until browned, about 5 minutes. Add eggplant, onion, bell pepper, celery, garlic, and remaining 1 tablespoon oil and cook 10 minutes or until eggplant is beginning to brown. Stir in flour and spices; cook 1 to 2 minutes longer.

2. Add tomatoes and liquid, zucchini, beans, and raisins to saucepan; heat to boiling. Reduce heat and simmer, covered, until vegetables and meat are tender, about 10 minutes. Season to taste with salt and cayenne pepper.

Caribbean Ginger Pork Stew

6 servings

1½ pounds boneless pork loin, cubed (¾-inch)
1 tablespoon olive oil
1 cup chopped onion
1 cup chopped red bell pepper
1 jalapeño chili, minced
1 tablespoon minced gingerroot
2 teaspoons minced garlic
½ teaspoon dried thyme leaves
½ teaspoon ground allspice
1 can (15 ounces) black-eyed peas, rinsed, drained
¾ cup fresh, *or* frozen, cut okra
⅓ cup orange juice
⅓ cup no-sugar-added orange marmalade
1 can (8 ounces) Mandarin orange segments, drained
Salt and pepper, to taste

Per Serving
Net Carbohydrate (gm): 21.6
Calories: 298
Fat (gm): 8.1
Saturated fat (gm): 2.3
Cholesterol (mg): 71
Sodium (mg): 277
Protein (gm): 29.7
Carbohydrate (gm): 26.1

1. Cook pork in oil in large skillet over medium heat until browned, 5 to 8 minutes. Add onion, bell pepper, jalapeño chili, gingerroot, and garlic and cook until onion is tender, about 5 minutes. Stir in thyme and allspice; cook 1 to 2 minutes longer.

2. Add black-eyed peas, okra, orange juice, and marmalade to skillet; heat to boiling. Reduce heat and simmer, covered, until pork is tender, about 10 minutes. Stir in orange segments; cook 1 to 2 minutes. Season to taste with salt and pepper.

Savory Pork and Chorizo

6 servings

1 pork tenderloin (about 12 ounces), cubed (1-inch)
Chorizo (recipe follows)
1 tablespoon olive oil
½ cup sliced onion
1 clove garlic, minced
2 cups chopped, seeded tomatoes
¼ teaspoon dried oregano leaves
¼ teaspoon dried thyme leaves
1 bay leaf
2–3 pickled jalapeño chilies, finely chopped
1 tablespoon pickled jalapeño chili juice
Salt and pepper, to taste
6 flour tortillas (6 inch), warm

Per Serving
Net Carbohydrate (gm): 22.1
Calories: 304
Fat (gm): 9.9
Saturated fat (gm): 2.6
Cholesterol (mg): 70.3
Sodium (mg): 475
Protein (gm): 28
Carbohydrate (gm): 25.2

1. Cover pork with water in medium saucepan; heat to boiling. Reduce heat and simmer, covered, until tender, 20 to 30 minutes. Cool; drain, reserving ½ cup broth. Finely shred pork with a fork; reserve.

2. Cook Chorizo in oil in large skillet over medium heat until browned, crumbling with a fork. Add onion and garlic to skillet; sauté 2 to 3 minutes. Add tomatoes and herbs and cook over medium heat 5 minutes, stirring occasionally. Add reserved pork, ½ cup reserved broth, bay leaf, jalapeño chilies, and jalapeño juice to skillet. Cook, uncovered, over medium heat, about 10 minutes, stirring occasionally (mixture should be moist, not dry). Discard bay leaf; season to taste with salt and pepper. Roll in tortillas.

Chorizo

Vegetable cooking spray
¼ teaspoon crushed coriander seeds
¼ teaspoon crushed cumin seeds, *or* ⅛ teaspoon ground cumin
1 dried ancho chili
12 ounces ground, *or* finely chopped, lean pork
2 cloves garlic, minced
1 tablespoon paprika
½ teaspoon dried oregano leaves
½–¾ teaspoon salt
1 tablespoon cider vinegar
1 tablespoon water

1. Spray small skillet with cooking spray; heat over medium heat until hot. Add coriander and cumin seeds; cook over medium heat, stirring frequently, until toasted. Remove from skillet.

2. Add ancho chili to skillet; cook over medium heat until softened, about 1 minute on each side, turning so that chili does not burn. Remove from skillet and discard stem, veins, and seeds. Chop chili finely.

3. Combine pork, toasted seeds, chopped chili, and remaining ingredients in small bowl, mixing thoroughly. Refrigerate, covered, at least 4 hours or overnight for flavors to blend.

Braised Pork Puerto Vallarta

8 servings

1½ cups chopped onions
¾ cup chopped poblano chili, *or* green bell pepper
4 cloves garlic, minced
2 tablespoons olive, *or* canola, oil
2 pounds boneless pork loin, cubed (¾-inch)
2 tablespoons all-purpose flour
¾ teaspoon dried oregano leaves
½ teaspoon ground cumin
¼ teaspoon dried thyme leaves
½ cup reduced-sodium fat-free chicken broth
2 cups chopped, seeded tomatoes
12 ounces Mexican green tomatoes (tomatillos), husked, chopped
1 can (4 ounces) mild, *or* hot, chopped green chilies
¼ cup minced cilantro, *or* parsley, leaves
1–2 teaspoons lime juice
Salt and pepper, to taste
3 tablespoons toasted pine nuts, *or* almonds

Per Serving
Net Carbohydrate (gm): 8.4
Calories: 245
Fat (gm): 10.3
Saturated fat (gm): 2.4
Cholesterol (mg): 72.6
Sodium (mg): 121
Protein (gm): 26.8
Carbohydrate (gm): 11.1

1. Sauté onions, poblano chili, and garlic in oil in large saucepan 2 to 3 minutes; add pork and sauté until browned, about 5 minutes. Stir in flour and herbs and cook 2 minutes longer.

2. Add broth, tomatoes, green tomatoes, and green chilies and heat to boiling; reduce heat and simmer, covered, until pork is tender, 40 to 50 minutes. Stir in cilantro and season to taste with lime juice, salt, and pepper. Spoon into serving bowl; sprinkle with pine nuts.

Pork with Tomatillo-Peanut Sauce

6 servings

1½ pounds boneless pork loin, cut into ½-inch slices
1 tablespoon minced garlic
Salt and pepper, to taste
1 tablespoon peanut oil
1 cup (½ recipe) Tomatillo Sauce (see p. 138)
½ cup finely chopped dry-roasted peanuts

Per Serving
Net Carbohydrate (gm): 4.2
Calories: 270
Fat (gm): 15.1
Saturated fat (gm): 3.5
Cholesterol (mg): 67.5
Sodium (mg): 63
Protein (gm): 27.4
Carbohydrate (gm): 5.8

1. Sprinkle pork on both sides with garlic, salt, and pepper. Cook pork in oil in large skillet over medium to medium-high heat until no longer pink in the center, 3 to 4 minutes on each side.

2. Add Tomatillo Sauce and peanuts to skillet; heat until hot.

Pork Oriental in Orange Sauce

4 servings

2 tablespoons peanut, *or* canola, oil
1 pound boneless pork loin, cubed (½-inch)
1 cup thinly sliced carrots
¾ cup chopped celery
½ cup orange juice
2 tablespoons soy sauce
1 tablespoon grated orange rind
2 teaspoons brown sugar
2 teaspoons cornstarch
⅛ teaspoon ground ginger
¼ cup coarsely chopped cashews

Per Serving
Net Carbohydrate (gm): 12.5
Calories: 270
Fat (gm): 15.5
Saturated fat (gm): 3.4
Cholesterol (mg): 46.6
Sodium (mg): 588
Protein (gm): 19.5
Carbohydrate (gm): 14.3

1. Heat oil in wok or large skillet until hot; stir-fry pork until browned, 3 to 4 minutes. Add carrots and celery; stir-fry until crisp tender, about 5 minutes. Stir in combined remaining ingredients; heat to boiling. Cook, stirring, until thickened, 1 to 2 minutes.

Pork and Vegetable Stir-Fry

4 servings

6 teaspoons cornstarch, divided
½ cup dry sherry, *or* chicken broth, divided
1 pound boneless pork loin, cut into 2 x ½-inch strips
2 tablespoons peanut, *or* canola, oil
2 cloves garlic, chopped
1 tablespoon chopped gingerroot
4 cups broccoli florets
2 cups sliced zucchini
¼ cup shredded carrots
2–3 teaspoons light soy sauce

Per Serving
Net Carbohydrate (gm): 10.3
Calories: 269
Fat (gm): 11.4
Saturated fat (gm): 2.7
Cholesterol (mg): 46.6
Sodium (mg): 167
Protein (gm): 20.8
Carbohydrate (gm): 13.9

1. Combine 4 teaspoons cornstarch and ¼ cup dry sherry; pour over pork in glass baking dish and toss to coat. Let stand 10 minutes.

2. Heat oil in wok or large skillet until hot; stir-fry pork mixture, garlic, and gingerroot 2 to 3 minutes. Add broccoli, zucchini, and carrots; stir-fry until broccoli is crisp-tender, 4 to 5 minutes. Stir in combined remaining ¼ cup dry sherry and 2 teaspoons cornstarch; heat to boiling. Cook, stirring until thickened, 1 to 2 minutes. Stir in soy sauce.

Sweet-and-Sour Pork

4 servings

1 tablespoon peanut, *or* canola, oil
½ cup thinly sliced red bell pepper
¼ cup sliced green onions and tops
¼ cup shredded carrots
2 cloves garlic, minced
1½ pounds boneless pork loin, cubed (¾-inch)
½ cup reduced-sodium fat-free chicken broth
2 teaspoons red wine vinegar
2 teaspoons soy sauce
1 teaspoon brown sugar
1 tablespoon water
2 teaspoons cornstarch
½ cup pineapple chunks

Per Serving
Net Carbohydrate (gm): 9.3
Calories: 245
Fat (gm): 10
Saturated fat (gm): 2.8
Cholesterol (mg): 73
Sodium (mg): 270
Protein (gm): 27.1
Carbohydrate (gm): 10.3

1. Heat oil in wok or large skillet over medium-high heat until hot; stir-fry vegetables until crisp-tender, 3 to 4 minutes. Move vegetables to side of wok; add pork and stir-fry until browned, about 5 minutes. Stir in combined remaining ingredients; heat to boiling. Cook, stirring until thickened, 1 to 2 minutes.

Chop Suey

4 servings

1 pork tenderloin (about 1 pound), cubed (1-inch)
1 tablespoon peanut, *or* canola, oil
2 cups thinly sliced Chinese cabbage
1 cup sliced celery
1 cup sliced mushrooms
1 cup chopped red, *or* green, bell pepper
⅓ cup sliced green onions and tops
2 cloves garlic, minced
½ cup reduced-sodium fat-free chicken broth
2 tablespoons cornstarch
½–1 tablespoon bead molasses
2 cups fresh, *or* canned, rinsed bean sprouts
½ can (8-ounce size) bamboo shoots, rinsed, drained
½ can (8-ounce size) water chestnuts, rinsed, drained
Soy sauce, to taste
Salt and pepper, to taste
1⅓ cups crisp chow mein noodles

Per Serving
Net Carbohydrate (gm): 23.3
Calories: 349
Fat (gm): 12.6
Saturated fat (gm): 2.7
Cholesterol (mg): 76.2
Sodium (mg): 269
Protein (gm): 30.7
Carbohydrate (gm): 28.6

1. Stir-fry pork in oil in wok or large skillet until browned, 3 to 5 minutes. Add cabbage, celery, mushrooms, bell pepper, green onions, and garlic; stir-fry until vegetables are crisp-tender, 3 to 5 minutes longer.

2. Mix broth, cornstarch, and molasses; stir into wok and heat to boiling. Boil, stirring constantly until thickened, 1 to 2 minutes. Stir in bean sprouts, bamboo shoots, and water chestnuts; cook until hot through, 1 to 2 minutes. Season to taste with soy sauce, salt, and pepper. Serve over chow mein noodles.

Jalapeño Pork Stir-Fry

4 servings

1 pound boneless pork loin, cubed (¾-inch)
1 tablespoon peanut oil
1½ cups thinly sliced carrots
2 cups shredded cabbage
1 cup sliced celery
¾ cup chopped onion
1 tablespoon chopped jalapeño chili
⅓ cup water
¼ cup soy sauce
¼ cup catsup
2 tablespoons packed brown sugar
1 tablespoon cornstarch

Per Serving
Net Carbohydrate (gm): 20.8
Calories: 307
Fat (gm): 12.3
Saturated fat (gm): 3.7
Cholesterol (mg): 71.9
Sodium (mg): 1320
Protein (gm): 24.6
Carbohydrate (gm): 24.5

1. Stir-fry pork in oil in wok or large skillet over medium-high heat until meat is browned, about 3 minutes. Add carrots; stir-fry 3 minutes longer. Add cabbage, celery, onion, and jalapeño chili; stir-fry until cabbage is wilted, about 5 minutes more.

2. Combine remaining ingredients in small bowl, whisking until smooth. Add mixture to wok; heat to boiling, stirring until sauce is thickened and pork is tender, about 5 minutes.

Cantonese Pork

6 servings

1½ pounds boneless pork steaks, ½ inch thick,
    cut into 1½-inch strips
2 tablespoons peanut oil
1 cup sliced onion
1 cup sliced red bell pepper
1 cup sliced mushrooms
1 can (8 ounces) tomato sauce
3 tablespoons packed dark brown sugar
1½ tablespoons cider vinegar
2 teaspoons Worcestershire sauce
1 tablespoon dry sherry, optional
Salt and pepper, to taste

Per Serving
Net Carbohydrate (gm): 12.7
Calories: 269
Fat (gm): 12.9
Saturated fat (gm): 3.7
Cholesterol (mg): 76.3
Sodium (mg): 303
Protein (gm): 23.3
Carbohydrate (gm): 14.3

1. Cook pork in oil in large skillet over medium-high heat until browned, 5 to 8 minutes. Stir in onion, bell pepper, and mushrooms and sauté 5 minutes more. Add remaining ingredients, except salt and pepper, and heat to boiling; reduce heat and simmer, covered, until meat is tender, about 20 minutes. Season to taste with salt and pepper.

Ham and Vegetables au Gratin

6 servings

4 cups thinly sliced, peeled red potatoes
1 pound smoked ham, cubed (1-inch)
1 cup chopped green bell pepper
1 cup thinly sliced zucchini
⅓ cup sliced green onions and tops
Cheddar Sauce (recipe follows)
¼ cup unseasoned dry bread crumbs

Per Serving
Net Carbohydrate (gm): 25.2
Calories: 350
Fat (gm): 16.1
Saturated fat (gm): 8.8
Cholesterol (mg): 72.7
Sodium (mg): 1346
Protein (gm): 24.6
Carbohydrate (gm): 27.1

1. Arrange potatoes in lightly greased 3-quart casserole, overlapping slightly. Top with ham, bell pepper, zucchini, and green onion. Pour Cheddar Sauce evenly over vegetables.

2. Bake at 375 degrees, covered, 45 minutes. Sprinkle with bread crumbs and bake, uncovered, until potatoes are tender and casserole is golden brown, about 20 minutes longer.

Cheddar Sauce

makes about 2½ cups

2 tablespoons butter
3 tablespoons all-purpose flour
¾ teaspoon dry mustard
2 cups reduced-fat milk
¼ teaspoon paprika
1 cup (4 ounces) shredded Cheddar cheese
Salt and pepper, to taste

1. Melt butter in small saucepan; whisk in flour and dry mustard. Whisk over medium heat 1 minute; gradually whisk in milk and paprika. Heat to boiling, whisking over medium heat until sauce thickens, 3 to 4 minutes. Add cheese, whisking until melted; season to taste with salt and pepper.

Sausage and Bean Stew

8 servings

Per Serving
Net Carbohydrate (gm): 18.9
Calories: 384
Fat (gm): 22.1
Saturated fat (gm): 7
Cholesterol (mg): 38.6
Sodium (mg): 1531
Protein (gm): 19.7
Carbohydrate (gm): 26.4

1 cup chopped onion
1 cup chopped green bell pepper
2 cloves garlic, minced
2 tablespoons olive oil
1 pound smoked pork sausage, sliced (½-inch)
½ teaspoon dried thyme leaves
½ teaspoon dried savory leaves
1 bay leaf
2 tablespoons all-purpose flour
1 quart water
2 cans (14½ ounces each) diced tomatoes, undrained
1 can (15½ ounces) light red kidney beans, rinsed, drained
1 can (15½ ounces) pinto beans, rinsed, drained
Salt and pepper, to taste

1. Sauté onion, bell pepper, and garlic in olive oil in large saucepan 3 to 4 minutes; add sausage, thyme, savory, and bay leaf and sauté until sausage is browned, about 5 minutes. Stir in flour and cook 1 minute longer.

2. Add remaining ingredients, except salt and pepper, and heat to boiling. Reduce heat and simmer, uncovered, until sauce is thickened, about 20 minutes. Discard bay leaf; season to taste with salt and pepper.

Roasted Eggplant, Tomatoes, and Sausage

6 servings

4 cups sliced (½-inch), unpeeled eggplant
3 cups onion wedges (½-inch)
2 tablespoons olive oil
½ teaspoon dried thyme leaves
½ teaspoon dried marjoram leaves
½ teaspoon dried savory leaves
Salt and pepper, to taste
1 pound Italian sausage
1 can (14½ ounces) diced tomatoes with roasted garlic, undrained

Per Serving
Net Carbohydrate (gm): 12
Calories: 365
Fat (gm): 12.2
Saturated fat (gm): 10.9
Cholesterol (mg): 51.1
Sodium (mg): 928
Protein (gm): 18.7
Carbohydrate (gm): 15.4

1. Line jelly roll pan with aluminum foil and grease lightly. Cut eggplant slices into fourths; toss with onions, oil, and herbs in large bowl. Arrange on jelly roll pan and sprinkle lightly with salt and pepper. Roast vegetables at 450 degrees until almost tender, about 25 minutes.

2. Cook sausage in medium skillet until browned, about 8 minutes; drain well and cut into 2-inch pieces. Spoon sausage and tomatoes with liquid and garlic over vegetables, and roast until eggplant is tender and juices are thickened, 5 to 10 minutes longer.

El Paso Lamb Kabobs

4 servings

2 pounds boneless lamb shoulder or leg, cubed (1½-inch)
Salt and pepper, to taste
1 tablespoon minced fresh, *or*
    1 teaspoon dried, oregano leaves
6 small plum tomatoes, halved
El Paso Sauce (recipe follows)

Per Serving
Net Carbohydrate (gm): 10.4
Calories: 255
Fat (gm): 9.7
Saturated fat (gm): 3.2
Cholesterol (mg): 90.6
Sodium (mg): 94
Protein (gm): 29.5
Carbohydrate (gm): 14

1. Sprinkle meat lightly with salt, pepper, and oregano. Thread meat onto skewers with tomatoes. Brush lamb with El Paso Sauce and grill over hot coals to desired degree of doneness, 3 to 4 minutes on each side for medium, brushing with additional sauce during cooking.

El Paso Sauce

makes about ½ cup

½ cup boiling water
3 small, dried, hot red chilies
2 teaspoons cumin seeds
2 teaspoons paprika
5 cloves garlic
¼ cup lemon juice
3 tablespoons chopped fresh cilantro
½ lemon, *or* lime, with rind, coarsely chopped

1. Combine boiling water and chilies in small bowl; let stand 10 minutes. Drain. Process chilies and remaining ingredients, except lemon, in food processor or blender until smooth. Add lemon and process until finely chopped.

Irish Lamb Stew

6 servings

1½ pounds boneless leg of lamb, cubed (¾-inch)
1½ cups sliced onions
2 tablespoons canola oil
3 tablespoons all-purpose flour
2 cups reduced-sodium fat-free chicken broth
½ teaspoon dried thyme leaves
1 bay leaf
1½ cups cubed, unpeeled red potatoes
1½ cups sliced carrots
1–1½ teaspoons Worcestershire sauce
Salt and pepper, to taste

Per Serving
Net Carbohydrate (gm): 12.1
Calories: 309
Fat (gm): 16.5
Saturated fat (gm): 5.1
Cholesterol (mg): 82.6
Sodium (mg): 160
Protein (gm): 25.3
Carbohydrate (gm): 14.2

1. Cook lamb and onions in oil in Dutch oven over medium heat until lamb is browned, about 8 minutes; sprinkle with flour and cook 1 minute longer.

2. Add broth and herbs and heat to boiling. Reduce heat and simmer, covered, until lamb is tender, 45 to 60 minutes, adding potatoes and carrots during last 20 minutes of cooking time. Discard bay leaf; season to taste with Worcestershire sauce, salt, and pepper.

Variations:

Irish Lamb Stew with Parsley Dumplings—Make lamb stew as above. Make Dill Dumplings (see p. 195), substituting 2 tablespoons finely chopped parsley for the dill weed; spoon dumpling mixture onto stew. Simmer, uncovered, 10 minutes; simmer, covered, 10 minutes, or until dumplings are dry.

Easy Shepherd's Pie—Make stew as above, omitting potatoes; add ¾ cup frozen peas to cooked stew and pour into 1½-quart casserole. Mash ¾ pound cooked, peeled Idaho potatoes with ¼ cup sour cream, 2 to 3 tablespoons milk, and 1 tablespoon butter; season to taste with salt and pepper. Spoon potatoes over top of stew. Bake at 400 degrees until potatoes are browned, about 10 minutes.

One-Step Lamb Stew

6 servings

2 pounds boneless lamb shoulder, cubed (1 inch)
2 cups cubed (1-inch), peeled potatoes
2 cups sliced (½-inch) carrots
1 cup thinly sliced onion
1 package (10 ounces) frozen peas
2 cups water
3 tablespoons quick-cooking tapioca
1 teaspoon dried Italian seasoning
½ teaspoon salt
¼ teaspoon pepper
1 bay leaf

Per Serving
Net Carbohydrate (gm): 23.3
Calories: 320
Fat (gm): 6.8
Saturated fat (gm): 2.5
Cholesterol (mg): 95.8
Sodium (mg): 325
Protein (gm): 35
Carbohydrate (gm): 28.6

1. Combine all ingredients in 2½-quart casserole; stir well. Bake, covered, at 325 degrees until lamb is tender, 1½ to 2 hours, stirring halfway through cooking time. Discard bay leaf.

Rosemary Lamb and Sweet Potato Stew

4 servings

1 pound boneless lamb shoulder, cubed (¾-inch)
2 tablespoons chopped fresh, *or*
    2 teaspoons dried, rosemary leaves
2 tablespoons chopped fresh, *or*
    2 teaspoons dried, thyme leaves
1 tablespoon olive oil
1 cup sliced onion
3 cups reduced-sodium fat-free beef broth
2 bay leaves
½ pound sweet potatoes, peeled, cubed (¾-inch)
1½ cups cut green beans
Salt and pepper, to taste

Per Serving
Net Carbohydrate (gm): 17.3
Calories: 403
Fat (gm): 23.8
Saturated fat (gm): 9.2
Cholesterol (mg): 77.8
Sodium (mg): 182
Protein (gm): 25.6
Carbohydrate (gm): 21.6

1. Toss lamb with herbs; sauté in oil in large saucepan until lightly browned, about 10 minutes. Add onion, broth, and bay leaves. Heat to boiling; reduce heat and simmer, covered, until meat is almost tender, about 45 minutes.

2. Stir sweet potatoes and green beans into stew; simmer, covered, until meat and vegetables are tender, about 10 minutes. Discard bay leaves; season to taste with salt and pepper.

Cognac-Spiked Lamb and Beef Stew

8 servings

1½ pounds boneless lamb shoulder, cubed (¾-inch)
1 pound boneless beef round steak, cubed (¾-inch)
¾ cup dry white wine, *or* apple juice
3 tablespoons cognac, *or* apple juice
½ teaspoon ground cinnamon
¼ teaspoon ground mace
2 tablespoons butter
2 tablespoons all-purpose flour
1 cup finely chopped celery
1 cup finely chopped carrots
1 cup finely chopped onion
¾ cup reduced-sodium fat-free chicken broth
8 ounces baby carrots
8 ounces small broccoli florets
8 ounces pearl onions, peeled
Salt and pepper, to taste

Per Serving
Net Carbohydrate (gm): 8.5
Calories: 328
Fat (gm): 13.9
Saturated fat (gm): 5.7
Cholesterol (mg): 100.3
Sodium (mg): 166
Protein (gm): 31.5
Carbohydrate (gm): 11.8

1. Combine meats, wine, cognac, cinnamon, and mace in glass bowl; refrigerate, covered, 6 hours or overnight, stirring occasionally. Drain, reserving marinade.

2. Sauté meats in butter in Dutch oven until browned, about 10 minutes; sprinkle with flour and cook 1 to 2 minutes longer. Remove meats from Dutch oven.

3. Add chopped vegetables to Dutch oven and sauté until lightly browned, about 8 minutes. Stir in meats, reserved marinade, and broth and heat to boiling. Bake, covered, at 350 degrees until meats are almost tender, about 50 minutes.

4. Stir in baby carrots, broccoli, and pearl onions. Bake, covered, until vegetables and meats are tender, about 10 minutes. Season to taste with salt and pepper.

Lamb with Roasted Ratatouille

6 servings

2 pounds boneless lamb shoulder, cubed (1-inch)
1 tablespoon olive oil
⅔ cup finely chopped celery
⅔ cup finely chopped green onions and tops
¾ cup tomato juice
¼ cup dry vermouth, *or* chicken broth
2 tablespoons lemon juice
½ teaspoon ground cumin
½ teaspoon garlic powder
⅛ teaspoon ground cloves
Salt and pepper, to taste
Roasted Ratatouille (recipe follows)

Per Serving
Net Carbohydrate (gm): 15.3
Calories: 373
Fat (gm): 16.3
Saturated fat (gm): 3.8
Cholesterol (mg): 95.8
Sodium (mg): 407
Protein (gm): 34.7
Carbohydrate (gm): 21.1

1. Sauté lamb in oil in Dutch oven until brown, about 8 minutes. Stir in remaining ingredients, except salt, pepper, and Roasted Ratatouille. Heat to boiling; reduce heat and simmer, covered, until lamb is tender and sauce is thickened, 45 to 60 minutes. Season to taste with salt and pepper.

2. Arrange Roasted Ratatouille on large serving platter; spoon lamb mixture over vegetables.

Roasted Ratatouille

4 cups cubed, peeled, and seeded tomatoes
3 cups cubed (1-inch), unpeeled eggplant
3 cups thickly sliced (¾-inch) zucchini
2 cups cubed (1-inch) green bell peppers
2 cups onion wedges
3 tablespoons olive oil
¾ teaspoon dried rosemary leaves
½ teaspoon dried thyme leaves
½ teaspoon salt
¼ teaspoon pepper

1. Toss all ingredients in large bowl; arrange on greased aluminum foil-lined jelly roll pan. Roast at 400 degrees until lightly browned and tender, 30 to 40 minutes.

Green Chili Lamb Stew

4 servings

1 cup sliced onion
2 tablespoons minced garlic
1 small jalapeño chili, minced
1 tablespoon canola oil
1½ pounds boneless lamb shoulder, cubed (¾-inch)
1 teaspoon dried oregano leaves
¼ teaspoon dried thyme leaves
2 tablespoons all-purpose flour
1 cup reduced-sodium fat-free chicken broth
2 cans (15 ounces each) diced tomatoes, undrained
2 cans (4 ounces each) chopped mild green chilies
2 cups cubed (½-inch) yellow summer squash
½ cup frozen whole kernel corn
Salt and pepper, to taste

Per Serving
Net Carbohydrate (gm): 17.8
Calories: 369
Fat (gm): 11.5
Saturated fat (gm): 3.1
Cholesterol (mg): 114
Sodium (mg): 1040
Protein (gm): 40.8
Carbohydrate (gm): 23.7

1. Sauté onion, garlic, and jalapeño chili in oil in large saucepan 2 minutes. Add lamb and cook until browned, about 5 minutes. Stir in herbs and flour and cook 1 minute longer.

2. Add chicken broth, tomatoes and liquid, and chilies and heat to boiling; reduce heat and simmer, covered, until lamb is tender, about 45 minutes, adding squash and corn during the last 5 minutes of cooking time. Season to taste with salt and pepper.

Lamb and Root Vegetable Stew

4 servings

1 pound boneless lamb shoulder, cubed (1-inch)
1 cup chopped onion
1 tablespoon olive oil
2½ cups tomato juice
½ cup dry red wine, *or* chicken broth
1 tablespoon minced garlic
1 tablespoon chopped fresh, *or* 1 teaspoon dried, sage leaves
1 cup cubed (¾-inch), peeled potatoes
1 cup cubed (¾-inch) turnips
½ cup chopped parsley
Salt and pepper, to taste

Per Serving
Net Carbohydrate (gm): 18.6
Calories: 421
Fat (gm): 25.8
Saturated fat (gm): 10.1
Cholesterol (mg): 78.8
Sodium (mg): 634
Protein (gm): 22.1
Carbohydrate (gm): 21.5

1. Sauté lamb and onion in oil in large saucepan until lightly browned, about 8 minutes; add tomato juice, wine, garlic, and sage. Heat to boiling; reduce heat and simmer, covered, until lamb is tender, about 1 hour, adding potatoes and turnip during last 20 minutes. Stir in parsley; season to taste with salt and pepper.

Moroccan Lamb Stew

8 servings

2 pounds boneless lamb shoulder, cubed (¾-inch)
1 tablespoon olive oil
½ cup chopped onion
2 large cloves garlic, minced
2 teaspoons minced gingerroot
1½ cups reduced-sodium fat-free chicken broth
1 cup tomato puree
½ teaspoon ground cinnamon
¼ teaspoon ground turmeric
Generous pinch ground cloves
1 bay leaf
¼ cup raisins
Salt and pepper, to taste
4 cups cooked couscous, warm
2–4 tablespoons whole almonds, toasted
2 hard-cooked eggs, chopped
Finely chopped mint, *or* parsley, as garnish

Per Serving
Net Carbohydrate (gm): 24.2
Calories: 321
Fat (gm): 10.1
Saturated fat (gm): 2.6
Cholesterol (mg): 130
Sodium (mg): 176
Protein (gm): 29.8
Carbohydrate (gm): 26.8

1. Sauté lamb in oil in Dutch oven until browned, 5 to 8 minutes. Add onion, garlic, and gingerroot; sauté until onion is tender, about 3 minutes.

2. Add broth, tomato puree, spices, and bay leaf to Dutch oven; heat to boiling. Reduce heat and simmer, covered, until lamb is tender, 45 to 60 minutes. Stir in raisins and simmer, uncovered, until sauce is thickened, about 10 minutes. Discard bay leaf; season to taste with salt and pepper.

3. Spoon stew over couscous on rimmed serving platter; sprinkle with almonds, eggs, and mint.

Lamb and Vegetable Tajine

8 servings

½ cup chopped onion
½ cup sliced celery
2 teaspoons minced gingerroot
2 teaspoons minced garlic
1 tablespoon olive oil
1 cinnamon stick
2 teaspoons ground cumin
2 teaspoons ground coriander
2 pounds cooked lean lamb, cubed (1-inch)
2 cans (14½ ounces each) diced tomatoes, undrained
1 can (15 ounces) garbanzo beans, rinsed, drained
2 cups cubed (2 inch) zucchini
1 cup cubed (1 inch) turnips
1 cup sliced carrots
1½ cups whole green beans, ends trimmed
½ cup pitted prunes
¼ cup pitted small black olives
½ cup reduced-sodium fat-free beef broth
Salt and pepper, to taste

Per Serving
Net Carbohydrate (gm): 23.1
Calories: 307
Fat (gm): 8.6
Saturated fat (gm): 2.3
Cholesterol (mg): 72.2
Sodium (mg): 621
Protein (gm): 28.2
Carbohydrate (gm): 29.3

1. Sauté onion, celery, gingerroot, and garlic in oil in Dutch oven until onion is tender, about 4 minutes. Stir in spices; cook 1 minute longer.

2. Add remaining ingredients, except salt and pepper, to Dutch oven. Bake, covered, at 350 degrees until vegetables are tender, 20 to 30 minutes. Season to taste with salt and pepper.

Marrakesh Lamb Stew

8 servings

1½ cups dried navy, *or* Great Northern, beans
2 pounds boneless leg of lamb, cubed (1-inch)
2 tablespoons olive oil
4 ounces portobello, *or*
    shittake, mushrooms, coarsely chopped
1 cup sliced carrots
1 cup sliced onion
3 large cloves garlic, minced
¼ cup all-purpose flour
1 teaspoon ground cumin
½ teaspoon dried thyme leaves
½ teaspoon dried savory leaves
2 bay leaves
1 quart reduced-sodium fat-free chicken broth
½ cup dry white wine, *or* chicken broth
1–2 tablespoons tomato paste
¾ cup sliced roasted red peppers
8 ounces fresh spinach, sliced
Salt and pepper, to taste

Per Serving
Net Carbohydrate (gm): 21.3
Calories: 486
Fat (gm): 24.6
Saturated fat (gm): 10.3
Cholesterol (mg): 84.3
Sodium (mg): 248
Protein (gm): 33
Carbohydrate (gm): 30.5

1. Cover beans with water in large saucepan; heat to boiling. Remove from heat and let stand, covered, 1 hour. Drain.

2. Sauté lamb in oil in Dutch oven until browned, about 5 minutes; add mushrooms, carrots, onion, and garlic and sauté 5 minutes. Add flour and herbs; cook 1 minute longer.

3. Add chicken broth, wine, and beans; heat to boiling. Reduce heat and simmer, covered, until lamb and beans are tender, 45 to 60 minutes. Stir in tomato paste, roasted red peppers, and spinach; cook until spinach is wilted, about 2 minutes. Discard bay leaves; season to taste with salt and pepper.

Curried Lamb Stew

12 servings

3 pounds boneless leg of lamb, cubed (1-inch)
1¼ cups plain yogurt
¼ teaspoon crushed red pepper
2 cups chopped onions
1 tablespoon minced gingerroot
2 cloves garlic, minced
2 teaspoons lightly crushed coriander seeds
1 teaspoon lightly crushed cumin seeds
½ teaspoon lightly crushed cardamom seeds
1 teaspoon ground turmeric
½ teaspoon ground cinnamon
Generous pinch ground cloves
2 tablespoons butter
1 cup reduced-sodium fat-free chicken broth
Salt and pepper, to taste
Turmeric Rice (recipe follows)
Condiments: toasted slivered almonds, chopped cucumber, finely chopped cilantro

Per Serving
Net Carbohydrate (gm): 26.8
Calories: 360
Fat (gm): 14.9
Saturated fat (gm): 6.5
Cholesterol (mg): 83.3
Sodium (mg): 161
Protein (gm): 26.4
Carbohydrate (gm): 28.6

1. Combine lamb, yogurt, and red pepper in bowl; refrigerate several hours or overnight, stirring occasionally.

2. Sauté onions, gingerroot, garlic, and spices in butter in Dutch oven until onions are tender, 5 to 8 minutes. Stir in lamb mixture and chicken broth; heat to boiling. Reduce heat and simmer, covered, until lamb is tender, 50 to 60 minutes. Season to taste with salt and pepper. Serve stew over Turmeric Rice; sprinkle with condiments (not included in nutritional data).

Turmeric Rice

makes 8 cups

4½ cups water
¾ teaspoon turmeric
¼ teaspoon salt
2 cups uncooked long-grain brown rice

1. Heat water, turmeric, and salt to boiling in large saucepan; stir in rice. Reduce heat and simmer, covered, until rice is tender, 45 to 50 minutes.

Lamb Biriani

6 servings

2 pounds boneless leg of lamb, cubed (1-inch)
1 tablespoon butter
1½ cups chopped onions
1 garlic clove, minced
1 teaspoon ground coriander
1 teaspoon ground ginger
½ teaspoon curry powder
¼ teaspoon ground cinnamon
¼ teaspoon ground cloves
1 cup reduced-sodium fat-free chicken broth
¾ cup plain yogurt
Salt and pepper, to taste
Basmati Rice Pilaf (recipe follows)

Per Serving
Net Carbohydrate (gm): 16.5
Calories: 397
Fat (gm): 20
Saturated fat (gm): 8.8
Cholesterol (mg): 118.3
Sodium (mg): 209
Protein (gm): 34.4
Carbohydrate (gm): 18.3

1. Cook lamb in butter in Dutch oven over medium heat until browned, about 8 minutes. Remove and reserve.

2. Add onion and garlic to Dutch oven and sauté until tender. Add spices and sauté 2 minutes. Stir in reserved lamb and broth and heat to boiling. Reduce heat and simmer, covered, until meat is tender, about 40 minutes. Stir in yogurt; season to taste with salt and pepper.

3. Spoon Basmati Rice Pilaf onto serving platter; spoon Biriani over.

Basmati Rice Pilaf

makes 2 cups

¼ cup chopped onion
¼ cup shredded carrot
½ teaspoon cumin seeds
2 teaspoons butter
½ cup uncooked brown basmati rice
1 cup reduced-sodium fat-free chicken broth

1. Sauté onion, carrot, and cumin in butter in large saucepan until onion is tender, about 5 minutes; stir in rice and cook until lightly browned, about 3 minutes. Add broth and heat to boiling. Reduce heat and simmer, covered, 40 minutes or until rice is tender.

Gingered Lamb, Indian Style

4 servings

1 pound boneless lamb shoulder, cubed (1-inch)
3 tablespoons all-purpose flour
1 tablespoon olive oil
¾ cup chopped onion
¼ cup finely chopped gingerroot
4 cloves garlic, minced
1 tablespoon curry powder, mild *or* hot
½ teaspoon ground cumin
¼ teaspoon ground turmeric
¼ teaspoon celery seeds
1 can (15 ounces) diced tomatoes, undrained
3 tablespoons lemon juice
1 cup frozen peas
¼ cup plain yogurt
Salt and pepper, to taste

Per Serving
Net Carbohydrate (gm): 16.7
Calories: 310
Fat (gm): 12.2
Saturated fat (gm): 3.5
Cholesterol (mg): 76.3
Sodium (mg): 276
Protein (gm): 27.2
Carbohydrate (gm): 21.4

1. Coat lamb with flour. Sauté lamb in oil in large saucepan until browned, about 5 minutes. Add onion, gingerroot, garlic, curry powder, cumin, turmeric, and celery seeds; cook until onion is tender, about 5 minutes. Add tomatoes and liquid and lemon juice; heat to boiling. Reduce heat and simmer, covered, until lamb is tender, 30 to 45 minutes.

2. Stir in peas; simmer 5 minutes. Stir in yogurt and season to taste with salt and pepper.

Shepherd's Pie

6 servings

1½ pounds boneless leg of lamb, cubed (½-inch)
1 tablespoon butter
¾ cup chopped onion
¾ cup chopped green bell pepper
½ cup chopped celery
3 cloves garlic, minced
3 tablespoons all-purpose flour
2½ cups reduced-sodium fat-free beef broth
1½ cups sliced carrots
1 tablespoon tomato paste
½ teaspoon dried rosemary leaves
½ teaspoon dried thyme leaves
1 bay leaf
¾ cup frozen peas
Salt and pepper, to taste
2 cups (½ recipe) Real Mashed Potatoes (see p. 353)

Per Serving
Net Carbohydrate (gm): 21.7
Calories: 310
Fat (gm): 9.9
Saturated fat (gm): 4.7
Cholesterol (mg): 84.9
Sodium (mg): 225
Protein (gm): 29.2
Carbohydrate (gm): 26

1. Sauté lamb in butter in large saucepan until browned, 5 to 8 minutes; remove from pan. Add onion, bell pepper, celery, and garlic; sauté until tender, about 5 minutes. Stir in flour; cook over medium heat 1 to 2 minutes, stirring constantly.

2. Return lamb to saucepan; add broth, carrots, tomato paste, and herbs. Heat to boiling; reduce heat and simmer, covered, until lamb is tender, about 25 minutes, adding peas during last 5 minutes cooking time. Discard bay leaf; season to taste with salt and pepper.

3. Pour lamb mixture into 1½-quart casserole. Spoon Real Mashed Potatoes around edge of casserole. Bake at 400 degrees until potatoes are browned, about 10 minutes.

Savory Lamb Shanks

6 servings

4 pounds lamb shanks
¼ cup all-purpose flour
1 tablespoon olive oil
2 cups sliced carrots
1½ cups chopped onions
1 cup chopped green bell pepper
2 cloves garlic, minced
2 cups reduced-sodium fat-free chicken broth
1 can (14½ ounces) tomatoes, undrained, coarsely chopped
½ cup uncooked brown lentils
¼ cup chopped parsley
2 bay leaves
2 teaspoons dried thyme leaves
¼ teaspoon ground cinnamon
¼ teaspoon ground cloves
Salt and pepper, to taste

Per Serving
Net Carbohydrate (gm): 17.8
Calories: 424
Fat (gm): 18.5
Saturated fat (gm): 6.7
Cholesterol (mg): 107.3
Sodium (mg): 270
Protein (gm): 38
Carbohydrate (gm): 26.3

1. Coat lamb shanks lightly with flour; cook in oil in Dutch oven over medium heat until browned, about 10 minutes. Stir in carrots, onions, bell pepper, and garlic and cook until lightly browned, about 5 minutes. Stir in remaining ingredients, except salt and pepper, and heat to boiling. Reduce heat and simmer, covered, 1½ hours or until lamb shanks are tender. Discard bay leaves.

2. Remove lamb shanks from Dutch oven; remove lean meat and cut into bite-sized pieces. Discard bones. Skim fat from surface of stew. Return meat to stew; season to taste with salt and pepper.

Pastitsio

6 servings

1½ pounds ground lean lamb, *or* extra-lean beef
1 tablespoon olive oil
½ cup chopped onion
½ cup chopped green bell pepper
1 can (8 ounces) tomato paste
⅓ cup water
Salt and pepper, to taste
⅓ cup grated Parmesan cheese
¼–½ teaspoon ground cinnamon
¼ teaspoon ground nutmeg
1 cup whole wheat elbow macaroni, cooked
2⅓ cups reduced-fat milk
2 tablespoons butter
4 eggs, lightly beaten
Minced parsley, as garnish

Per Serving
Net Carbohydrate (gm): 24.1
Calories: 413
Fat (gm): 17.8
Saturated fat (gm): 7.5
Cholesterol (mg): 235.6
Sodium (mg): 566
Protein (gm): 36.8
Carbohydrate (gm): 27.6

1. Cook lamb in oil in large skillet until browned, about 8 minutes; add onion and bell pepper and cook until tender, 5 to 8 minutes. Drain any fat. Stir in tomato paste and water; cook 2 to 3 minutes longer. Season to taste with salt and pepper.

2. Spoon lamb mixture into lightly greased 13 x 9-inch baking pan. Combine cheese and spices; sprinkle over meat. Top with macaroni.

3. Heat milk and butter in medium saucepan, stirring until butter is melted. Whisk milk into eggs; pour over macaroni. Bake, uncovered, at 350 degrees until casserole is bubbly, 50 to 60 minutes. Sprinkle with parsley.

Lamb and Vegetable Moussaka

12 servings

4 cups sliced, unpeeled eggplant
1 tablespoon olive oil
2 pounds ground lean lamb, *or* extra-lean beef
2 cups chopped onions
2 cups sliced, peeled potatoes
2 cups sliced carrots
3 cloves garlic, minced
1 teaspoon ground cinnamon
1 teaspoon dried oregano leaves
½ teaspoon dried thyme leaves
¾ cup reduced-sodium fat-free beef broth
2 cups chopped tomatoes
2 cups sliced mushrooms
1 cup sliced zucchini
1 cup cooked barley
Salt and pepper, to taste
Custard Topping (recipe follows)
Ground nutmeg, to taste

Per Serving
Net Carbohydrate (gm): 20.1
Calories: 291
Fat (gm): 11.9
Saturated fat (gm): 5.6
Cholesterol (mg): 102.8
Sodium (mg): 155
Protein (gm): 21.8
Carbohydrate (gm): 24.5

1. Toss eggplant with olive oil in large bowl; arrange on greased aluminum foil-lined jelly roll pan. Bake at 350 degrees until eggplant is tender but still firm to touch, about 20 minutes. Arrange eggplant on bottom of lightly greased 13 x 9-inch baking pan.

2. Cook lamb in Dutch oven over medium-high heat until browned, about 10 minutes; drain well. Add onions, potatoes, carrots, garlic, cinnamon, oregano, thyme, and broth to Dutch oven. Heat to boiling; reduce heat and simmer, uncovered, 5 minutes. Add tomatoes, mushrooms, zucchini, and barley; simmer, uncovered, until potatoes are tender and mixture is thick, about 8 minutes. Season to taste with salt and pepper.

3. Spoon lamb mixture over eggplant in baking pan. Pour Custard Topping over and sprinkle lightly with nutmeg. Bake at 350 degrees until lightly browned, about 45 minutes. Cool 5 to 10 minutes before cutting.

Custard Topping

⅓ cup butter
½ cup whole wheat flour
3 cups reduced-fat milk
2 eggs, lightly beaten
Salt and white pepper, to taste

1. Melt butter in medium saucepan; stir in flour. Cook over medium heat until bubbly, about 2 minutes, stirring constantly. Stir in milk; heat to boiling. Boil, stirring constantly, until thickened, about 1 minute.

2. Whisk about 1 cup milk mixture into eggs; stir egg mixture back into saucepan. Cook over low heat until thickened, 2 to 3 minutes. Season to taste with salt and white pepper.

Grilled Minted Lamb Patties

4 servings

1½ pounds ground lean lamb
¾ cup chopped onion
¼ cup minced parsley
¼ tablespoon salt
¼ teaspoon pepper
2 tablespoons lemon juice
⅓ cup cooked brown rice
1 cup (4 ounces) crumbled feta cheese
¼ teaspoon ground cinnamon
¼ teaspoon ground allspice
2 tablespoons chopped fresh, *or* 1 teaspoon dried, mint
Sliced cucumbers, as garnish
Halved cherry tomatoes, as garnish

Per Serving
Net Carbohydrate (gm): 7.6
Calories: 237
Fat (gm): 11
Saturated fat (gm): 5.9
Cholesterol (mg): 88.6
Sodium (mg): 673
Protein (gm): 25
Carbohydrate (gm): 8.8

1. Combine ground lamb with all ingredients, except cucumbers and tomatoes, in medium bowl. Form into patties. Grill over hot coals, or broil 6 inches from heat source, to desired doneness, 4 to 5 minutes on each side for medium. Garnish with cucumbers and tomatoes.

Gyros Burgers

4 servings

½ pound extra-lean ground beef
½ pound extra-lean ground lamb, *or* extra-lean ground beef
2 tablespoons chopped onion
2 cloves garlic, minced
½ teaspoon dried oregano leaves
½ teaspoon dried dill weed
1 teaspoon salt
2 pita breads, halved
Gyros Relish (recipe follows)

Per Serving
Net Carbohydrate (gm): 21.5
Calories: 385
Fat (gm): 20.6
Saturated fat (gm): 8.4
Cholesterol (mg): 79.3
Sodium (mg): 840
Protein (gm): 25.5
Carbohydrate (gm): 23

1. Combine all ingredients, except pita breads and Gyros Relish, in medium bowl until blended; shape into 4 patties. Cook in large skillet over medium heat to desired degree of doneness, about 5 minutes on each side for medium.

2. Place burgers in pitas; spoon Gyros Relish into sandwiches.

Gyros Relish

makes about 1½ cups

⅔ cup chopped, seeded cucumber
⅔ cup chopped, seeded tomato
1 green onion and top, sliced
⅔ cup plain yogurt
½ teaspoon dried mint leaves
½ teaspoon dried oregano leaves

1. Mix all ingredients.

FIVE

Seafood

Fisherman's Catch Chowder

6 servings

½ cup chopped onion
½ cup chopped celery
½ cup chopped carrot
⅓ cup chopped parsley
1 teaspoon dried rosemary leaves
1 tablespoon butter
3 tablespoons all-purpose flour
1 can (14½ ounces) diced tomatoes, undrained
2 cups dry white wine, *or* vegetable broth
1 bottle (8 ounces) clam juice
8 ounces flounder, *or* ocean perch, fillets, cut into 1-inch pieces
8 ounces walleye, *or* trout, fillets, cut into 1-inch pieces
8 ounces grouper, haddock, *or* halibut fillets, cut into 1-inch pieces
⅓ cup half-and-half
Salt and pepper, to taste

Per Serving
Net Carbohydrate (gm): 8.3
Calories: 232
Fat (gm): 5.1
Saturated fat (gm): 2.5
Cholesterol (mg): 74.9
Sodium (mg): 536
Protein (gm): 26.2
Carbohydrate (gm): 9.5

1. Sauté onion, celery, carrot, parsley, and rosemary in butter in large saucepan until onion is tender, about 10 minutes. Sprinkle with flour and cook 1 to 2 minutes. Stir in tomatoes and liquid, wine, and clam juice; heat to boiling. Reduce heat and simmer, covered, 10 minutes.

2. Stir in fish; simmer until fish flakes with a fork, about 10 minutes. Stir in half-and-half; simmer 2 to 3 minutes. Season to taste with salt and pepper.

Fish Soup Anise

6 servings

1 cup chopped onion
1 cup thinly sliced fennel bulb
1 tablespoon minced garlic
2 teaspoons olive oil
1 can (14½ ounces) Italian-style stewed tomatoes, undrained
4 cups reduced-sodium fat-free chicken broth
½ cup uncooked whole wheat orzo *or* small soup pasta
8 ounces firm, white-fleshed fish, cut into 1-inch pieces
8 ounces peeled, deveined small shrimp
Salt and pepper, to taste

Per Serving
Net Carbohydrate (gm): 12.6
Calories: 199
Fat (gm): 5.4
Saturated fat (gm): 0.7
Cholesterol (mg): 95.8
Sodium (mg): 381
Protein (gm): 21.9
Carbohydrate (gm): 14.7

1. Sauté onion, fennel, and garlic in oil in large saucepan until tender, about 8 minutes. Stir in stewed tomatoes and liquid and chicken broth. Heat to boiling; stir in orzo and reduce heat. Simmer, covered, until orzo is almost tender, about 8 minutes.

2. Add fish and shrimp; simmer, uncovered, until fish is tender and flakes with a fork and shrimp are pink, 5 to 10 minutes. Season to taste with salt and pepper.

Portuguese-Style Fisherman's Pot

6 servings

1 cup chopped onions
1 cup chopped carrots
½ cup chopped celery
½ cup chopped red bell pepper
¼ cup chopped parsley
1 large garlic clove, minced
¼ teaspoon crushed red pepper
1 tablespoon olive oil
1½ cups reduced-sodium fat-free chicken broth
2 cups cubed (½-inch), unpeeled red potatoes
1 can (28 ounces) diced tomatoes, undrained
¾ cup dry white wine
1 bay leaf
1¾ teaspoons chili powder
1¾ teaspoons paprika
¼ teaspoon celery seeds
¼ teaspoon dried thyme leaves
Pinch of saffron threads, crumbled, optional
18–24 fresh mussels, scrubbed
1½ pounds skinless cod, haddock, *or* lean whitefish fillets, cut into 1-inch pieces
8 ounces medium shrimp, peeled, deveined
Salt and pepper, to taste

Per Serving
Net Carbohydrate (gm): 19.5
Calories: 321
Fat (gm): 5.7
Saturated fat (gm): 0.8
Cholesterol (mg): 125.3
Sodium (mg): 676
Protein (gm): 38.8
Carbohydrate (gm): 23.2

1. Sauté onions, carrot, celery, bell pepper, parsley, garlic, and crushed red pepper in oil in large saucepan until onions are tender, about 10 minutes. Add broth and potatoes and heat to boiling. Reduce heat and simmer, covered, until potatoes are tender, about 10 minutes.

2. Add tomatoes and liquid, wine, seasonings, and herbs; simmer, uncovered, until slightly thickened, about 20 minutes. Add mussels and fish and simmer, covered, 5 minutes. Stir in shrimp and simmer, covered, until mussels open and fish and shrimp are tender, about 5 minutes. Discard bay leaf and any mussels that did not open; season to taste with salt and pepper.

Mediterranean Fish Soup

6 servings

1½ cups chopped carrots
1 cup thinly sliced onion
1 tablespoon minced garlic
1 teaspoon lightly crushed fennel seeds
2 tablespoons olive oil
1 tablespoon all-purpose flour
1 tablespoon minced orange rind
1 quart Fish Stock (see p. 21)
1 cup dry white wine, *or* clam juice
4 cups chopped, peeled and seeded tomatoes
2 pounds firm fish fillets (cod, red snapper, orange roughy, halibut, etc.),
    cut into 1½-inch pieces
¼ cup chopped parsley
Salt and pepper, to taste

Per Serving
Net Carbohydrate (gm): 10.2
Calories: 248
Fat (gm): 6
Saturated fat (gm): 0.9
Cholesterol (mg): 64.5
Sodium (mg): 1175
Protein (gm): 39.6
Carbohydrate (gm): 13.3

1. Sauté carrots, onion, garlic, and fennel seeds in oil in large saucepan until onion is tender, about 8 minutes; add flour and orange rind and cook 1 to 2 minutes longer.

2. Add Fish Stock, wine, and tomatoes; heat to boiling. Reduce heat and simmer, covered, 10 minutes. Add fish and simmer, uncovered, until fish is tender and flakes with a fork, about 10 minutes. Stir in parsley; season to taste with salt and pepper.

Tuscan Fish Soup

8 servings

1½ cups chopped onions
1 tablespoon minced garlic
¾ teaspoon crushed red pepper
1 tablespoon olive oil
1 cup dry red wine
6 cups chopped, peeled and seeded tomatoes
1 quart reduced-sodium fat-free chicken broth
1½ pounds mixed skinless fish fillets
    (sole, flounder, rockfish, snapper, tuna, *or* halibut), cut into ¾-inch pieces
8 ounces medium shrimp, peeled, deveined
2 tablespoons chopped parsley
2 tablespoons fresh, *or* 1 teaspoon dried, oregano leaves
2 tablespoons fresh, *or* 1 teaspoon dried, sage leaves
2 tablespoons fresh, *or* 1 teaspoon dried, rosemary leaves
Salt and pepper, to taste
8 thin slices crusty whole-grain French bread, toasted
2 cloves garlic, halved

Per Serving
Net Carbohydrate (gm): 17.7
Calories: 275
Fat (gm): 5.6
Saturated fat (gm): 0.7
Cholesterol (mg): 96.4
Sodium (mg): 343
Protein (gm): 30.1
Carbohydrate (gm): 24.9

1. Sauté onions, minced garlic, and crushed red pepper in oil in large saucepan until onions are tender, about 5 minutes; add wine and cook 2 minutes.

2. Add tomatoes and broth and heat to boiling. Reduce heat and simmer, covered, 20 minutes; add fish and shrimp and cook, uncovered, until fish is tender and flakes with a fork, about 10 minutes. Stir in herbs; season to taste with salt and pepper.

3. Rub toasted bread with halved garlic cloves. Place a slice in each serving bowl and ladle soup over.

Very Easy Fish Stew

4 servings

1 cup chopped onion
1 teaspoon minced garlic
1 tablespoon olive oil
1 cup clam juice, *or* chicken broth
3 tablespoons chopped, softened sun-dried tomatoes
1 teaspoon dried marjoram leaves
½ teaspoon dried oregano leaves
1½ pounds halibut steaks, cut into 1-inch pieces
1 can (8 ounces) tomato sauce
Salt and pepper, to taste

Per Serving
Net Carbohydrate (gm): 7.4
Calories: 257
Fat (gm): 7.5
Saturated fat (gm): 1
Cholesterol (mg): 54.1
Sodium (mg): 889
Protein (gm): 41.1
Carbohydrate (gm): 9.4

1. Sauté onion and garlic in oil in large skillet until tender and well-browned, about 8 minutes. Stir in clam juice, sun-dried tomatoes, and herbs; heat to boiling. Reduce heat and simmer, covered, 5 minutes.

2. Add fish and tomato sauce; simmer gently until fish is tender and flakes with a fork, about 5 minutes. Season to taste with salt and pepper.

Savory Fish Stew

6 servings

1 cup chopped onion
4 cloves garlic, minced
1 tablespoon butter
2 teaspoons dried basil leaves
1½ teaspoons dried oregano leaves
½ teaspoon ground turmeric
¼ teaspoon crushed red pepper
2 bay leaves
1 can (28 ounces) stewed tomatoes, undrained
2 cups clam juice, *or* chicken broth
¾ cup white wine, *or* chicken broth
1 pound cod, *or* other firm white fish, fillets, cut into 1-inch pieces
12 ounces peeled, deveined shrimp
12 ounces bay scallops
Salt and pepper, to taste

Per Serving
Net Carbohydrate (gm): 11.9
Calories: 262
Fat (gm): 4.2
Saturated fat (gm): 1.6
Cholesterol (mg): 142.6
Sodium (mg): 1066
Protein (gm): 41.7
Carbohydrate (gm): 14.6

1. Sauté onion and garlic in butter in large saucepan until tender, about 5 minutes. Stir in basil, oregano, turmeric, crushed red pepper, and bay leaves; cook 1 to 2 minutes longer.

2. Add tomatoes and liquid, clam juice, and wine; heat to boiling. Reduce heat and simmer, covered, 20 minutes.

3. Add fish and shellfish and simmer, covered, until cod is tender and flakes with a fork, 5 to 8 minutes. Discard bay leaves; season to taste with salt and pepper.

Fish Stew Marsala

4 servings

1 cup chopped onion
1 cup chopped red and green bell peppers
½ cup chopped celery
1 teaspoon minced garlic
1½ tablespoons olive oil
2¼ cups reduced-sodium fat-free chicken broth
⅓ cup dry Marsala wine, *or* chicken broth
¼ cup tomato paste
1 teaspoon dried thyme leaves
1¼ pounds haddock steaks, *or* other lean white fish, cut into 1½-inch pieces
2 tablespoons lemon juice
Salt and pepper, to taste

Per Serving
Net Carbohydrate (gm): 8.5
Calories: 252
Fat (gm): 7.1
Saturated fat (gm): 0.9
Cholesterol (mg): 94.5
Sodium (mg): 383
Protein (gm): 32.4
Carbohydrate (gm): 11

1. Sauté onion, bell peppers, celery, and garlic in oil in large skillet until tender and lightly browned, about 5 minutes. Add broth, wine, tomato paste, and thyme. Heat to boiling; reduce heat and simmer, uncovered, 10 minutes.

2. Stir in fish and lemon juice; simmer, covered, until fish is tender and flakes with a fork, about 5 minutes. Season to taste with salt and pepper.

Savory Fish and Vegetable Stew

8 servings

⅔ cup chopped red onion
4–6 cloves garlic, minced
2 tablespoons olive oil
1 pound small red potatoes, cut into ½-inch slices
⅔ cup sliced carrots (½-inch)
⅓ cup sliced celery (½-inch)
1 teaspoon dried basil leaves
1 tablespoon all-purpose flour
2–3 cups clam juice, *or* chicken broth
2½ pounds fish fillets (salmon, snapper, halibut, *or* cod) cut into 2-inch pieces
3–4 tablespoons lemon juice
Salt and pepper, to taste

Per Serving
Net Carbohydrate (gm): 11.2
Calories: 345
Fat (gm): 18.7
Saturated fat (gm): 3.5
Cholesterol (mg): 82.9
Sodium (mg): 496
Protein (gm): 33.8
Carbohydrate (gm): 12.9

1. Sauté onion and garlic in oil in large saucepan 3 to 4 minutes. Add potatoes, carrots, celery, and basil; sauté 5 minutes. Stir in flour and cook 1 minute longer. Add clam juice to almost cover vegetables; heat to boiling. Reduce heat and simmer, covered, until vegetables are crisp-tender, about 8 minutes.

2. Add fish and simmer, covered, until fish is tender and flakes with a fork, about 5 minutes. Season to taste with lemon juice, salt, and pepper.

Lobster and Shrimp Stew

6 servings

⅔ cup chopped onion
½ cup chopped leeks (white part only)
2 cloves garlic, minced
1 tablespoon butter
½ teaspoon dried oregano leaves
¼ teaspoon dried thyme leaves
¼ teaspoon lightly crushed fennel seeds
¼ teaspoon ground turmeric
3 cups chopped, seeded tomatoes
1 cup clam juice
1 pound peeled, deveined shrimp
12 ounces shelled lobster tail, cut into ¾-inch pieces
Salt and pepper, to taste
2 cups cooked brown rice

Per Serving
Net Carbohydrate (gm): 20.4
Calories: 254
Fat (gm): 4.8
Saturated fat (gm): 1.8
Cholesterol (mg): 174.3
Sodium (mg): 581
Protein (gm): 31.6
Carbohydrate (gm): 23.2

1. Sauté onion, leek, and garlic in butter in large saucepan until tender, 5 to 8 minutes; stir in herbs and cook 1 to 2 minutes longer.

2. Add tomatoes and clam juice; heat to boiling. Reduce heat and simmer, covered, 20 minutes. Add shrimp and lobster; simmer, covered, until shrimp and lobster are cooked, 5 to 8 minutes. Season to taste with salt and pepper; serve with rice.

Variation:

Shrimp, Chicken, and Sausage Stew—Make recipe as above, substituting chicken broth for the clam juice, and cubed chicken breast for the lobster. Sauté 4 ounces sliced smoked sausage with the onion, leek, and garlic. Season to taste with hot pepper sauce.

Shrimp, Artichoke, and Peppers Stew

4 servings

2 cups thinly sliced red and green bell peppers
⅔ cup thinly sliced onion
1 teaspoon minced garlic
1 tablespoon olive oil
1 can (14½ ounces) roasted garlic diced tomatoes, undrained
½ can (14 ounces) quartered artichoke hearts, drained
3 tablespoons dry sherry, *or* chicken broth
2 teaspoons Italian seasoning
1 pound medium shrimp, peeled, deveined
¼ cup chopped parsley
Salt and pepper, to taste

Per Serving
Net Carbohydrate (gm): 14.3
Calories: 298
Fat (gm): 13.3
Saturated fat (gm): 2.4
Cholesterol (mg): 172.4
Sodium (mg): 717
Protein (gm): 25.4
Carbohydrate (gm): 17

1. Sauté bell peppers, onion, and garlic in oil in large skillet until tender; add tomatoes and liquid, artichoke hearts, sherry, and seasoning. Heat to boiling; reduce heat and simmer, covered, 5 minutes.

2. Stir in shrimp and simmer, uncovered, until shrimp are cooked and pink, about 5 minutes. Stir in parsley; season to taste with salt and pepper.

California Cioppino

4 servings

Per Serving
Net Carbohydrate (gm): 15
Calories: 319
Fat (gm): 7.2
Saturated fat (gm): 1
Cholesterol (mg): 72.4
Sodium (mg): 768
Protein (gm): 39.8
Carbohydrate (gm): 19.1

1 cup chopped green bell pepper
1 cup chopped onion
1 cup sliced mushrooms
4 cloves garlic, minced
1 tablespoon olive oil
3 cups chopped, peeled and seeded tomatoes
½ cup dry white wine, *or* clam juice
1 tablespoon tomato paste
2 tablespoons finely chopped parsley
2 teaspoons dried oregano leaves
2 teaspoons dried basil leaves
½ teaspoon ground turmeric
8 ounces sea scallops
8 ounces crabmeat
8 ounces halibut, *or* haddock, steaks, cut into 1-inch pieces
12 mussels, scrubbed
Salt and pepper, to taste

1. Sauté bell pepper, onion, mushrooms, and garlic in oil in large saucepan until onion is tender, about 5 minutes.

2. Stir in tomatoes, wine, tomato paste, and herbs; heat to boiling. Reduce heat and simmer, covered, 5 minutes. Simmer, uncovered, 20 minutes or until thickened to desired consistency.

3. Add fish and shellfish; simmer, covered, until halibut is tender and flakes with a fork, about 10 minutes. Discard any mussels that have not opened; season to taste with salt and pepper.

Creole Shrimp and Ham Stew

6 servings

Per Serving
Net Carbohydrate (gm): 10.6
Calories: 250
Fat (gm): 8.3
Saturated fat (gm): 1.2
Cholesterol (mg): 185.7
Sodium (mg): 1150
Protein (gm): 31.8
Carbohydrate (gm): 13.2

6 ounces thinly sliced ham, cut into thin strips
2 tablespoons canola oil
½ cup chopped onion
½ cup chopped celery
½ cup chopped red, *or* green, bell pepper
3 cloves garlic, minced
1 can (28 ounces) stewed tomatoes, undrained
2–3 tablespoons tomato paste
½ cup bottled clam juice, *or* water
2–4 tablespoons dry sherry, optional
¼–½ teaspoon hot pepper sauce
1½ pounds peeled, deveined shrimp
Salt and pepper, to taste

1. Cook ham in oil in large saucepan over medium-high heat until browned and crisp, 3 to 4 minutes; remove ham and reserve. Add onion, celery, bell pepper, and garlic to pan and sauté until vegetables are tender, 5 to 8 minutes.

2. Add tomatoes and liquid, tomato paste, clam juice, sherry, and hot pepper sauce; heat to boiling. Reduce heat and simmer, covered, 30 minutes.

3. Add shrimp and reserved ham and simmer, covered, until shrimp are cooked and pink, about 5 minutes. Season to taste with salt and pepper; serve over rice (not included in nutritioanl data) in bowls.

Southern-Style Fish Stew

6 servings

2 cups chopped onions
1 large garlic clove, minced
2 teaspoons butter
2½ cups reduced-sodium fat-free chicken broth
1 cup bottled clam juice
2 cups cubed (¾-inch), peeled potatoes
2 cups coarsely chopped cauliflower
⅓ cup dry sherry, *or* chicken broth
1 bay leaf
2 teaspoons lemon juice
1½ teaspoons dried thyme leaves
1 teaspoon dried basil leaves
¼ teaspoon dry mustard
¾ cup reduced-fat milk
8 ounces lean white fish such as flounder, turbot, *or* haddock, cut into 1-inch pieces
8 ounces medium shrimp, peeled, deveined
8 ounces bay scallops
Salt and white pepper, to taste

Per Serving
Net Carbohydrate (gm): 18.2
Calories: 249
Fat (gm): 4.2
Saturated fat (gm): 1.5
Cholesterol (mg): 104.6
Sodium (mg): 562
Protein (gm): 30.1
Carbohydrate (gm): 21.2

1. Sauté onions and garlic in butter in Dutch oven until onions are tender, about 5 minutes. Add broth, clam juice, potatoes, cauliflower, sherry, bay leaf, lemon juice, thyme, basil, and dry mustard; heat to boiling. Reduce heat and simmer, covered, 12 to 15 minutes or until vegetables are tender. Discard bay leaf.

2. Process 3 cups mixture in blender or food processor until smooth. Return mixture to Dutch oven and stir in milk. Add seafood and simmer, uncovered, until fish is tender and flakes with a fork, 5 to 8 minutes. Season to taste with salt and white pepper.

Bayou Red Snapper Stew

4 servings

1 cup chopped onion
1 cup chopped green bell pepper
½ cup chopped carrot
2 cloves garlic, minced
2 tablespoons olive oil
1 can (14½ ounces) stewed tomatoes, undrained
½ cup frozen cut okra
½ cup bottled clam juice, *or* water
1½ pounds red snapper fillets, cut into 1-inch pieces
2–3 teaspoons Worcestershire sauce
⅛ teaspoon cayenne pepper
Hot pepper sauce, to taste
Salt and pepper, to taste

Per Serving
Net Carbohydrate (gm): 13.4
Calories: 301
Fat (gm): 9.3
Saturated fat (gm): 1.4
Cholesterol (mg): 62.4
Sodium (mg): 554
Protein (gm): 39.3
Carbohydrate (gm): 16.8

1. Sauté onion, bell pepper, carrot, and garlic in oil in large saucepan until onion is tender, about 5 minutes. Add tomatoes and liquid, okra, and clam juice; heat to boiling. Reduce heat and simmer, covered, 10 minutes.

2. Add fish, Worcestershire sauce, and cayenne pepper; simmer, uncovered, until fish is tender and flakes with a fork, about 10 minutes. Season to taste with hot pepper sauce, salt, and pepper.

Easy Jambalaya

4 servings

1 cup diced smoked ham
½ cup chopped green bell pepper
½ cup chopped onion
2 cloves garlic, minced
1–2 tablespoons olive oil
1 can (15 ounces) diced tomatoes with
    Italian herbs, undrained
½ cup water
1 bay leaf
¾ teaspoon Italian seasoning
1 pound peeled, deveined shrimp
¼ teaspoon salt
Hot red pepper sauce, to taste
Pepper, to taste
1½ cups cooked brown rice, warm

Per Serving
Net Carbohydrate (gm): 23.3
Calories: 318
Fat (gm): 8.5
Saturated fat (gm): 1.8
Cholesterol (mg): 188.8
Sodium (mg): 1220
Protein (gm): 32.6
Carbohydrate (gm): 26.1

1. Sauté ham, green pepper, onion, and garlic in oil in large saucepan until tender, about 5 minutes. Add tomatoes and liquid, water, bay leaf and Italian seasoning; heat to boiling. Reduce heat and simmer, covered, 15 minutes.

2. Add shrimp; simmer until cooked and pink, 2 to 3 minutes. Discard bay leaf, add salt and season to taste with hot pepper sauce and pepper. Serve over rice with additional red pepper sauce.

Shrimp and Sausage Gumbo

4 servings

4 ounces smoked turkey sausage, halved, thinly sliced
1 teaspoon butter
1 cup chopped red bell pepper
2 cloves garlic, minced
1 dried cayenne chili, minced, *or*
    ½ teaspoon crushed red pepper
8 ounces fresh, *or* frozen, thawed, okra, cut into ½-inch slices
2 cans (14 ounces each) stewed tomatoes, undrained
12 ounces medium shrimp, peeled, deveined
1 cup cooked brown rice
Salt and pepper, to taste

Per Serving
Net Carbohydrate (gm): 26.2
Calories: 279
Fat (gm): 6.1
Saturated fat (gm): 1.8
Cholesterol (mg): 149.5
Sodium (mg): 980
Protein (gm): 26.6
Carbohydrate (gm): 32.3

1. Sauté sausage in butter in large saucepan until browned, about 5 minutes; add bell pepper, garlic, and cayenne chili and sauté 3 to 4 minutes. Stir in okra and tomatoes and liquid; heat to boiling. Reduce heat and simmer, covered, until vegetables are tender, about 10 minutes. Add shrimp and rice and simmer, uncovered, until shrimp is cooked and pink, about 5 minutes. Season to taste with salt and pepper.

Catfish Creole

6 servings

2 pounds catfish fillets
1 tablespoon minced garlic
½ teaspoon paprika
¼ teaspoon cayenne pepper
1 cup chopped onion
1 cup chopped green bell pepper
½ cup sliced green onions and tops
½ cup thinly sliced celery
2 tablespoons canola oil
1 can (28 ounces) diced tomatoes, undrained
2 tablespoons tomato paste
1 teaspoon brown sugar
1 teaspoon dried thyme leaves
1 bay leaf
Hot pepper sauce, to taste
Salt and pepper, to taste
2 cups cooked brown rice, warm

Per Serving
Net Carbohydrate (gm): 24
Calories: 373
Fat (gm): 16.9
Saturated fat (gm): 3.1
Cholesterol (mg): 70.5
Sodium (mg): 469
Protein (gm): 27.7
Carbohydrate (gm): 27.5

1. Rub fish fillets with combined garlic, paprika, and cayenne pepper; refrigerate, covered, 1 hour; cut fillets into 1-inch pieces.

2. Sauté onion, bell pepper, green onions, and celery in oil in large saucepan until tender, about 5 minutes. Add tomatoes and liquid, tomato paste, sugar, and herbs and heat to boiling; reduce heat and simmer, covered, 10 minutes.

3. Add fish; simmer, uncovered, until fish is tender and flakes with a fork, about 10 minutes. Discard bay leaf; season to taste with hot pepper sauce, salt, and pepper. Serve over rice in bowls.

Caribbean Sweet-Sour Salmon Stew

6 servings

2 cups thinly sliced red and green bell peppers
1 cup sliced green onions and tops
1 tablespoon minced garlic
2 teaspoons minced gingerroot
1–2 teaspoons minced jalapeño chilies
1 tablespoon peanut oil
1 can (12 ounces) pineapple tidbits in juice, undrained
2 tablespoons packed light brown sugar
2–3 teaspoons curry powder
2–3 tablespoons apple cider vinegar
1½ tablespoons cornstarch
¼ cup cold water
1 pound salmon steaks, cut into 1½-inch pieces
1 can (15 ounces) black beans, rinsed, drained
Salt and pepper, to taste

Per Serving
Net Carbohydrate (gm): 26
Calories: 297
Fat (gm): 10.7
Saturated fat (gm): 2.1
Cholesterol (mg): 44.2
Sodium (mg): 275
Protein (gm): 19.6
Carbohydrate (gm): 30.9

1. Sauté bell peppers, green onions, garlic, gingerroot, and jalapeño chilies in oil in large skillet until onions are tender, about 5 minutes.

2. Drain pineapple, adding enough water to juice to make 1½ cups. Add pineapple mixture, brown sugar, curry powder, and vinegar to skillet; heat to boiling. Stir in combined cornstarch and water; boil, stirring until thickened, about 1 minute.

3. Stir in salmon and beans; simmer, uncovered, until salmon is tender and flakes with a fork, about 5 minutes. Season to taste with salt and pepper.

South American Fish Stew

8 servings

Per Serving
Net Carbohydrate (gm): 29.7
Calories: 279
Fat (gm): 5.4
Saturated fat (gm): 0.9
Cholesterol (mg): 54.4
Sodium (mg): 357
Protein (gm): 24.5
Carbohydrate (gm): 33.2

1 cup sliced onion
2 cloves garlic, minced
1 tablespoon chopped jalapeño chili, *or*
    ½ teaspoon cayenne pepper
1 bay leaf
2 tablespoons olive oil
3 tablespoons all-purpose flour
1 quart water
2 cups chopped, seeded tomatoes
½ cup finely chopped parsley
3 cups thinly sliced red cabbage
2½ cups cubed, peeled sweet potatoes
2 pounds fish fillets (flounder, orange roughy, *or* halibut), cut into 1-inch pieces
Salt and pepper, to taste

1. Sauté onion, garlic, jalapeño chili, and bay leaf in oil in large saucepan until onion is browned, about 5 minutes. Add flour and cook 1 minute; stir in water, tomatoes, and parsley. Heat to boiling, stirring until thickened.

2. Stir in cabbage and sweet potatoes. Heat to boiling; reduce heat and simmer, covered, until potatoes are almost tender, about 20 minutes. Add fish and simmer, uncovered, until fish is tender and flakes with a fork, about 10 minutes. Discard bay leaf; season to taste with salt and pepper.

Bouillabaisse

8 servings

Per Serving
Net Carbohydrate (gm): 7.3
Calories: 266
Fat (gm): 7.8
Saturated fat (gm): 1
Cholesterol (mg): 79.3
Sodium (mg): 922
Protein (gm): 39.5
Carbohydrate (gm): 8.5

½ cup chopped onion
½ cup chopped leek (white part only)
½ cup chopped celery
1 clove garlic, minced
2 tablespoons olive oil
1½ cups clam juice, *or* chicken broth
½ cup dry white wine, clam juice, *or* chicken broth
2 cans (15 ounces each) small diced tomatoes, undrained
1 bay leaf
1 teaspoon dried thyme leaves
1 teaspoon grated orange rind
2 pounds halibut, *or* other lean white fish, cut into 1-inch pieces
½ pound crabmeat, flaked into large pieces
½ pound bay scallops
12 mussels, scrubbed
¼ cup chopped parsley
Salt and pepper, to taste

1. Sauté onion, leek, celery, and garlic in olive oil in Dutch oven until tender, about 7 minutes. Add clam juice and wine. Stir in tomatoes and liquid, herbs, and orange rind; heat to boiling. Reduce heat to low and simmer, covered, 10 minutes.

2. Stir in halibut, crab, scallops, and mussels; simmer, covered, until fish is tender and flakes with a fork, 5 to 8 minutes. Discard any mussels that do not open. Discard bay leaf and stir in parsley; season to taste with salt and pepper.

Bouillabaisse St. Tropez

8 servings

½ cup chopped onion
2 cloves garlic, minced
1 teaspoon dried basil leaves
½ teaspoon dried thyme leaves
½ teaspoon crushed red pepper
⅛ teaspoon crushed fennel seeds
1 bay leaf
⅛ teaspoon crushed saffron threads
2 tablespoons olive oil
2 tablespoons all-purpose flour
1 can (14½ ounces) diced tomatoes, undrained
1 quart water
12 ounces haddock, *or* halibut, fillets
12 ounces cod, sole, *or* flounder fillets
8 ounces crabmeat
8 ounces lobster meat
8 ounces shucked oysters
Salt and pepper, to taste
8 lemon slices
8 slices whole-grain French bread
Aioli (recipe follows)

Per Serving
Net Carbohydrate (gm): 17.9
Calories: 415
Fat (gm): 22.6
Saturated fat (gm): 3.5
Cholesterol (mg): 107.5
Sodium (mg): 784
Protein (gm): 32.8
Carbohydrate (gm): 20.9

1. Sauté onion, garlic, and herbs and seasonings in oil in large Dutch oven until onion is tender, about 5 minutes. Add flour and cook 1 minute. Stir in tomatoes and liquid and water and heat to boiling. Reduce heat and simmer, covered, 15 minutes.

2. Add fish and shellfish to Dutch oven. Heat just to boiling; reduce heat and simmer, covered, until haddock and cod are tender and flake with a fork, 5 to 8 minutes. Discard bay leaf; season to taste with salt and pepper. Stir in lemon slices.

3. Spread bread slices with Aioli and place in bottoms of soup bowls; ladle stew over bread. Serve with remaining Aioli.

Aioli

makes about ¾ cup

¾ cup mayonnaise
1 teaspoon tarragon vinegar
1 teaspoon lemon juice
½–1 teaspoon Dijon mustard
3 cloves garlic, minced
Salt and white pepper, to taste

1. Mix all ingredients, except salt and white pepper; season to taste with salt and white pepper.

Mediterranean Fishermen's Stew

4 servings

1 cup chopped onion
4 teaspoons minced garlic
1 tablespoon olive oil
1 can (28 ounces) plum tomatoes, undrained, chopped
1 cup thinly sliced carrots
1 cup clam juice
1½ pounds cod, cut into 1-inch cubes
1½ cups sliced zucchini
½ cup chopped parsley
1 tablespoon finely chopped fresh basil leaves
1 teaspoon grated lemon rind
Salt and pepper, to taste

Per Serving
Net Carbohydrate (gm): 13.5
Calories: 248
Fat (gm): 4.9
Saturated fat (gm): 0.7
Cholesterol (mg): 72.5
Sodium (mg): 803
Protein (gm): 37.8
Carbohydrate (gm): 18

1. Sauté onion and garlic in oil in large saucepan until tender, about 5 minutes. Add tomatoes, carrots, and clam juice; heat to boiling. Reduce heat and simmer, covered, until carrots are tender, about 10 minutes.

2. Add cod and zucchini; simmer, uncovered, until cod is tender and flakes with a fork, 5 to 10 minutes. Stir in parsley, basil, and lemon rind; season to taste with salt and pepper.

Seafood Stew Milanese

4 servings

⅔ cup chopped onion
⅓ cup quick-cooking brown rice
1 teaspoon minced garlic
½ teaspoon dried thyme leaves
¼ teaspoon crushed saffron threads
1 tablespoon butter
2½ cups reduced-sodium fat-free chicken broth
1 can (14½ ounces) diced tomatoes, undrained
1 cup diced zucchini
8 ounces bay scallops
8 ounces medium shrimp, peeled, deveined
¼ cup grated Parmesan cheese
Salt and pepper, to taste

Per Serving
Net Carbohydrate (gm): 19.5
Calories: 280
Fat (gm): 7.6
Saturated fat (gm): 3.2
Cholesterol (mg): 132.7
Sodium (mg): 715
Protein (gm): 30.5
Carbohydrate (gm): 21.4

1. Sauté onion, rice, garlic, thyme, and saffron in butter in large saucepan until onion is tender, about 5 minutes. Add broth, tomatoes and liquid, and zucchini; heat to boiling. Reduce heat and simmer, covered, 10 minutes.

2. Stir in scallops and shrimp and simmer, uncovered, until shrimp and scallops are cooked and rice is tender, about 5 minutes. Stir in Parmesan cheese; season to taste with salt and pepper.

Italian Scallop Stew

4 servings

1 cup chopped onion
1 teaspoon minced garlic
1 cup chopped green bell pepper
1 tablespoon olive oil
1 tablespoon all-purpose flour
1 can (14½ ounces) Italian-seasoned tomatoes, undrained
¼ cup reduced-sodium fat-free chicken broth
½ cup dry sherry, *or* chicken broth
1 teaspoon dried basil leaves
1 bay leaf
2 cups small broccoli florets
1 pound bay, *or* sea, scallops
Salt and pepper, to taste

Per Serving
Net Carbohydrate (gm): 14.9
Calories: 239
Fat (gm): 4.7
Saturated fat (gm): 0.6
Cholesterol (mg): 39
Sodium (mg): 400
Protein (gm): 22.8
Carbohydrate (gm): 18.7

1. Sauté onion, garlic, and bell pepper in oil in large saucepan until onion is tender, about 5 minutes. Add flour and cook 1 minute. Stir in tomatoes and liquid, broth, sherry, basil, and bay leaf; heat to boiling. Stir in broccoli and simmer, covered, until broccoli is crisp-tender, about 5 minutes.

2. Heat stew to boiling; add scallops. Reduce heat, and simmer, covered, until scallops are cooked and opaque, about 5 minutes. Discard bay leaf; season to taste with salt and pepper.

Italian-Style Fish Stew

4 servings

1 cup sliced mushrooms
3 large garlic cloves, minced
1 tablespoon dried oregano leaves
1 teaspoon dried thyme leaves
¼ teaspoon crushed red pepper
1 tablespoon olive oil
1½ pounds tomatoes, peeled, chopped
1 cup chopped parsley
½ cup dry white wine, *or* clam juice
1¼ pounds grouper, *or* other firm-fleshed fish, cut into serving pieces
Salt and pepper, to taste

Per Serving
Net Carbohydrate (gm): 8.3
Calories: 234
Fat (gm): 5.7
Saturated fat (gm): 0.9
Cholesterol (mg): 52.2
Sodium (mg): 102
Protein (gm): 30.2
Carbohydrate (gm): 11.6

1. Sauté mushrooms, garlic, oregano, thyme, and red pepper in oil in Dutch oven until tender, about 5 minutes. Add tomatoes, parsley, and wine; heat to boiling. Reduce heat and simmer, covered, 10 minutes.

2. Add fish and simmer, uncovered, until fish is tender and flakes with a fork, about 10 minutes. Season to taste with salt and pepper.

Trout with Vegetable Garni

4 servings

4 fresh, *or* frozen, thawed, pan-dressed rainbow trout, *or*
    lake perch (about 6 ounces each)
Pepper, to taste
½ cup dry white wine, *or* clam juice
¼ cup clam juice
1 tablespoon lemon juice
½ teaspoon dried thyme leaves
½ teaspoon dried oregano leaves
1 cup sliced mushrooms
⅓ cup chopped carrot
⅓ cup chopped green onions and tops
1 clove garlic, minced
1 tablespoon canola oil

Per Serving
Net Carbohydrate (gm): 2.5
Calories: 299
Fat (gm): 12.6
Saturated fat (gm): 2.9
Cholesterol (mg): 99.9
Sodium (mg): 167
Protein (gm): 37.4
Carbohydrate (gm): 3.4

1. Place fish in shallow baking dish and sprinkle with pepper. Pour combined wine, clam juice, lemon juice, thyme, and oregano over fish. Cover and refrigerate 2 hours. Drain fish, reserving marinade.

2. Sauté mushrooms, carrot, green onions, and garlic in oil in large skillet until tender but not brown, about 5 minutes. Push vegetables to side of skillet. Add fish and cook over medium heat until browned, 2 to 3 minutes on each side. Add reserved marinade; simmer, covered, until fish is tender and flakes with a fork, about 5 minutes.

3. Transfer fish and vegetables to platter; keep warm. Boil marinade mixture until reduced to ¼ cup, 2 to 3 minutes; spoon over fish.

Pan-Fried Trout

4 servings

1½ pounds trout fillets
⅓ cup yellow cornmeal
¼ teaspoon anise seeds
¼ teaspoon pepper
½ cup minced cilantro, *or* parsley
1 tablespoon canola oil
1 tablespoon butter
Lemon wedges

Per Serving
Net Carbohydrate (gm): 7.2
Calories: 329
Fat (gm): 15.9
Saturated fat (gm): 4.8
Cholesterol (mg): 108.1
Sodium (mg): 94
Protein (gm): 36.4
Carbohydrate (gm): 8

1. Coat fish with combined cornmeal, spices, and cilantro, pressing gently into fish. Fry fish in oil and butter in large skillet over medium heat until fish is tender and flakes with a fork, about 5 minutes on each side. Serve with lemon wedges.

Sole with Rosemary Potatoes

4 servings

2 Idaho potatoes (about 6 ounces each), cut into wedges
Vegetable cooking spray
2 tablespoons dried rosemary leaves
½ teaspoon garlic powder
¼ teaspoon pepper
¼ cup chopped red onion
4 shallots, minced
1 large clove garlic, minced
1 tablespoon butter
1½ pounds sole fillets

Per Serving
Net Carbohydrate (gm): 19.2
Calories: 258
Fat (gm): 5.1
Saturated fat (gm): 2.4
Cholesterol (mg): 86
Sodium (mg): 174
Protein (gm): 31
Carbohydrate (gm): 22

1. Place potatoes on baking sheet; spray lightly with cooking spray and sprinkle with rosemary, garlic powder, and pepper. Bake potatoes at 400 degrees until fork-tender, about 45 minutes.

2. About 15 minutes before potatoes are done, sauté onion, shallots, and garlic in butter in large skillet until tender, about 5 minutes. Fold each sole fillet in half and add to skillet. Cook, uncovered, over medium heat until fish is tender and flakes with a fork, about 6 minutes, turning once. Arrange fish and potatoes on serving platter; spoon shallot mixture over fish.

Microwave Sole Oriental

4 servings

4 sole, *or* flounder, fillets (about 6 ounces each)
2 tablespoons soy sauce
3 tablespoons frozen orange juice concentrate
2 cloves garlic, minced
1½ tablespoons sesame oil
1 tablespoon chopped gingerroot
Pepper, to taste
2 teaspoons toasted sesame seeds
Chopped parsley, as garnish

Per Serving
Net Carbohydrate (gm): 6.5
Calories: 216
Fat (gm): 7.6
Saturated fat (gm): 1.2
Cholesterol (mg): 77.8
Sodium (mg): 648
Protein (gm): 29.5
Carbohydrate (gm): 6.9

1. Arrange fish in glass baking dish, tucking under any thin edges. Combine soy sauce, orange juice, garlic, sesame oil, and gingerroot in small bowl; drizzle over fish. Let stand 15 minutes.

2. Microwave, loosely covered, on High 3 to 4 minutes or until fish flakes with a fork. Let stand 1 minute. Sprinkle with pepper, sesame seeds, and parsley.

Sole, Mediterranean Style

4 servings

2 cups sliced red and green bell peppers
½ cup sliced onion
4 cloves garlic, minced
1 tablespoon olive oil
½ cup reduced-sodium fat-free chicken broth
¼ cup softened, chopped, sun-dried tomatoes (not in oil)
1 teaspoon dried basil leaves
Salt and pepper, to taste
4 ounces whole wheat penne, *or* mostaccioli, cooked, warm
¼ cup grated Parmesan cheese
4 skinless sole fillets (about 4 ounces each)
Chopped parsley, as garnish

Per Serving
Net Carbohydrate (gm): 26.3
Calories: 302
Fat (gm): 7.1
Saturated fat (gm): 1.8
Cholesterol (mg): 61.5
Sodium (mg): 291
Protein (gm): 30.1
Carbohydrate (gm): 31.1

1. Sauté bell peppers, onion, and garlic in olive oil in large skillet until tender, about 5 minutes; add chicken broth, sun-dried tomatoes, and basil. Heat to boiling; reduce heat and simmer, stirring frequently, until vegetables are very tender, about 5 minutes; season to taste with salt and pepper. Toss with pasta and cheese in large bowl; keep warm.

2. Cook sole, covered, in greased large skillet over medium heat until fish is tender and flakes with fork, 5 to 8 minutes. Sprinkle lightly with salt and pepper. Spoon pasta mixture onto serving platter; top with fish. Sprinkle with chopped parsley.

Wine-Poached Cod with Asparagus

4 servings

1 tablespoon chopped shallots, *or* green onion
2 cloves garlic, chopped
2 tablespoons butter
⅔ cup dry white wine
1 tablespoon lemon juice
2 tablespoons chopped parsley
1 tablespoon chopped fresh, *or* 1 teaspoon dried, basil leaves
4 cod fillets (about 6 ounces each)
Salt and pepper, to taste
1 pound fresh asparagus, ends trimmed, cooked, warm

Per Serving
Net Carbohydrate (gm): 4.3
Calories: 251
Fat (gm): 7.4
Saturated fat (gm): 4
Cholesterol (mg): 89
Sodium (mg): 160
Protein (gm): 33.2
Carbohydrate (gm): 6.9

1. Sauté shallots and garlic in butter in large skillet, until tender, about 2 minutes. Add wine, lemon juice, and herbs. Sprinkle fish lightly with salt and pepper and add to skillet. Heat to boiling; reduce heat and simmer, covered, until fish is tender and flakes with a fork, 8 to 10 minutes.

2. Arrange fish and asparagus on platter. Boil fish poaching liquid, uncovered, until slightly thickened, about 2 minutes; pour over fish and asparagus.

Baked Cod Provençal

4 servings

¾ cup chopped onion
2 cloves garlic, chopped
1 tablespoon olive oil
4 cups chopped, seeded tomatoes
¼ cup sliced, pitted black olives
2 tablespoons drained capers
¼ cup chopped fresh, *or* 1 tablespoon dried, basil leaves
1 tablespoon lemon juice
1 teaspoon dried oregano leaves
Salt and pepper, to taste
4 cod fillets (about 6 ounces each)

Per Serving
Net Carbohydrate (gm): 9.6
Calories: 233
Fat (gm): 6
Saturated fat (gm): 0.9
Cholesterol (mg): 72.5
Sodium (mg): 310
Protein (gm): 32.6
Carbohydrate (gm): 12.9

1. Sauté onion and garlic in oil in large skillet until onion is tender, about 5 minutes. Add tomatoes, olives, capers, basil, lemon juice, and oregano; heat to boiling. Reduce heat and simmer, uncovered, until sauce is thickened, 8 to 10 minutes, stirring occasionally. Season to taste with salt and pepper.

2. Spoon sauce into greased baking dish; arrange fish on sauce and sprinkle lightly with salt and pepper. Bake, covered, at 450 degrees until fish is tender and flakes with a fork, about 10 minutes.

Poached Halibut with Sun-Dried Tomato Sauce

4 servings

¾ cup chopped onion
1 teaspoon minced garlic
1 tablespoon olive oil
1 cup clam juice, *or* chicken broth
¼ cup chopped softened, sun-dried tomatoes (not in oil)
1 teaspoon dried marjoram leaves
½ teaspoon dried oregano leaves
4 halibut steaks (about 6 ounces each)
1 can (16 ounces) diced tomatoes, drained
Salt and pepper, to taste

Per Serving
Net Carbohydrate (gm): 7.6
Calories: 260
Fat (gm): 7.6
Saturated fat (gm): 1
Cholesterol (mg): 54.2
Sodium (mg): 847
Protein (gm): 41.5
Carbohydrate (gm): 9.3

1. Sauté onion and garlic in oil in large skillet until tender and well-browned, about 5 minutes. Stir in clam juice, sun-dried tomatoes, and herbs and heat to boiling. Reduce heat and simmer, uncovered, until liquid is almost evaporated, about 5 minutes.

2. Add fish and tomatoes and liquid to skillet; simmer gently until fish is tender and flakes with a fork, 3 to 5 minutes. Season to taste with salt and pepper.

Stuffed Flounder with Orange Sauce

6 servings

⅔ cup chopped onion
1 clove garlic, minced
2 teaspoons butter
1 cup chopped orange sections
½ cup fresh whole wheat bread crumbs
6 flounder fillets (6 ounces each)
Orange Sauce (recipe follows)

Per Serving
Net Carbohydrate (gm): 11.4
Calories: 224
Fat (gm): 3.7
Saturated fat (gm): 1.4
Cholesterol (mg): 85
Sodium (mg): 177
Protein (gm): 33.2
Carbohydrate (gm): 13

1. Sauté onion and garlic in butter in small skillet until tender, about 5 minutes. Remove from heat; stir in orange sections and bread crumbs. Spoon crumb mixture onto thick end of each fillet. Roll up fillets, beginning at large ends; fasten with wooden picks.

2. Arrange rolls, seam sides down, in greased baking dish. Bake, covered, at 400 degrees until fish is tender and flakes with a fork, 10 to 12 minutes. Spoon Orange Sauce over fish.

Orange Sauce

makes about 1 cup

1 cup fresh orange juice
1½ tablespoons grated orange rind
¼ teaspoon ground ginger
¼ teaspoon dry mustard
1 tablespoon cornstarch

1. Whisk together all ingredients in small saucepan. Heat to boiling over medium heat, whisking constantly until sauce thickens, about 2 minutes.

Flounder with Mixed Herb Pesto in Parchment

4 servings

4 sole, *or* flounder, fillets (about 6 ounces each)
Mixed Herb Pesto (recipe follows)

Per Serving
Net Carbohydrate (gm): 3.2
Calories: 305
Fat (gm): 16.6
Saturated fat (gm): 2.7
Cholesterol (mg): 83.3
Sodium (mg): 188
Protein (gm): 34.5
Carbohydrate (gm): 4

1. Place each fillet at one side of a 12-inch square of parchment paper or heavy foil. Spread Mixed Herb Pesto evenly on each fillet. Fold parchment squares in half and seal by folding edges together; place packets on baking pan sheet. Bake at 400 degrees until packets puff slightly, about 15 minutes.

Mixed Herb Pesto

makes about ⅓ cup

¼ cup packed fresh parsley
¼ cup packed fresh, *or* 1 tablespoon dried, basil leaves
2 tablespoons packed fresh, *or* 2 teaspoons dried, oregano leaves
2 tablespoons chopped shallots
3 small cloves garlic
2 tablespoons grated Parmesan cheese
3 tablespoons chopped walnuts
3 tablespoons olive oil
2 tablespoons lemon juice
½ teaspoon pepper
Salt, to taste

1. Process all ingredients, except salt, in food processor or blender until very finely chopped. Season to taste with salt.

Cajun-Style Fish

4 servings

1 cup chopped onion
1 clove garlic, minced
2 tablespoons butter, divided
1 can (14½ ounces) diced tomatoes, undrained
1 cup chopped green bell pepper
2 cups cubed zucchini *and/or* yellow squash
½ teaspoon dried basil leaves
½ teaspoon dried thyme leaves
¼ teaspoon dried marjoram leaves
2–3 drops hot pepper sauce
1½ pounds skinless fish fillets (flounder, sole, halibut, *or* other lean white fish)
Salt and pepper, to taste

Per Serving
Net Carbohydrate (gm): 9.2
Calories: 371
Fat (gm): 9.4
Saturated fat (gm): 4.5
Cholesterol (mg): 98.1
Sodium (mg): 465
Protein (gm): 37.3
Carbohydrate (gm): 34.3

1. Sauté onion and garlic in 1 tablespoon butter in large skillet until almost tender, about 5 minutes. Add tomatoes and liquid, green pepper, zucchini, and herbs. Heat to boiling; reduce heat and cook, covered, until vegetables are tender, about 10 minutes. Season to taste with hot pepper sauce, salt, and pepper.

2. While vegetables are cooking, sauté fish in remaining 1 tablespoon butter over medium heat until fish is tender and flakes with a fork, about 4 minutes on each side. Season to taste with salt and pepper.

3. Arrange fish on serving platter; spoon vegetables over.

Curried Pineapple Flounder

6 servings

1½ pounds flounder, *or*
    other lean white fish, fillets *or* steaks
2 tablespoons butter
1 cup pineapple juice, divided
2 tablespoons minced onion
1 tablespoon diced pimiento
1 teaspoon salt
2 tablespoons minced parsley
½ teaspoon curry powder
2 tablespoons lemon juice
1 tablespoon packed light brown sugar
1 tablespoon cornstarch

Per Serving
Net Carbohydrate (gm): 9.9
Calories: 252
Fat (gm): 6.1
Saturated fat (gm): 3
Cholesterol (mg): 65.4
Sodium (mg): 526
Protein (gm): 23.3
Carbohydrate (gm): 25.1

1. Place fish in baking pan; dot with butter. Bake, uncovered, at 400 degrees until fish is tender and flakes with a fork, about 10 minutes.

2. While fish is baking, combine pineapple juice and remaining ingredients in small saucepan; heat to boiling, stirring until thickened, 1 to 2 minutes.

3. Arrange fish over rice (not included in nutritional data) on serving platter; spoon pineapple sauce over.

Caribbean-Style Flounder

4 servings

1 cup thinly sliced onion
1 tablespoon minced gingerroot
2 teaspoons minced garlic
2 teaspoons peanut oil
2 cups reduced-sodium fat-free chicken broth
1 cup cubed (½-inch) sweet potato
1 can (14½ ounces) diced tomatoes, undrained
1 teaspoon dried thyme leaves
1 cup frozen peas
1 pound flounder fillets, cut into ¾-inch pieces
4 teaspoons lemon juice
Salt and pepper, to taste

Per Serving
Net Carbohydrate (gm): 17.9
Calories: 251
Fat (gm): 4.8
Saturated fat (gm): 0.8
Cholesterol (mg): 66.7
Sodium (mg): 514
Protein (gm): 29.2
Carbohydrate (gm): 22.5

1. Sauté onion, ginger, and garlic in oil in large saucepan until tender, about 5 minutes. Add broth, sweet potato, tomatoes and liquid, and thyme. Heat to boiling; reduce heat and simmer, covered, until potato is tender, about 10 minutes.

2. Add peas and flounder; simmer until fish is tender and flakes with a fork, about 5 minutes. Stir in lemon juice; season to taste with salt and pepper.

Flounder Florentine

4 servings

1 can (14½ ounces) diced tomatoes, undrained
2 cups packed baby spinach leaves
1 tablespoon olive oil
½ teaspoon minced garlic
Salt and pepper, to taste
1¼ pounds skinless flounder fillets
4 ounces linguine, cooked, warm
3 tablespoons grated Parmesan cheese

Per Serving
Net Carbohydrate (gm): 16.6
Calories: 277
Fat (gm): 7
Saturated fat (gm): 1.6
Cholesterol (mg): 71
Sodium (mg): 507
Protein (gm): 33
Carbohydrate (gm): 19.3

1. Combine tomatoes and liquid, spinach, olive oil, and garlic in medium saucepan; heat to boiling. Reduce heat and simmer until thickened to desired consistency, about 10 minutes; season to taste with salt and pepper.

2. Sprinkle flounder lightly with salt and pepper; cook, covered, in greased skillet over medium heat until fish is tender and flakes with a fork, 5 to 8 minutes.

3. Place linguine on serving platter; top with tomato mixture and flounder. Sprinkle with Parmesan cheese.

Microwave Whitefish with Cumberland Sauce

4 servings

1½ pounds whitefish fillets
¼ cup thinly sliced green onions and tops
Paprika
Sliced cucumber, as garnish
Fresh dill sprigs, as garnish
1½ cups cooked brown rice, warm
Cumberland Sauce (recipe follows)

Per Serving
Net Carbohydrate (gm): 18.6
Calories: 228
Fat (gm): 9.4
Saturated fat (gm): 4
Cholesterol (mg): 47
Sodium (mg): 59
Protein (gm): 15.1
Carbohydrate (gm): 20.2

1. Arrange fish in glass baking dish, folding thin ends under; sprinkle with green onions and paprika. Cover with vented plastic wrap. Microwave 5 minutes on High, or until fish flakes with fork.

2. Arrange fish on serving platter; garnish with cucumbers and dill sprigs. Serve with rice and Cumberland Sauce.

Cumberland Sauce

makes about 1 cup

½ cup chopped, peeled and seeded cucumber
½ cup sour cream
¼ cup plain yogurt
1 tablespoon chopped fresh, *or* 2 teaspoons dried, dill weed
2 cloves garlic, minced

1. Process all ingredients in food processor or blender until smooth.

Whitefish and Linguine with Lemon-Caper Sauce

6 servings

6 whitefish fillets (about 5 ounces each)
1 tablespoon Dijon mustard
2 cloves garlic, minced
1 teaspoon dried tarragon leaves
2–3 tablespoons butter
3 tablespoons all-purpose flour
1 can (14½ ounces) reduced-sodium fat-free chicken broth
2–3 teaspoons lemon juice
3 tablespoons drained capers
¼ teaspoon salt
⅛ teaspoon white pepper
6 ounces herb linguine, cooked, warm

Per Serving
Net Carbohydrate (gm): 17.9
Calories: 332
Fat (gm): 12.7
Saturated fat (gm): 3.7
Cholesterol (mg): 99.5
Sodium (mg): 523
Protein (gm): 32.9
Carbohydrate (gm): 19

1. Brush tops of fish fillets with combined mustard, garlic, and tarragon. Place in baking pan; bake, uncovered, at 350 degrees until fish is tender and flakes with fork, 10 to 12 minutes.

2. Melt butter in small saucepan; stir in flour. Cook over medium heat, stirring constantly, 1 to 2 minutes. Stir in chicken broth and lemon juice; heat to boiling. Boil, stirring constantly until thickened, 1 to 2 minutes. Stir in capers, salt, and white pepper. Arrange fish on linguine on serving platter; spoon sauce over fish.

Baked Fish with Tomato Mélange

8 servings

Tomato Mélange (recipe follows)
1–2 whole whitefish, red snapper, *or*
    trout, pan-dressed (about 2 pounds)
¼ cup sliced almonds, toasted
2 cups cooked brown rice, warm

Per Serving
Net Carbohydrate (gm): 19.8
Calories: 292
Fat (gm): 10.9
Saturated fat (gm): 1.5
Cholesterol (mg): 65.5
Sodium (mg): 201
Protein (gm): 25.8
Carbohydrate (gm): 22.5

1. Spoon Tomato Mélange into greased baking dish; arrange fish on top. Bake, uncovered, at 400 degrees until fish is tender and flakes with a fork. Sprinkle fish with almonds; serve with rice.

Tomato Mélange

makes about 2 cups

½ cup thinly sliced green onions and tops
¼ cup minced shallots, *or* onions
½ cup chopped celery
1 tablespoon olive oil
½ cup sun-dried tomatoes (not in oil) softened, chopped
2 cups chopped tomatoes
½ cup unseasoned dry bread crumbs
½ teaspoon dried chervil, *or* tarragon, leaves
¼ teaspoon white pepper

1. Sauté green onions, shallots, and celery in oil in large skillet over medium heat until tender, about 5 minutes. Add sun-dried and chopped tomatoes and continue cooking 5 minutes. Mix in bread crumbs, chervil, and white pepper.

Red Snapper with Cayenne Tomato Relish

4 servings

4 red snapper fillets (about 6 ounces each)
Juice of 1 lemon
½ cup dry white wine, *or* clam juice
Cayenne Tomato Relish (recipe follows)
2 tablespoons chopped parsley

Per Serving
Net Carbohydrate (gm): 3.4
Calories: 223
Fat (gm): 4.1
Saturated fat (gm): 0.7
Cholesterol (mg): 62.4
Sodium (mg): 246
Protein (gm): 36
Carbohydrate (gm): 4.4

1. Place fish in greased baking pan; pour lemon juice and wine over. Bake, uncovered, at 400 degrees until fish flakes with a fork, about 10 minutes. Remove fish to serving platter and spoon Cayenne Tomato Relish over. Sprinkle with parsley.

Cayenne Tomato Relish

makes about 2 cups

½ cup chopped green onions and tops
1 clove garlic, minced
1 tablespoon olive oil
1 can (15 ounces) small diced tomatoes, drained
½ cup finely chopped green bell pepper
½ cup sliced mushrooms
1 tablespoon dried basil leaves
1 teaspoon cayenne pepper
1 tablespoon lemon juice
Salt, to taste

1. Sauté green onions and garlic in oil until tender, 3 to 4 minutes. Add remaining ingredients, except lemon juice and salt, and heat to boiling. Reduce heat and simmer until mixture thickens slightly, about 12 to 15 minutes. Stir in lemon juice; season to taste with salt.

Grilled Red Snapper with Jalapeño Mayonnaise

6 servings

1 lemon, sliced
1 whole red snapper (about 3 pounds), pan-dressed
2 tablespoons tarragon wine vinegar
1 tablespoon chopped fresh, *or*
    1 teaspoon dried, tarragon leaves
Jalapeño Mayonnaise (recipe follows)

Per Serving
Net Carbohydrate (gm): 2.2
Calories: 386
Fat (gm): 19.9
Saturated fat (gm): 3.5
Cholesterol (mg): 94.8
Sodium (mg): 312
Protein (gm): 48.6
Carbohydrate (gm): 2.5

1. Place lemon slices in fish cavity; sprinkle inside of fish with vinegar and tarragon. Place fish on greased grill and cook, covered, until fish is tender and flakes with a fork, about 20 minutes; turn fish once during cooking. Arrange fish on serving platter; serve with Jalapeño Mayonnaise.

Jalapeño Mayonnaise

makes about 1 cup

½ cup mayonnaise
½ cup plain yogurt
2 jalapeño chilies, seeded, chopped
¼ cup chopped cilantro
¼ teaspoon ground cumin

1. Combine all ingredients in small bowl; refrigerate, covered, until ready to serve. Stir before serving.

Red Snapper Veracruz

6 servings

1 whole red snapper (about 3 pounds), pan-dressed
3 tablespoons lime juice
3 cloves garlic, minced
Veracruz Sauce (recipe follows)
6 lime wedges

Per Serving
Net Carbohydrate (gm): 7.4
Calories: 304
Fat (gm): 8.4
Saturated fat (gm): 1.5
Cholesterol (mg): 82
Sodium (mg): 380
Protein (gm): 48.7
Carbohydrate (gm): 9.5

1. Pierce surfaces of fish with long-tined fork; rub with lime juice and garlic. Refrigerate, covered, in large glass baking dish 2 hours.

2. Spoon Veracruz Sauce over fish. Bake, uncovered, at 400 degrees until fish is tender and flakes with a fork, 25 to 35 minutes. Place fish on serving plate; garnish with lime wedges.

Veracruz Sauce

makes about 2 cups

1 cup chopped onion
3 cloves garlic, minced
1 jalapeño chili, seeds discarded, minced
1–2 -inch piece cinnamon stick
1 bay leaf
½ teaspoon dried oregano leaves
¼ teaspoon dried thyme leaves
½ teaspoon ground cumin
1 tablespoon olive oil
3 cups chopped tomatoes
¼ cup sliced, pitted green olives
1–2 tablespoons drained capers
Salt and pepper, to taste

1. Sauté onion, garlic, jalapeño chili, cinnamon, and herbs in oil in large skillet until onion is tender, 5 to 8 minutes. Add tomatoes, olives, and capers; cook, covered, over medium-high heat until tomatoes release juice. Reduce heat and simmer, uncovered, until sauce is of medium consistency, about 10 minutes. Discard bay leaf; season to taste with salt and pepper.

Red Snapper Baked with Cilantro

4 servings

4 red snapper fillets (about 6 ounces each)
⅓ cup lime juice
1½ tablespoons pickled jalapeño chili juice
1 teaspoon ground cumin
½ cup thinly sliced onion
2 pickled jalapeño chilies, minced
2 cloves garlic, minced
½ cup coarsely chopped cilantro
Salt and pepper, to taste
6 lime wedges

Per Serving
Net Carbohydrate (gm): 5
Calories: 202
Fat (gm): 3.8
Saturated fat (gm): 0.8
Cholesterol (mg): 61.5
Sodium (mg): 255
Protein (gm): 36
Carbohydrate (gm): 6.3

1. Arrange fish in glass baking dish. Combine lime juice, jalapeño juice, and cumin; pour over fish. Arrange onion, jalapeño chilies, garlic, and cilantro over fish. Refrigerate, covered, 2 hours, turning fish once.

2. Bake, uncovered, at 400 degrees until fish is tender and flakes with a fork, about 10 minutes. Sprinkle fish lightly with salt and pepper. Arrange fish on serving platter; garnish with lime wedges.

Grilled Red Snapper with Tropical Salsa

6 servings

1 whole red snapper (about 3 pounds), dressed
3 tablespoons lime juice
2 cloves garlic, minced
Tropical Salsa (recipe follows)
Lime wedges, as garnish
Cilantro, *or* parsley, sprigs, as garnish

Per Serving
Net Carbohydrate (gm): 7.8
Calories: 276
Fat (gm): 5
Saturated fat (gm): 1.1
Cholesterol (mg): 82
Sodium (mg): 196
Protein (gm): 48.3
Carbohydrate (gm): 9.1

1. Pierce surfaces of fish with long-tined fork; rub with lime juice and garlic. Refrigerate, covered, in large glass baking dish 2 hours.

2. Grill fish over medium-hot coals, or bake, uncovered, at 400 degrees until fish is tender and flakes with a fork, 25 to 30 minutes. Arrange fish on serving platter; spoon Tropical Salsa around fish. Garnish with lime wedges and cilantro.

Tropical Salsa

makes about 1½ cups

½ cup cubed papaya, *or* mango
½ cup cubed pineapple
½ cup chopped tomato
¼ cup chopped, seeded cucumber
¼ cup cooked black beans
½ teaspoon minced jalapeño chili
2 tablespoons finely chopped cilantro
¼ cup orange juice
1 tablespoon lime juice
2–3 teaspoons packed brown sugar

1. Combine all ingredients and toss.

Grilled Swordfish with Jalapeño Tomato Relish

4 servings

1 tablespoon olive oil
2 tablespoons lime juice
¼ teaspoon pepper
4 swordfish steaks (about 6 ounces each)
Jalapeño Tomato Relish (recipe follows)

Per Serving
Net Carbohydrate (gm): 5.5
Calories: 260
Fat (gm): 9.9
Saturated fat (gm): 2.3
Cholesterol (mg): 64
Sodium (mg): 358
Protein (gm): 34.5
Carbohydrate (gm): 7

1. Mix olive oil, lime juice, and pepper in small bowl; brush onto swordfish. Refrigerate, covered, 1 hour.

2. Grill fish over hot coals until fish is tender and flakes with a fork, about 8 minutes, turning once. Serve fish with Jalapeño Tomato Relish.

Jalapeño Tomato Relish

makes about 1 cup

¼ cup chili sauce
1 cup chopped tomato
½–1 small jalapeño chili, seeded, chopped
1–2 tablespoon lime juice

1. Mix all ingredients.

Balsamic-Glazed Salmon Fillets

6 servings

6 salmon fillets (about 6 ounces each)
Balsamic Glaze (recipe follows)
1 tablespoon chopped fresh, *or*
    1 teaspoon dried, oregano leaves
Salt and pepper, to taste
12 fresh basil leaves, julienned

Per Serving
Net Carbohydrate (gm): 9.1
Calories: 353
Fat (gm): 18.3
Saturated fat (gm): 3.7
Cholesterol (mg): 99.5
Sodium (mg): 159
Protein (gm): 34
Carbohydrate (gm): 9.2

1. Arrange fish in greased baking pan. Brush with warm Balsamic Glaze and sprinkle with oregano. Bake, uncovered, at 475 degrees until fish flakes with a fork, 10 to 14 minutes. Brush with any remaining glaze. Sprinkle lightly with salt and pepper; sprinkle with basil.

Balsamic Glaze

makes about ½ cup

½ cup balsamic vinegar
1 tablespoon Dijon mustard
1 tablespoon dry white wine, *or* water
2 tablespoons honey
4 cloves garlic, minced

1. Heat all ingredients to boiling in small saucepan; reduce heat and simmer, uncovered, until slightly thickened, 2 to 3 minutes.

Salmon with Spinach and Mushrooms

4 servings

1 tablespoon minced shallots
1½ cups sliced red and yellow bell peppers
1 cup sliced mushrooms
1 tablespoon butter
1½ pounds salmon steaks, cut into 1½-inch pieces
½ pound baby spinach leaves
Juice of 2 lemons
Salt and pepper, to taste

Per Serving
Net Carbohydrate (gm): 4.9
Calories: 369
Fat (gm): 21.7
Saturated fat (gm): 5.6
Cholesterol (mg): 107.7
Sodium (mg): 201
Protein (gm): 36.7
Carbohydrate (gm): 6.5

1. Sauté shallots, bell peppers, and mushrooms in butter in large skillet until tender, about 5 minutes. Move vegetables to side of skillet. Add salmon and cook over medium heat until fish is tender and flakes with a fork, turning pieces occasionally, about 8 minutes. Add spinach and lemon juice; cook, covered, just until spinach wilts, about 2 minutes. Season to taste with salt and pepper.

Salmon Steaks Baked with Herbed Yogurt

4 servings

4 salmon steaks (about 5 ounces each)
1 cup plain yogurt
½ teaspoon dry mustard
½ teaspoon dried dill weed
½ teaspoon dried thyme leaves
1 tablespoon lemon juice
½ teaspoon pepper
Paprika, as garnish
2 tablespoons minced parsley
1½ cups cooked brown rice, warm

Per Serving
Net Carbohydrate (gm): 20.4
Calories: 382
Fat (gm): 17
Saturated fat (gm): 3.8
Cholesterol (mg): 86.6
Sodium (mg): 132
Protein (gm): 33.6
Carbohydrate (gm): 22

1. Arrange salmon in greased baking pan. Combine remaining ingredients, except paprika, parsley, and rice, and spread over fish. Bake, uncovered, at 375 degrees until fish is tender and flakes easily with fork, about 20 minutes; sprinkle with paprika and parsley. Serve with rice.

Fish Teriyaki

4 servings

4 salmon, orange roughy, *or*
    red snapper fillets or steaks (6 ounces each)
¼ cup light soy sauce
1 teaspoon brown sugar
2 tablespoons sake, *or* dry white wine
2 cloves garlic, minced
2 teaspoons minced fresh ginger
¼ teaspoon red pepper flakes

Per Serving
Net Carbohydrate (gm): 4.2
Calories: 342
Fat (gm): 18.3
Saturated fat (gm): 3.7
Cholesterol (mg): 99.5
Sodium (mg): 606
Protein (gm): 35.5
Carbohydrate (gm): 4.3

1. Arrange fish in greased broiling pan. Brush both sides of fish with combined remaining ingredients and let stand 15 minutes. Broil fish 6 inches from heat source until fish flakes easily when tested with fork, 8 to 10 minutes.

Poached Salmon with Cream Cheese Hollandaise Sauce

6 servings

¾ cup dry white wine, *or* clam juice
½ cup water
2 thin slices lemon
4 dill, *or* parsley, sprigs
½ teaspoon dried thyme leaves
½ teaspoon dried tarragon leaves
1 bay leaf
4 peppercorns
½ teaspoon salt
6 salmon steaks (5 ounces each)
Cream Cheese Hollandaise Sauce (see p. 4)
Finely chopped parsley leaves, as garnish
6 lemon wedges, as garnish

Per Serving
Net Carbohydrate (gm): 2.4
Calories: 408
Fat (gm): 27.7
Saturated fat (gm): 10.8
Cholesterol (mg): 120.1
Sodium (mg): 382
Protein (gm): 31.1
Carbohydrate (gm): 2.7

1. Heat wine, water, lemon slices, herbs, peppercorns, and salt to boiling in medium skillet. Reduce heat and simmer, covered, 5 minutes. Add salmon to skillet; simmer, covered, until fish is cooked and flakes with a fork, 6 to 10 minutes, depending upon thickness of fish. Carefully remove fish from skillet with slotted pancake turner.

2. Arrange salmon on serving platter and spoon Cream Cheese Hollandaise Sauce over; sprinkle with parsley. Serve with lemon wedges.

Salmon with Cilantro Pesto and Fettuccine

4 servings

4 salmon steaks (about 5 ounces each)
1 tablespoon Dijon mustard
4 ounces fettuccine, cooked, warm
Cilantro Pesto (recipe follows)

Per Serving
Net Carbohydrate (gm): 17.7
Calories: 468
Fat (gm): 27.6
Saturated fat (gm): 5.6
Cholesterol (mg): 107.5
Sodium (mg): 376
Protein (gm): 35.6
Carbohydrate (gm): 18.6

1. Brush salmon with mustard; place on broiler pan. Broil 6 inches from heat source until salmon is tender and flakes with fork, 10 to 15 minutes, turning once.

2. Toss fettuccine with Cilantro Pesto; arrange around salmon on serving platter.

Cilantro Pesto

makes about ¾ cup

1½ cups packed cilantro leaves
½ cup packed parsley
1 clove garlic, minced
¼ cup grated Parmesan cheese
3 tablespoons pine nuts, *or* walnuts
2 tablespoons olive oil
1–2 tablespoons lemon juice
¼ teaspoon salt
¼ teaspoon pepper

1. Combine herbs, garlic, Parmesan cheese, and pine nuts in food processor or blender. Process, adding oil and lemon juice gradually, until mixture is very finely chopped. Stir in salt and pepper.

Salmon and Pasta Salad

8 servings

1½ pounds cooked salmon steaks, cubed *or* flaked
1½ cups chopped tomatoes
¼ cup thinly sliced onion
½ cup shredded carrot
¼ cup sliced, pitted black olives
2 cloves garlic, minced
3 tablespoons olive oil
¼ cup minced parsley
1½ teaspoons dried oregano leaves
¾ teaspoon dried basil leaves
8 ounces bowties, *or* shells, cooked, room temperature
Salt and pepper, to taste

Per Serving
Net Carbohydrate (gm): 23.1
Calories: 326
Fat (gm): 15.4
Saturated fat (gm): 2.7
Cholesterol (mg): 50.2
Sodium (mg): 95
Protein (gm): 21.2
Carbohydrate (gm): 24.8

1. Mix all ingredients, except salt and pepper, in large bowl; season to taste with salt and pepper.

Niçoise Platter

4 servings

4 small artichokes (about 2 ounces each)
6 ounces small red potatoes
1 cup cut (2-inch) green beans
1 cup cubed (¾-inch) beets
2 hard-cooked eggs, halved
1½ cups tomato wedges
12 ounces tuna steaks, cooked, flaked, *or*
    2 cans (6 ounces each) tuna in water, drained
4 cups torn mixed salad greens
2 tablespoons sliced ripe olives
4 teaspoons drained capers
½ cup Italian dressing
1 tablespoon minced shallot
1 clove garlic, minced
Salt and pepper, to taste
Aioli (see p. 284)

Per Serving
Net Carbohydrate (gm): 22.2
Calories: 691
Fat (gm): 51.3
Saturated fat (gm): 8.1
Cholesterol (mg): 156.2
Sodium (mg): 1022
Protein (gm): 31
Carbohydrate (gm): 30.3

1. Steam artichokes, potatoes, green beans, and beets until tender; cool to room temperature. Arrange cooked vegetables, eggs, tomatoes, and tuna on plates lined with salad greens. Sprinkle with olives and capers.

2. Combine Italian dressing, shallot, and garlic; drizzle over vegetables and sprinkle lightly with salt and pepper. Serve with Aioli.

Tuna Steaks with Garlic Pasta

4 servings

4 tuna steaks (about 5 ounces each)
⅓ cup slivered garlic
1 tablespoon olive oil
2 tablespoons minced parsley
1 tablespoon minced fresh rosemary, *or*
    1 teaspoon crushed dried rosemary leaves
4 ounces whole wheat fettuccine, cooked, warm
¼ cup shredded Parmesan cheese
Salt and pepper, to taste

Per Serving
Net Carbohydrate (gm): 22.7
Calories: 373
Fat (gm): 12.3
Saturated fat (gm): 3.3
Cholesterol (mg): 57.5
Sodium (mg): 153
Protein (gm): 40.1
Carbohydrate (gm): 25.5

1. Broil tuna steaks 6 inches from heat source until fish is tender and flakes with a fork, 4 to 5 minutes on each side.

2. While fish is cooking, sauté garlic over very low heat in oil in small skillet until very tender but not browned, about 10 minutes; stir in herbs. Toss garlic mixture with pasta and cheese in serving bowl. Season to taste with salt and pepper; serve with tuna.

Tuna and Tortellini Salad with Artichokes

8 servings

6 ounces cheese tortellini, cooked, room temperature
½ cup fresh, *or* frozen, thawed, peas
½ chopped green bell pepper
½ cup chopped green onions and tops
½ can (14 ounces) artichoke hearts, drained and quartered
1½ pounds tuna steaks, cooked, flaked
¼ cup (1 ounce) grated Parmesan cheese
Tomato Dressing (recipe follows)
Salt and pepper, to taste

Per Serving
Net Carbohydrate (gm): 11.5
Calories: 246
Fat (gm): 9.6
Saturated fat (gm): 2.3
Cholesterol (mg): 40.1
Sodium (mg): 243
Protein (gm): 25
Carbohydrate (gm): 13.1

1. Combine all ingredients, except Tomato Dressing, salt, and pepper, in large salad bowl; pour Tomato Dressing over and toss. Season to taste with salt and pepper.

Tomato Dressing

makes about 1¼ cups

1 cup coarsely chopped tomato
2 tablespoons olive oil
2 tablespoons white wine vinegar
2 teaspoons Dijon mustard
3 tablespoons sliced green onions and tops
1 clove garlic, minced
½ cup fresh parsley sprigs
¼ cup fresh, *or* 1 tablespoon dried, basil leaves
1 tablespoon fresh, *or* 1 teaspoon dried, oregano leaves

1. Process all ingredients in food processor or blender until finely chopped.

Tuna, Fennel, and Pasta Salad with Orange Vinaigrette

6 servings

1¼ cups (5 ounces) whole wheat pasta shells,
    cooked, room temperature
4 cups mixed salad greens
¾ cup orange segments
½ cup very thinly sliced fennel bulb, *or* celery
½ cup thinly sliced red bell pepper
Orange Vinaigrette (recipe follows)
1 pound tuna steaks, grilled *or* broiled, warm

Per Serving
Net Carbohydrate (gm): 22.3
Calories: 258
Fat (gm): 8
Saturated fat (gm): 1.2
Cholesterol (mg): 33.7
Sodium (mg): 134
Protein (gm): 22.3
Carbohydrate (gm): 26.2

1. Combine pasta shells, greens, orange segments, fennel, and bell pepper in salad bowl. Pour Orange Vinaigrette over and toss. Break fish into 1-inch pieces with fork; add to salad and toss.

Orange Vinaigrette

makes about ⅔ cup

¼ cup orange juice
3 tablespoons olive oil
3 tablespoons balsamic vinegar, *or* red wine vinegar
2 tablespoons finely chopped shallots, *or* red onion
2 cloves garlic, minced
1 teaspoon dried rosemary leaves
½ teaspoon crushed fennel seeds
¼ teaspoon salt
⅛ teaspoon white pepper

1. Mix all ingredients.

Microwave Hot Garlic Shrimp

4 servings

1½ pounds large shrimp, peeled, deveined
1 tablespoon olive oil
4 cloves garlic, minced
½–1 teaspoon red pepper flakes
1 teaspoon ground cumin
¼ cup lemon juice
Minced parsley, as garnish

Per Serving
Net Carbohydrate (gm): 3.8
Calories: 222
Fat (gm): 6.5
Saturated fat (gm): 1
Cholesterol (mg): 258.6
Sodium (mg): 254
Protein (gm): 34.9
Carbohydrate (gm): 4.2

1. Combine shrimp, olive oil, and garlic in 1-quart glass casserole; sprinkle with red pepper flakes, cumin, and lemon juice. Cover with plastic wrap and vent edge. Microwave on High until shrimp are pink and cooked, 3 to 4 minutes, stirring once. Let stand, covered, 1 minute. Sprinkle with parsley.

Herbed Shrimp in Tomato Sauce

4 servings

1 cup chopped onion
½ cup chopped celery
2 garlic cloves, minced
1 tablespoon olive oil
1 can (15 ounces) tomato sauce
½ cup chopped parsley
2 tablespoons chopped, *or* 1 teaspoon dried, basil leaves
1 tablespoon chopped, *or* ½ teaspoon dried, thyme leaves
1¼ pounds medium shrimp, peeled, deveined
Salt and pepper, to taste

Per Serving
Net Carbohydrate (gm): 11.2
Calories: 236
Fat (gm): 6.2
Saturated fat (gm): 1
Cholesterol (mg): 215.5
Sodium (mg): 872
Protein (gm): 31.2
Carbohydrate (gm): 14.1

1. Sauté onion, celery, and garlic in oil in large saucepan until tender, about 5 minutes. Add remaining ingredients, except salt and pepper, and heat to boiling. Reduce heat and simmer, covered, until shrimp are cooked and pink, about 5 minutes. Season to taste with salt and pepper.

Variation:

Shrimp with Caramelized Garlic—Cook 25 peeled cloves of garlic in 3 tablespoons olive oil in small skillet over medium-low heat until garlic is golden, 20 to 25 minutes. Coarsely mash garlic with 1 to 2 tablespoons dry white wine. Make recipe as above, omitting the 2 cloves garlic. Stir caramelized garlic in at simmering stage.

Creole Shrimp and Brown Rice

6 servings

¾ cup uncooked brown rice
½ cup sliced green onions and tops
2 large garlic cloves, minced
½ teaspoon crushed red pepper
1 tablespoon olive oil
3 cups reduced-sodium fat-free chicken broth
1 can (14½ ounces) diced tomatoes, undrained
1 cup chopped celery
1 chopped green bell pepper
½ cup chopped carrot
1 large bay leaf
1½ teaspoons dried thyme leaves
¾ teaspoon paprika
1½ pounds medium shrimp, peeled, deveined
Salt and pepper, to taste

Per Serving
Net Carbohydrate (gm): 23.6
Calories: 282
Fat (gm): 6
Saturated fat (gm): 0.9
Cholesterol (mg): 184.9
Sodium (mg): 489
Protein (gm): 29.9
Carbohydrate (gm): 26.4

1. Sauté rice, green onions, garlic, and crushed red pepper in oil in large saucepan until lightly browned, about 3 minutes. Add remaining ingredients, except shrimp, salt, and pepper, and heat to boiling. Reduce heat and simmer, covered, until rice is almost tender, about 40 minutes. Add shrimp; simmer, covered, until shrimp is cooked and pink. Discard bay leaf; season to taste with salt and pepper.

Shrimp with Artichokes

4 servings

½ cup thinly sliced mushrooms
2 tablespoons finely chopped shallots
1 tablespoon butter
¼ cup dry white wine, *or* chicken broth
8 canned drained artichokes, halved
¼ cup snipped chives
¼ cup chopped pimiento
1¼ pounds medium shrimp, peeled, deveined
Salt and pepper, to taste
1 lemon, sliced
Parsley sprigs, as garnish

Per Serving
Net Carbohydrate (gm): 11.1
Calories: 258
Fat (gm): 5.8
Saturated fat (gm): 2.4
Cholesterol (mg): 223.7
Sodium (mg): 352
Protein (gm): 33.7
Carbohydrate (gm): 18.8

1. Sauté mushrooms and shallots in butter in medium skillet until tender, about 5 minutes. Add wine, artichoke hearts, chives, and pimiento; heat just to boiling. Add shrimp and reduce heat; simmer, covered, until shrimp are cooked and pink, 3 to 4 minutes. Season to taste with salt and pepper. Garnish with lemon and parsley.

Microwave Creole Shrimp

4 servings

1 can (16 ounces) Italian plum tomatoes,
   undrained, coarsely chopped
½ cup chopped onion
½ cup chopped green bell pepper
1 teaspoon chili powder
⅛ teaspoon red pepper flakes
1 bay leaf
1¼ pounds medium shrimp, peeled, deveined
Salt, to taste
1½ cups cooked brown rice, warm

Per Serving
Net Carbohydrate (gm): 20.3
Calories: 268
Fat (gm): 3.5
Saturated fat (gm): 0.7
Cholesterol (mg): 215.5
Sodium (mg): 389
Protein (gm): 32.2
Carbohydrate (gm): 26.5

1. Combine all ingredients, except shrimp, salt, and rice in 2-quart glass measure or casserole. Cover with vented plastic wrap, and microwave on High until onion is tender and mixture is bubbly, 5 to 8 minutes, stirring once. Add shrimp and microwave, covered, on High 2 to 3 minutes or until shrimp are pink. Remove bay leaf and let stand 3 minutes; season to taste with salt. Serve over rice.

Shrimp Tostadas

4 servings

4 corn tortillas
1 pound medium shrimp, peeled, deveined
⅓ cup thinly sliced green onions and tops
½ serrano chili, seeds and veins discarded, finely chopped
1 tablespoon olive oil
1 cup tomato sauce
1 tablespoon chili powder
1 teaspoon dried oregano leaves
2 cloves garlic, minced
2 cups chopped romaine lettuce
½ cup chopped tomato
½ cup crumbled Mexican white, *or* feta, cheese
⅓ cup Guacamole (½ recipe) (see p. 420)

Per Serving
Net Carbohydrate (gm): 18.8
Calories: 334
Fat (gm): 14.1
Saturated fat (gm): 4.2
Cholesterol (mg): 187.3
Sodium (mg): 790
Protein (gm): 30
Carbohydrate (gm): 23.7

1. Cook tortillas in greased large skillet until crisp and browned, about 1 minute on each side; place on serving plates.

2. Leave 8 shrimp whole for garnish; cut remaining shrimp into halves or thirds. Cook whole and cut-up shrimp, onion, and serrano chili in oil in large skillet until shrimp are cooked and pink, 3 to 5 minutes. Remove the 8 whole shrimp and reserve. Stir tomato sauce, chili powder, oregano, and garlic into skillet; cook until hot, 2 to 3 minutes.

3. Top tortillas with chopped lettuce and tomato; spoon shrimp mixture over. Sprinkle with crumbled cheese; top with dollops of Guacamole and reserved whole shrimp.

Shrimp de Jonghe

6 servings

2 tablespoons finely chopped shallots, *or* onion
4 cloves garlic, minced
3 tablespoons butter
2 tablespoons dry sherry, optional
1 tablespoon lemon juice
¼ teaspoon dried marjoram leaves
¼ teaspoon dried tarragon leaves
⅛ teaspoon ground nutmeg
⅛ teaspoon cayenne pepper
1 cup fresh whole wheat bread crumbs
¼ cup finely chopped parsley leaves
Salt and pepper, to taste
1½ pounds shrimp, peeled, deveined
2 cups cooked brown rice, warm

Per Serving
Net Carbohydrate (gm): 19.4
Calories: 274
Fat (gm): 9.1
Saturated fat (gm): 4.4
Cholesterol (mg): 188.9
Sodium (mg): 286
Protein (gm): 25.7
Carbohydrate (gm): 21.3

1. Sauté shallots and garlic in butter in medium skillet until tender, 2 to 3 minutes. Stir in sherry, lemon juice, marjoram, tarragon, nutmeg, and cayenne pepper. Pour mixture over combined bread crumbs and parsley in bowl and toss. Season to taste with salt and pepper.

2. Arrange shrimp in single layer in shell dishes or in 10 x 7-inch baking dish; top with crumb mixture. Bake at 450 degrees until shrimp are cooked, about 10 minutes. Serve with rice.

Shrimp with Feta Cheese

4 servings

¾ cup chopped green bell pepper
4 green onions and tops, finely chopped
1–2 teaspoons minced hot red, *or* jalapeño, chili
1 tablespoon olive oil
1½ cups chopped tomatoes
½ cup finely chopped parsley
1½ teaspoons dried oregano leaves
1 teaspoon brown sugar
1¼ pounds medium shrimp, peeled, deveined
¼ cup (1 ounce) crumbled feta cheese
3 tablespoons reduced-fat milk
Salt and pepper, to taste

Per Serving
Net Carbohydrate (gm): 8.1
Calories: 246
Fat (gm): 8.4
Saturated fat (gm): 2.5
Cholesterol (mg): 224.6
Sodium (mg): 333
Protein (gm): 31.9
Carbohydrate (gm): 10.3

1. Sauté bell pepper, green onions, and chili in oil in large skillet until tender, 4 to 5 minutes. Add tomatoes, parsley, oregano, and sugar; simmer 5 minutes. Add shrimp and simmer until shrimp are cooked, 3 to 4 minutes. Stir in cheese and milk and simmer 2 minutes longer. Season to taste with salt and pepper.

Sesame Shrimp Stir-Fry

4 servings

⅓ cup chopped red bell pepper
¼ cup thinly sliced green onions and tops
2 large cloves garlic, minced
1 tablespoon sesame oil
2 drops hot chili oil
8 ounces snow peas, ends trimmed
1 pound medium shrimp, peeled, deveined
⅓ cup chicken broth
2 tablespoons dry sherry, *or* chicken broth
2 tablespoons soy sauce
1–2 tablespoons hoisin sauce
2 teaspoons cornstarch
Salt and pepper, to taste
1½ cups cooked brown rice, warm

Per Serving
Net Carbohydrate (gm): 24.5
Calories: 292
Fat (gm): 6.5
Saturated fat (gm): 1.1
Cholesterol (mg): 172.4
Sodium (mg): 817
Protein (gm): 27.6
Carbohydrate (gm): 27.7

1. Stir-fry bell pepper, green onions, and garlic in sesame oil in wok or large skillet, 2 to 3 minutes. Add hot chili oil and snow peas; cook over medium heat, covered, until snow peas are crisp-tender, about 5 minutes. Add shrimp and stir-fry until pink, 2 to 3 minutes.

2. Stir in combined chicken broth, sherry, soy sauce, hoisin sauce, and cornstarch; heat to boiling, stirring until thickened, 1 to 2 minutes. Season to taste with salt and pepper. Serve over rice.

Shrimp Kyoto

4 servings

6 dried black mushrooms
4 green onions and tops, diagonally sliced
16 snow peas, ends trimmed, halved
2 teaspoons finely chopped garlic
1–2 tablespoons canola oil
1½ pounds medium shrimp, peeled, deveined
½ cup chicken broth
2 teaspoons cornstarch
2 ounces soba noodles, cooked

Per Serving
Net Carbohydrate (gm): 19.4
Calories: 333
Fat (gm): 7.3
Saturated fat (gm): 1
Cholesterol (mg): 258.6
Sodium (mg): 415
Protein (gm): 38.5
Carbohydrate (gm): 26.4

1. Soak mushrooms in hot water 20 minutes or until soft; drain. Remove and discard stems; cut caps into thin strips.

2. Stir-fry onions, snow peas, and garlic in oil in wok or large skillet until crisp-tender, about 4 minutes. Add shrimp; stir-fry until shrimp are pink, 2 to 4 minutes. Stir in combined chicken broth and cornstarch; stir until thickened, about 1 minute. Stir in mushrooms and noodles; cook until hot, 2 to 3 minutes.

Thai Coconut Shrimp

6 servings

1 cup chopped red and green bell peppers
½ cup chopped onion
2 cloves garlic, minced
1 jalapeño chili, minced
2–3 teaspoons chopped gingerroot
2 teaspoons dark sesame oil
1 can (14 ounces) unsweetened coconut milk
3–4 tablespoons smooth peanut butter
1 can (15 ounces) kidney beans, rinsed, drained
2 cups cubed (1-inch), seeded tomatoes
1 pound shrimp, peeled, deveined
1–2 tablespoons lime juice
1 tablespoon chopped cilantro
½–1 teaspoon salt

Per Serving
Net Carbohydrate (gm): 15.5
Calories: 390
Fat (gm): 24.1
Saturated fat (gm): 16.2
Cholesterol (mg): 114.9
Sodium (mg): 602
Protein (gm): 23.7
Carbohydrate (gm): 23.5

1. Sauté bell peppers, onion, garlic, chili, and gingerroot in sesame oil in large saucepan until tender, about 5 minutes. Stir in coconut milk and peanut butter; heat to boiling over medium heat, stirring until smooth. Reduce heat and simmer, uncovered, 5 minutes.

2. Stir in beans and tomatoes; heat to boiling. Stir in shrimp. Simmer, uncovered, until shrimp curl and turn pink, about 5 minutes. Stir in lime juice, cilantro, and salt. Serve in shallow bowls.

Seafood Newburg

4 servings

8 ounces shrimp, peeled, deveined
8 ounces bay scallops
½ cup water
¼ cup finely chopped shallots, *or* onion
2 tablespoons butter
¼ cup all-purpose flour
1½ cups half-and-half
1 egg yolk
1–2 tablespoons dry sherry, optional
Generous pinch ground nutmeg
Generous pinch cayenne pepper
Salt and white pepper, to taste
4 pieces thin-sliced whole wheat toast, cut diagonally into halves
Finely chopped parsley, as garnish

Per Serving
Net Carbohydrate (gm): 22.1
Calories: 387
Fat (gm): 19.9
Saturated fat (gm): 11
Cholesterol (mg): 207.8
Sodium (mg): 420
Protein (gm): 28.1
Carbohydrate (gm): 25.7

1. Simmer shrimp and scallops in water in medium saucepan, covered, until cooked, 3 to 5 minutes. Drain, reserving liquid.

2. Sauté shallots in butter in medium saucepan until tender, 2 to 3 minutes. Mix in flour and cook 1 to 2 minutes. Whisk in half-and-half and reserved cooking liquid; heat to boiling. Boil, whisking constantly, until thickened, about 1 minute. Whisk about half the mixture into egg yolk in small bowl; whisk egg mixture back into saucepan. Cook over very low heat, whisking constantly, 30 seconds.

3. Stir in shrimp, scallops, sherry, nutmeg, and cayenne pepper; cook 2 to 3 minutes. Season to taste with salt and white pepper. Serve over toast; sprinkle with parsley.

Shrimp and Scallops with Bell Pepper Mélange

4 servings

2 cups cubed (1-inch) red, yellow, and green bell peppers
1 cup chopped onion
1 tablespoon minced garlic
2 tablespoons olive oil
1½ cups clam juice, *or* chicken broth
⅓ cup chopped parsley
1½ tablespoons lemon juice
1 teaspoon grated lemon rind
½ teaspoon dried thyme leaves
Pinch crushed red pepper
1½ cups chopped, peeled tomatoes
8 ounces medium shrimp, peeled, deveined
8 ounces bay scallops
Salt and pepper, to taste

Per Serving
Net Carbohydrate (gm): 11.7
Calories: 226
Fat (gm): 8.7
Saturated fat (gm): 1.2
Cholesterol (mg): 104.9
Sodium (mg): 787
Protein (gm): 29.1
Carbohydrate (gm): 14.9

1. Sauté bell peppers, onion, and garlic in oil in large saucepan until onion begins to brown, 8 to 10 minutes. Add clam juice, parsley, lemon juice and rind, thyme, red pepper, and tomatoes to saucepan; heat to boiling. Reduce heat and simmer, uncovered, 5 minutes. Add shrimp and scallops; simmer until shellfish are cooked, 5 to 8 minutes. Season to taste with salt and pepper.

Scallops and Mushrooms in White Wine

4 servings

8 ounces sliced mushrooms
1 tablespoon chopped shallots
1 teaspoon dried tarragon leaves
1 teaspoon dried thyme leaves
3 tablespoons butter
⅓ cup dry white wine, *or* chicken broth
1¼ pounds sea scallops
3 tablespoons minced parsley
Salt and pepper, to taste

Per Serving
Net Carbohydrate (gm): 5.9
Calories: 238
Fat (gm): 10.5
Saturated fat (gm): 5.8
Cholesterol (mg): 71.4
Sodium (mg): 327
Protein (gm): 25.8
Carbohydrate (gm): 6.8

1. Sauté mushrooms, shallots, tarragon, and thyme in butter in large skillet until mushrooms are tender, about 5 minutes; add wine and heat to boiling. Reduce heat and simmer 1 to 2 minutes. Add scallops; cook over medium heat until scallops are tender and cooked, about 5 minutes. Stir in parsley. Season to taste with salt and pepper.

Scallops with Linguine

6 servings

½ cup chopped onion
½ cup shredded carrots
1–2 tablespoons olive oil
1½ pounds bay scallops
¼ cup minced basil, *or* cilantro
¼ cup minced parsley
2–3 teaspoons white Worcestershire sauce
Salt and pepper, to taste
4 ounces whole wheat linguine, cooked, warm

Per Serving
Net Carbohydrate (gm): 13.1
Calories: 185
Fat (gm): 3.6
Saturated fat (gm): 0.4
Cholesterol (mg): 37.4
Sodium (mg): 247
Protein (gm): 21.5
Carbohydrate (gm): 15.5

1. Sauté onion and carrots in oil in large skillet until onion is tender, 5 to 8 minutes. Move vegetables to side of skillet; add scallops and sauté until cooked and tender, about 5 minutes. Stir in basil and parsley; season to taste with Worcestershire sauce, salt, and pepper. Serve over linguine.

Scallops with Crisp Snow Peas

4 servings

½ cup chopped green onions and tops
½ cup chopped red bell pepper
3 cloves garlic, minced
2 tablespoons canola oil, divided
1 cup snow peas, ends trimmed
1 pound sea scallops, halved
¼ cup apple cider, *or* apple juice
1 tablespoon tamari soy sauce
2 teaspoons cornstarch
Salt and pepper, to taste

Per Serving
Net Carbohydrate (gm): 7.9
Calories: 189
Fat (gm): 7.8
Saturated fat (gm): 0.6
Cholesterol (mg): 37.4
Sodium (mg): 438
Protein (gm): 20.5
Carbohydrate (gm): 9.1

1. Stir-fry green onions, bell pepper, and garlic in 1 tablespoon oil in wok or large skillet 3 to 4 minutes; add snow peas and stir-fry 3 to 4 minutes longer. Move vegetable mixture to side of wok; add remaining 1 tablespoon oil and scallops.

2. Stir-fry until scallops are cooked and tender, 5 to 8 minutes. Stir in combined apple cider, soy sauce, and cornstarch; cook over medium-high heat until thickened, 1 to 2 minutes. Season to taste with salt and pepper.

Tuna Steaks with Sweet-Sour Tomato Relish

4 servings

1 tablespoon olive oil
1 teaspoon minced garlic
1 teaspoon lemon juice
4 tuna steaks (about 5 ounces each)
Salt and pepper, to taste
Sweet-Sour Tomato Relish (recipe follows)

Per Serving
Net Carbohydrate (gm): 8.3
Calories: 291
Fat (gm): 12.7
Saturated fat (gm): 2.6
Cholesterol (mg): 53.5
Sodium (mg): 126
Protein (gm): 33.8
Carbohydrate (gm): 9.2

1. Combine olive oil, garlic, and lemon juice in small bowl. Brush tuna with oil mixture and broil 6 inches from heat source for 8 minutes; turn. Brush other side with oil mixture; sprinkle lightly with salt and pepper. Broil until fish is tender and flakes with a fork, 6 to 8 minutes longer. Serve with Sweet-Sour Tomato Relish.

Sweet-Sour Tomato Relish

makes about 1 cup

1 cup chopped tomato
2 teaspoons olive oil
2 tablespoons tomato paste
1½ tablespoons red wine vinegar
1½ tablespoons packed light brown sugar
½ teaspoon dried basil leaves
¼ teaspoon dried thyme leaves

1. Sauté tomato in oil in small saucepan until just softened, 2 to 3 minutes. Stir in remaining ingredients and cook over medium heat until warm, 1 to 2 minutes.

Tuna Patties with Creamed Pea Sauce

4 servings

2 cans (6 ounces each) light tuna packed in water, drained
⅔ cup unseasoned dry bread crumbs, divided
¼ cup finely chopped onion
¼ cup finely chopped celery
¼ cup finely chopped red, *or* green, bell pepper
3 tablespoons mayonnaise
2 teaspoons Worcestershire sauce
Salt and cayenne pepper, to taste
1 egg
Creamed Pea Sauce (recipe follows)

Per Serving
Net Carbohydrate (gm): 22.4
Calories: 389
Fat (gm): 18.5
Saturated fat (gm): 6.6
Cholesterol (mg): 106.6
Sodium (mg): 650
Protein (gm): 29.9
Carbohydrate (gm): 24.5

1. Combine tuna, ½ cup bread crumbs, onion, celery, bell pepper, mayonnaise, and Worcestershire sauce in medium bowl; season to taste with salt and cayenne pepper. Add egg, mixing until ingredients are well blended. Shape into 4 patties.

2. Coat patties with remaining bread. Cook over medium-low heat until browned, about 5 minutes on each side. Serve with Creamed Pea Sauce.

Creamed Pea Sauce

makes about 1 cup

2 tablespoons butter
2 tablespoons all-purpose flour
1 cup reduced-fat milk
½ cup frozen, thawed peas
Salt and pepper, to taste

1. Melt butter in small saucepan. Stir in flour and cook, stirring constantly, over medium-low heat 1 minute. Whisk in milk and heat to boiling. Boil, whisking constantly, until thickened, about 1 minute. Stir in peas; cook over low heat 2 to 3 minutes. Season to taste with salt and pepper.

Salmon Cakes with Yogurt Dill Sauce

6 servings

1 pound potatoes, peeled, cooked, mashed
1 can (15½ ounces) salmon, drained,
    bones and skin discarded
¼ cup plain yogurt
¼ cup sliced green onions and tops
3 tablespoons chopped parsley
2 tablespoons lemon juice
¼ teaspoon pepper
¾ cup fresh whole wheat bread crumbs
2 tablespoons olive oil
1 teaspoon butter
Yogurt Dill Sauce (recipe follows)

Per Serving
Net Carbohydrate (gm): 20.9
Calories: 311
Fat (gm): 15.3
Saturated fat (gm): 5.8
Cholesterol (mg): 43.5
Sodium (mg): 448
Protein (gm): 20.6
Carbohydrate (gm): 22.9

1. Combine all ingredients, except olive oil, butter, and Yogurt Dill Sauce, in large bowl; mix well. Shape into 6 patties. Cook patties in oil and butter in large skillet over medium heat until browned, about 5 minutes per side. Serve with Yogurt Dill Sauce.

Yogurt Dill Sauce

makes about 1½ cups

¾ cup plain yogurt
¾ cup sour cream
1 tablespoon dried dill weed
Salt and pepper, to taste

1. Mix all ingredients.

Salmon Loaf with Cucumber-Dill Sauce

6 servings

1 can (16 ounces) salmon, undrained
1 egg, lightly beaten
2 tablespoons minced onion
½ cup chopped celery
2 tablespoons finely chopped green bell pepper
2 tablespoons snipped chives
1 tablespoon chopped fresh, *or* 1 teaspoon dried, dill weed
1 cup fresh whole wheat bread crumbs
1 tablespoon lemon juice
Cucumber-Dill Sauce (recipe follows)

Per Serving
Net Carbohydrate (gm): 9.4
Calories: 175
Fat (gm): 5.6
Saturated fat (gm): 1.6
Cholesterol (mg): 31.5
Sodium (mg): 506
Protein (gm): 19.9
Carbohydrate (gm): 10.9

1. Drain salmon, reserving juice; discard skin and bones. Add water to salmon juice to make ½ cup. Combine liquid, salmon, and remaining ingredients, except Cucumber Sauce, in large bowl. Shape mixture into loaf in greased 9 x 5-inch loaf pan. Bake at 350 degrees until golden, 30 to 40 minutes.

2. Unmold onto serving platter. Serve with Cucumber-Dill Sauce.

Cucumber-Dill Sauce

makes about 1½ cups

¾ cup plain yogurt
¾ cup finely chopped, seeded cucumber
1 teaspoon dried dill weed

1. Mix all ingredients.

Salmon and Corn Soufflé

6 servings

⅔ cup coarsely chopped red and green bell peppers
1 tablespoon butter
¼ cup all-purpose flour
1½ cups reduced-fat milk
½ package (10-ounce size) frozen whole kernel corn
¾ teaspoon dried dill weed
¼ teaspoon salt
⅛ teaspoon white pepper
2 egg yolks, lightly beaten
1 can (6½ ounces) salmon, drained, skin and bones discarded, flaked
5 egg whites
Pinch cream of tartar

Per Serving
Net Carbohydrate (gm): 12
Calories: 167
Fat (gm): 7.4
Saturated fat (gm): 3.1
Cholesterol (mg): 88.3
Sodium (mg): 342
Protein (gm): 12.2
Carbohydrate (gm): 13.1

1. Sauté bell peppers in butter in large saucepan until tender, about 5 minutes. Stir in flour and cook over medium heat 1 to 2 minutes. Gradually blend in milk, corn, dill weed, salt, and pepper; heat to boiling over medium heat. Remove from heat.

2. Gradually stir a small amount of vegetable mixture into egg yolks; stir yolk mixture back into mixture in saucepan. Mix in salmon.

3. Beat egg whites and cream of tartar in large bowl to stiff, but not dry, peaks; fold into salmon mixture. Pour into lightly greased 2-quart soufflé dish. Bake, uncovered, at 350 degrees until golden brown and knife inserted near center comes out clean, about 45 minutes. Serve immediately.

Salmon Risotto

6 servings

¼ cup sliced green onions and tops
2 cloves garlic, minced
1 tablespoon olive oil
1 cup arborio rice
3½ cups reduced-sodium fat-free chicken broth
¼ cup dry sherry, *or* chicken broth
¾ cup sour cream
¾ cup reduced-fat milk
2 teaspoons dried dill weed
1 pound salmon steaks, cooked, flaked
Salt and pepper, to taste

Per Serving
Net Carbohydrate (gm): 14.8
Calories: 312
Fat (gm): 16.6
Saturated fat (gm): 5.2
Cholesterol (mg): 70.6
Sodium (mg): 210
Protein (gm): 21.5
Carbohydrate (gm): 15.1

1. Sauté green onions and garlic in oil in large saucepan 3 to 4 minutes; add rice and cook until lightly browned, 2 to 3 minutes. Heat chicken broth and sherry to boiling in small saucepan; reduce heat to low to keep broth hot.

2. Add broth to rice mixture, ½ cup at a time, stirring constantly until broth is absorbed before adding next ½ cup. Continue process until rice is al dente and mixture is creamy, 20 to 25 minutes. Stir in sour cream, milk, and dill weed. Stir in salmon; cook over low heat until hot through, about 5 minutes. Season to taste with salt and pepper.

Crab Cakes with Poblano Chili Sauce

4 servings

1½ pounds crabmeat, *or* peeled and
    deveined shrimp, cooked and finely chopped
½ cup finely chopped onion
½ cup finely chopped tomato
1 small jalapeño chili, seeds and veins discarded, minced
1 egg
¼ cup unseasoned dry bread crumbs
1 teaspoon dried oregano leaves
½ teaspoon salt
Flour, *or* unseasoned dry bread crumbs
Poblano Chili Sauce (recipe follows)

Per Serving
Net Carbohydrate (gm): 11.3
Calories: 248
Fat (gm): 5.6
Saturated fat (gm): 1
Cholesterol (mg): 124.6
Sodium (mg): 1813
Protein (gm): 35.1
Carbohydrate (gm): 13.6

1. Combine crabmeat, onion, tomato, jalapeño chili, and egg in small bowl; mix in bread crumbs, oregano, and salt. Form mixture into 8 patties about ½ inch thick; coat lightly with flour or bread crumbs.

2. Cook patties in greased large skillet over medium heat until cooked through and lightly browned, 3 to 4 minutes on each side.

3. Arrange crab cakes on serving dish; spoon Poblano Chili Sauce over.

Poblano Chili Sauce

makes about 1 cup

⅓ cup finely chopped, seeded poblano chili
⅓ cup finely chopped onion
2 cloves garlic, minced
2 teaspoons olive oil
½ cup chopped tomato
1 tablespoon chili powder

1. Sauté poblano chili, onion, and garlic in oil in small skillet until chili is tender, 4 to 5 minutes. Stir in tomato and chili powder. Cook over medium heat until chili and onion are very tender. Process mixture in food processor or blender until smooth.

Sweet-Sour Grouper

4 servings

4 large grouper fillets (about 6 ounces each)
Salt and pepper, to taste
1½ tablespoons olive oil, divided
1 cup sliced onions
⅓ cup red wine vinegar
1½ teaspoons brown sugar
1 tablespoon chopped parsley
½ teaspoon dried mint leaves

Per Serving
Net Carbohydrate (gm): 4.4
Calories: 223
Fat (gm): 6.8
Saturated fat (gm): 1.1
Cholesterol (mg): 62.8
Sodium (mg): 93
Protein (gm): 33.5
Carbohydrate (gm): 5.2

1. Sprinkle grouper lightly with salt and pepper. Sauté fish in 1 tablespoon oil in large skillet until fish is tender and flakes with a fork, about 10 minutes, turning once.
2. While fish is cooking, sauté onion in remaining ½ tablespoon oil in medium skillet until tender, about 5 minutes. Stir in vinegar, sugar, parsley, and mint. Simmer, covered, 4 to 5 minutes. Season to taste with salt and pepper; serve over fish.

Microwave Lemon Halibut

4 servings

1½ pounds halibut, *or* haddock, fillets, cut into 4 pieces
Juice of 2 lemons
Dill weed, to taste
Paprika, to taste
Pepper, to taste
Parsley sprigs, as garnish

Per Serving
Net Carbohydrate (gm): 1.2
Calories: 190
Fat (gm): 3.8
Saturated fat (gm): 0.5
Cholesterol (mg): 53.9
Sodium (mg): 92
Protein (gm): 35.5
Carbohydrate (gm): 1.3

1. Place fish in lightly greased glass baking dish. Drizzle lemon juice over fish; sprinkle lightly with dill weed, paprika, and pepper. Cover with vented plastic wrap, and microwave on High for 4 minutes or until fish flakes easily with fork. Garnish with parsley sprigs.

Dilled Orange Roughy in Parchment

4 servings

1½ pounds orange roughy fillets, cut into 6 serving pieces
½ cup thinly sliced red bell pepper
½ cup thinly sliced mushrooms
¼ cup chopped parsley
1½ teaspoons dried dill weed
Salt and pepper, to taste
1½ cups cooked brown rice

Per Serving
Net Carbohydrate (gm): 16.8
Calories: 208
Fat (gm): 1.9
Saturated fat (gm): 0.2
Cholesterol (mg): 33.7
Sodium (mg): 114
Protein (gm): 27.5
Carbohydrate (gm): 18.8

1. Cut 6 pieces of cooking parchment to about 18 x 12 inches. Fold each sheet in half and round off unfolded edges to form half circles. Unfold each sheet. Place fish fillets in center of each sheet and top with bell peppers and mushrooms; sprinkle with parsley, dill weed, salt, and pepper.

2. Fold parchment over fish and roll edges tightly to seal. Place packets on baking sheet. Bake at 425 degrees until packets puff, about 10 minutes. Serve with rice.

Microwave Salmon with Herbs

4 servings

1½ pounds salmon fillets, cut into 4 pieces
Salt and pepper, to taste
¼ cup lemon juice
1 teaspoon dried tarragon leaves
1 teaspoon chopped chives
2 tablespoons finely chopped parsley
1 tablespoon chopped pimiento

Per Serving
Net Carbohydrate (gm): 1.6
Calories: 316
Fat (gm): 18.3
Saturated fat (gm): 3.7
Cholesterol (mg): 99.5
Sodium (mg): 102
Protein (gm): 34.1
Carbohydrate (gm): 1.8

1. Arrange fish in glass baking dish with thick sides toward the outside of dish; sprinkle lightly with salt and pepper. Drizzle lemon juice over fish and sprinkle with tarragon and chives. Microwave, loosely covered, on Medium-High 5 to 6 minutes or until fish flakes easily with fork. Sprinkle with parsley and pimiento.

Dilled Salmon Burgers

4 servings

1 can (12½ ounces) salmon, drained, bones and skin discarded
1 egg white, lightly beaten
½ cup seasoned dry bread crumbs
¼ cup chopped onion
½ teaspoon dried thyme leaves
½ teaspoon pepper
1 tablespoon canola oil
¼ cup sliced plum tomatoes
Yogurt Dill Sauce (see p. 317)

Per Serving
Net Carbohydrate (gm): 14.4
Calories: 255
Fat (gm): 10.3
Saturated fat (gm): 2.5
Cholesterol (mg): 38.3
Sodium (mg): 598
Protein (gm): 24.4
Carbohydrate (gm): 15.3

1. Combine all ingredients, except oil, tomatoes, and Dill Sauce; shape into 4 patties, ½ inch thick. Cook patties in oil in large skillet over medium heat until browned, 2 to 3 minutes on each side. Garnish plates with sliced tomatoes. Spoon Yogurt Dill Sauce over patties.

Microwave Fillet of Sole Dijon

4 servings

1½ pounds fillet of sole
8 stalks asparagus, cut diagonally into 2-inch pieces
Salt and pepper, to taste
2 tablespoons mayonnaise
2 tablespoons Dijon mustard
Juice of 1 lemon
2 tablespoons chopped chives
Paprika, to taste
Chopped chives, as garnish

Per Serving
Net Carbohydrate (gm): 1.6
Calories: 200
Fat (gm): 7.2
Saturated fat (gm): 1.2
Cholesterol (mg): 81.9
Sodium (mg): 345
Protein (gm): 29.2
Carbohydrate (gm): 2.4

1. Place fillets in single layer in glass baking dish, tucking under thin edges and arranging thick parts toward outside of dish. Arrange asparagus around outside edges of dish. Sprinkle fish and asparagus lightly with salt and pepper.

2. Mix mayonnaise, mustard, lemon juice, and 2 tablespoons chives in small bowl; spread over fish. Sprinkle lightly with paprika. Microwave, loosely covered, on High 4 minutes. Rotate dish; tightly cover and microwave 1 minute longer, or until fish flakes easily with fork. Let stand 1 to 2 minutes. Sprinkle with chives.

Basque-Style Fish Fillets

4 servings

1½ pounds fish fillets, *or* fish steaks (sole, grouper,
   orange roughy, cod, swordfish, salmon, *or* flounder)
¼ cup clam juice
½ cup dry white wine, *or* clam juice
½ cup canned crushed tomatoes
2 tablespoons chopped parsley
1–3 tablespoons chopped scallions
1 teaspoon dried thyme leaves
1 bay leaf
¼ teaspoon pepper
1½ cups cooked brown rice

Per Serving
Net Carbohydrate (gm): 17.2
Calories: 245
Fat (gm): 2.4
Saturated fat (gm): 0.5
Cholesterol (mg): 77.8
Sodium (mg): 334
Protein (gm): 31.7
Carbohydrate (gm): 19.3

1. Arrange fish in oiled skillet; add combined remaining ingredients and heat to boiling. Reduce heat and simmer, covered, until fish is tender and flakes with a fork, 10 to 15 minutes. Discard bay leaf.

2. Remove fish to heated platter and keep warm. Simmer tomato sauce, uncovered, until slightly thickened; spoon over fish. Serve with rice.

Quick 'n Easy Spiced Shrimp

4 servings

1 can (15 ounces) tomato puree
½ cup water
3 tablespoons white vinegar
3 tablespoons Worcestershire sauce
2 tablespoons grated orange rind
1 tablespoon prepared mustard
¼ teaspoon red pepper sauce
½ teaspoon garlic powder
¼ teaspoon salt
1¼ pounds cooked peeled, deveined shrimp
1½ cups cooked brown rice, warm

Per Serving
Net Carbohydrate (gm): 25.9
Calories: 291
Fat (gm): 3.8
Saturated fat (gm): 0.6
Cholesterol (mg): 215.5
Sodium (mg): 616
Protein (gm): 32.7
Carbohydrate (gm): 30.2

1. Place all ingredients, except shrimp and rice, in medium saucepan; heat to boiling. Reduce heat and simmer, covered, 5 minutes. Add shrimp and simmer until hot through, 2 to 3 minutes. Serve over rice.

Scallop Kabobs with Tomato-Ginger Sauce

4 servings

1 tablespoon minced gingerroot
4 large cloves garlic, minced
¼ cup chopped green onions
1 tablespoon canola oil
½ teaspoon crushed red pepper
2 tablespoons packed light brown sugar
2 teaspoons soy sauce
3 tablespoons catsup
¼ cup dry white wine, *or* reduced-sodium fat-free chicken broth
1 teaspoon distilled white vinegar
1¼ pounds sea scallops

Per Serving
Net Carbohydrate (gm): 14.4
Calories: 211
Fat (gm): 4.6
Saturated fat (gm): 0.4
Cholesterol (mg): 46.8
Sodium (mg): 530
Protein (gm): 24.5
Carbohydrate (gm): 14.9

1. Sauté ginger, garlic, and onion in oil in large skillet 2 minutes; stir in combined red pepper, sugar, soy sauce, catsup, wine, and vinegar. Heat to boiling; reduce heat and simmer 1 to 2 minutes.

2. Thread scallops on skewers. Place scallops on greased broiler pan and broil 6 inches from heat source until scallops are tender and cooked, 6 to 8 minutes, turning once. Serve with warm sauce.

Steamed Clams and Pasta

4 servings

½ cup finely chopped onion
4 cloves garlic, minced
2 teaspoons canola oil
¼ cup minced parsley
½ teaspoon dried oregano leaves
¼ teaspoon white pepper
24 fresh clams, scrubbed
1 cup clam juice, *or* chicken broth
1½ cups cooked spaghetti, warm
2 tablespoons grated Parmesan cheese

Per Serving
Net Carbohydrate (gm): 21
Calories: 246
Fat (gm): 5.1
Saturated fat (gm): 0.9
Cholesterol (mg): 59.8
Sodium (mg): 546
Protein (gm): 29.8
Carbohydrate (gm): 22.5

1. Sauté onion and garlic in oil in large skillet 3 to 4 minutes; add parsley, oregano, and white pepper. Add clams and clam juice; heat to boiling. Reduce heat and simmer, covered, until clams open, about 5 minutes. Discard any unopened clams. Arrange clams on spaghetti; pour broth over and sprinkle with Parmesan cheese.

SIX

Vegetables and Side Dishes

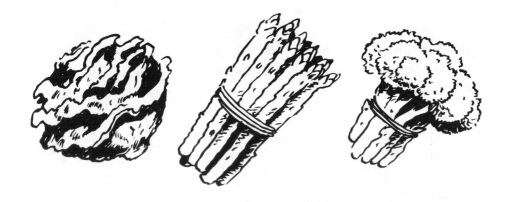

Braised Whole Artichokes

4 servings

4 medium artichokes
Salt
1–2 tablespoons extra-virgin olive oil

Per Serving
Net Carbohydrate (gm): 6.9
Calories: 90
Fat (gm): 3.6
Saturated fat (gm): 0.5
Cholesterol (mg): 0
Sodium (mg): 114
Protein (gm): 4.2
Carbohydrate (gm): 13.4

1. Cut 1 inch from tops of artichokes and cut off stems. Place artichokes in medium saucepan and sprinkle lightly with salt; add 1 inch water. Heat to boiling; reduce heat and simmer, covered, until artichokes are tender, about 30 minutes (bottom leaves will pull out easily).

2. Remove artichokes from pan; discard any remaining water. Holding artichokes with a towel or hot pad, brush bottom of each with olive oil; return to saucepan. Cook, uncovered, over medium to medium-low heat until bottoms of artichokes are deeply browned, 10 to 15 minutes.

Wine-Braised Artichoke Hearts

4 servings

1 package (10 ounces) frozen artichoke hearts
2 tablespoons finely chopped shallots
2 tablespoons finely chopped onion
1 clove garlic, minced
2 tablespoons canola oil
2 tablespoons white wine vinegar
¼ cup dry white wine, *or* vegetable broth
Salt and pepper, to taste

Per Serving
Net Carbohydrate (gm): 5.7
Calories: 115
Fat (gm): 6.9
Saturated fat (gm): 0.5
Cholesterol (mg): 0
Sodium (mg): 69
Protein (gm): 2.7
Carbohydrate (gm): 9.6

1. Sauté artichoke hearts, shallots, onion, and garlic in oil in large skillet until artichokes are separated and onion is softened but not browned. Stir in vinegar and wine and heat to boiling; reduce heat and simmer, covered, until artichoke hearts are tender, about 10 minutes. Season to taste with salt and pepper.

Artichokes with Cream Cheese Hollandaise Sauce

4–6 servings

4–6 whole artichokes, stems trimmed
Cream Cheese Hollandaise Sauce (see p. 4)

Per Serving
Net Carbohydrate (gm): 9.5
Calories: 250
Fat (gm): 18.6
Saturated fat (gm): 11.6
Cholesterol (mg): 54.7
Sodium (mg): 269
Protein (gm): 8.3
Carbohydrate (gm): 16.1

1. Slice 1 inch off tops of artichokes and discard. Trim tips of remaining leaves with scissors. Place artichokes in medium saucepan with 2 inches of water; heat to boiling. Reduce heat and simmer, covered, until artichoke leaves pull off easily and bottom is tender when pierced with a fork, about 30 minutes.

2. Place artichokes on serving plates with Cream Cheese Hollandaise Sauce on the side for dipping.

Asparagus with Lemon-Wine Sauce

6 servings

2 tablespoons minced shallots, *or*
    green onions (white parts only)
1–2 tablespoons butter
¼ cup dry white wine, *or* vegetable broth
¾ cup light cream
2 tablespoons all-purpose flour
½ teaspoon dried thyme leaves
½ teaspoon dried marjoram leaves
1 tablespoon lemon juice
Salt and white pepper, to taste
1 pound asparagus spears, cooked until crisp-tender, warm

Per Serving
Net Carbohydrate (gm): 5.8
Calories: 113
Fat (gm): 8
Saturated fat (gm): 4.9
Cholesterol (mg): 25.3
Sodium (mg): 35
Protein (gm): 2.9
Carbohydrate (gm): 7.5

1. Cook shallots in butter in small saucepan over medium to medium-low heat until tender but not browned, 2 to 3 minutes. Add wine and heat to boiling; reduce heat and simmer, uncovered, until wine is evaporated, 3 to 4 minutes. Stir in combined light cream, flour, and herbs; heat to boiling. Boil, stirring constantly, until sauce is thickened, about 1 minute. Stir in lemon juice; season to taste with salt and pepper. Arrange asparagus in serving dish; spoon sauce over.

Asparagus with Peanut Sauce

8 servings

2 tablespoons creamy peanut butter
2–3 tablespoons packed light brown sugar
2–3 tablespoons reduced-sodium tamari soy sauce
3–4 teaspoons rice wine (sake), dry sherry, *or* water
1 teaspoon grated gingerroot
1½ pounds asparagus spears, cooked until
    crisp-tender, chilled

Per Serving
Net Carbohydrate (gm): 6.3
Calories: 62
Fat (gm): 2.2
Saturated fat (gm): 0.5
Cholesterol (mg): 0
Sodium (mg): 273
Protein (gm): 3.4
Carbohydrate (gm): 8.4

1. Mix peanut butter, brown sugar, soy sauce, rice wine, and gingerroot until smooth.

2. Arrange asparagus on serving platter; spoon peanut sauce over.

Microwave Asparagus with Pimiento

4 servings

1 pound asparagus
2 tablespoons lemon juice
2 tablespoons chopped pimiento
Salt and pepper, to taste
2 tablespoons toasted walnut pieces

Per Serving
Net Carbohydrate (gm): 3.8
Calories: 54
Fat (gm): 2.7
Saturated fat (gm): 0.3
Cholesterol (mg): 0
Sodium (mg): 3
Protein (gm): 3.3
Carbohydrate (gm): 6.6

1. Arrange asparagus in single layer in glass baking dish; drizzle with lemon juice and sprinkle with pimiento. Microwave, loosely covered, on High 5 to 6 minutes or until tender, turning dish once. Season to taste with salt and pepper; sprinkle with walnuts.

Green Bean Casserole

8 servings

1 can (10¾ ounces) reduced-fat
    reduced-sodium cream of mushroom soup
½ cup sour cream
¼ cup reduced-fat milk
1¼ pounds green beans,
    cut into 1½-inch pieces, cooked until crisp-tender
¼–½ cup canned French-fried onions

Per Serving
Net Carbohydrate (gm): 8.1
Calories: 88
Fat (gm): 4.5
Saturated fat (gm): 2.3
Cholesterol (mg): 9.1
Sodium (mg): 180
Protein (gm): 2.3
Carbohydrate (gm): 10.4

1. Mix soup, sour cream, and milk in 2-quart casserole; stir in beans.

2. Bake, uncovered, at 350 degrees until mixture is bubbly, 30 to 45 minutes. Sprinkle onions on top during last 5 minutes of baking time.

Green Beans in Mustard Sauce

8 servings

2 tablespoons butter
2 tablespoons all-purpose flour
1 teaspoon dry mustard
¾ cup reduced-fat milk
3 tablespoons spicy brown, *or* Dijon, mustard
2 teaspoons apple cider vinegar
2 teaspoons packed light brown sugar
1 tablespoon chopped fresh, *or* 1 teaspoon dried, dill weed
Salt and pepper, to taste
1½ pounds green beans, cooked until crisp-tender, warm

Per Serving
Net Carbohydrate (gm): 7.1
Calories: 84
Fat (gm): 4.2
Saturated fat (gm): 2.3
Cholesterol (mg): 10
Sodium (mg): 136
Protein (gm): 3.2
Carbohydrate (gm): 10.3

1. Melt butter in small saucepan over medium heat. Whisk in flour and dry mustard; cook 1 minute. Whisk in milk; heat to boiling, whisking until thickened and smooth, 2 to 3 minutes. Stir in brown mustard, vinegar, brown sugar, and dill. Season to taste with salt and pepper.

2. Place beans in serving bowl; pour sauce over.

Greek-Style Green Beans

6 servings

4 cloves garlic, minced
1 tablespoon olive oil
¾ teaspoon dried oregano leaves
½ teaspoon dried basil leaves
1 can (16 ounces) tomatoes, undrained, coarsely chopped
1 pound green beans
Salt and pepper, to taste

Per Serving
Net Carbohydrate (gm): 6.8
Calories: 65
Fat (gm): 2.6
Saturated fat (gm): 0.4
Cholesterol (mg): 0
Sodium (mg): 115
Protein (gm): 2.3
Carbohydrate (gm): 10.1

1. Sauté garlic in oil in large skillet until tender, 3 to 4 minutes. Stir in herbs and cook 1 to 2 minutes longer.

2. Add tomatoes with liquid and green beans and heat to boiling; reduce heat and simmer, covered, until beans are very tender, 30 to 40 minutes. Season to taste with salt and pepper.

Oriental Green Beans

6 servings

¼ cup chopped green onions and tops
¼ cup chopped red bell pepper
2 teaspoons finely chopped gingerroot
2 cloves garlic, minced
1–2 tablespoons peanut, *or* canola, oil
1 pound green beans, halved
½ cup sliced water chestnuts
1 tablespoon rice wine vinegar
1–2 teaspoons tamari soy sauce
Salt and pepper, to taste

Per Serving
Net Carbohydrate (gm): 5.1
Calories: 55
Fat (gm): 2.5
Saturated fat (gm): 0.4
Cholesterol (mg): 0
Sodium (mg): 60
Protein (gm): 1.8
Carbohydrate (gm): 7.9

1. Stir-fry green onions, bell pepper, gingerroot, and garlic in oil in wok or large skillet until tender, 3 to 4 minutes.

2. Add green beans and water chestnuts to wok; stir-fry until beans are crisp-tender, 5 to 8 minutes. Stir in vinegar, and soy sauce; cook 1 to 2 minutes longer. Season to taste with salt and pepper.

Italian Green Beans

6 servings

1 pound green beans, cut into 2-inch pieces,
    cooked crisp-tender
2 teaspoons olive oil
¼ cup seasoned dry bread crumbs
¼ cup (1 ounce) grated Parmesan, *or* Romano, cheese
6 basil leaves, chopped
¼ cup sun-dried tomatoes (not oil-packed), softened, sliced
Salt and pepper, to taste

Per Serving
Net Carbohydrate (gm): 7.2
Calories: 76
Fat (gm): 2.8
Saturated fat (gm): 0.9
Cholesterol (mg): 2.7
Sodium (mg): 246
Protein (gm): 3.8
Carbohydrate (gm): 10.3

1. Sauté beans in oil in large skillet 3 minutes. Stir in bread crumbs, cheese, basil, and sun-dried tomatoes. Season to taste with salt and pepper.

Microwave Green Beans with Pine Nuts

6 servings

1 pound green beans
½ cup chopped, seeded Italian plum tomatoes
Salt and pepper, to taste
3 tablespoons toasted pine nuts

Per Serving
Net Carbohydrate (gm): 3.7
Calories: 52
Fat (gm): 2.3
Saturated fat (gm): 0.4
Cholesterol (mg): 0
Sodium (mg): 41
Protein (gm): 2.6
Carbohydrate (gm): 6.7

1. Combine green beans and tomatoes in 8-inch
glass baking dish. Microwave, loosely covered, on High 7 to 9 minutes or until tender, stirring twice. Season to taste with salt and pepper. Sprinkle with pine nuts.

Refried Beans

8 servings

1¼ cups dried pinto beans
⅓ cup chopped onion
3 cloves garlic, minced
½–¾ teaspoon ground cumin
1 tablespoon canola oil
Salt and pepper, to taste
Chopped cilantro, as garnish

Per Serving
Net Carbohydrate (gm): 12.1
Calories: 118
Fat (gm): 2.1
Saturated fat (gm): 0.2
Cholesterol (mg): 0
Sodium (mg): 3
Protein (gm): 6.2
Carbohydrate (gm): 19.4

1. Wash and sort beans, discarding any stones. Cover beans with 2 inches water in large saucepan; heat to boiling and boil, uncovered, 2 minutes. Remove from heat; let stand, covered, 1 hour. Drain beans, cover with 2 inches water, and heat to boiling. Reduce heat and simmer, covered, until beans are tender, 30 to 45 minutes. Drain, reserving 2 cups liquid.

2. Sauté onion, garlic, and cumin in oil in large skillet until tender, 3 to 5 minutes. Add 1 cup beans and 1 cup reserved liquid to skillet. Cook over high heat, mashing beans until almost smooth with end of meat mallet or potato masher. Add half the remaining beans and liquid; continue cooking and mashing beans. Repeat with remaining beans and liquid. Season to taste with salt and pepper. Sprinkle with cilantro.

Curried Microwave Lentils

8 servings

1 tablespoon olive oil
3 shallots, minced
⅓ cup chopped carrot
¼ cup chopped celery
2 cloves garlic, minced
¾ cup dried lentils
3 cups reduced-sodium fat-free chicken broth
½ teaspoon chopped gingerroot
1 teaspoon curry powder
Few dashes reduced-sodium soy sauce
Few dashes sesame oil

Per Serving
Net Carbohydrate (gm): 6.2
Calories: 100
Fat (gm): 2.5
Saturated fat (gm): 0.3
Cholesterol (mg): 9.4
Sodium (mg): 101
Protein (gm): 7.9
Carbohydrate (gm): 12

1. Microwave olive oil, shallots, carrot, celery, and garlic in 2-quart glass casserole, covered, on High 3 minutes or until tender, stirring once. Add lentils, broth, and gingerroot. Cover with vented plastic wrap and microwave on High until lentils are tender, but not mushy, about 30 minutes, stirring several times. Drain excess liquid. Stir in curry powder, soy sauce and sesame oil.

Harvard Beets

6 servings

2–3 tablespoons packed light brown sugar
1½ tablespoons cornstarch
¾ cup water
3–4 tablespoons cider vinegar
2 teaspoons butter
Salt and white pepper, to taste
1 pound beets, cooked, sliced or julienned, warm

Per Serving
Net Carbohydrate (gm): 11.8
Calories: 70
Fat (gm): 1.5
Saturated fat (gm): 0.9
Cholesterol (mg): 3.6
Sodium (mg): 72
Protein (gm): 1.2
Carbohydrate (gm): 14

1. Mix brown sugar and cornstarch in small saucepan; whisk in water and vinegar. Heat to boiling, whisking constantly until thickened, about 1 minute. Add butter, whisking until melted. Season to taste with salt and pepper.

2. Pour sauce over beets in serving bowl and toss gently.

Beets Dijon

8 servings

¼ cup finely chopped green onions and tops
2 cloves garlic, minced
1–2 tablespoons butter, *or* canola oil
⅓ cup sour cream
2 tablespoons Dijon-style mustard
2–3 teaspoons lemon juice
Salt and white pepper, to taste
1½ pounds beets, cooked, cubed or sliced, warm
Parsley, minced, as garnish

Per Serving
Net Carbohydrate (gm): 6.6
Calories: 73
Fat (gm): 3.3
Saturated fat (gm): 2
Cholesterol (mg): 7.6
Sodium (mg): 170
Protein (gm): 1.7
Carbohydrate (gm): 9.1

1. Sauté green onions and garlic in butter in small saucepan until tender, 3 to 4 minutes. Stir in sour cream, mustard, and lemon juice; cook over low heat until hot. Season to taste with salt and pepper.

2. Spoon sauce over beets; stir gently. Sprinkle with parsley.

Honey-Roasted Beets

8 servings

1½ pounds medium beets
4 tablespoons honey, divided
2–3 tablespoons red wine vinegar
1 tablespoon canola oil
4 cloves garlic, minced
⅓ cup chopped toasted walnuts
Salt and pepper, to taste
Parsley, minced, as garnish

Per Serving
Net Carbohydrate (gm): 15.2
Calories: 118
Fat (gm): 5.1
Saturated fat (gm): 0.5
Cholesterol (mg): 0
Sodium (mg): 64
Protein (gm): 2.3
Carbohydrate (gm): 18

1. Simmer beets in water to cover in large saucepan 15 minutes; drain and rinse in cold water. Peel beets; cut into fourths.

2. Line jelly roll pan with aluminum foil and grease lightly. Arrange beets on pan; drizzle with 2 tablespoons honey. Roast at 400 degrees until beets are tender, about 40 minutes.

3. Transfer beets to serving bowl. Combine remaining 2 tablespoons honey, vinegar, oil, and garlic; drizzle over beets and toss. Add walnuts and toss; season to taste with salt and pepper. Sprinkle with parsley.

Grilled Beet Puree

4 servings

12 ounces beets
¼ cup orange juice
3 tablespoons sour cream
2 teaspoons grated orange rind
1½ tablespoons minced cilantro
Salt and pepper, to taste
8 orange segments
Cilantro sprigs, as garnish

Per Serving
Net Carbohydrate (gm): 10.2
Calories: 75
Fat (gm): 2.1
Saturated fat (gm): 1.2
Cholesterol (mg): 4
Sodium (mg): 68
Protein (gm): 2
Carbohydrate (gm): 13.3

1. Grill beets over medium-hot coals, covered, until tender, about 30 minutes. Let stand until cool enough to handle. Peel beets.

2. Process beets, orange juice, sour cream, and orange rind in food processor or blender until smooth. Stir in minced cilantro; season to taste with salt and pepper.

3. Spoon beets into serving bowl; garnish with orange segments and cilantro sprigs.

Broccoli Parmesan

6 servings

3 tablespoons chopped shallots, *or* green onions and tops
1 clove garlic, minced
1 tablespoon olive oil
1 pound broccoli florets and cut stems,
    cooked until crisp-tender
2 teaspoons balsamic vinegar, *or* lemon juice
⅓ cup shredded Parmesan cheese
Salt and pepper, to taste
2 tablespoons toasted pine nuts, *or* almonds

Per Serving
Net Carbohydrate (gm): 4.9
Calories: 80
Fat (gm): 5.3
Saturated fat (gm): 1.4
Cholesterol (mg): 3.5
Sodium (mg): 104
Protein (gm): 4.9
Carbohydrate (gm): 5.2

1. Sauté shallots and garlic in oil in large skillet until tender, about 2 minutes. Stir in broccoli and sauté until warm, about 3 minutes. Stir in vinegar and cheese; season to taste with salt and pepper. Spoon into serving bowl and sprinkle with pine nuts.

Herb-Crumbed Broccoli

8 servings

¼ cup chopped pecans
1 tablespoon butter
¼ cup unseasoned dry bread crumbs
½ teaspoon dried marjoram leaves
2 teaspoon dried chervil leaves
2 tablespoons finely chopped parsley
1½ pounds broccoli, cut into florets, cooked, warm
Salt and pepper, to taste

Per Serving
Net Carbohydrate (gm): 4.5
Calories: 75
Fat (gm): 4.4
Saturated fat (gm): 1.2
Cholesterol (mg): 4.1
Sodium (mg): 68
Protein (gm): 3.3
Carbohydrate (gm): 7.5

1. Cook pecans in butter in small skillet over medium heat until toasted, 2 to 3 minutes, stirring frequently. Add bread crumbs, marjoram, and chervil to skillet; cook until crumbs are toasted, 3 to 4 minutes, stirring frequently. Remove from heat and stir in parsley.

2. Season broccoli with salt and pepper to taste; arrange in serving bowl. Spoon crumb mixture over broccoli.

Broccoli Rabe Sautéed with Garlic

6 servings

1 pound broccoli rabe, cooked until crisp-tender
4 cloves garlic, minced
1–2 tablespoons olive oil
Salt and pepper, to taste

Per Serving
Net Carbohydrate (gm): 2.4
Calories: 32
Fat (gm): 2.3
Saturated fat (gm): 0.3
Cholesterol (mg): 0
Sodium (mg): 9
Protein (gm): 1.5
Carbohydrate (gm): 2.5

1. Sauté broccoli rabe and garlic in oil in large skillet over medium heat until broccoli rabe is beginning to brown, 4 to 5 minutes. Season to taste with salt and pepper.

Sugar-Glazed Brussels Sprouts and Pearl Onions

6 servings

12 ounces medium Brussels sprouts, halved
4 ounces small pearl onions
1–2 tablespoons butter
3–4 tablespoons packed light brown sugar
Salt and white pepper, to taste

Per Serving
Net Carbohydrate (gm): 10.7
Calories: 74
Fat (gm): 2.2
Saturated fat (gm): 1.3
Cholesterol (mg): 5.5
Sodium (mg): 41
Protein (gm): 2
Carbohydrate (gm): 13.3

1. Cook Brussels sprouts and onions in 2 inches boiling water in 2 separate covered saucepans until vegetables are crisp-tender, 8 to 10 minutes. Drain well.

2. Heat butter in medium skillet until melted; stir in brown sugar. Cook over medium heat until mixture is bubbly; add vegetables and toss to coat. Season to taste with salt and white pepper.

Microwave Brussels Sprouts Almondine

6 servings

1 pound Brussels sprouts, cut into halves
1 clove garlic, minced
¼ cup chicken broth
1–2 tablespoons lemon juice
1–2 teaspoons Dijon mustard
Salt and pepper, to taste
3 tablespoons toasted slivered almonds

Per Serving
Net Carbohydrate (gm): 4.6
Calories: 59
Fat (gm): 2.4
Saturated fat (gm): 0.2
Cholesterol (mg): 0
Sodium (mg): 80
Protein (gm): 3.5
Carbohydrate (gm): 8

1. Microwave Brussels sprouts, garlic, and broth in 1-quart glass casserole, loosely covered, on High until tender, about 6 minutes, stirring once. Combine lemon juice and mustard in small bowl; drizzle over Brussels sprouts and toss. Season to taste with salt and pepper. Sprinkle with almonds.

Microwave Bok Choy

4 servings

6 cups thinly sliced bok choy
2 teaspoons soy sauce
1 clove garlic, minced
1 tablespoon frozen apple juice concentrate
½ teaspoon dark sesame oil
½ teaspoon ground ginger
Salt and pepper, to taste
1–2 tablespoons toasted pumpkin seeds

Per Serving
Net Carbohydrate (gm): 6.4
Calories: 34
Fat (gm): 1
Saturated fat (gm): 0.2
Cholesterol (mg): 0
Sodium (mg): 241
Protein (gm): 2
Carbohydrate (gm): 5.3

1. Combine all ingredients, except salt, pepper, and pumpkin seeds, in 2-quart glass measure. Cover with vented plastic wrap, and microwave on High 3 to 4 minutes or until bok choy is wilted, stirring once. Season to taste with salt and pepper. Toss with pumpkin seeds.

Wine-Braised Cabbage

6 servings

½ cup chopped green bell pepper
3 cloves garlic, minced
1–2 tablespoons light olive, *or* canola, oil
2 tablespoons dried onion flakes
½ teaspoon caraway seeds, crushed
½ teaspoon anise seeds, crushed
1 medium head cabbage (1 pound), thinly sliced
½ cup dry white wine, *or* chicken broth
½ cup canned chicken broth
3 slices bacon, fried crisp, crumbled
Salt and pepper, to taste

Per Serving
Net Carbohydrate (gm): 5
Calories: 85
Fat (gm): 4.3
Saturated fat (gm): 0.9
Cholesterol (mg): 2.7
Sodium (mg): 149
Protein (gm): 2.7
Carbohydrate (gm): 7.2

1. Sauté green pepper and garlic in oil in large skillet 3 to 4 minutes; add onion flakes, caraway, and anise seeds and cook 1 minute longer.

2. Add cabbage, wine, and broth to skillet; heat to boiling. Reduce heat and simmer, covered, until cabbage is wilted, about 5 minutes. Simmer, uncovered, until cabbage is tender, 10 to 15 minutes. Stir in bacon; season to taste with salt and pepper.

Microwave Ruby Red Cabbage

6 servings

½ cup chopped onion
4 cloves garlic, minced
2 teaspoons olive oil
1 pound red cabbage, shredded
¼ cup balsamic vinegar
1 cup reduced-sodium fat-free chicken broth
3 tablespoons raisins
1 tablespoon chopped gingerroot
½ teaspoon ground cloves
1 bay leaf
2–3 tablespoons lemon juice
Salt and pepper, to taste

Per Serving
Net Carbohydrate (gm): 11
Calories: 74
Fat (gm): 2
Saturated fat (gm): 0.3
Cholesterol (mg): 1.7
Sodium (mg): 12
Protein (gm): 2.2
Carbohydrate (gm): 13.2

1. Microwave onion, garlic, and oil in 2-quart glass casserole on High 3 minutes. Stir in remaining ingredients, except salt and pepper; microwave, loosely covered on High until cabbage is tender, about 8 minutes, stirring once. Discard bay leaf; season to taste with salt and pepper.

Baby Carrots à l'Orange

4 servings

¼ cup chopped onion
1 tablespoon butter
1 tablespoon packed light brown sugar
12 ounces baby carrots, cooked until crisp-tender
½ cup diced, peeled orange
Ground cinnamon, to taste
Salt, to taste

Per Serving
Net Carbohydrate (gm): 11.7
Calories: 87
Fat (gm): 3.5
Saturated fat (gm): 2
Cholesterol (mg): 8.2
Sodium (mg): 62
Protein (gm): 1.1
Carbohydrate (gm): 13.8

1. Sauté onion in butter in small skillet 2 to 3 minutes; stir in brown sugar, carrots, and orange. Cook over medium heat until carrots are hot through. Season to taste with cinnamon and salt.

Carrots Parisienne

6 servings

¼ cup chopped sweet onion
¼ cup thinly sliced green onions and tops
1 tablespoon butter
1 pound carrots, sliced ½ inch thick,
    cooked until crisp-tender
Salt and pepper, to taste
2 tablespoons chopped parsley

Per Serving
Net Carbohydrate (gm): 6.1
Calories: 55
Fat (gm): 2.2
Saturated fat (gm): 1.3
Cholesterol (mg): 5.5
Sodium (mg): 49
Protein (gm): 1
Carbohydrate (gm): 8.6

1. Sauté sweet and green onions in butter in large skillet until tender and lightly browned, about 8 minutes, stirring frequently. Add carrots and cook over medium heat until hot through. Season to taste with salt and pepper; stir in parsley.

Gingered Carrot Puree

8 servings (about ⅓ cup each)

2 pounds carrots, sliced
1 small Idaho potato (4 ounces), peeled, cubed
1–2 tablespoons butter
¼–½ cup whipping cream, heated
¼–½ teaspoon ground ginger
Salt and white pepper, to taste
Ground nutmeg, as garnish

Per Serving
Net Carbohydrate (gm): 8.9
Calories: 98
Fat (gm): 4.5
Saturated fat (gm): 2.7
Cholesterol (mg): 14.4
Sodium (mg): 58.9
Protein (gm): 1.6
Carbohydrate (gm): 14

1. Cook carrots and potato in 2 inches simmering water until very tender, about 15 minutes; drain.

2. Process carrots and potato in food processor until smooth; transfer mixture to large skillet. Cook mixture over medium to medium-low heat, stirring frequently, until mixture is the consistency of thick mashed potatoes (do not brown), about 15 minutes.

3. Beat butter and enough cream into carrot mixture to make creamy consistency. Stir in ginger; season to taste with salt and white pepper. Spoon into serving bowl; sprinkle with nutmeg.

Cauliflower with Creamy Cheese Sauce

8 servings

1 whole large cauliflower (1½ pounds)
Creamy Cheese Sauce (recipe follows)
Paprika, as garnish
Parsley, finely chopped, as garnish

Per Serving
Net Carbohydrate (gm): 3.2
Calories: 79
Fat (gm): 4.7
Saturated fat (gm): 2.8
Cholesterol (mg): 14
Sodium (mg): 101
Protein (gm): 4.7
Carbohydrate (gm): 5.4

1. Place cauliflower in saucepan with 2 inches of water; heat to boiling. Reduce heat and simmer, covered, until cauliflower is tender, 20 to 25 minutes.

2. Place cauliflower on serving plate; spoon Creamy Cheese Sauce over and sprinkle with paprika and parsley.

Creamy Cheese Sauce

makes about 1¼ cups

2 tablespoons minced onion
1 tablespoon butter
2 tablespoons all-purpose flour
1 cup reduced-fat milk
½ cup (2 ounces) shredded Cheddar cheese
¼ teaspoon dry mustard
2–3 drops red pepper sauce
Salt and white pepper, to taste

1. Sauté onion in butter in small saucepan 2 to 3 minutes. Stir in flour; cook over medium-low heat, stirring constantly, 1 minute. Whisk in milk and heat to boiling; boil, whisking constantly, until thickened, about 1 minute.

2. Reduce heat to low. Add cheese, dry mustard, and pepper sauce, whisking until cheese is melted. Season to taste with salt and white pepper.

Cauliflower Siciliano

6 servings

½ cup thinly sliced leeks (white parts only), *or* onion
½ cup thinly sliced green bell pepper
3 cloves garlic, minced
2 tablespoons olive oil
1 pound cauliflower florets
½ cup sliced tomato
½ cup dry white wine, *or* chicken broth
½ teaspoon dried oregano leaves
2 tablespoons chopped parsley
2 tablespoons chopped fresh, *or* 1 teaspoon dried, basil leaves
2 tablespoons drained capers
2 tablespoons chopped, pitted Italian black olives
Salt and pepper, to taste
6 lemon wedges, as garnish

Per Serving
Net Carbohydrate (gm): 4.9
Calories: 90
Fat (gm): 5.1
Saturated fat (gm): 0.7
Cholesterol (mg): 0
Sodium (mg): 137
Protein (gm): 2.1
Carbohydrate (gm): 7.6

1. Sauté leek, bell pepper, and garlic in oil in large skillet until leeks are lightly browned, about 5 minutes. Add cauliflower, and cook over medium heat, stirring constantly, 3 minutes. Reduce heat to low, and cook, covered, 5 minutes longer.

2. Stir in remaining ingredients, except salt, pepper, and lemon wedges; simmer, covered, until cauliflower is tender, about 5 minutes. Season to taste with salt and pepper. Spoon into serving bowl; garnish with lemon wedges.

Cauliflower Fennel Puree

8 servings (about ⅓ cup each)

2 pounds cauliflower, cut into florets
1½ cups cubed, unpeeled Idaho potato
1–1½ teaspoons fennel, *or* caraway, seeds, crushed
1–2 tablespoons butter
¼–½ cup whipping cream, heated
Salt and white pepper, to taste
Parsley, finely chopped, as garnish

Per Serving
Net Carbohydrate (gm): 4.2
Calories: 83
Fat (gm): 4.6
Saturated fat (gm): 2.7
Cholesterol (mg): 14.4
Sodium (mg): 54
Protein (gm): 2.8
Carbohydrate (gm): 9.6

1. Cook cauliflower and potato in 2 inches simmering water, covered, until very tender, 10 to 12 minutes. Drain.

2. Process vegetables in food processor until smooth; transfer mixture to large skillet and stir in fennel seeds. Cook mixture over medium to medium-low heat, stirring frequently, until mixture is the consistency of very thick mashed potatoes (do not brown), about 15 minutes.

3. Beat butter and enough cream into mixture to make creamy consistency. Season to taste with salt and white pepper. Spoon into serving bowl; sprinkle with parsley.

Microwave Cauliflower Medley

6 servings

1 pound cauliflower florets
1 cup chopped green bell pepper
1 cup sliced carrots
1 teaspoon caraway seeds
¼ cup water
Salt and pepper, to taste

Per Serving
Net Carbohydrate (gm): 4.7
Calories: 35
Fat (gm): 0.3
Saturated fat (gm): 0
Cholesterol (mg): 0
Sodium (mg): 30
Protein (gm): 2
Carbohydrate (gm): 7.8

1. Combine cauliflower, bell pepper, and carrots in l-quart glass casserole; sprinkle with caraway seeds. Add water and microwave, covered, on High until tender, 5 to 7 minutes, stirring once; drain. Season to taste with salt and pepper.

Celery Root Puree

8 servings (about ⅓ cup each)

2 pounds peeled celery root, cubed
1½ cups cubed, unpeeled Idaho potato
¼ cup coarsely chopped sweet onion
1–2 tablespoons butter
¼–½ cup whipping cream, heated
Nutmeg, ground, to taste
Salt and white pepper, to taste
Parsley, finely chopped, as garnish

Per Serving
Net Carbohydrate (gm): 6.8
Calories: 87
Fat (gm): 4.5
Saturated fat (gm): 2.8
Cholesterol (mg): 14.4
Sodium (mg): 89
Protein (gm): 1.7
Carbohydrate (gm): 10.7

1. Cook celery root, potato, and onion in 2 inches simmering water, covered, until very tender, about 15 minutes; drain.

2. Process vegetables in food processor until smooth; transfer mixture to large skillet. Cook mixture over medium to medium-low heat, stirring frequently, until mixture is the consistency of thick mashed potatoes (do not brown), about 15 minutes.

3. Beat butter and enough cream into mixture to make creamy consistency. Stir in nutmeg, salt, and white pepper to taste. Spoon into serving bowl; sprinkle with parsley.

Corn Pudding

6 servings

2 tablespoons plain, unseasoned bread crumbs
2 cups fresh, *or* frozen, thawed, whole kernel corn
½ cup whipping cream
½ cup sour cream
1 tablespoon butter, melted
2 eggs
½ teaspoon baking powder
½ teaspoon dried savory leaves
½ teaspoon dried thyme leaves
½ teaspoon salt
⅛ teaspoon cayenne pepper
¼ teaspoon black pepper

Per Serving
Net Carbohydrate (gm): 12.6
Calories: 200
Fat (gm): 14.8
Saturated fat (gm): 8.5
Cholesterol (mg): 110.7
Sodium (mg): 314
Protein (gm): 4.8
Carbohydrate (gm): 14.1

1. Process all ingredients in blender or food processor until mixture is coarsely chopped. Pour into ungreased soufflé dish. Bake at 350 degrees until puffed and set in the center, 45 to 50 minutes. Serve immediately.

Succotash

8 servings

¼ cup sliced green onions and tops
1–2 tablespoons butter
2 cups frozen, *or* canned, drained baby lima beans
2 cups fresh, *or* frozen, whole kernel corn
½ cup canned vegetable broth
½ cup light cream
Salt and pepper, to taste

Per Serving
Net Carbohydrate (gm): 15.8
Calories: 132
Fat (gm): 4.8
Saturated fat (gm): 2.8
Cholesterol (mg): 14
Sodium (mg): 108
Protein (gm): 4.8
Carbohydrate (gm): 19.3

1. Sauté onions in butter in medium saucepan until tender, about 3 minutes. Stir in lima beans, corn, broth, and cream; heat to boiling. Reduce heat and simmer, covered, until vegetables are tender, about 5 minutes. Season to taste with salt and pepper.

Microwave Southwest-Style Corn

6 servings

¼ cup diced green bell pepper
¼ cup diced red bell pepper
2 teaspoons olive oil
½ pound whole kernel corn, cooked, drained
½ teaspoon ground cumin
½ teaspoon chili powder
Salt and pepper, to taste

Per Serving
Net Carbohydrate (gm): 7.1
Calories: 48
Fat (gm): 1.8
Saturated fat (gm): 0.2
Cholesterol (mg): 0
Sodium (mg): 5
Protein (gm): 1.2
Carbohydrate (gm): 8.4

1. Microwave bell peppers and oil in 1-quart glass casserole on High 3 minutes. Add corn, cumin, and chili powder; microwave, loosely covered on High until hot, 2 to 4 minutes. Season to taste with salt and pepper.

Pesole

8 servings

Per Serving
Net Carbohydrate (gm): 11.3
Calories: 79
Fat (gm): 1.3
Saturated fat (gm): 0.2
Cholesterol (mg): 0
Sodium (mg): 312
Protein (gm): 2.1
Carbohydrate (gm): 15

1 can (20 ounces) pesole (white hominy), drained
½ cup chopped onion
1 tablespoon chili powder
3 cloves garlic, minced
2 tablespoons ground cumin
1 tablespoon dried oregano leaves
2 cups chopped, peeled tomatoes, *or* 1 can (16 ounces) diced tomatoes, drained
½ teaspoon salt
¼ teaspoon pepper

1. Combine all ingredients in large saucepan; add water just to cover. Heat to boiling; reduce heat and simmer, covered, until tender, about 15 minutes. Uncover and simmer until thickened, about 5 minutes.

Seasoned Eggplant Sauté

6 servings

Per Serving
Net Carbohydrate (gm): 6.2
Calories: 63
Fat (gm): 2.6
Saturated fat (gm): 0.4
Cholesterol (mg): 0
Sodium (mg): 43
Protein (gm): 1.6
Carbohydrate (gm): 9.7

1 large eggplant (about 1½ pounds),
    unpeeled, cut into scant ¾-inch cubes
¼ cup chopped onion
½ cup chopped red bell pepper
4 large cloves garlic, minced
1 tablespoon olive oil
1 teaspoon dried oregano leaves
½ teaspoon dried thyme leaves
¼ teaspoon crushed red pepper
½ cup reduced-sodium vegetable, *or* chicken broth
Salt and pepper, to taste
2 tablespoons finely chopped parsley

1. Sauté vegetables in oil in large skillet until crisp-tender, 8 to 10 minutes; add dried herbs and red pepper and cook 1 to 2 minutes longer.

2. Add broth to skillet and heat to boiling; reduce heat and simmer, covered, until vegetables are tender and broth is absorbed, 15 to 20 minutes. Season to taste with salt and pepper; stir in parsley.

Eggplant and Tomato Casserole

8 servings

1 large eggplant (1½ pounds), peeled, cut into 1-inch cubes
½ cup seasoned dry bread crumbs
¼ cup chopped onion
3 cloves garlic, minced
1½ teaspoons dried oregano leaves, divided
½ teaspoon dried basil leaves
½ teaspoon dried thyme leaves
Salt and pepper, to taste
2 eggs, lightly beaten
2 medium tomatoes, sliced
¼ cup grated Parmesan cheese

Per Serving
Net Carbohydrate (gm): 9.9
Calories: 90
Fat (gm): 2.7
Saturated fat (gm): 1
Cholesterol (mg): 55.1
Sodium (mg): 126
Protein (gm): 4.8
Carbohydrate (gm): 12.8

1. Cook eggplant in 2 inches simmering water in covered medium saucepan until tender, 5 to 8 minutes. Drain well. Mash eggplant with fork; mix in bread crumbs, onion, garlic, 1 teaspoon oregano, basil, and thyme. Season to taste with salt and pepper. Mix in eggs.

2. Spoon eggplant mixture into baking dish, 11 x 7 inches. Arrange tomatoes in rows over eggplant; sprinkle with cheese and remaining ½ teaspoon oregano.

3. Bake, uncovered, at 350 degrees until casserole is hot and tomatoes tender, about 20 minutes.

Roasted Eggplant

6 servings

1 medium eggplant (1–1¼ pounds)
1 cup chopped, seeded tomato
4 green onions and tops, sliced
2–3 tablespoons balsamic, *or* red wine, vinegar
1 tablespoon olive oil
1–2 teaspoons lemon juice
1 tablespoon finely chopped parsley
Salt and pepper, to taste

Per Serving
Net Carbohydrate (gm): 5
Calories: 51
Fat (gm): 2.5
Saturated fat (gm): 0.3
Cholesterol (mg): 0
Sodium (mg): 7
Protein (gm): 1.2
Carbohydrate (gm): 7.5

1. Pierce eggplant 6 to 8 times with fork; place in baking pan. Bake, uncovered, at 425 degrees until tender, about 40 minutes. Cool until eggplant can be handled easily. Cut eggplant in half; scoop out pulp with large spoon, and cut into ¾-inch pieces.

2. Combine eggplant and remaining ingredients, except salt and pepper, in bowl; season to taste with salt and pepper.

Cajun Eggplant

4 servings

1 medium eggplant (about 1 pound),
    unpeeled, cut into ½-inch slices
1–2 tablespoons olive oil
Cajun Seasoning (recipe follows)

Per Serving
Net Carbohydrate (gm): 4.5
Calories: 62
Fat (gm): 3.8
Saturated fat (gm): 0.5
Cholesterol (mg): 0
Sodium (mg): 149
Protein (gm): 1.3
Carbohydrate (gm): 7.2

1. Lightly brush both sides of eggplant with oil;
sprinkle with Cajun Seasoning, pressing mixture onto eggplant.

2. Grill eggplant over medium-hot coals until tender, about 5 minutes per side, or roast in oven at 425 degrees until tender, about 15 minutes.

Cajun Seasoning

makes about 2 tablespoons

2 teaspoons paprika
1 teaspoon onion powder
1 teaspoon garlic powder
½ teaspoon dried thyme leaves
½ teaspoon dried oregano leaves
½ teaspoon cayenne pepper
½ teaspoon black pepper
¼ teaspoon salt

1. Mix all ingredients; store in airtight container until ready to use.

Mediterranean Roasted Eggplant and Tomatoes

6 servings

1 medium eggplant (about 1 pound), unpeeled
8 ounces tomatoes, cut into wedges
½ teaspoon dried dill weed
½ teaspoon dried mint leaves
Salt and pepper, to taste
1–2 tablespoons olive oil

Per Serving
Net Carbohydrate (gm): 4.1
Calories: 48
Fat (gm): 2.5
Saturated fat (gm): 0.3
Cholesterol (mg): 0
Sodium (mg): 6
Protein (gm): 1.1
Carbohydrate (gm): 6.4

1. Line jelly roll pan with aluminum foil and grease lightly. Cut eggplant into ½-inch-thick slices; cut slices into fourths. Arrange eggplant and tomatoes on jelly roll pan; sprinkle with herbs.

2. Roast vegetables at 425 degrees until browned and very tender, 30 to 40 minutes. Transfer to serving bowl; season to taste with salt and pepper. Drizzle with olive oil.

Braised Fennel

6 servings

½ cup thinly sliced leek (white parts only)
3 cloves garlic, minced
2 tablespoons canola oil
1 pound fennel bulbs, cut into 1-inch wedges
1 cup reduced-sodium vegetable broth, *or*
    reduced-sodium fat-free chicken broth
1 teaspoon dried oregano leaves
½ teaspoon fennel seeds
Salt and pepper, to taste
1 tablespoon chopped parsley

Per Serving
Net Carbohydrate (gm): 6.3
Calories: 81
Fat (gm): 4.9
Saturated fat (gm): 0.3
Cholesterol (mg): 0
Sodium (mg): 120
Protein (gm): 1.5
Carbohydrate (gm): 9.2

1. Sauté leek and garlic in oil in large saucepan until lightly browned, about 3 minutes. Stir in fennel and sauté 2 minutes.

2. Stir in broth, oregano, and fennel seeds. Heat to boiling; reduce heat and simmer, covered, until fennel is crisp-tender, 10 to 12 minutes. Season to taste with salt and pepper. Spoon into serving dish; sprinkle with parsley.

Braised Kale

4 servings

¼ cup sliced leek (white part only)
2 teaspoons olive oil
1 pound kale, rinsed, torn into pieces
½ cup water
½ teaspoon vegetable bouillon crystals
½ cup sour cream
1 teaspoon Dijon mustard
2 slices bacon, fried crisp, crumbled
Salt and pepper, to taste

Per Serving
Net Carbohydrate (gm): 10.9
Calories: 151
Fat (gm): 9.6
Saturated fat (gm): 4.1
Cholesterol (mg): 13.2
Sodium (mg): 262
Protein (gm): 5.5
Carbohydrate (gm): 13.2

1. Sauté leek in oil in large saucepan until tender, 3 to 4 minutes. Add kale, water, and bouillon crystals; heat to boiling. Reduce heat and simmer, covered, until kale is wilted and tender, about 5 minutes. Drain and discard any excess liquid.

2. Stir sour cream, mustard, and bacon into kale mixture; cook over low heat 2 to 3 minutes. Season to taste with salt and pepper.

Microwave Kale

4 servings

¾ cup chopped onion
3 cloves garlic, minced
1 tablespoon grated gingerroot
3–4 leaves fresh basil, chopped, *or*
    1 teaspoon dried basil leaves
½ teaspoon crushed red pepper
1 teaspoon canola, *or* olive, oil
1 pound kale, *or* turnip greens, sliced
1 cup Chicken Stock (see p. 20), *or* canned reduced-sodium fat-free chicken broth
4 dashes dark sesame oil
1 tablespoon lemon juice
Salt and pepper, to taste
1 tablespoon toasted pine nuts

Per Serving
Net Carbohydrate (gm): 12.8
Calories: 107
Fat (gm): 3.5
Saturated fat (gm): 0.5
Cholesterol (mg): 2.5
Sodium (mg): 51
Protein (gm): 5.7
Carbohydrate (gm): 15.9

1. Microwave onion, garlic, ginger, basil, crushed red pepper, and oil in 2-quart glass baking dish on High 2 minutes. Stir in kale and Chicken Stock; cover with vented plastic wrap, and microwave on High until kale is wilted and tender, 3 to 5 minutes, stirring once. Stir in sesame oil and lemon juice; season to taste with salt and pepper. Sprinkle with pine nuts.

Lemon-Spiked Garlic Greens

6 servings

¼ cup finely chopped onion
¼ cup finely chopped red bell pepper
4 cloves garlic, minced
2 tablespoons light olive, *or* canola, oil
1½ pounds greens (kale, Swiss chard, collard, turnip),
    washed and stems removed, coarsely chopped
⅓ cup water
1–2 tablespoons lemon juice
Salt and pepper, to taste
1 hard-cooked egg, chopped

Per Serving
Net Carbohydrate (gm): 10.7
Calories: 117
Fat (gm): 6.2
Saturated fat (gm): 1
Cholesterol (mg): 35.4
Sodium (mg): 58
Protein (gm): 5.1
Carbohydrate (gm): 13.3

1. Sauté onion, bell pepper, and garlic in oil in large saucepan until tender, 3 to 4 minutes.

2. Add greens and water to saucepan; heat to boiling. Reduce heat and simmer, covered, until greens are wilted and tender, about 3 to 5 minutes, adding more water if necessary. Season to taste with lemon juice, salt, and pepper.

3. Spoon greens into serving bowl; sprinkle with egg.

Spinach-Stuffed Mushrooms

8 servings (2 mushrooms each)

16 large mushrooms (about 12 ounces)
1 clove garlic, crushed
1 tablespoon butter
1 package (10 ounces) frozen chopped, *or*
    fresh, spinach, cooked, well-drained
1 teaspoon Worcestershire sauce
½ cup seasoned dry bread crumbs
1 teaspoon Dijon mustard
2 tablespoons mayonnaise
2 tablespoons grated Parmesan cheese
Salt and pepper, to taste

Per Serving
Net Carbohydrate (gm): 6.6
Calories: 92
Fat (gm): 5
Saturated fat (gm): 1.7
Cholesterol (mg): 7.2
Sodium (mg): 325
Protein (gm): 3.8
Carbohydrate (gm): 8.3

1. Remove and chop mushroom stems; reserve caps. Sauté mushroom stems and garlic in butter in medium skillet until tender, about 5 minutes. Stir in remaining ingredients, except mushroom caps, salt, and pepper; season to taste with salt and pepper.

2. Spoon spinach mixture into reserved mushroom caps. Place mushrooms, stuffed sides up, in lightly greased 11 x 7-inch baking pan. Bake, uncovered, at 350 degrees 20 minutes or until mushrooms are tender.

Mushrooms with Sour Cream

4 servings

12 ounces shiitake, *or*
    cremini, mushrooms, tough stems discarded, sliced
2 large cloves garlic, minced
1 tablespoon olive oil
¼ cup vegetable, *or* chicken, broth
¼ teaspoon dried thyme leaves
½ cup sour cream
Salt and cayenne pepper, to taste

Per Serving
Net Carbohydrate (gm): 12.2
Calories: 132
Fat (gm): 8.6
Saturated fat (gm): 3.6
Cholesterol (mg): 10.6
Sodium (mg): 45
Protein (gm): 2.3
Carbohydrate (gm): 14

1. Sauté mushrooms and garlic in oil in large skillet until tender, 3 to 4 minutes. Add broth and thyme to skillet; heat to boiling. Reduce heat and simmer, covered, until mushrooms are very tender, 8 to 10 minutes. Cook, uncovered, on low heat until mushrooms are dry and well browned, 20 to 25 minutes longer. Stir in sour cream; season to taste with salt and pepper.

Stuffed Portobello Mushrooms with Basil Pesto

4 servings

4 large (5–6 inches diameter)
    portobello mushrooms (8–10 ounces)
½ cup finely chopped zucchini
½ cup shredded carrots
2 green onions and tops, thinly sliced
1 tablespoon olive oil
2 tablespoons unseasoned dry bread crumbs
¼ cup prepared basil pesto
Salt and pepper, to taste
¼ cup (1 ounce) shredded mozzarella cheese

Per Serving
Net Carbohydrate (gm): 7.4
Calories: 163
Fat (gm): 12.3
Saturated fat (gm): 2.5
Cholesterol (mg): 6.5
Sodium (mg): 181
Protein (gm): 5.5
Carbohydrate (gm): 9.1

1. Remove and chop mushroom stems. Sauté mushroom stems, zucchini, carrots, and green onions in oil in medium skillet until crisp-tender, 8 to 10 minutes. Stir in bread crumbs and pesto. Season to taste with salt and pepper. Spoon mixture into mushroom caps.

2. Line baking pan with aluminum foil and grease lightly; arrange mushrooms in pan. Bake, uncovered, at 425 degrees until mushrooms are tender, about 20 minutes, sprinkling with cheese during the last 5 minutes of baking time.

Gulfport Okra

8 servings

1½ pounds fresh, *or* frozen, thawed, okra, tops trimmed
2 tablespoons olive oil
Garlic powder, to taste
Salt and pepper, to taste

Per Serving
Net Carbohydrate (gm): 3.8
Calories: 58
Fat (gm): 3.5
Saturated fat (gm): 0.5
Cholesterol (mg): 0
Sodium (mg): 7
Protein (gm): 1.7
Carbohydrate (gm): 6.5

1. Trim okra stems without cutting into tops of okra; cook in boiling water 1 to 2 minutes; drain well.

2. Sauté okra in oil in large skillet over medium heat until well browned, almost black, stirring occasionally. Sprinkle okra generously with garlic powder; season to taste with salt and pepper.

Microwave Okra Provençal

6 servings

1 pound small okra, tops trimmed
1 can (15 ounces) stewed tomatoes, drained,
    coarsely chopped
¼ cup chopped green onions and tops
2 cloves garlic, minced
½ cup chopped green bell pepper
6 small pimiento-stuffed olives, sliced
¼ cup chopped parsley
¼ teaspoon dried thyme leaves
¼ teaspoon dried marjoram leaves
2 teaspoons dried basil leaves
Salt and pepper, to taste

Per Serving
Net Carbohydrate (gm): 9.8
Calories: 64
Fat (gm): 0.6
Saturated fat (gm): 0.1
Cholesterol (mg): 0
Sodium (mg): 243
Protein (gm): 2.7
Carbohydrate (gm): 13.6

1. Place okra on paper towels in glass baking dish. Microwave on High 2 to 3 minutes until tender, turning once.

2. Microwave remaining ingredients, except salt and pepper, in 1-quart glass measure, loosely covered, on High 5 to 6 minutes. Stir in okra and microwave 1 minute longer on High. Season to taste with salt and pepper.

Sautéed Leeks and Peppers

6 servings

1 cup sliced (½-inch) leeks (white parts only)
⅓ cup sliced yellow bell pepper
⅓ cup sliced red bell pepper
⅓ cup sliced green bell pepper
2 tablespoons olive oil
2 tablespoons water
½ teaspoon bouquet garni
Salt and pepper, to taste

Per Serving
Net Carbohydrate (gm): 9
Calories: 86
Fat (gm): 4.8
Saturated fat (gm): 0.6
Cholesterol (mg): 0
Sodium (mg): 10
Protein (gm): 1.3
Carbohydrate (gm): 10.8

1. Sauté vegetables in oil in large skillet 1 minute; add water and cook, covered, over medium heat until vegetables are wilted, 5 to 8 minutes.

2. Stir in bouquet garni and cook, uncovered, over medium to medium-low heat until vegetables are tender. Season to taste with salt and pepper.

Trio of Onions

8 servings

2 pounds sweet onions, sliced
4 ounces shallots, finely chopped
½ cup sliced green onions and tops
2 tablespoons olive oil
½ cup vegetable broth
1 teaspoon dried mint leaves
½ teaspoon dried sage leaves
Salt and white pepper, to taste

Per Serving
Net Carbohydrate (gm): 10.7
Calories: 87
Fat (gm): 3.6
Saturated fat (gm): 0.5
Cholesterol (mg): 0
Sodium (mg): 35
Protein (gm): 1.9
Carbohydrate (gm): 13

1. Sauté onions, shallots, and green onions in oil in large skillet 3 to 4 minutes, stirring frequently. Stir in broth and heat to boiling; reduce heat and simmer, covered, 5 minutes.

2. Stir in herbs and cook, uncovered, over medium-low heat until onion mixture is golden, about 15 minutes. Season to taste with salt and white pepper.

Onions Stuffed with Mushrooms

6 servings

6 small red onions (3 ounces each), peeled
1½ cups finely chopped mushrooms
2 cloves garlic, minced
¼ cup seasoned dry bread crumbs
3 tablespoons grated Parmesan cheese
2 tablespoons chopped parsley
2 tablespoons chopped fresh, *or*
    2 teaspoons dried, oregano leaves
Salt and pepper, to taste

Per Serving
Net Carbohydrate (gm): 9.6
Calories: 66
Fat (gm): 1.1
Saturated fat (gm): 0.5
Cholesterol (mg): 2
Sodium (mg): 183
Protein (gm): 3.3
Carbohydrate (gm): 11.4

1. Place onions in large saucepan with 1 inch water; heat to boiling. Reduce heat and simmer until onions are crisp-tender, 10 to 15 minutes. Drain onions; let stand until cool enough to handle. Cut tops off onions; scoop out pulp in centers, leaving solid shells of 3 or 4 layers of onion with bottoms intact.

2. Chop enough onion pulp to measure ½ cup; save remaining pulp for another use. Combine chopped onion and remaining ingredients, except salt and pepper, in small bowl; season to taste with salt and pepper. Fill onions with stuffing. Place snugly side by side in lightly greased baking dish. Bake, loosely covered, at 350 degrees until tender and browned, about 30 minutes. Serve warm or at room temperature.

Green Peas, Valencia Style

4 servings

½ cup chopped onion
2 cloves garlic, minced
1 tablespoon olive oil
⅓ cup finely chopped yellow bell pepper
8 ounces fresh, *or* frozen, thawed, green peas
½ cup chicken broth, *or* dry white wine
2 tablespoons chopped parsley
1 tablespoon chopped fresh, *or* 1 teaspoon dried, thyme leaves
1 bay leaf
⅛ teaspoon saffron threads, optional
Salt and pepper, to taste
Pimiento strips, as garnish

Per Serving
Net Carbohydrate (gm): 8
Calories: 94
Fat (gm): 3.9
Saturated fat (gm): 0.6
Cholesterol (mg): 0
Sodium (mg): 177
Protein (gm): 3.8
Carbohydrate (gm): 11.8

1. Sauté onion and garlic in oil in large skillet until softened, about 3 minutes. Stir in bell pepper, peas, broth, and herbs; heat to boiling. Reduce heat and simmer, covered, until peas are tender, about 10 minutes; drain. Stir in saffron (if using) and cook 1 minute longer. Season to taste with salt and pepper; discard bay leaf. Garnish with pimiento.

Tricolored Bell Pepper Stir-Fry

4 servings

3 cups thinly sliced mixed green, red, and yellow bell peppers
¾ cup sliced onion
¼ cup sliced green onions and tops
2 tablespoons peanut, *or* canola, oil
1 tablespoon minced fresh, *or* 1 teaspoon dried, basil leaves
1 teaspoon fresh, *or* ½ teaspoon dried, thyme leaves
1 teaspoon garlic powder
3 tablespoons dry white wine, *or* water
2 tablespoons chopped fresh parsley
Salt and pepper, to taste

Per Serving
Net Carbohydrate (gm): 8.9
Calories: 117
Fat (gm): 7.1
Saturated fat (gm): 1.2
Cholesterol (mg): 0
Sodium (mg): 6
Protein (gm): 1.8
Carbohydrate (gm): 11.6

1. Stir-fry bell peppers and onions in oil in wok or large skillet 2 to 3 minutes. Sprinkle with herbs and garlic powder; stir-fry until vegetables are crisp-tender, 3 to 5 minutes longer. Stir in wine; cook 1 minute. Sprinkle with parsley; season to taste with salt and pepper..

Potatoes Gratin

10–12 servings

2 tablespoons butter
3 tablespoons all-purpose flour
1¾ cups whipping cream
1 cup (4 ounces) shredded Cheddar cheese
Salt and pepper, to taste
2 pounds Idaho potatoes, peeled, cut into scant ¼-inch slices
¼ cup very thinly sliced onion
Ground nutmeg, to taste

Per Serving
Net Carbohydrate (gm): 19.8
Calories: 300
Fat (gm): 21.8
Saturated fat (gm): 13.6
Cholesterol (mg): 76
Sodium (mg): 116
Protein (gm): 5.5
Carbohydrate (gm): 21.6

1. Melt butter in medium saucepan; stir in flour and cook over medium heat, stirring constantly, 2 minutes. Whisk in cream and heat to boiling; boil, stirring constantly, until thickened. Remove from heat; add cheese, stirring until melted. Season to taste with salt and pepper.

2. Layer ⅓ of the potatoes and onion in bottom of 2-quart casserole; sprinkle lightly with salt, pepper, and nutmeg. Spoon ⅔ cup sauce over. Repeat layers 2 times, using remaining ingredients.

3. Bake, covered, at 350 degrees for 45 minutes; uncover and bake until potatoes are fork-tender and browned, 20 to 30 minutes more.

Variations:

Scalloped Potatoes—Make white sauce as above, increasing butter to 3 tablespoons, flour to ¼ cup, and cream to 2¼ cups; omit cheese. Assemble and bake as directed.

Rosemary-Scented Potatoes Gratin

12 servings

4 cloves garlic, minced
1 tablespoon minced shallots
¼ cup chopped parsley
2 tablespoons chopped fresh, *or*
   2 teaspoons dried, rosemary leaves
¼ cup grated Parmesan cheese
2¼ pounds Idaho potatoes, peeled, sliced
Salt and pepper, to taste
2 cups reduced-sodium fat-free chicken broth

Per Serving
Net Carbohydrate (gm): 20
Calories: 97
Fat (gm): 0.9
Saturated fat (gm): 0.4
Cholesterol (mg): 5.5
Sodium (mg): 82
Protein (gm): 4.1
Carbohydrate (gm): 18.7

1. Combine garlic, shallots, parsley, rosemary, and Parmesan cheese in small mixing bowl. Slightly overlap ⅓ of the potato slices to cover bottom of lightly greased 12-inch gratin or baking dish. Sprinkle about ⅓ of cheese mixture over potatoes; sprinkle lightly with salt and pepper. Repeat layers twice using remaining potatoes and cheese mixture. Pour chicken broth over potatoes. Bake at 350 degrees 45 minutes or until potatoes are tender. Cool 5 minutes before serving.

Real Mashed Potatoes

10 servings

2 pounds Idaho potatoes, peeled,
   quartered, cooked until tender
½ cup sour cream
¼ cup reduced-fat milk, hot
2 tablespoons butter
Salt and pepper, to taste

Per Serving
Net Carbohydrate (gm): 17.2
Calories: 123
Fat (gm): 4.7
Saturated fat (gm): 2.9
Cholesterol (mg): 11.3
Sodium (mg): 37
Protein (gm): 2.1
Carbohydrate (gm): 18.9

1. Mash potatoes, or beat until smooth, in medium bowl, adding sour cream, milk, and butter. Season to taste with salt and pepper.

Variations:

Garlic Mashed Potatoes—Cook 10 peeled cloves of garlic with the potatoes. Follow recipe above, mashing garlic with potatoes.

Horseradish Mashed Potatoes—Make Real or Garlic Mashed Potatoes, beating in 2 teaspoons horseradish.

Potato Pancakes—Make any of the mashed potato recipes above; refrigerate until chilled. Mix in 1 egg, 4 chopped green onions and tops, and ¼ cup grated Parmesan cheese. Form mixture into 10 patties, using about ½ cup mixture for each. Coat patties in flour, dip in beaten egg white, and coat lightly with plain dry bread crumbs. Cook over medium-high heat in lightly greased large skillet until browned, 3 to 5 minutes on each side.

Smashed Potatoes and Greens

6 servings

3 cloves garlic, minced
2 teaspoons canola oil
2 cups thinly sliced greens (kale, mustard, turnip greens)
¼ cup water
1 pound Idaho potatoes, peeled, cubed, cooked
⅓ cup sour cream
2–4 tablespoons reduced-fat milk
2 tablespoons butter, softened
Salt and pepper, to taste
Paprika, as garnish

Per Serving
Net Carbohydrate (gm): 16.7
Calories: 153
Fat (gm): 8.1
Saturated fat (gm): 4.1
Cholesterol (mg): 16
Sodium (mg): 63
Protein (gm): 2.7
Carbohydrate (gm): 18.6

1. Sauté garlic in oil in small skillet until tender, 2 to 3 minutes. Add greens and water to skillet; heat to boiling. Cook, covered, until greens are tender about 5 minutes. Cook, uncovered, until water has evaporated and greens are almost dry.

2. Mash potatoes in bowl; mix in sour cream, milk, and butter. Mix in greens mixture; season to taste with salt and pepper. Spoon potato mixture into serving bowl; sprinkle lightly with paprika.

Veggie-Stuffed Bakers

6 servings

3 medium Idaho potatoes (about 5 ounces each)
½ cup thinly sliced green onions and tops
⅓ cup chopped red bell pepper
4 cloves garlic, minced
1 tablespoon canola oil
⅓ cup sour cream
¾–1 cup (3–4 ounces) shredded Cheddar cheese, divided
Salt and pepper, to taste
1 cup broccoli florets, cooked until crisp-tender

Per Serving
Net Carbohydrate (gm): 17.1
Calories: 181
Fat (gm): 9.4
Saturated fat (gm): 4.6
Cholesterol (mg): 19.5
Sodium (mg): 103
Protein (gm): 6.1
Carbohydrate (gm): 19.2

1. Grease potatoes lightly and pierce in several places with a fork; bake at 400 degrees until tender, 45 to 60 minutes. Let stand until cool enough to handle. Cut potatoes lengthwise into halves; scoop out insides of potatoes, leaving shells intact.

2. Sauté onions, bell pepper, and garlic in oil in medium skillet until tender, about 5 minutes.

3. Mash potatoes, adding sour cream and half the Cheddar cheese. Mix in sautéed vegetables; season to taste with salt and pepper. Spoon mixture into potato shells; arrange broccoli on top and sprinkle with remaining cheese.

4. Arrange potatoes in baking pan; bake, uncovered, at 350 degrees until hot through, 20 to 30 minutes.

Garden-Topped Potatoes

8 servings

4 Idaho baking potatoes (6–7 ounces each)
¼ cup chopped green bell pepper
¼ cup chopped green onions and tops
2 cloves garlic, minced
2 tablespoons butter
½ cup sliced mushrooms
1 cup cubed zucchini
½ cup chopped tomato
Salt and pepper, to taste
¼ cup shredded Parmesan cheese
Chopped parsley, as garnish

Per Serving
Net Carbohydrate (gm): 20.8
Calories: 125
Fat (gm): 3.9
Saturated fat (gm): 2.4
Cholesterol (mg): 10
Sodium (mg): 84
Protein (gm): 3.6
Carbohydrate (gm): 20

1. Pierce potatoes several times with tip of sharp knife or fork. Set potatoes on baking sheet. Bake at 425 degrees 45 minutes to 1 hour or until tender.

2. Sauté bell pepper, onions, and garlic in butter in large skillet until softened, about 3 minutes. Stir in mushrooms and zucchini and sauté until lightly browned, about 5 minutes. Add tomato and cook 2 minutes; season to taste with salt and pepper.

3. Split potatoes lengthwise and fluff pulp with fork. Spoon vegetable mixture over potatoes; sprinkle with Parmesan cheese and parsley.

Twice-Baked Potatoes with Cheese

4 servings

2 medium Idaho potatoes (about 6 ounces each)
⅓ cup sour cream
½–¾ cup (3–4 ounces) shredded sharp, *or* mild, Cheddar cheese, divided
Salt and pepper, to taste
Paprika, as garnish

Per Serving
Net Carbohydrate (gm): 16.4
Calories: 164
Fat (gm): 8.1
Saturated fat (gm): 5.1
Cholesterol (mg): 21.9
Sodium (mg): 100
Protein (gm): 5.5
Carbohydrate (gm): 17.9

1. Pierce potatoes with a fork and bake at 400 degrees until tender, about 1 hour. Cut into halves; let stand until cool enough to handle.

2. Scoop out insides of potatoes, being careful to leave shells intact. Mash warm potatoes, or beat until smooth, in medium bowl, adding sour cream and ¼ cup of cheese. Season to taste with salt and pepper.

3. Spoon potato mixture into potato shells; sprinkle with remaining ¼ cup cheese and paprika. Bake at 400 degrees until hot through, 15 to 20 minutes.

Spanakopita Baked Potatoes

8 servings

4 Idaho potatoes (6–7 ounces each)
¼ cup chopped green onions and tops
4 cloves garlic, minced
2 tablespoons olive oil
2 cups chopped spinach leaves
½ cup ricotta cheese
½ teaspoon dried basil leaves
½ teaspoon dried oregano leaves
¼ teaspoon ground nutmeg
Salt and pepper, to taste

Per Serving
Net Carbohydrate (gm): 20.6
Calories: 141
Fat (gm): 5.6
Saturated fat (gm): 1.8
Cholesterol (mg): 7.8
Sodium (mg): 28
Protein (gm): 4.3
Carbohydrate (gm): 19.6

1. Pierce potatoes several times with tip of sharp knife or fork. Set potatoes on baking sheet. Bake at 425 degrees 45 minutes to 1 hour or until tender.

2. Sauté onion and garlic in oil in large skillet until onion is soft, about 5 minutes. Stir in spinach and cook, stirring occasionally, until spinach is wilted. Stir in ricotta cheese and herbs; season to taste with salt and pepper.

3. Cut hot baked potatoes in half horizontally and fluff pulp with a fork. Place potatoes on serving plates and spoon spinach mixture over.

Dilly Baked Potatoes with Bacon

8 servings

4 Idaho potatoes (6–7 ounces each)
1 cup sour cream
¼ cup chopped, seeded cucumber
1 tablespoon dried dill weed
4 slices bacon, cooked crisp, crumbled

Per Serving
Net Carbohydrate (gm): 18.3
Calories: 155
Fat (gm): 7.1
Saturated fat (gm): 3.9
Cholesterol (mg): 14
Sodium (mg): 82
Protein (gm): 3.7
Carbohydrate (gm): 19.7

1. Pierce potatoes several times with tip of sharp knife or fork. Set potatoes on baking sheet. Bake at 425 degrees 45 minutes to 1 hour or until tender.

2. Cut warm baked potatoes in half horizontally and fluff pulp with a fork. Combine sour cream, cucumber, and dill weed; spoon over potato halves and sprinkle with bacon. (Nutritional data does not include potato skins).

Baked Potatoes with Avocado Sour Cream

8 servings

4 Idaho potatoes (6–7 ounces each)
½ cup coarsely mashed avocado
1 tablespoon lemon juice
¾ cup sour cream
4 slices bacon, fried crisp, crumbled

Per Serving
Net Carbohydrate (gm): 20.5
Calories: 155
Fat (gm): 7.3
Saturated fat (gm): 3.2
Cholesterol (mg): 10.6
Sodium (mg): 70
Protein (gm): 3.9
Carbohydrate (gm): 19.7

1. Pierce potatoes several times with tip of sharp knife or fork. Set potatoes on baking sheet. Bake at 425 degrees 45 minutes to 1 hour or until tender.

2. Cut warm baked potatoes in half horizontally and fluff pulp with a fork. Mix avocado and lemon juice; stir gently into sour cream. Spoon mixture over potato halves and sprinkle with bacon.

Stir-Fry Potatoes and Asian Vegetables

8 servings

4 cloves garlic, minced
½ teaspoon grated gingerroot
1 cup chopped green onions and tops
2 tablespoons peanut, *or* canola, oil
1 pound red potatoes, unpeeled, cooked,
    cut into ½-inch cubes
3 cups sliced bok choy
8 shittake mushrooms, stems discarded, sliced
2 cups bean sprouts
½ cup reduced-sodium fat-free chicken broth
1 tablespoon cornstarch
2 tablespoons reduced-sodium soy sauce
½ teaspoon curry powder
Salt and pepper, to taste

Per Serving
Net Carbohydrate (gm): 14.2
Calories: 109
Fat (gm): 3.7
Saturated fat (gm): 0.6
Cholesterol (mg): 1.6
Sodium (mg): 167
Protein (gm): 3.7
Carbohydrate (gm): 16.7

1. Stir-fry garlic, gingerroot, and green onions in oil in wok or large skillet about 2 minutes or until tender. Add potatoes and stir-fry until beginning to brown, 3 to 4 minutes. Add remaining vegetables and stir-fry until crisp-tender, about 5 minutes.

2. Stir in combined remaining ingredients, except salt and pepper. Heat to boiling, stirring until thickened, 1 to 2 minutes. Season to taste with salt and pepper.

Sweet Potato-Veggie Cake

4 servings

1 cup shredded sweet potatoes
¼ cup shredded carrot
¼ cup shredded zucchini
¼ cup shredded, peeled Idaho potato
¼ cup chopped green onions and tops
½ teaspoon dried sage leaves
Salt and pepper, to taste
1 egg
2 tablespoons all-purpose flour
4 tablespoons sour cream

Per Serving
Net Carbohydrate (gm): 12.7
Calories: 106
Fat (gm): 4
Saturated fat (gm): 2
Cholesterol (mg): 58.4
Sodium (mg): 31
Protein (gm): 3.4
Carbohydrate (gm): 14.8

1. Combine vegetables and sage in medium bowl; season to taste with salt and pepper. Mix in egg and flour.

2. Place mixture in greased medium skillet, pressing down firmly to make an 8-inch cake. Cook over medium heat until browned on the bottom, 8 to 10 minutes. Loosen cake with spatula and invert onto plate. Slide cake back into greased skillet and cook until browned on the bottom, 8 to 10 minutes. Cut cake into wedges; serve with sour cream.

Grilled Sweet Potato Kabobs

8 servings

1½ pounds sweet potatoes, peeled,
    cooked until crisp-tender, cut into 1½-inch cubes
1½ cups cubed (¾-inch) banana peppers, *or*
    green bell peppers
4 ounces cherry tomatoes
1–2 tablespoons butter, melted
½ teaspoon ground cumin
½ teaspoon ground cinnamon
¼ cup chopped cilantro, *or* chives

Per Serving
Net Carbohydrate (gm): 19.1
Calories: 113
Fat (gm): 2
Saturated fat (gm): 1
Cholesterol (mg): 4.1
Sodium (mg): 31
Protein (gm): 2
Carbohydrate (gm): 22.7

1. Thread skewers with sweet potatoes, peppers, and cherry tomatoes. Brush with combined butter, cumin, cinnamon, and cilantro.

2. Place kabobs on lightly greased grill rack 6 inches over hot coals. Cook until tender and browned, about 10 minutes, turning frequently.

Tiny Peas and Onions

6 servings

1 package (8 ounces) frozen petit peas
½ package (16 ounces) frozen small whole onions
¼ cup water
1 tablespoon butter
½ teaspoon dried mint leaves
½ teaspoon dried dill weed
Salt and pepper, to taste

Per Serving
Net Carbohydrate (gm): 5.7
Calories: 59
Fat (gm): 2.2
Saturated fat (gm): 1.3
Cholesterol (mg): 5.5
Sodium (mg): 72
Protein (gm): 2.4
Carbohydrate (gm): 8.3

1. Heat peas, onions, and water to boiling in medium saucepan; reduce heat and simmer until vegetables are tender, 8 to 10 minutes. Drain. Add butter and herbs to vegetables, stirring until butter is melted. Season to taste with salt and pepper.

Peperonata

6 servings

2 cups sliced onions
1 cup sliced green bell pepper
1 cup sliced red bell pepper
6 cloves garlic, minced
2 tablespoons olive oil
¼ cup water
Salt and pepper, to taste

Per Serving
Net Carbohydrate (gm): 6.8
Calories: 78
Fat (gm): 4.7
Saturated fat (gm): 0.6
Cholesterol (mg): 0
Sodium (mg): 3
Protein (gm): 1.3
Carbohydrate (gm): 8.8

1. Cook onions, bell peppers, and garlic in oil in large skillet over medium heat 5 minutes, stirring occasionally. Add water to skillet; cook, covered, over medium-low to low heat until vegetables are very tender and soft, 20 to 25 minutes, stirring occasionally. Season to taste with salt and pepper.

Roasted Peperonata

6 servings

½ pound green bell peppers, sliced
½ pound red bell peppers, sliced
½ pound yellow bell peppers, sliced
12 ounces onions, sliced
2 tablespoons olive oil
1 teaspoon dried oregano leaves
¾ teaspoon dried sage leaves
¾ teaspoon dried thyme leaves
Salt and pepper, to taste

Per Serving
Net Carbohydrate (gm): 9.5
Calories: 93
Fat (gm): 4.9
Saturated fat (gm): 0.7
Cholesterol (mg): 0
Sodium (mg): 4
Protein (gm): 1.8
Carbohydrate (gm): 12.5

1. Line jelly roll pan with aluminum foil and grease lightly. Toss vegetables with oil and arrange on pan; sprinkle with herbs.

2. Roast vegetables at 425 degrees until browned and very soft, about 45 minutes. Combine in serving bowl; season to taste with salt and pepper.

Creamed Spinach

4 servings

2 packages (10 ounces each) fresh spinach, stems trimmed
¼ cup finely chopped onion
2 teaspoons butter
2 tablespoons all-purpose flour
1 cup light cream, *or* reduced-fat milk
¼ cup sour cream
Nutmeg, ground, to taste
Salt and pepper, to taste

Per Serving
Net Carbohydrate (gm): 7.7
Calories: 213
Fat (gm): 16.6
Saturated fat (gm): 10.1
Cholesterol (mg): 50.4
Sodium (mg): 156
Protein (gm): 6.7
Carbohydrate (gm): 12.2

1. Rinse spinach and place in large saucepan with water clinging to leaves. Cook, covered, over medium-high heat until spinach is wilted, 3 to 4 minutes. Drain excess liquid.

2. Sauté onion in butter in small saucepan until tender, 3 to 5 minutes. Stir in flour; cook over medium-low heat 1 minute, stirring constantly. Whisk in milk; heat to boiling. Boil, whisking constantly, until thickened, about 1 minute. Remove from heat and stir in sour cream.

3. Pour sauce over spinach and mix lightly; season to taste with nutmeg, salt, and pepper.

Variation:

Spinach au Gratin—Prepare recipe through Step 2. Mix spinach and sauce and spoon into a small casserole; sprinkle with ¼ cup grated Parmesan cheese *or* shredded Cheddar cheese. Bake, uncovered, at 375 degrees until cheese is melted, 5 to 8 minutes.

Microwave Sesame Spinach

6 servings

1 teaspoon sesame oil
2 cloves garlic, minced
½ teaspoon minced gingerroot
¼ cup chopped onion
1½ pounds fresh spinach, stems removed
1 teaspoon soy sauce
¼ cup sliced water chestnuts
2–3 teaspoons toasted sesame seeds

Per Serving
Net Carbohydrate (gm): 2.1
Calories: 43.2
Fat (gm): 1.7
Saturated fat (gm): 0.2
Cholesterol (mg): 0
Sodium (mg): 148
Protein (gm): 3.7
Carbohydrate (gm): 5.5

1. Microwave oil, garlic, gingerroot, and onion in 4-quart glass casserole on High 1 minute. Stir in spinach; cover with vented plastic wrap, and microwave on High 4 to 6 minutes until wilted, stirring once. Drain excess liquid. Stir in soy sauce and water chestnuts, and microwave on High 1 minute longer. Toss with sesame seeds.

Baked Acorn Squash

4 servings

1 medium acorn, *or*
    Hubbard, squash (about 1 pound), quartered, seeded
2 tablespoons honey
2 tablespoons grated orange rind
Ground cinnamon, to taste
Ground nutmeg, to taste

Per Serving
Net Carbohydrate (gm): 18.7
Calories: 78
Fat (gm): 0.1
Saturated fat (gm): 0
Cholesterol (mg): 0
Sodium (mg): 4
Protein (gm): 0.9
Carbohydrate (gm): 20.6

1. Place squash, cut sides up, in baking dish; drizzle centers with honey and sprinkle with orange rind and spices. Bake, uncovered, at 350 degrees until tender, about 1 hour. Sprinkle with cinnamon and nutmeg.

Microwave Acorn Squash with Walnuts

4 servings

1 medium squash (about 1 pound) quartered, seeded
¼ cup water
½ cup walnuts
½ cup sugar-free maple-flavored pancake syrup

Per Serving
Net Carbohydrate (gm): 14.7
Calories: 153
Fat (gm): 9.9
Saturated fat (gm): 0.9
Cholesterol (mg): 0
Sodium (mg): 46
Protein (gm): 3.2
Carbohydrate (gm): 17.4

1. Place squash, cut sides down, in glass baking dish; add water. Microwave, loosely covered, on High 8 to 10 minutes, rotating dish halfway through cooking time. Drain and turn squash cut sides up. Sprinkle squash with walnuts and drizzle with pancake syrup. Microwave at High, loosely covered, until syrup is hot, 1 to 2 minutes.

Chayote with Pepitas

4 servings

¼ cup pepitas (pumpkin seeds)
1 tablespoon light olive oil, divided
½ cup finely chopped onion
2 cloves garlic, minced
1 pound chayote squash, peeled, pitted,
     cut into ½-inch cubes
Salt and pepper, to taste

Per Serving
Net Carbohydrate (gm): 6.2
Calories: 108
Fat (gm): 7.5
Saturated fat (gm): 1.2
Cholesterol (mg): 0
Sodium (mg): 5
Protein (gm): 3.4
Carbohydrate (gm): 8.9

1. Cook pumpkin seeds in 1 teaspoon oil in small skillet over medium heat until they are toasted and begin to pop, 3 to 5 minutes. Reserve.

2. Sauté onion and garlic in remaining 2 teaspoons oil in large skillet until tender, 3 to 5 minutes. Add squash and cook over medium heat until squash is crisp-tender, about 20 minutes, stirring occasionally. Season to taste with salt and pepper. Spoon squash into serving bowl; sprinkle with reserved pepitas.

Sweet-Spiced Spaghetti Squash

6 servings

2 tablespoons butter, melted
2 tablespoons honey
½ teaspoon ground cinnamon
¼ teaspoon salt
1 spaghetti squash (about 1½ pounds), halved, seeded
1 cup coarsely chopped orange segments
½ cup coarsely chopped walnuts, *or* pecans

Per Serving
Net Carbohydrate (gm): 17.1
Calories: 172
Fat (gm): 11.3
Saturated fat (gm): 3.3
Cholesterol (mg): 10.9
Sodium (mg): 158
Protein (gm): 2.6
Carbohydrate (gm): 18.7

1. Combine butter, honey, cinnamon, and salt in small bowl.

2. Place squash halves, cut sides down, on shallow baking pan. Bake at 375 degrees 35 to 45 minutes or until tender. Scrape squash pulp into serving bowl with a fork, forming spaghetti-like strands. Toss with butter mixture and orange. Sprinkle tops with walnuts.

Spaghetti Squash with Mushrooms

4 servings

1 small spaghetti squash (1½–1¾ pounds), halved, seeded
2 cups sliced mushrooms
½ cup chopped onion
4 cloves garlic, minced
1 tablespoon olive oil
1 tablespoon butter
¾ cup halved cherry tomatoes
1½ teaspoons dried basil leaves
Salt and pepper, to taste
¼ cup grated Parmesan cheese

Per Serving
Net Carbohydrate (gm): 10.7
Calories: 135
Fat (gm): 8.7
Saturated fat (gm): 3.4
Cholesterol (mg): 12.2
Sodium (mg): 144
Protein (gm): 4.5
Carbohydrate (gm): 12.1

1. Place squash halves, cut sides down, in baking pan; add ½ inch water. Bake, covered, at 350 degrees until tender, 30 to 40 minutes. Using fork, scrape squash to separate into strands.

2. Sauté mushrooms, onion, and garlic in oil and butter in large skillet until tender, 5 to 8 minutes. Add tomatoes and basil; cook over medium heat 3 to 4 minutes. Season to taste with salt and pepper. Toss mushroom mixture and spaghetti squash in large serving bowl; sprinkle with cheese.

Spaghetti Squash Parmesan

4 servings

1 small spaghetti squash (1½–1¾ pounds),
   cut lengthwise into halves, seeded
2 tablespoons sliced green onions and tops
1 teaspoon minced garlic
1–2 tablespoons butter
¼ cup canned vegetable, *or* chicken, broth
1 teaspoon dried Italian seasoning
⅓ cup grated Parmesan cheese
Salt and pepper, to taste

Per Serving
Net Carbohydrate (gm): 6.7
Calories: 87
Fat (gm): 5.6
Saturated fat (gm): 3.3
Cholesterol (mg): 13.5
Sodium (mg): 232
Protein (gm): 3.6
Carbohydrate (gm): 6.8

1. Place squash, cut sides down, in baking pan; add ½ inch hot water. Bake, covered, at 400 degrees until squash is fork-tender, 30 to 40 minutes. Transfer squash, cut sides up, to serving dish. Fluff strands of squash with tines of fork.

2. Sauté green onions and garlic in butter in small saucepan until tender, 3 to 4 minutes. Stir in broth and Italian seasoning; heat to boiling. Season to taste with salt and pepper. Pour over squash and sprinkle with Parmesan cheese.

Sautéed Summer Squash with Snow Peas

4 servings

2 tablespoons sliced green onions and tops
2 cloves garlic, minced
1 tablespoon canola oil
3 cups sliced yellow summer squash
2 ounces snow peas, strings trimmed
2 tablespoons finely chopped tarragon, *or* parsley
Salt and white pepper, to taste

Per Serving
Net Carbohydrate (gm): 3.8
Calories: 59
Fat (gm): 3.7
Saturated fat (gm): 0.3
Cholesterol (mg): 0
Sodium (mg): 4
Protein (gm): 1.7
Carbohydrate (gm): 6

1. Sauté green onions and garlic in oil in medium skillet 2 to 3 minutes; add squash, snow peas, and tarragon to skillet and cook over medium heat until vegetables are crisp-tender, about 5 minutes. Season to taste with salt and pepper.

Microwave Green and Yellow Squash

4 servings

1 cup sliced yellow summer squash
1 cup sliced zucchini
¼ cup chopped pimiento
2 cloves garlic, minced
½ teaspoon dried oregano leaves
1 bay leaf
2 tablespoons lemon juice
1 teaspoon olive oil
Salt and pepper, to taste
Chopped chives, as garnish

Per Serving
Net Carbohydrate (gm): 2.4
Calories: 25
Fat (gm): 1.3
Saturated fat (gm): 0.2
Cholesterol (mg): 0
Sodium (mg): 2
Protein (gm): 0.8
Carbohydrate (gm): 3.4

1. Combine all ingredients, except salt, pepper, and chives, in 2-quart glass casserole. Cover with vented plastic wrap and microwave on High 4 to 5 minutes, stirring halfway through cooking time. Let stand covered 2 minutes. Remove bay leaf; season to taste with salt and pepper. Sprinkle with chives.

Zucchini Provençal

4 servings

4 small zucchini (about 12 ounces), cubed
1 cup coarsely chopped tomatoes
¾ cup chopped sweet onion
6 cloves garlic, minced, divided
1½–2 teaspoons dried Italian seasoning
Salt and pepper, to taste
½ cup dry white wine, *or* vegetable broth, warm

Per Serving
Net Carbohydrate (gm): 6.7
Calories: 60
Fat (gm): 0.3
Saturated fat (gm): 0.1
Cholesterol (mg): 0
Sodium (mg): 10
Protein (gm): 2
Carbohydrate (gm): 8.9

1. Combine all ingredients, except salt, pepper, and wine, in 11 x 7-inch baking pan. Sprinkle lightly with salt and pepper; pour wine over. Bake, covered, at 350 degrees until zucchini is crisp-tender, about 25 minutes.

Zucchini with Garlic and Tomato

6 servings

1½ pounds zucchini, sliced into ½-inch rounds
4 cloves garlic, minced
1 tablespoon olive oil
1 cup chopped tomato, peeled and seeded
1 tablespoon chopped fresh, *or*
    1 teaspoon dried, basil leaves
1 tablespoon chopped fresh, *or* 1 teaspoon dried, oregano leaves
2 tablespoons chopped parsley
Salt and pepper, to taste

Per Serving
Net Carbohydrate (gm): 3.7
Calories: 46
Fat (gm): 2.5
Saturated fat (gm): 0.4
Cholesterol (mg): 0
Sodium (mg): 7
Protein (gm): 1.8
Carbohydrate (gm): 5.5

1. Sauté zucchini and garlic in oil in large skillet until lightly browned, about 5 minutes. Stir in tomatoes, basil, and oregano; cook 5 minutes longer. Stir in parsley; season to taste with salt and pepper.

Herbed Zucchini and Tomato Gratin

6 servings

1 can (14½ ounces) diced tomatoes, undrained
¼ cup chopped fresh, *or* 1 tablespoon dried, basil leaves
¼ cup chopped parsley
2 tablespoons chopped cilantro
2 cups sliced zucchini
Salt and pepper, to taste
¼ cup seasoned dry bread crumbs
¼ cup grated Parmesan cheese
1 tablespoon butter, melted

Per Serving
Net Carbohydrate (gm): 6
Calories: 70
Fat (gm): 3.3
Saturated fat (gm): 1.9
Cholesterol (mg): 8.2
Sodium (mg): 438
Protein (gm): 3.3
Carbohydrate (gm): 7.3

1. Heat tomatoes and herbs to boiling in medium saucepan. Reduce heat and simmer, uncovered, 5 minutes. Pour half the tomato mixture into 11 x 7-inch baking dish. Arrange zucchini on top; sprinkle lightly with salt and pepper. Spoon remaining tomato mixture over top.

2. Bake, covered, at 375 degrees until zucchini is tender, about 30 minutes. Combine bread crumbs, Parmesan cheese, and butter; sprinkle over casserole. Bake, uncovered, until browned, about 10 minutes.

Zucchini from Pueblo

6 servings

Per Serving
Net Carbohydrate (gm): 9.3
Calories: 96
Fat (gm): 4
Saturated fat (gm): 1.1
Cholesterol (mg): 4.5
Sodium (mg): 132
Protein (gm): 4.2
Carbohydrate (gm): 13.2

1 cup chopped onion
1 tablespoon olive, *or* canola, oil
2 pounds zucchini, cut diagonally into ¼-inch slices
4 roasted medium red bell peppers, cut into strips
½ cup vegetable broth
½–1 teaspoon ground cumin
½ cup reduced-fat milk
Salt and pepper, to taste
2 tablespoons crumbled Mexican white cheese, *or* farmer's cheese

1. Sauté onion in oil in large skillet until tender, 5 to 8 minutes. Stir in zucchini, roasted peppers, broth, and cumin. Heat to boiling. Reduce heat and simmer, covered, just until zucchini is crisp-tender, 5 to 8 minutes.

2. Add milk; cook until hot, 1 to 2 minutes. Season to taste with salt and pepper. Spoon zucchini and broth into serving bowl; sprinkle with cheese.

Fried Tomatoes

4 servings

Per Serving
Net Carbohydrate (gm): 9.2
Calories: 109
Fat (gm): 7
Saturated fat (gm): 0.5
Cholesterol (mg): 0
Sodium (mg): 11
Protein (gm): 1.8
Carbohydrate (gm): 10.3

4 medium green, *or*
    red, tomatoes (about 12 ounces), sliced ¼ inch thick
¼ cup all-purpose flour
2 tablespoons canola, *or* light olive, oil
Salt and pepper, to taste

1. Coat tomato slices lightly with flour; cook in oil in large skillet over medium heat until browned, 2 to 3 minutes on each side. Sprinkle lightly with salt and pepper.

Variations:

Sugar-Glazed Fried Tomatoes—Cook tomatoes as above, but do not coat with flour. After tomatoes are browned, sprinkle lightly with 2 tablespoons packed light brown sugar and cook until caramelized, about 1 minute on each side. Do not season with salt and pepper.

Cornmeal-Fried Tomatoes—Cook tomatoes as in main recipe, substituting yellow cornmeal for the flour.

Tomato Pudding

4 servings

½ cup thinly sliced celery
½ cup chopped green bell pepper
¼ cup chopped onion
1 tablespoon canola oil
1 can (16 ounces) whole tomatoes,
    undrained, coarsely chopped
½ teaspoon celery seeds
½ teaspoon dried marjoram leaves
1 tablespoon packed light brown sugar
Salt and pepper, to taste
1¼ cups cubed toasted whole wheat bread

Per Serving
Net Carbohydrate (gm): 12.8
Calories: 101
Fat (gm): 4.2
Saturated fat (gm): 0.4
Cholesterol (mg): 0.1
Sodium (mg): 243
Protein (gm): 2.2
Carbohydrate (gm): 15.4

1. Sauté celery, bell pepper, and onion in oil in medium skillet until tender, about 8 minutes. Stir in tomatoes, celery seeds, marjoram, and brown sugar and heat to boiling. Reduce heat and simmer, covered, 2 to 3 minutes. Pour mixture into 1-quart soufflé dish or casserole; season to taste with salt and pepper.

2. Stir bread cubes into tomato mixture, leaving some of the cubes on the top. Bake at 425 degrees until hot through, about 20 minutes.

Herbed Tomato Halves

4 servings

4 medium tomatoes (about 12 ounces), halved
¼ cup grated Parmesan cheese
1 tablespoon unseasoned dry bread crumbs
½ teaspoon dried basil leaves
½ teaspoon dried marjoram leaves
½ teaspoon dried thyme leaves
¼ teaspoon garlic powder
⅛ teaspoon pepper

Per Serving
Net Carbohydrate (gm): 4.6
Calories: 49
Fat (gm): 1.9
Saturated fat (gm): 1
Cholesterol (mg): 3.9
Sodium (mg): 116
Protein (gm): 3.1
Carbohydrate (gm): 5.8

1. Place tomato halves, cut sides up, in baking pan. Combine remaining ingredients and sprinkle over tomatoes.

2. Bake at 375 degrees until tomatoes are hot and topping is browned, 15 to 20 minutes.

Greens-Stuffed Baked Tomatoes

6 servings

6 medium tomatoes (about 1¼ pounds)
10 ounces fresh, *or*
    frozen, turnip greens, cooked, coarsely chopped
½ teaspoon dried chervil leaves
½ teaspoon dried marjoram leaves
Salt and pepper, to taste
3 tablespoons grated Parmesan cheese
1 tablespoon unseasoned dry bread crumbs

Per Serving
Net Carbohydrate (gm): 5.5
Calories: 49
Fat (gm): 1.3
Saturated fat (gm): 0.6
Cholesterol (mg): 2
Sodium (mg): 84
Protein (gm): 2.7
Carbohydrate (gm): 8.1

1. Cut thin slice from top of each tomato; scoop pulp from tomatoes, discarding seeds. Chop tomato pulp and mix with turnip greens and herbs; season to taste with salt and pepper.

2. Fill tomato shells with turnip greens mixture and place in baking pan. Sprinkle tops of tomatoes with combined cheese and bread crumbs. Bake at 350 degrees until tender, about 20 minutes.

Tomatoes Stuffed with Mushrooms

4 servings

4 large tomatoes (about 1½ pounds)
8 ounces mushrooms, chopped
½ cup chopped onion
¼ cup chopped green bell pepper
3 cloves garlic, minced
1–2 tablespoons olive, *or* canola, oil
¼ cup chopped parsley
¾ teaspoon dried oregano leaves
¼ teaspoon cayenne pepper
Salt, to taste
¼ cup grated Parmesan cheese

Per Serving
Net Carbohydrate (gm): 10.4
Calories: 117
Fat (gm): 5.7
Saturated fat (gm): 1.5
Cholesterol (mg): 3.9
Sodium (mg): 112
Protein (gm): 5.7
Carbohydrate (gm): 13.7

1. Slice ¾ to 1 inch off top of each tomato. Scoop out pulp; coarsely chop tops and pulp.

2. Sauté mushrooms, onion, bell pepper, and garlic in oil in large skillet until tender, about 10 minutes. Stir in chopped tomato, herbs, and cayenne pepper; cook 5 minutes longer. Season to taste with salt.

3. Place tomato shells in lightly greased baking pan and fill with vegetable mixture. Sprinkle with Parmesan cheese and bake, uncovered, at 350 degrees until tomatoes are tender, 10 to 15 minutes.

Microwave Tomatoes with Onion-Rice Stuffing

4 servings

4 large tomatoes (about 1½ pounds)
3 tablespoons olive, *or* canola, oil
½ cup chopped onion
½ cup sliced green onions and tops
⅓ cup chopped mushrooms
1 cup cooked brown rice
1 teaspoon dried Italian seasoning
Salt and pepper, to taste
¼ cup shredded Parmesan cheese

Per Serving
Net Carbohydrate (gm): 18.6
Calories: 213
Fat (gm): 12.6
Saturated fat (gm): 2.4
Cholesterol (mg): 3.6
Sodium (mg): 105
Protein (gm): 5.2
Carbohydrate (gm): 22.1

1. Slice ¾ to 1 inch off top of each tomato. Scoop out pulp; coarsely chop tops and pulp.

2. Microwave oil, onions, and mushrooms in glass casserole on High 3½ to 4 minutes or until soft. Stir in chopped tomato, rice, and Italian seasoning; season to taste with salt and pepper. Microwave, loosely covered, on High until hot, 2 to 3 minutes. Spoon mixture into tomato shells; sprinkle with cheese. Place in small glass baking dish and microwave, uncovered, on High until cheese is melted and tomatoes are soft, about 4 minutes.

Braised Winter Vegetables

6 servings

¼ cup finely chopped onion
2 large cloves garlic, minced
2 tablespoons olive, *or* canola, oil
2 cups sliced carrots
2 cups thinly sliced red, *or* green, cabbage
1 cup cubed celery root, *or* sliced celery
½ cup vegetable broth, *or* dry white wine
2 tablespoons packed light brown sugar
1 teaspoon balsamic, *or* red wine, vinegar
1 teaspoon dried sage leaves
½ teaspoon dried thyme leaves
Salt and pepper, to taste

Per Serving
Net Carbohydrate (gm): 10.8
Calories: 95
Fat (gm): 4.8
Saturated fat (gm): 0.7
Cholesterol (mg): 0
Sodium (mg): 73
Protein (gm): 1.2
Carbohydrate (gm): 13.1

1. Sauté onion and garlic in oil in large skillet 2 to 3 minutes; add carrots, cabbage, and celery root and sauté until beginning to brown, 4 to 5 minutes.

2. Add remaining ingredients, except salt and pepper, to skillet. Heat to boiling; reduce heat and simmer, covered, until vegetables are tender, 8 to 10 minutes. Season to taste with salt and pepper.

Vegetable Puff

6 servings

4 ounces mushrooms, sliced
½ cup chopped red bell pepper
¼ cup finely chopped shallots
2 cloves garlic, minced
1 tablespoon canola oil
1 pound broccoli, cooked, coarsely chopped
1 cup chopped carrots, cooked
½ cup frozen whole kernel corn, thawed
2 teaspoons lemon juice
¾ teaspoon dried thyme leaves
½ teaspoon salt
½ teaspoon pepper
1 cup reduced-fat milk
2 tablespoons all-purpose flour
4 eggs, lightly beaten
4 egg whites
½ teaspoon cream of tartar

Per Serving
Net Carbohydrate (gm): 12.9
Calories: 168
Fat (gm): 6.9
Saturated fat (gm): 1.8
Cholesterol (mg): 144.9
Sodium (mg): 323
Protein (gm): 11.9
Carbohydrate (gm): 16.8

1. Sauté mushrooms, bell pepper, shallots, and garlic in oil in large skillet until tender, about 4 minutes. Stir in broccoli, carrots, corn, lemon juice, thyme, salt, and pepper; sauté 5 minutes longer. Transfer vegetables to large bowl.

2. Whisk milk and flour in small saucepan until smooth. Heat to boiling; boil, whisking constantly, until thickened, about 1 minute. Whisk milk mixture into whole eggs in large bowl; stir in vegetable mixture.

3. Beat egg whites in large mixing bowl until foamy. Add cream of tartar and continue beating until stiff, but not dry, peaks form; fold into vegetable mixture and spoon all into lightly greased 1½-quart casserole. Place casserole in a large roasting pan on center rack of oven; add 2 inches hot water to pan.

4. Bake, uncovered, at 375 degrees, 35 minutes or until casserole is puffed and lightly browned on top. Serve immediately.

Vegetable Crepes

8 servings (1 crepe each)

2 cups thinly sliced cabbage
1 cup thinly sliced celery
½ cup thinly sliced green bell pepper
½ cup sliced mushrooms
¼ cup chopped green onions and tops
1 tablespoon packed light brown sugar
2 tablespoons water
2–3 teaspoons lemon juice
Salt and pepper, to taste
8 Crepes (recipe follows), warm
Cream Cheese Hollandaise Sauce (see p. 4)

Per Serving
Net Carbohydrate (gm): 13.4
Calories: 189
Fat (gm): 12.2
Saturated fat (gm): 7.2
Cholesterol (mg): 84.9
Sodium (mg): 209
Protein (gm): 5.8
Carbohydrate (gm): 15.3

1. Cook cabbage, celery, bell pepper, mushrooms, green onions, sugar, and water in large, lightly greased large skillet, covered, over medium heat until cabbage and mushrooms are wilted, about 5 minutes. Cook, uncovered, until vegetables are tender, about 5 minutes longer. Season to taste with lemon juice, salt, and pepper.

2. Spoon vegetable mixture along centers of cooked Crepes; roll up and arrange, seam sides down, on serving plates. Serve with Cream Cheese Hollandaise Sauce.

Crepes

makes 8

½ cup whole wheat pastry flour
½ cup reduced-fat milk
2 eggs
1 tablespoon canola oil, *or* melted butter
¼ teaspoon salt

1. Combine all ingredients in small bowl, beating until smooth (batter will be very thin).

2. Pour ⅛ batter into greased 8-inch crepe pan or small skillet, tilting pan to coat bottom evenly with batter. Cook over medium heat until browned on the bottom, 2 to 3 minutes. Turn crepe and cook until browned on other side, 2 to 3 minutes.

Vegetable Strudel with Wild Mushroom Sauce

8 servings

½ cup chopped red bell pepper
½ cup chopped yellow bell pepper
¼ cup chopped shallots, *or* green onions and tops
2 cloves garlic, minced
2 tablespoons canola oil, divided
1½ cups cubed butternut, *or* acorn, squash, cooked
1½ cups broccoli florets, cooked
Wild Mushroom Sauce (recipe follows), divided
¾ cup (3 ounces) shredded brick, *or* mozzarella, cheese
Salt and pepper, to taste
1 egg white, lightly beaten
5 sheets frozen fillo pastry, thawed

Per Serving
Net Carbohydrate (gm): 16.2
Calories: 197
Fat (gm): 9.5
Saturated fat (gm): 2.5
Cholesterol (mg): 16.1
Sodium (mg): 197
Protein (gm): 7.7
Carbohydrate (gm): 18.4

1. Sauté bell peppers, shallots, and garlic in 1 tablespoon oil in large skillet until tender, 5 to 8 minutes. Stir in squash, broccoli, 1 cup Wild Mushroom Sauce, and the cheese; season to taste with salt and pepper.

2. Mix remaining 1 tablespoon oil and egg white in small bowl. Lay 1 sheet of fillo on clean towel on table; brush with oil mixture. Cover with second sheet of fillo and brush with oil mixture; repeat with remaining fillo and all but 1½ teaspoons oil mixture.

3. Spoon vegetable mixture along long edge of fillo, 3 to 4 inches from the edge. Fold edge of fillo over filling and roll up, using towel to help lift and roll; place rool, seam side down, on greased cookie sheet. Brush top of fillo with remaining oil mixture.

4. Bake at 375 degrees until golden, about 30 minutes. Let stand 5 minutes before cutting. Cut strudel into 8 pieces and arrange on plates. Spoon remaining Wild Mushroom Sauce over each serving.

Wild Mushroom Sauce

makes about 2½ cups

¼ cup finely chopped shallots, *or* green onions and tops
2 cloves garlic, minced
1 tablespoon canola oil
2 cups chopped *or* sliced wild mushrooms (portobello, shiitake, cremini)
⅓ cup dry sherry, *or* reduced-sodium fat-free chicken broth
2–3 tablespoon lemon juice
½ teaspoon dried thyme leaves
2 cups reduced-sodium fat-free chicken broth
2 tablespoons cornstarch
Salt and pepper, to taste

1. Sauté shallots and garlic in oil in medium saucepan until tender, 3 to 4 minutes. Stir in mushrooms; cook, covered, over medium-low heat until mushrooms are wilted, about 5 minutes. Stir in sherry, lemon juice, and thyme; heat to boiling. Reduce heat and simmer, uncovered, until mushrooms are tender and excess liquid is gone, about 5 minutes.

2. Mix broth and cornstarch; stir into saucepan and heat to boiling. Boil, stirring constantly, until thickened, about 1 minute. Season to taste with salt and pepper.

Microwave Pearl Barley with Pecans

4 servings

2 cups water
½ cup pearl barley
¼ cup chopped toasted pecans
¼ cup finely chopped celery
Pinch ground cardamom
Salt and pepper, to taste

Per Serving
Net Carbohydrate (gm): 16
Calories: 136
Fat (gm): 5.2
Saturated fat (gm): 0.5
Cholesterol (mg): 0
Sodium (mg): 9
Protein (gm): 3.2
Carbohydrate (gm): 20.6

1. Heat water to boiling in 2-quart glass measure; stir in barley and pecans and microwave on High until tender, about 30 minutes, stirring several times. Drain and stir in celery and cardamom; season to taste with salt and pepper.

Savory Herbed Bulgur

6 servings

¼ cup chopped green onions and tops
¼ cup chopped celery
1 tablespoon olive oil
¾ cup bulgur (cracked wheat)
1½ cups reduced-sodium fat-free chicken broth
¼ cup dark raisins
¾ teaspoon dried tarragon leaves
½ teaspoon dried marjoram leaves
½ teaspoon ground cinnamon
Salt and pepper, to taste

Per Serving
Net Carbohydrate (gm): 15.8
Calories: 116
Fat (gm): 2.9
Saturated fat (gm): 0.4
Cholesterol (mg): 6.2
Sodium (mg): 72
Protein (gm): 4.3
Carbohydrate (gm): 19.6

1. Sauté onion and celery in oil in medium saucepan until tender, about 5 minutes. Stir in bulgur and continue cooking until grain is golden brown. Stir in remaining ingredients, except salt and pepper. Heat to boiling; reduce heat and simmer, covered, 15 minutes or until liquid has been absorbed. Season to taste with salt and pepper.

Microwave Bulgur Pilaf à l'Orange

6 servings

2 tablespoons sunflower seeds, *or* slivered almonds
2 tablespoon grated orange rind
⅓ cup orange juice
¾ cup bulgur (cracked wheat)
1 teaspoon sesame oil
¼ cup chopped onion
1½ cups boiling water
Salt and pepper, to taste

Per Serving
Net Carbohydrate (gm): 12.6
Calories: 95
Fat (gm): 2.5
Saturated fat (gm): 0.3
Cholesterol (mg): 0
Sodium (mg): 3
Protein (gm): 3.1
Carbohydrate (gm): 16.5

1. Process sunflower seeds, orange rind, and juice in food processor or blender until smooth; reserve.

2. Microwave bulgur, sesame oil, and onion in 2-quart glass casserole, uncovered, on High 2 minutes. Stir in boiling water and microwave on High 5 minutes longer. Stir in orange mixture and microwave on Medium until bulgur is tender, about 12 minutes. Let stand until liquid is absorbed. Season to taste with salt and pepper.

Curried Couscous

6 servings

4 ounces fresh, *or* frozen, thawed, whole okra, tops trimmed
¼ cup chopped onion
2 cloves garlic, minced
2 tablespoons chopped parsley
1 tablespoon olive oil
½ cup sliced mushrooms
⅓ cup sliced carrots
¾ teaspoon curry powder
½ cup vegetable broth
⅓ cup couscous
½ cup chopped tomato
¼ cup chopped peanuts
¼ cup dark raisins
Salt and pepper, to taste
Cucumber Sauce (recipe follows)

Per Serving
Net Carbohydrate (gm): 12
Calories: 117
Fat (gm): 5.9
Saturated fat (gm): 1
Cholesterol (mg): 1.2
Sodium (mg): 106
Protein (gm): 4.2
Carbohydrate (gm): 14.2

1. Sauté okra, onion, garlic, and parsley in oil in medium skillet until onion is tender, about 5 minutes. Stir in mushrooms, carrots, and curry powder; cook 2 minutes longer.

2. Add broth to saucepan and heat to boiling; reduce heat and simmer, covered, until vegetables are tender, 8 to 10 minutes. Stir in couscous, tomato, peanuts, and raisins. Remove from heat and let stand, covered, until couscous is tender and broth absorbed, about 5 minutes. Season to taste with salt and pepper. Serve with Cucumber Sauce.

Cucumber Sauce

makes 1 cup

⅔ cup finely chopped, seeded cucumber
½ cup plain yogurt, *or* sour cream
1 teaspoon dried dill weed

1. Mix all ingredients; refrigerate until serving time.

Basic Polenta

6 servings (about ½ cup each)

3 cups water
¾ cup yellow cornmeal
Salt and pepper, to taste

Per Serving
Net Carbohydrate (gm): 12.1
Calories: 63
Fat (gm): 0.3
Saturated fat (gm): 0
Cholesterol (mg): 0
Sodium (mg): 1
Protein (gm): 1.5
Carbohydrate (gm): 13.4

1. Heat water to boiling in medium saucepan; gradually stir in cornmeal. Cook over medium to medium-low heat, stirring constantly, until polenta thickens enough to hold its shape but is still soft, 5 to 8 minutes. Season to taste with salt and pepper.

Variations:

Blue Cheese-Onion Polenta—Stir ½ cup (2 ounces) crumbled blue cheese and ⅓ cup sautéed chopped onion into the cooked polenta.

Rosemary-Goat Cheese Polenta—Stir ¼ to ½ cup (1 to 2 ounces) crumbled goat cheese and 1 teaspoon dried rosemary leaves into the cooked polenta.

Garlic Polenta—Sauté ¼ cup finely chopped onion and 4 to 6 cloves minced garlic in 1 tablespoon olive oil in medium saucepan. Add water, as above, and complete recipe.

Microwave Sesame Kasha

4 servings

2 teaspoons sesame oil
½ cup kasha (buckwheat groats)
1 egg white
1¾ cups boiling water
2 cloves garlic, minced
1 teaspoon soy sauce
2 teaspoons sesame seeds
Salt and pepper, to taste

Per Serving
Net Carbohydrate (gm): 14.1
Calories: 107
Fat (gm): 3.6
Saturated fat (gm): 0.5
Cholesterol (mg): 0
Sodium (mg): 102
Protein (gm): 3.7
Carbohydrate (gm): 16.5

1. Microwave sesame oil and kasha in 2-quart glass casserole, uncovered, on High 1 to 2 minutes until toasted. Stir in egg white and microwave on High 30 seconds longer.

2. Stir in boiling water, garlic, and soy sauce; microwave, loosely covered, on High 2 minutes. Let stand, covered, 5 minutes. Stir in sesame seeds; season to taste with salt and pepper.

Microwave Millet with Vegetables

8 servings

¾ cup millet
2 tablespoons olive oil
½ cup chopped celery
½ cup chopped zucchini
¼ cup chopped onion
¼ cup chopped green, *or* red, bell pepper
¼ cup chopped carrot
2 cloves garlic, minced
1 teaspoon chopped gingerroot
2½ cups reduced-sodium fat-free chicken broth
1–2 teaspoons curry powder
½ teaspoon dried dill weed
Salt and pepper, to taste

Per Serving
Net Carbohydrate (gm): 13.5
Calories: 124
Fat (gm): 4.7
Saturated fat (gm): 0.6
Cholesterol (mg): 7.8
Sodium (mg): 88
Protein (gm): 4.6
Carbohydrate (gm): 15.7

1. Spread millet over 9-inch glass pie plate, and microwave on High until toasted, about 1 minute.

2. Combine oil, celery, zucchini, onion, bell pepper, carrot, garlic, and gingerroot in 2-quart glass casserole. Microwave, covered, on High until slightly softened, 3 to 4 minutes.

3. Add toasted millet, broth, curry powder, and dill weed. Cover with vented plastic wrap and microwave on High until tender, about 20 minutes, stirring several times. Season to taste with salt and pepper.

Rice Louisiana

8 servings

¼ pound ground chicken breast
2 tablespoons butter, divided
½ cup finely chopped onion
½ cup finely chopped celery
½ cup finely chopped green bell pepper
2 teaspoons minced garlic
2 teaspoons cayenne pepper
1½ teaspoons black pepper
1½ teaspoons sweet paprika
1 teaspoon dry mustard
1 teaspoon ground cumin
½ teaspoon ground thyme
½ teaspoon dried oregano leaves
2 bay leaves
2 cups reduced-sodium fat-free chicken broth
¾ cup quick-cooking brown rice
Salt, to taste

Per Serving
Net Carbohydrate (gm): 14.9
Calories: 139
Fat (gm): 5.4
Saturated fat (gm): 2
Cholesterol (mg): 14.5
Sodium (mg): 110
Protein (gm): 6.2
Carbohydrate (gm): 16.5

1. Cook chicken in 1 tablespoon butter in large skillet until browned, crumbling chicken with a fork. Add remaining butter, vegetables, seasonings, and herbs to skillet and sauté until vegetables are tender, about 5 minutes, stirring frequently and scraping bottom of skillet occasionally. Reduce heat to low; continue cooking 5 to 10 minutes, stirring occasionally.

2. Add broth and heat to boiling; add rice. Reduce heat to low and simmer, covered, until rice is tender, about 20 minutes. Discard bay leaves. Season to taste with salt.

Rice Acapulco

6 servings

¾ cup quick-cooking brown rice
1 tablespoon canola oil
2 cloves garlic, minced
¼ cup finely chopped onion
2 cups chopped tomatoes
1½ cups reduced-sodium fat-free chicken broth
1 teaspoon chili powder
½ teaspoon cumin seeds, lightly crushed
Salt and pepper, to taste
¼ cup chopped cilantro

Per Serving
Net Carbohydrate (gm): 19.3
Calories: 131
Fat (gm): 3.6
Saturated fat (gm): 0.3
Cholesterol (mg): 6.2
Sodium (mg): 73
Protein (gm): 4.1
Carbohydrate (gm): 20.9

1. Cook rice in oil in small skillet over medium heat until rice begins to brown, 3 to 4 minutes, stirring occasionally. Mix in garlic, onion, and tomato; sauté 2 to 3 minutes longer. Stir in broth and remaining ingredients, except salt, pepper, and cilantro; heat to boiling. Reduce heat and simmer, covered, 20 to 30 minutes or until rice is tender. Season to taste with salt and pepper; stir in cilantro.

Microwave Mushroom Risotto

8 servings

1 cup arborio rice
2 cloves garlic, minced
½ cup sliced mushrooms
2 tablespoons olive oil
3 cups reduced-sodium fat-free chicken broth, hot
¼ cup grated Parmesan cheese
Salt and pepper, to taste

Per Serving
Net Carbohydrate (gm): 17.9
Calories: 90
Fat (gm): 4
Saturated fat (gm): 0.5
Cholesterol (mg): 9.5
Sodium (mg): 97
Protein (gm): 3.6
Carbohydrate (gm): 9.4

1. Microwave rice, garlic, and mushrooms in oil in 2-quart glass measure on High until rice is opaque, about 4 minutes. Stir in broth and microwave on High, covered, until liquid is almost absorbed and rice is *al dente*, about 15 minutes. Let stand, uncovered, 5 minutes for rice to absorb remaining liquid, stirring several times. Stir in Parmesan cheese; season to taste with salt and pepper.

SEVEN

Salads and Dressings

Cottage Cheese Lime Mold

6 servings

1 package (3 ounces) sugar-free lime-flavored gelatin
½ cup plain yogurt
½ cup mayonnaise
1 teaspoon lemon juice
1 tablespoon packed light brown sugar
2 cups cottage cheese
½ small cantaloupe, finely diced

Per Serving
Net Carbohydrate (gm): 8.6
Calories: 248
Fat (gm): 18.3
Saturated fat (gm): 4.6
Cholesterol (mg): 20.1
Sodium (mg): 446
Protein (gm): 10.7
Carbohydrate (gm): 9.6

1. Prepare gelatin according to package directions, but do not add cold water. With electric mixer, mix in yogurt, mayonnaise, and lemon juice; refrigerate until mixture is the consistency of unbeaten egg whites, about 20 minutes.

2. Combine sugar, cottage cheese, and cantaloupe in small bowl. Fold cottage cheese mixture into gelatin mixture. Pour into greased l-quart mold. Refrigerate until set, 3 to 4 hours or overnight.

3. To unmold, dip mold briefly in warm water; loosen edge of gelatin with tip of sharp knife. Unmold onto serving plate.

Waldorf Salad

6 servings

2 cups cubed, unpeeled red and green apples
½ cup sliced celery
⅓ cup coarsely chopped, toasted walnuts, *or* pecans
3 tablespoons raisins
¼ cup mayonnaise
¼ cup sour cream
2–3 teaspoons lemon juice
1 tablespoon honey

Per Serving
Net Carbohydrate (gm): 12.7
Calories: 176
Fat (gm): 13.5
Saturated fat (gm): 2.6
Cholesterol (mg): 8.9
Sodium (mg): 66
Protein (gm): 1.7
Carbohydrate (gm): 14.6

1. Combine apples, celery, walnuts, and raisins in medium bowl. Mix in combined remaining ingredients.

Green Bean Salad Vinaigrette

6 servings

1 pound green beans, cut into 2-inch pieces,
    cooked crisp-tender
1 cup sliced Italian plum tomatoes
½ cup sliced green onions and tops
½ cup sliced mushrooms
¼ cup chopped parsley
½ cup Italian dressing

Per Serving
Net Carbohydrate (gm): 5.6
Calories: 158
Fat (gm): 13.8
Saturated fat (gm): 1
Cholesterol (mg): 13.2
Sodium (mg): 321
Protein (gm): 2.1
Carbohydrate (gm): 8.8

1. Combine green beans, tomatoes, green onions, mushrooms, and parsley in salad bowl; toss with Italian dressing.

Three-Bean and Corn Salad

12 servings

1 can (16 ounces) whole green beans, rinsed, drained
1 can (15 ounces) garbanzo beans, rinsed, drained
1 can (15 ounces) kidney beans, rinsed, drained
1 cup frozen whole kernel corn, thawed
½ cup chopped red bell pepper
½ cup sliced green onions and tops
½ cup French salad dressing
¾ cup (3 ounces) shredded Mexican-blend cheese
12 pieces lettuce leaves

Per Serving
Net Carbohydrate (gm): 15.6
Calories: 167
Fat (gm): 7.2
Saturated fat (gm): 2.6
Cholesterol (mg): 6.2
Sodium (mg): 520
Protein (gm): 6.2
Carbohydrate (gm): 20.7

1. Toss all ingredients, except cheese and lettuce; refrigerate 1 hour for flavors to blend. Add cheese and toss; serve on lettuce leaves.

Mediterranean Garbanzo Salad

12 servings

2 cans (15½ ounces each) garbanzo beans, rinsed, drained
3 cups chopped parsley
1 cup chopped green bell pepper
1 cup seeded chopped tomato
½ cup sliced green onions and tops
¼ cup lemon juice
1 clove garlic, minced
¼ cup olive oil
Salt and pepper, to taste

Per Serving
Net Carbohydrate (gm): 15.6
Calories: 142
Fat (gm): 5.6
Saturated fat (gm): 0.7
Cholesterol (mg): 0
Sodium (mg): 230
Protein (gm): 4.4
Carbohydrate (gm): 19.8

1. Combine beans, parsley, green pepper, tomato, and green onions in bowl. Combine lemon juice and garlic in small bowl; gradually whisk in olive oil. Pour dressing over salad and toss; season to taste with salt and pepper.

Mandarin Beets with Citrus Dressing

6 servings

1 pound medium beets, cooked, cooled, thinly sliced
⅓ cup thinly sliced red onion
Citrus Dressing (recipe follows)
Lettuce leaves, as garnish
½ cup Mandarin orange segments, drained

Per Serving
Net Carbohydrate (gm): 9.9
Calories: 72
Fat (gm): 2.4
Saturated fat (gm): 0.2
Cholesterol (mg): 0
Sodium (mg): 251
Protein (gm): 1.5
Carbohydrate (gm): 12.3

1. Combine beets and onion in medium bowl; pour dressing over and toss. Serve salad on lettuce leaves; arrange orange segments on top.

Citrus Dressing

makes about ⅓ cup

1 tablespoon canola oil
2 tablespoons sugar-free orange marmalade
2 tablespoons lemon juice
½ teaspoon salt
Dash pepper

1. Combine all ingredients.

Pickled Beet Salad

4 servings

1 can (15 ounces) sliced beets, undrained
1 tablespoon red wine vinegar
1 bay leaf
1 whole clove
1 tablespoon packed light brown sugar
Shredded lettuce, as garnish
¼ cup sliced red onion

Per Serving
Net Carbohydrate (gm): 9.8
Calories: 49
Fat (gm): 0.2
Saturated fat (gm): 0
Cholesterol (mg): 0
Sodium (mg): 208
Protein (gm): 1.1
Carbohydrate (gm): 11.8

1. Drain beet juice into small skillet; add vinegar, bay leaf, clove, and brown sugar. Heat to boiling; reduce heat and simmer until sugar is dissolved, about 1 minute. Cool.

2. Pour cooled juice over beets in small bowl; refrigerate several hours or overnight for flavors to blend. Drain beets; discard bay leaf. Serve on shredded lettuce; sprinkle onion slices over.

Crunchy Broccoli Salad

12 servings

2 pounds broccoli florets, cooked crisp-tender, cooled
½ pound sliced mushrooms
1 can (8 ounces) sliced water chestnuts, drained
¾ cup mayonnaise
½ cup plain yogurt
¼ cup finely chopped onion
1 tablespoon packed light brown sugar
1 clove garlic, minced
Salt and pepper, to taste

Per Serving
Net Carbohydrate (gm): 7.9
Calories: 142
Fat (gm): 11.4
Saturated fat (gm): 1.8
Cholesterol (mg): 8.8
Sodium (mg): 108
Protein (gm): 3.6
Carbohydrate (gm): 8.5

1. Combine broccoli, mushrooms, and water chestnuts in bowl. Add combined mayonnaise, yogurt, onion, brown sugar, and garlic and mix well. Season to taste with salt and pepper. Cover and refrigerate 2 hours or more to blend flavors.

Cactus Salad

6 servings

2 quarts water
1½ pounds cactus paddles, cut into ½-inch pieces
1 tablespoon salt
¼ teaspoon baking soda
1½ cups halved cherry tomatoes
½ cup thinly sliced red onion
Lime Dressing (recipe follows)
Lettuce leaves, as garnish

Per Serving
Net Carbohydrate (gm): 5.4
Calories: 58
Fat (gm): 2.6
Saturated fat (gm): 0.3
Cholesterol (mg): 0
Sodium (mg): 151
Protein (gm): 2
Carbohydrate (gm): 8.7

1. Heat water to boiling in large saucepan; add cactus, salt, and baking soda. Reduce heat and simmer, uncovered, until cactus is crisp-tender, about 20 minutes. Rinse well in cold water and drain well.

2. Combine cactus, tomatoes, and onion in small bowl; pour Lime Dressing over and toss. Serve on lettuce-lined plates.

Lime Dressing

makes about ⅓ cup

2 tablespoons lime juice
1–2 tablespoons olive, *or* vegetable, oil
1 tablespoon water
1 teaspoon cider vinegar
2 teaspoons packed brown sugar
½ teaspoon dried oregano leaves

1. Combine all ingredients.

Tip: The tender cactus paddles, *nopales*, are readily available in large supermarkets today—be sure all the thorns have been removed! If not, they can be pulled out easily with tweezers.

Family Favorite Coleslaw

6 servings

¼ cup Dijon mustard
¼ cup mayonnaise
2 teaspoons brown sugar
1 pound cabbage, shredded
1–2 teaspoons lemon juice
Salt and pepper, to taste

Per Serving
Net Carbohydrate (gm): 4.2
Calories: 101
Fat (gm): 7.5
Saturated fat (gm): 1.1
Cholesterol (mg): 5.4
Sodium (mg): 296
Protein (gm): 1.2
Carbohydrate (gm): 5.9

1. Mix mustard, mayonnaise, and brown sugar; spoon over cabbage in bowl and toss well. Season to taste with lemon juice, salt, and pepper.

Sweet-Sour Coleslaw

6 servings

1 tablespoon olive oil
½ cup white distilled vinegar
3 tablespoons packed light brown sugar
2 tablespoons thinly sliced green onions and tops
1 pound cabbage, shredded
½ cup sliced radishes
Salt and pepper, to taste

Per Serving
Net Carbohydrate (gm): 9.3
Calories: 67
Fat (gm): 2.5
Saturated fat (gm): 0.3
Cholesterol (mg): 0
Sodium (mg): 19
Protein (gm): 1.2
Carbohydrate (gm): 11.3

1. Combine oil, vinegar, brown sugar, and green onions; pour over cabbage and radishes in bowl and mix well. Season to taste with salt and pepper. Refrigerate 1 hour for flavors to blend.

Poppy Seed Slaw

6 servings

¾ cup plain yogurt
¼ cup buttermilk
2 teaspoons packed brown sugar
2 tablespoons minced dill pickle
2 tablespoons poppy seeds
1 teaspoon garlic powder
1 pound cabbage, shredded
Salt and pepper, to taste
Paprika, as garnish

Per Serving
Net Carbohydrate (gm): 6.7
Calories: 64
Fat (gm): 2.4
Saturated fat (gm): 0.8
Cholesterol (mg): 4.3
Sodium (mg): 81
Protein (gm): 3.1
Carbohydrate (gm): 8.8

1. Mix yogurt, buttermilk, brown sugar, dill pickle, poppy seeds, and garlic powder; spoon over cabbage in bowl and toss. Season to taste with salt and pepper; sprinkle with paprika.

Pasta Coleslaw

8 servings

1½ cups (4 ounces) whole wheat rotini, *or* macaroni, cooked, room temperature
1 cup thinly sliced green cabbage
⅔ cup chopped tomato
⅔ cup chopped green bell pepper
¼ cup sliced celery
Creamy Slaw Dressing (recipe follows)
Salt and pepper, to taste

Per Serving
Net Carbohydrate (gm): 8.9
Calories: 98
Fat (gm): 5.9
Saturated fat (gm): 0.9
Cholesterol (mg): 4.5
Sodium (mg): 52
Protein (gm): 2.4
Carbohydrate (gm): 10.3

1. Combine all ingredients, except Creamy Slaw Dressing, salt, and pepper in bowl; stir in Creamy Slaw Dressing. Season to taste with salt and pepper.

Creamy Slaw Dressing

makes about ½ cup

¼ cup mayonnaise
¼ cup plain yogurt
1 tablespoon lemon juice
2 cloves garlic, minced
1 teaspoon dried tarragon leaves

1. Mix all ingredients.

Carrot-Raisin Salad

6 servings

2 cups shredded carrots
⅓ cup chopped celery
¼ cup raisins
¼ cup coarsely chopped walnuts
⅔ cup mayonnaise
½–1 teaspoon Dijon mustard
1 teaspoon packed brown sugar
⅛ teaspoon salt

Per Serving
Net Carbohydrate (gm): 9.7
Calories: 249
Fat (gm): 22.9
Saturated fat (gm): 3.2
Cholesterol (mg): 14.5
Sodium (mg): 217
Protein (gm): 1.7
Carbohydrate (gm): 11.5

1. Combine carrots, celery, raisins, and walnuts in medium bowl. Stir in combined remaining ingredients, mixing well.

Crisp Cucumber and Onion Salad

6 servings

2½ cups thinly sliced, peeled cucumbers
½ cup thinly sliced red onion
½ cup white distilled vinegar
3 tablespoons packed light brown sugar
½ teaspoon ground ginger
1 tablespoon chopped chives
½ teaspoon dried oregano leaves
Salt and pepper, to taste

Per Serving
Net Carbohydrate (gm): 8.3
Calories: 36
Fat (gm): 0.1
Saturated fat (gm): 0
Cholesterol (mg): 0
Sodium (mg): 4
Protein (gm): 0.5
Carbohydrate (gm): 8.9

1. Combine cucumbers and onion in bowl. Combine remaining ingredients, except salt and pepper; pour over cucumbers and toss. Season to taste with salt and pepper. Refrigerate several hours for flavors to blend.

Jicama Salad

8 servings

2 cups julienned jicama
½ cup julienned zucchini
⅓ cup orange segments
2 tablespooons finely chopped red onion
Cilantro Lime Dressing (recipe follows)
Salt and pepper, to taste
Lettuce leaves, as garnish

Per Serving
Net Carbohydrate (gm): 4.1
Calories: 42
Fat (gm): 1.8
Saturated fat (gm): 0.2
Cholesterol (mg): 0
Sodium (mg): 2
Protein (gm): 0.5
Carbohydrate (gm): 6.4

1. Combine jicama, zucchini, orange, and onion in bowl. Pour Cilantro Lime Dressing over and toss; season to taste with salt and pepper. Serve on lettuce-lined plates.

Cilantro Lime Dressing

makes about ¼ cup

2 tablespoons lime juice
1 tablespoon orange juice
1–2 tablespoons olive oil
2 tablespoons finely chopped cilantro
2 teaspoons brown sugar

1. Combine all ingredients.

Sprouted Lentil Salad

8 servings

Sprouted Lentils (recipe follows)
1 cup torn radicchio, *or* lettuce, leaves
1 cup chopped tomato
½ cup chopped, seeded cucumber
½ cup chopped yellow bell pepper
½–⅔ cup garlic ranch dressing
Salt and pepper, to taste

Per Serving
Net Carbohydrate (gm): 6.8
Calories: 103
Fat (gm): 8.1
Saturated fat (gm): 1.2
Cholesterol (mg): 0.7
Sodium (mg): 183
Protein (gm): 2.2
Carbohydrate (gm): 7.2

1. Combine lentils and vegetables in salad bowl; spoon garlic ranch dressing over and toss. Season to taste with salt and pepper.

Tip: Any favorite sprouted beans or grains can be used in this salad.

Sprouted Lentils

makes about 2 cups

½ cup dried lentils
Water

1. Place lentils in quart jar; add water to cover lentils by 2 to 3 inches and soak overnight. Drain.

2. Return drained lentils to jar and cover with cheesecloth. Let stand at room temperature, rinsing lentils and draining them well 3 to 4 times a day, each time returning them to the cheesecloth-covered jar, until they have sprouted, about 2 days.

3. Refrigerate sprouted lentils until ready to use. Check the sprouts daily; if they appear dry, rinse and drain, then return to refrigerator.

Wheat berries—½ cup dry wheat berries yields about 1½ cups sprouted wheat berries.

Chickpeas—½ cup dry chickpeas yields about 1½ cups sprouted chickpeas.

Tip: Most grains and beans can be sprouted according to the directions above, although they may require shorter or longer times to sprout. They will also yield different amounts.

Roasted Mushroom and Orzo Salad

12 servings

1½ pounds assorted mushrooms
   (portobello, cremini, shiitake, etc.)
1 tablespoon olive oil
2 cups cooked orzo, room temperature
½ cup chopped tomato
3 tablespoons red wine vinaigrette dressing
3 tablespoons minced fresh, *or* 1½ teaspoons dried, dill weed
3 tablespoons minced chives
Salt and pepper, to taste
Lettuce leaves, as garnish

Per Serving
Net Carbohydrate (gm): 9.5
Calories: 68
Fat (gm): 2
Saturated fat (gm): 0.2
Cholesterol (mg): 0
Sodium (mg): 3.9
Protein (gm): 2.7
Carbohydrate (gm): 10.7

1. Line jelly roll pan with aluminum foil and grease lightly. Arrange mushrooms in single layer in pan; drizzle with olive oil.

2. Roast mushrooms at 425 degrees until tender, about 20 minutes; cool to room temperature. Slice mushrooms; combine in bowl with orzo, tomato, vinaigrette, and herbs. Season to taste with salt and pepper. Serve salad on lettuce-lined plates.

New Potato Salad with Mustard Dressing

8 servings

1¼ pounds new potatoes, peeled, cooked, cubed
4 hard-cooked eggs, chopped
1 cup diced celery
1 cup chopped roasted red peppers
¼ cup plain yogurt
¼ cup mayonnaise
2 teaspoons whole grain mustard
½ teaspoon garlic powder
Salt and pepper, to taste

Per Serving
Net Carbohydrate (gm): 16.6
Calories: 164
Fat (gm): 8.2
Saturated fat (gm): 1.7
Cholesterol (mg): 110.8
Sodium (mg): 154
Protein (gm): 5
Carbohydrate (gm): 18.2

1. Combine potatoes, eggs, celery, and red peppers in bowl. Mix yogurt, mayonnaise, mustard, and garlic powder; spoon over salad and mix well. Season to taste with salt and pepper.

Creamy Potato Salad

12 servings

1½ pounds russet potatoes, peeled, cooked, cubed
½ cup thinly sliced celery
½ cup thinly sliced green onions and tops
1 cup chopped red, *or* green, bell pepper
⅓ cup chopped sweet pickle, *or* pickle relish
3 hard-cooked eggs, chopped
6 slices bacon, fried crisp, crumbled
1 cup mayonnaise
½ cup sour cream
2 tablespoons cider vinegar
1 tablespoon prepared mustard
½ teaspoon celery seeds
Salt and pepper, to taste

Per Serving
Net Carbohydrate (gm): 13.9
Calories: 252
Fat (gm): 19.7
Saturated fat (gm): 4.3
Cholesterol (mg): 70.9
Sodium (mg): 255
Protein (gm): 4.5
Carbohydrate (gm): 15.4

1. Combine potatoes, celery, green onions, bell pepper, sweet pickle, eggs, and bacon in large bowl. Mix remaining ingredients, except salt and pepper; spoon over potato mixture and toss. Season to taste with salt and pepper.

Caribbean Potato Salad

12 servings

1½ pounds russet potatoes, peeled, cooked, cubed
1 pound sweet potatoes, peeled, cooked, cubed
⅔ cup mayonnaise
⅓ cup reduced-fat milk
2 teaspoons lime juice
1 teaspoon ground cumin
⅛ teaspoon red cayenne pepper
Salt, to taste
¼ cup halved small pimiento-stuffed olives
Minced parsley, as garnish

Per Serving
Net Carbohydrate (gm): 19.1
Calories: 184
Fat (gm): 10.4
Saturated fat (gm): 1.6
Cholesterol (mg): 7.8
Sodium (mg): 144
Protein (gm): 2
Carbohydrate (gm): 21.4

1. Combine potatoes in large bowl. Mix mayonnaise, milk, lime juice, cumin, and cayenne pepper; spoon over potatoes and mix gently. Season to taste with salt; mix in olives. Spoon salad into serving bowl; sprinkle with parsley.

German Potato Salad

8 servings

3 slices bacon
½ cup chopped green onions and tops
1 tablespoon all-purpose flour
½ cup vegetable broth
¼ cup cider vinegar
1 tablespoon packed light brown sugar
½ teaspoon celery seeds
1½ pounds small russet potatoes, peeled, cooked, sliced, warm
Salt and pepper, to taste

Per Serving
Net Carbohydrate (gm): 18.9
Calories: 105
Fat (gm): 1.7
Saturated fat (gm): 0.6
Cholesterol (mg): 2.6
Sodium (mg): 117
Protein (gm): 2.7
Carbohydrate (gm): 20.6

1. Fry bacon in medium skillet until crisp; drain all but 1 tablespoon bacon fat from skillet. Drain bacon, crumble, and reserve.

2. Sauté green onions in bacon fat until tender, 2 to 3 minutes; sprinkle with flour and cook 1 minute longer. Stir in broth, vinegar, brown sugar, and celery seeds and heat to boiling; boil, stirring constantly, until thickened, 1 to 2 minutes. Pour mixture over warm potatoes in bowl and toss. Season to taste with salt and pepper; sprinkle with reserved bacon.

Tomato-Cucumber Salad with Mozzarella

6 servings

2 cups sliced tomatoes
½ cup sliced peeled cucumber
4 ounces sliced mozzarella cheese
Salt and pepper, to taste
Dijonnaise Sauce (recipe follows)
Basil sprigs, as garnish

Per Serving
Net Carbohydrate (gm): 3.6
Calories: 206
Fat (gm): 18.7
Saturated fat (gm): 4.7
Cholesterol (mg): 21.7
Sodium (mg): 396
Protein (gm): 5
Carbohydrate (gm): 4.5

1. Arrange tomato, cucumber, and cheese slices attractively on serving platter; sprinkle lightly with salt and pepper. Spoon dollops of Dijonnaise Sauce over; garnish with basil sprigs.

Dijonnaise Sauce

makes about ½ cup

½ cup mayonnaise
1½ tablespoons Dijon mustard
2 tablespoons lemon juice
2 tablespoons drained capers
2 tablespoons finely chopped fresh, *or* 2 teaspoons dried, basil leaves

1. Mix all ingredients.

Tomatoes Vinaigrette

8 servings

4 cups sliced small tomatoes
¼ cup sliced Greek, *or* ripe, olives
Salt and pepper, to taste
¼ cup chopped parsley
1 tablespoon olive oil
1 tablespoon tarragon vinegar
1 teaspoon Dijon mustard
1 clove garlic, minced

Per Serving
Net Carbohydrate (gm): 3.4
Calories: 40
Fat (gm): 2.5
Saturated fat (gm): 0.3
Cholesterol (mg): 0
Sodium (mg): 119
Protein (gm): 0.9
Carbohydrate (gm): 4.5

1. Arrange tomatoes on serving plate and sprinkle with olives; season to taste with salt and pepper. Sprinkle with parsley. Drizzle with combined remaining ingredients.

Tomato Aspic with Herbed Mayonnaise

6 servings

1 envelope unflavored gelatin
¼ cup cold water
1¼ cups boiling water
3 tablespoons basil, *or* tarragon, wine vinegar
2 tablespoons onion juice
1 can (4 ounces) tomato paste
1 teaspoon packed brown sugar
Salt and pepper, to taste
2 cups shredded lettuce
Parsley sprigs, as garnish
Herbed Mayonnaise (recipe follows)

Per Serving
Net Carbohydrate (gm): 5.1
Calories: 206
Fat (gm): 19.8
Saturated fat (gm): 3
Cholesterol (mg): 14.9
Sodium (mg): 296
Protein (gm): 2.4
Carbohydrate (gm): 6.3

1. Sprinkle gelatin over cold water in small bowl; let stand 5 minutes. Add boiling water and stir until gelatin is dissolved. Stir in vinegar, onion juice, tomato paste, and brown sugar; season to taste with salt and pepper. Pour into 6 greased individual molds and chill until set, about 3 hours.

2. To unmold, dip molds briefly into warm water; loosen edges of gelatin with sharp knife. Unmold on lettuce. Garnish with parsley and serve with Herb Mayonnaise.

Herbed Mayonnaise

makes about ¾ cup

⅔ cup mayonnaise
2–3 tablespoons reduced-fat milk
1 tablespoon chopped fresh, *or* 1 teaspoon dried, dill weed
1 tablespoon chopped fresh, *or* 1 teaspoon dried, rosemary leaves

1. Mix all ingredients.

Spinach and Melon Salad

6 servings

4 cups torn spinach
1½ cups watermelon, honeydew, and cantaloupe balls
¼ cup thinly sliced cucumber
2 tablespoons finely chopped red onion
Honey Dressing (recipe follows)

1. Combine all ingredients and toss.

Per Serving
Net Carbohydrate (gm): 9.5
Calories: 61
Fat (gm): 2.5
Saturated fat (gm): 0.3
Cholesterol (mg): 0
Sodium (mg): 29
Protein (gm): 1
Carbohydrate (gm): 10.1

Honey Dressing

makes ⅓ cup

2 tablespoons honey
1 tablespoon red wine vinegar
1 tablespoon olive oil
1 tablespoon orange juice
2 teaspoons lime juice
1 teaspoon dried tarragon, *or* mint, leaves
2–3 dashes salt

1. Mix all ingredients.

Easy Wilted Spinach Salad

4 servings

6 cups spinach leaves
4 green onions and tops, sliced
4 slices bacon, fried crisp, crumbled
½ cup French salad dressing
1 hard-cooked egg, chopped
Salt and pepper, to taste

Per Serving
Net Carbohydrate (gm): 6
Calories: 208
Fat (gm): 18.2
Saturated fat (gm): 4.7
Cholesterol (mg): 59.9
Sodium (mg): 630
Protein (gm): 5.8
Carbohydrate (gm): 6.8

1. Combine spinach, green onions, and bacon in salad bowl. Heat French dressing to boiling in small saucepan; immediately pour over salad and toss. Sprinkle chopped egg over salad. Season to taste with salt and pepper.

Wilted Spinach Salad Oriental

6 servings

1 tablespoon canola oil
1 tablespoon lemon juice
1½ tablespoons hoisin sauce
1–2 teaspoons sesame oil
1 teaspoon packed brown sugar
3 quarts baby spinach leaves
1 cup sliced mushrooms
2 teaspoons toasted sesame seeds

Per Serving
Net Carbohydrate (gm): 2.5
Calories: 53
Fat (gm): 3.8
Saturated fat (gm): 0.4
Cholesterol (mg): 0.1
Sodium (mg): 142
Protein (gm): 2.4
Carbohydrate (gm): 3.5

1. Heat oil, lemon juice, hoisin sauce, sesame oil, and sugar to simmering in small skillet, stirring until sugar is melted. Pour warm dressing over spinach and mushrooms in large bowl and toss. Sprinkle with sesame seeds.

Mixed Vegetable Salad

6 servings

2 cups broccoli florets and diced stalks
¾ cup sliced zucchini
¾ cup chopped red, *or* green, bell pepper
¾ cup sliced mushrooms
12 cherry tomatoes, cut into halves
3 green onions and tops, sliced
2 tablespoons dark raisins
Sour Cream-Mayonnaise Dressing (recipe follows)
Salt and pepper, to taste

Per Serving
Net Carbohydrate (gm): 7.9
Calories: 138
Fat (gm): 10.6
Saturated fat (gm): 3
Cholesterol (mg): 12.5
Sodium (mg): 130
Protein (gm): 3.3
Carbohydrate (gm): 9.3

1. Combine all ingredients, except Sour Cream-Mayonnaise Dressing, salt, and pepper in salad bowl. Toss with Sour Cream-Mayonnaise Dressing and season to taste with salt and pepper.

Sour Cream-Mayonnaise Dressing

makes about ¾ cup

¼ cup sour cream
¼ cup mayonnaise
2 cloves garlic, minced
2 tablespoons reduced-fat milk
3 tablespoons crumbled blue cheese

1. Mix all ingredients.

Caesar Salad

4 servings

2 slices French bread (½ inch thick)
1 clove garlic, cut in half
4 cups torn romaine lettuce
2 tablespoons lemon juice
2 tablespoons real egg product
1 tablespoon olive oil
½ teaspoon Worcestershire sauce
2 tablespoons grated Parmesan cheese
⅛ teaspoon dry mustard
Dash red pepper sauce
Pepper, to taste

Per Serving
Net Carbohydrate (gm): 7.8
Calories: 99
Fat (gm): 5.5
Saturated fat (gm): 1.2
Cholesterol (mg): 2.1
Sodium (mg): 145
Protein (gm): 4
Carbohydrate (gm): 9.2

1. Rub both sides of bread slices with cut sides of garlic; mince remaining garlic and reserve. Cut bread into ½– ¾-inch cubes. Bake on jelly roll pan at 425 degrees until croutons are toasted, about 5 minutes.

2. Place lettuce in salad bowl. Beat lemon juice, reserved garlic, and remaining ingredients, except pepper, in small bowl. Pour dressing over lettuce and toss; season to taste with pepper. Add croutons and toss again.

Tip: Real egg product is a pasteurized product and is used instead of raw egg to protect against the possibility of salmonella.

Sprouts and Vegetable Salad

8 servings

1½ cups broccoli florets
1½ cups chopped tomato
1½ cups sprouted lentils, wheat berries, *or* chickpeas (see p. 387)
2 green onions and tops, thinly sliced
Salt and pepper, to taste
½ cup ranch, *or* blue cheese, salad dressing
¼ cup (1 ounce) crumbled blue cheese

Per Serving
Net Carbohydrate (gm): 7.7
Calories: 123
Fat (gm): 9.4
Saturated fat (gm): 2
Cholesterol (mg): 3.8
Sodium (mg): 246
Protein (gm): 3
Carbohydrate (gm): 8.2

1. Combine tomato, broccoli, sprouted lentils, and green onions in salad bowl; sprinkle lightly with salt and pepper. Pour dressing over salad and toss; sprinkle with blue cheese.

12-Layer Salad

12 servings

2 cups sliced spinach leaves
½ cup sliced, *or* shredded, carrots
2 cups thinly sliced red cabbage
2 cups small broccoli florets
2 cups chopped iceberg lettuce
½ cup sliced yellow, *or* red, bell pepper
½ cup thinly sliced small tomato
1 cup cut green beans, cooked until crisp-tender, cooled
1 can (15 ounces) dark red kidney beans, rinsed, drained
½ cup thinly sliced red onion
Garlic Dressing (recipe follows)
¼ cup finely chopped parsley
3 hard-cooked eggs, cut into wedges

Per Serving
Net Carbohydrate (gm): 7.5
Calories: 195
Fat (gm): 15.1
Saturated fat (gm): 3.6
Cholesterol (mg): 66.5
Sodium (mg): 237
Protein (gm): 5.3
Carbohydrate (gm): 11.1

1. Layer spinach, carrots, cabbage, broccoli, lettuce, bell pepper, tomato, green beans, kidney beans, and onion in 2½-quart glass salad bowl. Spread Garlic Dressing over top and sprinkle with parsley. Serve immediately, or refrigerate up to 24 hours.

2. At the table, toss salad and garnish with egg wedges.

Garlic Dressing

makes about 1½ cups

¾ cup mayonnaise
¾ cup sour cream
4 cloves garlic, minced
1 teaspoon dried basil leaves
1 teaspoon dried oregano leaves
¾ teaspoon dried tarragon leaves

1. Combine all ingredients.

Greek Islands Salad

6 servings

2 cups torn lettuce leaves
4 tomatoes, cut into wedges
1 cup sliced, peeled cucumber
½ cup quartered artichoke hearts
⅓ cup thinly sliced green bell pepper
⅓ cup thinly sliced yellow bell pepper
⅓ cup thinly sliced red bell pepper
2–3 anchovies, optional
12 Greek olives
¼ cup thinly sliced red onion
½ cup crumbled feta cheese
¾ cup garlic vinaigrette dressing
Basil sprigs, as garnish

Per Serving
Net Carbohydrate (gm): 7.8
Calories: 191
Fat (gm): 15.3
Saturated fat (gm): 4
Cholesterol (mg): 11
Sodium (mg): 535
Protein (gm): 3.6
Carbohydrate (gm): 10.5

1. Arrange lettuce leaves on serving platter; arrange remaining ingredients, except feta cheese, garlic dressing, and basil sprigs, on lettuce. Sprinkle with feta cheese, drizzle with vinaigrette, and garnish with basil sprigs.

Mixed Vegetable and Orzo Salad

12 servings

1½ cups thinly sliced zucchini
1 cup cut asparagus spears (1½-inch pieces),
    cooked until crisp-tender
½ cup frozen peas, thawed
½ cup halved cherry tomatoes
½ cup sliced carrots, cooked until crisp-tender
6 ounces orzo, cooked
Mustard-Turmeric Vinaigrette (recipe follows)
Salt and pepper, to taste

Per Serving
Net Carbohydrate (gm): 12.4
Calories: 98
Fat (gm): 3.7
Saturated fat (gm): 0.5
Cholesterol (mg): 0
Sodium (mg): 29
Protein (gm): 2.7
Carbohydrate (gm): 13.7

1. Combine all vegetables and orzo in a bowl; pour Mustard-Turmeric Vinaigrette over and toss. Season to taste with salt and pepper.

Mustard-Turmeric Vinaigrette

makes about ¾ cup

⅓ cup red wine vinegar
3 tablespoons olive oil
¾ teaspoon ground turmeric
2–3 tablespoons lemon juice
2–3 teaspoons Dijon-style mustard
2 cloves garlic, minced

1. Shake all ingredients in covered jar.

Roasted Vegetable and Wild Rice Salad

8 servings

1½ cups sliced (½-inch) yellow summer squash
1½ cups sliced (½-inch) zucchini
1 pound eggplant, peeled, cubed (¾-inch)
½ cup cubed red bell pepper
3 cloves garlic, peeled
2–3 teaspoons olive oil
1 tablespoon herbs de Provence
½ cup honey Dijon salad dressing
¼ cup plain yogurt
3 tablespoons orange juice
2 teaspoons grated orange rind
3 cups cooked wild rice
Salt and pepper, to taste

Per Serving
Net Carbohydrate (gm): 19.8
Calories: 120
Fat (gm): 1.7
Saturated fat (gm): 0.3
Cholesterol (mg): 0.5
Sodium (mg): 250
Protein (gm): 4.1
Carbohydrate (gm): 23.2

1. Line jelly roll pan with aluminum foil and grease lightly. Cut vegetables, except garlic, into ¾ to 1-inch pieces. Arrange vegetables in single layer on pan; brush or drizzle with olive oil and sprinkle with herbs.

2. Roast vegetables at 425 degrees until browned and tender, about 40 minutes, removing garlic when soft, after about 20 minutes. Cool to room temperature.

3. Mash garlic in small bowl; mix in salad dressing, yogurt, orange juice, and rind. Combine vegetables and wild rice in serving bowl; drizzle dressing over and toss. Season to taste with salt and pepper.

Oriental Noodle and Vegetable Salad

12 servings

1 package (3 ounces) ramen noodles
1 cup trimmed snow peas, cooked until crisp-tender
1 cup halved Brussels sprouts, cooked until crisp-tender
½ cup sliced red bell pepper
1 cup sliced mushrooms
1 cup bean sprouts
½ cup frozen peas, thawed
⅓ cup sliced carrots
1 can (11 ounces) Mandarin orange segments, drained
¼ cup finely chopped parsley
Orange-Sesame Dressing (recipe follows)

Per Serving
Net Carbohydrate (gm): 9.5
Calories: 72
Fat (gm): 2.6
Saturated fat (gm): 0.3
Cholesterol (mg): 4.4
Sodium (mg): 213
Protein (gm): 2.4
Carbohydrate (gm): 11.3

1. Lightly break noodles apart and cook according to package directions, but do not use flavoring packet; cool.

2. Combine noodles, vegetables, orange segments, and parsley in large salad bowl; pour Orange-Sesame Dressing over and toss.

Orange-Sesame Dressing

makes about ⅔ cup

½ cup orange juice
1–2 tablespoons sesame oil
2 cloves garlic, minced
½ teaspoon five-spice powder
2 teaspoons toasted sesame seeds
½ teaspoon salt
¼ teaspoon white pepper

1. Mix all ingredients.

Pasta Egg Salad

8 servings

4 ounces whole wheat macaroni, *or*
    other shaped pasta, cooked, cooled
5 hard-cooked eggs, coarsely chopped
½ cup sliced snow peas
½ cup chopped, seeded tomato
¼ cup finely chopped onion
¼ cup chopped red bell pepper
Mayonnaise Dressing (recipe follows)
Salt and pepper, to taste
Lettuce leaves, as garnish

Per Serving
Net Carbohydrate (gm): 11.5
Calories: 207
Fat (gm): 14.4
Saturated fat (gm): 2.6
Cholesterol (mg): 141
Sodium (mg): 164
Protein (gm): 6.6
Carbohydrate (gm): 13.2

1. Combine pasta, eggs, snow peas, tomato, onion, and bell pepper in large bowl; spoon Mayonnaise Dressing over and toss. Season to taste with salt and pepper. Serve salad on lettuce-lined plates.

Mayonnaise Dressing

makes about ⅔ cup

½ cup mayonnaise
3 tablespoons white wine vinegar
1 tablespoon Dijon mustard
¼ cup finely chopped parsley
¼ cup finely chopped chives
2 tablespoons finely chopped lovage, *or* celery, leaves

1. Mix all ingredients.

Macaroni Salad

8 servings

4 ounces whole wheat elbow macaroni, cooked, cooled
½ cup frozen baby peas, thawed
½ cup chopped celery
¼ cup chopped onion
¼ cup shredded carrot
¼ cup chopped red bell pepper
¼ cup sliced ripe, *or* pimiento-stuffed, olives
¾ cup mayonnaise
2 teaspoons prepared mustard
1 teaspoon packed brown sugar
Salt and pepper, to taste

Per Serving
Net Carbohydrate (gm): 12.5
Calories: 218
Fat (gm): 17.2
Saturated fat (gm): 2.5
Cholesterol (mg): 12.2
Sodium (mg): 187
Protein (gm): 3.1
Carbohydrate (gm): 14.6

1. Combine macaroni, peas, celery, onion, carrot, bell pepper, and olives in medium bowl. Mix in combined mayonnaise, mustard, and sugar; season to taste with salt and pepper.

Macaroni-Blue Cheese Salad

8 servings

1 cup (4 ounces) cooked whole wheat
   elbow macaroni, room temperature
¾ cup chopped red bell pepper
½ cup chopped cucumber
½ cup shredded carrot
¼ cup thinly sliced green onions and tops
Blue Cheese Dressing (recipe follows)

Per Serving
Net Carbohydrate (gm): 10.8
Calories: 195
Fat (gm): 15.5
Saturated fat (gm): 2.6
Cholesterol (mg): 12.4
Sodium (mg): 284
Protein (gm): 2.9
Carbohydrate (gm): 12.6

1. Combine macaroni, bell pepper, cucumber, carrot, and green onions in bowl; stir in Blue Cheese Dressing.

Blue Cheese Dressing

makes about ⅔ cup

⅔ cup mayonnaise
2–3 tablespoons crumbled blue cheese
1 tablespoon red wine vinegar
1 teaspoon celery seeds
½ teaspoon salt
⅛ teaspoon cayenne pepper
⅛ teaspoon black pepper

1. Mix all ingredients.

Macaroni Chicken Salad

8 servings

1½ cups cooked whole wheat elbow macaroni, cold
1 pound cooked skinless chicken breast,
    cut into scant ½-inch cubes
1 can (15 ounces) kidney beans, rinsed, drained
1 cup cubed zucchini
½ cup sliced celery
½ cup sliced carrots
½ cup chopped red bell pepper
Honey-Mustard Dressing (recipe follows)
Salt and pepper, to taste

Per Serving
Net Carbohydrate (gm): 17.3
Calories: 321
Fat (gm): 16.8
Saturated fat (gm): 2.7
Cholesterol (mg): 54.5
Sodium (mg): 346
Protein (gm): 21.3
Carbohydrate (gm): 22.2

1. Combine all ingredients, except salt and pepper, in large bowl, mixing well. Season to taste with salt and pepper.

Honey-Mustard Dressing

makes about ¾ cup

⅔ cup mayonnaise
2 tablespoons honey
2–3 teaspoons prepared mustard

Mix all ingredients.

Rotini and Tuna Salad

6 servings

6 ounces whole wheat rotini, cooked, cooled
2 cans (6½ ounces each) water-packed white tuna,
    drained, chunked
1 cup chopped tomato
1 jar (4 ounces) marinated artichoke hearts, drained, quartered
½ cup chopped red, *or* green, bell pepper
½ cup chopped radishes
½ cup (2 ounces) shredded mozzarella cheese
½–¾ cup Italian salad dressing
Salt and pepper, to taste

Per Serving
Net Carbohydrate (gm): 23.7
Calories: 318
Fat (gm): 14.7
Saturated fat (gm): 2.9
Cholesterol (mg): 31.2
Sodium (mg): 490
Protein (gm): 21.5
Carbohydrate (gm): 27.5

1. Mix all ingredients, except salt and pepper, in large bowl; season to taste with salt and pepper.

Tabbouleh

8 servings

¾ cup bulgur
1½ cups coarsely chopped seeded tomatoes
¾ cup finely chopped parsley
½ cup sliced green onions and tops
¼ cup finely chopped mint leaves
⅓–⅔ cup plain yogurt
¼–⅓ cup lemon juice
2 tablespoons olive oil
Salt and pepper, to taste

Per Serving
Net Carbohydrate (gm): 10.7
Calories: 95
Fat (gm): 3.9
Saturated fat (gm): 0.6
Cholesterol (mg): 0.6
Sodium (mg): 17
Protein (gm): 2.8
Carbohydrate (gm): 13.9

1. Place bulgur in large bowl; pour boiling water over to cover. Let stand 15 minutes or until bulgur is tender but still slightly chewy. Drain excess water.

2. In large salad bowl, mix bulgur, tomatoes, parsley, green onions, and mint; stir in combined yogurt, lemon juice, and oil. Season to taste with salt and pepper. Refrigerate 2 to 3 hours for flavors to blend.

Wheat Berry and Garden Tomato Salad

12 servings

3 cups cooked wheat berries
4 cups coarsely chopped ripe tomatoes
1½ cups cubed, seeded cucumbers
½ cup sliced green onions and tops
¼ cup finely chopped parsley
½ cup (2 ounces) crumbled feta cheese
Roasted Garlic Vinaigrette (recipe follows)
Salt and pepper, to taste
Curly endive, *or* escarole

Per Serving
Net Carbohydrate (gm): 10.1
Calories: 101
Fat (gm): 4.7
Saturated fat (gm): 1.2
Cholesterol (mg): 4.2
Sodium (mg): 62
Protein (gm): 2.8
Carbohydrate (gm): 13.1

1. Combine wheat berries, vegetables, parsley, and feta cheese in salad bowl; pour Roasted Garlic Vinaigrette over and toss. Season to taste with salt and pepper. Serve on endive-lined plates.

Roasted Garlic Vinaigrette

makes about ½ cup

3 tablespoons olive oil
¼ cup balsamic vinegar
2–3 teaspoons minced roasted garlic
1 teaspoon dried mint leaves
1 teaspoon dried oregano leaves

1. Mix all ingredients.

Chicken and Summer Berry Salad

8 servings

4 cups mixed salad greens, torn into bite-size pieces
¼ cup thinly sliced red onion
3 cups julienned cooked skinless chicken breast
Raspberry Dressing (recipe follows)
1 cup fresh raspberries
½ cup halved small strawberries
½ cup blueberries

Per Serving
Net Carbohydrate (gm): 3.2
Calories: 133
Fat (gm): 5.1
Saturated fat (gm): 0.9
Cholesterol (mg): 40.4
Sodium (mg): 126
Protein (gm): 15.8
Carbohydrate (gm): 5.4

1. Combine salad greens, onion, and chicken in salad bowl; toss with Raspberry Dressing. Add berries and toss gently.

Raspberry Dressing

makes about ½ cup

⅓ cup raspberry vinegar
2 tablespoons olive oil
1 tablespoon honey mustard
¼ teaspoon salt
¼ teaspoon pepper

1. Mix all ingredients.

Chicken, Spinach, and Raspberry Salad

4 servings

2½ cups water
¼ cup raspberry vinegar
1 pound boneless, skinless chicken breast
1½ cups fresh raspberries
4 cups spinach
Honey-Raspberry Vinaigrette (recipe follows)

Per Serving
Net Carbohydrate (gm): 11.9
Calories: 245
Fat (gm): 8.5
Saturated fat (gm): 1.2
Cholesterol (mg): 65.7
Sodium (mg): 98
Protein (gm): 27.5
Carbohydrate (gm): 15.3

1. Heat water and vinegar to boiling in large skillet; add chicken. Reduce heat and simmer, covered, until chicken is cooked, about 10 minutes. Drain. Cut chicken into cubes and cool.

2. Combine chicken, raspberries, and spinach in bowl; drizzle with Honey-Raspberry Vinaigrette and toss gently.

Honey-Raspberry Vinaigrette

makes about ⅔ cup

⅓ cup raspberry vinegar
2 tablespoons canola oil
2 tablespoons honey
1 tablespoon water

1. Whisk all ingredients in small bowl. Refrigerate, covered.

Confetti Chicken Salad

4 servings

1 pound boneless, skinless chicken breast, cooked, cubed
1 cup chopped red, green, and yellow bell peppers
1 cup cubed zucchini
½ cup chopped carrot
½ cup whole kernel corn
4 green onions and top, sliced
1 clove garlic, minced
⅓ cup sun-dried tomato salad dressing
1 teaspoon dried oregano leaves
Salt and pepper, to taste

Per Serving
Net Carbohydrate (gm): 8.4
Calories: 235
Fat (gm): 8.8
Saturated fat (gm): 1.4
Cholesterol (mg): 65.7
Sodium (mg): 104
Protein (gm): 28.1
Carbohydrate (gm): 11.1

1. Combine all ingredients, except salt and pepper, in large bowl; toss well. Season to taste with salt and pepper.

Chicken Salad Louisiana

4 servings

1 pound boneless, skinless chicken breast
Creole Seasoning (recipe follows)
4 cups Boston lettuce, torn into pieces
1 cup halved cherry tomatoes
⅓ cup thinly sliced onion
Louisiana Dressing (recipe follows)
Salt, to taste

Per Serving
Net Carbohydrate (gm): 12.2
Calories: 299
Fat (gm): 13.2
Saturated fat (gm): 2.1
Cholesterol (mg): 73.9
Sodium (mg): 327
Protein (gm): 28.3
Carbohydrate (gm): 14.8

1. Coat chicken breasts generously with Creole Seasoning. Broil or grill chicken until cooked, 5 to 6 minutes on each side; cool. Cut chicken into 1-inch pieces.

2. Combine chicken, lettuce, tomatoes, and onion in salad bowl; pour Louisiana Dressing over and toss. Season to taste with salt.

Creole Seasoning

makes about ¼ cup

4 teaspoons cayenne pepper
1 tablespoon paprika
2 teaspoons pepper
1 teaspoon chili powder
1 teaspoon garlic powder

1. Mix all ingredients.

Louisiana Dressing

makes about ½ cup

¼ cup mayonnaise
2–4 tablespoons Dijon-style mustard
2 tablespoons dry white wine
1 tablespoon honey
2 teaspoons packed brown sugar

1. Mix all ingredients in small bowl.

Smoked Chicken Salad

4 servings

2 slices bacon, cut into ½-inch pieces
⅓ cup Dijon mustard
2 tablespoons red wine vinegar
2 tablespoons water
¼ cup (1 ounce) crumbled feta cheese
4 cups spinach
2 cups romaine lettuce, torn into bite-size pieces
12 ounces smoked boneless, skinless chicken breast, cut into thin strips
Salt and pepper, to taste

Per Serving
Net Carbohydrate (gm): 3.3
Calories: 164
Fat (gm): 5.6
Saturated fat (gm): 2.1
Cholesterol (mg): 48.9
Sodium (mg): 1562
Protein (gm): 20.3
Carbohydrate (gm): 4.1

1. Cook bacon in large skillet until crisp. Stir in mustard, vinegar, and water. Add feta cheese, stirring over medium heat until warm (do not boil).

2. Combine spinach, romaine, and chicken in large bowl. Pour dressing over, tossing until well mixed. Season to taste with salt and pepper.

Bangkok Chicken Salad

6 servings

1½ pounds boneless, skinless chicken breast, cooked,
    coarsely chopped or shredded
3 cups romaine lettuce, torn into bite-size pieces
1 cup thinly sliced Chinese cabbage
1 can (8 ounces) sliced water chestnuts, drained
6 ounces snow peas, cooked until crisp-tender
¼ cup diagonally sliced green onions and tops
Oriental Dressing (recipe follows)
½ cup chow mein noodles
Salt and pepper, to taste

Per Serving
Net Carbohydrate (gm): 10.3
Calories: 241
Fat (gm): 7.4
Saturated fat (gm): 1.2
Cholesterol (mg): 65.7
Sodium (mg): 775
Protein (gm): 29.7
Carbohydrate (gm): 12.8

1. Combine all ingredients, except Oriental Dressing, chow mein noodles, salt, and pepper, in bowl; toss with Oriental Dressing and chow mein noodles. Season to taste with salt and pepper.

Oriental Dressing

makes about ⅔ cup

¼ cup tamari soy sauce
2 tablespoons canola oil
3 tablespoons balsamic vinegar
1 tablespoon packed light brown sugar
2 cloves garlic, minced
2 tablespoons chopped chives

1. Whisk all ingredients in small bowl.

Curried Chicken and Fruit Salad

8 servings

1½ pounds boneless, skinless chicken breast,
    cooked, shredded, or cubed
1 can (15¼ ounces) pineapple tidbits in juice, drained
1½ cups halved red, *or* green, seedless grapes
¾ cup diced red and green bell pepper
¼ cup sliced green onions and tops
Curry Dressing (recipe follows)
Salt and pepper, to taste

Per Serving
Net Carbohydrate (gm): 14.7
Calories: 255
Fat (gm): 12.3
Saturated fat (gm): 2
Cholesterol (mg): 57.7
Sodium (mg): 133
Protein (gm): 20.7
Carbohydrate (gm): 16

1. Combine all ingredients, except salt and pepper, in large bowl, tossing well. Season to taste with salt and pepper.

Curry Dressing

makes about ¾ cup

½ cup mayonnaise
¼ cup buttermilk
2 teaspoons mild curry powder, *or* to taste

1. Mix all ingredients.

Chicken and Wild Rice Salad with Curried Chutney Dressing

8 servings

1 cup wild rice, cooked
1½ pounds boneless, skinless chicken breast,
    cooked, cubed or shredded
2 cups cut asparagus spears,
    cooked until crisp-tender (1½-inch pieces)
½ cup sliced green onions and tops
½ cup walnut pieces
Curried Chutney Dressing (recipe follows)
Salt and pepper, to taste

Per Serving
Net Carbohydrate (gm): 7.9
Calories: 223
Fat (gm): 10.7
Saturated fat (gm): 2
Cholesterol (mg): 51.9
Sodium (mg): 60
Protein (gm): 22.8
Carbohydrate (gm): 9.8

1. Combine wild rice, chicken, vegetables, and walnuts; spoon Curried Chutney Dressing over and toss. Season to taste with salt and pepper.

Curried Chutney Dressing

makes about 1 cup

¼ cup sour cream
¼ cup finely chopped cilantro
2 tablespoons mango chutney
2 tablespoons olive oil
2 tablespoons lemon juice
1 tablespoon white distilled vinegar
1–2 tablespoons water
1 clove garlic, minced

1. Process all ingredients in food processor until almost smooth.

Chicken Salad with Brown Rice and Tarragon Dressing

8 servings

2 cups cooked brown rice
3 cups shredded or diced cooked skinless chicken breast
1 cup halved cherry tomatoes
⅓ cup chopped green bell pepper
⅓ cup sliced radishes
⅓ cup thinly sliced celery
⅓ cup sliced green onions and tops
Tarragon Dressing (recipe follows)
Salt and pepper, to taste

Per Serving
Net Carbohydrate (gm): 11.8
Calories: 188
Fat (gm): 7.2
Saturated fat (gm): 1.2
Cholesterol (mg): 40.4
Sodium (mg): 44
Protein (gm): 16.9
Carbohydrate (gm): 13.3

1. Combine all ingredients, except Tarragon Dressing and salt and pepper, in serving bowl; drizzle with Tarragon Dressing and toss. Season to taste with salt and pepper.

Tarragon Dressing

makes about ½ cup

¼ cup tarragon wine vinegar
3 tablespoons olive oil
1 tablespoon chopped fresh, *or*
    1½ teaspoons dried, tarragon leaves

1. Mix all ingredients.

Smoked Turkey Potato Salad

8 servings

3 cups sliced, peeled and cooked small red potatoes
1–2 tablespoons butter
3 cups shredded or cubed smoked turkey breast
½ cup chopped celery
¼ cup chopped onion
¼ cup chopped parsley
2 teaspoons dried basil leaves
½ cup mayonnaise
¼ cup sour cream
Salt and pepper, to taste
2 hard-cooked eggs, chopped
Paprika, as garnish

Per Serving
Net Carbohydrate (gm): 20.2
Calories: 255
Fat (gm): 15.9
Saturated fat (gm): 3.9
Cholesterol (mg): 74.8
Sodium (mg): 364
Protein (gm): 7
Carbohydrate (gm): 22

1. Fry potatoes in butter in large skillet until lightly browned, 3 to 5 minutes (potatoes will break into pieces). Toss potatoes, turkey, celery, onion, parsley, and basil in large bowl; mix in combined mayonnaise and sour cream. Season to taste with salt and pepper. Spoon into serving bowl; sprinkle with eggs and paprika.

Island Fish Salad with Tarragon Guacamole

4 servings

1¼ pounds mahi mahi, *or* monkfish, fillets
2 tablespoons grated orange rind
2 tablespoons butter
1 cup tomato wedges
¼ cup thinly sliced orange slices
Lettuce leaves, as garnish
Tarragon Guacamole (recipe follows)
¼ cup thinly sliced red onion

Per Serving
Net Carbohydrate (gm): 4.9
Calories: 431
Fat (gm): 32.8
Saturated fat (gm): 7.9
Cholesterol (mg): 135.8
Sodium (mg): 498
Protein (gm): 27.7
Carbohydrate (gm): 7.2

1. Sprinkle fish with orange rind. Cook fish in butter in large skillet over medium-high heat until fish is tender and flakes with a fork, 6 to 8 minutes, turning once; cool. Refrigerate, covered, until well chilled. Cut fish into slices or chunks.

2. Arrange fish, tomato wedges, and orange slices on lettuce-lined plates; spoon Tarragon Guacamole next to fish; top with onion slices.

Tarragon Guacamole

makes about 1 cup

½ cup diced avocado
½ cup mayonnaise
2 teaspoons red wine vinegar
1 teaspoon dried tarragon leaves
¼ teaspoon hot pepper sauce
¼ teaspoon salt

1. Mash avocado coarsely; mix in remaining ingredients.

Sausalito Crab Salad

4 servings

12 ounces crabmeat, flaked
½ cup cut asparagus spears,
    cooked until crisp tender (1-inch pieces)
½ cup diced water chestnuts
¼ cup sliced green onions and tops
Sausalito Dressing (recipe follows)
Salt and pepper, to taste
4 large Boston lettuce leaves
1 cup alfalfa sprouts
8 canned, drained, *or* fresh cooked, artichoke bottoms
¼ cup chopped roasted red pepper
Finely chopped parsley, as garnish

Per Serving
Net Carbohydrate (gm): 15.7
Calories: 256
Fat (gm): 7.8
Saturated fat (gm): 1.3
Cholesterol (mg): 51.4
Sodium (mg): 1234
Protein (gm): 25.8
Carbohydrate (gm): 23.5

1. Combine crabmeat, asparagus, water chestnuts, and green onions in medium bowl; pour Sausalito Dressing over and toss. Season to taste with salt and pepper.

2. Place lettuce leaves on salad plates; top with alfalfa sprouts and artichoke bottoms. Fill artichoke bottoms with crabmeat mixture. Sprinkle with roasted red pepper and parsley.

Sausalito Dressing

makes about ¾ cup

½ cup cottage cheese
2 tablespoons prepared horseradish
2 tablespoons mayonnaise
1 tablespoon lemon juice
1 tablespoon packed brown sugar
1–2 teaspoons Worcestershire sauce
½ teaspoon dry mustard

1. Process all ingredients in blender or food processor until smooth.

Crab Salad Louis

4 servings

12 ounces crabmeat, flaked
¼ cup chopped green bell pepper
¼ cup chopped green onions and tops
¼ cup chopped green olives
2 tablespoons lemon juice
⅔ cup mayonnaise
⅓ cup plain yogurt
2 tablespoons reduced-fat milk
¼ cup chili sauce
Salt and pepper, to taste
¼ cup minced chives

Per Serving
Net Carbohydrate (gm): 7
Calories: 385
Fat (gm): 31.6
Saturated fat (gm): 4.9
Cholesterol (mg): 59.3
Sodium (mg): 1343
Protein (gm): 18
Carbohydrate (gm): 8.4

1. Combine crabmeat, bell pepper, green onions, olives, and lemon juice in bowl; stir in combined mayonnaise, yogurt, milk, and chili sauce. Season to taste with salt and pepper. Spoon salad into serving bowl and sprinkle with chives.

EIGHT

Snacks, Appetizers, and Pizza

Gorp, by Golly

16 servings (about ¼ cup each)

1½ cups granola
1 cup pretzel goldfish
½ cup sesame sticks, broken into halves
1 cup coarsely chopped mixed dried fruit
Vegetable cooking spray
¾ teaspoon ground cinnamon
½ teaspoon ground nutmeg
¼ teaspoon ground allspice

Per Serving
Net Carbohydrate (gm): 16.7
Calories: 121
Fat (gm): 4.6
Saturated fat (gm): 0.9
Cholesterol (mg): 0
Sodium (mg): 140
Protein (gm): 2.9
Carbohydrate (gm): 18.8

1. Mix granola, pretzel goldfish, sesame sticks, and dried fruit on jelly roll pan; spray generously with cooking spray. Sprinkle with combined spices and toss. Bake at 350 degrees 15 to 20 minutes, stirring after 10 minutes. Cool; store in covered container at room temperature.

Hot Stuff

16 servings (about ⅓ cup each)

2 cups oyster crackers
2 cups baked pita chips
½ cup dry-roasted smoked almonds
⅔ cup coarsely chopped dried apples
⅔ cup coarsely chopped dried apricots
Vegetable cooking spray
1 teaspoon dried oregano leaves
1 teaspoon garlic powder
1 teaspoon chili powder
1–1¼ teaspoons cayenne pepper
1–1¼ teaspoons black pepper

Per Serving
Net Carbohydrate (gm): 18
Calories: 139
Fat (gm): 5.1
Saturated fat (gm): 0.5
Cholesterol (mg): 0
Sodium (mg): 178
Protein (gm): 3.2
Carbohydrate (gm): 20.3

1. Mix crackers, pita chips, almonds, and fruit on large jelly roll pan; spray generously with cooking spray. Sprinkle with combined remaining ingredients and toss. Bake at 350 degrees 15 to 20 minutes, stirring after 10 minutes. Cool; store in covered container at room temperature.

Chili Bonzos

8 servings (about ¼ cup each)

2 cans (15 ounces each) garbanzo beans
Olive oil cooking spray
1 tablespoon Worcestershire sauce
1–2 teaspoons chili powder
1–2 teaspoons garlic powder
1–2 teaspoons onion powder
1 teaspoon paprika
2–3 dashes red pepper sauce
Salt, to taste

Per Serving
Net Carbohydrate (gm): 20.3
Calories: 132
Fat (gm): 1.3
Saturated fat (gm): 0.1
Cholesterol (mg): 0
Sodium (mg): 329
Protein (gm): 5.4
Carbohydrate (gm): 25.2

1. Rinse beans, drain, and dry well on paper toweling. Arrange beans in large skillet; spray generously with cooking spray. Cook over medium heat, stirring frequently, until beans begin to brown, about 10 minutes. Remove from heat.

2. Combine remaining ingredients, except salt; add to beans and stir to coat evenly. Sprinkle lightly with salt.

3. Transfer beans to jelly roll pan; bake at 325 degrees until beans are very crisp on the outside, 20 to 25 minutes, stirring twice. Cool; store in airtight container.

Veggie Crisps

8 servings (about ½ cup each)

1½ pounds assorted vegetables, peeled
    (russet potatoes, large radishes, butternut squash,
    large carrots, turnips, beets etc.)
Salt, to taste
Vegetable cooking spray

Per Serving
Net Carbohydrate (gm): 7.8
Calories: 42
Fat (gm): 0.3
Saturated fat (gm): 0
Cholesterol (mg): 0
Sodium (mg): 18
Protein (gm): 0.9
Carbohydrate (gm): 9.6

1. Cut vegetables into $1/16$-inch slices. Sprinkle vegetable slices lightly and evenly with salt. Let stand 20 to 30 minutes, allowing vegetables to release moisture. Rinse well in cold water and dry completely on paper toweling.

2. To dry vegetables in the microwave, arrange slices in single layer on large microwave-safe plate sprayed with cooking spray. Spray vegetables lightly with cooking spray. Microwave on High power until vegetables are dried, 5 to 7 minutes, checking and rearranging after 4 or 5 minutes and removing vegetables as they are dry. The vegetables will become crisper as they cool.

3. To dry vegetables in the oven, arrange slices in single layer on jelly roll pan sprayed with cooking spray. Spray vegetables lightly with cooking spray. Bake at 275 degrees for 40 to 50 minutes, checking occasionally and removing vegetables as they are dry. The vegetables will become crisper as they cool.

4. Store cooled chips in airtight container at room temperature.

Tip: Different kinds of vegetables cook in different amounts of time, so it is important to check frequently for doneness. In microwave cooking it is better to cook one kind of vegetable at a time.

Fruit Nuggets

10 servings (2 each)

1 cup graham cracker crumbs
¼ cup finely ground ginger snaps
½ teaspoon ground cinnamon
¼ teaspoon ground nutmeg
⅛ teaspoon ground ginger
½ cup dried apples
¼ cup pitted dates
¼ cup raisins
¼ cup orange juice
1 tablespoon honey
¼ cup finely chopped pecans, *or* walnuts

Per Serving
Net Carbohydrate (gm): 19.6
Calories: 117
Fat (gm): 3.3
Saturated fat (gm): 0.5
Cholesterol (mg): 0
Sodium (mg): 101
Protein (gm): 1.8
Carbohydrate (gm): 21.1

1. Combine graham cracker and ginger snap crumbs and spices in medium bowl. Process fruit in food processor until finely chopped; add to crumb mixture. Mix in orange juice and honey, stirring until mixture holds together. Roll into 20 balls; roll in nuts to coat.

Toasted Onion Dip with Veggies

12 servings (about 2 tablespoons each)

3–4 tablespoons dried minced onion
1 package (8 ounces) cream cheese, softened
⅓ cup plain yogurt
⅓ cup mayonnaise
2 small green onions and tops, chopped
2 cloves garlic, minced
¼ teaspoon instant beef bouillon
2–3 tablespoons reduced-fat milk
1 teaspoon lemon juice
2–3 drops red pepper sauce
Salt and white pepper, to taste
1 cup small cherry tomatoes
1 cup sliced large radishes
1 cup sliced cucumber

Per Serving
Net Carbohydrate (gm): 3.4
Calories: 128
Fat (gm): 11.7
Saturated fat (gm): 5
Cholesterol (mg): 25
Sodium (mg): 117
Protein (gm): 2.4
Carbohydrate (gm): 4

1. Cook dried onion in small skillet over medium to medium-low heat until toasted, 3 to 4 minutes, stirring frequently. Cool.

2. Mix cream cheese, yogurt, mayonnaise, green onions, garlic, and bouillon in medium bowl until smooth, adding enough milk to make desired dipping consistency. Stir in toasted onions. Season to taste with lemon juice, pepper sauce, salt, and white pepper. Serve with vegetables for dipping.

Baked Artichoke Dip

16 servings (about 3 tablespoons each)

1 can (15 ounces) artichoke hearts, rinsed, drained
½ package (8-ounce size) cream cheese, softened
½ cup grated Parmesan cheese
½ cup mayonnaise
½ cup sour cream
1–2 teaspoons lemon juice
1 green onion and top, thinly sliced
2 teaspoons minced garlic
2–3 drops red pepper sauce
Salt and cayenne pepper, to taste
1 cup celery sticks
1 cup baby carrots
1 cup sliced zucchini
1 cup halved medium mushrooms

Per Serving
Net Carbohydrate (gm): 3.6
Calories: 116
Fat (gm): 10
Saturated fat (gm): 3.6
Cholesterol (mg): 16.5
Sodium (mg): 199
Protein (gm): 2.9
Carbohydrate (gm): 4.4

1. Process artichoke hearts, cream cheese, Parmesan cheese, mayonnaise, sour cream, and lemon juice in food processor until almost smooth. Stir in green onion, garlic, and red pepper sauce. Season to taste with salt and cayenne pepper.

2. Spoon dip into small casserole or baking dish. Bake, uncovered, at 350 degrees until hot through and lightly browned on the top, 20 to 25 minutes. Serve warm with vegetables for dipping.

Curry Dip

12 servings (about 2 tablespoons each)

1½ cups mayonnaise
½ cup sour cream
¼ cup thinly sliced green onions and tops
1½–2 teaspoons prepared horseradish
1½–2 teaspoons curry powder
2 teaspoons packed brown sugar
2–4 teaspoons lemon juice
Salt and white pepper, to taste
1 cup baby carrots
1 cup sliced cucumber
1 cup red, *or* green, bell pepper strips (½ inch thick)

Per Serving
Net Carbohydrate (gm): 3.7
Calories: 230
Fat (gm): 23.7
Saturated fat (gm): 4.3
Cholesterol (mg): 19.8
Sodium (mg): 169
Protein (gm): 0.9
Carbohydrate (gm): 4.5

1. Mix mayonnaise, sour cream, green onions, horseradish, curry powder, and brown sugar. Season to taste with lemon juice, salt, and white pepper. Refrigerate several hours for flavors to blend. Serve with vegetables for dipping.

Green Tomato Salsa and Chips

8 servings (about ¼ cup each)

1½ pounds Mexican green tomatoes (tomatillos)
¼ cup chopped green onions and tops
2 cloves garlic, minced
½–1 teaspoon minced jalapeño chili
¼ cup finely chopped cilantro
½ teaspoon ground cumin
¼ teaspoon dried oregano leaves
¼ teaspoon brown sugar
Salt, to taste
Baked Tortilla Chips (recipe follows)

Per Serving
Net Carbohydrate (gm): 12
Calories: 76
Fat (gm): 1.4
Saturated fat (gm): 0.2
Cholesterol (mg): 0
Sodium (mg): 35
Protein (gm): 2.1
Carbohydrate (gm): 15

1. Remove and discard husks from tomatoes; simmer tomatoes in water to cover in large saucepan until tender, 5 to 8 minutes. Cool; drain, reserving liquid.

2. Process tomatoes, green onions, garlic, jalapeño chili, cilantro, cumin, and oregano in food processor or blender until almost smooth, adding enough reserved liquid to make medium dipping consistency. Mix in brown sugar; season to taste with salt. Serve with Baked Tortilla Chips for dipping.

Baked Tortilla Chips

makes 8 servings (6 chips each)

6 corn, *or* whole wheat, flour tortillas (6 inch)
Vegetable cooking spray
½ teaspoon ground cumin
½ teaspoon dried oregano leaves
Salt, to taste

1. Cut each tortilla into 8 wedges; arrange in single layer on jelly roll pan. Spray tortillas with cooking spray and sprinkle lightly with cumin, oregano, and salt. Bake at 350 degrees until lightly browned, 5 to 7 minutes.

Red Tomato Salsa

8 servings (about ¼ cup each)

1½ cups chopped tomatoes
⅓ cup chopped poblano chili
½–1 teaspoon minced jalapeño chili
¼ cup chopped green onions and tops
1 clove garlic, minced
¼ cup finely chopped cilantro
Salt, to taste
Baked Tortilla Chips (see p. 416)

Per Serving
Net Carbohydrate (gm): 9.9
Calories: 55
Fat (gm): 0.7
Saturated fat (gm): 0.1
Cholesterol (mg): 0
Sodium (mg): 37
Protein (gm): 1.7
Carbohydrate (gm): 11.6

1. Process tomatoes, chilies, green onions, and garlic in food processor or blender until finely chopped. Mix in cilantro; season to taste with salt. Serve with Baked Tortilla Chips for dipping.

Mexican Bean Dip

12 servings (about 2 tablespoons each)

½ cup thinly sliced green onions and tops
1–2 cloves garlic, minced
1 tablespoon canola oil
1 can (15 ounces) pinto beans, rinsed, drained
¾ cup (3 ounces) shredded Cheddar cheese
¾ teaspoon salt
⅓ cup vegetable broth, *or* water
2 tablespoons finely chopped cilantro
Baked Tortilla Chips (see p. 416)
½ cup carrot sticks
½ cup celery sticks

Per Serving
Net Carbohydrate (gm): 9.8
Calories: 103
Fat (gm): 4.1
Saturated fat (gm): 1.7
Cholesterol (mg): 7.4
Sodium (mg): 273
Protein (gm): 4.8
Carbohydrate (gm): 12.6

1. Sauté onions and garlic in oil in small skillet until tender, about 3 minutes.

2. Process beans, cheese, and salt in food processor until almost smooth, adding enough broth to make desired dipping consistency. Mix in onion mixture and cilantro. Serve with Baked Tortilla Chips and vegetables for dipping.

Pinto Bean and Avocado Dip

12 servings (about 2 tablespoons each)

1 can (15 ounces) pinto beans, rinsed, drained
½ cup finely chopped onion
2 cloves garlic
½–1 teaspoon minced jalapeño chili
3 tablespoons finely chopped cilantro
1 cup chopped tomato
½ cup chopped avocado
2–3 tablespoons medium, *or* hot, tomato salsa
Salt and pepper, to taste
1 cup sliced zucchini
1 cup red, *or* green, bell pepper strips (½ inch thick)

Per Serving
Net Carbohydrate (gm): 5.8
Calories: 55
Fat (gm): 1.6
Saturated fat (gm): 0.3
Cholesterol (mg): 0
Sodium (mg): 113
Protein (gm): 2.4
Carbohydrate (gm): 8.5

1. Process beans in food processor until smooth; add onion, garlic, jalapeño chili, and cilantro and process until blended. Mix in tomato, avocado, and salsa; season to taste with salt and pepper. Refrigerate 1 to 2 hours for flavors to blend. Serve with zucchini and bell pepper for dipping.

Chile con Queso

12 servings (about 2 tablespoons each)

⅔ cup chopped poblano chili
⅓ cup chopped onion
1 tablespoon olive oil
⅓ cup chopped tomato
½ teaspoon dried oregano leaves
2 cups (8 ounces) shredded processed cheese product
1 cup (4 ounces) shredded Cheddar cheese
2–4 tablespoons reduced-fat milk
1 cup carrot sticks
⅔ cup cherry tomatoes
⅔ cup sliced jicama
⅔ cup red and green bell pepper strips (½ inch thick)

Per Serving
Net Carbohydrate (gm): 4.2
Calories: 127
Fat (gm): 9.1
Saturated fat (gm): 5.1
Cholesterol (mg): 22.2
Sodium (mg): 290
Protein (gm): 6.6
Carbohydrate (gm): 5.1

1. Cook poblano chili and onion in oil in medium saucepan over medium heat until very tender, about 10 minutes; add tomato and oregano and cook 5 minutes longer. Add cheeses and cook over low heat until melted, stirring in milk for desired consistency.

2. Serve warm with vegetables for dipping.

Tip: Chile con Queso can also be served with Baked Tortilla Chips (p. 416).

Queso Fundido

8 servings

¼ cup chopped red bell pepper
1 teaspoon canola oil
¾ cup (3 ounces) shredded Cheddar cheese
½ cup (2 ounces) cubed processed cheese product
¼–⅓ cup reduced-fat milk
8 corn tortillas, warm (6 inch)
½ cup crumbled, cooked chorizo
2 tablespoons finely chopped green onions and tops
2 tablespoons finely chopped cilantro

Per Serving
Net Carbohydrate (gm): 12.2
Calories: 167
Fat (gm): 9.3
Saturated fat (gm): 4.6
Cholesterol (mg): 22.5
Sodium (mg): 283
Protein (gm): 7.5
Carbohydrate (gm): 13.7

1. Sauté bell pepper in oil in small saucepan until tender, 2 to 3 minutes. Add cheeses; cook over low heat until melted, stirring in milk for desired consistency.

2. Spoon about 2 tablespoons cheese mixture in the center of each tortilla. Sprinkle with chorizo, green onions, and cilantro and roll up.

Sombrero Dip

12 servings

¼ cup chopped poblano chili, *or* green bell pepper
¼ cup chopped green onions and tops
1 tablespoon canola oil
2–3 large romaine leaves
1 can (15 ounces) vegetarian refried beans
½ cup mild, *or* hot, tomato salsa
½ cup cooked crumbled chorizo
½ cup chopped romaine lettuce
½ cup chopped tomato
Guacamole (recipe follows)
¼ cup (1 ounce) shredded Cheddar cheese
½ cup sour cream
2 tablespoons finely chopped cilantro
Baked Tortilla Chips (see p. 416)

Per Serving
Net Carbohydrate (gm): 10.8
Calories: 143
Fat (gm): 7.6
Saturated fat (gm): 2.6
Cholesterol (mg): 10.1
Sodium (mg): 271
Protein (gm): 5.1
Carbohydrate (gm): 14.6

1. Sauté poblano chili and green onions in oil in small skillet until tender, 3 to 5 minutes; reserve.

2. Line a dinner-size serving plate with romaine lettuce; cover with refried beans to within 2 inches of edge of lettuce. Spoon salsa over beans, leaving edge of bean layer showing. Combine chorizo and reserved poblano chili mixture; sprinkle over salsa. Sprinkle chopped lettuce and tomato over chorizo mixture, leaving edge of chorizo layer showing.

3. Spoon Guacamole over lettuce and tomato, leaving edge of previous layer showing; sprinkle with Cheddar cheese. Spoon sour cream in large dollop on top; sprinkle with cilantro. Serve with Baked Tortilla Chips for dipping.

Guacamole

makes about ⅔ cup

⅔ cup chopped avocado
3 tablespoons finely chopped onion
1 teaspoon minced jalapeño chili
1 tablespoon finely chopped cilantro
Salt and white pepper, to taste

1. Coarsely mash avocado in small bowl; mix in onion, jalapeño chili, and cilantro. Season to taste with salt and white pepper.

Pine Nut Spinach Pâté

12 servings (about 2 tablespoons each)

1 package (10 ounces) frozen chopped spinach, thawed
¼ cup coarsely chopped onion
¼ cup coarsely chopped celery
1 clove garlic
2–3 teaspoons lemon juice
½ teaspoon dried dill weed
2 tablespoons toasted pine nuts, *or* slivered almonds
½ package (8-ounce size) cream cheese, softened
Salt and pepper, to taste
Bruschetta (recipe follows)

Per Serving
Net Carbohydrate (gm): 8.5
Calories: 116
Fat (gm): 7.1
Saturated fat (gm): 2.7
Cholesterol (mg): 10.4
Sodium (mg): 146
Protein (gm): 3.7
Carbohydrate (gm): 10.7

1. Dry spinach well between layers of paper toweling. Process spinach, onion, celery, garlic, lemon juice, and dill weed in food processor until almost smooth; add pine nuts and process until coarsely chopped, using pulse technique. Stir in cream cheese; season to taste with salt and pepper. Refrigerate several hours for flavors to blend.

2. Spoon pâté into crock or bowl; serve with Bruschetta.

Bruschetta

makes 12 servings (1 each)

12 pieces thin-sliced whole wheat, *or* multigrain, bread
2–3 tablespoons olive oil
2 cloves garlic, cut into halves

1. Cut bread into rounds using 2-inch round cutter (remaining bread can be used to make croutons or bread crumbs). Brush both sides of rounds very lightly with olive oil. Broil on cookie sheet 4 inches from heat source until browned, 2 to 3 minutes on each side.

2. Rub top sides of Bruschetta rounds with cut sides of garlic.

Tip: Size and shape of the bread slices will determine whether you can cut 1 or 2 rounds from each slice.

If desired, bread rounds can be sprinkled with herbs, such as dried basil, oregano, or Italian seasoning, before broiling. Bread can also be sprinkled with grated Parmesan cheese before broiling.

Soybean-Vegetable Spread

12 servings (about 3 tablespoons each)

¾ cup finely chopped carrot
½ cup finely chopped green onions and tops
2 cloves garlic, minced
3 tablespoons water
1 can (15 ounces) soybeans, rinsed, drained
1 cup sour cream
2 tablespoons minced parsley
2–3 teaspoons lemon juice
Salt and pepper, to taste
¾ cup sliced zucchini
¾ cup sliced cucumber
¾ cup sliced daikon, *or* red radishes
¾ cup sliced large carrots

Per Serving
Net Carbohydrate (gm): 4.1
Calories: 108
Fat (gm): 6.6
Saturated fat (gm): 2.6
Cholesterol (mg): 7
Sodium (mg): 101
Protein (gm): 6.9
Carbohydrate (gm): 7.1

1. Heat chopped carrot, green onions, garlic, and water to boiling in small skillet; reduce heat and simmer until vegetables are tender and dry, 5 to 8 minutes. Cool.

2. Process soybeans and sour cream in food processor until smooth; stir in cooked vegetable mixture and parsley; season to taste with lemon juice, salt, and pepper. Refrigerate several hours for flavors to blend. Spread on sliced vegetables to serve.

Wild Mushroom Pâté

8 servings (about 2 tablespoons each)

12 ounces coarsely chopped shiitake, *or*
    portobello, mushrooms
½ cup chopped green onion
2–4 cloves garlic, minced
¼ cup dry sherry, *or* chicken broth
2 tablespoons grated Parmesan cheese
2–3 teaspoons lemon juice
Salt and pepper, to taste
16 small endive leaves, *or* zucchini slices

Per Serving
Net Carbohydrate (gm): 6.9
Calories: 46
Fat (gm): 0.5
Saturated fat (gm): 0.3
Cholesterol (mg): 1
Sodium (mg): 27
Protein (gm): 1.5
Carbohydrate (gm): 8.1

1. Heat mushrooms, green onions, garlic, and sherry to boiling in large skillet; reduce heat and simmer, covered, until mushrooms are wilted, 5 minutes. Cook, uncovered, over medium to medium-low heat until mushrooms are very tender and all liquid is absorbed, 8 to 10 minutes. Cool.

2. Process mushroom mixture and Parmesan cheese in food processor until smooth. Season to taste with lemon juice, salt, and pepper. Refrigerate 2 to 3 hours for flavors to blend. Spoon onto endive leaves or zucchini slices.

Roasted Garlic and Herb Cannellini Dip

12 servings (about 2 tablespoons each)

1 can (15 ounces) cannellini, *or*
   Great Northern, beans, rinsed, drained
1 teaspoon minced roasted garlic
1 tablespoon olive oil
1 tablespoon prepared horseradish
2 tablespoons minced chives
½ teaspoon dried oregano leaves
½ teaspoon dried basil leaves
2–3 drops red pepper sauce
2–3 teaspoons lemon juice
Salt and white pepper, to taste
Pita Chips (recipe follows)

Per Serving
Net Carbohydrate (gm): 8.9
Calories: 67
Fat (gm): 1.6
Saturated fat (gm): 0.2
Cholesterol (mg): 0
Sodium (mg): 134
Protein (gm): 2.5
Carbohydrate (gm): 11.2

1. Process beans, garlic, olive oil, and horseradish in food processor until smooth. Mix in chives, herbs, and red pepper sauce. Season to taste with lemon juice, salt, and white pepper. Refrigerate 1 to 2 hours for flavors to blend. Serve with Pita Chips for dipping.

Pita Chips

makes 32 to 40

2 whole wheat pita breads

1. Open pita breads and separate each into 2 halves. Stack pita halves and cut into 8 to 10 wedges. Arrange pita wedges, soft sides up, in single layer on jelly roll pan. Bake at 425 degrees until pita wedges are browned and crisp, 5 to 10 minutes.

Tip: Jarred roasted garlic can be found in the produce department of a grocery store.

Variation:

Seasoned Pita Chips—Arrange pita wedges on jelly roll pan as above; spray generously with vegetable spray and sprinkle with any desired herb or chili powder or grated Parmesan cheese. Bake as above.

Sun-Dried Tomato Hummus

8 servings (about 2 tablespoons each)

1 can (15 ounces) chickpeas, rinsed, drained
⅓ cup plain yogurt
2–3 tablespoons tahini (sesame seed paste)
3 cloves garlic
3 tablespoons finely chopped sun-dried tomatoes
   (not packed in oil)
1 teaspoon dried oregano leaves
1 teaspoon dried mint leaves
2–3 teaspoons lemon juice
Salt and white pepper, to taste
Pita Chips (see p. 422)

Per Serving
Net Carbohydrate (gm): 19.8
Calories: 140
Fat (gm): 3.1
Saturated fat (gm): 0.4
Cholesterol (mg): 0.2
Sodium (mg): 280
Protein (gm): 5.7
Carbohydrate (gm): 23.8

1. Process chickpeas, yogurt, tahini, and garlic in food processor until smooth. Stir in sun-dried tomatoes and herbs; season to taste with lemon juice, salt, and white pepper. Refrigerate 1 to 2 hours for flavors to blend. Serve with Pita Chips for dipping.

Spicy Orange Hummus

8 servings (about ¼ cup each)

1 can (15 ounces) chickpeas, rinsed, drained
3 cloves garlic, minced
¼ cup orange juice
2 teaspoons soy sauce
1 teaspoon Dijon mustard
½ teaspoon curry powder
¼–½ teaspoon ground ginger
2 teaspoons grated orange rind
Salt and white pepper, to taste
1 cup celery sticks
1 cup carrot sticks
1 cup red and green bell pepper strips (½ inch thick)

Per Serving
Net Carbohydrate (gm): 13.6
Calories: 86
Fat (gm): 0.8
Saturated fat (gm): 0.1
Cholesterol (mg): 0
Sodium (mg): 280
Protein (gm): 3.3
Carbohydrate (gm): 17

1. Process chickpeas, garlic, orange juice, soy sauce, mustard, curry powder, and ginger in food processor until smooth; stir in orange rind. Season to taste with salt and white pepper. Refrigerate 1 to 2 hours for flavors to blend. Serve with vegetables for dipping.

Black Bean Hummus

12 servings (about 2 tablespoons each)

1 can (15 ounces) black beans, rinsed, drained
¼ cup water
2–3 tablespoons tahini (sesame seed paste)
3 cloves garlic
2–2½ tablespoons lemon juice
1½ tablespoons soy sauce
Salt and cayenne pepper, to taste
Pita Chips (see p. 422)

Per Serving
Net Carbohydrate (gm): 9.7
Calories: 74
Fat (gm): 1.6
Saturated fat (gm): 0.2
Cholesterol (mg): 0
Sodium (mg): 298
Protein (gm): 3.3
Carbohydrate (gm): 12.1

1. Process beans, water, tahini, garlic, lemon juice, and soy sauce in food processor until smooth; season to taste with salt and cayenne pepper. Refrigerate 1 to 2 hours for flavors to blend. Serve with Pita Chips for dipping.

Eggplant Caviar

6 servings (about 2 tablespoons each)

1 large eggplant (1½ pounds)
½ cup chopped tomato
¼ cup finely chopped onion
3 cloves garlic, minced
¼ cup plain yogurt
2 teaspoons olive oil
1 teaspoon dried oregano leaves
1–2 tablespoons lemon juice
Salt and pepper, to taste
½ recipe Pita Chips, *or* Bruschetta (see pp. 422, 420)

Per Serving
Net Carbohydrate (gm): 10.9
Calories: 81
Fat (gm): 2.1
Saturated fat (gm): 0.3
Cholesterol (mg): 0.2
Sodium (mg): 69
Protein (gm): 2.9
Carbohydrate (gm): 14.4

1. Pierce eggplant in several places with fork; place in baking pan. Bake at 350 degrees until eggplant is soft, 45 to 50 minutes. Cool.

2. Cut eggplant in half; scoop out pulp with spoon. Mash pulp coarsely with a fork; mix with tomato, onion, garlic, yogurt, olive oil, and oregano in bowl. Season to taste with lemon juice, salt, and pepper. Refrigerate 3 to 4 hours for flavors to blend. Serve with Pita Chips for dipping.

Roasted Zucchini and Garlic Spread

12 servings (about 2 tablespoons each)

1¼ pounds zucchini, cut into 1-inch pieces
¼ cup coarsely chopped onion
2 cloves garlic
⅓ cup plain yogurt
2 tablespoons chopped parsley
Lemon juice, to taste
Salt and cayenne pepper, to taste
Pita Chips (see p. 422)

Per Serving
Net Carbohydrate (gm): 6.8
Calories: 42
Fat (gm): 0.5
Saturated fat (gm): 0.1
Cholesterol (mg): 0.4
Sodium (mg): 63
Protein (gm): 2
Carbohydrate (gm): 8.2

1. Line jelly roll pan with aluminum foil and grease lightly. Arrange zucchini, onion, and garlic in single layer on pan. Bake at 425 degrees until vegetables are very tender, about 15 to 20 minutes for garlic, 25 to 30 minutes for zucchini and onion. Cool 15 to 20 minutes; process in food processor until coarsely chopped. Stir in yogurt and parsley; season to taste with lemon juice, salt, and cayenne pepper. Refrigerate several hours for flavors to blend. Serve with Pita Chips for dipping.

Artichoke Pâté in Mushroom Caps

16 servings

1 can (15 ounces) artichoke hearts or bottoms, drained
½ package (8-ounce size) cream cheese, softened
⅓ cup grated Parmesan cheese
2–4 tablespoons mayonnaise
1–1½ teaspoons minced roasted garlic
2 tablespoons chopped parsley
1–2 teaspoons lemon juice
Salt and cayenne pepper, to taste
32 medium mushroom caps

Per Serving
Net Carbohydrate (gm): 2.4
Calories: 60
Fat (gm): 4.7
Saturated fat (gm): 2.1
Cholesterol (mg): 10.1
Sodium (mg): 141
Protein (gm): 2.5
Carbohydrate (gm): 2.9

1. Process artichokes, cream cheese, Parmesan cheese, mayonnaise, and garlic in food processor until smooth. Stir in parsley; season to taste with lemon juice, salt, and cayenne pepper. Refrigerate several hours for flavors to blend. Fill mushroom caps with pâté.

Tip: Jarred roasted garlic can be purchased in the produce department of a grocery store.

Garden Mushroom Spread

12 servings (about 2 tablespoons each)

½ cup chopped onion
½ cup chopped carrot
1–2 teaspoons grated lemon rind
2–3 cloves garlic, minced
1 tablespoon olive oil
12 ounces cremini, *or* white, mushrooms, chopped
2 tablespoons dry sherry, *or* water
½ teaspoon dried thyme leaves
½ teaspoon dried savory leaves
½ package (8-ounce size) cream cheese, softened
2 tablespoons grated Parmesan cheese
2 tablespoons chopped parsley
Salt, cayenne, and black pepper, to taste
1 cup sliced cucumber
1 cup sliced large radishes
1 cup celery sticks

Per Serving
Net Carbohydrate (gm): 2.4
Calories: 70
Fat (gm): 4.8
Saturated fat (gm): 2.4
Cholesterol (mg): 11.1
Sodium (mg): 68
Protein (gm): 2.7
Carbohydrate (gm): 3.8

1. Sauté onion, carrot, lemon rind, and garlic in oil in medium skillet until tender, about 5 minutes. Remove from skillet. Add mushrooms, sherry, and herbs. Cook, covered, over medium heat until mushrooms are wilted, about 5 minutes. Cook, uncovered, until mushrooms are tender and liquid absorbed, about 5 minutes longer. Cool.

2. Process cream cheese, Parmesan cheese, and half the mushroom mixture in food processor until smooth. Stir in onion mixture, remaining mushroom mixture, and parsley. Season to taste with salt and peppers. Refrigerate 2 to 3 hours for flavors to blend. Spread on vegetable slices.

Lentil-Walnut Stuffed Veggies

12 servings (2 tablespoons each)

1¾ cups vegetable, *or* chicken, broth
½ cup dried lentils
½ cup finely chopped onion
1 clove garlic, minced
¼–½ teaspoon dried thyme leaves
2 teaspoons olive oil
⅓ cup chopped walnuts
Salt and pepper, to taste
1 hard-cooked egg, chopped
1½ cups medium mushroom caps, stems removed
1½ cups halved large cherry tomatoes, seeded
Minced parsley, as garnish

Per Serving
Net Carbohydrate (gm): 4.6
Calories: 75.7
Fat (gm): 3.6
Saturated fat (gm): 0.5
Cholesterol (mg): 17.7
Sodium (mg): 76
Protein (gm): 3.9
Carbohydrate (gm): 7.8

1. Heat vegetable broth and lentils to boiling in medium saucepan; reduce heat and simmer, covered, until lentils are tender but not mushy, and liquid is absorbed, about 45 minutes. Sauté onion, garlic, and thyme in oil in small skillet until onion is tender, 5 to 8 minutes.

2. Process lentil and onion mixtures and walnuts in food processor until almost smooth. Season to taste with salt and pepper. Refrigerate 2 to 3 hours for flavors to blend. Mix in hard-cooked egg. Fill mushroom caps and cherry tomatoes with lentil mixture. Garnish with parsley.

Eggplant Marmalade

12 servings (about 2 tablespoons each)

1 medium eggplant (1¼ pounds), unpeeled
¼ cup coarsely chopped onion
1 tablespoon minced roasted garlic
1–1½ tablespoons minced gingerroot
1 tablespoon packed light brown sugar
1 teaspoon fennel seeds, crushed
1 tablespoon red wine vinegar
1 teaspoon dark sesame oil
¼ cup raisins
¼ cup vegetable, *or* chicken, broth
¼ cup toasted pine nuts, *or* slivered almonds
24 small endive leaves

Per Serving
Net Carbohydrate (gm): 6.3
Calories: 51
Fat (gm): 2
Saturated fat (gm): 0.3
Cholesterol (mg): 0
Sodium (mg): 14
Protein (gm): 1.5
Carbohydrate (gm): 8.1

1. Cut eggplant into ½-inch cubes; toss eggplant with onion, garlic, gingerroot, brown sugar, and fennel seeds; arrange in single layer on greased foil-lined jelly roll pan. Drizzle with combined vinegar and oil.

2. Bake at 400 degrees until eggplant is dark brown and wrinkled, about 1 hour, stirring every 20 minutes. Stir raisins into mixture; drizzle with broth and toss. Bake until broth is absorbed, 10 to 15 minutes longer. Stir in pine nuts and cool. Refrigerate overnight for flavors to blend. Spoon eggplant onto endive leaves.

Chutney-Cheese Appetizers

8 servings

1 package (8 ounces) cream cheese, softened
1 cup (4 ounces) shredded Cheddar cheese
3 tablespoons chopped mango chutney
¼ cup thinly sliced green onions and tops
2 tablespoons chopped raisins
1–2 teaspoons finely chopped gingerroot
1 clove garlic, minced
½–1 teaspoon curry powder
2 tablespoons chopped dry-roasted cashews
¾ cup celery sticks
¾ cup small mushroom caps

Per Serving
Net Carbohydrate (gm): 6.6
Calories: 191
Fat (gm): 15.7
Saturated fat (gm): 9.4
Cholesterol (mg): 46
Sodium (mg): 199
Protein (gm): 6.5
Carbohydrate (gm): 7.3

1. Beat cheeses in small bowl until well blended; mix in chutney, green onions, raisins, gingerroot, garlic, curry powder, and cashews. Refrigerate 1 to 2 hours for flavors to blend. Fill celery sticks and mushroom caps with cheese mixture.

Roasted Garlic and Three-Cheese Spread

12 servings (about 2 tablespoons each)

1 small garlic bulb
Olive oil
1 package (8 ounces) cream cheese, softened
1½–2 ounces goat cheese
¼ cup (2 ounces) grated Parmesan cheese
⅛ teaspoon white pepper
2–4 tablespoons reduced-fat milk
1½ cups zucchini slices
1½ cups red, *or* green, bell pepper pieces (1-inch)

Per Serving
Net Carbohydrate (gm): 2.7
Calories: 96
Fat (gm): 8
Saturated fat (gm): 5
Cholesterol (mg): 23.9
Sodium (mg): 103
Protein (gm): 3.4
Carbohydrate (gm): 3.3

1. Cut off top of garlic bulb to expose cloves; brush lightly with olive oil and wrap in aluminum foil; bake at 400 degrees until very tender, 35 to 40 minutes. Cool; gently press cloves to remove from skins. Mash cloves with fork in medium bowl.

2. Mix cheeses, garlic, and white pepper in medium bowl, adding enough milk to make desired spread consistency. Refrigerate 2 to 3 hours for flavors to blend. Spread on vegetable slices.

Artichoke-Cheese Spread

12 servings (about 3 tablespoons each)

1 package (8 ounces) cream cheese, softened
1 can (14 ounces) artichoke hearts, drained, chopped
½ cup chopped red bell pepper
¼ cup chopped pitted green, *or* black, olives
1 large clove garlic, minced
1 teaspoon Italian seasoning
1 cup sliced cucumber
1 cup sliced large carrots
1 cup sliced yellow zucchini

Per Serving
Net Carbohydrate (gm): 3.9
Calories: 90
Fat (gm): 7.1
Saturated fat (gm): 4.2
Cholesterol (mg): 20.8
Sodium (mg): 224
Protein (gm): 2.6
Carbohydrate (gm): 4.9

1. Mix softened cream cheese with remaining ingredients, except sliced cucumber, carrots, and zucchini. Refrigerate 2 to 3 hours for flavors to blend. Spread on sliced vegetables.

Goat Cheese Quesadillas

8 servings

3 ounces cream cheese, softened
2 ounces goat cheese
1 teaspoon minced jalapeño chili
¼ cup chopped cilantro
4 whole wheat flour tortillas (6 inch)
Tropical Fruit Salsa (recipe follows)

Per Serving
Net Carbohydrate (gm): 4.6
Calories: 105
Fat (gm): 5.9
Saturated fat (gm): 3.8
Cholesterol (mg): 17.3
Sodium (mg): 159
Protein (gm): 3.5
Carbohydrate (gm): 9.4

1. Combine cheeses, jalapeño chili, and cilantro; spread mixture on 2 tortillas and top with remaining tortillas.

2. Cook quesadillas in greased large skillet over medium to medium-low heat until browned, 2 to 3 minutes on each side. Cut into wedges and serve with Tropical Fruit Salsa.

Tropical Fruit Salsa

makes about 1¼ cups

⅓ cup cubed mango
⅓ cup cubed pineapple
¼ cup chopped tomato
¼ cup chopped, seeded cucumber
½ teaspoon minced jalapeño chili
2 tablespoon minced cilantro
2 tablespoons orange juice
1 tablespoon lime juice

1. Combine all ingredients.

Black Bean Quesadillas

12 servings

½ cup canned black beans, rinsed, drained
⅓ cup mild, *or* hot, tomato salsa, divided
¼ cup thinly sliced green onions and tops
¼ cup finely chopped cilantro
1–1½ teaspoons minced jalapeño chili
6 whole wheat flour tortillas (6 inch)
1 cup (4 ounces) shredded Mexican cheese blend

Per Serving
Net Carbohydrate (gm): 3
Calories: 78
Fat (gm): 3.1
Saturated fat (gm): 2
Cholesterol (mg): 8.3
Sodium (mg): 172
Protein (gm): 3.7
Carbohydrate (gm): 8.3

1. Mash beans slightly; combine with salsa, green onions, cilantro, and jalapeño chili. Divide mixture on 3 tortillas, spreading almost to edges. Sprinkle with cheese and top with remaining tortillas.

2. Cook quesadillas in large greased skillet over medium to medium-low heat until browned, 2 to 3 minutes on each side. Cut quesadillas into wedges and serve warm.

Poblano Quesadillas

6 servings

¾ cup sliced poblano chili, *or* green bell pepper
½ cup sliced green onions and tops
½ teaspoon ground cumin
1 tablespoon canola oil
2 tablespoons finely chopped cilantro
½ cup (2 ounces) shredded Cheddar cheese
3 whole wheat flour tortillas (6 inch)
¾ cup mild, *or* hot, tomato salsa
6 tablespoons sour cream

Per Serving
Net Carbohydrate (gm): 11.2
Calories: 149
Fat (gm): 9.2
Saturated fat (gm): 4
Cholesterol (mg): 15.2
Sodium (mg): 213
Protein (gm): 4.8
Carbohydrate (gm): 12.3

1. Sauté poblano chili, green onions, and cumin in oil greased skillet until vegetables are tender, 5 to 7 minutes; stir in cilantro.

2. Sprinkle cheese on half of each tortilla; spoon vegetable mixture over and fold tortillas in half. Cook quesadillas in large greased skillet over medium to medium-low heat until browned, 2 to 3 minutes on each side. Cut into wedges and serve warm with salsa and sour cream.

Mexican-Style Pizza

2 servings

½ cup crumbled chorizo
½ cup chopped green bell pepper
½ cup chopped green onions and tops
1 tablespoon canola oil
3 large whole wheat flour tortillas (10 inch)
2 cups (8 ounces) shredded Colby-Jack cheese
1 cup mild, *or* hot, tomato salsa
¾ cup sour cream

Per Serving
Net Carbohydrate (gm): 11.3
Calories: 195
Fat (gm): 12.8
Saturated fat (gm): 6.6
Cholesterol (mg): 26.1
Sodium (mg): 325
Protein (gm): 7.4
Carbohydrate (gm): 12.3

1. Cook chorizo, bell pepper, and green onions in oil in medium skillet until chorizo is cooked and vegetables are tender, about 5 minutes.

2. Place tortillas on cookie sheets; sprinkle evenly with chorizo mixture and cheese. Bake at 450 degrees until edges of tortillas are browned and cheese is melted, 6 to 8 minutes. Top with salsa and sour cream. Cut into wedges and serve warm.

Nachos

8 servings

Baked Tortilla Chips (see p. 416)
½ cup canned pinto beans, rinsed, drained
¼ cup mild, *or* hot, tomato salsa
¾ teaspoon chili powder
¾ teaspoon dried oregano leaves
2–3 cloves garlic, minced
½ cup (2 ounces) shredded Cheddar, *or* Monterey Jack, cheese
½ cup chopped seeded tomato
½ cup chopped avocado
¼ cup sliced green onions and tops
4 pitted ripe olives, sliced
¼ cup sour cream

Per Serving
Net Carbohydrate (gm): 11.4
Calories: 126
Fat (gm): 6.4
Saturated fat (gm): 2.7
Cholesterol (mg): 10.1
Sodium (mg): 162
Protein (gm): 4.4
Carbohydrate (gm): 14.2

1. Spread Baked Tortilla Chips in a single layer on jelly roll pan. Mix beans, salsa, chili powder, oregano, and garlic and mash lightly; spoon over Baked Tortilla Chips and sprinkle with cheese. Bake at 350 degrees until beans are hot and cheese is melted, 5 to 10 minutes. Sprinkle with tomato, avocado, onions, and olives; finish with dollops of sour cream.

Jicama with Lime and Cilantro

4 servings

1 medium (8 ounces) jicama, peeled, thinly sliced
Salt, to taste
1–2 tablespoons lime juice
2 tablespoons finely chopped cilantro

Per Serving
Net Carbohydrate (gm): 2.6
Calories: 23
Fat (gm): 0.1
Saturated fat (gm): 0
Cholesterol (mg): 0
Sodium (mg): 2
Protein (gm): 0.4
Carbohydrate (gm): 5.4

1. Arrange jicama slices on large serving plate; sprinkle very lightly with salt. Sprinkle with lime juice and cilantro.

Fruit Empanadas

12 servings (2 each)

½ cup chopped dried apples
¼ cup raisins
½ cup water
3 tablespoons packed light brown sugar
½ teaspoon ground cinnamon
⅛ teaspoon ground nutmeg
Empanada Pastry (recipe follows)
2–3 tablespoons reduced-fat milk, for glaze

Per Serving
Net Carbohydrate (gm): 16.8
Calories: 108
Fat (gm): 3.3
Saturated fat (gm): 0.8
Cholesterol (mg): 0.2
Sodium (mg): 42
Protein (gm): 1.9
Carbohydrate (gm): 18.9

1. Heat dried apples, raisins, and water to boiling in small saucepan. Reduce heat and simmer, covered, until fruit is very soft, about 5 minutes. Mash fruit with fork until almost smooth; stir in brown sugar and spices.

2. Roll Empanada Pastry on lightly floured surface until ⅛ inch thick; cut into circles with 3-inch cookie cutter. Place slightly rounded teaspoon of fruit mixture in center of each pastry circle; fold pastries in half and crimp edges with tines of fork. Make slit in top of each pastry with knife. Place pastries on greased cookie sheet; brush lightly with milk; and bake at 350 degrees until golden, 12 to 15 minutes. Cool on wire racks.

Empanada Pastry

1¼ cups whole wheat pastry flour
1 tablespoon packed brown sugar
¼ teaspoon baking powder
⅛ teaspoon salt
3 tablespoons vegetable shortening
1 teaspoon distilled white vinegar
3–4 tablespoons water

1. Combine flour, brown sugar, baking powder, and salt in small bowl; cut in shortening until mixture resembles coarse crumbs. Mix in vinegar and water, a tablespoon at a time, to form soft dough. Refrigerate until ready to use.

Ricotta-Stuffed Shells with Basil Pesto

6 servings (2 shells each)

¼ cup finely chopped onion
2–3 cloves garlic, minced
1 teaspoon olive oil
½ teaspoon dried basil leaves
½ cup chopped fresh spinach
¾ cup ricotta cheese
¼ teaspoon ground nutmeg
¼ teaspoon salt
¼ teaspoon pepper
12 whole wheat jumbo pasta shells (about 4 ounces), cooked
6 tablespoons basil pesto

Per Serving
Net Carbohydrate (gm): 15.2
Calories: 155
Fat (gm): 7
Saturated fat (gm): 3
Cholesterol (mg): 16.3
Sodium (mg): 139
Protein (gm): 6.4
Carbohydrate (gm): 16.5

1. Sauté onion and garlic in oil in small skillet until tender, 2 to 3 minutes; sprinkle with basil. Add spinach; cook over medium heat until spinach is wilted, about 5 minutes. Combine spinach mixture, ricotta cheese, nutmeg, salt, and pepper; spoon into shells and place in baking pan. Bake, covered, at 350 degrees until hot through, about 20 minutes. Serve with basil pesto.

Stuffed Mushrooms

4 servings (3 mushrooms each)

12 large mushrooms
2 tablespoons finely chopped shallots, *or* onion
2 cloves garlic, minced
2 teaspoons olive oil
¾ cup cooked brown rice
1 teaspoon dried basil leaves
½ teaspoon dried oregano leaves
¼ teaspoon dried thyme leaves
¼ cup (1 ounce) goat cheese, *or* cream cheese, softened

Per Serving
Net Carbohydrate (gm): 10.9
Calories: 107
Fat (gm): 4.9
Saturated fat (gm): 1.9
Cholesterol (mg): 5.6
Sodium (mg): 42
Protein (gm): 4.3
Carbohydrate (gm): 12.5

1. Remove stems from mushrooms and chop coarsely. Reserve caps. Sauté mushroom stems, shallots, and garlic in oil in medium skillet until tender 3 to 4 minutes. Stir in rice, herbs, and goat cheese.

2. Spoon rice mixture into mushroom caps and place in 13 x 9-inch baking pan. Bake at 350 degrees, covered with aluminum foil, until mushroom caps are tender, about 15 minutes. Remove foil and bake 5 minutes longer. Serve warm.

Curried Onion Croustades

8 servings (2 each)

1 cup chopped onion
1 cup chopped green onions and tops
2 cloves garlic, minced
1 teaspoon curry powder
½ teaspoon ground cumin
1 tablespoon olive oil
2 tablespoons all-purpose flour
1 cup half-and-half
2 tablespoons minced cilantro
Salt, cayenne, and black pepper, to taste
Croustades (recipe follows)
2 tablespoons chopped almonds

Per Serving
Net Carbohydrate (gm): 15.8
Calories: 167
Fat (gm): 9
Saturated fat (gm): 2.9
Cholesterol (mg): 11.1
Sodium (mg): 148
Protein (gm): 4.4
Carbohydrate (gm): 18.1

1. Cook onions, garlic, curry powder, and cumin in oil in large skillet over medium-low heat until onions are very soft, about 20 minutes. Stir in flour and cook 2 minutes longer. Stir in half-and-half and heat to boiling. Reduce heat and simmer, stirring, until thickened. Stir in cilantro; season to taste with salt, cayenne, and black pepper.

2. Spoon onion mixture into Croustades; sprinkle with almonds. Bake at 425 degrees 10 minutes.

Croustades

makes 8 servings (2 each)

16 pieces thin-sliced soft whole wheat bread
1–2 tablespoons olive oil

1. Cut 2½-inch rounds out of bread slices with cookie cutter (remaining bread can be used for croutons or bread crumbs). Brush tops of rounds lightly with olive oil. Gently press bread rounds into cups of lightly greased muffin tins. Bake at 350 degrees until browned and crisp, 10 to 12 minutes.

Curried Pinwheels

8 servings (3 each)

3 small whole wheat lavoshes (5 inch)
2 packages (3 ounces each) cream cheese, softened
1 tablespoon mayonnaise
1 teaspoon spicy brown mustard
1 clove garlic, minced
¾ teaspoon curry powder
¼ teaspoon ground cumin
¼ teaspoon cayenne pepper
6 tablespoons no-sugar-added apricot preserves
¼ cup finely chopped, cored apple
¼ cup finely chopped green onions and tops
¼ cup chopped dry-roasted peanuts

Per Serving
Net Carbohydrate (gm): 18.4
Calories: 206
Fat (gm): 11.8
Saturated fat (gm): 5.2
Cholesterol (mg): 24.4
Sodium (mg): 188
Protein (gm): 5.4
Carbohydrate (gm): 20.5

1. Brush lavoshes lightly with water and place between damp kitchen towels until softened enough to roll, 20 to 30 minutes. Do not roll.

2. Mix cream cheese, mayonnaise, mustard, garlic, curry, cumin, and cayenne pepper in small bowl; spread about 3 tablespoons mixture on each lavosh. Spread preserves over cream cheese mixture; combine remaining ingredients and sprinkle over preserves. Roll each lavosh tightly; wrap each in plastic wrap and refrigerate until firm, 2 to 3 hours. Cut each roll into 8 pieces.

Mushroom Bruschetta

12 servings (1 each)

⅓ cup chopped red, *or* yellow, bell pepper
2 green onions and tops, thinly sliced
2 cloves garlic, minced
1 tablespoon olive oil
2 cups chopped portobello, shiitake, *or* white mushrooms
1 teaspoon dried basil leaves
¼ teaspoon dried thyme leaves
2–3 tablespoons grated Parmesan cheese
Few drops balsamic vinegar
Salt and pepper, to taste
Bruschetta (see p. 420)
½ cup (2 ounces) shredded mozzarella cheese

Per Serving
Net Carbohydrate (gm): 8.3
Calories: 101
Fat (gm): 5.4
Saturated fat (gm): 1.4
Cholesterol (mg): 4.3
Sodium (mg): 134
Protein (gm): 3.7
Carbohydrate (gm): 10.3

1. Sauté bell pepper, green onions, and garlic in oil in large skillet 2 to 3 minutes. Add mushrooms; cook, covered, over medium heat until wilted, about 5 minutes. Stir in herbs and cook until mushrooms are tender and all liquid is gone, 8 to 10 minutes. Stir in Parmesan cheese; season to taste with balsamic vinegar, salt, and pepper.

2. Spoon mushroom mixture on Bruschettas and sprinkle with mozzarella cheese; broil until cheese is melted, 1 to 2 minutes. Serve warm.

Spinach and Cheese Mini-Quiches

8 servings (2 each)

1¼ cups cottage cheese
¼ cup grated Parmesan cheese
2 tablespoons reduced-fat milk
2 tablespoons all-purpose flour
½ cup finely chopped spinach leaves
½ teaspoon dried oregano leaves
¼ teaspoon dried thyme leaves
Salt and white pepper, to taste
2 eggs
16 frozen mini-fillo shells, thawed

Per Serving
Net Carbohydrate (gm): 7
Calories: 116
Fat (gm): 4.8
Saturated fat (gm): 1.3
Cholesterol (mg): 58.4
Sodium (mg): 230
Protein (gm): 8.9
Carbohydrate (gm): 8.3

1. Mix cottage cheese, Parmesan cheese, milk, flour, spinach, oregano, and thyme in medium bowl; season to taste with salt and pepper. Stir in eggs.

2. Arrange fillo shells on cookie sheet or in mini-muffin tins; fill with cheese mixture. Bake at 325 degrees until puffed and beginning to brown on the tops, about 20 minutes.

Cheese and Spinach Squares

12 servings (2 squares each)

1–2 tablespoons unseasoned dry bread crumbs
2 cups cottage cheese
1½ cups (6 ounces) shredded Cheddar cheese
2 eggs
⅓ cup whole wheat flour
1 package (10 ounces) frozen chopped spinach,
    thawed, well drained
¼ cup thinly sliced green onions and tops
¼ cup chopped roasted red bell pepper, *or* pimiento
¼ cup finely chopped parsley
¼ teaspoon cayenne pepper
½ teaspoon black pepper
⅛ teaspoon ground nutmeg

Per Serving
Net Carbohydrate (gm): 4.4
Calories: 128
Fat (gm): 7.3
Saturated fat (gm): 4.3
Cholesterol (mg): 55.5
Sodium (mg): 264
Protein (gm): 10.3
Carbohydrate (gm): 5.8

1. Coat bottom and sides of greased 13 x 9-inch baking pan with bread crumbs.

2. Combine cheeses and eggs in bowl; stir in remaining ingredients and mix well. Pour into prepared pan and bake at 350 degrees until set and lightly browned, 35 to 40 minutes. Cool 10 minutes before cutting into squares.

Spinach Balls with Mustard Sauce

12 servings (2 balls each)

2 cups herb-seasoned bread stuffing cubes
¼ cup grated Parmesan cheese
¼ cup chopped green onions and tops
2 cloves garlic, minced
⅛ teaspoon ground nutmeg
1 package (10 ounces) frozen chopped spinach,
    thawed, well drained
¼–⅓ cup vegetable, *or* chicken, broth
2 tablespoons butter, melted
Salt and pepper, to taste
1 egg, beaten
Mustard Sauce (recipe follows)

Per Serving
Net Carbohydrate (gm): 8
Calories: 99
Fat (gm): 5.8
Saturated fat (gm): 3.3
Cholesterol (mg): 29.8
Sodium (mg): 233
Protein (gm): 3.1
Carbohydrate (gm): 9

1. Combine stuffing cubes, Parmesan cheese, green onions, garlic, and nutmeg in medium bowl. Mix in spinach, broth, and butter; season to taste with salt and pepper. Mix in egg.

2. Shape mixture into 24 balls. Bake at 350 degrees until spinach balls are browned, about 15 minutes. Serve with Mustard Sauce for dipping.

Mustard Sauce

makes about 1 cup

¾ cup sour cream
3–4 teaspoons Dijon mustard
1½ tablespoons honey
1 tablespoon chopped chives

1. Mix all ingredients.

Five-Spice Potstickers

12 servings (2 potstickers each)

1 cup sliced Chinese cabbage
¼ cup shredded carrot
2 tablespoons thinly sliced green onions and tops
2 tablespoons thinly sliced celery
1 teaspoon minced gingerroot
1 small clove garlic, minced
1 tablespoon dark sesame oil
1 tablespoon tamari soy sauce
¼ teaspoon hot chili paste
½ teaspoon five-spice powder
24 wonton wrappers
1 egg white, beaten
Tamari Dipping Sauce (recipe follows)

Per Serving
Net Carbohydrate (gm): 11.1
Calories: 69
Fat (gm): 1.4
Saturated fat (gm): 0.2
Cholesterol (mg): 1.5
Sodium (mg): 839
Protein (gm): 3
Carbohydrate (gm): 11.7

1. Stir-fry cabbage, carrot, green onions, celery, gingerroot, and garlic in sesame oil in wok or large skillet over medium to medium-high heat until cabbage is wilted, 2 to 3 minutes. Remove from heat; stir in soy sauce, chili paste, and five-spice powder and cool.

2. Spoon ½ tablespoon filling on wonton wrapper; brush edges of wrapper with egg white. Fold wrapper in half and press edges to seal. Repeat with remaining filling, wrappers, and egg white. Add wontons 6 or 8 at a time to simmering water in large saucepan; simmer, uncovered, until wontons rise to the surface, 2 to 3 minutes. Remove from water with slotted spoon and drain. Repeat with remaining wontons.

3. Cook wontons in greased large skillet over medium heat until browned, 2 to 3 minutes on each side. Serve hot with Tamari Dipping Sauce.

Tamari Dipping Sauce

makes ¾ cup

½ cup tamari soy sauce
2 tablespoons rice wine vinegar
4 teaspoons lemon juice
2 teaspoons honey

1. Mix all ingredients.

Cranberry-Cheese Wontons

6 servings (2 wontons each)

1 package (3 ounces) cream cheese, softened
2 tablespoons chopped dried cranberries
1 tablespoon finely chopped chives
½ teaspoon minced gingerroot
1 tablespoon minced parsley
Salt and white pepper, to taste
12 wonton wrappers
1 egg white, beaten
Vegetable oil, for frying
Tamari Dipping Sauce (see above)

Per Serving
Net Carbohydrate (gm): 16.3
Calories: 151
Fat (gm): 7.4
Saturated fat (gm): 3.4
Cholesterol (mg): 17.1
Sodium (mg): 1434
Protein (gm): 5.3
Carbohydrate (gm): 16.8

1. Mix cream cheese, cranberries, chives, gingerroot, and parsley in small bowl; season to taste with salt and white pepper.

2. Spoon ½ tablespoon filling on wonton wrapper; brush edges of wrapper with egg white. Fold wrapper in half and press edges to seal. Repeat with remaining filling, wrappers, and egg white.

3. Heat 2 inches of oil to 375 degrees in large saucepan. Fry wontons, 6 to 8 at a time, until golden, 1 to 2 minutes. Drain very well on paper toweling. Serve hot with Tamari Dipping Sauce.

Shrimp and Vegetable Egg Rolls

12 servings (1 each)

1 tablespoon sesame seeds
2–3 teaspoons dark sesame oil
2 green onions and tops, sliced
1 tablespoon minced gingerroot
2 cloves garlic, minced
2 cups thinly sliced spinach
¼ cup chopped water chestnuts
¼ cup shredded carrot
¼ diced celery
½ cup sliced small mushrooms
1 cup coarsely chopped cooked shrimp
1–1½ teaspoons tamari soy sauce
Salt and pepper, to taste
2 egg whites
1 cup alfalfa sprouts
12 egg roll wrappers
1 tablespoon vegetable, *or* peanut, oil
Tamari Dipping Sauce (see p. 438)

Per Serving
Net Carbohydrate (gm): 16.1
Calories: 115
Fat (gm): 2.7
Saturated fat (gm): 0.4
Cholesterol (mg): 20.8
Sodium (mg): 802
Protein (gm): 6.2
Carbohydrate (gm): 16.9

1. Sauté sesame seeds in sesame oil in large skillet until beginning to brown, 1 to 2 minutes. Add green onions, gingerroot, and garlic; sauté until onions are tender, 1 to 2 minutes. Add spinach, water chestnuts, carrot, celery, and mushrooms; cook, covered, over medium heat until spinach and mushrooms are wilted. Stir in shrimp and tamari sauce; season to taste with salt and pepper. Cool 5 to 10 minutes; stir in egg whites and alfalfa sprouts.

2. Spoon about ⅓ cup vegetable mixture near corner of 1 egg roll wrapper. Brush edges of wrapper with water. Fold bottom corner of egg roll wrapper up over filling; fold sides in and roll up. Repeat with remaining filling and wrappers.

3. Heat oil to 375 degrees in deep skillet or large saucepan. Fry egg rolls until golden, 4 to 5 minutes. Drain on paper toweling. Serve hot with Tamari Dipping Sauce.

Bean Patties with Cucumber-Cilantro Sauce

12 servings (2 patties each)

1 can (15 ounces) pinto beans, rinsed, drained
1 cup mashed, cooked potato
¼ cup finely chopped green onions and tops
¼ cup minced parsley
1 teaspoon ground cumin
5 drops red pepper sauce
Salt and pepper, to taste
2 egg whites
⅓ cup unseasoned dry bread crumbs
1–2 tablespoons olive oil
Cucumber-Cilantro Sauce (recipe follows)

Per Serving
Net Carbohydrate (gm): 10.6
Calories: 93
Fat (gm): 2.9
Saturated fat (gm): 1
Cholesterol (mg): 3.3
Sodium (mg): 210
Protein (gm): 4.4
Carbohydrate (gm): 12.9

1. Mash beans with fork; combine with potato, green onions, parsley, cumin, and red pepper sauce. Season to taste with salt and pepper; mix in egg whites and bread crumbs. Shape mixture into 24 patties.

2. Cook patties in oil in large skillet over medium to medium-low heat until browned and crisp on both sides; drain well. Serve hot with Cucumber-Cilantro Sauce.

Cucumber-Cilantro Sauce

makes about 1½ cups

1 cup plain yogurt
¼ cup sour cream
½ cup finely chopped, peeled, seeded cucumber
2 cloves garlic, minced
3 tablespoons finely chopped cilantro
Salt and white pepper, to taste

1. Combine all ingredients, except salt and pepper; season to taste with salt and pepper.

Indonesian-Style Satay

6 servings

1 pound boneless, skinless chicken breast, cubed (¾-inch)
2–3 tablespoons soy sauce, divided
2 tablespoons peanut butter
2 tablespoons honey
1 tablespoon unsulphured molasses
1 tablespoon lemon juice
1 tablespoon chopped gingerroot
1 tablespoon finely chopped serrano, *or* jalapeño, chili
3 cloves garlic, minced
1 teaspoon chili powder
1 teaspoon dark oriental sesame oil
2 tablespoons thinly sliced green onions and tops

Per Serving
Net Carbohydrate (gm): 10.2
Calories: 160
Fat (gm): 4.5
Saturated fat (gm): 0.9
Cholesterol (mg): 43.8
Sodium (mg): 414
Protein (gm): 19.4
Carbohydrate (gm): 10.9

1. Arrange chicken cubes on 6 skewers. Place in single layer in baking dish; brush with 1 to 2 tablespoons soy sauce. Refrigerate, covered, 1 hour or longer.

2. Process 1 tablespoon soy sauce and remaining ingredients, except green onions, in food processor or blender until smooth. Stir in green onions.

3. Bake chicken kabobs at 400 degrees until cooked, about 20 minutes. Arrange kabobs on serving plate; spoon sauce over.

Tortellini Kabobs with Garlic Sauce

8 servings (2 kabobs each)

1 package (9 ounces) cheese tortellini, cooked
¾ cup medium mushroom caps
¾ cup medium cherry tomatoes
¾ cup green bell pepper pieces (1-inch),
   cooked until crisp-tender
¾ cup sliced zucchini (½-inch)
Olive oil
Garlic Sauce (recipe follows)

Per Serving
Net Carbohydrate (gm): 17.5
Calories: 129
Fat (gm): 3.8
Saturated fat (gm): 0.7
Cholesterol (mg): 9
Sodium (mg): 207
Protein (gm): 5.2
Carbohydrate (gm): 18.8

1. Alternate tortellini and vegetables on 16-inch-long skewers and arrange on broiler pan. Brush lightly with olive oil and broil 6 inches from heat source, 4 minutes; turn kabobs, brush with olive oil, and broil 3 to 4 minutes longer. Serve with Garlic Sauce.

Garlic Sauce

makes about 2 cups

24 cloves garlic, peeled
1 tablespoon olive oil
2 cups vegetable broth
2 tablespoons all-purpose flour
2 tablespoons chopped parsley
Salt and pepper, to taste

1. Cook garlic in oil in medium skillet, covered, over medium to medium-low heat until tender, about 10 minutes. Uncover and continue cooking until garlic is golden brown, about 10 minutes. Mash cloves slightly with a fork.

2. Add 1¾ cups broth to skillet and heat to boiling. Mix flour and remaining ¼ cup broth and stir into boiling mixture. Boil, stirring, until thickened, about 1 minute. Stir in parsley; season to taste with salt and pepper.

Apricot Cheese Melt

4 servings

1 package (3 ounces) cream cheese, softened
¼ cup (1 ounce) shredded smoked Gouda, *or* Swiss, cheese
¼ cup chopped walnuts
4 pieces thin-sliced whole wheat bread
¼ cup no-sugar-added apricot preserves
2 ounces thinly sliced Cheddar cheese

Per Serving
Net Carbohydrate (gm): 14.7
Calories: 273
Fat (gm): 19.5
Saturated fat (gm): 9.1
Cholesterol (mg): 44.9
Sodium (mg): 326
Protein (gm): 10
Carbohydrate (gm): 18.2

1. Mix cream cheese, Gouda cheese, and walnuts; spread on 4 slices bread. Top with apricot preserves and Cheddar cheese. Place sandwiches in greased large skillet; cook, covered, over medium heat until bread is browned on the bottom and cheese is melted, about 5 minutes.

Sun-Dried Tomato Pesto and Cheese Grill

4 servings

4 pieces thin-sliced Italian, *or* sourdough, bread
½ cup sun-dried tomato pesto
6 ounces thinly sliced mozzarella cheese
⅓ cup thinly sliced tomato

Per Serving
Net Carbohydrate (gm): 12
Calories: 297
Fat (gm): 20.7
Saturated fat (gm): 7.2
Cholesterol (mg): 20.2
Sodium (mg): 649
Protein (gm): 13.8
Carbohydrate (gm): 15.9

1. Spread each slice bread with 2 tablespoons pesto; top with cheese and tomato slices. Place open-face sandwiches in greased large skillet; cook, covered, over medium heat until bread is browned on the bottom and cheese is melted, about 5 minutes.

Gourmet Turkey Melt

4 servings

1 package (3 ounces) cream cheese, softened
2 tablespoons crumbled blue cheese
4 pieces thin-sliced multigrain bread
¼ cup no-sugar-added orange marmalade
¼ cup thinly sliced seeded cucumber
4 ounces shaved smoked turkey
2 ounces thinly sliced Swiss cheese

Per Serving
Net Carbohydrate (gm): 16.9
Calories: 253
Fat (gm): 14
Saturated fat (gm): 8.2
Cholesterol (mg): 49.4
Sodium (mg): 463
Protein (gm): 14.6
Carbohydrate (gm): 22.3

1. Mix cream cheese and blue cheese; spread on bread slices. Top with marmalade, cucumber slices, turkey, and Swiss cheese. Place open-face sandwiches in greased large skillet; cook, covered, over medium heat until bread is browned on the bottom and cheese is melted, about 5 minutes.

Swiss Cheese, Ham, and Spinach Pinwheels

8 servings (2 slices each)

1 large whole wheat lavosh (about 16 inches diameter)
1 package (8 ounces) cream cheese, softened
1 tablespoon sour cream
2 tablespoons minced onion
1 teaspoon fennel seeds, crushed
8 ounces shaved smoked ham
4 ounces thinly sliced Alpine Lace Swiss cheese
4 cups loosely packed spinach leaves
1 cup thinly sliced tomatoes
¼ cup sliced, pitted ripe olives

Per Serving
Net Carbohydrate (gm): 14.7
Calories: 266
Fat (gm): 15.9
Saturated fat (gm): 9
Cholesterol (mg): 61.8
Sodium (mg): 494
Protein (gm): 13.7
Carbohydrate (gm): 16.6

1. Place lavosh between 2 damp clean kitchen towels; let stand until lavosh is softened enough to roll, 10 to 15 minutes.

2. Mix cream cheese, sour cream, onion, and fennel seeds in small bowl; spread mixture on lavosh. Arrange ham, Swiss cheese, spinach, tomatoes, and olives on cheese. Roll up lavosh tightly; wrap in plastic wrap and refrigerate at least 4 hours but no longer than 2 days. Trim ends; cut into scant 1-inch slices to serve.

Chicken and Mushroom Pinwheels

8 servings (2 slices each)

1 large whole wheat lavosh (about 16 inches diameter)
4 ounces mushrooms
1 package (8 ounces) cream cheese, softened
1 tablespoon sour cream
1 teaspoon minced garlic
2 teaspoons Dijon mustard
½ cup thinly sliced green onions and tops
⅓ cup thinly sliced red bell pepper
3 tablespoons Italian salad dressing
6 ounces shaved chicken, *or* turkey, breast

Per Serving
Net Carbohydrate (gm): 14.7
Calories: 224
Fat (gm): 13.9
Saturated fat (gm): 7
Cholesterol (mg): 39.3
Sodium (mg): 441
Protein (gm): 8.7
Carbohydrate (gm): 16.4

1. Place lavosh between 2 damp clean kitchen towels; let stand until lavosh is softened enough to roll, 10 to 15 minutes.

2. Remove mushroom stems and chop; slice mushroom caps. Mix cream cheese, chopped mushroom stems, sour cream, garlic, and mustard in small bowl; spread mixture on lavosh. Toss sliced mushrooms, onions, and bell pepper with salad dressing. Spoon vegetable mixture over cheese mixture and press lightly into surface; top with chicken. Roll up lavosh tightly; wrap in plastic wrap and refrigerate at least 4 hours, but no longer than 2 days. Trim ends; cut into scant 1-inch slices to serve.

Spinach and Ricotta Pizza

8 servings

¼ cup finely chopped onion
1 clove garlic, minced
1 tablespoon olive oil
1 package (10 ounces) baby spinach leaves
Salt and pepper, to taste
Whole Wheat Pizza Dough (recipe follows)
¼ cup tomato sauce
1 cup ricotta cheese
½ cup (2 ounces) shredded mozzarella cheese
2 tablespoons shredded Parmesan cheese
2 tablespoons sour cream
¾ teaspoon dried oregano leaves
½ cup sliced tomato
½ teaspoon Italian seasoning
¼ cup (1 ounce) crumbled blue cheese

Per Serving
Net Carbohydrate (gm): 13.1
Calories: 183
Fat (gm): 9.7
Saturated fat (gm): 5
Cholesterol (mg): 24.4
Sodium (mg): 311
Protein (gm): 10.3
Carbohydrate (gm): 15.9

1. Sauté onion and garlic in oil in large skillet until tender, 2 to 3 minutes; add spinach and cook, covered, until wilted. Season to taste with salt and pepper.

2. Roll dough on floured surface to circle 13 inches in diameter; spread dough on greased 12-inch pizza pan, making rim around the edge. Spread tomato sauce on dough. Spoon combined cheeses, sour cream, and oregano onto dough and top with spinach mixture. Top with tomato slices and sprinkle with Italian seasoning and blue cheese.

3. Bake pizza at 400 degrees until dough is browned, about 20 to 30 minutes. Let stand 5 to 10 minutes before cutting.

Whole Wheat Pizza Dough

makes one 12-inch crust (8 slices)

1 cup whole wheat pastry flour, divided
1 package fast-rising yeast
¼ teaspoon salt
½ cup very hot water (120 degrees)
2 teaspoons honey

1. Combine ¾ cup flour, yeast, and salt in medium bowl; add hot water and honey, stirring until smooth. Mix in enough remaining flour to make a soft dough. Knead dough on floured surface until smooth and elastic, about 5 minutes. Cover and let stand 15 minutes before using.

Ranch-Style Pizza

8 servings

Whole Wheat Pizza Dough (see above)
⅓ cup ranch salad dressing
1½ cups (6 ounces) shredded mozzarella cheese
1 cup thinly sliced spinach
½ cup sliced mushrooms

Per Serving
Net Carbohydrate (gm): 11.7
Calories: 167
Fat (gm): 10.1
Saturated fat (gm): 3.6
Cholesterol (mg): 16.6
Sodium (mg): 274
Protein (gm): 6.7
Carbohydrate (gm): 13.8

1. Spread dough on greased 12-inch pizza pan, making rim around edge. Brush dough with salad dressing; sprinkle with cheese. Toss spinach and mushrooms together; mound in center of pizza.

2. Bake pizza at 425 degrees until crust is browned, 15 to 20 minutes.

Reuben Pizza

8 servings

4 slices bacon
¼ cup thinly sliced red onion
1½ teaspoons caraway seeds, crushed, divided
1 cup fresh sauerkraut, well drained
Whole Wheat Pizza Dough (see p. 445)
½ cup rye flour
¼ cup thousand island salad dressing
1 cup (4 ounces) shredded mozzarella cheese

Per Serving
Net Carbohydrate (gm): 16.5
Calories: 173
Fat (gm): 7.9
Saturated fat (gm): 2.9
Cholesterol (mg): 15.6
Sodium (mg): 336
Protein (gm): 6.9
Carbohydrate (gm): 20.1

1. Fry bacon in large skillet until crisp; drain and crumble. Return bacon and 1 tablespoon bacon fat to skillet; add onion and 1 teaspoon caraway seeds; sauté 2 to 3 minutes. Stir in sauerkraut; cook, uncovered, over medium-low heat until warm.

2. Make Whole Wheat Pizza Dough, substituting rye flour for ½ cup of the whole wheat flour, and adding remaining ½ teaspoon caraway seeds.

3. Spread dough on greased 12-inch pizza pan, making rim around edge. Spread salad dressing on dough. Spread sauerkraut mixture evenly over dough; sprinkle with cheese.

4. Bake pizza at 425 degrees until crust is browned, 15 to 20 minutes.

Tip: Fresh sauerkraut is packaged in cellophane bags and can be found in the produce section of the supermarket.

Fresh Tomato and Basil Pizza

8 servings

Whole Wheat Pizza Dough (see p. 445)
¾ cup pizza sauce
1 cup (4 ounces) shredded mozzarella cheese
¾ cup thinly sliced tomatoes
12 basil leaves, *or* 1 teaspoon dried basil leaves

Per Serving
Net Carbohydrate (gm): 12.7
Calories: 111
Fat (gm): 3.6
Saturated fat (gm): 1.9
Cholesterol (mg): 10.8
Sodium (mg): 138
Protein (gm): 5.6
Carbohydrate (gm): 15.3

1. Spread dough on greased 12-inch pizza pan, making rim around edge. Spread pizza sauce over dough; sprinkle with cheese and top with tomato slices and basil.

2. Bake pizza at 425 degrees until crust is browned, 15 to 20 minutes.

Artichoke and Roasted Peppers Pizza

8 servings

1 cup sliced red bell pepper (½-inch)
Whole Wheat Pizza Dough (see p. 445)
½ can (15-ounce size) diced tomatoes, drained
½ can (15-ounce size) artichoke hearts, rinsed,
    drained, cut into fourths
½ teaspoon Italian seasoning
¾ cup (3 ounces) shredded mozzarella cheese
¼ cup (1 ounce) shredded Parmesan cheese

Per Serving
Net Carbohydrate (gm): 13.5
Calories: 128
Fat (gm): 5.2
Saturated fat (gm): 1.9
Cholesterol (mg): 10.1
Sodium (mg): 321
Protein (gm): 5.8
Carbohydrate (gm): 17

1. Arrange pepper slices on greased aluminum foil-lined baking pan; bake at 425 degrees until pepper slices are just tender and lightly browned, 20 to 30 minutes.

2. Spread dough on greased 12-inch pizza pan, making a rim around edge. Arrange pepper slices, tomatoes, and artichoke hearts on dough; sprinkle with Italian seasoning and cheeses. Bake pizza at 425 degrees until crust is browned, 15 to 20 minutes.

Gazpacho Pizza

8 servings

1 package (8 ounces) cream cheese, softened
2 tablespoons mayonnaise
½ teaspoon dry mustard
2 teaspoons finely chopped parsley
2 teaspoons finely chopped chives
1 large whole wheat lavosh (about 16 inches diameter)
½ cup chopped avocado
1 cup chopped, seeded tomato
1 cup chopped, seeded cucumber
⅓ cup chopped green onions and tops
⅓ cup chopped yellow bell pepper
⅓ cup chopped green bell pepper
¼ cup Italian salad dressing
1 teaspoon minced garlic
1 teaspoon minced jalapeño chili
Salt and pepper, to taste

Per Serving
Net Carbohydrate (gm): 15.8
Calories: 259
Fat (gm): 18.8
Saturated fat (gm): 7.4
Cholesterol (mg): 33.2
Sodium (mg): 272
Protein (gm): 5.5
Carbohydrate (gm): 18.3

1. Mix cream cheese, mayonnaise, dry mustard, parsley, and chives. Spread mixture on lavosh.

2. Combine vegetables in large bowl. Combine salad dressing, garlic, and jalapeño chili; pour over vegetables and toss. Season to taste with salt and pepper. Spoon mixture onto lavosh and serve immediately.

Tomato Fillo Pie

8 servings

8 sheets frozen fillo pastry, thawed
2–3 tablespoons olive oil
2 cups (8 ounces) shredded mozzarella cheese
½ cup thinly sliced onion
3 cups thinly sliced tomatoes
Salt and pepper, to taste
¼ cup (1 ounce) grated Parmesan cheese
¾ teaspoon dried dill weed
½ teaspoon dried basil leaves

Per Serving
Net Carbohydrate (gm): 13.5
Calories: 194
Fat (gm): 11.5
Saturated fat (gm): 4.9
Cholesterol (mg): 23.5
Sodium (mg): 248
Protein (gm): 8.5
Carbohydrate (gm): 14.8

1. Place sheet of fillo on greased jelly roll pan; brush lightly with olive oil. Repeat with remaining sheets of fillo and oil.

2. Sprinkle mozzarella cheese and onion over fillo; arrange tomato slices on top. Sprinkle lightly with salt and pepper. Sprinkle with Parmesan cheese and herbs.

3. Bake at 375 degrees until fillo is browned and cheese melted, about 15 minutes.

Mushroom-Zucchini Fillo Pie

8 servings

½ cup thinly sliced leek
½ cup thinly sliced green onions and tops
3–4 tablespoons olive oil, divided
3 cups sliced cremini, shiitake, *or* portobello mushrooms
1 teaspoon minced garlic
1½ cups thinly sliced zucchini
¾ teaspoon dried thyme leaves
Salt and pepper, to taste
8 sheets frozen fillo pastry, thawed
1 cup (4 ounces) crumbled feta cheese

Per Serving
Net Carbohydrate (gm): 12.2
Calories: 168
Fat (gm): 10.2
Saturated fat (gm): 3.7
Cholesterol (mg): 16.5
Sodium (mg): 312
Protein (gm): 5.6
Carbohydrate (gm): 13.7

1. Cook leek and green onions in 1 tablespoon oil in large skillet, covered, over medium heat until wilted, 3 to 4 minutes. Add mushrooms and garlic; cook, covered, 5 minutes. Add zucchini and cook, uncovered, until vegetables are tender, 5 to 8 minutes. Stir in thyme; season to taste with salt and pepper.

2. Place sheet of fillo on greased jelly roll pan; brush lightly with olive oil. Repeat with remaining fillo and oil. Spoon vegetable mixture evenly over fillo; sprinkle with cheese. Bake at 375 degrees until fillo is browned and cheese melted, about 15 minutes.

Artichoke Pie

8 servings

1 package (8 ounces) cream cheese, softened
1 cup (4 ounces) shredded mozzarella cheese
¼ cup (1 ounce) grated Parmesan cheese
2½ teaspoons minced roasted garlic, divided
1 can (14 ounces) artichoke hearts, rinsed, drained, sliced
1 cup reduced-fat milk
¼ cup mayonnaise
¼ cup sour cream, *or* plain yogurt
2 eggs
¾ cup biscuit baking mix

Per Serving
Net Carbohydrate (gm): 12.2
Calories: 330
Fat (gm): 27.4
Saturated fat (gm): 11.3
Cholesterol (mg): 106.2
Sodium (mg): 537
Protein (gm): 9.6
Carbohydrate (gm): 14.2

1. Mix cheeses and ½ teaspoon roasted garlic; spread in bottom of lightly greased 10-inch pie pan. Mix artichoke hearts with remaining 2 teaspoons roasted garlic; spoon over cheese mixture.

2. Mix milk, mayonnaise, sour cream, and eggs in small bowl; mix in baking mix until blended. Pour batter over artichoke mixture in pie pan. Bake at 400 degrees until set and browned on the top, 35 to 40 minutes. Let stand 5 minutes before cutting.

Mushroom Rolls

12 servings

12 pieces thin-sliced whole wheat bread, crusts removed
1 pound mushrooms, minced
3 green onions and tops, minced
1 tablespoon olive oil
3 tablespoons all-purpose flour
½ teaspoon salt
¾ cup whipping cream

Per Serving
Net Carbohydrate (gm): 11.9
Calories: 135
Fat (gm): 7.8
Saturated fat (gm): 3.8
Cholesterol (mg): 20.6
Sodium (mg): 223
Protein (gm): 3.9
Carbohydrate (gm): 14.1

1. Roll each slice of bread with rolling pin until very thin; set aside.

2. Sauté mushrooms and green onions in oil in large skillet until mushrooms are very tender and liquid evaporates, 8 to 10 minutes. Stir in flour and salt and cook over medium heat, stirring, 1 minute. Stir in cream and cook, stirring, over medium heat until thickened.

3. Spread mixture evenly on bread slices; roll up jelly-roll style. Arrange, seam sides down, on cookie sheet. Bake at 400 degrees until lightly browned, about 10 minutes. Slice rolls into thirds.

Sweet-Sour Cocktail Dogs

8 servings

2 tablespoons cornstarch
¾ cup apple juice, *or* cider
½ cup red wine vinegar
¼ cup pineapple juice
¼ cup chopped pimiento
2 tablespoons soy sauce
½ teaspoon garlic powder
½ teaspoon ground ginger
2 tablespoons packed light brown sugar
1 pound cocktail hot dogs

Per Serving
Net Carbohydrate (gm): 10.8
Calories: 199
Fat (gm): 14.4
Saturated fat (gm): 5.3
Cholesterol (mg): 29.5
Sodium (mg): 801
Protein (gm): 6.2
Carbohydrate (gm): 11

1. Combine cornstarch and apple juice in small saucepan. Stir in remaining ingredients, except hot dogs. Heat to boiling; reduce heat and simmer, stirring, until thickened, about 1 minute. Add hot dogs and simmer until warm, 2 to 3 minutes.

Microwave Potato Cheezees

8 servings

1 pound medium Idaho potatoes
½ cup (2 ounces) shredded mozzarella cheese
½ teaspoon garlic powder
¼ teaspoon chili powder
¼ teaspoon dried basil leaves
Pepper, to taste

Per Serving
Net Carbohydrate (gm): 10.7
Calories: 70
Fat (gm): 1.6
Saturated fat (gm): 0.9
Cholesterol (mg): 5.5
Sodium (mg): 30
Protein (gm): 2.5
Carbohydrate (gm): 11.8

1. Wash potatoes and pierce with a fork. Microwave potatoes on High until tender, 4 to 7 minutes. Cool; refrigerate until chilled.

2. Cut potatoes into ¼-inch slices. Arrange on microwave-safe platter. Sprinkle with cheese, combined herbs, and pepper. Microwave for 30 to 40 seconds, just until cheese melts.

Baked Spinach Balls

12 servings (2 each)

2 cups herb-seasoned bread stuffing cubes
¼ cup (1 ounce) grated Parmesan cheese
¼ cup chopped green onions and tops
2 cloves garlic, minced
⅛ teaspoon ground nutmeg
1 package (10 ounces) frozen chopped spinach,
     thawed, well drained
¼–⅓ cup vegetable, *or* chicken, broth
2 tablespoons butter, melted
Salt and pepper, to taste
1 egg, beaten
Mustard Sauce (recipe follows)

Per Serving
Net Carbohydrate (gm): 10.4
Calories: 113
Fat (gm): 5.9
Saturated fat (gm): 3.3
Cholesterol (mg): 29.8
Sodium (mg): 256
Protein (gm): 3.6
Carbohydrate (gm): 11.8

1. Combine stuffing cubes, Parmesan cheese, onions, garlic, and nutmeg in medium bowl. Mix in spinach, broth, and butter; season to taste with salt and pepper. Mix in egg.

2. Shape mixture into 24 balls. Bake on greased cookie sheet at 350 degrees until browned, about 15 minutes. Serve warm with Mustard Sauce.

Mustard Sauce

makes about 1 cup

¾ cup sour cream
3–4 teaspoons Dijon mustard
1½ tablespoons honey
1 tablespoon chopped chives

1. Mix all ingredients.

Eggplant-Mushroom Spread

8 servings (about ¼ cup each)

1 eggplant (about 1 pound)
½ cup minced green onions and tops
2 cloves garlic, minced
2 ribs celery, finely chopped
½ cup chopped mushrooms
1 cup chopped, peeled tomato
2 tablespoons lemon juice
⅓ cup tomato juice
½ teaspoon salt
½ teaspoon pepper
1 tablespoon chopped fresh, *or* 1½ teaspoons dried, basil leaves
½ teaspoon dried oregano leaves
1 cup celery pieces (¾-inch)
1 cup sliced large carrots
1 cup sliced zucchini

Per Serving
Net Carbohydrate (gm): 5.7
Calories: 40
Fat (gm): 0.3
Saturated fat (gm): 0.1
Cholesterol (mg): 0
Sodium (mg): 218
Protein (gm): 1.7
Carbohydrate (gm): 8.8

1. Pierce eggplant with fork; place on greased aluminum foil-lined baking sheet. Bake at 400 degrees about 30 minutes or until tender. Cool.

2. Cut eggplant in half and scoop out flesh with a spoon; mash eggplant and place in large mixing bowl. Mix in remaining ingredients except celery, carrots, and zucchini. Refrigerate 1 to 2 hours for flavors to blend; spread on vegetable slices.

Mediterranean Eggplant Dip

8 servings

1 eggplant (about 1½ pounds)
2 large cloves garlic, minced
1 tablespoon paprika
2 teaspoons dried oregano leaves
1 teaspoon ground cumin
1 tablespoon olive oil
2 tablespoons lemon juice
Salt and pepper, to taste
½ recipe Pita Chips (see p. 422)
1 cup halved medium mushrooms
1 cup sliced cucumber

Per Serving
Net Carbohydrate (gm): 7.3
Calories: 64
Fat (gm): 2.2
Saturated fat (gm): 0.3
Cholesterol (mg): 0
Sodium (mg): 43
Protein (gm): 2.4
Carbohydrate (gm): 10.7

1. Pierce eggplant with fork; place on greased aluminum foil-lined baking sheet. Bake at 400 degrees until tender, 30 to 45 minutes. Cool.

2. Cut eggplant in half and scoop out flesh with a spoon; mash eggplant and place in large mixing bowl. Stir in garlic, herbs, and olive oil. Cook eggplant mixture in greased large skillet over medium heat until all liquid evaporates, stirring often to avoid scorching. Stir in lemon juice and season to taste with salt and pepper; cool. Serve at room temperature with Pita Chips, mushrooms, and cucumber for dipping.

Chicken Salad Croustades

8 servings (2 each)

1½ cups finely chopped cooked skinless chicken breast
1 cup finely chopped apple
½ cup sour cream
¼ cup chopped green onions and tops
Salt and pepper, to taste
Croustades (see p. 434)

Per Serving
Net Carbohydrate (gm): 12.2
Calories: 151
Fat (gm): 6.1
Saturated fat (gm): 2.3
Cholesterol (mg): 25.5
Sodium (mg): 155
Protein (gm): 10.5
Carbohydrate (gm): 14.4

1. Mix all ingredients, except Croustades, in small bowl; serve in Croustades.

Tip: Chicken mixture can also be spread on Bruschetta (see p. 420).

Dilled Salmon Croustades

8 servings (2 each)

1 can (15½ ounces) salmon, skin and bones discarded
1 tablespoon lemon juice
1 tablespoon prepared horseradish
1 package (8 ounces) cream cheese, softened
2–4 tablespoons mayonnaise
1 tablespoon dried dill weed
4 green onions and tops, chopped
¼ cup finely chopped parsley
Croustades (see p. 434)

Per Serving
Net Carbohydrate (gm): 11.5
Calories: 283
Fat (gm): 18.4
Saturated fat (gm): 7.9
Cholesterol (mg): 54.6
Sodium (mg): 512
Protein (gm): 16.7
Carbohydrate (gm): 13.6

1. Combine all ingredients, except Croustades, in medium bowl; serve in Croustades.

Tip: Salmon mixture can also be served on Bruschetta (see p. 420).

Smoked Salmon Cream Cheese Rolls

8 servings

2 packages (3 ounces each) cream cheese, softened
3 tablespoons drained capers
4 ounces thinly sliced smoked salmon
16 endive leaves
1 small lemon, cut into wedges

Per Serving
Net Carbohydrate (gm): 1
Calories: 94
Fat (gm): 8.1
Saturated fat (gm): 4.8
Cholesterol (mg): 26.6
Sodium (mg): 271
Protein (gm): 4.4
Carbohydrate (gm): 1.3

1. Mix cream cheese and capers in small bowl. Spread smoked salmon slices with cream cheese mixture; roll up jelly roll style and cut into ¾-inch slices. Arrange salmon slices on endive leaves; squeeze lemon juice over and serve.

Salmon-Filled Mushroom Caps

6 servings (3 each)

18 medium mushrooms
1 can (7½ ounces) salmon and skin discarded, chopped
2 tablespoons unseasoned dry bread crumbs
2 tablespoons chopped green onions and tops
2 tablespoons chopped parsley
2 tablespoons diced pimiento

Per Serving
Net Carbohydrate (gm): 3
Calories: 76
Fat (gm): 3.1
Saturated fat (gm): 0.7
Cholesterol (mg): 13.8
Sodium (mg): 196
Protein (gm): 9.8
Carbohydrate (gm): 3.6

1. Remove stems from mushrooms and chop finely. Combine chopped stems, salmon, bread crumbs, green onions, and parsley; fill mushroom caps with mixture and top each with pimiento. Bake in greased baking pan at 350 degrees until mushrooms are tender, 15 to 20 minutes. Serve warm.

Mushrooms in Vermouth

6 servings

½ cup dry vermouth
1 tablespoon olive oil
⅓ cup red wine vinegar
2 tablespoons lemon juice
1 large clove garlic, minced
2 tablespoons chopped shallots, *or* onion
1 tablespoon chopped fresh, *or* 2 teaspoons dried, basil leaves
1 teaspoon brown sugar
½ teaspoon dry mustard
½ teaspoon salt
⅛ teaspoon pepper
1 pound medium mushrooms

Per Serving
Net Carbohydrate (gm): 4.3
Calories: 68
Fat (gm): 2.6
Saturated fat (gm): 0.3
Cholesterol (mg): 0
Sodium (mg): 198
Protein (gm): 2.4
Carbohydrate (gm): 5.3

1. Place all ingredients, except mushrooms, in a jar with a tight-fitting lid; shake well and pour over mushrooms in large bowl. Refrigerate 1 or 2 days for flavors to develop; drain and serve with wooden picks.

Tomato-Herb Croustades

6 servings (2 each)

1½ cups chopped, peeled seeded plum tomatoes
½ cup chopped fresh, *or* 1 tablespoon dried, basil leaves
1 tablespoon chopped fresh, *or* 1
    teaspoon dried, oregano leaves
Salt and pepper, to taste
Bruschetta (p. 420)

Per Serving
Net Carbohydrate (gm): 7.6
Calories: 72
Fat (gm): 3.7
Saturated fat (gm): 0.5
Cholesterol (mg): 4
Sodium (mg): 158
Protein (gm): 2.7
Carbohydrate (gm): 8.3

1. Mix tomatoes and herbs in bowl; season to taste with salt and pepper. Top Bruschetta with tomato mixture and serve immediately.

Tortellini-Vegetable Kabobs

12 servings (2 each)

24 cooked small spinach with cheese, *or*
    plain cheese, tortellini
24 medium mushrooms
6 artichoke hearts, cut into quarters
12 cherry tomatoes, halved
½ cup garlic vinaigrette

Per Serving
Net Carbohydrate (gm): 7.6
Calories: 72
Fat (gm): 3.7
Saturated fat (gm): 0.5
Cholesterol (mg): 4
Sodium (mg): 158
Protein (gm): 2.7
Carbohydrate (gm): 8.3

1. Alternate tortellini, mushrooms, artichokes, and tomatoes on 6-inch skewers; place in a 13 x 9-inch glass baking dish. Drizzle vinaigrette dressing over kabobs.

2. Bake, uncovered, at 350 degrees until mushrooms are tender and kabobs are warm, about 15 minutes.

Artichokes with Green Sauce

4 servings

¼ cup dry white wine, *or* vegetable broth
2 tablespoons lemon juice
1 tablespoon finely chopped parsley
½ teaspoon dried marjoram leaves
¼ teaspoon dried tarragon leaves
1 can (8½ ounces) artichoke hearts, drained

Per Serving
Net Carbohydrate (gm): 4.5
Calories: 35
Fat (gm): 0
Saturated fat (gm): 0
Cholesterol (mg): 0
Sodium (mg): 178
Protein (gm): 1.6
Carbohydrate (gm): 5.3

1. Combine wine, lemon juice, and herbs. Pour mixture over artichoke hearts; refrigerate 1 to 2 hours for flavors to blend. Serve with wooden picks.

Mini Cheese Quiches

15 servings (2 each)

1 egg
16 ounces small-curd cottage cheese
3 tablespoons plain yogurt
1 cup (4 ounces) shredded Swiss cheese
½ cup biscuit baking mix
¾ teaspoon dried dill weed
¼ teaspoon pepper
1 tablespoon butter, melted

Per Serving
Net Carbohydrate (gm): 4
Calories: 88
Fat (gm): 4.5
Saturated fat (gm): 2.4
Cholesterol (mg): 25.6
Sodium (mg): 203
Protein (gm): 7.2
Carbohydrate (gm): 4.1

1. Combine all ingredients in medium bowl. Spoon mixture into lightly greased miniature muffin cups, filling each ⅔ full. Bake at 375 degrees until set, 25 to 30 minutes. Let stand in pans on wire racks 5 to 10 minutes; remove from pans. Serve warm.

Easy Microwave Nachos

4 servings

16 baked tortilla chips
¼ cup (1 ounce) shredded mozzarella cheese
2 green onions and tops, thinly sliced
1–2 teaspoons minced jalapeño chili
2 tablespoons chopped cilantro
¼ cup mild, *or* medium, tomato salsa

Per Serving
Net Carbohydrate (gm): 7.1
Calories: 59
Fat (gm): 1.2
Saturated fat (gm): 0.6
Cholesterol (mg): 3.4
Sodium (mg): 222
Protein (gm): 3.1
Carbohydrate (gm): 8.1

1. Arrange tortilla chips on glass dinner plate; sprinkle with cheese, green onions, and jalapeño chili. Microwave on High just until cheese melts, 30 to 60 seconds. Sprinkle with cilantro and serve warm with salsa.

Sweet-and-Sour Chicken Chunks

12 servings

½ cup chopped onion
½ cup chopped green bell pepper
1 clove garlic, minced
1 tablespoon olive oil
1½ pounds cooked boneless, skinless chicken breast,
    cut into ¾-inch pieces
Sweet-and-Sour Sauce (recipe follows)

Per Serving
Net Carbohydrate (gm): 4
Calories: 115
Fat (gm): 2.9
Saturated fat (gm): 0.6
Cholesterol (mg): 44.3
Sodium (mg): 129
Protein (gm): 16.9
Carbohydrate (gm): 4.3

1. Sauté onion, green pepper, and garlic in oil until tender, about 5 minutes. Add chicken and sauté until browned, 3 to 4 minutes. Stir in Sweet-and-Sour Sauce; cook until sauce is bubbly, about 5 minutes. Spoon into serving bowl; serve with wooden picks.

Sweet-and-Sour Sauce

makes about 1 cup

1 tablespoon cornstarch
⅓ cup chicken broth
⅓ cup red wine vinegar
2 tablespoons frozen pineapple juice concentrate
1 tablespoon soy sauce
¼ teaspoon garlic powder
¼ teaspoon ground ginger
1 tablespoon packed brown sugar

1. Mix cornstarch and chicken broth in small saucepan until smooth; stir in remaining ingredients and heat to boiling. Boil, stirring, until thickened, about 1 minute.

Baked Clams

6 servings (2 each)

12 clams in shells
¾ cup unseasoned dry bread crumbs
6 tablespoons dry white wine, *or* clam juice
¼ cup chopped parsley
3 cloves garlic, finely chopped
1 teaspoon Italian seasoning
¼ teaspoon pepper

Per Serving
Net Carbohydrate (gm): 10.9
Calories: 88
Fat (gm): 1
Saturated fat (gm): 0.2
Cholesterol (mg): 9.6
Sodium (mg): 135
Protein (gm): 5.5
Carbohydrate (gm): 11.3

1. Open clams above bowl, reserving clam liquor. Arrange clams in shells in a single layer in a shallow baking dish.

2. Combine remaining ingredients in bowl; spoon mixture over clams and drizzle with reserved clam liquor. Bake, uncovered, at 375 degrees for 15 to 20 minutes or until browned.

Mussels in Red Sauce

6 servings

12 ounces canned mussels, drained
3 jars (2½ ounces each) chopped pimiento, drained
⅓ cup mayonnaise
1–2 tablespoons Dijon mustard
1 tablespoon dry sherry, optional
1½ teaspoons lemon juice

Per Serving
Net Carbohydrate (gm): 5.4
Calories: 156
Fat (gm): 9.8
Saturated fat (gm): 1.5
Cholesterol (mg): 7.3
Sodium (mg): 623
Protein (gm): 10.9
Carbohydrate (gm): 6

1. Place mussels on platter. Combine remaining ingredients and serve with mussels.

Shrimp with Horseradish Cocktail Sauce

8 servings

2 quarts water
¼ cup sliced onion
1 clove garlic, quartered
1 bay leaf
2 small ribs celery with leaves
½ lemon, sliced
1½ pounds medium shrimp, shelled, deveined
Horseradish Cocktail Sauce (recipe follows)

Per Serving
Net Carbohydrate (gm): 8.4
Calories: 123
Fat (gm): 1.6
Saturated fat (gm): 0.3
Cholesterol (mg): 129.3
Sodium (mg): 415
Protein (gm): 18
Carbohydrate (gm): 9.5

1. Heat water, onion, garlic, bay leaf, celery, and lemon to boiling in large saucepan; add shrimp. Reduce heat and simmer, uncovered, until shrimp turn pink, 3 to 4 minutes; drain. Refrigerate shrimp until chilled, about 1 hour. Serve with Horseradish Cocktail Sauce.

Horseradish Cocktail Sauce

makes about 1 cup

¾ cup catsup
1 tablespoon prepared horseradish
2 tablespoons lemon juice
¼ cup finely chopped celery
2 tablespoons minced parsley
1 teaspoon Worcestershire sauce
¼ teaspoon red pepper sauce

1. Combine all ingredients.

Oriental Skewered Shrimp

8 servings

1½ pounds medium shrimp, peeled, deveined
8 cherry tomatoes
8 yellow pickled peppers
¾ cup dry sherry, *or* chicken broth
¼ cup soy sauce
½ teaspoon ground ginger
1 teaspoon brown sugar

Per Serving
Net Carbohydrate (gm): 5
Calories: 135
Fat (gm): 1.5
Saturated fat (gm): 0.3
Cholesterol (mg): 129.3
Sodium (mg): 833
Protein (gm): 18
Carbohydrate (gm): 5.3

1. Thread shrimp lengthwise on eight 9-inch skewers. Thread a cherry tomato and a yellow pickled pepper at the end of each skewer. Place skewers in a glass baking dish; pour combined remaining ingredients over. Refrigerate 1 hour, turning skewers occasionally. Drain and reserve marinade.

2. Broil kabobs 6 inches from heat source until shrimp are cooked, 4 to 5 minutes, turning once. Heat reserved marinade to boiling; serve with kabobs.

Cheeseburgers Supreme

4 servings

1 pound ground beef eye of round steak, *or*
    95% lean ground beef
¼ cup finely chopped onion
3 tablespoons water
½ teaspoon salt
¼ teaspoon pepper
4 slices (1 ounce each) Cheddar, *or* Swiss, cheese
4 pieces thin-sliced whole wheat bread, toasted

Per Serving
Net Carbohydrate (gm): 8
Calories: 322
Fat (gm): 16.6
Saturated fat (gm): 7.8
Cholesterol (mg): 87.7
Sodium (mg): 635
Protein (gm): 33.6
Carbohydrate (gm): 11

1. Mix ground beef, onion, water, salt, and pepper in medium bowl just until blended. Shape mixture into four 1-inch-thick patties.

2. Cook burgers in lightly greased skillet to desired degree of doneness, 3 to 4 minutes per side for medium. Top each burger with slice of cheese; cover skillet and cook until cheese is beginning to melt, 1 to 2 minutes. Serve burgers on toasted bread.

Crab Melt

2 servings

4 ounces cooked crabmeat, flaked
2 tablespoons chopped red bell pepper
1 green onion and top, thinly sliced
2 tablespoons mayonnaise
2 tablespoons sour cream
¼–½ teaspoon dried dill weed
1–2 teaspoons lemon juice
Salt and pepper, to taste
2 pieces thin-sliced whole wheat bread
2 slices (¾ ounce each) processed American cheese

Per Serving
Net Carbohydrate (gm): 9.5
Calories: 311
Fat (gm): 21.6
Saturated fat (gm): 7.5
Cholesterol (mg): 63.4
Sodium (mg): 1115
Protein (gm): 18.6
Carbohydrate (gm): 12.7

1. Mix crabmeat, red bell pepper, green onion, mayonnaise, sour cream, and dill weed in small bowl; season to taste with lemon juice, salt, and pepper. Spread on bread slices and top with cheese.

2. Bake at 400 degrees, or broil 6 inches from heat source, until sandwiches are warm and cheese melted, 4 to 5 minutes.

Fried Egg and Bacon Sandwich

2 servings

2 pieces thin-sliced whole wheat bread
1 tablespoon butter, softened
2 tablespoons chili sauce
4 slices bacon, fried crisp
2 eggs, fried
Chopped chives, as garnish

Per Serving
Net Carbohydrate (gm): 10.8
Calories: 279
Fat (gm): 19.8
Saturated fat (gm): 8
Cholesterol (mg): 238.3
Sodium (mg): 744
Protein (gm): 12.6
Carbohydrate (gm): 14.5

1. Spread both sides of bread slices very lightly with butter; cook in large skillet over medium heat until browned, 1 to 2 minutes on each side. Spread bread with chili sauce; top with bacon and eggs; sprinkle with chives.

Mock Monte Cristo Sandwiches

4 servings

4 pieces thin-sliced whole wheat bread
2 eggs, beaten
3 ounces thinly sliced lean smoked ham
3 ounces thinly sliced turkey
4 slices (4 ounces) Cheddar cheese

Per Serving
Net Carbohydrate (gm): 8.8
Calories: 263
Fat (gm): 16.4
Saturated fat (gm): 7.5
Cholesterol (mg): 162.1
Sodium (mg): 928
Protein (gm): 20
Carbohydrate (gm): 11.6

1. Dip bread slices in beaten egg, coating both sides well. Cook in greased large skillet over medium to medium-low heat until browned on the bottom, 3 to 5 minutes. Turn bread browned side up. Arrange meats and cheese on bread; cook, covered, until bread is browned on the bottom and cheese is melted, 3 to 5 minutes.

NINE

Desserts

Glazed Applesauce-Raisin Cake

24 servings

1 cup unsweetened applesauce
⅔ cup canola oil
2 eggs
1 teaspoon maple, *or* vanilla, extract
½ cup raisins
½ cup coarsely chopped walnuts, optional
2 cups whole wheat pastry flour
7¼ teaspoons Equal® for Recipes, *or* 24 packets Equal® sweetener
1 teaspoon baking soda
½ teaspoon salt
1½ teaspoons ground cinnamon
¼ teaspoon ground nutmeg
⅛ teaspoon ground cloves
Vanilla Cream Cheese Glaze (recipe follows)

Per Serving
Net Carbohydrate (gm): 10.8
Calories: 130
Fat (gm): 8.3
Saturated fat (gm): 2
Cholesterol (mg): 22.9
Sodium (mg): 121
Protein (gm): 2.4
Carbohydrate (gm): 12.5

1. Mix applesauce, oil, eggs, maple extract, raisins, and walnuts in large bowl. Add combined flour, Equal® for Recipes, baking soda, salt, and spices, mixing until blended.

2. Spoon batter into greased 13 x 9-inch baking pan. Bake at 350 degrees until cake is browned and toothpick inserted in center comes out clean, 18 to 20 minutes (do not overbake!). Cool on wire rack. Drizzle with Vanilla Cream Cheese Glaze.

Vanilla Cream Cheese Glaze

makes about ½ cup

½ package (8-ounce size) cream cheese, softened
½ teaspoon vanilla
1 teaspoon Equal® for Recipes, *or* 3 packets Equal® sweetener
Reduced-fat milk

1. Beat cream cheese, vanilla, Equal® for Recipes, and enough milk to make desired consistency.

Blueberry Crumb Cake

9–12 servings

Per Serving
Net Carbohydrate (gm): 16.6
Calories: 194
Fat (gm): 11.9
Saturated fat (gm): 7
Cholesterol (mg): 53.4
Sodium (mg): 349
Protein (gm): 3.9
Carbohydrate (gm): 19.5

4 tablespoons butter
1 egg
5½ teaspoons Equal® for Recipes, *or*
    18 packets Equal® sweetener
1 cup whole wheat pastry flour
1½ teaspoons baking powder
½ teaspoon baking soda
¼ teaspoon salt
1 teaspoon ground cinnamon
½ cup buttermilk
½ teaspoon vanilla
Blueberry Crumb Topping (recipe follows)

1. Beat butter, egg, and Equal® for Recipes in medium bowl until smooth. Mix in combined flour, baking powder, baking soda, salt, and cinnamon alternately with combined buttermilk and vanilla, beginning and ending with dry ingredients.

2. Pour batter into greased and floured 8-inch square cake pan; sprinkle Blueberry Crumb Topping evenly over batter. Bake at 350 degrees until toothpick inserted in cake comes out clean, 35 to 40 minutes. Serve warm.

Blueberry Crumb Topping

⅓ cup whole wheat pastry flour
3½ teaspoons Equal® for Recipes, *or* 12 packets Equal® sweetener
1 teaspoon ground cinnamon
½ teaspoon maple extract
4 tablespoons cold butter, cut into pieces
1 cup fresh, *or* frozen, blueberries

1. Combine flour, Equal® for Recipes, and cinnamon in small bowl; sprinkle with maple extract. Cut in butter until mixture resembles coarse crumbs. Add blueberries and toss.

Carrot Snack Bars

18 bars (1 per serving)

4 tablespoons butter, softened
⅔ cup packed light brown sugar
¾ cup reduced-fat milk
1 egg
1 tablespoon lemon juice
1 teaspoon vanilla
1¼ cups quick-cooking oats
¾ cup whole wheat pastry flour
2 teaspoons baking powder
¼ teaspoon baking soda
1 teaspoon ground cinnamon
¼ teaspoon salt
1 cup shredded carrots
½ cup chopped walnuts
⅓ cup raisins
Whipped Cream Cheese Topping (recipe follows)

Per Serving
Net Carbohydrate (gm): 19.9
Calories: 192
Fat (gm): 10.8
Saturated fat (gm): 5.3
Cholesterol (mg): 35
Sodium (mg): 186
Protein (gm): 3.9
Carbohydrate (gm): 21.6

1. Beat butter and brown sugar in large bowl until blended; beat in milk, egg, lemon juice, and vanilla. Mix in combined oats, flour, baking powder, baking soda, cinnamon, and salt; mix in carrots, walnuts, and raisins.

2. Pour batter into greased 11 x 7-inch baking pan. Bake at 350 degrees until toothpick inserted in center comes out clean, about 30 minutes. Cool on wire rack. Cut into 18 bars. Serve with Whipped Cream Cheese Topping.

Whipped Cream Cheese Topping

makes about 1¼ cups

1 package (8 ounces) cream cheese, softened
2 tablespoons packed light brown sugar
¼ cup sour cream

Mix all ingredients.

Oatmeal Date Bars

24 bars (1 per serving)

¾ cup chopped dates
½ cup boiling water
6 tablespoons butter, softened
¾ cup packed light brown sugar
2 eggs
2 tablespoons honey
1 teaspoon vanilla
1½ cups quick-cooking oats
1 cup whole wheat pastry flour
½ teaspoon baking soda
½ teaspoon salt
1 teaspoon ground cinnamon
⅛ teaspoon ground nutmeg
Whipped topping, optional

Per Serving
Net Carbohydrate (gm): 17.9
Calories: 116
Fat (gm): 4
Saturated fat (gm): 2.1
Cholesterol (mg): 25.9
Sodium (mg): 114
Protein (gm): 2
Carbohydrate (gm): 19.4

1. Process dates and boiling water in food processor or blender until smooth. Beat butter and brown sugar in large bowl until blended; beat in eggs, honey, vanilla, and date mixture. Mix in combined remaining ingredients, except whipped topping.

2. Spread batter in greased 13 x 9-inch baking pan. Bake at 375 degrees until wooden pick inserted in center comes out clean, 15 to 18 minutes. Cool on wire rack. Cut into 24 bars. Serve with whipped topping if desired.

Chocolate-Marmalade Cake Squares

24 servings

½ cup quick-cooking oats
1¼ cups packed light brown sugar
1¼ cups whole wheat pastry flour
¾ cup unsweetened cocoa
1½ teaspoons baking powder
1½ teaspoons baking soda
½ teaspoon salt
1 cup reduced-fat milk
⅓ cup vegetable oil
2 teaspoons vanilla
1 egg
1 egg white
1 cup boiling water
1 ounce unsweetened chocolate, melted
½ cup no-sugar-added orange marmalade

Per Serving
Net Carbohydrate (gm): 20.2
Calories: 132
Fat (gm): 4.3
Saturated fat (gm): 0.8
Cholesterol (mg): 9.7
Sodium (mg): 185
Protein (gm): 2.4
Carbohydrate (gm): 21.8

1. Process oats in blender until finely chopped, but not ground. Combine oats, brown sugar, flour, cocoa, baking powder, baking soda, and salt in large bowl. Mix milk, oil, vanilla, egg, and egg whites, beating lightly to blend; add to flour mixture and beat 2 minutes at medium speed. Mix in boiling water and melted chocolate.

2. Pour batter into greased 13 x 9-inch baking pan; bake at 350 degrees until cake springs back when touched lightly, about 35 minutes. Cool on wire rack; spread with orange marmalade.

Cheesecake Cupcakes

20 cupcakes (1 per serving)

¾ cup whole wheat pastry flour
⅔ cup packed light brown sugar
⅓ cup unsweetened cocoa
¾ teaspoon baking soda
½ teaspoon salt
¾ cup buttermilk
¼ cup vegetable shortening
1 egg
1 teaspoon vanilla
Cheesecake Topping (recipe follows)

Per Serving
Net Carbohydrate (gm): 14.8
Calories: 135
Fat (gm): 7.2
Saturated fat (gm): 3.3
Cholesterol (mg): 34.1
Sodium (mg): 130
Protein (gm): 2.7
Carbohydrate (gm): 15.6

1. Combine all ingredients, except Cheesecake Topping, in large bowl. Beat at low speed until blended; beat at high speed 3 minutes, scraping side of bowl occasionally.

2. Pour batter into paper-lined muffin cups, filling each about ½ full. Spread about 1 tablespoon Cheesecake Topping over batter in each cup, covering batter completely. Bake at 350 degrees until golden, about 30 minutes. Cool in pans on wire rack.

Cheesecake Topping

1 package (8 ounces) cream cheese, softened
⅓ cup packed light brown sugar
1 egg

1. Mix all ingredients until smooth.

Macaroon Cupcakes

24 cupcakes (1 per serving)

6 egg whites
½ teaspoon cream of tartar
1¼ cups packed light brown sugar, divided
½ teaspoon vanilla
¾ cup whole wheat pastry flour
½ teaspoon baking powder
½ teaspoon salt
1¼ cups flaked coconut
Sliced almonds, as garnish

Per Serving
Net Carbohydrate (gm): 16.3
Calories: 91
Fat (gm): 2.1
Saturated fat (gm): 2.1
Cholesterol (mg): 0
Sodium (mg): 96
Protein (gm): 1.7
Carbohydrate (gm): 16.8

1. Beat egg whites and cream of tartar to soft peaks in large bowl; beat to stiff peaks, adding ¼ cup brown sugar gradually. Beat in vanilla. Combine remaining 1 cup brown sugar, flour, baking powder, and salt; fold into beaten egg white mixture. Fold in coconut.

2. Spoon batter into paper-lined muffin cups; top each with 2 or 3 almond slices. Bake at 300 degrees until just beginning to brown, about 30 minutes. Cool on wire rack.

Old-Fashioned Custard Pie

10 servings

Pie Pastry (see p. 471)
4 eggs
¼ teaspoon salt
2½ cups reduced-fat milk
5½ teaspoons Equal® for Recipes, *or*
    18 packets Equal® sweetener
1½ teaspoons vanilla
¼ teaspoon ground cinnamon
⅛ teaspoon ground nutmeg

Per Serving
Net Carbohydrate (gm): 14.2
Calories: 164
Fat (gm): 8.3
Saturated fat (gm): 4.4
Cholesterol (mg): 103
Sodium (mg): 222
Protein (gm): 6.7
Carbohydrate (gm): 16

1. Roll Pie Pastry on floured surface into circle 1½ inches larger than inverted 9-inch pie pan; ease pastry into pan, flute, and trim.

2. Beat eggs and salt in large bowl until thick and lemon colored, about 5 minutes. Mix in milk, Equal® for Recipes, and remaining ingredients; pour into pastry.

3. Bake at 425 degrees 15 minutes; reduce temperature to 350 degrees and bake until sharp knife inserted halfway between center and edge comes out clean, about 12 minutes. Cool on wire rack. Serve at room temperature, or refrigerate and serve chilled.

Variation:

Coconut Custard Pie—Make recipe as above, reducing milk to 2 cups, adding ½ cup flaked coconut, and substituting 1 to 2 teaspoons coconut extract for the vanilla.

Black Bottom Pie

10 servings

Pie Pastry (recipe follows)
Pastry Cream (recipe follows)
1 ounce unsweetened chocolate, melted
2 tablespoons unsweetened cocoa
4 teaspoons vanilla, divided
1 envelope unflavored gelatin
¼ cup plus 2 tablespoons water, divided
2 teaspoons meringue powder
¼ cup packed light brown sugar
1½ cups whipped topping
Grated unsweetened chocolate, as garnish

Per Serving
Net Carbohydrate (gm): 10.6
Calories: 96
Fat (gm): 4.2
Saturated fat (gm): 3.2
Cholesterol (mg): 12.4
Sodium (mg): 24
Protein (gm): 2.2
Carbohydrate (gm): 11.4

1. Roll Pie Pastry into circle 1½ inches larger than inverted 9-inch pie pan; ease pastry into pan and trim. Pierce bottom of pastry with tines of a fork. Bake at 425 degrees until browned, about 15 minutes. Cool on wire rack.

2. Mix 1 cup warm Pastry Cream with melted chocolate, cocoa, and 2 teaspoons vanilla in small bowl. Spread evenly in cooled crust and refrigerate. Transfer remaining Pastry Cream to bowl and cover surface with plastic wrap; cool. Refrigerate until chilled, about 1 hour.

3. Sprinkle gelatin over ¼ cup water in small saucepan; let stand 3 to 4 minutes to soften. Cook over low heat, stirring, until dissolved; add to chilled Pastry Cream. Refrigerate, stirring occasionally, until mixture mounds slightly when dropped from spoon.

4. Beat meringue powder with remaining 2 tablespoons water until foamy; beat to stiff peaks, gradually adding brown sugar. Beat in remaining 2 teaspoons vanilla. Fold gelatin mixture into meringue. Spread over chocolate layer in crust. Refrigerate until set, 2 to 3 hours. Top with whipped topping; sprinkle with grated chocolate.

Variation:

Banana Black Bottom Pie—Make pie through Step 2. Arrange 1 cup sliced bananas over chocolate layer. Stir 1 tablespoon banana liqueur, *or* ½ teaspoon banana extract, into remaining Pastry Cream. Complete pie as above; sprinkle with chopped pecans and grated chocolate.

Pie Pastry

makes one 9- or 10-inch pastry crust

1¼ cups whole wheat pastry flour
2 tablespoons Splenda® sweetener, *or* 3 packets Equal® sweetener
¼ teaspoon salt
4–5 tablespoons cold butter, cut into pieces
3–5 tablespoons ice water

1. Combine flour, Splenda®, and salt in medium bowl. Cut in butter with pastry blender or 2 knives until mixture resembles coarse crumbs. Sprinkle with water, 1 tablespoon at a time, mixing lightly with a fork after each addition until pastry just holds together. Refrigerate, covered, 30 minutes.

Pastry Cream

makes about 2 cups

1 cup Splenda® sweetener
¼ cup all-purpose flour
2 cups reduced-fat milk
4 egg yolks, lightly beaten
1 tablespoon vanilla

1. Combine Splenda® and flour in small saucepan; whisk in milk. Whisk over medium-high heat until mixture boils and thickens, 2 to 3 minutes. Whisk ½ the milk mixture into egg yolks; whisk yolk mixture back into saucepan. Whisk over low heat until smooth and thick, about 1 minute. Stir in vanilla.

Tip: Meringue powder replaces raw egg whites in the pie filling. Meringue powder can be purchased in large supermarkets, gourmet, or specialty stores.

Strawberry Cream Pie

8 servings

Graham Cracker Crust (recipe follows)
1 package (8 ounces) cream cheese, softened
5¼ teaspoons Equal® for Recipes, *or*
   16 packets Equal® sweetener, divided
1 teaspoon vanilla
1 cup boiling water
1 package (.3 ounces) sugar-free strawberry gelatin
2 cups sliced strawberries
Whipped topping, as garnish

Per Serving
Net Carbohydrate (gm): 15
Calories: 245
Fat (gm): 17.8
Saturated fat (gm): 10.4
Cholesterol (mg): 47.6
Sodium (mg): 299
Protein (gm): 4.7
Carbohydrate (gm): 16.3

1. Prepare Graham Cracker Crust.

2. Beat cream cheese, 1¾ teaspoons Equal® for Recipes, and vanilla in small bowl until smooth; spread evenly in bottom of crust.

3. Pour boiling water over gelatin and remaining 3½ teaspoons Equal® for Recipes in bowl, whisking until gelatin is dissolved. Refrigerate until mixture is the consistency of unbeaten egg whites, 20 to 30 minutes.

4. Arrange half the strawberries over the cream cheese; spoon half the gelatin mixture over strawberries. Arrange remaining strawberries over pie and spoon remaining gelatin mixture over. Refrigerate until pie is set and chilled, 2 to 3 hours. Serve with whipped topping.

Graham Cracker Crust

makes one 9-inch crust

1¼ cups graham cracker crumbs
4–5 tablespoons butter, melted
1 teaspoon Equal® for Recipes, *or* 3 packets Equal® sweetener

1. Mix all ingredients and transfer to 9-inch pie pan; pat evenly on bottom and sides of pan. Bake at 350 degrees until lightly browned, 6 to 8 minutes. Cool.

Variations:

Double Berry Pie—Make recipe as above, substituting 1 cup blueberries for 1 cup of the strawberries. Arrange 1 cup blueberries over cream cheese in pie crust; spoon half the gelatin mixture over berries. Top with 1 cup sliced strawberries, and spoon remaining gelatin mixture over.

Strawberry Banana Pie—Make recipe as above, substituting sugar-free strawberry-banana gelatin for the strawberry gelatin and 1 small sliced banana for 1 cup of the strawberries. Arrange banana slices over cream cheese; spoon half the gelatin mixture over. Top with 1 cup sliced strawberries and spoon remaining gelatin mixture over.

Lemon Cream Pie

10 servings

Pie Pastry (see p. 471)
Lemon Cream (recipe follows)
Whipped topping, as garnish
Lemon slices, halved, as garnish

Per Serving
Net Carbohydrate (gm): 18.7
Calories: 177
Fat (gm): 8.9
Saturated fat (gm): 4.9
Cholesterol (mg): 84.1
Sodium (mg): 148
Protein (gm): 4.9
Carbohydrate (gm): 20.6

1. Roll Pie Pastry on floured surface into circle 1½ inches larger than inverted 9-inch pie pan; ease pastry into pan and trim. Pierce bottom of pastry with tines of a fork. Bake at 425 degrees until browned, about 15 minutes. Cool on wire rack.

2. Spoon Lemon Cream into baked crust and refrigerate until chilled, 2 to 3 hours. Garnish pie with rosettes or dollops of whipped topping and lemon slices.

Lemon Cream

makes about 3 cups

¼ cup cornstarch
2 tablespoons all-purpose flour
5½ teaspoons Equal® for Recipes, *or* 18 packets Equal® sweetener
2 cups reduced-fat milk
½ cup lemon juice
1 teaspoon finely grated lemon rind
3 egg yolks
1–2 tablespoons butter
½ teaspoon lemon extract

1. Combine cornstarch, flour, Equal® for Recipes, milk, lemon juice, and rind in medium saucepan; heat to boiling over medium heat, whisking until thickened, about 1 minute. Whisk about 1 cup milk mixture into egg yolks; whisk yolk mixture back into saucepan. Whisk over low heat until thickened, about 1 minute. Whisk in butter and lemon extract. Cool 15 minutes, whisking occasionally.

Key Lime Pie

8 servings

Graham Cracker Crust (see p. 472)
1 envelope unflavored gelatin
1¾ cups reduced-fat milk, divided
1 package (8 ounces) cream cheese, softened
½ cup key lime, *or* Persian lime, juice
3½ teaspoons Equal® for Recipes, *or*
    12 packets Equal® sweetener
Whipped topping, as garnish
Mint sprigs, as garnish

Per Serving
Net Carbohydrate (gm): 12.4
Calories: 210
Fat (gm): 15.9
Saturated fat (gm): 9.5
Cholesterol (mg): 44
Sodium (mg): 236
Protein (gm): 4.6
Carbohydrate (gm): 12.8

1. Make Graham Cracker Crust, decreasing graham cracker crumbs to 1 cup and melted butter to 3 to 4 tablespoons. Pat mixture evenly on bottom and ½ inch up sides of 7-inch springform pan. Do not bake.

2. Sprinkle gelatin over ½ cup of the milk in small saucepan; let stand 2 to 3 minutes. Heat just to simmering, stirring constantly; cool.

3. Beat cream cheese until fluffy in medium bowl; beat in remaining 1¼ cups milk and gelatin mixture. Mix in lime juice and Equal® for Recipes. Pour into pie crust; refrigerate until set, 3 to 4 hours.

4. Remove sides of pan; place pie on serving plate. Garnish with whipped topping and mint.

Peach Chiffon Pie

10 servings

Gingersnap Crumb Crust (recipe follows)
1 can (8 ounces) sliced peaches in juice, drained
1 carton (8 ounces) sugar-free peach yogurt
1 tablespoon honey
1 teaspoon lemon juice
1 envelope unflavored gelatin
½ cup cold water, divided
4 teaspoons meringue powder
2 tablespoons packed light brown sugar
Ground nutmeg, as garnish

Per Serving
Net Carbohydrate (gm): 17
Calories: 110
Fat (gm): 3.3
Saturated fat (gm): 0.7
Cholesterol (mg): 0.5
Sodium (mg): 128
Protein (gm): 3.1
Carbohydrate (gm): 17.6

1. Make Gingersnap Crumb Crust, using 9-inch pie pan.

2. Reserve 3 peach slices to use as garnish. Process remaining peaches, yogurt, honey, and lemon juice in blender or food processor until smooth.

3. Sprinkle gelatin over ¼ cup water in small saucepan; let stand until gelatin is softened. Cook over low heat, stirring, until gelatin is dissolved; add to peach mixture with blender running.

4. Beat meringue powder with remaining ¼ cup water until foamy; continue beating, gradually adding brown sugar, until stiff peaks form. Fold peach mixture into meringue. Pour filling into crust. Chill 2 to 3 hours before serving. Garnish with reserved peach slices and sprinkle with nutmeg.

Gingersnap Crumb Crust

makes one 9-inch crust

½ cup graham cracker crumbs
½ cup gingersnap cookie crumbs
2–3 tablespoons butter
1–2 tablespoons honey

1. Combine graham cracker crumbs, gingersnap crumbs, and butter in 9-inch pie pan; add enough honey for mixture to stick together. Pat mixture evenly on bottom and sides of pan. Bake at 350 degrees 8 to 10 minutes or until edge of crust is lightly browned. Cool on wire rack.

Tip: Meringue powder replaces raw egg whites in this recipe. Meringue powder can be purchased in large supermarkets, gourmet shops, or specialty stores.

Pumpkin Chiffon Pie

10 servings

Pie Pastry (see p. 471)
2½ teaspoons Equal® for Recipes, *or*
    9 packets Equal® sweetener
1 envelope unflavored gelatin
1 teaspoon cornstarch
½ cup reduced-fat milk
2 egg yolks
2 cups canned pumpkin
1 teaspoon pumpkin pie spice
1 teaspoon vanilla
⅛ teaspoon salt
1 cup whipped topping
Whipped topping, as garnish

Per Serving
Net Carbohydrate (gm): 15.3
Calories: 158
Fat (gm): 8.2
Saturated fat (gm): 5.2
Cholesterol (mg): 56.6
Sodium (mg): 153
Protein (gm): 4.3
Carbohydrate (gm): 18.6

1. Roll Pie Pastry into circle 1½ inches larger than inverted 9-inch pie pan; ease pastry into pan, flute, and trim. Pierce bottom of pastry with tines of a fork. Bake at 425 degrees until browned, about 15 minutes. Cool on wire rack.

2. Whisk Equal® for Recipes, gelatin, cornstarch, and milk in medium saucepan over medium heat until mixture boils and thickens, 2 to 3 minutes. Whisk half the milk mixture into the egg yolks; whisk egg mixture back into saucepan. Whisk over low heat until thickened, 1 to 2 minutes. Remove from heat and stir in pumpkin, pumpkin pie spice, vanilla, and salt. Cool to room temperature; refrigerate until mixture mounds when dropped from a spoon, about 20 minutes.

3. Whisk mixture gently until smooth; fold in 1 cup whipped topping and spoon into pie crust, smoothing top. Refrigerate until set, 3 to 4 hours. Garnish slices with dollops of whipped topping.

Apple Walnut Streusel Tart

10 servings

Pie Pastry (see p. 471)
3 cups sliced (¼ inch), peeled baking apples
1¾ teaspoons Equal® for Recipes, *or*
    6 packets Equal® sweetener
Walnut Streusel (recipe follows)
⅓ cup no-sugar-added apricot preserves, warm

Per Serving
Net Carbohydrate (gm): 19.1
Calories: 170
Fat (gm): 8.7
Saturated fat (gm): 4.7
Cholesterol (mg): 19.7
Sodium (mg): 133
Protein (gm): 2.7
Carbohydrate (gm): 22.3

1. Roll Pie Pastry into circle 1½ inches larger than inverted 10-inch tart pan or quiche dish. Ease pastry into pan and trim.

2. Arrange apples in circles on pastry; sprinkle with 1¾ teaspoons Equal® for Recipes; sprinkle with Walnut Streusel.

3. Bake at 400 degrees until pastry is golden and apples are tender, 25 to 30 minutes. Cool on wire rack. Drizzle or brush preserves over apples.

Walnut Streusel

makes about ⅓ cup

2 tablespoons all-purpose pastry flour
1¾ teaspoons Equal® for Recipes, *or* 6 packets Equal® sweetener
½ teaspoon ground cinnamon
2 tablespoons cold butter, cut into pieces
2–4 tablespoons coarsely chopped walnuts

1. Combine flour, Equal® for Recipes, and cinnamon in small bowl; cut in butter until mixture resembles coarse crumbs. Stir in walnuts.

Pineapple Crumb Tart

12 servings

1¼ cups whole wheat pastry flour
5½ teaspoons Equal® for Recipes, *or*
    18 packets Equal® sweetener
4 teaspoons cornstarch
¼ teaspoon salt
10 tablespoons cold butter, cut into pieces
1½ teaspoons vanilla
2 cans (8 ounces each) sliced pineapple in juice, well drained
¼ cup no-sugar-added apricot preserves, warm

Per Serving
Net Carbohydrate (gm): 17.4
Calories: 173
Fat (gm): 10.4
Saturated fat (gm): 6.4
Cholesterol (mg): 27.4
Sodium (mg): 153
Protein (gm): 2
Carbohydrate (gm): 19.4

1. Combine flour, Equal® for Recipes, cornstarch, and salt in medium bowl; cut in butter until mixture resembles coarse crumbs. Sprinkle vanilla over mixture and stir with fork to combine. Reserve ½ cup crumb mixture. Pat remaining mixture evenly on bottom of ungreased 10-inch tart pan or quiche dish. Bake at 350 degrees until browned, about 15 minutes. Cool on wire rack.

2. Cut pineapple slices in half and arrange on crust; sprinkle with reserved ½ cup crumb mixture. Bake at 400 degrees until topping is browned, about 10 minutes. Cool on wire rack; drizzle with preserves.

Raspberry Cream Tart

12 servings

Pie Pastry (see p. 471)
2½ teaspoons Equal® for Recipes, *or*
    8 packets Equal® sweetener
⅓ cup cornstarch
1½ cups reduced-fat milk
3 eggs, lightly beaten
2 teaspoons finely grated lemon, *or* orange, rind
¼ teaspoon lemon extract, optional
2 pints raspberries
¼ cup no-sugar-added seedless raspberry preserves, warm

Per Serving
Net Carbohydrate (gm): 17.2
Calories: 158
Fat (gm): 6.4
Saturated fat (gm): 3.3
Cholesterol (mg): 66.5
Sodium (mg): 122
Protein (gm): 4.8
Carbohydrate (gm): 21.7

1. Roll Pie Pastry into circle 1½ inches larger than inverted 10-inch tart pan or quiche dish; ease pastry into pan and trim. Pierce bottom of pastry with tines of a fork. Bake at 425 degrees until crust is browned, about 10 minutes. Cool on wire rack.

2. Mix Equal® for Recipes and cornstarch in medium saucepan; whisk in milk and heat to boiling, whisking until thickened. Whisk about ½ of the milk mixture into the eggs; whisk egg mixture back into saucepan. Whisk in lemon rind and extract; whisk over low heat until thickened, 1 to 2 minutes. Cool to room temperature, stirring occasionally. Spoon into pie crust.

3. Arrange raspberries, pointed ends up, on custard. Brush raspberries with preserves. Refrigerate until chilled, 1 to 2 hours.

Variation:

Banana Cream Tart—Make recipe as above, substituting 3 medium bananas, sliced, for the raspberries and omitting the raspberry preserves. Cover bottom of baked crust with layer of sliced bananas; cover with custard and refrigerate until chilled, 2 to 3 hours. Before serving, garnish top of tart with remaining bananas and dollops of whipped topping.

Rich Chocolate Cheesecake

16 servings

Graham Cracker Crust (see p. 472)
3 packages (8 ounces each) cream cheese, softened
5½ teaspoons Equal® for Recipes, *or*
    18 packets Equal® sweetener
3 eggs
2 tablespoons cornstarch
1 cup sour cream
⅓ cup Dutch process cocoa
1 teaspoon vanilla
1 cup whipped topping
Chocolate shavings, as garnish

Per Serving
Net Carbohydrate (gm): 10.7
Calories: 277
Fat (gm): 23.3
Saturated fat (gm): 14.3
Cholesterol (mg): 100.1
Sodium (mg): 240
Protein (gm): 6
Carbohydrate (gm): 11.3

1. Make Graham Cracker Crust using 9-inch springform pan. Do not bake.

2. Beat cream cheese and Equal® for Recipes in large bowl until smooth; beat in eggs and cornstarch. Beat in sour cream, cocoa, and vanilla, blending well; pour into crust.

3. Bake cheesecake at 300 degrees just until set in the center, 45 to 50 minutes. Turn oven off and let cheesecake cool in oven with door ajar for 3 hours. Refrigerate 8 hours or overnight.

4. Remove sides of pan; place cheesecake on serving plate. Spread whipped topping over top and garnish with chocolate shavings.

Creamy Cheesecake Melba

16 servings

Vanilla Crumb Crust (recipe follows)
5½ teaspoon Equal® for Recipes, *or*
    18 packets Equal® sweetener
3 packages (8 ounces each) cream cheese, softened
3 eggs
2 tablespoons cornstarch
1½ cups sour cream, divided
1 teaspoon vanilla
Melba Sauce (recipe follows)

Per Serving
Net Carbohydrate (gm): 6.3
Calories: 255
Fat (gm): 22.8
Saturated fat (gm): 13.9
Cholesterol (mg): 102.8
Sodium (mg): 179
Protein (gm): 5.3
Carbohydrate (gm): 8.4

1. Make Vanilla Crumb Crust.

2. Beat cream cheese and Equal® for Recipes in large bowl until fluffy; beat in eggs and cornstarch. Mix in ¾ cup sour cream and vanilla. Pour mixture into crust.

3. Bake at 300 degrees until just set in the center, 45 to 60 minutes. Turn oven off; let cheesecake cool in oven with door ajar 3 hours. Refrigerate 8 hours or overnight.

4. Remove sides of pan; place cheesecake on serving plate. Spread top of cheesecake with remaining ¾ cup sour cream and drizzle with 2 to 3 tablespoons Melba Sauce. Drizzle remaining Melba Sauce on serving plates and top with cheesecake slices.

Vanilla Crumb Crust

makes one 9-inch crust

1¼ cups vanilla wafer crumbs
4–5 tablespoons butter, melted
1 teaspoon Equal® for Recipes, *or* 3 packets Equal® sweetener

1. Mix vanilla wafer crumbs, butter, and Equal® for Recipes in bottom of 9-inch springform pan. Pat mixture evenly on bottom and ½ inch up sides of pan. Bake at 350 degrees until lightly browned, about 8 minutes. Cool on wire rack.

Melba Sauce

makes about 2 cups

4 cups fresh, *or* frozen, thawed, unsweetened raspberries
3½–5 teaspoons Equal® for Recipes, *or* 12–16 packets Equal® sweetener

1. Process raspberries in food processor or blender until smooth; strain and discard seeds. Stir in Equal® for Recipes.

Pumpkin Cheesecake

12–14 servings

Gingersnap Crumb Crust (see p. 474)
3 packages (8 ounces each) cream cheese, softened
1 cup canned pumpkin
3 eggs
7½ teaspoons Equal® for Recipes, *or*
     22 packets Equal® sweetener
2 teaspoons ground cinnamon
1 teaspoon ground cloves
1 teaspoon ground ginger
2 tablespoons cornstarch
1 cup whipped topping
Chopped toasted pecans, as garnish

Per Serving
Net Carbohydrate (gm): 7.8
Calories: 293
Fat (gm): 26.6
Saturated fat (gm): 16.8
Cholesterol (mg): 126.4
Sodium (mg): 233
Protein (gm): 6.3
Carbohydrate (gm): 8.7

1. Make Gingersnap Crumb Crust, using ¾ cup each graham cracker crumbs and gingersnap cookies, and increasing butter to 4 to 5 tablespoons; substitute 1 teaspoon Equal® for Recipes or 3 packets Equal® sweetener for the honey. Reserve 2 tablespoons crumb mixture. Pat remaining mixture evenly on bottom and ½ inch up sides of 9-inch springform pan. Bake at 350 degrees until lightly browned, about 8 minutes. Cool on wire rack.

2. Beat cream cheese until smooth in large bowl; beat in pumpkin and eggs. Mix in Equal® for Recipes, spices, and cornstarch. Pour mixture into crust.

3. Bake at 300 degrees just until set in the center, 45 to 60 minutes; sprinkle with reserved crumbs and return to oven. Turn oven off and let cheesecake cool in oven with door ajar for 3 hours. Refrigerate 8 hours or overnight.

4. Remove sides of springform pan; place cheesecake on serving plate. Spread with whipped topping and sprinkle with pecans.

Almond Cheesecake Squares

24 servings

3 packages (8 ounces each) cream cheese, softened
5½ teaspoons Equal® for Recipes, *or*
     18 packets Equal® sweetener
3 eggs
2 tablespoons cornstarch
1 cup sour cream
¾ teaspoon vanilla
¼ teaspoon almond extract
Chocolate Crumb Crust
(recipe follows)
¼ cup sliced almonds

Per Serving
Net Carbohydrate (gm): 7.3
Calories: 191
Fat (gm): 16.2
Saturated fat (gm): 9.3
Cholesterol (mg): 68.1
Sodium (mg): 172
Protein (gm): 4.4
Carbohydrate (gm): 7.9

1. Beat cream cheese until smooth in large bowl; beat in remaining ingredients, except Chocolate Crumb Crust and almonds, until smooth. Pour filling into Chocolate Crumb Crust; sprinkle with almonds.

2. Bake cheesecake at 300 degrees until set, about 30 minutes. Cool on wire rack; refrigerate until chilled, 6 hours or overnight. Cut into squares to serve.

Chocolate Crumb Crust

1½ cups graham cracker crumbs
¼ cup Dutch process cocoa
2½ teaspoons Equal® for Recipes, *or* 8 packets Equal® sweetener
5 tablespoons butter, melted
½–¾ teaspoon chocolate extract

1. Mix graham cracker crumbs, cocoa, and Equal® for Recipes in bottom of 13 x 9-inch baking pan; mix in butter and chocolate extract. Pat mixture evenly on bottom of pan.

Chocolate Chip Cookies

60 cookies (1 per serving)

8 tablespoons butter, softened
1½ cups packed light brown sugar
1 egg
1 teaspoon vanilla
2 cups whole wheat pastry flour
½ cup soy flour
½ teaspoon baking soda
½ teaspoon salt
½ cup reduced-fat milk
1 package (6-ounce size) semisweet chocolate morsels

Per Serving
Net Carbohydrate (gm): 9.7
Calories: 68
Fat (gm): 2.8
Saturated fat (gm): 1.6
Cholesterol (mg): 8.1
Sodium (mg): 51
Protein (gm): 1.1
Carbohydrate (gm): 10.4

1. Beat butter and brown sugar in medium bowl until fluffy; beat in egg and vanilla. Mix in combined flours, baking soda, and salt alternately with milk, beginning and ending with dry ingredients. Mix in chocolate morsels.

2. Drop cookies by tablespoonfuls onto greased cookie sheets. Bake at 375 degrees until browned, about 10 minutes. Cool on wire racks.

Raisin Oatmeal Cookies

30 cookies (1 per serving)

6 tablespoons butter, softened
¼ cup sour cream
1 egg
1 teaspoon vanilla
1 cup packed light brown sugar
1½ cups quick-cooking oats
1 cup whole wheat pastry flour
½ teaspoon baking soda
¼ teaspoon baking powder
1 teaspoon ground cinnamon
½ cup raisins

Per Serving
Net Carbohydrate (gm): 14.1
Calories: 92
Fat (gm): 3.3
Saturated fat (gm): 1.8
Cholesterol (mg): 14.4
Sodium (mg): 56
Protein (gm): 1.5
Carbohydrate (gm): 15.1

1. Mix butter, sour cream, egg, and vanilla in large bowl; beat in brown sugar. Mix in combined oats, flour, baking soda, baking powder, and cinnamon. Mix in raisins.

2. Drop dough onto greased cookie sheets, using 2 tablespoons for each cookie. Bake at 350 degrees until browned, 12 to 15 minutes. Cool on wire racks.

Mom's Sugar Cookies

72 cookies (1 per serving)

10 tablespoons butter, softened
2 tablespoons sour cream
1 egg
1 teaspoon lemon extract
¾ cup packed light brown sugar
1½ cups whole wheat pastry flour
½ cup soy flour
1 teaspoon baking powder
¼ teaspoon salt
Ground cinnamon, as garnish

Per Serving
Net Carbohydrate (gm): 3.9
Calories: 37
Fat (gm): 2
Saturated fat (gm): 1.1
Cholesterol (mg): 7.7
Sodium (mg): 34
Protein (gm): 0.7
Carbohydrate (gm): 4.3

1. Beat butter, sour cream, egg, and lemon extract in medium bowl until smooth; mix in brown sugar. Mix in combined flours, baking powder, and salt. Refrigerate dough 4 to 6 hours.

2. Roll dough on floured surface to ¼ inch thickness. Cut cookies into decorative shapes with 2-inch cookie cutters. Bake at 375 degrees on greased cookie sheets until lightly browned, 8 to 10 minutes. Sprinkle warm cookies generously with cinnamon; cool on wire racks.

Nutty Nutmeg Sugar Cookies

36 cookies (1 per serving)

6 tablespoons butter, softened
⅔ cup packed light brown sugar
1 egg
1½ tablespoons lemon juice
1¼ cups whole wheat pastry flour
½ cup soy flour
½ teaspoon baking soda
¾–1 teaspoon ground nutmeg
½ cup very finely chopped pecans, *or* walnuts

Per Serving
Net Carbohydrate (gm): 6.9
Calories: 65
Fat (gm): 3.6
Saturated fat (gm): 1.5
Cholesterol (mg): 11.4
Sodium (mg): 42
Protein (gm): 1.3
Carbohydrate (gm): 7.7

1. Beat butter in large bowl until fluffy. Beat in brown sugar, egg, and lemon juice. Mix in combined flours, baking soda, and nutmeg. Refrigerate until dough is firm enough to roll, 15 to 30 minutes (dough will be sticky).

2. Roll dough into ¾-inch balls; roll balls lightly in pecans and place on ungreased cookie sheets. Flatten to 2 inch diameter with bottom of glass. Bake at 375 degrees until very lightly browned, about 10 minutes. Cool on wire racks.

Soft Molasses Cookies

36 cookies (1 per serving)

¼ cup vegetable shortening
½ cup packed dark brown sugar
1 egg yolk
1 cup whole wheat pastry flour
¼ cup soy flour
2 teaspoons baking soda
½ teaspoon ground cinnamon
½ teaspoon ground ginger
¼ teaspoon ground nutmeg
¼ teaspoon salt
¼ cup light molasses
2 tablespoons water
⅓ cup currants, *or* chopped raisins

Per Serving
Net Carbohydrate (gm): 6.8
Calories: 46
Fat (gm): 1.7
Saturated fat (gm): 0.4
Cholesterol (mg): 5.9
Sodium (mg): 89
Protein (gm): 0.8
Carbohydrate (gm): 7.3

1. Beat shortening, brown sugar, and egg yolk in bowl until blended. Mix in combined flours, baking soda, spices, and salt alternately with combined molasses and water, beginning and ending with dry ingredients. Mix in currants.

2. Drop mixture by rounded teaspoons onto greased cookie sheets. Bake at 350 degrees until lightly browned on the bottoms (cookies will be soft), 8 to 10 minutes. Cool on wire racks.

Shortbread

12 cookies (1 per serving)

1 cup whole wheat pastry flour
3½ teaspoons Equal® for Recipes, *or*
    12 packets Equal® sweetener
1 tablespoon cornstarch
⅛ teaspoon salt
8 tablespoons cold butter, cut into pieces
½–1 teaspoon butter extract
½ teaspoon vanilla

Per Serving
Net Carbohydrate (gm): 7.6
Calories: 113
Fat (gm): 8.3
Saturated fat (gm): 5.1
Cholesterol (mg): 21.9
Sodium (mg): 107
Protein (gm): 1.5
Carbohydrate (gm): 8.8

1. Combine flour, Equal® for Recipes, cornstarch, and salt in medium bowl; cut in butter until mixture resembles coarse crumbs. Sprinkle butter extract and vanilla over mixture and mix by hand briefly until dough begins to hold together.

2. Pat dough evenly in bottom of greased 8-inch round cake pan with removable bottom. Lightly cut dough into 12 wedges with sharp knife, cutting about halfway through dough. Pierce each wedge 3 to 4 times with tines of fork.

3. Bake at 325 degrees until lightly browned, 25 to 30 minutes. Cool 10 to 15 minutes on wire rack; remove from pan and cut into wedges while warm.

Variations:

Almond Shortbread—Make recipe as above, substituting almond extract for the butter extract and omitting vanilla. Separate 6 whole blanched almonds into halves; press 1 half into each shortbread wedge before baking.

Chocolate Shortbread—Make recipe as above, adding ¼ cup Dutch process cocoa, increasing Equal® for Recipes to 5½ teaspoons or 18 packets, and substituting vanilla for butter extract.

Almond Tuiles

36 cookies (1 per serving)

½ cup quick-cooking oats
¼ cup finely chopped blanched almonds
4 tablespoons buttter, melted
⅓ cup light corn syrup
⅓ cup packed light brown sugar
1 teaspoon almond extract
½ cup whole wheat pastry flour
¼ teaspoon salt

Per Serving
Net Carbohydrate (gm): 6
Calories: 44
Fat (gm): 2
Saturated fat (gm): 1
Cholesterol (mg): 3.6
Sodium (mg): 35
Protein (gm): 0.6
Carbohydrate (gm): 6.4

1. Place oats and almonds in separate pie pans. Bake at 350 degrees until toasted, 5 to 8 minutes for the almonds and about 10 minutes for the oats. Cool.

2. Mix butter and corn syrup in bowl; mix in brown sugar and almond extract. Mix in combined oats, almonds, flour, and salt.

3. Drop batter by well-rounded teaspoons, 3 inches apart, onto parchment-lined cookie sheets (4 to 6 cookies per pan). Bake at 350 degrees until golden and bubbly, 7 to 10 minutes. Let cookies cool until just firm enough to remove from cookie sheet, about 1 minute. Working quickly, remove each cookie and roll or fold it over the handle of a wooden spoon, or leave flat; cool on wire rack. If cookies have cooled too much to shape, return to warm oven for about 1 minute to soften.

Variations:

Cream-Filled Tuiles—Remove warm tuiles from cookie sheet 1 at a time and roll loosely around handle of wooden spoon; transfer to wire rack and cool. Using pastry bag with medium star tip, use 3 cups whipped topping to fill tuiles.

Chocolate Tuiles—Make tuiles, leaving them flat. Flip half the tuiles over and drizzle bottoms with 2 to 3 ounces melted semisweet baking chocolate. Top with remaining tuiles, bottom sides down, while chocolate is still warm. Let stand in cool place, or refrigerate briefly, until chocolate is set.

Beany Bites

48 cookies (1 per serving)

1 can (15 ounces) garbanzo beans, rinsed, drained
¼ cup water
½ cup butter, softened
⅔ cup packed light brown sugar
1 egg
½ teaspoon vanilla
1¼ cups whole wheat pastry flour
¼ cup soy flour
2 teaspoons baking powder
¼ teaspoon salt
½ teaspoon ground cinnamon
¼ teaspoon ground nutmeg
⅓ cup reduced-fat milk
Ground nutmeg, as garnish

Per Serving
Net Carbohydrate (gm): 6.8
Calories: 55
Fat (gm): 2.4
Saturated fat (gm): 1.4
Cholesterol (mg): 10
Sodium (mg): 83
Protein (gm): 1.2
Carbohydrate (gm): 7.6

1. Process beans and water in food processor or blender until smooth. Beat butter, brown sugar, egg, and vanilla in large bowl until blended; mix in bean mixture. Mix in combined flours, baking powder, salt, and spices alternately with milk, beginning and ending with dry ingredients.

2. Drop dough by scant tablespoons onto greased cookie sheets. Bake at 375 degrees until lightly browned, 12 to 15 minutes. Sprinkle warm cookies generously with nutmeg; cool on wire racks.

Granola-Pecan Nuggets

24 cookies (1 per serving)

6 tablespoons butter, softened
⅓ cup packed light brown sugar
1 egg white
1 tablespoon finely grated orange rind
1 tablespoon finely grated lemon rind
2 teaspoons lemon juice
¼ teaspoon salt
1 cup whole wheat pastry flour
1 cup granola, divided
1 egg white
2 tablespoons water
24 pecan halves

Per Serving
Net Carbohydrate (gm): 8.3
Calories: 89
Fat (gm): 5.2
Saturated fat (gm): 2.2
Cholesterol (mg): 8.2
Sodium (mg): 62
Protein (gm): 1.9
Carbohydrate (gm): 9.6

1. Beat butter, brown sugar, egg white, citrus rinds, lemon juice, and salt until well blended; beat at medium speed 2 minutes. Mix in flour and ½ cup granola. Refrigerate dough until firm enough to roll, 15 to 30 minutes (dough will be sticky).

2. Beat egg white and water in shallow bowl until foamy. Shape dough into 24 balls; roll in egg white mixture, then roll in remaining ½ cup granola and place on greased cookie sheet. Press pecan halves into tops of cookies. Bake at 325 degrees until nuggets are lightly browned, 25 to 30 minutes. Cool on wire racks.

Peach Streusel Bars

36 bars (1 per serving)

1¼ cups whole wheat pastry flour
½ cup soy flour
2 cups quick-cooking oats
¾ cup packed light brown sugar
12 tablespoons cold butter, cut into pieces
2 tablespoons honey
1¼ cups no-sugar-added peach preserves

Per Serving
Net Carbohydrate (gm): 14.3
Calories: 106
Fat (gm): 4.7
Saturated fat (gm): 2.6
Cholesterol (mg): 10.9
Sodium (mg): 44
Protein (gm): 1.7
Carbohydrate (gm): 15.5

1. Combine flours, oats, and brown sugar in large bowl; cut in butter until mixture resembles coarse crumbs. Reserve ⅓ mixture. Mix honey into remaining mixture; pat evenly in bottom of greased 13 x 9-inch baking pan.

2. Spread preserves over mixture in pan; sprinkle with reserved crumb mixture. Bake at 350 degrees until bubbly and golden, about 35 minutes. Cool on wire rack.

Apricot-Almond Bars

24 bars (1 per serving)

2 cups whole wheat pastry flour
3½ teaspoons Equal® for Recipes, *or*
    12 packets Equal® sweetener
⅛ teaspoon salt
8 tablespoons cold butter, cut into pieces
1 large egg, beaten
1 tablespoon reduced-fat milk, *or* water
⅔ cup no-sugar-added apricot preserves
1 teaspoon cornstarch
¼–⅓ cup finely chopped almonds, walnuts, *or* pecans, toasted

Per Serving
Net Carbohydrate (gm): 9.5
Calories: 95
Fat (gm): 5.2
Saturated fat (gm): 2.7
Cholesterol (mg): 19.9
Sodium (mg): 57
Protein (gm): 2
Carbohydrate (gm): 11

1. Combine flour, Equal® for Recipes, and salt in medium bowl; cut in butter until mixture resembles coarse crumbs. Mix in egg and milk.

2. Press mixture evenly in bottom of greased 11 x 7-inch baking dish. Bake at 400 degrees until edges of crust are browned, about 15 minutes. Cool on wire rack.

3. Mix preserves and cornstarch in small saucepan; heat to boiling. Boil, stirring constantly, until thickened, about 1 minute; cool 5 minutes. Spread mixture evenly over cooled crust; sprinkle with almonds. Bake at 400 degrees until preserves are thick and bubbly, about 15 minutes. Cool on wire rack.

Lemon Squares

12 squares (1 per serving)

2 eggs
5½ teaspoons Equal® for Recipes, *or*
    18 packets Equal® sweetener
¼ cup plus 2 tablespoons lemon juice
4 tablespoons butter, melted, cooled
1 tablespoon grated lemon rind
Rich Pastry Crust (recipe follows)

Per Serving
Net Carbohydrate (gm): 7.7
Calories: 140
Fat (gm): 11.1
Saturated fat (gm): 6.6
Cholesterol (mg): 62.8
Sodium (mg): 139
Protein (gm): 2.3
Carbohydrate (gm): 8.7

1. Beat together eggs and Equal® for Recipes; mix in lemon juice, butter, and lemon rind. Pour mixture into baked Rich Pastry Crust.

2. Bake at 350 degrees until filling is set, about 15 minutes. Cool on wire rack.

Rich Pastry Crust

¾ cup whole wheat pastry flour
2½ teaspoons Equal® for Recipes, *or* 8 packets Equal® sweetener
2¼ teaspoons cornstarch
⅛ teaspoon salt
6 tablespoons cold butter, cut into pieces
¾ teaspoon vanilla
1 teaspoon lemon rind

1. Combine flour, Equal® for Recipes, cornstarch, and salt in medium bowl; cut in butter until mixture resembles coarse crumbs. Sprinkle with vanilla and lemon rind; mix by hand to form dough.

2. Press dough evenly on bottom and ¼ inch up sides of 8-inch square baking pan. Bake at 350 degrees until lightly browned, about 10 minutes. Cool on wire rack.

Chocolate Mousse Squares

16 squares (1 per serving)

6 tablespoons butter
4 ounces unsweetened chocolate
⅓ cup reduced-fat milk
⅓ cup no-sugar-added apricot preserves
1 egg yolk
1 teaspoon vanilla
½ cup whole wheat pastry flour
10¾ teaspoons Equal® for Recipes, *or* 36 packets Equal® sweetener
½ teaspoon baking powder
⅛ teaspoon salt
3 egg whites
⅛ teaspoon cream of tartar
½ cup coarsely chopped walnuts, *or* pecans, optional

Per Serving
Net Carbohydrate (gm): 8.4
Calories: 151
Fat (gm): 12.2
Saturated fat (gm): 5.9
Cholesterol (mg): 27.7
Sodium (mg): 101
Protein (gm): 3.2
Carbohydrate (gm): 10.4

1. Heat butter, chocolate, milk, and preserves in small saucepan, stirring frequently, until chocolate is almost melted. Remove from heat; continue stirring until chocolate is melted. Stir in egg yolk and vanilla; mix in combined flour, Equal® for Recipes, baking powder, and salt.

2. Beat egg whites and cream of tartar to stiff, but not dry, peaks in medium bowl; fold chocolate mixture into egg whites. Fold in walnuts, if using. Pour batter into greased 8-inch square baking pan.

3. Bake at 350 degrees until top of mousse squares are firm to touch and toothpick comes out clean, 18 to 20 minutes (do not overbake). Cool on wire rack. Serve warm or at room temperature.

Cocoa Brownies

25 brownies (1 per serving)

¾ cup whole wheat pastry flour
¼ cup soy flour
1 cup packed light brown sugar
¼ cup unsweetened cocoa
5 tablespoons butter, melted
¼ cup reduced-fat milk
2 eggs
¼ cup honey
1 teaspoon vanilla
Unsweetened cocoa, as garnish

Per Serving
Net Carbohydrate (gm): 14.1
Calories: 90
Fat (gm): 3.2
Saturated fat (gm): 1.8
Cholesterol (mg): 23.8
Sodium (mg): 35
Protein (gm): 1.6
Carbohydrate (gm): 14.9

1. Combine flours, brown sugar, and cocoa in medium bowl; add butter, milk, eggs, honey, and vanilla, mixing until smooth. Pour batter into greased and floured 8-inch square baking pan.

2. Bake at 350 degrees until brownies spring back when touched, about 30 minutes. Cool in pan on wire rack; sprinkle lightly with cocoa.

Marbled Cheesecake Brownies

24 brownies (1 per serving)

1¼ cups packed light brown sugar
5 tablespoons butter, melted
¼ cup buttermilk
2 eggs
1 teaspoon vanilla
1 cup whole wheat pastry flour
½ cup Dutch process cocoa
½ teaspoon salt
Cheesecake Topping (recipe follows)

Per Serving
Net Carbohydrate (gm): 18.3
Calories: 143
Fat (gm): 6.8
Saturated fat (gm): 4
Cholesterol (mg): 43.9
Sodium (mg): 119
Protein (gm): 2.6
Carbohydrate (gm): 19.5

1. Beat brown sugar, butter, buttermilk, eggs, and vanilla until smooth. Mix in combined flour, cocoa, and salt.

2. Spread half the batter in greased 11 x 7-inch baking pan. Pour Cheesecake Topping evenly over chocolate batter; dollop remaining chocolate batter over Cheesecake Topping. Swirl knife through mixtures to create marbled effect.

3. Bake at 350 degrees until brownies are set and firm to touch, 45 to 55 minutes. Cool on wire rack.

Cheesecake Topping

makes about 1½ cups

1 package (8 ounces) cream cheese, softened
⅓ cup packed light brown sugar
1 tablespoon all-purpose flour
1 egg
1 teaspoon vanilla

1. Beat cream cheese, brown sugar, and flour in large bowl until smooth; beat in egg and vanilla.

Variation:

Banana Split Brownies—Make brownies as above, mixing ½ cup mashed banana into the Cheesecake Topping and substituting ¼ teaspoon banana extract for the vanilla in both the brownie and topping recipes. Serve brownies with a drizzle of sugar-free chocolate sauce; sprinkle lightly with walnut pieces.

Anise-Almond Biscotti

60 biscotti (1 per serving)

4 tablespoons butter, softened
¾ cup packed light brown sugar
3 eggs
2 cups whole wheat pastry flour
½ cup soy flour
2 teaspoons crushed anise seeds
1½ teaspoons baking powder
½ teaspoon baking soda
¼ teaspoon salt
⅓ cup whole blanched almonds

Per Serving
Net Carbohydrate (gm): 5.4
Calories: 43
Fat (gm): 1.7
Saturated fat (gm): 0.6
Cholesterol (mg): 12.8
Sodium (mg): 45
Protein (gm): 1.3
Carbohydrate (gm): 6.1

1. Beat butter, brown sugar, and eggs in large bowl until smooth. Mix in combined flours, anise seeds, baking powder, baking soda, and salt. Mix in almonds.

2. Shape dough on greased cookie sheets into 4 slightly flattened rolls, each 1½ inches in diameter. Bake at 350 degrees until lightly browned, about 20 minutes. Let stand on wire rack until cool enough to handle; cut rolls into ½-inch slices. Arrange slices, cut sides down, on ungreased cookie sheets.

3. Bake biscotti again at 350 degrees until toasted on the bottoms, 7 to 10 minutes; turn and bake until biscotti are golden on the bottoms and feel almost dry, 7 to 10 minutes longer. Cool on wire racks.

Variations:

Chocolate-Walnut Biscotti—Make biscotti as above, omitting anise seeds, substituting walnuts for the almonds, adding 1 teaspoon vanilla, and adding ½ cup finely chopped unsweetened baking chocolate.

Apple-Apricot Newtons

30 bars (1 per serving)

½ cup chopped dried apples
½ cup chopped dried apricots
5¼ teaspoons Equal® for Recipes, *or*
    18 packets Equal® sweetener, divided
¾ cup water
5 tablespoons butter, softened
2 eggs
1 teaspoon vanilla
1½ cups whole wheat pastry flour flour
¼ cup soy flour
½ teaspoon baking soda
¼ teaspoon salt
Reduced-fat milk

Per Serving
Net Carbohydrate (gm): 6.4
Calories: 58
Fat (gm): 2.6
Saturated fat (gm): 1.4
Cholesterol (mg): 19.6
Sodium (mg): 54
Protein (gm): 1.6
Carbohydrate (gm): 7.5

1. Heat apples, apricots, 3½ teaspoons Equal® for Recipes, and water to boiling in small saucepan; reduce heat and simmer, uncovered, until fruit is tender and water is absorbed, about 10 minutes. Process mixture in food processor or blender until smooth; cool.

2. Beat butter and remaining 1¾ teaspoons Equal® for Recipes in medium bowl until smooth; beat in eggs and vanilla. Mix in combined flours, baking soda, and salt. Divide dough into 4 equal parts; roll each into a log about 5 inches long. Refrigerate, covered, until firm, about 2 hours.

3. Roll 1 piece dough on floured surface into rectangle 12 x 4 inches. Spread one-fourth of the fruit filling along a 1½-inch strip in center of dough. Fold sides of dough over filling, pressing edges to seal. Cut filled dough in half and place seam sides down on greased cookie sheet. Repeat with remaining dough and fruit filling.

4. Brush top of dough lightly with milk; bake at 400 degrees until lightly browned, 10 to 12 minutes. Remove from pan and cool on wire racks; cut into 1½-inch bars. Store in airtight container.

Orange-Almond Meringues

24 cookies (1 per serving)

3 egg whites
½ teaspoon orange extract
½ teaspoon cream of tartar
¼ teaspoon salt
⅔ cup packed light brown sugar
½ cup chopped toasted almonds

Per Serving
Net Carbohydrate (gm): 6.3
Calories: 41
Fat (gm): 1.4
Saturated fat (gm): 0.1
Cholesterol (mg): 0
Sodium (mg): 34
Protein (gm): 1
Carbohydrate (gm): 6.6

1. Beat egg whites, orange extract, cream of tartar, and salt to soft peaks in medium bowl. Beat to stiff peaks, adding brown sugar gradually. Fold in almonds.

2. Drop mixture by tablespoons onto parchment- or aluminum foil-lined cookie sheets. Bake at 300 degrees until cookies begin to brown and feel crisp when touched, 20 to 25 minutes. Cool on pans on wire racks.

Variations:

Lemon-Poppy Seed Meringues—Make cookies, substituting lemon extract for the orange extract and omitting almonds. Fold 2 teaspoons finely chopped lemon rind and 2 tablespoons poppy seeds into meringue mixture.

Black Walnut Meringues—Make cookies as above, substituting ¼ teaspoon black walnut extract for the orange extract and ½ cup finely chopped black or English walnuts for the almonds.

Cinnamon Bread Pudding

8 servings

2 cups reduced-fat milk
4 tablespoons butter, cut into pieces
2 eggs
3½ teaspoons Equal® for Recipes, *or*
    12 packets Equal® sweetener
1½ teaspoons ground cinnamon
⅛ teaspoon ground cloves
3 dashes ground nutmeg
¼ teaspoon salt
6 cups cubed (¾-inch) day-old whole wheat bread

Per Serving
Net Carbohydrate (gm): 15.6
Calories: 180
Fat (gm): 10.2
Saturated fat (gm): 5.3
Cholesterol (mg): 74.7
Sodium (mg): 357
Protein (gm): 5.9
Carbohydrate (gm): 17.6

1. Heat milk and butter to simmering in medium saucepan; remove from heat and stir until butter is melted. Cool 10 minutes.

2. Beat eggs in large bowl until foamy; mix in Equal® for Recipes, spices, and salt. Mix in milk mixture and bread. Spoon mixture into ungreased 1½-quart casserole. Place casserole in roasting pan on middle oven rack; pour 1 inch hot water into pan. Bake, uncovered, at 350 degrees until pudding is set and sharp knife inserted halfway between center and edge comes out clean, 40 to 45 minutes.

Creamy Lemon Pudding

6 servings (about ½ cup each)

3 tablespoons cornstarch
2 tablespoons all-purpose flour
Pinch salt
3 cups reduced-fat milk
1 egg
1 egg white
3–4 tablespoons lemon juice
½–¾ teaspoon lemon extract
3½ teaspoons Equal® for Recipes, *or* 12 packets Equal® sweetener

Per Serving
Net Carbohydrate (gm): 14
Calories: 111
Fat (gm): 3.2
Saturated fat (gm): 1.7
Cholesterol (mg): 45.2
Sodium (mg): 81
Protein (gm): 6.1
Carbohydrate (gm): 14.1

1. Mix cornstarch, flour, and salt in medium saucepan; stir in milk. Whisk over medium to medium-high heat until mixture boils and thickens. Whisk about ½ of the milk mixture into combined egg and egg white; whisk egg mixture back into saucepan. Whisk over low heat 1 to 2 minutes.

2. Strain pudding into a bowl; cool to room temperature. Stir in lemon juice and extract and Equal® for Recipes. Refrigerate 1 to 2 hours.

Peach Custard

6 servings (⅔ cup each)

3 tablespoons cornstarch
2½ teaspoons Equal® for Recipes, *or*
   8 packets Equal® sweetener
2 cups reduced-fat milk
½ cup peach nectar
2 egg yolks, lightly beaten
1–2 tablespoons butter, softened
1½ cups diced peaches
Whipped topping, as garnish
Ground nutmeg, as garnish

Per Serving
Net Carbohydrate (gm): 19.6
Calories: 148
Fat (gm): 5.4
Saturated fat (gm): 2.8
Cholesterol (mg): 82.9
Sodium (mg): 64
Protein (gm): 4.4
Carbohydrate (gm): 21.4

1. Mix cornstarch and Equal® for Recipes in medium saucepan; whisk in milk and peach nectar. Whisk over medium to medium-high heat until mixture boils and thickens. Whisk about 1 cup milk mixture into the egg yolks; whisk egg yolk mixture back into saucepan. Whisk over low heat until thickened, 1 to 2 minutes. Stir in butter and cool to room temperature. Refrigerate until chilled, about 2 hours.

2. Whisk chilled custard until fluffy; fold in peaches. Spoon into dishes; garnish with dollops of whipped topping and sprinkle lightly with nutmeg.

Orange Flan

10 servings

⅔ cup packed light brown sugar, divided
3¾ cups reduced-fat milk
¼ cup orange juice
6 eggs, lightly beaten
¼ teaspoon orange extract

Per Serving
Net Carbohydrate (gm): 19.7
Calories: 149
Fat (gm): 4.8
Saturated fat (gm): 2
Cholesterol (mg): 134.8
Sodium (mg): 89
Protein (gm): 6.8
Carbohydrate (gm): 19.7

1. Heat ⅓ cup brown sugar in small skillet over medium-high heat until sugar melts and turns golden, stirring occasionally (watch carefully as the sugar can burn easily!). Quickly pour syrup into bottom of 2-quart soufflé dish or casserole and tilt bottom to spread caramel. Set aside to cool.

2. Heat milk, orange juice, and remaining ⅓ cup brown sugar in medium saucepan until steaming and just beginning to bubble at edges. Whisk hot milk mixture into eggs; add orange extract. Strain into soufflé dish.

3. Place soufflé dish in roasting pan on middle oven rack. Cover soufflé dish with lid or aluminum foil. Pour 2 inches hot water into roasting pan. Bake at 350 degrees 1 hour or until sharp knife inserted halfway between center and edge of custard comes out clean. Remove soufflé dish from roasting pan and cool to room temperature on wire rack. Refrigerate 8 hours or overnight.

4. To unmold, loosen edge of custard with sharp knife. Place rimmed serving dish over soufflé dish and invert.

Coeur à la Crème

6 servings

2 envelopes unflavored gelatin
¾ cup reduced-fat milk
2 cups cottage cheese
1 package (8 ounces) cream cheese
3 tablespoons packed light brown sugar
1 teaspoon vanilla
Whole strawberries, as garnish
2 cups sliced strawberries, *or* fresh raspberries

Per Serving
Net Carbohydrate (gm): 13.4
Calories: 269
Fat (gm): 17.1
Saturated fat (gm): 10.7
Cholesterol (mg): 54.5
Sodium (mg): 418
Protein (gm): 14.9
Carbohydrate (gm): 14.5

1. Sprinkle gelatin over milk in small saucepan; let stand 1 minute. Stir over low heat to just simmering.

2. Process cottage cheese in food processor until smooth. Add cream cheese, brown sugar, vanilla, and gelatin mixture and process until smooth. Pour cheese mixture into lightly greased 5-cup heart mold or cake pan. Cover; refrigerate until firm, 3 to 4 hours.

3. Dip mold briefly in warm water and loosen edge of cheese mixture with sharp knife; unmold onto serving platter. Garnish with whole strawberries; serve with sliced strawberries.

Strawberry Cloud Pudding

4 servings

1 package (3 ounces) sugar-free strawberry-flavored gelatin
1 cup boiling water
1 cup cold water
1 cup strawberry yogurt
Fresh strawberries, as garnish

Per Serving
Net Carbohydrate (gm): 10.9
Calories: 67
Fat (gm): 0.5
Saturated fat (gm): 0.3
Cholesterol (mg): 2.7
Sodium (mg): 93
Protein (gm): 3.5
Carbohydrate (gm): 10.9

1. In small bowl, dissolve gelatin in boiling water. Add cold water and chill until mixture mounds on spoon. Place bowl in larger bowl filled with ice and water. Add yogurt and beat at high speed until fluffy. Spoon into serving bowl or dishes; refrigerate until set, 2 to 3 hours. Garnish with strawberries.

Citrus Pumpkin Pudding

8 servings

1 package (3.9 ounces) sugar-free instant lemon, *or* orange, pudding and pie filling
1 cup sugar-free lemon, *or* orange, yogurt
1 cup canned pumpkin
1 tablespoon grated lemon, *or* orange, rind
1 teaspoon pumpkin pie spice
1 cup whipped topping
Whipped topping, as garnish
Chopped pecans, *or* walnuts, as garnish

Per Serving
Net Carbohydrate (gm): 15.7
Calories: 91
Fat (gm): 2.1
Saturated fat (gm): 2.1
Cholesterol (mg): 0.6
Sodium (mg): 594
Protein (gm): 1.4
Carbohydrate (gm): 16.9

1. Beat pudding and pie filling and lemon yogurt in medium bowl on low speed 1 minute. Beat in pumpkin, lemon rind, and pumpkin pie spice; fold in 1 cup whipped topping. Spoon into serving bowl or dishes. At serving time, top with dollops of whipped topping and sprinkle with pecans.

Lemon Yogurt Crepes

8 servings (1 per serving)

½ cup whole wheat pastry flour
½ cup reduced-fat milk
2 eggs
1 tablespoon butter, melted
2 tablespoons packed brown sugar
¼ teaspoon salt
Lemon Yogurt Pastry Cream (recipe follows)
Grated lemon rind, as garnish
Mint sprigs, as garnish

Per Serving
Net Carbohydrate (gm): 14.4
Calories: 123
Fat (gm): 4.4
Saturated fat (gm): 2.1
Cholesterol (mg): 88.1
Sodium (mg): 148
Protein (gm): 5.5
Carbohydrate (gm): 15.5

1. Combine all ingredients, except Lemon Yogurt Pastry Cream, lemon rind, and mint in small bowl; beat until smooth (batter will be thin). Heat greased 8-inch crepe pan or small skillet over medium heat until hot. Pour scant ¼ cup batter into pan, tilting to coat bottom evenly with batter. Cook over medium heat until browned on the bottom, 2 to 3 minutes. Turn crepe and cook until browned on the other side, 2 to 3 minutes. Repeat with remaining batter. Cool crepes.

2. Fill each crepe with about ¼ cup Lemon Yogurt Pastry Cream and roll up. Place seam sides down on serving plates; garnish with grated lemon rind and mint.

Lemon Yogurt Pastry Cream

makes about 2¼ cups

¼ cup Splenda® sweetener
2 tablespoons cornstarch
1 cup reduced-fat milk
1 egg yolk, beaten
¼ teaspoon vanilla
1 container (8 ounces) sugar-free lemon yogurt

1. Combine Splenda® and cornstarch in small saucepan; whisk in milk. Whisk over medium-high heat until mixture boils and thickens, 2 to 3 minutes. Whisk ½ the milk mixture into egg yolk; whisk yolk mixture back into saucepan. Whisk over low heat 1 minute.

2. Transfer pastry cream to bowl; stir in vanilla. Cover surface with plastic wrap. Cool; refrigerate until chilled, 1 to 2 hours. Stir in yogurt.

Chocolate Soufflé Crepes

8 servings

4 tablespoons packed light brown sugar, divided
3 tablespoons unsweetened cocoa
1 tablespoon all-purpose flour
⅓ cup reduced-fat milk
2 egg yolks
1 tablespoon coffee liqueur, *or* strong coffee
2 teaspoons vanilla
4 egg whites
Crepes (see p. 370)
Mint sprigs, as garnish

Per Serving
Net Carbohydrate (gm): 18.6
Calories: 148
Fat (gm): 4.7
Saturated fat (gm): 2.1
Cholesterol (mg): 111.5
Sodium (mg): 151
Protein (gm): 6.4
Carbohydrate (gm): 20.1

1. Mix 3 tablespoons brown sugar, cocoa, and flour in small saucepan; whisk in milk and egg yolks. Whisk over low heat, stirring constantly until thick, about 5 minutes. Remove from heat; stir in liqueur and vanilla.

2. Beat egg whites to soft peaks in large bowl; gradually add remaining 1 tablespoon brown sugar, beating to stiff peaks. Fold into chocolate mixture.

3. Place crepes on greased baking sheet; spoon about ⅓ cup soufflé mixture in center of each crepe and fold in half. Bake at 350 degrees until puffed, about 10 minutes. Sprinkle with powdered sugar; serve immediately. Garnish with mint sprigs.

Variation:

Lemon Soufflé Crepes—Make recipe as above, omitting cocoa, coffee liqueur, and vanilla. Add 1 tablespoon grated lemon rind, 1 tablespoon lemon juice, and ½ teaspoon lemon extract to yolk mixture. Complete recipe as above.

Chocolate Soufflé with White Chocolate Sauce

10 servings

½ cup unsweetened applesauce
3 ounces unsweetened chocolate, grated
2 tablespoons unsweetened cocoa
2 teaspoons instant espresso powder, *or*
 instant coffee granules
1 egg yolk
5 egg whites
¼ cup packed light brown sugar
White Chocolate Sauce (recipe follows)

Per Serving
Net Carbohydrate (gm): 13.3
Calories: 138
Fat (gm): 8.2
Saturated fat (gm): 4.9
Cholesterol (mg): 23
Sodium (mg): 43
Protein (gm): 3.9
Carbohydrate (gm): 15.1

1. Mix applesauce, chocolate, cocoa, espresso, and egg yolk until well blended.

2. Beat egg whites in large bowl to soft peaks; beat to stiff peaks, adding brown sugar gradually. Fold ¼ of the egg white mixture into chocolate mixture. Fold chocolate mixture back into egg white mixture. Pour into 1½-quart soufflé dish that has been lightly greased and sprinkled with sugar.

3. Place soufflé dish in square baking pan on middle shelf of oven. Pour 2 inches boiling water into pan. Bake at 350 degrees until puffed and set, about 55 minutes. Serve immediately with White Chocolate Sauce.

White Chocolate Sauce

makes about ½ cup

2 tablespoons reduced-fat milk
3 ounces white chocolate, chopped
1 tablespoon coffee, *or* chocolate liqueur, optional

1. Heat milk over low heat in small saucepan to simmering; add white chocolate and whisk over very low heat until melted. Remove from heat; stir in coffee or liqueur.

Baked Banana Soufflés

6 servings

2 ripe bananas, peeled
2 teaspoons lemon juice
1 teaspoon vanilla
¼ cup packed light brown sugar, divided
¼ teaspoon ground nutmeg
2 egg yolks
4 egg whites
½ teaspoon cream of tartar

Per Serving
Net Carbohydrate (gm): 17.9
Calories: 105
Fat (gm): 1.9
Saturated fat (gm): 0.6
Cholesterol (mg): 70.9
Sodium (mg): 43
Protein (gm): 3.7
Carbohydrate (gm): 18.9

1. Process bananas, lemon juice, vanilla, 2 tablespoons brown sugar, and nutmeg in food processor or blender until smooth. Add egg yolks, one at a time, blending until smooth.

2. Beat egg whites and cream of tartar in medium bowl to soft peaks; beat to stiff peaks, adding remaining 2 tablespoons brown sugar gradually. Fold in banana mixture. Spoon into 6 lightly greased 1-cup soufflé dishes or custard cups. Place dishes on cookie sheet.

3. Bake at 450 degrees 7 minutes; reduce heat to 425 degrees and bake until soufflés are lightly browned and sharp knife inserted near centers comes out clean, about 7 minutes. Remove from oven; serve immediately.

498 Best Low-Carb Recipes

498   *1,001 Best Low-Carb Recipes*

Peach-Allspice Soufflés

6 servings

1½ cups chopped fresh, *or* frozen, thawed, peaches, *or*
    canned peaches in water, drained
2 teaspoons lemon juice
1 teaspoon vanilla
¼ cup packed light brown sugar, divided
⅛ teaspoon ground allspice
2 egg yolks
4 egg whites
⅛ teaspoon cream of tartar

Per Serving
Net Carbohydrate (gm): 17.3
Calories: 105
Fat (gm): 1.8
Saturated fat (gm): 0.5
Cholesterol (mg): 70.9
Sodium (mg): 43
Protein (gm): 3.9
Carbohydrate (gm): 19.1

1. Process peaches, lemon juice, vanilla, 2 tablespoons brown sugar, and allspice in food processor or blender until smooth. Add egg yolks, one at a time, processing until smooth.

2. Beat egg whites and cream of tartar in large bowl until soft peaks form. Beat to stiff peaks, adding remaining 2 tablespoons brown sugar gradually. Fold in peach mixture. Spoon into greased 1-cup soufflé dishes or custard cups and place on baking sheet.

3. Bake at 450 degrees 7 minutes; reduce heat to 425 degrees and bake 7 minutes longer or until soufflés are lightly browned and sharp knife inserted near centers comes out clean. Serve immediately.

Raspberry Rhubarb Mousse

8 servings

4 cups sliced rhubarb
¼ cup water
⅓ cup packed light brown sugar
1 package (3 ounces) sugar-free raspberry-flavored gelatin
1 package (12 ounces) frozen unsweetened raspberries
3 cups whipped topping

Per Serving
Net Carbohydrate (gm): 19.7
Calories: 144
Fat (gm): 6.1
Saturated fat (gm): 6
Cholesterol (mg): 0
Sodium (mg): 48
Protein (gm): 1.2
Carbohydrate (gm): 21.5

1. Cook rhubarb, water, and brown sugar in large saucepan until tender, about 10 minutes. Add gelatin and stir until dissolved. Stir in raspberries until well mixed. Fold in whipped topping. Pour into serving bowl. Chill until set, about 4 hours.

Chilled Raspberry Chiffon

6 servings

¼ cup packed light brown sugar
½ cup water
1 tablespoon lemon juice
1 envelope unflavored gelatin
2 cups fresh, *or* frozen, thawed, raspberries
2 envelopes (1.3 ounces each) whipped topping mix
1 cup reduced-fat milk
Fresh raspberries, as garnish
Mint sprigs, as garnish

Per Serving
Net Carbohydrate (gm): 18.4
Calories: 119
Fat (gm): 3.7
Saturated fat (gm): 3.2
Cholesterol (mg): 3.3
Sodium (mg): 26
Protein (gm): 2.7
Carbohydrate (gm): 21.2

1. Combine brown sugar, water, and lemon juice in small saucepan; sprinkle gelatin over and let stand 2 to 3 minutes. Heat to simmering over medium heat, stirring constantly until sugar and gelatin are dissolved. Cool; refrigerate until mixture is consistency of unbeaten egg whites.

2. Process 2 cups raspberries in food processor or blender until smooth; strain and discard seeds. Blend whipped topping mix and milk in large bowl; beat at high speed until topping forms soft peaks, about 4 minutes. Stir raspberry puree into gelatin mixture; fold into whipped topping.

3. Spoon soufflé mixture into serving bowl or individual stemmed dishes. Chill 2 to 4 hours or until set. Garnish with fresh raspberries and mint.

Frozen Lemon Soufflé

8 servings

1 egg yolk
3 tablespoons packed light brown sugar
1½ tablespoons all-purpose flour
½ cup reduced-fat milk
⅓ cup lemon juice
2 tablespoons grated lemon rind
2 tablespoons meringue powder
⅓ cup water
3 cups whipped topping
Grated lemon rind, as garnish
Mint leaves, as garnish

Per Serving
Net Carbohydrate (gm): 14
Calories: 128
Fat (gm): 7
Saturated fat (gm): 6.4
Cholesterol (mg): 27.8
Sodium (mg): 58
Protein (gm): 3.1
Carbohydrate (gm): 14.2

1. Whisk egg yolk and brown sugar in small bowl until smooth; whisk in flour. Heat milk to boiling in small saucepan. Whisk small amount of hot milk into yolk mixture; whisk yolk mixture into saucepan. Whisk constantly over medium heat until thick, about 3 minutes. Stir in lemon juice and rind. Cool to room temperature.

2. Beat meringue powder and water to stiff peaks; fold into lemon mixture. Fold in whipped topping. Pour into 2-quart soufflé dish or serving bowl. Freeze until firm, 6 to 8 hours. Garnish with lemon rind and mint.

Variation:

Frozen Orange Soufflés—Make recipe as above, substituting orange juice and rind for the lemon juice and rind, and adding 1 tablespoon orange liqueur, *or* ½ teaspoon orange extract, with the juice in Step 1. Cut the top quarter off 8 large navel oranges. Remove fruit from shells, using a grapefruit spoon or knife (reserve fruit for another use). Dry insides of shells. Spoon soufflé mixture into shells and freeze until firm, about 4 hours.

Pineapple-Champagne Ice

8 servings

1 envelope unflavored gelatin
2 cups unsweetened pineapple juice
½ cup dry champagne, *or* sparkling white wine
⅛ teaspoon ground nutmeg
8 slices (½ inch thick) fresh pineapple
Mint sprigs, as garnish

Per Serving
Net Carbohydrate (gm): 19
Calories: 93
Fat (gm): 0.5
Saturated fat (gm): 0
Cholesterol (mg): 0
Sodium (mg): 3
Protein (gm): 1.3
Carbohydrate (gm): 20.2

1. Sprinkle gelatin over pineapple juice in medium saucepan; let stand 2 to 3 minutes. Cook over low heat, stirring constantly, until gelatin is dissolved. Cool to room temperature. Stir in champagne and nutmeg.

2. Freeze mixture in ice cream maker according to manufacturer's directions. Or pour mixture into 9-inch square baking pan and freeze until slushy, about 2 hours; spoon into bowl and beat until fluffy. Return to pan and freeze until firm, 6 hours or overnight.

3. To serve, place pineapple slices on dessert plates. Top each with a scoop of Pineapple-Champagne Ice. Garnish with mint.

Sweet Cherry Soup with Yogurt Swirl

6 servings (about ½ cup each)

2 cups canned sweet pitted cherries, water packed
1½ cups vanilla yogurt, divided
¼ cup dry red wine, *or* cranberry juice
2 tablespoons lemon juice

Per Serving
Net Carbohydrate (gm): 17.5
Calories: 98
Fat (gm): 0.9
Saturated fat (gm): 0.5
Cholesterol (mg): 3.1
Sodium (mg): 42
Protein (gm): 3.7
Carbohydrate (gm): 18.8

1. Process cherries in food processor or blender until finely chopped. Add 1 cup yogurt, wine, and lemon juice; process until smooth (mixture will be frosty). Pour into chilled soup bowls; dollop remaining ½ cup yogurt onto top of soup in each bowl and swirl with a skewer or spoon.

Tropical Ambrosia

8 servings

Per Serving
Net Carbohydrate (gm): 14.4
Calories: 76
Fat (gm): 1.3
Saturated fat (gm): 1
Cholesterol (mg): 0.6
Sodium (mg): 23
Protein (gm): 1.6
Carbohydrate (gm): 16

2 cups cubed pineapple
½ cup sliced kiwi
1 cup cubed mango, *or* papaya
1 cup cubed cantaloupe, *or* honeydew melon
1 carton (8 ounces) sugar-free lemon, *or* orange, yogurt
½ cup whipped topping
2 tablespoons no-sugar-added orange marmalade
Toasted coconut, as garnish
Macadamia nuts, *or* slivered almonds, as garnish
Mint sprigs, as garnish

1. Combine fruits and spoon into serving dishes. Combine yogurt, whipped topping, and marmalade in medium bowl; spoon dollops of topping over fruit. Garnish with toasted coconut, macadamia nuts, and mint.

Honey-Lime Melon

4 servings

Per Serving
Net Carbohydrate (gm): 12
Calories: 47
Fat (gm): 0.1
Saturated fat (gm): 0
Cholesterol (mg): 0
Sodium (mg): 4
Protein (gm): 0.4
Carbohydrate (gm): 12.4

2 tablespoons honey
2 cups cantaloupe, *or* honeydew melon, balls or cubes
4 lime wedges
Ground nutmeg, as garnish

1. Drizzle honey over melon; squeeze juice from lime wedges over and sprinkle lightly with nutmeg.

Spiced Orange Slices

8 servings

Per Serving
Net Carbohydrate (gm): 13.5
Calories: 66
Fat (gm): 0.1
Saturated fat (gm): 0
Cholesterol (mg): 0
Sodium (mg): 2
Protein (gm): 0.7
Carbohydrate (gm): 15.1

⅓ cup orange juice
3 tablespoons packed light brown sugar
2–3 tablespoons orange-flavored liqueur
4 whole allspice
1 cinnamon stick
3 cups sliced, peeled oranges
Mint springs, as garnish

1. Heat orange juice, brown sugar, liqueur, allspice, and cinnamon stick to boiling in small saucepan; pour over orange slices in glass serving bowl. Refrigerate, covered, 8 hours or overnight for flavors to blend. Garnish with mint.

Honey-Broiled Pineapple Slices

8 servings

8 slices (½-inch) pineapple
3 tablespoons honey
2 tablespoons unsweetened orange juice concentrate
2 tablespoons minced fresh cilantro, *or* mint

Per Serving
Net Carbohydrate (gm): 17.5
Calories: 72
Fat (gm): 0.4
Saturated fat (gm): 0
Cholesterol (mg): 0
Sodium (mg): 1
Protein (gm): 0.5
Carbohydrate (gm): 18.6

1. Arrange pineapple on broiler pan; brush with combined honey and orange juice. Broil 6 inches from heat source 3 minutes; turn and baste with honey mixture. Broil 2 to 3 minutes more or until golden. Sprinkle with cilantro.

Stewed Rhubarb and Berries

6 servings (about ⅔ cup each)

1 pound fresh, *or* frozen, rhubarb, cut into 1-inch pieces
¼ cup water
2 cups sliced strawberries
2½ teaspoons Equal® for Recipes, *or*
   8 packets Equal® sweetener

Per Serving
Net Carbohydrate (gm): 5.5
Calories: 35
Fat (gm): 0.3
Saturated fat (gm): 0
Cholesterol (mg): 0
Sodium (mg): 4
Protein (gm): 1
Carbohydrate (gm): 8

1. Combine rhubarb and water in medium saucepan; cook, covered, over medium heat until soft, about 10 minutes. Stir in strawberries and Equal® for Recipes; cook until hot through, 1 to 2 minutes. Serve warm, or refrigerate and serve chilled.

Mixed Berries with Mock Mascarpone Cream

8 servings

4 cups mixed berries
   (raspberries, blackberries, strawberries, blueberries, etc.)
½ cup no-sugar-added strawberry preserves, warm
Mock Mascarpone Cream (recipe follows)
Mint leaves, as garnish

Per Serving
Net Carbohydrate (gm): 11.3
Calories: 72
Fat (gm): 1.7
Saturated fat (gm): 0.9
Cholesterol (mg): 4.2
Sodium (mg): 12
Protein (gm): 0.9
Carbohydrate (gm): 14.5

1. Drizzle berries with preserves and toss; spoon into bowl. Top each serving with Mock Mascarpone Cream; garnish with mint.

Mock Mascarpone Cream

makes about 1¼ cups

1 package (8 ounces) cream cheese, room temperature
3 tablespoons sour cream
2–3 tablespoons reduced-fat milk

1. Beat cream cheese until fluffy; mix in sour cream and milk. Refrigerate several hours or up to several days.

Strawberries with Brown sugar and Balsamic Vinegar

8 servings

4 cups halved, *or* quartered, strawberries
3 tablespoons packed light brown sugar
2–3 teaspoons balsamic vinegar
⅛ teaspoon pepper
½ cup sour cream
Mint leaves, as garnish

Per Serving
Net Carbohydrate (gm): 9.3
Calories: 68
Fat (gm): 2.8
Saturated fat (gm): 1.6
Cholesterol (mg): 5.3
Sodium (mg): 9
Protein (gm): 0.8
Carbohydrate (gm): 11

1. Sprinkle strawberries with brown sugar, vinegar, and pepper; toss and let stand 15 to 20 minutes. Serve with dollops of sour cream; garnish with mint.

Peaches and Blueberries with Lime Cream Sauce

8 servings

2 cups sliced peaches
1 cup blueberries
Lime Cream Sauce (recipe follows)
Mint sprigs, as garnish

Per Serving
Net Carbohydrate (gm): 17.6
Calories: 173
Fat (gm): 10
Saturated fat (gm): 6.2
Cholesterol (mg): 31.2
Sodium (mg): 88
Protein (gm): 2.9
Carbohydrate (gm): 19.9

1. Arrange peaches and blueberries in bowls; spoon Lime Cream Sauce over and garnish with mint.

Lime Cream Sauce

makes about 1¼ cups

1 package (8 ounces) cream cheese, softened
¼ cup packed light brown sugar
2–3 tablespoons lime juice

1. Beat cream cheese until smooth; beat in brown sugar and lime juice.

Berries Romanoff

8 servings (about ½ cup each)

2 cups whipped topping
1 container (8 ounces) custard-style lemon yogurt
1–2 tablespoons lemon juice
1¾ teaspoons Equal® for Recipes, *or*
    6 packets Equal® sweetener
1½ cup blueberries
1½ cups raspberries
Ground nutmeg, as garnish
Mint sprigs, as garnish

Per Serving
Net Carbohydrate (gm): 14.3
Calories: 111
Fat (gm): 4.8
Saturated fat (gm): 4.3
Cholesterol (mg): 2.5
Sodium (mg): 27
Protein (gm): 1.6
Carbohydrate (gm): 16.6

1. Mix whipped topping, yogurt, lemon juice, and Equal® for Recipes; fold in berries. Spoon into stemmed goblets; sprinkle lightly with nutmeg and garnish with mint.

Berry Meringues

4 servings

4 egg whites
½ teaspoon cream of tartar
1 cup plus 2 tablespoons Splenda® sweetener, divided
1½ cups sliced strawberries
½ cup blueberries

Per Serving
Net Carbohydrate (gm): 11.9
Calories: 70
Fat (gm): 0.3
Saturated fat (gm): 0
Cholesterol (mg): 0
Sodium (mg): 62
Protein (gm): 4
Carbohydrate (gm): 13.7

1. Beat egg whites and cream of tartar in medium bowl to soft peaks. Gradually beat in 1 cup Splenda®, beating to stiff peaks. Spoon mixture into 4 mounds on greased and floured cookie sheet; shape into "nests" with back of spoon. Bake at 350 degrees until meringues are firm to touch and very lightly browned, about 40 minutes. Cool on wire rack.

2. Mix berries and remaining 2 tablespoons Splenda®. Spoon into meringues.

Chocolate Fondue

8 servings (about ¼ cup each)

1 package (8 ounces) unsweetened baking chocolate,
    coarsely chopped
1 cup reduced-fat milk
14½ teaspoons Equal® for Recipes, *or*
    48 packets Equal® sweetener
1 teaspoon vanilla, *or* ½ to ¾ teaspoon rum *or* mint extract
1½ cups small strawberries
1 cup cubed (¾-inch) melon
1 cup sliced apple

Per Serving
Net Carbohydrate (gm): 15
Calories: 210
Fat (gm): 16.5
Saturated fat (gm): 9.7
Cholesterol (mg): 2.4
Sodium (mg): 21
Protein (gm): 4.5
Carbohydrate (gm): 20.5

1. Heat chocolate and milk in medium saucepan over low heat until chocolate is melted and mixture is smooth, stirring frequently. Stir in Equal® for Recipes and vanilla.

2. Pour chocolate mixture into serving bowl; serve with fruit for dipping. If chocolate mixture becomes too thick, stir in 1 to 2 tablespoons warm milk.

Index